Selling Today

PARTNERING TO CREATE VALUE

FOURTEENTH
EDITION

Selling Today

PARTNERING TO CREATE VALUE

GERALD MANNING

Des Moines Area Community College

MICHAEL AHEARNE

University of Houston

BARRY L. REECE

Virginia Polytechnic Institute and State University

FOURTEENTH EDITION

330 Hudson Street, NY NY 10013

Vice President, Business Publishing: Donna Battista
Director of Portfolio Management: Stephanie Wall
Portfolio Manager: Emily Tamburri
Editorial Assistant: Eric Santucci
Vice President, Product Marketing: Roxanne McCarley
Director of Strategic Marketing: Brad Parkins
Strategic Marketing Manager: Deborah Strickland
Product Marketer: Becky Brown
Field Marketing Manager: Lenny Ann Kucenski
Product Marketing Assistant: Jessica Quazza
**Vice President, Production and Digital Studio,
    Arts and Business:** Etain O'Dea
Director of Production, Business: Jeff Holcomb
Managing Producer, Business: Ashley Santora
Content Producer: Lauren Russell

Operations Specialist: Carol Melville
Creative Director: Blair Brown
Manager, Learning Tools: Brian Surette
Content Developer, Learning Tools: Sarah Peterson
Managing Producer, Digital Studio, Arts and Business:
    Diane Lombardo
Digital Studio Producer: Monique Lawrence
Digital Studio Producer: Alana Coles
Full-Service Project Management and Composition:
    Thistle Hill Publishing Services/Cenveo® Publisher
    Services
Cover Design: Cenveo® Publisher Services
Cover Art: Getty Images
Printer/Binder: LSC Communications
Cover Printer: LSC Communications

Library of Congress Cataloging-in-Publication Data
Names: Manning, Gerald L., author. | Ahearne, Michael, author. | Reece, Barry
    L., author.
Title: Selling today : partnering to create value / Gerald Manning, Des
    Moines Area Community College, Michael Ahearne, University of Houston,
    Barry L. Reece, Virginia Polytechnic Institute and State University.
Description: Fourteenth edition. | New York, NY : Pearson, [2018] | Includes
    bibliographical references and index.
Identifiers: LCCN 2016043126| ISBN 9780134477404 (hardcover) | ISBN
    0134477405 (hardcover)
Subjects: LCSH: Selling.
Classification: LCC HF5438.25 .M35 2018 | DDC 658.85—dc23
LC record available at https://lccn.loc.gov/2016043126

3   17

ISBN 10: 0-13-447740-5
ISBN 13: 978-0-13-447740-4

Brief Contents

Contents

Preface

Much of the Western world has experienced a rapid shift from a production-focused to a sales- and service-focused economy. Approximately one in nine people in the U.S. workforce hold sales-related positions. In fact, selling is the second largest employment category in the United States, offering an enormous variety of different employment contexts and opportunities to more than 21 million salespeople nationwide. Moreover, as sales researchers predict, this figure will go up by the year 2020, as more than two million more workers will be added to the sales profession. Despite these staggering numbers conveying the importance of the sales function, business education has been slow to act to the market's increased demand for highly trained salespeople. Fortunately, in the last decade, many business schools have either developed or begun to develop specialized courses and programs in sales and sales management. Given the high demand for skilled sales professionals, senior sales managers are highly enthusiastic about recruiting students from these programs, where many of these students are receiving multiple job offers with excellent earning potential.

Those seeking a job in sales are not the only ones who will benefit from learning how to sell. In fact, almost everyone these days uses traditional sales-related activities in their professional and social lives. People use a whole assortment of selling techniques in everyday life to persuade decision makers and advance their causes. According to Daniel Pink, the author of the recent best-selling book, *To Sell Is Human*, people are using about 40 percent of their time at work to engage in what he calls "non-sales selling"—persuading, convincing, influencing, and moving others in ways that do not involve anybody making a purchase. Moreover, people across a wide variety of professions spend about 24 minutes of every hour influencing or moving others, and they consider this time investment crucial to their success.[1] Selling is increasingly becoming a master skill for success in the 21st century.

This paradigm shift in which selling has become an integral part of the social and business life has coincided with another major revolution—the dramatic change in which people access information. The information age has transferred the power from sellers to customers. Today's customers can easily compare the offerings of different sellers through various online methods and choose those offerings that best suit their needs. For example, a recent Google shopper sciences study discovered that, on average, customers gather information from ten different sources before making a decision. In the business-to-business selling context, research estimates that approximately 60 percent of a customer's buying decision has been completed digitally by decision makers before they reach out to a sales rep. Given this shift, the true value of a salesperson lies in the co-creation of value with the customer.

Another phenomenon that has received less attention in the press is the shift in sales force composition from field sales to inside sales, thereby lowering the sales costs by more than 50% (on average, an outside sales call costs $308 whereas an inside sales call costs only $50). Research by ZS Associates indicates that 40 percent of large companies in the technology arena are shifting from the field to inside sales. In the coming five years, the expected number of jobs to be created in inside sales is nearly three times the job creation for field sales. The primary enablers of this change are the new easy-to-use online videoconferencing and webinar communication tools, which are a good substitute for face-to-face meetings and give customers the comfort of purchasing and collaborating remotely.

The simultaneous shift towards co-creation of value and inside sales represents a dichotomy in sales function and is a manifestation of changing customer preferences. In order to lock their customers in and *create and deliver superior value* in times when customers have more choices and fewer switching costs, salespeople are adopting a partnering style of selling to build long-term, strategic relationships with their customers. Having these long-term relationships is important, as it is more profitable for companies to retain existing customers than it is to acquire new customers. The pivotal role of a *partnering style of selling* in today's highly competitive business environment is a common theme throughout the 14th edition of *Selling Today: Partnering to Create Value*.

[1] Daniel Pink, *To Sell Is Human: The Surprising Truth about Persuading, Convincing, and Influencing Others.* (NY: Riverhead Books, 2012), pp. 19–25.

The primary goal of each revision of *Selling Today* is to develop the premier research-backed text available, and the most practical and applied text available in the marketplace. The revision process begins with a thorough review of several hundred articles, books, and research reports. The authors also study popular sales training programs such as Conceptual Selling, SPIN Selling, Integrity Selling, Trusted Advisor and Solution Selling. Major corporations throughout the world such as Microsoft, Marriott, Principal Financial Group, UPS, Wells Fargo, and Xerox use these training programs. Of course, reviews and suggestions by professors and students influence decisions made during the revision process as well.

Staying on the Cutting Edge: New to This Edition

Since the 13th edition, the business environment and research on personal selling and sales force management have experienced significant changes. Our primary goal as researchers, practitioners, and consultants in the field of selling is to provide a cutting-edge treatment of the field. The 14th edition of *Selling Today* describes what ramifications the information age has for the selling world and how sales professionals must cope with new issues arising from the information revolution with an ethical, customer-centered mindset. The most significant changes in the new edition include the following:

Neil Rackham
Source: Michael Ahearne

- *Exclusive to 14e Selling Today! New Neil Rackham Selling Today/SPIN Selling Video.* Utilizing the extensive research, writing, and worldwide consulting work of Neil Rackham, the authors have partnered with him to produce an exclusive video new to the 14th edition of *Selling Today.* Neil Rackham is one of the most recognized sales authors of all time. Celebrated for his pioneering book titled *SPIN Selling,* Neil is a sought-after expert who consults with global organizations on improving and streamlining their sales functions.

  Presented in Chapter 11 "Determining Customer Needs with a Consultative Questioning Strategy," this new to the Adaptive Selling Today Video Series that features Rackham providing cutting-edge information on the effective use of questions in *Selling Today.* (Also see boxed insert on p. 228.) Additionally, Neil shares his insights on the changing role of salespeople in an increasingly competitive marketplace. He further emphasizes the importance of sales education in the business curriculum.

  In addition to this being a "first custom-produced Neil Rackham video for a college textbook," *Selling Today* was the first text to present an entire chapter on the critically important skill of using questions to partner with customers. Another first for *Selling Today* was an entire chapter devoted to the important process of building partnering relationships using communication or behavioral style principles. This kind of relationship is important for developing the right context for the effective use of the questions Rackham advocates in his SPIN Selling research, writings, and consulting work.

- *New Entrepreneurial and Inside Sales Reality Selling Videos for the 14th Edition* With the rapid increase in college graduates starting careers in Entrepreneurship and Inside Sales, new Reality *Selling Today* Videos, with accompanying Case Problems and Role Plays, covering these important career areas were created for the 14th edition.

Ryan Guillory
Source: Michael Ahearne

  The new Chapter 2 Reality Selling Video features Entrepreneur Ryan Guillory, an **owner/agent** of an independent insurance agency. He is his company—responsible for building a successful organization that relies on developing and maintaining customer relationships, being an expert regarding both his many products and his competition, understanding the needs of his clientele and partnering with them in finding and delivering value adding solutions to their buying problems. How well Ryan, a recent college graduate, executes and manages these important company functions will determine the future growth and success of his agency (see pp. 29–30 for more information).

Khalid Naziruddin
Source: Michael Ahearne

  The new Chapter 14 Reality Selling Video showcases Khalid Naziruddin, a big-ticket **sales representative** for a highly acclaimed luxury brand Audi automobile dealership that is "Obsessed with Service." Khalid, a recent graduate of Texas Tech University, was tested by his company during the hiring process for intelligence and aptitude. The goal was to find the kind of individual, such as Kahlid, that is friendly, well groomed, highly trainable, and able to personalize and create value during the buying experience. Kahlid engages and partners with his clients in an attractive setting of fresh flowers, original art, an ultra clean facility, and a large inventory of high quality luxury products. His goal is to provide legendary customer service, create moments of magic, and develop a highly satisfied lifetime customer base (see p. 312 for more information).

   Selling Today **is the only personal selling text to bring this type of sales training support to the classroom.** With these two new videos, there are now a total of 12 Reality *Selling Today* videos. These unique learning tools feature successful recent college graduates making sales calls as they do on a daily basis in their professional personal selling careers. The videotaped presentations are introduced in a chapter-opening vignette, related to the material presented in the chapter, applied with a case problem at the end of the chapter, and further used as a setting for detailed role play scenarios presented in Appendix 1. The two new videos were shot "on-site" in settings where these successful young salespeople make their sales presentations.

- *Introducing CRM (Customer Relationship Management) Systems Boxed Inserts.* The 14e CRM has been updated and enhanced by exposing users to a broad-based application of today's best-selling CRM applications. The 14e introduces the use of popular CRM systems, such as Salesforce, NetSuite, Siebel, and Sugar CRM in Chapter 1 through our popular boxed inserts. Then in Chapter 2 we provide instructions for the use of a regularly updated 30-day Salesforce.com free trial, as well as access to training videos for the software. Additional CRM boxed inserts appearing throughout the text show how salespeople apply customer relationship management software to improve their partnering strategies.

Additionally, students can experience the importance of CRM Contact Reports and accompanying Notes Windows with the 20 regional accounts presented in Appendix 2, Regional Accounts Management Case Study. They soon realize the value of information entered into CRM systems as they analyze account metrics, prepare reports, and move their new accounts successfully through the sales process.

- *Updated Social Media and* **Selling Today** *Boxed Inserts*. Social media is playing a larger role in *Selling Today*. The 14e boxed inserts have been carefully updated and expanded to reflect strategies utilizing social media for selling in today's information-driven business world.
- *Latest Research and Trends from Academic Journals and Trade References.* Extensive referencing of academic articles found in the *Journal of Personal Selling and Sales Management, Journal of Marketing, Harvard Business Review,* and others has been brought up to date. Topics and trends in selling garnered from numerous trade publications such as *Selling Power, ThinkSales, Value Added 21 Selling, Sales and Marketing Management,* and *The American Salesperson* have been integrated throughout the 14th edition.
- *An updated glossary appears at the end of the book for quick reference*.
- *Revised Set of Annotated PowerPoint Slides*. These provide additional insights for presenting important points in the text.
- *New Study Guides.* These are added to maximize student learning when viewing both the Reality Selling Today and Adaptive Selling Today videos. With more video support than any text on the market, these new study guides ensure in-depth student learning.

Building on Traditional Strengths

Selling Today: Partnering to Create Value has been successful because the authors continue to build on strengths that have been enthusiastically praised by instructors and students. Speaking to these strengths, *Selling Today* has become the standard for personal-selling textbooks internationally, significantly exceeding all other textbooks in terms of worldwide sales. International editions of the book have been sold in over 30 different countries, including Canada, China, Croatia, Indonesia, the Netherlands, Mexico, and Spain. *Selling Today* is the premier research-backed textbook in the marketplace for personal selling.

   Previous editions of *Selling Today* have evolved by tracing the trends in professional selling and highlighting the most critical areas for salesperson success. This edition provides new material on a number of evolving and important concepts.

1. **The partnering era** is described in detail. Partnership selling principles, so important to today's successful selling and marketing strategies, are presented and clearly illustrated throughout the text. Strategic alliances—the highest form of partnering—are discussed in detail.

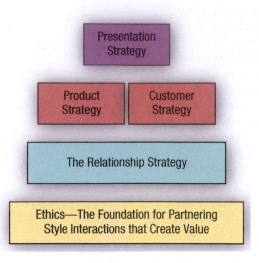

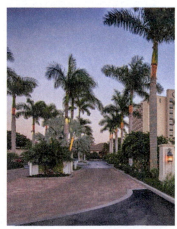

Park Shores Resort and Convention Center.

Source: Courtesy of Beach Resort

2. **Value-added selling strategies** are presented throughout the text. Salespeople today are guided by a new principle of personal selling: *Partnerships are established and maintained only when the salesperson creates customer value.* Customers have fundamentally changed their expectations. They want to partner with salespeople who can create value, not just communicate it. Value creation involves a series of improvements in the sales process that enhance the customer's experience.

3. **Ethics as the Foundation of Selling Today** Ethical selling is highlighted in Chapter 3, "Ethics: The Foundation for Partnering Relationships that Create Value," as well as throughout the book. Chapter 3 addresses the many ethical lapses existing in the business world and emphasizes the need for a highly ethical interaction with customers as the starting point of all relationship development, if one is to build long-term, partnering-style selling relationships. Moreover, the ethics assessment at the end of the chapter and new text models are used to highlight an emphasis on ethical selling.

4. **The NewNet Systems Regional Accounts Management Case Study.** For the first time in a personal-selling textbook, students are exposed to the strategic sales-planning responsibilities associated with moving multiple accounts successfully through the sales process for a company called NewNet Systems. Appendix 2 features the challenges and responsibilities of a regional account manager selling to 20 accounts with a projected total sales of $1.8 million. Training future salespeople on these planning responsibilities is extremely important as the demand for account managers in today's businesses is burgeoning. Moreover, a recent study suggests that account managers spend 74 percent of their time engaging in non-sales activities such as administrative tasks, traveling and waiting, and sales preparation. These figures attest to the fact that training and practicing effective management of these activities is crucial for future salespeople in today's business context. These account management responsibilities are coded to each of the six chapters in Part 5, Developing a Presentation Strategy, a sales process unit which makes it easy for professors to assign and monitor, and excellent for in-class or online courses.

5. **Popular Appendix 3 Role-Play.** This revision includes an exciting luxury beachfront resort and convention center as the setting for the Partnership Role Play. A highly interactive simulated website is also included for use in student sales presentations. *Selling Today* is the only textbook that provides student exposure and experience to role-playing the entire consultative sales process from acquiring easy-to-learn product knowledge, initial building of sales relationships, discovering customer needs, and creating and delivering a technology-rich sales presentation. Appendix 3 is a perfect fit for both in-class or online courses. Serving as an excellent capstone experience, students develop the critical skills needed to apply relationship, product, customer, and presentation strategies.

6. **Real-world examples**, a hallmark of previous editions and a continued focus in this edition, build the reader's interest in personal selling and promote an understanding of the major topics and concepts. With opening vignettes at the beginning of each chapter that put students in the shoes of the salesperson, and role-plays that allow students to utilize the skills they have learned, the real-world examples truly enrich the overall learning experience.

7. **The Reality Selling Video Series** features successful young salespeople, which provides real-world examples of sales careers and presentations. Additional real-selling examples have been obtained from a range of progressive organizations, large and small, such as Emeco Ltd., Whirlpool Corporation, UPS, BKM Total Office, Mutual of Omaha, Design Display, Inc., Baxter Healthcare, Marriott Hotels, and Nordstrom.

8. **The Reality Selling Video Role-Plays**, in addition to the role-play exercises and video case problems, remain an invaluable resource for instructors. Found in Appendix 1, each scenario gives students the chance to assume the role of a salesperson in selling scenarios that are relevant to today's competitive environment. These role-play scenarios build on what students learned in the Reality Selling Video sales presentations and interviews. The detailed salesperson/customer role-play scenarios use the actual products and sales positions of the

salespeople who appeared in the Reality Selling Videos. Websites of the companies the students will be using to role-play their sales presentations are supplied in order to learn appropriate amounts of product and company information. The Reality Selling Video interviews and sales presentations provide the necessary background and contextual information for students to use in both selecting the scenario and conducting the role-play. The Reality Selling Role-Plays are also specifically designed to prepare students for professional selling role-play competitions at annual college and university competitive event conventions. Refer to the following links for more information on the leading sales competitions at the college and university level:

- http://coles.kennesaw.edu/ncsc/
- www.universitysalescenteralliance.org/sales_competitions.html
- https://www.deca.org/wp-content/uploads/2016/09/CGuide_2016-17_ProfSales.pdf
- http://rbisaleschallenge.wpunj.edu/
- https://kelley.iu.edu/GlobalSales/students/competitions/page15657.html

9. **The Professionally Produced Adaptive Selling Training Video Series** is the only custom-produced video series available to accompany a textbook on selling. The four-part series is produced and directed by Arthur Bauer, a well-known and widely acclaimed award-winning training-video professional. Concepts in the text are presented based on carefully written scripts, utilization of professional actors, and are filmed in real, contemporary business settings. These high-cost, professionally produced videos available to professors who adopt the *Selling Today* text are also marketed and sold to sales training directors throughout the world, and are used to train their salespeople in the skills critical to success in the profession of selling.

    The first video on building relationships, "Communication Styles: The Key to Adaptive Selling," describes how to use behavioral psychology to build strong, mutually rewarding relationships. Designed to be shown when presenting Chapter 5, it discusses how to avoid style bias by understanding and flexing one's style to adapt and communicate effectively with the customer's style. A web-based style assessment exercise titled Communication Style Assessment at www.pearsonhighered.com is designed to discover one's own preferred style, as well as to discover the styles of those clients in the prospect database. To access the Communication Style Assessment and share with your students, go to www.pearsonhighered.com, search for this text, click on Resources and locate the Student Resources supplement. The second video on "Questioning" presents a widely researched approach to discovering customer needs using the consultative model. Shown when covering Chapter 11, application exercises at the end of the chapter apply and enhance the development of this critical, consultative selling skill. Closely aligned with the four questions in the Spin Selling Model, professional actors show how each of these questions are effectively used in the sales process. The third Adaptive Selling Video titled "Negotiations: Solving the Tough Points," supports the principles in Chapter 13 on negotiation. Using a medical equipment sales setting, professional negotiation strategies are dramatically presented for moving through the sometimes difficult process of answering customer concerns, moving the sale forward, and achieving a win-win solution. The fourth video titled "Ask for the Order and Get It" is built on the concepts in Chapter 14, "Adapting the Close and Confirming the Partnership." This video is designed to visually and dramatically present the many methods for moving the sales process to a successful conclusion.

10. **The following high-interest boxed inserts** are updated for the 14th edition; new and interesting material regarding the role of social media selling as well as global selling has been added to the social media and global selling inserts:

- *Selling Is Everyone's Business.* These real-world examples explain how selling skills affect the success of persons who do not consider themselves salespeople.
- *Selling in Action.* These concise inserts feature contemporary issues in selling to keep the readers of *Selling Today* abreast of the latest developments.
- *Global Business Insight.* These brief inserts provide practical tips on how to build global relationships. Each insert focuses on a different country.
- *Customer Relationship Management with Technology.* These application exercises help the student learn how to use technology to add value to the sales process.
- *Social Media and Selling Today.* Informing students how social networking applies to personal selling, these succinct inserts identify how social media networks, such as Facebook, Twitter, LinkedIn, and YouTube can be used effectively in the selling process.

Organization of This Book

The material in *Selling Today* continues to be organized around the four pillars of personal selling: relationship strategy, product strategy, customer strategy, and presentation strategy. Moreover, in the 14th edition, we emphasize ethical selling as an important factor within which all the four strategies should be embedded. Part 1, "Developing a Personal Selling Philosophy," includes Chapters 1 and 2 and sets the stage for an in-depth study of these strategies. The first chapter provides a contemporary definition of selling and gives students the opportunity to explore career opportunities in the information age, while the second chapter describes the evolution of personal selling associated with the information revolution.

Research indicates that high-performance salespeople are better able to build and maintain relationships than are moderate performers. Part 2, "Developing a Relationship Strategy," focuses on several important person-to-person relationship-building practices that contribute to success in personal selling. The influence of ethical selling as the foundation of successful relationships is discussed in Chapter 3. Creating value with a relationship strategy is discussed in Chapter 4. Chapter 5, "Communication Styles: A Key to Adaptive Selling Today," with its accompanying website style assessment at www.pearsonhighered.com introduces communication styles, explains how to build strong relationships with style flexing, and provides a web-based assessment that enables one to discover their own style and the style of others they will be working with. To access the Communication Styles: A Key to Adaptive Selling Today assessment and share with your students, go to www.pearsonhighered.com, search for this text, click on Resources and locate the Student Resources supplement.

Part 3, "Developing a Product Strategy," examines the importance of complete and accurate product, company, and competitive knowledge in personal selling. A well-informed salesperson is in a strong position to configure value-added product solutions for a customer's unique needs. The importance of having expert product knowledge as well as knowledge of competition and industry trends is discussed in Chapter 6, while Chapter 7 explains how to sell with a value-added strategy.

Part 4, "Developing a Customer Strategy," presents information on why and how customers buy, and also explains how to identify prospects. With increased knowledge of the customer, salespeople are in a better position to understand a customer's unique wants and needs and to create customer value in the multi-call, lifetime customer setting. Chapter 8 sheds light on consumer- and business-buying behaviors, while Chapter 9 describes the strategies used to develop prospects and accounts. Appendix 2 provides students the opportunity to assume a new sales position as Regional Account Manager, taking over an account base with 20 existing clients/prospects. Students assume responsibility for developing sales strategies and tactics to move these prospects through the six-step sales process presented in the text. Regional Account Management Case Study exercises at the end of Chapters 9–15 challenge students to properly apply the sales process they are studying to the their new role as a Regional Account Manager.

The concept of a salesperson as an advisor, consultant, value creator, and partner to buyers is stressed in Part 5, "Developing a Presentation Strategy." Emphasis is placed on the need-satisfaction presentation model as well as on ways to provide outstanding service after the sale. Chapter 10 introduces the concept of adaptive selling as a useful strategy to approach customers. Chapter 11 explains how to identify customer needs with a consultative questioning strategy and Chapter 12 discusses the role of a consultative presentation in delivering value to the customers. The principles of formal negotiations as a part of a win-win strategy are discussed in Chapter 13, while Chapter 14 focuses on proper attitudes and strategies to close the sales. Chapter 15 finishes Part 5 by discussing the role of customer service in building sustaining, profitable relationships with the customer.

Personal selling is one of the few professions that inherently require a great deal of self-discipline. Part 6 focuses on managing self as well as others by discussing the four dimensions of opportunity management in Chapter 16 and the fundamentals of sales force management in Chapter 17.

The 14th edition features three appendices. Appendix 1, "The Reality *Selling Today* Role-Play and Video Scenarios," includes 12 role-play scenarios that provide students with the opportunity to, of course, sell. Due to the rise of multiple-account management as one of the key sales roles in many organizations today, the 14e includes Appendix 2, which is devoted to a multi-chapter case study on regional account managers' daily challenges and responsibilities.

The popular Appendix 3 allows students to integrate and apply what they have learned from this textbook in all four strategic areas of personal selling. The 14th edition features the luxury beachfront resort and convention center with an interactive simulated website for use in student sales presentations. To access additional materials for Appendix 3, go to www.pearsonhighered .com, search for this text, click on Resources and locate the Student Resources supplement.

A Special Note to Students on How to Use the Book

This 14th edition of *Selling Today* has several new features that distinguish it from other texts. Here we offer students of sales a few tips to make the most out of the materials presented in the new edition.

Selling is fun. That does not mean it is easy to close a deal. Each chapter in this new edition has been reorganized with the sole goal of providing you with a systematic summary of key concepts related to the topic area and ample application exercises. While there are different ways you can approach the text, we believe it is most effective to start each chapter with a concrete understanding of how the chapter fits into the big picture of selling through value creation, the overriding theme of this textbook. In this regard, we have extensively revised and updated the chapter previews, chapter summaries, key terms, review questions, and cross references among the chapters to assist you in integrating key concepts.

Practice makes perfect. We have created numerous role-play exercises that resemble real-life selling situations and applications to provide you with hands-on experience. From our experience, some students may dismiss these exercises as easy. Try one of the exercises, and you will see how these students could not be more wrong. Do not get us wrong. The exercises are not that difficult, but we do inject a great deal of reality into them to make them complex enough to provide you with the opportunity to hone your selling skills. So practice them with a friend, a family member, or in front of a video camera or mirror.

Observe, analyze, and think about your experiences with salespeople in everyday life. Use the concepts and themes you have learned from the text. Think about how those salespeople sell to you, or how you would do it differently if you were they.

We encourage you to write to us regarding your experience with this new edition.

Selling Today Supplements

At www.pearsonhighered.com, instructors can access a variety of print, digital, and presentation resources available with this text in downloadable format. Registration is simple and gives you immediate access to new titles and new editions. As a registered faculty member, you can download resource files and receive immediate access and instructions for installing course management content on your campus server.

If you need assistance, our dedicated technical support team is ready to help with the media supplements that accompany this text. Visit support.pearson.com/getsupport for answers to frequently asked questions and toll-free user-support phone numbers.

The following supplements are available to adopting instructors:

- *Instructor's Manual.* This downloadable Instructor's Manual includes lecture outlines, answers to all end-of-chapter questions and case questions, detailed teaching instructions and answers for the three appendices, and additional activities and assignments for your students.
- *Test Item File.* This downloadable Test Item File contains over 1,200 questions, including multiple-choice, true/false, and essay-type questions. Each question is followed by the correct answer, the learning objective it ties to, the AACSB category when appropriate, the question type (concept, application, critical thinking, or synthesis), and a difficulty rating.
- *PowerPoint Presentations.* This downloadable deck of PowerPoint presentations includes basic outlines and key points with corresponding figures and art from each chapter. These presentations are ready to use or completely customizable for individual course needs. The notes section of each slide provides additional explanations written for your students.
- *TestGen.* Pearson Education's test-generating software is PC/Mac compatible and preloaded with all of the Test Item File questions. You can manually or randomly view test questions and drag-and-drop to create a test. You can add or modify test-bank questions as needed.
- *Learning Management Systems.* Our TestGens are converted for use in BlackBoard, WebCT, Moodle, D2L, Angel, and Respondus. These conversions can be found on the Instructor's Resource Center. Respondus can be downloaded by visiting www.respondus.com.
- *Video Library.* Pearson-lead content videos are featured within MyMarketingLab alongside four sets of text specific videos, illustrating the most important subject topics. These Selling Today videos include Adaptive Selling Today videos, Adaptive Selling Training videos, Reality Selling Today videos, and Reality Selling Today Role-Play videos.
- *eBook:* This title is available as an ebook and can be purchased at most ebook retailers.

- *Website for Appendix 3.* Since its debut in previous editions, Appendix 3 has remained one of the most popular role-play supplements for any selling course. The 14th edition luxury beachfront resort and convention center role-play in this appendix provides an excellent opportunity for students to apply their understanding of the four major strategic areas of personal selling in a simulation of reality. In this 14th edition, this appendix is augmented with an interactive, simulated website assisting students in sales presentations. This material prepares students to catch up with the new technology-rich selling techniques in the information age. To access this material to share with your students go to www.pearsonhighered.com, search for this text, click on Resources and locate the Student Resources supplement.

The Search for Wisdom in the Age of Information

The search for the fundamentals of personal selling has become more difficult in the age of information. The glut of information (information explosion) threatens our ability to identify what is true, right, or lasting. The search for knowledge begins with a review of information, and wisdom is gleaned from knowledge. Books continue to be one of the best sources of wisdom as are online links and videos. We provide an excellent array of support videos for various parts such as the Reality Selling section, making the 14th edition more practical and hands-on than any other textbook in the market. Many new books, and several classics, were used as references for the 14th edition of *Selling Today: Partnering to Create Value*. A sample of the more than 40 books used to prepare this edition follows:

To Sell Is Human by Daniel H. Pink

Working with Emotional Intelligence by Daniel Goleman

The Tipping Point by Malcolm Gladwell

Integrity Selling for the 21st Century by Ron Willingham

The Platinum Rule by Tony Alessandra and Michael J. O'Connor

A Whole New Mind by Daniel H. Pink

Rethinking the Sales Force by Neil Rackham and John R. DeVincentis

Business Ethics by O. C. Ferrell, John Fraedrich, and Linda Ferrell

Negotiating Genius by Deepak Malhotra and Max H. Baserman

52 Sales Management Tips: The Sales Manager's Success Guide by Steven Rosen

Blur: The Speed of Change in the Connected Economy by Stan Davis and Christopher Meyer

Close the Deal by Sam Deep and Lyle Sussman

Complete Business Etiquette Handbook by Barbara Pachter and Marjorie Brody

Effective Human Relations—Personal and Organizational Applications by Barry L. Reece and Monique Reece

Emotional Intelligence for Sales Success: Connect with Customers and Get Results by Colleen Stanley and Jill Konrath

First Impressions—What You Don't Know About How Others See You by Ann Demarais and Valerie White

Hug Your Customers by Jack Mitchell

Insightful Selling: Learn the S.A.L.E.S. Formula to Differentiate Yourself and Create Customer Value by Adon T. Rigg

Keeping the Funnel Full by Don Thomson

LinkedIn Marketing: An Hour a Day by Viveka von Rosen

Marketing Imagination by Ted Levitt

Marketing—Real People, Real Choices by Michael R. Solomon, Greg W. Marshall, and Elnora W. Stuart.

Megatrends by John Naisbitt

New Sales, Simplified: The Essential Handbook of Prospecting and New Business Development by Mike Weinberg and S. Anthony Iannarino

Personal Styles and Effective Performance by David W. Merrill and Roger H. Reid

Psycho-Cybernetics by Maxwell Maltz

Questions—The Answer to Sales by Duane Sparks

Re-Imagine! Business Excellence in a Disruptive Age by Tom Peters

Rules of the Hunt: Real-World Advice for Entrepreneurial and Business Success by Michael Dalton Johnson

Self Matters by Phillip C. McGraw

Selling Fearlessly: A Master Salesman's Secrets for the One-Call-Close Salesperson by Robert Terson

Small Message, Big Impact: The Elevator Speech Effect by Terri L. Sjodin

SPIN Selling by Neil Rackham

SPIN Selling Fieldbook by Neil Rackham

Strategic Sales Presentations by Jack Malcolm

Strategic Selling by Robert B. Miller and Stephen E. Heiman

The 7 Habits of Highly Effective People by Stephen R. Covey

The Customer Revolution by Patricia Seybold

The Wow Factor by Tom Peters

The Double Win by Denis Waitley

The New Conceptual Selling by Stephen E. Heiman and Diane Sanchez

The New Professional Image by Susan Bixler and Nancy Nix-Rice

The New Solution Selling by Keith M. Eades

The Power of 5 by Harold H. Bloomfield and Robert K. Cooper

The Sedona Method by Hale Dwoskin

The Speed of Change in the Connected Economy by Stan Davis and Christopher Meyer

The Success Principles by Jack Canfield

To Sell Is Human: The Surprising Truth about Moving Others by Daniel H. Pink

Value-Added Selling by Tom Reilly

Winning the Battle for Sales: Lessons on Closing Every Deal from the World's Greatest Military Victories by John Golden

Working with Emotional Intelligence by Daniel Goleman

Zero-Resistance Selling by Maxwell Maltz, Dan S. Kennedy, William T. Brooks, Matt Oechsli, Jeff Paul, and Pamela Yellen

Zero-Time Selling: 10 Essential Steps to Accelerate Every Company's Sales by Andy Paul

Acknowledgments

Many people have made contributions to the 14th edition of *Selling Today: Partnering to Create Value*. We are very appreciative of the creative assistance and design work Rick Giudicessi did on the new Park Shores Resort and Convention Center promotional sales tools in Appendix 3, and the design for the NewNet Systems logo. We also appreciate his work on the new hotel and convention center website, enabling users to prepare technology-rich sales tools and presentations.

We also are very grateful to Jack Linge for his original work on the Appendix 2 NewNet Systems database and Regional Accounts Management Case Study Exercises. We thank award-winning video producer Art Bauer for his creativity, dedication, and attention to detail in the production of the Adaptive Selling Training Video Series. We thank Shashank Vaid, Raguram Bommaraju, and Yashar Atefi for their help and contributions with the new 14th edition Reality Selling Video Series, Cases, and Role-Play exercises.

We would also like to thank all those who contributed to the revisions of the supplements for this edition. This includes Barbara Sue Faries, M.B.A., CEO, SciMed Partners, Inc. and Mission College for her work on the instructor's manual, Richard A. Rocco, DePaul University for his work on the PowerPoint presentations, Magda Pecsenye for her work on the test bank, and Julie Boyles for accuracy checking this work and the MyLab content. A special thank you as well to our MyLab Contributors for this edition—Susan Carder, The W.A. Franke College of Business, Northern Arizona University; Dr Jefrey R Woodall, York College of Pennsylvania; S. Arlene Green; and Barbara Sue Faries, M.B.A., CEO, SciMed Partners, Inc. and Mission College, and thank you to Kim Norbuta for her project management!

Throughout the years the text has improved as a result of numerous helpful comments and recommendations by both students and faculty. We extend special appreciation to the following reviewers:

Kate Bailey, *South Valley Bank and Trust*

Jurgita Baltrusaitye, *University of Illinois at Chicago*

Susan Baxter, *Bethune-Cookman University*

Alex Birkholz, *Wisconsin Indianhead Technical College*

Robert Bochrath, *Gateway Technical Institute*

Jim Boespflug, *Arapahoe Community College*

Jerry Boles, *Western Kentucky University*

Jim Boles, *Georgia State University*

Jerry Bradley, *Saint Joseph's University*

Duane Brickner, *South Mountain Community College*

Don Brumlow, *St. John's College*

Jeff Bruns, *Bacone College*

Murray Brunton, *Central Ohio Technical College*

Larry P. Butts, *Southwest Tennessee Community College*

John C. Calhoun, *State Community College, Alabama*

Alan Canton, *California State University, Fresno*

John J. Carlisle, *New Hampshire Community Technical College, Nashua*

Mark Chock, *Marian College*

William R. Christensen, *Community College of Denver (North Campus)*

Patricia W. Clarke, *Boston College*

Cindy Claycomb, *Wichita State University*

Gloria Cockerell, *Collin College*

Lori Connors, *Delgado Community College*

David Corbett, *Ohio Valley University*

Douglas A. Cords, *California State University, Fresno*

Robert Cosenza, *The University of Mississippi*

Larry Davis, *Youngstown State University*

Lynn Dawson, *Louisiana Technical University—Ruston*

De'Arno De'Armond, *West Texas A&M University*

Dayle Dietz, *North Dakota State School of Science*

Gary Donnelly, *Casper College*

Casey Donoho, *Northern Arizona University*

Robert Dunn, *Cuesta Community College*

Mimi Eglin, *Fulton-Montgomery Community College*

Susan Emens, *Kent State University*

Joyce Ezrow, *Anne Arundel Community College*

Wendal Ferguson, *Richland College*

Dean Flowers, *Waukesha County Technical College*

Stefanie Garcia, *University of Central Florida*

Deb Gaspard, *Southeast Community College*

Richard Geyer, *Tiffin University*

Connie Golden, *Lakeland Community College*

Victoria Griffis, *University of South Florida*

David Grypp, *Milwaukee Area Technical College*

Andrew Haaland, *Tompkins Cortland Community College*

Donald Hackett, *Wichita State University*

Robert Hausladen, *University of Louisville*

Jon Hawes, *The University of Akron*

Ken Hodge, *Marketing Manager, Nordson*

Norm Humble, *Kirkwood Community College*

Phil Hupfer, *Elmhurst College*

Kathy Illing, *Greenville Technical College*

Karen James, *Louisiana State University, Shreveport*

Mark Johlke, *Bradley University*

Michael Johnson, *Chippewa Valley Tech College*

Peter Johnson, *Pace University*

Richard Jones, *Marshall University*

Jim Kaempfer, *Century College*

Ali Kara, *Pennsylvania State University, York*

Jaciel Keltgen, *Augustana College*

Katy Kemp, *Middle Tennessee State University*

Davis King, *Pennsylvania State University, Delaware County*

Wesley Koch, *Illinois Central College*

Stephen Koernig, *University of Illinois—Chicago*

Bruce Kusch, *Brigham Young University*

Bernard Kyle, *Westchester Community College*

Wilburn Lane, *Lambuth University*

James Lawson, *Mississippi State University*

R. Dale Lounsburg, *Emporia State College*

Marvin Lovett, *University of Texas, Brownsville*

George H. Lucas, Jr., *Texas A&M University*

Alice Lupinacci, *University of Texas at Arlington*

Jennifer Malarski, *Lake Superior College*

Lynnea Mallalieu, *University of North Carolina—Wilmington*

Jack Maroun, *Herkimer County Community College*

Leslie E. Martin, *University of Wisconsin, Whitewater*

Lee McCain, *Seminole Community College*

Tammy McCullough, *Eastern Michigan University*

Norman McElvany, *Johnson State College*

Kimberly McMahill, *Carl Sandburg College*

Bob McMahon, *Appalachian State University*

Robert McMurrian, *University of Tampa*

Darrel Millard, *Kirkwood Community College*

Chip Miller, *Drake University*

Ron Milliaman, *Western Kentucky University*

Irene Mittlemark, *Kingsborough Community College*

Rita Mix, *Our Lady of the Lake University—Dallas*

Russ Movritsem, *Brigham Young University*

Mark Mulder, *Grand Rapids Junior College*

Lynn Muller, *University of South Dakota*

Gordon Myron, *Lucent Technologies*

Lewis Neisner, *University of Maryland*

John Odell, *Marketing Catalysts*

Robert Owen, *Texas A&M University, Texarkana*

Mark Pantaleo, *Pensacola Christian College*

Jim Parr, *Louisiana State University*

Nancy Patterson, *University of Arkansas Community College*

Robert Perrella, *Piedmont College*

Ron Pimentel, *California State University—Bakersfield*

Richard Plank, *University of Southern Florida*

Ray Polchow, *Zane State College*

Quenton Pullman, *Nashville Technical Community College*

Walter Purvis, *Coastal Carolina Community College*

James Randall, *Georgia Southern University*

Adam Rapp, *Kent State University*

Peter Reday, *Youngstown State University*

Judy Reinders, *Milwaukee Area Technical College*

Daniel Ricica, *Sinclair Community College*

Richard Riesbeck, *West Liberty State College*

Carol Robarge, *Chippewa Valley Technical College*

Sandra Robertson, *Thomas Nelson Community College*

Mark Ryan, *Hawkeye Community College*

Stan Salzman, *American River College*

Nicholas A. Santarone, *Penn State University, Abington*

Gary Schirr, *University of Illinois at Chicago*

Donald T. Sedik, *William Rainey Harper College*

Rick Shannon, *Western Kentucky University*

C. David Shepherd, *Kennesaw State University*

Scott Sherwood, *Metropolitan State College of Denver*

Kent Sickmeyer, *Kaskaskia College*

Robert E. Smiley, *Indiana State University, Terra Haute*

C. Phillip Smith, *State Community College, Alabama*

Diane Smith, *Henry Ford Community College*

David Snyder, *Canisius College*

Karl Sooder, *University of Central Florida*

Forrest Stegelin, *University of Georgia*

Thomas Stevenson, *University of North Carolina, Charlotte*

Philip Stillitano, *Stark State College*

Phil Straniero, *Western Michigan University*

Carol Sullinger, *University of Toledo*

Michael Swenson, *Brigham Young University*

Leslie Thompson, *Hutchinson Community College*

Robert Thompson, *Indiana State University*

Ronald Tibbles, *University of North Florida*

Gary Tucker, *Oklahoma City Community College*

Sven Tuzovic, *Murray State University*

Rae Verity, *Southern Alberta Institute of Technology*

Douglas Vorhies, *University of Mississippi*

Donna Waldron, *Manchester Community College*

Jeff Walls, *Indiana Tech*

Joan Weiss, *Bucks County Community College*

Stanley "Martin" Welc, *Saddleback College*

Stacia Wert-Gray, *University of Central Oklahoma*

Scott Widmier, *University of Akron*

Jim Wilkinson, *Stark State College*

Thomas Williamson, *Ohio State ATI*

Raymond Wimer, *Syracuse University*

Susan Van Winkle, *Milwaukee Area Technical College*

Amy Wojciechowski, *West Shore Community College*

John Wolper, *The University of Findlay*

Andy Wood, *West Virginia University*

Lauren Wright, *California State University, Chico*

Curtis W. Youngman, *Salt Lake Community College*

Raymond Zagorski, *University of Alaska/Kenai Penonsula College*

Donald A. Zimmerman, *University of Akron*

About the Authors

(in alphabetical order)

Michael Ahearne
University of Houston

Michael Ahearne is Professor of Marketing and C. T. Bauer Chair in Marketing at the University of Houston. He is also Executive Director of the Sales Excellence Institute (SEI). The SEI is widely recognized as the leading university-based sales institute in the world, training more than 2,000 sales students, placing Ph.D. students at top research universities and working with more than 200 major corporations annually. He earned his Ph.D. in marketing from Indiana University. He has also served on the faculty at the University of Connecticut and at Pennsylvania State University. In addition, he has lectured internationally about sales and sales management in such countries as Austria, Belgium, France, Germany, India, Italy, Russia, and Spain.

Dr. Ahearne's research has focused primarily on improving the performance of salespeople and sales organizations. He has published over 40 articles in leading journals such as *Journal of Marketing, Journal of Marketing Research, Management Science, Strategic Management Journal, Journal of Applied Psychology,* and *Organizational Behavior and Human Decision Processes.* He was recently recognized by the American Marketing Association as one of the 20 most research-productive scholars in the field of marketing. His research has been profiled in the *Wall Street Journal, Business 2.0, Business Investors Daily, Fox News, INC Magazine,* and many other news outlets.

Before entering academia, Mike played professional baseball for the Montreal Expos and worked in marketing research and sales operations for Eli Lilly and PCS Healthcare. He actively consults in many industries including insurance, health care, consumer packaged goods, technology, and transportation.

Gerald L. Manning
Des Moines Area Community College

Gerald Manning is an international author, consultant, speaker, and successful businessperson. Professor Manning's book *Selling Today: Partnering to Create Value,* now in its 14th edition, is today's international number-one selling textbook on negotiations and partnering. With Chinese, Spanish, International English–Speaking, Canadian, Croatian, and U.S. editions, millions have profited from the strategies and tactics presented. He is author of four additional books on management and sales, all published by large, international publishing companies.

Gerald Manning also serves as a sales and marketing consultant to senior management and owners of more than 500 businesses, including both national and international companies. He appears regularly as a speaker at national sales and management conferences, and is featured regularly in training videos on sales and management.

Professor Manning served as chair of the Marketing/Management Department of one of the leading colleges in the country for more than 30 years. In addition to his administrative duties, he has served as lead instructor in negotiations and sales. Mr. Manning received the "Outstanding Professor of the Year" award given annually by his college.

He has also applied numerous negotiation and personal selling principles and practices as owner of a very successful commercial and residential real estate investment, development, and management company.

Professor Manning's speaking and classroom experience, along with his consulting and the management of his company, have provided him a unique opportunity to research, study, test, refine, and write about personal selling. With this background, and a long-term partnership-type relationship with acclaimed training video producer Arthur Bauer, the Adaptive Selling Training Video Series was produced.

Barry Reece
Virginia Polytechnic Institute and State University

Barry Reece is Professor Emeritus at Virginia Polytechnic Institute and State University. Prior to joining the faculty at Virginia Tech, he held faculty positions at Ellsworth Community College and the University of Northern Iowa. Over the years, he has served as visiting professor at the University of Iowa, University of Missouri, University of Nebraska, University of Colorado, and Wayne State College. He is the author or coauthor of six college textbooks that have been through a total of 41 editions since 1980.

Dr. Reece received his Ed.D. from the University of Nebraska. He has been actively involved in teaching, research, consulting, and designing training programs throughout his career. He has conducted more than 500 workshops and seminars devoted to leadership, human relations, communications, sales, customer service, and small business operations. He has received the "Excellence in Teaching Award" for classroom teaching at Virginia Tech and the "Trainer of the Year Award" presented by the Valleys of Virginia Chapter of the American Society for Training and Development.

Selling Today

PARTNERING TO CREATE VALUE

FOURTEENTH
EDITION

PART 1

DEVELOPING A PERSONAL SELLING PHILOSOPHY

The two chapters that make up Part 1 establish a foundation for the entire textbook. Chapter 1 provides a contemporary definition and description of personal selling and describes information-age personal-selling career opportunities. Sales-training programs offered by academic institutions, sales-training companies, and employer-provided sales training are also presented. Chapter 2, in response to the developments associated with the information economy, presents the evolution of contemporary selling models that complement the marketing concept. Chapter 2 also introduces the major themes that connect all of the chapters.

1

Relationship Selling Opportunities in the Information Economy

Learning Objectives

When you finish reading this chapter, you should be able to

1.1 Define personal selling and describe the three prescriptions of a personal selling philosophy

1.2 Describe the emergence of relationship selling in the age of information

1.3 Discuss the rewarding aspects of a career in selling today

1.4 Discuss the different employment settings in selling today

1.5 Explain how personal selling skills have become one of the master skills needed for success in the information age and how personal selling skills contribute to the work performed by knowledge workers

1.6 Identify the four major sources of sales training

MyMarketingLab™
⭐ **Improve Your Grade!**
Over 10 million students improved their results using the Pearson MyLabs. Visit **mymktlab.com** for simulations, tutorials, and end-of-chapter problems.

Source: Michael Ahearne

▶ Reality Selling Video—Alex Homer/Tom James Company

Job seekers who visit websites like Monster.com are usually surprised to discover that sales careers represent one of the largest job-posting categories. The next big surprise comes when they discover the great variety of companies that hire salespeople. Alex Homer (pictured above) is a professional clothier for the Tom James Company (www.tomjames.com), one of the world's largest manufacturers and retailers of custom-made, luxury clothing. Each Tom James client purchases directly from one of the company's well-trained professional clothiers who provide clients with wardrobe consultation on a variety of fashion topics such as wardrobe coordination, current trends, proper fit, pattern and cloth selection, necessary collection pieces, and attire for specific occasions. Tom James clothiers like Homer always come to their clients, because appointments are conducted at the client's location of choice.

Alex Homer discovered the Tom James Company after he placed second in the National Collegiate Sales Competition as a student representing the University of Central Florida. Tom James took interest in Homer, and Homer decided to learn more about Tom James by participating in ride-alongs with their existing sales representatives. He liked it and decided to accept the job offer. Before starting to actually call on customers, Homer received training in selling, product knowledge, and prospecting. Regarding career development, Tom James offers new hires the necessary training to build a successful selling career regardless of their level of past experience. They also offer opportunities for net worth building, such as profit sharing, 401(k), and stock plans. In a recent report, 30 percent of Tom James sales professionals earned $100,000 or more in commissions, leadership pay, bonuses, and stock dividends. ●

Personal Selling Today—A Definition and a Philosophy

1.1 Define personal selling and describe the three prescriptions of a personal selling philosophy

Most people are aware of Arthur Miller's very successful Pulitzer Prize–winning stage and screenplay, and its title "The Death of a Salesman." The reality of **personal selling** today is that there is a "Rebirth of the Salesperson." Between 2000 and today, when many thought the computer and Internet were causing a reduction in the need for salespeople, the number of selling jobs increased. Selling is the second-largest employment category in the United States (government jobs are the largest) and research indicates there will be two million more salespeople added to the U.S. sales force by 2020. One out of every nine people in the United States is employed in selling, a number that has remained constant for many years. According to Neil Rackham, author of the best-selling *SPIN Selling* and *Rethinking the Sales Force*, "personal selling today employs more people than any other business function—more than accounting, engineering and law put together."[1]

This ratio of salespeople to the total number in the workforce is true for many developed countries. In less developed countries such as China and Brazil, as their economies grow wealthier, the need for salespeople will increase substantially. One study done by McKinsey and Company projects that India's growing pharmaceutical industry will triple its cadre of drug representatives to 300,000 by 2020.[2]

Personal selling occurs when a company representative interacts directly with a customer or prospective customer to present information about a product or service.[3] It is a process of developing relationships, discovering needs, matching the appropriate products with these needs, and communicating benefits through informing, reminding, or persuading. The term **product** should be broadly interpreted to encompass information, services, ideas, and issues. Increasingly, personal selling is viewed as a process that adds value. In an ideal situation, the salesperson builds a mutually rewarding relationship, diagnoses the customer's needs, and custom fits the product to meet these needs. Having knowledge of these customer needs will lead to higher customer satisfaction and willingness to purchase a product.[4]

Preparation for a career in personal selling begins with the development of a personal philosophy or set of beliefs that provides guidance. To some degree, this philosophy is like the rudder that steers a ship. Without a rudder, the ship's direction is unpredictable. Without a personal philosophy, the salesperson's behavior also is unpredictable.

The development of a **personal selling philosophy** involves three prescriptions: adopt the marketing concept, value personal selling, and assume the role of a problem solver or partner in helping customers make informed and intelligent buying decisions (Figure 1.1). These three prescriptions for success in personal selling are presented here as part of the Strategic/Consultative–Selling Model. This model is expanded in future chapters to include additional strategic steps in the selling process. Chapter 2 will illustrate how the marketing concept has produced an evolving set of improvements to the sales process, moving it from peddling to value-added partnering.

Emergence of Relationship Selling in the Information Economy

1.2 Describe the emergence of relationship selling in the age of information

The restructuring of America from an industrial economy to an **information economy** began approximately 50 years ago (Figure 1.2). During this period, our economy began shifting from an emphasis on industrial activity to an emphasis on information processing. America was giving

Strategic/Consultative Selling Model	
Strategic Step	**Prescription**
Develop a Personal Selling Philosophy	☐ Adopt Marketing Concept
	☐ Value Personal Selling
	☐ Become a Problem Solver/Partner

FIGURE 1.1

Today, salespeople use a strategic plan based on a personal philosophy that emphasizes adopting the marketing concept, valuing personal selling, and becoming a problem solver/partner.

FIGURE 1.2

The age of information has greatly influenced personal selling. Today, salespeople use a variety of information technology tools to gather and process information of value to the customer. They recognize that information is a strategic resource and relationship skills are needed to build a conduit of trust for information acceptance.

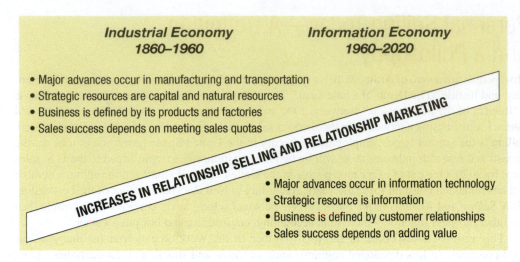

way to a new society where most of us would work with information instead of producing goods.[5] Today, we live in an age in which the effective exchange of information is the foundation of most economic transactions, and the implications for personal selling are profound. We will describe the four major developments that have shaped the information economy and discuss the implications for personal selling.

Major Advances in Information Technology and Electronic Commerce

The information age has spawned the information technology revolution. Technology as well as globalization and speed of change influence almost everything we do.[6] Salespeople and other marketing-related players in today's information age use personal computers, mobile phones, smartphones, websites, customer relationship management (CRM) applications with cloud computing, e-mail, instant messaging, blogging, and social media such as Facebook, YouTube, Twitter, and others. Frequently referred to today as **Selling 2.0**, these information technology tools, along with innovative sales practices, are used to create value for both the buyer and seller by improving the speed, collaboration, customer engagement, and accountability of the sales process.

The explosive growth of electronic commerce and other Internet activities has changed the way in which computers are used. Stan Davis, futurist and coauthor of *Blur: The Speed of Change in the Connected Economy*, notes that in today's information economy we use computers less for data crunching and more for connecting. These connections involve people-to-people, company-to-customer, machine-to-machine, product-to-service, organization-to-organization, and all these in combination.[7] The jobs of information-age workers depend on these connections. People who work extensively with information, such as salespeople, need these electronic connections to conduct their information gathering, information sharing, and information management responsibilities.

Strategic Resource Is Information

Advances in information technology have increased the speed at which we acquire, process, and disseminate information. David Shenk, author of *Data Smog: Surviving the Information Glut*, notes that we have moved from a state of information scarcity to one of information overload.[8] In an era of limitless data, informed salespeople can help us decide which information has value and which information should be ignored. Salespeople are the eyes and ears of today's marketplace. They collect a wide range of product, customer, and competitive intelligence.[9]

Business Is Defined by Customer Relationships

Michael Hammer, consultant and author of *The Agenda*, says the *real* new economy is the customer economy. As scarcity gave way to abundance, as supply exceeded demand, and as customers became better informed, we have seen a power shift. Customers have taken more control of their own destinies.[10]

On the surface, the major focus of the age of information seems to be the accumulation of more and more information and the never-ending search for new forms of information technology. It's easy to overlook the importance of the human element. Humans, not computers, have the ability to think, feel, and create ideas. It is no coincidence that relationship selling and relationship marketing, which emphasize long-term, mutually satisfying buyer–seller partnering

SOCIAL MEDIA AND SELLING TODAY

Creating Customer Value with Social Media

Popular business strategies such as "Selling Is a Contact Sport" and "Speed Is Life" describe the value of social media in the selling process. Being immediately available to a customer is essential to a salesperson's success for many reasons, including providing information at the moment the customer needs it, responding to a customer's relationship-building contact, and obtaining and following up on leads. Instant outreach to one or more customers is also critical for high-performing salespeople. This instant contact capability empowers salespeople to quickly send notices of price changes, product modifications, product operation tips, service alerts, website updates, and invitations to business and social events.

Advances in communication technology enhance the value of salesperson availability and outreach by dramatically reducing the time required for salesperson and customer interactions. Among these advances is the category generally referred to as "social media." Facebook, Twitter, LinkedIn, YouTube, Whatsapp and smartphones are frequently identified as key components of this category.

Facebook can be used by a salesperson to expand his or her personal information that may be found on the company's website. Products or services are also found on Facebook, allowing customers and others to learn about and discuss a salesperson's offerings. LinkedIn allows registered users to maintain a list of contact details of people they know and trust in business. Social media may also be put to use for instant messaging (Twitter, Whatsapp etc.), live streaming (Periscope, Blab etc.), image sharing (Snapchat), communication with B2B customers (Slack), etc. Other ways to streamline content is by letting customers, especially influencers, know that they have been mentioned in the content that has been created (Notifier helps connect with influencers), while apps such as Quuu.co and Crate help find and build curated content. Social media image creation tools such as Pablo 2.0 are particularly helpful for image management apps such as Pinterest and Instagram. Smartphones and similar mobile devices allow communications to include still and moving images designed to improve recipients' understanding and acceptance of the accompanying messages.

High-performing salespeople and their organizations are well advised to carefully study the continuous advances in communication technologies and rapidly adopt the advantages they offer.[11] Playing the serious "sport" of customer contact at the fastest possible speed is now a critical necessity in a salesperson's life.

relationships, began to gain support at the beginning of the information age. Companies such as DuPont, Kraft Foods, and General Electric have adopted a philosophy that focuses on customer satisfaction, team selling, and relationship selling.[12]

Sales Success Depends on Creating and Adding Value

Value-added selling can be defined as a series of creative improvements within the sales process that enhance the customer experience. Salespeople can create value by developing a quality relationship, carefully identifying the customer needs, and then configuring and presenting the best possible product solution. Value is also created when the salesperson provides excellent service after the sale. Neil Rackham, author of *Rethinking the Sales Force*, and other experts in sales and marketing say that success no longer depends on merely communicating the value of products and services. **Success in personal selling rests on the critical ability to create value for customers.**

The value added by salespeople today is increasingly derived from intangibles such as the quality of the advice offered and the level of trust that underlies the relationship between the customer and the salesperson. The value of these intangibles can erode with shocking speed when the customer feels deceived or discovers that the competition is able to add more value to the sales process.[13]

Considerations for a Future in Personal Selling

1.3 Discuss the rewarding aspects of a career in selling today

Job seekers who visit Monster.com or Careerbuilder.com are usually surprised to discover that sales careers represent one of the largest job-posting categories. Many thousands of entry-level sales positions are listed every day. The next big surprise comes when they discover the great variety of companies that hire salespeople. Some companies, such as Marriott and United Parcel Service (UPS), are well known throughout the nation. Other companies, such as SpeechPhone, LLC (www.speechphone.net), and World Golf Hospitality, Inc. (www.worldgolf.com), may be unfamiliar to the job seeker. SpeechPhone, LLC, sells call-forwarding, message retrieval, and other phone services. World Golf Hospitality, Inc., plans corporate-travel events and meetings that typically involve golf. The company has created travel programs for major events including the Masters, the Ryder Cup, and the U.S. Open tournaments.[14]

From a personal and economic standpoint, selling can be a rewarding career. Careers in selling offer financial rewards, recognition, security, and opportunities for advancement to a degree that is unique, when compared with other occupations.

Wide Range of Employment Opportunities

The 500 largest sales forces in America employ more than 24 million salespeople.[15] These companies will seek to recruit 500,000 college graduates. A large number of additional salespeople are employed by smaller companies. In addition, the number of new sales positions is consistently increasing and sales positions commonly rank among the jobs considered most in demand.[16] A close examination of these positions reveals that there is no single "selling" occupation. Our labor force includes hundreds of different selling careers and, chances are, there are positions that match your interests, talents, and ambitions. The diversity within selling becomes apparent as you study the career options discussed in this chapter.

Although two-thirds of college graduates take jobs as salespeople,[17] often it's not their first career choice. Students tend to view sales as dynamic and active, but believe a selling career requires them to engage in deceitful or dishonest practices. The good news is that old stereotypes about sales are gradually going by the wayside. Students who study the careers of highly successful relationship salespeople discover that ethical sales practices represent the key to long-term success.

Activities Performed by Salespeople

A professional selling position encompasses a wide range of tasks and, therefore, salespeople must possess a variety of skills. Figure 1.3 provides important insight about how many outside salespeople spend their time on the job. Note the time spent on administrative tasks, servicing, and telephoning. This, along with face-to-face selling and traveling time, provides a large amount of variety for salespeople. In some selling positions, such as retail selling, more time may be spent in face-to-face selling.

A salesperson representing Federal Express (FedEx) makes numerous sales calls each day in an attempt to establish new accounts and provide service to established accounts. A wide range of potential customers can use FedEx delivery services. A salesperson working for a Caterpillar

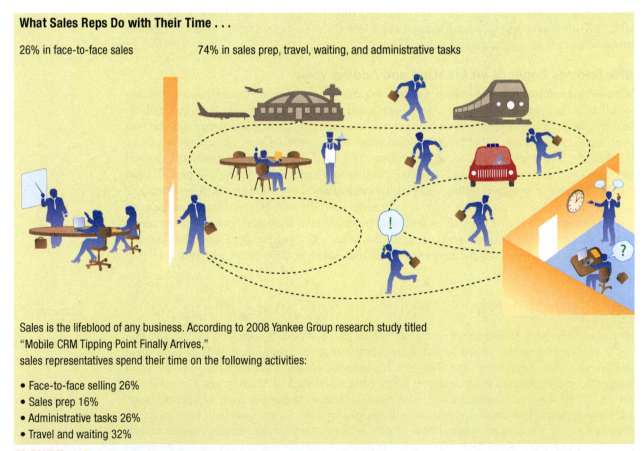

What Sales Reps Do with Their Time . . .

26% in face-to-face sales   74% in sales prep, travel, waiting, and administrative tasks

Sales is the lifeblood of any business. According to 2008 Yankee Group research study titled "Mobile CRM Tipping Point Finally Arrives," sales representatives spend their time on the following activities:

- Face-to-face selling 26%
- Sales prep 16%
- Administrative tasks 26%
- Travel and waiting 32%

FIGURE 1.3

How Salespeople Spend Their Time

A professional selling position encompasses a wide range of tasks and, therefore, salespeople must possess a variety of skills.

Source: Data from Sybase Inc., www.sybase.com/files/Thankyou_Pages/Sybase_Mobile_Solutions_for_SAP_Sales_Reps_print.pdf (accessed June 21, 2010).

construction equipment dealer may make only two or three sales calls per day. The products offered by the dealer are expensive and are not purchased frequently.

Freedom to Manage One's Own Time and Activities

Because of the wide range of activities, most selling positions allow salespeople to be in control of how they use their time, decide what activities they will prioritize in their work schedules, and interact with a wide range of people. This is in contrast to many careers where one is confined to a particular location and team of people, assigned very specific tasks, and directly supervised by others. This freedom to plan activities and prioritize the use of time, not unlike that of an entre-preneur, is high on the list of why many successful people have chosen sales as a career.

However, the ability to manage one's time, set priorities, and execute successfully on these priorities is critical to success in selling. More on this subject of opportunity management will be presented in Chapter 16.

Titles Used in Selling Today

Just as selling occupations differ, so do the titles by which salespeople are known. Many of these titles and careers are represented in the careers described in the Reality Selling Videos presented throughout the book. A survey of current job announcements indicates that companies are us-ing such titles as these (the abbreviations shown are commonly used by salespeople with these titles):

Account Executive (AE)	Sales Consultant
Account Representative	Business Development Representative (BDR)
Account Manager	Sales Associate
Relationship Manager	Marketing Representative
District Representative	Territory Manager
Marketing Partner	Channel Partner
Regional Accounts Manager (RAM)	National Accounts Manager (NAM)
Key Accounts Manager (KAM)	Global Accounts Manager (GAM)
Strategic Accounts Manager (SAM)	Account Development Representative (ADR)

Two factors have contributed to the creation of new titles. First, we have seen a shift from "selling" to "consulting" and "partnering." When salespeople assume a consulting or partnering role, the value of the relationship often exceeds the value of the transaction. Second, the new titles reflect a difference in education and skill sets needed for the position.[18] Both of these fac-tors, along with the newer definition and philosophy of selling noted earlier in this chapter, have brought about the increasing use of the title "Account Manager" to describe the responsibilities of today's sales personnel. The account manager's role in creating and adding value has resulted in the Bureau of Labor Statistics projecting the Strategic Account Manager field as one of the fastest growing in the management, scientific, and technology industry. The bureau recently projected an 83 percent increase in employment in this field by the year 2018. It is important to recognize, however, that there is still a large number of individuals employed in selling who prefer, and are proud, to be called "salespeople."

Salespeople, regardless of title, play an important role in sustaining the growth and prof-itability of organizations of all sizes. They also support the employment of many nonselling employees.

Above-Average Income

Studies dealing with incomes in the business community indicate that salespeople earn signifi-cantly higher incomes than most other workers. Some salespeople actually earn more than their sales managers and other executives within the organization. In fact, a successful career in sales and sales management can result in earnings similar to doctors, lawyers, and chief executives. [19, 20] U.S. companies spend more than $800 billion on sales force compensation each year—three times what they spend on advertising.[21] This high level of compensation (whether from base salary, bonus, or incentives) is justified for good performance. Table 1.1 provides a summary of a recent compensation survey by the Sales Account Management Association. Executive and sales force compensation continues to climb despite uncertain economic conditions.[22]

In recent years, we have seen new ways to report compensation for salespeople. The Hay Group, working with C&C Market Research, developed a reporting method that tracks earnings

TABLE 1.1 Sales Force Compensation

	LOW PERFORMERS	AVERAGE PERFORMERS	TOP PERFORMERS
Salespeople	$57,403	$ 73,213	$101,629
Sales Managers	$68,887	$ 84,525	$111,922
Strategic Account Managers	$99,133	$121,246	$161,627

Source: Ahearne, Michael, Jeffrey Boichuk, Craig Chapman, and Thomas Steenburgh, "The 2012 Earnings Management Practices in Sales and Strategic Accounts Survey," *Strategic Account Management Association,* April 2012, p. 43.

for different types of sales approaches. Research indicates that salespeople involved in transactional sales, which generally focus on selling products at the lowest price, also earned the lowest compensation.

Sales personnel involved in value-added sales earned the highest level of compensation. These highly paid salespeople created improvements and, therefore, value in the sales process that enhanced the customer experience.[23]

Above-Average Psychic Income

Two major psychological needs common to all people are recognition and security. **Psychic income,** which consists of factors that provide psychological rewards, helps satisfy these important needs and motivates persons to achieve higher levels of performance. The need for recognition has been established in numerous studies that have examined human motivation. Workers from all employment areas indicate that recognition for work well done is an important morale-building factor.

In selling, recognition occurs more frequently and with greater intensity than it does in most other occupations. Because selling contributes so visibly to the success of most business firms, the accomplishments of sales personnel seldom go unrecognized. Most people want to achieve some measure of security in their work. Selling is one of those occupations that usually provide job security during both good and bad times.

Opportunity for Advancement

Each year, thousands of openings appear in the ranks of supervision and management. Because salespeople work in positions of high visibility, they are in an excellent position to be chosen for advancement to positions of greater responsibility. The top executives of many of today's companies began their careers in the ranks of the sales force. As noted in a business article written by Theodore B. Kinni, "Today's C-suites are literally bursting with sales professionals."[24]

Of course, not all salespeople can become presidents of large corporations, but in the middle-management ranks there are numerous interesting and high-paying positions in which experience in selling is a prime requisite for advancement. Information on careers in sales management is presented in Chapter 17.

Opportunities for Women

Prodded by a growing awareness that gender is not a barrier to success in selling, business firms are recruiting qualified women in growing numbers. The percentage of women in the sales force has increased considerably. In fact, in sales and related occupations, women comprise approximately 50 percent of the workforce.[25] Although women are still relative newcomers to industrial sales, they have enjoyed expanded career opportunities in such areas as real estate, insurance, advertising services, investments, and travel services. A growing number of women are turning to sales employment because it offers excellent economic rewards[26] and, in many cases, a flexible work schedule. Flexible schedules are very appealing to women who want to balance career and family.

At Pitney Bowes, the nation's largest provider of corporate mail services, about 24 percent of the top employees are women. Many of the top salespeople are women who were formerly teachers.[27] Nationally, about 20 percent of all financial advisers are women.[28]

SELLING IN ACTION

Opportunities for Women in Sales

In a world that is beginning to value diversity, we are seeing growing opportunities for women in sales. However, some misinformation concerning women in sales still exists. Four common myths follow:

Myth: Women will not relocate or stick around long enough to repay the firm's hiring and training expenses. Today, working women make up nearly half of the workforce and they have made significant gains in a wide range of traditionally male-dominated areas. About 50 percent of the working women contribute more than half of their family's income. Most of the women in this group, who also outnumber male students in many business schools today, need to work, want to work, and seek rewarding career opportunities.

Myth: Women earn significantly less in sales than their male counterparts. Although a pay gap between men and women exists in the field of sales, it is relatively small compared with the earnings gap for women who work full time in the workforce as a whole.

Myth: Buyers are less accepting of female salespeople. In the field of personal selling, perceived expertise, likability, and trustworthiness can have a major influence on purchase decisions. Women who project these qualities seldom face rejection based on gender.

Myth: Women face special problems when assigned to selling positions in foreign countries. The truth is that recent research suggests that businesswomen often enjoy a significant edge over their male counterparts when given overseas assignments.[a]

Source: racorn/Shutterstock

In recent years, the labor market has become a place of churning dislocation caused by the heavy volume of mergers, acquisitions, business closings, bankruptcies, and downsizings. Personal-selling careers, as well as those career areas that value selling skills, have become attractive employment options to the thousands of professionals who walk away from—or are pushed out of—corporate jobs.

Employment Settings in Selling Today

1.4 Discuss the different employment settings in selling today

Careers in sales include both inside and outside sales positions. **Inside salespeople** are those who perform selling activities at the employer's location, typically using the telephone and e-mail. Many manufacturers and wholesalers have developed inside sales forces to take orders, make calls on customers, and provide support for field salespeople. In some cases, the inside salespeople are called customer service representatives (CSRs) and provide a number of support services on behalf of field salespeople.

Inside sales can be either "inbound" or "outbound." Inbound inside salespeople respond to calls initiated by the customer. For more insight on outside sales, see Appendix 2: The NewNet Systems Regional Accounts Management Case Study. Telemarketing is a common form of outbound inside sales that serves several purposes, including sales and service. In some cases, this includes technical support personnel who provide technical information and answer questions. Some companies utilize sales assistants to confirm appointments, conduct credit checks, and follow up on deliveries.[29] The use of telemarketing, websites, and the Internet has grown rapidly as businesses use these methods to contact potential new customers and to follow up on current customers or customers in distant areas.

Unlike inside sales, **outside salespeople** travel to meet prospects and customers in their places of business or residence. Information technology companies like Hewlett-Packard employ thousands of salespeople to sell computer systems, peripherals, and integrated technology solutions to other companies, large and small. Wholesalers, like Super Value, employ outside salespeople who, in addition to selling products, offer a variety of services to their customers, such as maintaining inventories, merchandising, providing promotional support, gathering and interpreting market information, extending credit, and distributing goods. In addition, many direct-to-consumer salespeople, such as interior designers, engage at least partially in outside sales; for example, financial services, life insurance, or direct sales.

Inside and outside salespeople for the same company often work together and rely heavily upon each other. For example, inside salespeople often prospect, generating and qualifying leads for outside salespeople to call on personally. Also, once an initial sale is made by an outside salesperson, inside salespeople are asked to provide ongoing customer contact and service, taking responsibility for meeting customer needs while being alert for opportunities to sell additional products or services.

Selling through Channels

Many times, people mistakenly think of selling jobs as being limited to the interaction between the company and the end user of the good or service. However, goods and services flow from manufacturer to end user through a "channel of distribution."

As can be seen in Figure 1.4, sales jobs exist throughout this supply chain.[30] In fact, many of the most promising sales careers in terms of career advancement and compensation exist at the beginning of the channel flow in the form of business-to-business, or "B2B," sales. **Trade selling** refers to the sale of a product or service to another member of the supply chain. For example, a manufacturer of household goods may employ sales representatives to sell his or her products to retailers. The manufacturer may instead (or also) sell the products to wholesalers who warehouse the product; in turn, the wholesaler employs sales representatives to sell these and other products to retailers whom the manufacturer does not want to service directly. In the latter part of the channel flow, we find retail salespeople and, in some cases, service salespeople selling to consumers. This is often referred to as "business-to-consumer," or "B2C" sales. As you can see, selling careers may be classified in several ways.

Similar scenarios exist with industrial products where the end user is a business rather than an individual consumer, and with services where the end user is either a consumer or business user. Another example of B2B sales is **missionary, or detail, sales**. Rather than selling directly to the end user, the missionary salesperson attempts to generate goodwill and stimulate demand for the manufacturer's product among channel members.

Career Opportunities in the Service Channel

Sales careers in service sales include both business-to-business and business-to-consumer sales. Today, approximately 80 percent of the U.S. labor force is employed in some capacity in the service sector of the economy. The growth rate for the service industry is much higher than the growth rate for product companies. Service companies provide career opportunities in a variety of settings.

HOTEL, MOTEL, AND CONVENTION CENTER SERVICES Every year in the United States, thousands of seminars, conferences, weddings, and business meetings take place in hotels, motels, and convention centers. According to the JW Marriott chain, the MICE market (meetings, incentives, conferences, and exhibitions) is worth about $106 billion in sales revenue.[31] The salespeople employed by these companies, often referred to as account managers, sales managers, or account executives, play important roles in attracting clients to utilize these facilities. Salespeople build relationships; carefully analyze needs; configure solutions; often upgrade services to sell room space, food, beverages, and entertainment; and can offer services to create an attractive atmosphere for potential clients. (For more insight into personal selling opportunities in the MICE market, refer to Appendix 3, Partnership Selling: A Role-Play.)

Typical of the salespeople employed in this service sector is Brian Moon, sales manager of the Renaissance Indian Wells Resort and Spa located in Indian Wells, California. This resort is a world-class facility located in the desert and includes exquisite swimming pools.[32] When Brian and his sales force encounter resistance from a client, they work diligently to identify the sources of the resistance, clarify the issues, and resolve the problems so as to consummate the sale. In the selling of hotel and convention center sales, as well as a number of the other types of service selling, salespeople may be involved in both B2B and B2C selling, depending upon whether they are selling to a business or to an individual. Buying motives and selling strategies described in later chapters will vary considerably depending upon whether the sale is B2B or B2C.

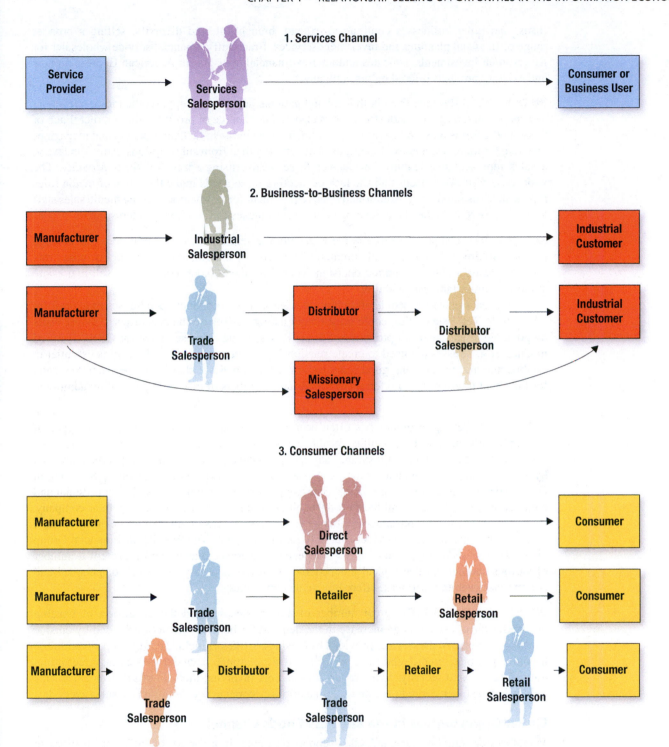

FIGURE 1.4

Shown here are salespeople in different channels.

TELECOMMUNICATIONS SERVICES The deregulation of telephone service resulted in the fragmentation of major telephone companies and the creation of numerous new communications companies. This has led to an increased need for telecommunications salespeople. These individuals must have a thorough knowledge of their system and a good understanding of competing telecommunications systems.

FINANCIAL SERVICES Today there are more than one million sales jobs in the securities and financial service field and employment continues to increase. Banks, credit unions, brokerage firms, and other businesses continue to expand, branch out, and diversify, selling a broader range of financial planning and investment services. Brad Duffy, financial service wholesaler for Riversource Investments, educates and advises financial advisors for American Express on new and existing products offered by his company.[33]

MEDIA SALES Revenue from both local and national advertising supports the radio, television, newspaper, and magazine industries and is also a major source of profit for the Internet. Each of these media forms must sell advertising to remain in business. In fact, newspapers and magazines generate far more revenue from the sales of advertising than from subscriptions. Amy Vandaveer, a sales representative featured in Chapter 6, sells advertising space for *Texas Monthly*. The wide variety of client needs and the task of meeting these needs make the work of media sales representatives interesting. Additionally, the requirement for the members of the media sales staff to develop or to help the client develop commercials makes this work very interesting.

REAL ESTATE The purchase of a home is usually the single-largest expenditure in the average person's lifetime. The purchase of commercial property by individual investors or business firms also represents a major economic decision. Therefore, the 800,000 people who sell real estate assume an important responsibility.

Busy real estate salespeople often hire sales associates to conduct open houses or to perform other tasks. Real estate salespeople must obtain listings, advertise the properties, conduct visits by potential clients, and sell properties. Susana Rosas, a sales representative for CBRE featured in Chapter 4, stresses the need to create relationships with her clients.[34] Honesty is essential in establishing and maintaining good relationships. Susana believes that if the experience is good for the client it will result in referrals to friends and members of the family, providing additional clients.

INSURANCE Selling insurance has often been a very rewarding career in sales. The types of insurance sold include fire, liability, health, automobile, casualty, homeowner, and business. There are two general types of insurance salespeople. One type consists of salespeople employed by major insurance companies such as Allstate, Farmers, Prudential, Travelers, State Farm, Geico, Hartford, and Mutual of Omaha. Salespeople for these companies sell both personal and commercial lines; however, all their product solutions are offered exclusively by their company. Ryan Guillory, whom we introduce in Chapter 2, is an excellent example of this type of salesperson who sells various insurance products but only for his company, The Woodlands Financial Group (TWFG). The second type consists of independent insurance agents who represent a number of various companies. The typical independent agency sells a very broad line of personal and commercial insurance services, offered by many companies.

BUSINESS SERVICES The great number of new businesses and the expansion of existing businesses have resulted in an increase in the demand for business services provided by outside contractors. Some of the services provided by outside contractors include computer programming, training, printing, credit reporting, payroll and accounting, payment processing, recruiting, transportation, and security. Many other sales careers involving the sale of services exist. This field is increasing at a rapid pace and sales positions become available in service sales every day.

Career Opportunities in the Business Goods Channel

Manufacturers employ sales and sales-support personnel in a variety of different positions in outside and inside sales. Outside salespeople interact with potential customers on a face-to-face basis. Some of the categories of outside salespeople include field salespeople, sales or application engineers, and missionary salespeople. Inside salespeople include customer service representatives (CSRs), who rely primarily on the telephone and the Internet to communicate with customers, to identify new prospects, and to carry out other sales activities.

INDUSTRIAL SALESPEOPLE Industrial salespeople include both technical salespeople (sales engineers or application engineers) and nontechnical salespeople. Sales engineers or technical salespeople sell heavy equipment, machinery, chemical products, aircraft, complex electronic equipment, and military equipment. Such salespeople must have a good technical understanding of their products and customer needs. Nontechnical salespeople generally sell office equipment; disposable goods such as adhesives, cleaners, and packaging; and office supplies.

What Motivates Salespeople?

A recent study of more than 40,000 salespeople worldwide reported that 36 percent of U.S. salespeople and 33 percent of the salespeople in the United Kingdom say they work primarily to earn substantial incomes. The same statistic for New Zealand and Norway peers was only 9 percent and 11 percent, respectively. Unlike their counterparts in other countries who considered sales a temporary step to being promoted to management, successful U.S. salespeople preferred to make more money in sales rather than be promoted into management.[b]

SALES ENGINEER OR APPLICATIONS ENGINEER Sales or applications engineers must possess a detailed and thorough technical knowledge of their products as well as competing products. These salespeople must be able to identify and analyze customer problems and develop solutions that meet the customer's needs. These sales engineers must be technically proficient in all aspects of their products and in communicating the merits and advantages of the products to the customer.

Steve Tice, president of Sim Graphics Engineering Corporation, and Steve Glenn, vice president for new business development, are the primary sales engineers for the corporation.[35] Sim Graphics develops automated graphic simulation systems for use in industries, hospitals, and educational institutions. Their company utilizes customized demonstration presentations for potential customers. Many potential customers fail to understand the complexity of the systems, so demonstrations are needed to show what actually is available. On some occasions, it is necessary to build and demonstrate a prototype or to make a full-blown presentation. Customers who do not understand the product will be reluctant to purchase something they don't comprehend.

FIELD SALESPEOPLE **Field salespeople** interact with new customers and current customers. They must be able to identify customer needs and requirements and to recommend the proper product or service to meet the customer's needs. Field salespeople who provide excellent service to their customers often receive information from their satisfied customers on new leads. These customers often provide recommendations to other potential customers for the field salesperson.

Betty Robertson, president of Lyncole Industries, is also the field sales representative for her company. Lyncole sells piping and associated supplies to contractors. Robertson states that following up on the installation of the equipment is very important. The contractors she sells to are potential repeat customers; it is essential to follow up and make certain that the customer is satisfied.[36]

Missionary salespeople, also known as "detail salespeople," serve to develop goodwill, provide information, and stimulate demand for the manufacturer's products. A missionary salesperson does not sell the product but receives recognition for increasing the sale of products indirectly. Missionary salespeople must be able to provide technical product information and offer sound advice in areas including credit policies, pricing, display, layout, and storage.

Deborah Karish, a sales representative for Amgen, stresses relationship selling in her work with medical facilities while selling to both medical staff and physicians. She had to learn the technology of her products, how they were manufactured, and how the medicines could be utilized most effectively in treating patients. She went through a pairing program with physicians to learn how the products are used. Karish knows it is necessary to establish good relationships with the medical staff. Failing to establish good relationships generally means that the people will not work with the salesperson.

Career Opportunities in the Consumer Goods Channel

Sales careers in the consumer goods channel, referred to earlier as "B2C" selling, include both retail-selling and direct-selling careers. Conventional retailers face increased competition from online retailers. Consumers spend billions of dollars on Internet purchases. Traditional retailers are forced to offer customers more than products in order to compete effectively against online sellers. Well-trained salespeople can add value to the traditional shopping experience.

RETAIL SELLING A large number of salespeople work in retail. Retail selling is probably an excellent area for gaining initial sales experience. Retail-selling careers abound in a number of product areas.

A well-trained retail salesperson can add significant value to the retail buying experience. Trainees after working 8 to 15 months for the Asbury Automotive Group earn between $45,000 and $60,000 per year in salary plus bonus. Significant management opportunities also exist for those who create value in the partnership selling process.

Source: goodluz/Fotolia

Asbury Automotive Group employs 1,440 sales personnel. These salespeople take pride in their work and are rewarded with a promising career. Many of the sales personnel were recruited at college and university job fairs. Some work as management trainees, selling cars for 8 to 15 months, making $45,000 to $60,000 per year in salary plus bonus. Then they are trained and certified to work in the finance and insurance department. Next, some are promoted to new- or used-car manager, earning $100,000 to $150,000 per year. The final promotion opportunity is general manager of the dealership.[37]

Mike Patterson, the owner of MP Yacht Services, provides specialized electrical repairs and installations for boats. His easy sales approach and high technical performance have attracted a large group of repeat customers to whom he offers electrical services that competitors are unable to provide. Patterson firmly believes that one should never bad-mouth a competitor, and his philosophy has resulted in competitors referring customers to MP Yacht Services.[38]

The sales staff at Julian's in Chapel Hill, North Carolina, take pride in their work. This family-owned business, founded in 1942, is located near the University of North Carolina (UNC). The store sells custom-order clothing to UNC alumni who live all over the South. Some buy private-label suits created by the founder's son, Alexander Julian, who is a noted fashion designer.[39]

Direct salespeople are independent contractors who generally represent manufacturers. In 2014, *Direct Selling News* reported there are 18.2 million direct salespeople in the United States and 78.2 million outside this country.[40] The top 15 countries each have more than $1 billion in direct sales revenue and are a combination of old and new markets. Together they account for $90.8 billion in annual revenues for the world's direct-selling companies, which translates to almost 90 percent of the industry's global sales. The United States is number one with $29.6 billion in revenues, Japan is a close second with $27 billion, and Korea is number three with $8 billion. According to Neil Offen, past-president of U.S. Direct Selling Association, the international growth rate of direct selling is exceeding domestic growth.

A rapidly growing form of direct sales is network (or multilevel) marketing. The three largest U.S.-based firms in direct marketing are Amway, Avon, and Mary Kay with $2.2 billion in sales

INTRODUCING CRM (CUSTOMER RELATIONSHIP MANAGEMENT SYSTEMS)

Learning about CRM Systems—Salesforce, NetSuite, Siebel, Sugar CRM, SalesLogic, etc.

Many technology tools are available to today's salespeople and marketing personnel because there is so much information to manage. There is one category of software specifically designed for a salesperson's responsibilities. **Customer relationship management (CRM)**, sometimes referred to as "sales automation," is software that records in one place the extensive information necessary to understand a customer and their needs and expectations. This type of software is becoming essential because it can be used to capture and rapidly display the information needed to work toward assuring the satisfaction of many customers at the same time. In addition to providing the basic data about a company and its products, CRM software offers information needed to build partnering relationships and add value throughout the sales process.

CRM enables its user to easily sort and store information so it can be quickly retrieved to enhance each customer contact. When a conversation is social, at a salesperson's fingertips is the name of a customer's spouse. One can be quickly reminded of a buyer's favorites when arranging lunch or golf. Product delivery and credit preferences are available in case the topics are raised in an e-mail. CRM keeps a salesperson intimately involved in a sale by identifying the customer's stage in the sales process, reminding the salesperson about tasks and due dates to move the sale along, keeping track of all previous steps in the process and information shared, and displaying personal information recorded about those involved in a purchase in order to improve relationships with them.

CRM has gone mobile. CRM mobile apps—predictive and less hierarchical in a big way—interact with map, image, content, and note-taking apps. The focus is on management of real-time data as salespeople lean towards showing demos, analytics, and dashboards on mobile phones and towards integration of information across platforms focused on sales automation, analytics software, and sales accounting system. As the sales profession becomes even more specialized and industry focused, we should also expect more vertical CRMs that focus on industry-specific CRM solutions. Examples include Veeva, which focuses on pharma and healthcare; Vlocity, which focuses on communications, media and insurance; and OpenGov, which focuses on public sector.

Leading CRM software company websites include www.Salesforce.com, www.NetSuite.com, www.SugarCRM.com, www.SalesLogic.com, and www.Siebel.com. Each of these companies supplies training videos and, in some cases, free trial demos. Their training videos can also be accessed on YouTube. To learn about these companies, and to access their videos and free trials, click on their website. *In Chapter 2, you will be provided instructions for signing up and accessing a free trial and videos for the Salesforce.com CRM Software. You will learn in future chapters how CRM enhances the effectiveness of high-performing salespeople in their efforts to establish relationships, partner with, and meet and exceed their customers' needs and expectations.*

and 1.1 million salespeople.[41] In this form of distribution, manufacturers eschew advertising and other trade/promotional spending, relying instead on a large network of independent consultants or distributors to sell the product or service directly to consumers or businesses. The independent consultant builds his or her business not only through the direct sales of the product or service to consumers, but also by sponsoring new consultants to sell the company's products or services. The sponsoring consultant then earns commissions on the product/service sales generated by the new consultant, in addition to what he or she personally sells. The number of levels on which a consultant is paid varies by company, but the benefit to the consultant is the ability to leverage his or her own efforts plus those of other consultants in his or her "downline." These types of organizations are highly reliant on socialization, communication, and cooperation between consultants for successful sales results.[42]

Selling Skills—One of the "Master Skills for Success" in the Information Age

1.5 Explain how personal selling skills have become one of the master skills needed for success in the information age and how personal selling skills contribute to the work performed by knowledge workers

In his best-selling book *Megatrends*, John Naisbitt noted **"the game of life in the information age is people interacting with other people."**[43] With its emphasis on effective and adaptive interpersonal interaction, selling has become one of the "master skills for success in the information economy."

A study reported in Daniel Pink's *To Sell Is Human* makes a similar observation concerning what he calls the rise of "nonsales selling." He reports in his statistically correct sample of 7,000 individuals in the workforce:

1. People are now spending about 40 percent of their time at work engaged in nonsales selling—persuading, influencing, and convincing others in ways that don't involve anyone making a purchase.

2. Across a range of professions, people are devoting roughly 24 minutes of every hour moving others—what Pink refers to as "nonsales selling."

3. Respondents consider moving others—that is, a nonsales-selling skill set—as crucial to their professional success.[44]

Knowledge Workers in the Information Economy

Stanley Marcus, founder of the prestigious Neiman Marcus Company, said, "Sooner or later in business, everybody has to sell something to somebody." He noted that even if you are not in sales, you must know how to sell a product, a service, an idea, or yourself.[45] Marcus's views have garnered a great deal of support among observers of the information age. Today's workforce is made up of millions of knowledge workers who succeed only when they add value to information. **Knowledge workers** are individuals whose work effort is centered around creating, using, sharing, and applying knowledge. The information economy is about the growing value of knowledge, making it the most important ingredient of what people buy and sell.[46] One way to add value to information is to collect it, organize it, clarify it, and present it in a convincing manner. This skill, used every day by professional salespeople, is invaluable in a world that is overloaded with information.

As noted earlier, relationships have become more important in the information age. In many cases, information does not have value unless people interact effectively. Creating networks with social ties allows knowledge workers to acquire and provide information more successfully.[47] For example, a salesperson may possess information concerning an important new technology, but that information has no value until it is communicated effectively to an investor, a customer, or someone else who can benefit from knowing more about his product. A bank loan officer may have the resources needed to assist a prospective homeowner in reaching her dream, but in the absence of a good relationship, communications may break down. Thus, in the information age, it becomes important for firms to create structures to encourage knowledge sharing.[48]

Individuals who have developed skills associated with careers in sales are more likely to be successful when they decide to go out on their own because, more often than not, those skills translate very well to other businesses.[49] Today, personal-selling skills contribute in a major way to four groups of knowledge workers who may not consider themselves salespeople:

- Managerial personnel
- Professionals (accountants, consultants, lawyers, architects, engineers, etc.)
- Entrepreneurs and small business owners
- Marketing personnel and customer service representatives

Managerial Personnel

People working in managerial occupations represent a large group of knowledge workers. They are given such titles as "executive," "manager," or "administrator." Leaders are constantly involved in capturing, processing, and communicating information. Some of the most valuable information is acquired from customers. This helps explain the rapid growth in what is being described as "executive selling." Chief executive officers and other executives often accompany salespeople on sales calls to learn more about customer needs and, in some cases, to assist with presentations. Manny Fernandez of the Gartner Group, a technology-consulting firm based in Stamford, Connecticut, spent more than half his time traveling on sales calls.[50] Leaders also must articulate their ideas in a persuasive manner and win support for their vision. Brian Tracy, author of *The 100 Absolutely Unbreakable Laws of Business Success*, says, "People who cannot present their ideas or sell themselves effectively have very little influence and are not highly respected."[51]

Professionals

Today's professional workers include lawyers, designers, programmers, engineers, consultants, dietitians, counselors, doctors, accountants, and many other specialized knowledge workers. Our labor force includes nearly 20 million professional service providers, persons who need many of the skills used by professional salespeople. Clients who purchase professional services are usually more interested in the person who delivers the service than in the firm that employs the professional. They seek expert diagnosticians who are truly interested in their needs. The

SELLING IS EVERYONE'S BUSINESS

Successful Entrepreneur's Early Start in Sales

At the age of 12, Michael Dell, CEO of Dell Computer Corporation, was displaying the characteristics of an opportunistic entrepreneur. He turned his stamp-collecting hobby into a mail-order business that netted $2,000. This money was used to purchase his first computer. He also developed his personal-selling skills at an early age. At age 16, he was selling subscriptions to his hometown paper, the *Houston Post.* Later, he enrolled in college but had difficulty focusing on his coursework. He often cut classes in order to spend more time assembling and selling computers. When Dell's parents discovered his newest enterprise, they pressured him to stay focused on completing his degree. Dell completed the spring semester and then spent the summer expanding his business. In the month prior to the fall semester, he sold $180,000 worth of computers. He did not return to college.[c]

Source: Bloomberg/Getty Images

professional must display good communication skills and be able to build a relationship built on trust.

Technical skills are not enough in the information age. Many employers expect the professional to bring in new business, often referred to as **business or client development**, in addition to keeping current customers satisfied. Employers often screen professional applicants to determine their customer focus, ability to interact well with people, and business and client development skills.

Many firms are providing their professional staff with sales training. The accounting firm Ernst & Young sets aside several days each year to train its professional staff in personal selling. The National Law Firm Marketing Association featured Neil Rackham, author of *SPIN Selling*, as keynote speaker at one of their national conferences. The Wicker Corporation, a manufacturer of equipment for the plastics industry, has initiated a program designed to motivate its researchers, engineers, and manufacturing staff members to get involved in sales. Faced with increased competition and more cost-conscious customers, a growing number of law, accounting, engineering, and architectural firms are discovering the merits of personal selling as an auxiliary activity.[52]

Entrepreneurs and Small Business Owners

About 400,000 people start new businesses each year in the United States.[53] As noted previously, people who want to start a new business frequently need to sell their plan to investors and others who can help get the firm established. Once the firm is open, owners rely on personal selling to build their businesses.

James Koch, chief executive officer of the Boston Beer Company (brewer of Samuel Adams beer), makes a strong case for personal selling. Like most new companies, his started with no customers. To get the new company established, he assumed the role of salesperson and set a goal of establishing one new account each week.

Today Koch continues to spend time on the street, visiting convenience stores, supermarkets, and taverns. Competition from popular craft beers such as Fat Tire and Magic Hat, and imports such as Stella Artois and Beck's, present a major challenge. He's also trying to get the attention of young men who think of Samuel Adams as their father's beer. He readily admits that selling his beer is the most rewarding part of his job. Koch could have sold his company to a megabrewer long ago, but that option is not appealing to this wealthy entrepreneur who loves to sell.[54]

SELLING IS EVERYONE'S BUSINESS

Job Sharing at the Vice President Level—Teaching Sales

Cynthia Cunningham and Shelley Murray worked 60-hour work-weeks to achieve success as BankBoston branch managers. They wanted more time with their children, but the long hours created a major barrier to motherhood. Then they came up with a novel plan: package themselves and share one job. Once the plan was developed, the selling began. They wrote a letter that described their accomplishments, attached a résumé, and delivered the package to several senior executives. Eventually they met with more than a dozen executives and finally hit pay dirt. They began sharing a vice president–level job that involved teaching branch personnel and small businesses how to sell their services to customers. Cunningham and Murray now work 20 to 25 hours each week at what has since become Fleet Bank.[d]

Marketing Personnel and Customer Service Representatives

Because of the close working relationships with customers, it is imperative that marketing directors, product managers, marketing research specialists, warehouse and shipping specialists, and others within marketing and sales must understand and, in most cases, acquire the skills of personal selling. This generally results in a much more productive effort for the company, and a satisfied customer base.

The assignment of selling duties to employees with customer service responsibilities has become quite common today. The term **customer service representative (CSR)** is used to describe knowledge workers who process reservations, accept orders by phone or other means, deliver products, handle customer complaints, provide technical assistance, and assist full-time sales representatives. Some companies are teaming CSRs and salespeople. After the sale is closed, the CSR helps process paperwork, check on delivery of the product, and engage in other customer follow-up duties. In addition to increased service quality, the improved customer expertise from this process improves customer loyalty.[55]

Assigning sales duties to customer service representatives makes sense when you consider the number of contacts customers have with CSRs. When a customer seeks assistance with a problem or makes a reservation, the CSR learns more about the customer and often provides the customer with needed information. Customer needs often surface as both parties exchange information. It is important to keep in mind the advice offered by the authors of *Selling the Invisible*: "Every act is a marketing act. Make every employee a marketing person."[56]

Increasingly, work in the information economy is understood as an expression of thought. At a time when people change their careers eight or more times during their lives, selling skills represent important transferable employment skills.

1.6 Identify the four major sources of sales training

Learning to Sell

"Are salespeople made or are they born?" This classic question seems to imply that some people are born with certain qualities that give them a special advantage in the selling field. This is not true. The principles of adaptive selling, listening, and customer orientation can be learned and applied by people whose personal characteristics are quite different.[57]

In the past few decades, sales training has been expanded on four fronts. These four sources of training are corporate-sponsored training, training provided by commercial vendors, certification programs, and courses provided by colleges and universities.

Corporate-Sponsored Training

Hundreds of business organizations, such as Apple Computer, IBM, Maytag, Western Electric, and Zenith, have established training programs. These large corporations spend millions of dollars each year to develop their salespeople. *Training* magazine, which conducts annual analyses of employer-provided training in U.S. organizations, indicates that salespeople are among the most intensively trained employee groups. A new salesperson preparing for a consultative-selling position may spend a few months to a year or more in training. For many salespeople, the training is as close as their laptop computer. Lucent Technologies, for example, uses web-based training for about one-third of its training courses.[58]

Training Provided by Commercial Vendors

The programs designed by firms specializing in the development of sales personnel are a second source of sales training. Some of the most popular courses are offered by Richardson E Learning, Acclivus Corporation, Wilson Learning Corporation, Miller Heiman Inc., Dale Carnegie Training, and AchieveGlobal (see Table 1.2). The legendary Professional Selling Skills (PSS) course, developed by Gene Keluche, is still offered by AchieveGlobal. This carefully designed course, once owned by Xerox, has been completed by millions of salespeople.[59]

Certification Programs

The trend toward increased professionalism in personal selling has been the stimulus for a third type of training and education initiative. Many salespeople are returning to the classroom to earn

TABLE 1.2 Sales Training Offered by Commercial Vendors

Training programs provided by commercial vendors are very popular. This table introduces a few of the well-established sales training programs offered throughout America.

COMPANY	TRAINING PROGRAMS	DESCRIPTION
Sales Performance International www.spisales.com	• Solution Selling • Opportunity Selling	Provides sales training based on concepts explained in *The New Solution Selling,* by Keith Eades
Integrity Systems, Inc. www.integritysystems .com	• Integrity Selling • The Customer	Provides sales training based on concepts explained in *Integrity Selling for the 21st Century,* by Ron Willingham
	• Spin Selling Certificate • Creating Client Value	Provides sales training based on concepts in *The SPIN Selling Fieldbook,* by Neil Rackham
Miller Heiman, Inc. www.millerheimangroup .com/sales-ready	• Strategic Selling • Conceptual Selling	Provides sales training based on concepts presented in *Strategic Selling* and *The New Conceptual Selling*
	• Professional Selling • Professional Sales	Provides the original Xerox *Professional Selling Skills* (PSS) sales training; *Course Content Coaching* has been updated
Wilson Learning Worldwide www.wilsonlearning.com	• The Versatile Salesperson	Provides updated sales training based on the original Larry Wilson *Counselor Selling Training Program*
Dale Carnegie Training, Inc. www.dalecarnegie.com	• Sales Advantage • How to Sell Like a Pro	One of the largest international training companies providing sales training using many of the concepts presented in the Dale Carnegie books, such as *How to Win Friends and Influence People*
Richardson E Learning www.richardson.com	• Richardson Quick Learning	*Richardson QuickSkills*™ 5.0 incorporates a set of online tools that allows for improved efficiency in developing and delivering customized and tailored online sales training courses

TABLE 1.3 Sales Training Offered by a Sample of Universities

A large number of two- and four-year colleges and universities have established extensive educational programs for students interested in sales. Sales programs have also recently become an important part of the MBA curriculum at several elite universities. This table from the Sales Education Foundation provides a representative sample of universities that offer a variety of sales-training program options.

	GRADUATE PROGRAM	SPECIALTY AREA	COMPETITION PARTICIPANT	INTERNSHIP REQUIRED	TOTAL FACULTY	% OF JOB PLACEMENT
Auburn University		▲	▲		2	*
Ball State University	▲	▲	▲		4	90
Baylor University			▲	▲	5	100
Bradley University			▲		3	100
California State University, Chico		▲	▲		9	90
California State University, Fullerton	▲	▲	▲		5	90
Central Michigan University			▲	▲	5	100
Clemson University			▲		3	100
The College of New Jersey		▲	▲		1	70
Concordia University, St. Paul			▲	▲	*	*
DePaul University	▲	▲	▲	▲	17	82
Douglas College		▲	▲		*	90
Duquesne University		▲	▲		5	92
Elon University		▲	▲	▲	3	90
Ferris State University		▲	▲	▲	10	85
Florida State University	▲	▲	▲	▲	4	100
Georgia Southern University		▲	▲		4	90
Georgia State University	▲	▲	▲		7	80
Illinois State University		▲	▲		4	100
Indiana State University	▲	▲	▲		4	75
Indiana University			▲	▲	3	93
Kansas State University			▲	▲	11	88
Kennesaw State University		▲	▲		7	98
Michigan State University		▲	▲	▲	4	100
Missouri State University			▲		3	*
Nicholls State University		▲	▲		1	85
North Carolina A&T State University			▲		3	90
Northern Illinois University	▲		▲		6	100
Nova Southeastern University	▲	▲			8	*
Ohio University			▲	▲	5	98
Plymouth State University			▲	▲	4	*
St. Catherine University		▲	▲	▲	6	98
Texas State University (San Marcos)			▲	▲	4	95
Tuskegee University			▲		6	66
University of Akron	▲	▲	▲	▲	5	100
University of Alabama	▲	▲	▲		5	100
University of Alabama at Birmingham			▲		7	80

	GRADUATE PROGRAM	SPECIALTY AREA	COMPETITION PARTICIPANT	INTERNSHIP REQUIRED	TOTAL FACULTY	% OF JOB PLACEMENT
University of Arkansas at Little Rock			▲		2	*
University of Central Florida			▲		5	100
University of Central Missouri		▲	▲		2	*
University of Central Oklahoma		▲	▲		7	100
University of Cincinnati	▲		▲		10	95
University of Connecticut		▲	▲	▲	4	100
University of Dayton		▲	▲		5	92
University of Georgia		▲	▲	▲	2	100
University of Houston	▲		▲		11	98
University of Louisville		▲	▲	▲	2	*
University of Nebraska at Kearney (IDSD)		▲	▲	▲	4	100
University of Nebraska at Kearney (PBSMB)					2	62
University of New Haven, The		▲	▲	▲	3	100
University of North Alabama		▲	▲	▲	7	100
University of North Carolina: Kenan-Flagler Business School	▲	▲	▲		2	90
University of Southern Mississippi, The		▲	▲		3	*
University of Toledo	▲	▲	▲	▲	10	100
University of Washington		▲	▲	▲	*	92
University of Wisconsin–Eau Claire		▲	▲		9	100
University of Wisconsin–Parkside		▲	▲		3	90
Virginia Tech		▲	▲		3	*
Washington State University		▲	▲		2	95
Weber State University	▲		▲	▲	12	100
West Virginia University			▲	▲	4	100
Western Carolina University			▲	▲	*	*
Western Kentucky University			▲		5	*
Western Michigan University			▲		4	90
Widener University			▲		1	80
William Paterson University		▲	▲		7	90
Winona State University			▲		2	94
Xavier University of Louisiana			▲		2	75

Source: Used with permission of the Chally Group Worldwide. Used with permission.

certification in a sales or sales-related area. In the pharmaceutical industry, many salespeople earn the Certified Medical Representative (CMR) designation. The CMR curriculum includes nearly 40 courses that are delivered to more than 9,000 students. The National Automobile Dealers Association sponsors the Code of Conduct Certification program for automotive sales representatives. Both of these certification programs require extensive study of modules and the completion of rigorous examinations. Sales & Marketing Executives–International offers the Certified Sales Executive (CSE) designation to sales professionals who meet the highest standards of education, experience, and ethical conduct.

Some companies have developed their own sales-training certification programs. The Pitney Bowes Certified Postal Consultant (CPC) program is designed to improve the level of assistance given to customers who want to upgrade their mail process. It is available to members of the 4,000-person Pitney Bowes sales force who sell both products (postage meters) and services. Freightliner developed a certification program for its 1,800-member sales force. The various courses include topics ranging from product knowledge to truck-selling skills.[60]

College and University Courses

The fourth source of sales training is personal-selling courses offered by colleges and universities throughout the United States (see Table 1.3). A large majority of the nation's community colleges and undergraduate business schools offer this course, and it is attracting more interest among business majors. Sales training has become an important part of the MBA curriculum at several elite universities as well.[61] Although there is no formulaic answer that can be applicable to all selling situations,[62] these courses provide students with a repertoire of skills that help them become more effective. Some two- and four-year colleges have developed extensive educational programs for students interested in a sales career. The Sales Center Alliance (www.salescenteralliance.com) was established to advance the sales profession through academic leadership. The University of Akron, the University of Houston, Ball State University, Baylor University, Kennesaw State University, and many other schools offer undergraduate programs for students who are preparing for a career in personal selling.

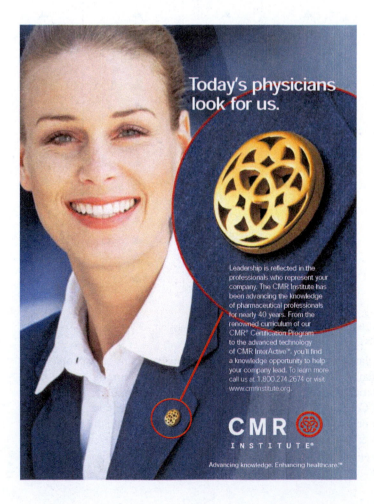

For over 35 years, the Certified Medical Representatives Institute has been empowering sales representatives who call on medical professionals. The CMR certification program is designed to increase sales performance.

Source: CMR Institute

CHAPTER LEARNING ACTIVITIES

Reviewing Key Concepts

Define personal selling and describe the three prescriptions of a personal selling philosophy

Personal selling occurs when a company representative interacts directly with a customer or prospective customer to present information about a product or service. Salespeople are encouraged to develop a personal-selling philosophy based on three prescriptions: adopt the marketing concept, value personal selling, and assume the role of a problem solver or partner.

Describe the emergence of relationship selling in the age of information

The restructuring of America from an industrial economy to an information economy began in the 1950s. We now live in an age in which the effective exchange of information is the foundation of most economic transactions. Salespeople use a variety of information technology tools to gather and process information of value to the customer.

Discuss the rewarding aspects of a career in selling today

Selling careers offer many rewards not found in other occupations. Income, both monetary and psychic, is above average, and there are many opportunities for advancement. Salespeople enjoy job security, mobility, and independence. Opportunities in selling for members of minority groups and for women are growing. In addition, selling is very interesting work, because a salesperson is constantly in contact with people. The adage "no two people are alike" reminds us that sales work is never dull or routine.

Discuss the different employment settings in selling today

The text describes each of the three major career options and employment opportunities in the field of personal selling, namely, services, business goods, and consumer goods. Keep in mind that each category features a wide range of selling positions, varying in terms of educational requirements, earning potential, and type of customer served. The discussion and examples should help you discover which kind of sales career best suits your talents and interests.

Explain how personal selling skills have become one of the master skills needed for success in the information age and how personal selling skills contribute to the work performed by knowledge workers

Today's workforce is made up of millions of *knowledge workers* who succeed only when they add value to information. The new economy rewards salespeople and other knowledge workers who collect, organize, clarify, and present information in a convincing manner. Selling skills contribute in a major way to four groups of knowledge workers who usually do not consider themselves salespeople: customer service representatives, professionals (accountants, consultants, lawyers, etc.), entrepreneurs, and managerial personnel.

Identify the four major sources of sales training

Sales training can be acquired from four key sources: corporate-sponsored training, training provided by commercial vendors, certification programs, and courses offered by colleges and universities. Many MBA programs are now including professional selling and sales management in the curriculum.

Key Terms

Personal selling, p. 5
Product, p. 5
Personal-selling philosophy,
  p. 5

Information economy, p. 5
Selling, p. 6
Value-added selling, p. 7
Psychic income, p. 10

Inside salespeople, p. 11
Outside
  salespeople, p. 11
Trade selling, p. 12

Missionary, or detail, sales, p. 12
Field salespeople, p. 15
Missionary salespeople, p. 15

Direct salespeople, p. 16
Customer relationship management, p. 17
Knowledge workers, p. 18

Business or client development, p. 19
Customer service representative (CSR), p. 20

MyMarketingLab

To complete the problems with the ⭐ in your MyLab, go to the EOC Discussion Questions.

Review Questions

1-1 Explain how personal selling can help solve the problem of information overload.

⭐ **1-2** According to the Strategic/Consultative–Selling Model (see Figure 1.1), what are the three prescriptions for developing a successful personal-selling philosophy?

1-3 List and describe the four employment settings for people who are considering a selling career.

1-4 What future for women is there in selling?

⭐ **1-5** Some salespeople have an opportunity to earn certification in a sales or sales-related area. How can a salesperson benefit from certification?

1-6 Explain why high-performance value-added salespeople earn much more than high-performance transactional salespeople.

1-7 List three titles commonly used to describe manufacturing salespeople. Describe the duties of each.

1-8 Develop a list of eight selling-career opportunities in the service field.

1-9 List and briefly describe the four major sources of sales training.

Application Exercises

1-10 Examine a magazine or newspaper ad for a new product or service that you have never seen. Evaluate its chances for receiving wide customer acceptance. Does this product require a large amount of personal-selling effort? What types of salespeople (service, manufacturing, wholesale, or retail) are involved in selling this product?

1-11 For each of the following job classifications, name at least one person you know in that field:
  a. Full-time person who sells a service
  b. Full-time inside wholesale salesperson
  c. Full-time manufacturer's salesperson
  d. Full-time retail salesperson
Interview one of the people you have listed, asking the following questions concerning their duties and responsibilities:
  a. What is your immediate supervisor's title?
  b. What would be a general description of your position?
  c. What specific duties and responsibilities do you have?
  d. What is the compensation plan and salary range for a position like yours?
Write a job description from this information.

1-12 Shelly Jones, a vice president and partner in the Chicago office of the consulting firm Korn/Ferry International, has looked into the future and sees some new challenges for salespeople. She recently shared the following predictions with *Selling Power* magazine:
  a. Salespeople will spend more time extending the range of applications or finding new markets for the products they sell.
  b. The selling function will be less of pitching your product and more of integrating your product into the business equation of your client. Understanding the business environment in which your client operates will be critical.

    c. In the future, you will have to be a financial engineer for your client. You need to understand how your client makes money and be able to explain how your product or service contributes to profitable operation of the client's firm.

Interview a salesperson who is involved in business-to-business selling—a manufacturer's representative, for example—and determine whether this person agrees with the views of Shelly Jones.

1-13 There are many information sources on selling careers and career opportunities on the Internet. Two examples include Monster.com and CareerBuilder.com. Search the Internet for information on selling careers.

    Use your search engine to find career information on a pharmaceutical representative, a field sales engineer, and a retail salesperson.

Role-Play Exercise

This role-play will give you experience in selling your knowledge, skills, and experience to a prospective employer. You will be meeting with a class member who will assume the role of an employer who is developing a new sales team. Prior to this interview, reflect on the courses you have completed, work experience, and other life experiences that may have value in the eyes of the employer. You may also want to reflect on any volunteer work you have completed and leadership roles you have held. Be prepared to discuss the personal-selling skills you are developing in this course, skills you have learned in previous employment settings, and related skills you have learned in other courses you have taken, such as psychology, communications, sociology, and so forth.

Reality Selling Case Problem—
Alex Homer/Tom James Company

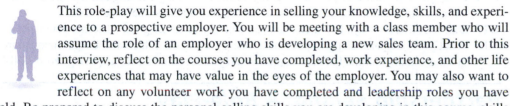

Alex Homer, featured at the beginning of this chapter, works as a professional clothier for the Tom James Company (www.tomjames.com). Alex sells a comprehensive collection of high-quality attire: formal (black tie/tuxedo), business (suits), business casual (sport coats, slacks, etc.), and weekend (jeans, sport shirts, shorts, khakis, etc.). His clients are typically gentlemen and ladies who do not have time to go to the store, dislike the idea of store shopping, or have fit characteristics that present challenges for purchasing clothing "off-the-peg."

For Alex, it is important to call on existing customers as well as prospects and to be aware of the different approaches used in each type of sales call. Typically, prior to visiting with an existing customer, he puts together clothing ideas for the season that make sense for the client based on how she/he dresses and how much her/his closet is lacking in a particular area (e.g., shirts or slacks). For new prospects, Alex contacts them by telephone. Realizing that cold-calling is an antiquated way of building a long-standing and fruitful sales career, the Tom James Company emphasizes the importance of referrals to build a business. Referrals tend to be easier to contact by phone and they typically purchase more in person, due to the strength of the referrer's name. All in all, referrals remove many obstacles to turning a person who is completely unaware of one's business into a client.

According to Alex, the biggest challenge in his business is getting in front of people. This challenge stems from many possible sources: lack of time for the prospect, perceived price/value imbalance, lack of experience in in-office clothing shopping, and being perceived as a "suit" company rather than an all-inclusive clothing provider.

Especially for repeat clients, who represent 80 percent of the company's annual business, Alex Homer describes solid call preparation as key for successful selling. If the salesperson is unprepared and shows up in the client's office with bag-in-hand and a "what-are-you-buying-today?" attitude, clients can sense this and become frustrated. They understand that professional clothiers provide a service and expect them to be prepared as a partner/problem solver regarding their wardrobes. As Alex puts it, "Stores provide clothing. Tom James provides a service."

When it comes to understanding the needs of a prospect, Alex follows a certain sales process: He first asks his clients what is most important to them when they go clothing shopping. For most of his clients, it is one of four things: price, quality, fit, and trend-sensitivity. Based on that, he determines what clothing the clients wear during the vital parts of their business (client meetings, board meetings, trial, close-the-sale presentations, speaking engagements, etc.). Then he asks how they would evaluate their closet (excellent, good, fair, or poor). Finally, if applicable, he finds out what it would take to make a slight improvement in their closet. (See the chapter opener on page 4 and Reality Selling Today Role-Play 1 in Appendix 1 for more information.)

Questions

1-14   Does it appear that Tom James and Alex Homer have a personal-selling philosophy like that described in this chapter? Provide examples that support each of the three prescriptions.

1-15   Put yourself in the position of Alex Homer. What might be the most rewarding and the most adverse aspects of his sales job?

1-16   Describe how Alex uses personal-selling skills in utilizing existing knowledge and gathering new information from the customer in order to advance the sales process.

1-17   Discuss different ways in which Alex can actively generate good customer referrals.

1-18   What skills are particularly important for Alex's sales job? Which of the four major sources of sales training outlined in this chapter would you recommend for acquiring those skills?

Partnership Selling: A Role-Play (see Appendix 3, page 419)

Learning about the new Upscale Park Shores Resort and Convention Center, Partnership Selling Role-Play

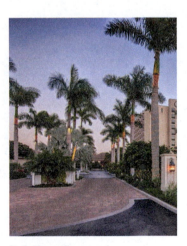

Park Shores Resort and Convention Center.

Source: Courtesy of Beach Resort

[If your instructor has chosen to use the Partnership-Selling Role-Play exercise that accompanies this text, these boxes alert you to your Role-Play assignments. Your instructor will also provide you with needed information.]

Preview the role-play materials in Appendix 3. The role-play materials are produced by the Southern California beachfront Park Shores Resort and Convention Center, and you will be using them in your role as a new salesperson (and, at times, as the customer) for the hotel and its convention services.

The role-play exercises begin in Chapter 6, as you begin to create your product strategy. However, in anticipation of the role-play, you can begin to imagine yourself in the role of an actual salesperson. Start to think about how you can develop your personal-selling philosophy. What are some ethical guidelines that you may wish to adopt for yourself? (Ethics is also the subject of Chapter 3, "Ethics: The Foundation for Relationships in Selling.") What skills do you need to develop to become a partner with your prospective customers? (Refer to the position description in Part I of Appendix 3.)

The Park Shores has implemented a quality improvement process. How does this affect your role as a sales representative? (Refer to the Total Quality Customer Service Glossary in Part I of Appendix 3.)

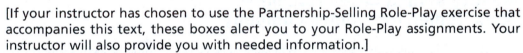

MyMarketingLab

Go to the Assignments section of your MyLab to complete these writing exercises.

1-19   Preparation for a career in personal selling begins with the development of a personal philosophy or set of beliefs that provide guidance. Discuss the development of the three prescriptions of a personal-selling philosophy and how these prescriptions apply to value-added selling.

1-20   The restructuring of America from an industrial economy to an information economy began approximately 60 years ago. Explain the key factors involved in the emergence of relationship selling in the information economy.

Evolution of Selling Models That Complement the Marketing Concept

Source: Michael Ahearne

MyMarketingLab™

⭐ Improve Your Grade!

Over 10 million students improved their results using the Pearson MyLabs. Visit **mymktlab.com** for simulations, tutorials, and end-of-chapter problems.

▶ Reality Selling Video—Ryan Guillory/Independent Consultant (TWFG)

Ryan Guillory, 33, a native of Houston, Texas, is a highly successful owner/agent of an independent insurance agency and branch owner of The Woodlands Financial Group (TWFG) (www.twfg.com), a privately held national firm that describes itself as a team of "caring, conscientious people" working through more than 300 TWFG retail branches and 3,000 independent agents in 38 states across the United States.

As an owner/agent of an Independent insurance agency founded in 2014, Guillory writes (sells) more than one insurance carrier. He represents about 75 different personal and commercial lines insurance carriers, allowing him to partner with his clients and sell many products that may not be directly associated with the main products he focuses on, that include home, auto, life, and commercial insurance. The partnering ability to meet additional customer needs regarding insurance protections is referred to as cross-selling.

Guillory's business philosophy is to get his customers the very best coverage available at the best rate available. His unique customer insight into relationship-selling is that, even though he may not always have the lowest price, going over the quote and policies with customers in detail has its advantages. Through this consultative-selling approach Guillory spends considerably more time discussing a client's insurance needs with them than his competitors might. He believes this helps the customer feel more comfortable buying the policies that he recommends.

Guillory's strategy to beat competition is to keep a tab on market information on captive agents (an agent who can only sell one carrier such as State Farm or Liberty Mutual) and companies that do not have agents and sell directly to the customer such as Geico or Esurance. He mainly markets to home owners while cross-selling the auto policy—the idea being that while almost every home owner has an automobile that will need insurance, every customer who has an automobile does not have a home as they may rent or live with parents

The first conversation with the customer is for gathering strategic information, mostly on the customer's property. Questions on personal details, past claims, acquaintances, experiences and primary concerns follow soon after.

Product presentation is always in person so that the client and Guillory review the quote together. Quotes are emailed before meetings that normally start by prodding the customer to ask questions to start the conversation. Thereafter, both sides go over the quote thoroughly focusing on exactly what the policy covers. To get additional information, Guillory peppers the meeting with open-ended questions. If the customer does not have any further questions, Guillory likes to say, "I can get this started as early as tonight for you." If the customer wants to think about the offer, he likes to get a commitment on the day he can come back. As Guillory puts it, the goal is always to get a commitment which will lead to the sell. ●

| 2.1 | Discuss the evolution of personal selling models as an extension of the marketing concept |

Marketing Concept Requires New Selling Models

A careful examination of personal selling practices during the past 50 years reveals some positive developments. We have seen the evolution of personal selling through several stages. The earlier "persuader stage" that was popular prior to the emergence of the marketing concept emphasized pushing or peddling products. At this stage, with little regard for long-term, mutually rewarding customer relationships, salespeople attempted to convince any and all market members to buy products offered. Over the years, personal selling evolved to the "problem-solver stage"—obtaining the participation of buyers in identifying their problems, which could be translated into needs. At this stage, the salesperson attempts to present products that correspond with customer needs.[1] Today, salespeople are no longer the flamboyant product "peddlers" of the past. Instead, they are increasingly becoming diagnosticians of customers' needs and problems. A growing

Salespeople who build partnering relationships are rewarded with repeat business and referrals. These relationships require a strategic approach to selling.

Source: Konstantin Chagin/Shutterstock

number of salespeople recognize that the quality of the partnerships they create is as important as the quality of the products they sell. This sweeping change in personal-selling models, from peddling to long-term consultative problem solving and value-added partnering, was prompted by the emergence of the marketing concept.

Evolution of the Marketing Concept

What is the **marketing concept**? It is a principle that holds that achieving organizational goals depends on knowing the needs and wants of target markets and delivering the desired products. Under the marketing concept, customer focus and value are the paths to sales and profits.[2]

The era of marketing and the age of information began in the 1950s (Table 2.1). A General Electric executive is credited with making one of the earliest formal statements indicating corporate interest in the marketing concept. In a paper heralding a new management philosophy, he observed that the principal marketing function of a company is to determine what the customer wants and then develop the appropriate product or service. This view contrasted with the prevailing practice of that period, which was to develop products and then build customer interest in those products.[3]

The foundation for the marketing concept is a business philosophy that leaves no doubt in the mind of every employee that customer satisfaction is of primary importance. All energies are directed toward satisfying the customer. As Peter Drucker once observed, "The customers define the business."

Although the marketing concept is a very basic business fundamental, some companies ignore it and suffer the consequences. Ford Motor Company was a leader in quality control during the 1980s and early 1990s but then seemed to shift its focus to other areas. The result was a drop in its J.D. Power and Associates quality rankings and a drop in sales. Ford also failed to stay in touch with consumer tastes.[4] With renewed insight into the marketing concept, Ford now appears to be reconnecting with their customers.[5]

TABLE 2.1 Evolution of Personal Selling (1950 to Present)

SALES AND MARKETING EMPHASIS	SELLING EMPHASIS
Marketing Era Begins (1950s) Organizations determine needs and wants of target markets and adapt themselves to delivering desired satisfaction; product orientation is replaced by a customer orientation	• More organizations recognize that the salesperson is in a position to collect product, market, and service information concerning the buyer's needs
Consultative-Selling Era Emerges (Late 1960s to early 1970s) Salespeople are becoming diagnosticians of customers' needs as well as consultants offering well-considered recommendations; mass markets are breaking into target markets	• Buyer needs are identified through two-way communication • Information giving and negotiation tactics replace manipulation
Strategic-Selling Era Emerges (Early 1980s) The evolution of a more complex selling environment and greater emphasis on market niches create the need for greater structure and more emphasis on planning	• Strategy is given as much attention as selling tactics • Product positioning is given more attention • Greater emphasis on account management and team selling
Partnering Era Emerges (1990 to the present) Salespeople are encouraged to think of everything they say or do in the context of their long-term, high-quality partnership with individual customers; sales force automation provides specific customer information	• Customer supplants the product as the driving force in sales • Greater emphasis on strategies that create customer value • Adaptive selling is given greater emphasis

Business firms vary in terms of how strongly they support the marketing concept. Some firms have gone the extra mile to satisfy the needs and wants of their customers:

- UPS founder Jim Casey adopted the marketing concept when the company was first established. He described the firm's customer focus this way: "Our real, primary objective is to serve—to render perfect service to our stores and their customers. If we keep that objective constantly in mind, our reward in money can be beyond our fondest dreams."[6]
- Marriott Hotels uses a blend of "high tech" and "high touch" to build customer goodwill and repeat business. Each of the 8,500 sales representatives can sell the services of 10 motel brands in Marriott's portfolio. The customer with a small-meeting budget might be encouraged to consider a Fairfield Inn property. The customer seeking luxury accommodations might be introduced to a Ritz-Carlton hotel (acquired a few years ago). All reservations go through the same system, so if one Marriott hotel is full, the sales representative can cross-sell rooms in another Marriott hotel in the same city.[7]

Marketing Concept Yields Marketing Mix

Once the marketing concept becomes an integral part of a firm's philosophy, its management seeks to develop a network of marketing activities that maximize customer satisfaction and ensure profitability. The combination of elements making up a program based on the marketing concept is known as the **marketing mix** (Figure 2.1). The marketing mix is a set of controllable, tactical marketing tools that consists of everything the firm can do to influence the demand for its product. The many possibilities can be organized into four groups of variables: *product, price, place*, and *promotion*.[8]

One of the four Ps shown in Figure 2.1—promotion—can be further subdivided into advertising, public relations, sales promotion, and personal selling. When a company adopts the marketing concept, it must determine how some combination of these elements can result in maximum customer satisfaction.

Important Role of Personal Selling

Every marketer must decide how much time and money to invest in each of the four areas of the marketing mix. The decision must be objective; no one can afford to invest money in a marketing strategy that does not provide a good return on money invested. *Personal selling is often the major promotional method used—whether measured by people employed, by total expenditures, or by expenses as a percentage of sales.* As noted in Chapter 1, there are more than 21 million field and retail salespeople in the United States. This represents about 11 percent of all of the people who are employed full time. Approximately 6 million of these salespeople have field responsibility. Full-time salespeople in the United States cost their companies more than a trillion dollars every year and represent by far the largest marketing expenditure. This is more than four times what is spent on advertising.[9]

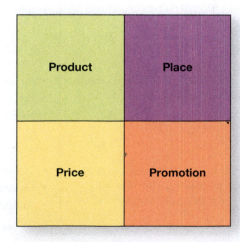

FIGURE 2.1

The Marketing Mix

Each of the elements that make up the marketing mix must be executed effectively for a marketing program to achieve the desired results.

Firms make large investments in personal selling in response to several major trends: Products and services are becoming increasingly sophisticated and complex; competition has greatly increased in most product areas; and demand for quality, value, and service by customers has risen sharply. In response to these trends, personal selling has evolved to a new level of professionalism. Since the beginning of the information age, personal selling has evolved through three distinct developmental periods: the consultative-selling era, the strategic-selling era, and the partnering era.

Evolution of Consultative Selling

2.2 Describe the evolution of consultative selling from the marketing era to the present

Consultative selling, which emerged in the late 1960s and early 1970s, is an extension of the marketing concept (see Table 2.1). This approach emphasizes need identification, which is achieved through effective communication between the salesperson and the customer. The salesperson establishes two-way communication by asking appropriate questions and listening carefully to the customer's responses. The salesperson assumes the role of consultant and offers well-considered recommendations. Negotiation replaces manipulation as the salesperson sets the stage for a long-term partnership. Salespeople who have adopted consultative selling possess a keen ability to listen, define the customer's problems, and offer one or more solutions.

Although consultative selling is emphasized throughout this text, it is helpful to understand the role of transactional selling in our economy. **Transactional selling** is a sales process that most effectively matches the needs of the value-conscious buyer who is primarily interested in price and convenience. Because of the emergence of e-commerce, most transactional buyers are well aware of their needs and may already know a great deal about the products or services they intend to purchase. Because the transaction-based buyer tends to focus primarily on low price, some marketers are adopting lower-cost selling channels. This approach to selling is usually used by marketers who do not see the need to spend very much time on customer need assessment, problem solving, relationship building, or sales follow-up.[10,11]

The decline in popularity of transactional sales approaches is due to two industry trends: the rise of e-commerce, which displaces transactional sales managed by people; and the increasing complexity of businesses. As more business supplier–related transactions are managed through portals and online bidding, businesses have a diminished demand for salespeople to manage the transactional sale.[12]

Service, retail, manufacturing, and wholesale firms that embrace the marketing concept already have adopted or are currently adopting consultative-selling practices. The major features of consultative selling are as follows:

1. The customer is seen as a *person to be served*, not a prospect to be sold. Consultative salespeople believe their function is to help the buyer make an intelligent decision. They use a four-step process that includes need discovery, selection of a solution, a need–satisfaction presentation, and servicing the sale (Figure 2.2). These customer-centered strategies are fully developed and explained in Chapters 10 to 15.
2. The consultative salesperson, unlike the peddler of an earlier era, does not try to overpower the customer with a high-pressure sales presentation. Instead, the buyer's needs are identified through *two-way* communication. The salesperson conducts precall research and asks questions during the sales call in an attempt to develop a relationship and learn as much as possible about the person's needs and perceptions.
3. Consultative selling emphasizes *need identification, problem solving*, and *negotiation instead of manipulation*. This approach is very compatible with the "problem-solver stage" of personal selling discussed in Chapter 1.[13] Helping the buyer make an informed and intelligent buying decision adds value to the sales process.

| Need discovery | → | Selection of solution | → | Need–satisfaction presentation | → | Servicing the sale |

FIGURE 2.2

The Consultative Sales Presentation Guide

This contemporary presentation guide emphasizes the customer as a person to be served.

The War between Sales and Marketing

Within many companies, there is little alignment between sales and marketing. In fact, a real turf war often exists between these two functions.[a] One source of friction is *economic*.

Senior management must make decisions regarding budget allocation for each function. The folks in marketing may want to spend large amounts of money on advertising to generate customer awareness of a new product. The folks in sales may feel this money would be better spent by increasing the size of the sales force.

The second source of conflict is *cultural*. Sales and marketing attract different types of people who spend their time in different ways. The marketing staff may be focused on program elements (product warranty, price, placement of the product, etc.). Salespeople, in contrast, want to focus their attention on existing and potential customers. One way to end the war between sales and marketing is to encourage more joint planning and information sharing. The leaders of both functions must try to achieve common ground in terms of philosophies and values.[b] Research indicates that greater collaboration between sales and marketing leads to superior business performance.[c]

4. Consultative selling emphasizes *service* at every phase of the personal-selling process. Several important research studies indicate the strong, positive impact of customer satisfaction on company profits.[14] The relationship between a seller and a buyer seldom ends when the sale is made. In most cases, customer expectations increase after the sale.

At first glance, it may appear that consultative-selling practices can be easily mastered. The truth is that consultative selling is a complex process that puts great demands on sales personnel. This approach to personal selling requires an understanding of concepts and principles borrowed from the fields of psychology, communications, and sociology. It takes a great deal of personal commitment and self-discipline to become a sales consultant/adviser.

From Peddling to Partnering—A Historical Perspective on Selling Today

Personal selling began in the very early ages of human history with the bargaining of goods and services as the first form of economic trade. In approximately 5000 B.C., money in the form of metal coins was introduced, enabling the exchange of goods for money—and the work of the peddler emerged.

The work of salespeople started to differentiate with the beginning of the industrial revolution in 1760. In 1892, American advertising and sales pioneer, Elmo Lewis, introduced the AIDA model, which stands for Attention, Interest, Desire, and Action. This model was applied to many sales situations. In 1916 the first world selling congress was held where salespeople were encouraged to earn customers' trust. This was the first move in the marketplace to start establishing customer trust among salespeople, with the idea that the customer was important and it was important to earn customer trust in order to establish a relationship.

In 1936, Dale Carnegie introduced the best-selling book titled "How to Win Friends and Influence People." This book continues to have a large impact on the selling profession even today. The decades of the '50s and '60s were the era of fast-talking, door-to-door salespeople. Due to the limited information about products and services, salespeople brought powerful messages about the benefits of the products that motivated customers to buy those products and services.

The 1970s witnessed the introduction of *SPIN Selling* by Neil Rackham that stems from the work of the Xerox Corporation. SPIN selling utilizing the consultative model focused on the concept of increasing the number of questions and customer involvement in the sales process. The 1980s witnessed the introduction of the Solution and Strategic Selling concepts while the next decades saw the emergence of more relationship-oriented selling, utilizing strategic selling and solution selling. The dot-com revolution changed the power to the more informed customer—and the Partnering era emerged. The challenge today is to better understand how to build long-term relationships, meet customer needs and create value in the marketplace.

Dale Carnegie's 1936 book, *How to Win Friends and Influence People,* had a huge impact on how professional salespeople, such as in this photo, managed their customer relationships.
Source: Classic Stock/Alamy Stock Photo

Evolution of Strategic Selling

Strategic selling began receiving considerable attention during the 1980s (see Table 2.1). During this period, we witnessed the beginning of several trends that resulted in a more complex selling environment. These trends, which include increased global competition, broader and more diverse product lines, more decision makers involved in major purchases, and greater demand for specific, custom-made solutions, continue to influence personal selling and sales training in the age of information.

As companies face increased levels of complexity in the marketplace, they must give more attention to strategic planning. The strategic planning done by salespeople is often influenced by the information included in their company's strategic market plan. **Strategic planning** is the process that matches the firm's resources to its market opportunities. It takes into consideration the various functional areas of the business that must be coordinated, such as financial assets, workforce, production capabilities, and marketing.[15] Almost every aspect of strategic planning directly or indirectly influences sales and marketing.

The strategic plan should be a guide for a strategic-selling plan. This plan includes strategies that you use to position yourself with the customer before the sales call even begins. The authors of *Strategic Selling* point out that there is a difference between a *tactic* and a *strategy*.[16] **Tactics** are techniques, practices, or methods you use when you are face-to-face with a customer. Examples are the use of questions to identify needs, presentation skills, and various types of closes. These and other tactics are discussed in Chapters 10 to 15.

A **strategy**, on the other hand, is a prerequisite to tactical success. If you develop the correct strategies, you are more likely to make your sales presentation to the right person, at the right time, and in a manner most likely to achieve positive results.

A selling strategy is a carefully conceived plan that is needed to accomplish a sales objective. Let's assume you are a sales representative employed by a pharmaceutical company. In an ideal situation, you want to establish a dialogue with the physician and learn about the types of patients she sees, diseases she treats, and challenges facing her practice. However, you do not want to call on busy doctors who may have no use for the drugs offered by your company. A strategy might include a careful study of the entire physician population in your territory. This analysis will help you identify those who need information about the drugs your company offers.[17] With this information, you can select the most appropriate selling tactic (method), which might be to present samples to doctors who are not currently prescribing your drug.

Strategic planning, an important element of the "problem-solver stage," sets the groundwork for a value-added form of consultative selling that is more structured, more focused, and more efficient. The result is better time allocation, more precise problem solving, and a greater chance that there will be a good match between your product and the customer's needs.

Adaptive selling is another key element of the "problem-solver stage." **Adaptive selling** can be defined as altering sales behaviors during a customer interaction in order to improve communication. It

Adaptive selling requires a strategic selling plan. Adaptive selling can be defined as altering sales behaviors during a customer interaction in order to improve communication. It relates to a salesperson's ability to collect information regarding the customer's needs and responding appropriately. Adaptive selling frequently requires complex behavioral adjustments.

Source: Rehan Qureshi/Shutterstock

Strategic/Consultative Selling Model*

Strategic Step	Prescription
Develop a Personal Selling Philosophy	☐ Adopt Marketing Concept ☐ Value Personal Selling ☐ Become a Problem Solver/Partner
Develop a Relationship Strategy	☐ Maintain High Ethical Standards ☐ Project Professional Image ☐ Manage the Relationship Process
Develop a Product Strategy	☐ Become a Product Expert ☐ Sell Benefits ☐ Configure Value-Added Solutions
Develop a Customer Strategy	☐ Understand the Buying Process ☐ Understand Buyer Behavior ☐ Develop Prospect Base
Develop a Presentation Strategy	☐ Prepare Objectives ☐ Develop Presentation Plan ☐ Provide Outstanding Service

*Strategic/consultative selling evolved in response to increased competition, more complex products, increased emphasis on customer needs, and growing importance of long-term relationships.

Product	Place
Price	**Promotion**

FIGURE 2.3

The Strategic/Consultative–Selling Model is an extension of the marketing concept.

relates to a salesperson's ability to collect information regarding the customer's needs and responding appropriately. Adaptive selling frequently requires complex behavioral adjustments.[18]

Many companies have discovered that specialized sales training is an effective strategy. When Microsoft wanted to build a stronger partnership with its customers, all 5,000 sales professionals completed the Solution Selling sales training course. This training, based on concepts presented in *The New Solution Selling*, by Keith Eades, helped Microsoft salespeople create greater value for its customers.[19]

Strategic/Consultative–Selling Model

When you study a value-added approach to personal selling that combines strategic planning, consultative-selling practices, and partnering principles, you experience a mental exercise that is similar to solving a jigsaw puzzle. You are given many pieces of information that ultimately must form a complete picture. Putting the parts together isn't nearly as difficult if you can see the total picture at the beginning. Therefore, a single model has been developed to serve as a source of reference throughout the entire text. Figure 2.3 shows this model.

The Strategic/Consultative–Selling Model features five steps, and each step is based on three prescriptions. The first step involves the development of a personal-selling philosophy, which was introduced in Chapter 1. Each of the other four steps relates to a broad strategic area of personal selling. Each step makes an important and unique contribution to the selling/buying process.

GLOBAL BUSINESS INSIGHT

Learning Different Business Cultures

If your company is going global and you need to deal with customers from China, Brazil, Germany or Russia, learning different ways of developing and maintaining business relationships is a must for you. Too often Americans rely on the "time is money" belief and they take shortcuts in some key areas. For example, they often fail to take the time needed to build a relationship with the client or learn how to approach different clients from different cultures.

- The negotiation process in China, Japan, and Latin American countries is very slow, with a lot of time spent on relationship-building activities.

- In Japan, great importance is placed on relationships, and building long-term business relationships is what matters most.
- The importance of relationships for Russians is low, and they mostly remain reserved until negotiations conclude.
- French approach to business interactions is formal; having etiquette is extremely important in dealing with French clients.[d]

DEVELOPING A RELATIONSHIP STRATEGY Success in selling depends heavily on the salesperson's ability to develop, manage, and enhance interpersonal relations with the customer. People seldom buy products or services from someone they dislike or distrust. Harvey B. Mackay, founder of Mackay Envelope Corporation, says, "People don't care how much you know until they know how much you care." Most customers are more apt to openly discuss their needs and wants with a salesperson with whom they feel comfortable.

A **relationship strategy** is a well-thought-out plan for establishing, building, and maintaining quality relationships. This type of plan is essential for success in today's marketplace, which is characterized by vigorous competition, look-alike products, and customer loyalty dependent on quality relationships as well as quality products. The relationship strategy must encompass every aspect of selling from the first contact with a prospect to servicing the sale once this prospect becomes an established customer. The relationship strategy is an integral dimension of **relationship selling**. Relationship selling is a form of personal selling that involves securing, developing, and maintaining long-term relationships with customers.[20] Increased support for relationship selling recognizes the growing importance of partnerships in selling. The primary goal of the relationship strategy is to create rapport, trust, and mutual respect, which ensures a long-term partnership. To establish this type of relationship, salespeople must *maintain high ethical standards, which forms the very foundation for long-term partnerships.* They must project and maintain high ethical standards, project a professional

SELLING IS EVERYONE'S BUSINESS

Sales Success Paves the Way for Hispanic Entrepreneur

At age 19, Deborah Rosado Shaw wanted to be a salesperson, but the company she worked for wouldn't let her sell. She had recently dropped out of elite Wellesley College and had taken a job with a company that makes umbrellas and tote bags. One day she took a sick day and called on the marketing staff at the Museum of Natural History. The result of this impromptu sales call was a $140,000 order. She then went to the president of the company and asked him, "Are you going to let me sell now, or what?" After two years in sales, Shaw moved to a rival firm, Umbrellas Plus, and acquired more experience. Years later she purchased controlling interest in the company and turned it into a $10 million enterprise. Over a twenty-year period she groomed her business know-how designing, negotiating, and closing deals with some of the smartest buyers in the world, including Costco, Toys 'R' Us, Walmart and The Walt Disney Company. www.debshaw.com/biography[e, f]

Source: Deborah Rosado Shaw

Patricia Seybold, CEO and founder of the Patricia Seybold Group, and best-selling author of *The Customer Revolution*, says we are in the midst of a profound revolution—the customer revolution.

Source: Patricia Seybold, President, Patricia Seybold Group, Inc.

image and manage their relationships by adapting their communication style (see Figure 3.1). Chapters 3, 4, and 5 provide important information on development of the relationship strategy.

Some people think that the concept of "relationships" is too soft and too emotional for a business application; these people think that it's too difficult to think about relationships in strategic terms. In fact, this is not the case at all. Every salesperson can and should formulate a strategic plan that builds and enhances relationships.

DEVELOPING A PRODUCT STRATEGY

Products and services represent problem-solving tools. The **product strategy** is a plan that helps salespeople make correct decisions concerning the selection and positioning of products to meet identified customer needs. The three prescriptions for the product strategy are *become a product expert*, *sell benefits*, and *configure value-added solutions*. The development of a product strategy begins with a thorough study of one's product (see Figure 2.3) using a feature–benefit analysis approach. Product features such as technical superiority, reliability, fashionableness, design integrity, or guaranteed availability should be converted to benefits that appeal to the customer. Today's high-performance salespeople strive to become product experts. Chapter 6 focuses on company, product, and competition knowledge needed by salespeople.

Product knowledge is not the only important element of a product strategy. In fact, salespeople who are too focused on selling products often fail to identify complete solutions to the customer's problem. Stephen Covey, author of the best-selling book, *The Seven Habits of Highly Effective People*, says, "Diagnose before you prescribe." If the salesperson does not deeply engage the customer and fails to diagnose the problem correctly, chances are the solution recommended may not be the best one.[21]

The development of a product strategy often requires thoughtful decision making. Today's more knowledgeable customers seek a cluster of satisfactions that arise from the product itself, from the manufacturer or distributor of the product, and from the salesperson. The "new" product that customers are buying today is the sum total of the satisfactions that emerge from all three sources. The cluster-of-satisfactions concept is discussed in more detail in Chapter 7.

DEVELOPING A CUSTOMER STRATEGY Patricia Seybold, author of *The Customer Revolution*, says we are in the midst of a profound revolution—the customer revolution. And it's bigger than the Internet revolution:

> Customers have taken control of our companies' destinies. Customers are transforming our industries. And customers' loyalty—or lack thereof—has become increasingly important. . . .[22]

Customers have become increasingly sophisticated in their buying strategies. More and more, they have come to expect value-added products and services and long-term commitments. Selling to today's customers starts with getting on the customers' agenda and carefully identifying their needs, wants, and buying conditions. Salespeople who have a better understanding of customer needs are better able to produce satisfied customers who are willing to pay more![23]

A **customer strategy** is a carefully conceived plan that results in maximum responsiveness to the customer's needs. This strategy is based on the fact that success in personal selling depends, in no small measure, on the salesperson's ability to learn as much as possible about the prospect. It involves the collection and analysis of specific information on each customer. When developing a customer strategy, the salesperson should *develop an understanding of the customer's buying process, understand buyer behavior, and develop a prospect base*. The first two parts of the customer strategy are introduced in Chapter 8. Suggestions concerning ways to develop and manage a solid prospect base are discussed in Chapter 9.

The customer strategy is dictated by the needs of the customer. For example, it's best to consider relationship formation from the customer's perspective. When a *consultative*-selling approach is required, the customer strategy will usually encompass a long-term relationship and ongoing collaboration. If a *transactional* approach is required, the customer strategy would not, in most cases, emphasize need assessment, problem solving, relationship building, and sales follow-up.[24]

DEVELOPING A PRESENTATION STRATEGY Typical salespeople spend about 30 percent of their time in actual face-to-face selling situations. However, the sales presentation is a critical part of the selling process. The **presentation strategy** is a well-developed plan that includes *preparing the sales presentation objectives, preparing a presentation plan that is needed to meet these objectives, and renewing one's commitment to provide outstanding customer service* (see Figure 2.3).

The presentation strategy usually involves developing one or more objectives for each sales call. For example, a salesperson might update personal information about the customer, provide information on a new product, and close a sale during one sales call. Multiple-objective sales presentations, which are becoming more common, are discussed in Chapter 10.

Presale presentation plans give salespeople the opportunity to consider those activities that take place during the sales presentation. For example, a salesperson might preplan a demonstration of product features to use when meeting with the customer. Presale planning ensures that salespeople are well organized during the sales presentation and prepared to offer outstanding service.

INTERRELATIONSHIP OF BASIC STRATEGIES The major strategies that form the Strategic/ Consultative–Selling Model are by no means independent. The relationship, product, and customer strategies all influence development of the presentation strategy (Figure 2.4). For example, one relationship-building practice might be developed for use during the initial face-to-face meeting with the customer and another for possible use during the negotiation of buyer resistance. Another relationship-building method might be developed for use after the sale has been closed. The discovery of customer needs (part of the customer strategy) greatly influences planning for the sales presentation.

FIGURE 2.4

The major strategies that form the Strategic/Consultative–Selling Model are by no means independent of one another. The focus of each strategy is to satisfy customer needs and build quality partnerships.

2.4 Describe the evolution of partnering and the nature of strategic account management

Evolution of Partnering

"Partnering" became a buzzword in the early 2000s and today it has become a business reality.[25] Partnering has been driven by several economic forces. One is the demise of the product solution in several industries. When products of one company are nearly identical to the competition, the product strategy becomes less important than the relationship, customer, and presentation strategies. By contrast, some partnerships grow out of the need for customized products or services. Many manufacturers have formed partnerships with companies that offer flexibility in terms of product configuration, scheduling of deliveries, or some other factor.

Today's customer wants a quality product *and* a quality relationship. Salespeople willing to abandon short-term thinking and invest the time and energy needed to develop a high-quality, long-term relationship with customers are greatly rewarded. A strong partnership serves as a barrier to competing salespeople who want to sell to your accounts. Salespeople who are able to build partnerships enjoy more repeat business and referrals. Keeping existing customers happy makes a great deal of sense from an economic point of view. Experts in the field of sales and marketing know that it costs four to five times more to get a new customer than to keep an existing one. Therefore, even small increases in customer retention can result in major increases in profits.[26]

Partnering is a strategically developed, long-term relationship that solves the customer's problems. A successful long-term partnership is achieved when the salesperson is able to skillfully apply the four major strategies and, thus, add value in various ways (Figure 2.5). Successful sales professionals stay close to the customer and constantly search for new ways to add value.

The salespeople at Mackay Envelope Corporation achieve this goal by making sure they know more about their customers than the competitors know. Salespeople who work for Xerox Corporation are responding to a sales orientation that emphasizes postal service. Bonuses are based on a formula that includes not only sales but also customer satisfaction.

Strategic Selling Alliances—The Highest Form of Partnering

Throughout the past decade, we have seen the growth of a new form of partnership that often is described as a strategic selling alliance.

The goal of a strategic selling alliance is to achieve a marketplace advantage by teaming up with another company whose products or services fit well with its own.[27] A strategic selling alliance, also called **strategic account management**, is usually led by a **Strategic Account Manager (SAM).** The SAM's job description is to execute an enterprise-wide sales strategy for growth, profitability, customer loyalty, and customer-driven innovation. A key element of strategic account management is involving senior level management on the sales and buying teams in relationship development, product configuration, and service after the sale. Technical sales-support personnel are also an important part of the strategic account management team.

In varying degrees of account management, additional titles are used to describe the process of aligning and partnering with today's customers and clients. As described in Chapter 1, the

FIGURE 2.5

Partnering is a strategically developed, long-term relationship that solves the customer's problems. A successful partnering effort results in repeat sales and referrals that expand the prospect base. The strength of the partnership increases each time the salesperson uses value-added selling strategies.

use of the title "account manager" has become commonplace in describing this process. For example:

The **Regional Account Manager (RAM)** is a part of a larger sales team and acts as the direct client contact and manager of a number of business accounts. These accounts usually encompass a certain territory. For example, one who works in the United States may have all the accounts she manages based in California (for more information on personal-selling opportunities and activities in this career area, see Appendix 2: The NewNet Systems Regional Accounts Management Case Study).

The **Key Account Manager (KAM)** is responsible for the coordination and management of a company's prioritized accounts. These customers may be given special treatment due to their long-term growth potential, current size of business, global presence, or strategic fit, among other factors.

The **National Account Manager (NAM)** is responsible for recruiting and negotiating various business transactions and signing on new regional and national retailers. They coordinate activities providing support to the Channel which includes market and account launches, key metrics, and communications with matrixes in departments like Operations, Field Sales, Marketing, and Supply Chain.

The **Global Account Manager (GAM)** is a key account manager who is specialized on a specific product portfolio and not on a given customer or geography. They are housed in a specific business unit, yet they span the globe. They are required to speak multiple languages and understand the intricacies of many different cultures.

These account manager positions are generally not considered entry-level sales positions. They represent senior sales positions in most firms that entry-level salespeople aspire to attain by mastering the strategic/consultative skills presented in this book.

Corning, a maker of glass products, has formed strategic account partnerships with several companies that need innovative glass technology. For example, Corning formed a partnership with Samsung, a Korean manufacturer of television screens. RadioShack has formed strategic partnerships with several leading consumer electronics manufacturers. This move helped the company avoid the costs of starting new divisions.[28]

ACCESSING AND EXPLORING SALESFORCE.COM'S 30-DAY FREE TRIAL

Selling Today offers you a unique opportunity to learn how software is redefining sales and marketing. The program you will be using is referred to as Customer Relationship Management (CRM) software. CRM systems support the sales force and marketing personnel by automating the functions essential to maintaining strong partnering relationships with customers.

Introducing Salesforce.com

Salesforce.com is both the name of the company and its Internet site (www.salesforce.com). The 15-year-old company generated $5.4 billion in revenue during its latest fiscal year. The company serves more than two million salespeople-users and their 97,000 employers. Companies or individuals may subscribe to the company's online service for a monthly fee.

The software you will be using is a demonstration version of Salesforce.com. The full fee-based version of the Salesforce.com software offers additional functions, some of which are disabled for our studies. According to Salesforce, sales representatives using Salesforce experience a 34 percent increase in sales productivity, a 29 percent increase in sales volume, and a 42 percent increase in forecast accuracy.

Registering with Salesforce.com

Go to www.salesforce.com. Click on the *Free Trial link* and follow the instructions to *Sign up for a free 30-day trial.* When completing

the registration, make sure you enter a valid e-mail address. It will be used to contact you to finish the registration process. You will be required to enter information in all the categories listed, including a company name, a title for you, number of employees, telephone number, and postal code. Also, you must check the box next to the statement, "I agree to the Master Subscription Agreement." It is always good to read these types of agreements on websites that are important to you.

Once you click "Start free trial," an information screen will be displayed to let you know a message will be sent to the e-mail address you entered. Follow all the instructions in the e-mail. You will need the link in this e-mail each time you access your Free Trial. You must also remember the e-mail address you used and the new password you are asked to create. This information will be used each time you access the free Salesforce.com Trial Demo link.

Becoming Familiar with Salesforce.com

After completing the registration process, Salesforce.com initially opens a home screen. You are encouraged to click on the various icons, tabs, and links to get acquainted with the layout of the software.

The first step in building a strategic account relationship is for the SAM to learn as much as possible about the proposed partner. This study takes place long before face-to-face contact. Alliances that are formed between companies that vary greatly in such areas as customer focus, financial stability, or ethical values will likely fail.[29] The second step is to meet with the proposed partner and explore mutual benefits of the alliance. At this point, the strategic account manager or salesperson is selling advice, assistance, and counsel, not specific products. Building win-win strategic partnerships requires the highest form of partnership selling. Very often, the strategic account manager is working with a company team made up of persons from such areas as research and development (R&D), finance, and distribution. Presentations and proposals usually focus on profit impact and other strategic alliance benefits.[30] Due to the low-cost threat from emerging nations, many Western-based companies have had to develop strategic account management. Its crucial importance will vastly continue to grow.[31]

Partnering Is Enhanced with High Ethical Standards

In the field of selling, there are certain pressures that can influence the ethical conduct of salespeople, and poor ethical decisions can weaken or destroy partnerships. To illustrate, let us assume a competitor makes exaggerated claims about a product. Do you counteract by promising more than your product can deliver? What action do you take when there is a time-management problem and you must choose between servicing past sales and making new sales? What if a superior urges you to use a strategy that you consider unethical? These and other pressures must be dealt with every day.

Although Chapter 3 is devoted entirely to ethical considerations in personal selling, it should be noted that ethics is a major theme of the text. The topic of ethics has been interwoven throughout several chapters. The authors believe that ethical decisions must be made every day in the life of a salesperson, so this important topic cannot be covered in a single chapter.

Partnering Is Enhanced with Customer Relationship Management

Many companies have adopted some form of customer relationship management software. **Customer relationship management (CRM)**, sometimes referred to as "sales automation," is the system used for building and maintaining strong customer relationships while adding customer value.[32] A modern CRM program relies on a variety of technologies to improve communications in a sales organization and enhance customer responsiveness. A variety of CRM applications will be discussed throughout the text.

FIGURE 2.6

Creating and Delivering Customer Value Model

The salesperson's role in value creation is illustrated in this figure.

Source: Solomon, Michael R.; Marshal, Greg W.; Stuart, Elnora W., *Marketing: Real People, Real Choices,* 6th ed., ©2009, p. 23. Reprinted and Electronically reproduced by permission of Pearson Education, Inc. Upper Saddle River, New Jersey.

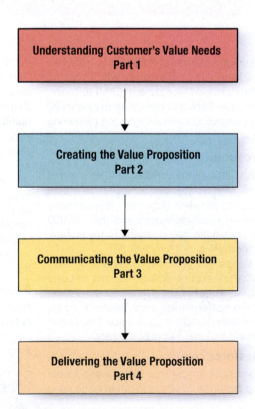

Value Creation—The New Selling Imperative

2.5 Explain how value-added selling strategies enhance personal selling

We have defined value-added selling as a series of creative improvements within the sales process that enhance the customer experience. The **information economy** will reward those salespeople who have the skills, the knowledge, and the motivation to determine how to create value at every step of the sales process.

As Figure 2.6 shows, value creation begins with an understanding of the customer's value needs. Salespeople can create value in many ways: establishing a relationship based on trust, carefully identifying the customer's needs, and identifying the best possible product solution. In the case of a complex sale, understanding the customer's value needs may take a great deal of time and may involve bringing in team members who have specific technical expertise.

Creating an appealing value proposition (Part 2) requires a detailed study of the customer's value needs. If you discover that timely delivery of your product is of critical importance, you must give clients what they want. And if you promise on-time delivery, you must back up your claims.

Communicating the value proposition (Part 3) presents another major challenge. Traditional selling has too often emphasized communicating only the value that lies in the product. The focus of the sales call has too often been the product, not creating value for the customer.[33]

Delivering value (Part 4) can be very challenging. It may require coordination of credit approval, training, installation, service, and other aspects of the sale. Of course, each element of the selling process provides an opportunity to add value.

CHAPTER LEARNING ACTIVITIES

Reviewing Key Concepts

Discuss the evolution of personal selling models as an extension of the marketing concept

The *marketing concept* is the belief that a firm should dedicate all its policies, planning, and operations to the satisfaction of the customer. Salespeople today are problem solvers who obtain the participation of buyers in identifying their problems, which can be translated into needs.

Describe the evolution of consultative selling from the marketing era to the present

The *marketing era* that began in the United States in the 1950s looked first at customer needs and wants and then created goods and services to meet those needs and wants. *Consultative selling* emerged in the late 1960s and early 1970s as an approach that emphasizes the identification of customer needs through effective communication between the salesperson and customer. The evolution of selling continued with the development of *strategic selling and partnering*.

Define strategic selling and name the four broad strategic areas in the Strategic/Consultative–Selling Model

Strategic selling evolved in the 1980s and involves the preparation of a carefully conceived plan to accomplish sales objectives. Strategic selling is based on a company's *strategic market plan*, which takes into consideration the coordination of all the major functional areas of the business—production, marketing, finance, and personnel. The four broad strategic areas in the Strategic/Consultative–Selling Model (after development of personal-selling philosophy) are developing a relationship strategy, developing a product strategy, developing a customer strategy, and developing a presentation strategy.

Describe the evolution of partnering and the nature of strategic account management

Partnering is a strategically developed, long-term relationship that solves the customer's problems. The long-term partnership is achieved when the salesperson is able to skillfully apply the four major strategies and therefore add value in various ways. *Strategic Selling Alliances* (or as it is sometimes called, *Strategic Account Management*) is the highest form of partnering. Strategic account management is an enterprise-wide initiative seeking the development of strategic partnering relationships with a limited number of key customers and focused on achieving long-term, significant, and measurable business.

Explain how value-added selling strategies enhance personal selling

Value-added selling has emerged as a major response to the customer economy. This approach to personal selling is defined as a series of creative improvements that enhance the customer's experience. The information economy rewards those salespeople who have the skills, the knowledge, and the motivation to determine how to create value at every step of the sales process.

Key Terms

Marketing concept, p. 31
Marketing mix, p. 31
Consultative selling, p. 33
Transactional selling, p. 33
Strategic planning, p. 35
Tactics, p. 35
Strategy, p. 35

Adaptive selling, p. 35
Relationship strategy, p. 37
Relationship selling, p. 37
Product strategy, p. 38
Customer strategy, p. 38
Presentation strategy, p. 39

Partnering, p. 40
Strategic Account Management, p. 40
Customer Relationship Management, p. 42
Information economy, p. 43

MyMarketingLab

To complete the problems with the ⭐ in your MyLab, go to the EOC Discussion Questions.

Review Questions

 2-1 Why is peddling or "pushing products" inconsistent with the marketing concept?

2-2 Describe how new models of selling emerged in response to the marketing concept.

 2-3 Describe the importance of personal selling as a part of the marketing concept.

2-4 What is consultative selling? Give examples.

2-5 Diagram and label the four-step Consultative Sales Presentation Guide.

2-6 List and briefly explain the four broad strategic areas that make up the selling process.

2-7 Briefly describe the evolution of partnering. Discuss the forces that contributed to this approach to selling.

2-8 Provide a brief description of value-added selling. What economic forces have motivated companies to adopt value-added selling?

 2-9 Explain why the ethical conduct of salespeople has become so important today.

Application Exercises

2-10 Assume that you are an experienced professional salesperson. A professor who teaches at a nearby university has asked you to speak to a consumer economics class about the benefits of personal selling to customers. Make an outline of what to say.

2-11 A friend of yours has invented a unique and useful new product. This friend, an engineer by profession, understands little about marketing and selling this new product. She does understand, however, that "nothing happens until somebody sells the product." She has asked you to describe the general factors that need to be considered when you market a product. Prepare an answer to her question.

2-12 Sharon Alverez has been teaching college biology courses. She is offered a position selling pharmaceutical products. This position requires that she call on doctors and pharmacists to explain her product line. Describe the similarities and the differences between personal selling and teaching.

2-13 To learn more about industry-based, global, sales-training programs, access www .wilsonlearning.com. Click on the "Sales Effectiveness" link and examine the content of the various sales courses offered throughout the world by this company. From this review, describe the similarities between what this company offers and the material in this chapter.

Role-Play Exercise

The purpose of this role-play is to provide you with an opportunity to engage in a basic-need identification exercise. You will be meeting with someone (a class member) who is preparing for an important job interview and needs a pen and/or pencil. Prior to the meeting, make a list of the questions you will ask. Then pair off with the class member and ask your questions. Be sure to take notes. At the end of the interview, be prepared to recommend the most appropriate pen and/or pencil.

Reality Selling Video Case Problem—Ryan Guillory/ Independent Consultant (TWFG)

This chapter started with an introduction to Ryan Guillory, owner/agent of an independent insurance agency and branch owner of The Woodlands Financial Group (TWFG). While representing about 75 different personal and commercial lines insurance carriers, Guillory focuses specifically on home, auto, life, and commercial insurance. As he keeps a tab on market information on captive agents and companies that sell directly to the customer, Guillory's philosophy is to get his customers the very best coverage available at the best rate available.

Source: Michael Ahearne

We now know how salespeople such as Guillory focus on value-added selling strategies to enhance personal selling. We also know that salespeople who strategically build partnering relationships are rewarded with repeat business and referrals. As a strategic seller, the salesperson understands that the customer supplants the product as the driving force in sales and that greater emphasis on adaptive selling and strategy that create customer value is needed.

High-performing consultative salespeople such as Guillory are constantly learning new product knowledge, competitive offerings, industry trends and customer needs. As a graduate of the Program in Excellence in Selling at the University of Houston, he takes time out to visit trade shows and do continuing education courses. He keeps in touch with friends who are also insurance agents to discuss what they are seeing in the industry. He also subscribes to *Insurance Journal* magazine and on a daily basis reads insurance articles online.

Questions

2-14 Does it appear that Ryan Guillory has adopted the three prescriptions of a personal selling philosophy? (See the Strategic/Consultative–Selling Model.) Explain.

2-15   What prescriptions of the relationship strategy (see the Strategic/Consultative–Selling Model) have been adopted by Guillory? Describe why a relationship strategy is especially important in personal selling.

2-16   Value-added selling is defined as a series of creative improvements in the sales process that enhance the customer's experience. Describe the various ways that Ryan Guillory can create value for his customers.

2-17   Why would it be important for the marketing-support personnel (marketing research, product managers, advertising and sales promotion, et al.) employed by TWFG to understand personal selling? Can you describe any marketing-support people who would benefit from the acquisition of personal-selling skills?

MyMarketingLab

Go to the Assignments section of your MyLab to complete these writing exercises.

2-18   A careful examination of personal-selling practices during the past 50 years reveals some positive developments with the evolution of personal selling through several stages. How has the evolution of the marketing concept required the use of new selling models?

2-19   Strategic selling evolved in the 1980s and involves the preparation of a carefully conceived plan to accomplish sales objectives. Discuss the four strategic areas in the Strategic/Consultative–Selling Model.

PART 1   ROLE-PLAY EXERCISE

Developing a Personal Selling Philosophy

Scenario

You are currently working part time at the Best Buy store located in Jordan Creek Town Center Mall. You are a full-time student majoring in marketing at Vista College. The manager of your store wants you to identify potential customers on your campus and sell Dell laptop computers to those who have a need for this product.

Customer Profile

Melissa Torres is a full-time commuter student who lives with her parents and shares one computer with her mom. Each morning, she drives about 20 miles to the campus (one way) and spends most of the day attending classes, working in the library, and visiting with friends. She currently spends about two hours each evening on the computer at home.

Salesperson Profile

You started working at the Best Buy store shortly after graduating from high school. The store manager was impressed with your computer expertise and your friendly manner. Although you are able to sell any type of computer, you tend to specialize in laptop computers, which are ideal for college students who have mobile computing needs. Your personal computer is a new Dell laptop, which replaced your desktop computer.

Product

You sell several different laptop computers that vary in price from $535 to $1,299 (type "Best Buy + Dell laptops computers" into your search engine for specific Dell laptop computers carried by Best Buy). Each laptop is equipped with specific, easily accessible ports to interact with a variety of external components. All of your notebooks offer both productivity and entertainment applications. Services offered by Dell include helpful assistance via telephone or online tutorials at www.support.dell.com. Dell's warranty also provides for service and support to be handled by the Geek Squad (www.geeksquad.com), which is located in the store.

Instructions

For this role-play, you will meet with Melissa Torres and determine her interest and need for a laptop computer. Prior to meeting with Ms. Torres, preplan your relationship strategy, product strategy, customer strategy, and presentation strategy. Chapter 2 provides a description of each strategic area. Be prepared to close the sale if you feel the customer will benefit from this purchase.

Sales success in the new economy requires us to think of ourselves as a problem solver/partner throughout the sales process.

PART 2

DEVELOPING A RELATIONSHIP STRATEGY

High-performance sales-people are generally better able to build and maintain relationships than moderate performers. Part 2 includes three chapters that focus on person-to-person relationship-building strategies. The influence of ethical decisions as the very foundation for relationships in selling is discussed in Chapter 3. Chapter 4 explains how to create value with a relationship strategy. Chapter 5 introduces communication style bias and explains how to build strong interpersonal relationships with style flexing.

Learning Objectives

When you finish reading this chapter, you should be able to

3.1 Explain the importance of developing a relationship strategy

3.2 Describe issues that challenge the ethical decision making of salespeople

3.3 Describe the factors that influence the ethical conduct of sales personnel

3.4 Describe how ethical decisions influence the building of partnering relationships in selling

3.5 Discuss guidelines for developing a personal code of ethics that creates value

Source: Michael Ahearne

▶ **Reality Selling Video—Edith Botello/Mattress Firm Edith**

Edith Botello (pictured above) started her career as a salesperson with Mattress Firm (www.mattressfirm.com), one of the world's largest and most successful retailers in the specialty bedding market. Edith, a recent university graduate, is currently the assistant manager of one of the company's 560 nationwide stores. She is responsible for the sales productivity, maintenance, and merchandising of the store. Within her district, she is also an in-market trainer, recruiter, and intern coordinator.

Edith believes that *qualifying* (the term Mattress Firm uses to describe needing identification) and *listening* are the most important skills to be a successful salesperson in her industry. Therefore, she really tries to understand why customers come to visit her and what will make them get a great night's sleep. People come into her store with a wide variety of different needs: Their bed is 20 years old; they are upgrading to a different size; they are buying a college bed; they need a bed for a guest bedroom; their current bed has dips and sags; they are going in for surgery next week and would like to recover on a supportive mattress, and so forth. Accordingly, Edith's goal is to ask the right questions so that she can sell them a solution based on their individual needs. Mattress Firm has taught Edith techniques on how to sell to different types of people. Edith believes that the main reason why many salespeople are successful is that they get their customer to believe in them by educating them and making them feel great about their purchase. Edith feels very fortunate to work for a company that values training and customer service.

Building relationships with customers is very important for Edith because people typically buy from salespeople they like and trust. One way she builds relationships is by getting to know her customers and talking to them about things that interest them. As Edith puts it, you cannot expect your customers to open up to you unless you kick things off by asking questions. Edith also makes use of testimonials to demonstrate how previous customers have resolved their needs with particular sleep products. Customers like to hear that their salesperson has experience dealing with, and finding solutions to, problems they are encountering. ●

Developing a Relationship Strategy for Partnering Style Selling

3.1 Explain the importance of developing a relationship strategy

Developing and applying the wide range of relationship skills needed in today's complex sales environment can be challenging. Daniel Goleman, author of the best-selling books *Emotional Intelligence* and *Working with Emotional Intelligence*, notes that there are many forms of intelligence that influence our actions throughout life.

EMOTIONAL INTELLIGENCE One of these, **emotional intelligence**, refers to the capacity for monitoring our own feelings and those of others, for motivating ourselves, and for managing emotions well in ourselves and in our relationships. People with a high level of emotional intelligence display many of the qualities needed in sales work: self-awareness, self-confidence, trustworthiness, adaptability, initiative, optimism, empathy, and well-developed social skills.[1]

Goleman and other researchers state that there are widespread exceptions to the rule that IQ predicts success. In the field of personal selling and most other business occupations, emotional intelligence is a much greater predictor of success.[2] The good news is that emotional intelligence can be enhanced with a variety of self-development activities, many of which are discussed in these chapters on developing a relationship strategy that results in partnering style relationships that add value.

Information-age selling involves three major relationship challenges. The first major challenge is building new relationships. Salespeople who can quickly build rapport with new prospects have a much greater chance of achieving success in personal selling. The second major challenge is transforming relationships from the personal level to the business level. Once rapport is established, the salesperson is in a stronger position to begin the "need identification" process. The third major challenge is the management of relationships. To achieve a high level of success, salespeople have to manage a multitude of different relationships.[3] Salespeople must develop relationship management strategies that focus on many individuals and key groups.

In this chapter, we introduce the importance of maintaining high ethical standards as the very foundation to building long-term partnering style relationships that create value. Chapter 4 focuses on a win-win philosophy and discusses the importance of projecting a professional image. Chapter 5, on adaptive selling, explains how an understanding of our own communication style and the communication style of the customer can help us better manage a relationship process that creates value (Figure 3.1).

Strategic/Consultative Selling Model	
Strategic Step	**Prescription**
Develop a Personal Selling Philosophy	☑ Adopt Marketing Concept
	☑ Value Personal Selling
	☑ Become a Problem Solver/Partner
Develop a Relationship Strategy	☐ Maintain High Ethical Standards
	☐ Project Professional Image
	☐ Manage the Relationship Process

FIGURE 3.1

Every salesperson should have an ongoing goal of developing a relationship strategy that adds value to the sale.

3.2 Describe issues that challenge the ethical decision making of salespeople

Issues Challenging the Ethics of Salespeople

In the field of personal selling, the temptation to maximize short-term gains by some type of unethical conduct is always present and occurs more often than in most other careers. Salespeople are especially vulnerable to *un*ethical decision making, because they are subject to many temptations. These temptations are often motivated by offers from clients, competitors, company personnel, and suppliers, and may involve personal gain on the part of the salesperson. While attractive to one or more of the stakeholders associated with the sale in the short run, they serve as the basis for the destruction of long-term relationship, product, customer, and presentation strategies. A few examples follow:

- A customer asks you to create a set of product specifications for completing a sales proposal. A new supplier of yours indicates a sizable direct cash payment would be made to you if you listed the supplier's technical data in the specifications. What would you do?
- You work with the research and development departments of the companies you call on, and therefore are trusted with confidential information about strategic new product development. One of your larger clients has asked if you could help them with a project by answering some questions about their competitor's research activities. How would you respond?
- Your competition whom you know well wants to meet with you to talk about a competitive bid you will be presenting. A suggestion is made that if you will bid this job a little higher than they do, they will definitely do you the same favor on the next purchase made by your customer. What should you do?
- You have visited the buyer twice, and each time the person displayed a great deal of interest in your proposal. During a recent negotiations meeting, the buyer hinted that the order might be signed if you could provide tickets to a national sporting event. Your company has a long-standing policy that gifts are not to be given under any circumstances. What do you do?
- The competition is using exaggerated claims to close the sale of its product. Should you counteract this action by using exaggerated claims of your own to build a stronger case for your product?
- A lucrative proposal you are scheduled to make will provide only a mediocre solution to your client's problem. Your client trusts you, and you know there are better solutions that are being provided by the competition that you cannot match. What would you do?
- Your sales manager is under great pressure to increase sales. At a recent meeting of the entire sales staff, this person said, "We have to hit our numbers no matter what it takes!" Does this emotional appeal change your way of dealing with customers?
- During a recent business trip, you met an old friend and decided to have dinner together. At the end of the meal, you paid for the entire bill and left a generous tip. Do you now put these nonbusiness-related expenses on your expense account?

These ethical dilemmas arise in the field of selling. How do salespeople respond? Some ignore company policy, disregard local, state, federal, and international laws, cast aside personal

FIGURE 3.2

Ethical decision making is the foundation for partnering style relationship, product, customer and presentation strategies.

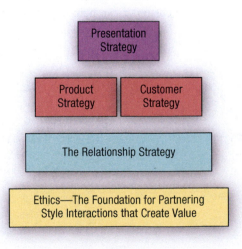

values and standards of conduct, and yield to the pressure. Yielding to this pressure often destroys long-term partnering relationships, and can result in fines, monetary damages, and, in some cases, prison time.

However, a large number of trusted salespersons are able to resist. They can be counted on by the various stakeholders to a sale to form highly ethical win-win relationships, fully understand the customers' buying strategies, make honest nonexaggerated claims about their product, and fully embrace a needs-based consultative presentation strategy. Therefore, in the partnering style seller/buyer relationship, a high level of ethical decision making becomes the foundation for creating value (see Figure 3.2).

Factors Influencing Ethical Decision Making of Salespeople

3.3 Describe the factors that influence the ethical conduct of sales personnel

A number of important factors influence ethical decision making. These factors help sales and marketing personnel to distinguish right from wrong. Figure 3.3 outlines the forces that can help salespeople deal honestly and openly with prospects at all times.

Influences in a Global Economy

Ethical and legal issues that are quite complex on the domestic scene become even more complicated at the international level. International business is growing, and the United States is deeply involved in the global marketplace. Thomas Friedman, author of the best-selling book *The World Is Flat: A Brief History of the Twenty-First Century*, says today's highly competitive and global marketplace is flattening the world of international business. In order to compete with China, India, and other dynamic economics, U.S.-based companies must adopt a more aggressive global focus.[4]

CULTURAL ISSUES Today's global marketplace reflects a kaleidoscope of cultures, each with its own unique qualities. **Culture** is the sum total of beliefs, values, knowledge, ethnic customs, and objects that people use to adapt to their environment. Cultural barriers can impede acceptance of products in foreign countries and weaken interpersonal relationships. When the salesperson understands the cultural background of the foreign customer, communication problems are less likely. Many people from Asia, Arab countries, and much of Africa prefer a more indirect style of communication and therefore value harmony, subtlety, sensitivity, and tact more than brevity.[5] The customer who seems to be agreeing with everything you say may have no intention of buying your product. This person may simply be displaying polite and tactful behaviors.

Perceptions of time differ from country to country. Americans value promptness, but businesspeople from other countries often approach meetings in a more relaxed manner. Arriving

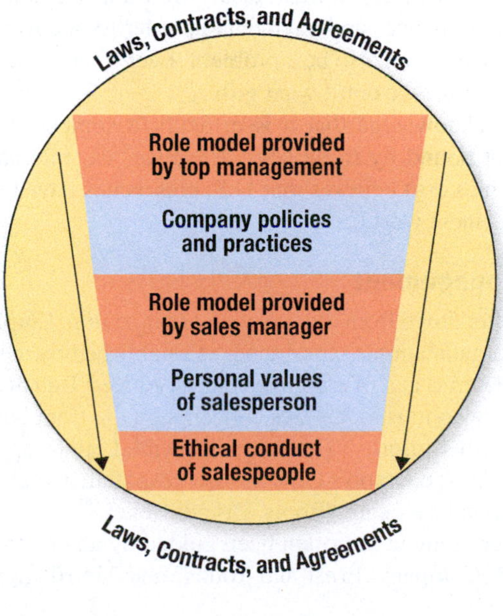

FIGURE 3.3

Factors Influencing the Ethical Behavior of Salespeople

In personal selling, the temptation to maximize short-term gains by some type of unethical conduct is always present. The forces in this figure can help salespeople deal honestly and openly with prospects at all times.

Doing Business in China

China has entered the World Trade Organization, and its leaders have promised to tear down the barriers that have frustrated foreign business representatives for so long. This country provides a huge market for foreign brands. However, doing business in China begins with a careful study of Chinese business customs.

- Patience is critical when doing business in China. Avoid taking the initiative until you fully understand the rules.
- Business entertaining is frequently done banquet style. If you host a banquet, plan your menu carefully because foods have different meanings. You will be in complete control and no one will eat or drink until you give the signal. Toasting is a ritual in China.
- Chinese businesspeople do not make deals quickly. They prefer to spend time building relationships that will last for years. Harmony is important.
- When making introductions, the oldest and highest-ranking person is introduced first. Chinese bow slightly when greeting another person and the handshake follows.
- Gift giving is a complex process in China. Gifts should be given after all business transactions have been completed. Avoid gifts that suggest death in the Chinese culture: clocks, knife openers, and handkerchiefs, for example.[a]

Source: alexsalo images/ Shutterstock

late for a meeting may not be viewed as a problem. Many companies are spending thousands of dollars to make sure that employees sent abroad are culturally prepared. Eastman Chemical Company, for example, has developed a highly successful orientation program for employees who have accepted overseas assignments.[6]

LEGAL ISSUES Doing business in the global marketplace continues to be an ethical minefield. Illegal demands for bribes, kickbacks, or special fees may stand in the way of successful transactions. The Foreign Corrupt Practices Act prohibits U.S. companies from using bribes or kickbacks to influence foreign officials. The new U.K. Anti-Bribery Act prohibits any kind of commercial bribery. Prosecution is aggressive and penalties are severe, ranging from multimillion-dollar fines for companies and jail time for individuals. But monitoring illegal activities throughout the world is a very difficult task.[7] Motorola and some other U.S. businesses are using software to analyze invoices and payments in order to uncover possible payoffs. Gifts from suppliers to U.S. companies can also be a problem. Each year, United Technologies sends a letter to foreign suppliers stating "we don't want gifts."[8]

American businesses acknowledge that it is difficult to compete with organizations from other countries that are not bound by these laws. However, the International Business Ethics Institute (www.business-ethics.org) believes that U.S. companies have been a very positive role model for the rest of the business world.

Influence of Senior Management

Ethical standards tend to filter down from the top of an organization. Employees look to company leaders for guidance. The organization's moral tone, as established by management personnel, is the most important single determinant of employee ethics. At Best Buy, Richard Schulze, founder and chairman, is the person who must put ethics concerns on the front burner and make sure that employees stay focused on that priority. The most influential ethics spokesman at Timberland is CEO Jeffrey Swartz, a third-generation CEO whose grandfather founded the company. With pride, he points out Timberland's slogan: "Boots, Brand, Belief."[9]

In recent years, top management has often been guided by advice from professional service firms such as McKinsey & Company, Ernst and Young, and Merrill Lynch and Company. Too

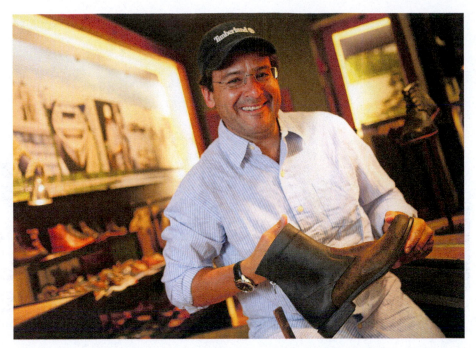

The most influential ethics spokesman at Timberland is CEO Jeffrey Swartz, a third-generation CEO whose grandfather founded the company. With pride, he points out Timberland's slogan: "Boots, Brand, Belief."

Source: ZUMA Press, Inc./Alamy

often these firms are recommending strategies that result in quick, short-term gains. Alan M. Webber, who has been studying professional service firms for 20 years, notes, "They want the money right now." He says, ". . . to make the most money, you actually have to believe in the product or service you offer and care for the customers or clients whom you serve."[10]

Influence of Company Policies and Practices

Company policies and practices can have a major impact on the ethical conduct of salespeople. Many employees do not have well-developed moral sensitivity and, therefore, need the guidance of ethics policies. These policies should cover distributor relations, customer service, pricing, product development, and related areas.[11]

Developing policy statements forces a firm to take a stand on various business practices. Distinguishing right from wrong can be a healthy activity for any organization. The outcome is a more clear-cut philosophy of how to conduct business transactions. Furthermore, the efforts of salespeople can be compromised by the unethical actions of their companies. Selling products for a company that condones unethical practices is very difficult for the salesperson who maintains high ethical standards.[12]

SOCIAL MEDIA AND SELLING TODAY

Ethical Social Networking

Are you an *active* social networker? A recent study was conducted by the Ethics Resource Center that provided some important results with implications for salespeople. Do you spend more than 30 percent of your time on social network sites? Then be careful, since a recent study has shown that active social networkers see many of those activities that other people find unethical as acceptable behaviors. For example this study shows that 59 percent of active social networkers believe that "friending" a client/customer on a social network is acceptable, while only 28 percent of other U.S. workers see it as an acceptable behavior. Forty-two percent of active social networkers believe that tweeting or blogging negatively about your company or colleagues is also acceptable, while only 6 percent of others believe so. This divide between active social networkers and others is crucial because if your client is from the other group, then what you think is acceptable, such as "friending" your customer on Facebook, might come across to your client as unprofessional.[13]

Another extremely important aspect of today's social media comes from the fact that what you post on these media can quickly go viral. For example tweeting about how you used your sales savvy to close a deal can easily spread and reach your customer/other customers and project the wrong image of you and your company as people with self-interest and little customer focus. Companies these days are very cautious about the kind of messages that spread out from the inside and make sure that everything is consistent with their overall corporate image.

Personal selling, by its nature, promotes close working relationships. It is important that salespeople preserve the confidentiality of information they receive. Violation of this ethical responsibility will quickly erode a relationship with the customer.

Source: Jeanette Dietl/ Fotolia

Mutual of Omaha executives provide their employees with a carefully worded document titled "Values for Success." Several of these values form the foundation for a corporate culture that encourages ethical behavior:[14]

- *Openness and Trust* We encourage an open sharing of ideas and information, displaying a fundamental respect for each other as well as our cultural diversity.
- *Honesty and Integrity* We are honest and ethical with others, maintaining the highest standards of personal and professional conduct.
- *Customer-Focus* We never lose sight of our customers, and constantly challenge ourselves to meet their requirements even better.

Most marketing companies provide salespeople with guidelines in such areas as sharing confidential information, reciprocity, bribery, gift giving, entertainment, interacting with competitors, and business defamation.

SHARING CONFIDENTIAL INFORMATION Personal selling, by its very nature, promotes close working relationships. Customers often turn to salespeople for advice. They disclose confidential information freely to someone they trust. It is important that salespeople preserve the confidentiality of the information they receive.

It is not unusual for a customer to disclose information that may be of great value to a competitor. This might include the development of new products, plans to expand into new markets, or anticipated changes in personnel. A salesperson may be tempted to share confidential information with a representative of a competing firm. This breach of confidence might be seen as a means of gaining favor. In most cases, this action backfires and can violate contractual or legal obligations. The person who receives the confidential information quickly loses respect for the salesperson. A gossipy salesperson seldom develops a trusting relationship with a customer.

RECIPROCITY **Reciprocity** is a mutual exchange of benefits, as when a firm buys products from its own customers. Some business firms actually maintain a policy of reciprocity. For example, the manufacturer of commercial sheets and blankets may purchase hotel services from firms that use its products.

Is there anything wrong with the "you scratch my back and I'll scratch yours" approach to doing business? The answer is sometimes yes. In some cases, the use of reciprocity borders on commercial blackmail. Salespeople have been known to approach firms that supply their company and encourage them to buy out of obligation. Reciprocity agreements are illegal when one company pressures another company to join in the agreement.

A business relationship based on reciprocity has other drawbacks. There is the ever-present temptation to take such customers for granted. A customer who buys out of obligation may take a backseat to customers who were won in the open market.

BRIBERY The book *Arrogance and Accords: The Inside Story of the Honda Scandal* describes one of the largest commercial corruption cases in U.S. history. Over a 15-year period, Honda officials received more than $50 million in cash and gifts from dealers eager to obtain fast-selling Honda cars and profitable franchises. Eighteen former Honda executives were convicted of obtaining kickbacks; most went to prison.[15]

In most cases, a bribe is wrong from a legal standpoint. In almost all cases, the bribe is wrong from an ethical point of view. However, bribery does exist, and a salesperson must be prepared to cope with it. It helps to have a well-established company policy to use as a reference point for what is not acceptable.[16]

Salespeople who sell products in foreign markets need to know that giving bribes is viewed as an acceptable business practice in some cultures. However, bribes or payoffs may violate the U.S. Foreign Corrupt Practices Act (FCPA) and other antibribery laws. Lucent Technologies Incorporated dismissed two high-ranking executives in China after it found potential violations of the FCPA.[17]

GIFT GIVING Gift giving is a common practice in America. However, some companies do maintain a "no gift" policy. Many companies report that their policy is either no gifts or nothing of real value. Some gifts, such as advertising novelties, planning calendars, or a meal, are of limited value and cannot be construed as a bribe or payoff.

There are some gray areas that separate a gift from a bribe. Most people agree that a token of insignificant price, such as a pen imprinted with a company logo or a desk calendar, is appropriate. These types of gifts are meant to foster goodwill. A bribe, on the other hand, is an attempt to influence the person receiving the gift.

Are there right and wrong ways to handle gift giving? The answer is yes. The following guidelines are helpful to any salesperson who is considering giving gifts to customers:

1. Do not give gifts before doing business with a customer. Do not use the gift as a substitute for effective selling methods.
2. Never convey the impression you are "buying" the customer's business with gifts. When this happens, the gift becomes nothing more than a bribe.
3. When gift giving is done correctly, the customer clearly views it as symbolic of your appreciation—a "no strings attached" goodwill gesture.
4. Be sure the gift is not a violation of the policies of your firm or of your customer's firm. Some firms do not allow employees to accept gifts at all. Other firms place a dollar limit on a gift's value.

In summary, if you have second thoughts about giving a gift, do not do it. When you are sure some token is appropriate, keep it simple and thoughtful.

ENTERTAINMENT Entertainment is a widespread practice in the field of selling and may be viewed as a bribe by some people. The line dividing gifts, bribes, and entertainment is often quite arbitrary.

Salespeople must frequently decide how to handle entertaining. A few industries see entertainment as part of the approach used to obtain new accounts. This is especially true when competing products are nearly identical. A good example is the cardboard box industry. These products vary little in price and quality. Winning an account may involve knowing who to entertain and how to entertain.

Entertainment is a highly individualized process. One prospect might enjoy a professional football game, while another would be impressed most by a quiet meal at a good restaurant. The key is to get to know your prospect's preferences. How does the person spend leisure time? How much time can the person spare for entertainment? You need to answer these and other questions before you invest time and money in entertainment.

BUSINESS DEFAMATION Salespeople frequently compare their product's qualities and characteristics with those of a competitor during the sales presentation. If such comparisons are inaccurate, misleading, or slander a company's business reputation, such conduct is illegal. Competitors have sued hundreds of companies and manufacturers' representatives for making slanderous statements while selling.

What constitutes business defamation? Steven M. Sack, coauthor of *The Salesperson's Legal Guide*, provides the following examples:

1. *Business slander.* This arises when an unfair and untrue oral statement is made about a competitor. The statement becomes actionable when it is communicated to a third party and can be interpreted as damaging the competitor's business reputation or the personal reputation of an individual in that business.
2. *Business libel.* This may be incurred when an unfair and untrue statement is made about a competitor in writing. The statement becomes actionable when it is communicated to a third party and can be interpreted as damaging the company.
3. *Product disparagement.* This occurs when false or deceptive comparisons or distorted claims are made concerning a competitor's product, services, or property.[18]

USE OF THE INTERNET Use of the Internet offers salespeople many advantages, but it can also create a number of ethical dilemmas. For example, e-mail abuse has become a modern-day problem because some employees forget that their employer owns the e-mail system. E-mail messages that contain inflammatory or abusive content, inappropriate jokes, embarrassing gossip, or breaches of confidentiality can lead to legal liabilities. A growing number of companies are developing policies that define permissible uses of their e-mail system.[19]

Some resourceful salespeople have created their own websites to alert, attract, or support clients. The rise of these "extranets" has created some problems because they often function outside of the company's jurisdiction. What should top management do if a top salesperson encourages her customers to participate in a special Web auction for a backlogged product? What if the salesperson makes exaggerated claims about a new product? Every marketing firm needs to carefully monitor the development and use of extranets.[20]

The effectiveness of company policies as a deterrent to unethical behavior depends on two factors. The first is the firm's attitude toward employees who violate these policies. If violations are routinely ignored, the policy's effect soon erodes. Second, policies that influence personal selling need the support of the entire sales staff. Salespeople should have some voice in policy decisions; they are more apt to support policies they have helped develop.

ETHICAL AND LEGAL ISSUES WITH RECORDING CRM DATA

Customer relationship management systems enable you to collect information about people with whom you maintain relationships, including the taking of notes. It is a good practice to record more than basic transaction information, such as personal details about your customers. Reviewing your observations about the customers' behavior and your recording of their statements can help you understand them and their needs. Rereading their comments about ethical issues can assist you in assessing the value of maintaining a business relationship with them.

To be fair, it is important to record only the facts concerning your observations, not necessarily your conclusions, especially if negative. Information in an electronic database can last a long time and, for reasons such as litigation or company acquisitions, can be "mobile." This means that others may form an opinion about your customer based on your recorded conclusions, with potential detrimental consequences for your customer. Because the customer may not be aware of the existence of the information in your database, that person does not have a fair opportunity to correct any erroneous conclusions. Another reason to carefully record only the facts is the possibility that any inappropriate information may come to the attention of the customer. For example, there are reported instances in which a customer later joined the sales organization and gained access to the customer relationship management (CRM) system.

Most CRM systems contain scheduling functions, which means that you can set aside time on your calendar to attend meetings, make phone calls, and perform tasks. The scheduling tools usually include alarms, which remind you that a deadline is approaching. The disciplined use of these features can help you get your work accomplished on time. Taking advantage of the system's reminder tools can be especially important when it involves fulfilling your commitments. The system can help you build trust by reminding you to always do what you said you would do.

Influence of the Sales Manager

The salesperson's actions often mirror the sales manager's behavior and expectations. This is not surprising when you consider the relationship between salespeople and their supervisors. They look to their supervisors for guidance and direction. The sales manager is generally the company's closest point of contact with the sales staff. This person is usually viewed as the chief spokesperson for top management.

Sales managers generally provide new salespeople with their first orientation to company operations. They are responsible for interpreting company policy. On a continuing basis, the sales manager monitors the salesperson's work and provides important feedback concerning conduct. If a salesperson violates company policy, it is usually the sales manager who is responsible for administering reprimands. If the moral fiber of a sales force begins to break down, the sales manager must shoulder a great deal of responsibility, even if it goes against "standard practice."[21]

Sales managers influence the ethical behavior of salespeople by virtue of what they say and what they do. From time to time, managers must review their expectations of ethical behavior. Salespeople are under continuous pressure to abandon their personal ethical standards to achieve sales goals. Values such as integrity and honesty must receive ongoing support from the sales manager. The role of the sales manager will be discussed in more detail in Chapter 17.

Influence of the Salesperson's Personal Values

Ann Kilpatrick, a sales representative in the transportation industry, encountered an unexpected experience when entertaining a potential client. The client said, "Let's go to Johnny's." She was not familiar with Johnny's, but on arrival discovered it was a raunchy bar. Kilpatrick related that she sat there for five minutes and then said, "This is not what I was expecting. This is a sleazy place. Let's go somewhere else where we can talk." She was not willing to compromise her personal values to win a new account.[22]

Values represent the ultimate reasons people have for acting as they do. Values are your deep personal beliefs and preferences that influence your behavior. To discover what really motivates you, carefully examine what you value.[23] Values serve as a foundation for our attitudes, and our attitudes serve as a foundation for our behavior (Figure 3.4). Destructive attitudes can result in unethical behaviors, where constructive attitudes generally create ethical behaviors. We do not adopt or discard values quickly. In fact, the development and refinement of values is a lifelong process.

Customers have a very negative view of salespeople who lack integrity. Yet, the temptation to lie about a product's features or benefits grows when you are trying to meet sales quotas. John Craig, a pharmacist at Hancock Drugs in Scottsburg, Indiana, describes a meeting with a pushy sales representative employed by a pharmaceutical company. The salesperson emphasized the wonders of a powerful, expensive painkiller but failed to describe its side effects. Craig said, "He was very pushy at the beginning," and this behavior revealed a character flaw.[24]

VALUES CONFLICT Values help us establish our own personal standards concerning what is right and what is wrong. Ron Willingham, author of *Integrity Selling for the 21st Century*, says, "Selling success is more an issue of who you are than what you know."[25] A salesperson's ethics and values contribute more to sales success than do techniques or strategies. Some salespeople discover a values conflict between themselves and their employer. If you view your employer's instructions or influence as improper, you have three choices:

1. Ignore the influence of your values and engage in the unethical behavior. However, even with success, inattention to values will result in a loss of self-respect and feelings of guilt and in some circumstances legal liability.[26] When salespeople experience conflicts between their actions and values, they also feel a loss of confidence and energy.[27] Positive energy is the result of creating value for the customer. Negative energy is experienced when salespeople fail to honor and embrace their ethical values.

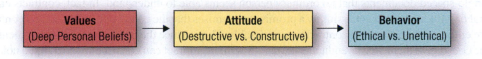

FIGURE 3.4

Values represent the ultimate reasons salespeople have for acting as they do. Values serve as a foundation for either constructive or destructive attitudes, and these attitudes serve as a foundation for ethical or unethical behavior.

2. Voice strong opposition to the practice that is in conflict with your values system. Take a stand and state your beliefs. When ethical infractions occur, it's best to bring them up internally and try to influence decisions made by your peers or superiors. In some cases, doing the right thing may not be popular with others. Price Pritchett, the author of *The Ethics of Excellence*, says, "Not everybody will be on your side in your struggle to do the right thing."[28] However, more and more companies are celebrating employees who come forward to identify questionable conduct.

3. Refuse to compromise your values and be prepared to deal with the consequences. This may mean leaving the job. It also may mean that you will be fired.

Salespeople face ethical problems and decisions every day. In this respect, they are no different from the doctor, the lawyer, the teacher, or any other professional. Ideally, they make decisions on the basis of the values they hold.[29]

Influence of Laws, Contracts, and Agreements

Take another look at Figure 3.3 and you will notice that all of the key elements, personnel, and policies are influenced by laws, contracts, and agreements. Everyone involved in sales and marketing is guided by legal as well as ethical standards. We live in a society in which the legal system plays a key role in preventing people from engaging in unethical behavior.

LAWS The specific obligations imposed by government on the way business operates take the form of "statutes," laws passed by Congress or state legislatures. Some of the most common laws deal with price competition, credit reporting, debt collection practices, contract enforcement, and land sales disclosure. The Uniform Commercial Code (UCC) is a major law influencing sales throughout the United States. The UCC is a legal guide to a wide range of transactions between the seller and the buyer. This law has been adopted throughout the United States.

Several areas featured in the UCC focus directly on the seller–buyer relationship. Some of the primary areas follow:

1. *Definition of a sale.* The code defines the legal dimensions of a sale. It clearly states that salespeople have the authority to legally obligate the company they represent.
2. *Warranties and guarantees.* The code distinguishes between express warranties and implied warranties. Express warranties are those that are described by the express language of the seller. Implied warranties are the obligations imposed by law on the seller that are not assumed in express language.
3. *Salesperson and reseller.* In many cases, the salesperson has resellers as customers or prospects. Salespeople must be aware of their employer's obligations to the reseller.
4. *Financing of sales.* Often salespeople work for firms that are directly involved in financing products or services or in arranging such financing from outside sources. A salesperson needs to be familiar with the legal aspects of these credit arrangements.
5. *Product consignment.* In some cases, goods are delivered to the buyer, but the title remains with the seller. This type of transaction can become complicated if the goods have a limited life span. Depreciation may occur with the passing of time. Salespeople should be familiar with the company's rights in cases where goods are sold on consignment.

A majority of the states have passed legislation that establishes a cooling-off period during which the consumer may void a contract to purchase goods or services. Although the provisions of **cooling-off laws** vary from state to state, their primary purpose is to give customers an opportunity to reconsider a buying decision made under a salesperson's persuasive influence. Many laws are designed to deal specifically with sales made in the consumer's home. For example, the Federal Trade Commission (FTC) established the National Do Not Call Registry in an attempt to reduce the number of telemarketing calls.

CONTRACTS AND AGREEMENTS The word "contract" may bring to mind the familiar, multipage, single-spaced documents that no ordinary person seems able to understand. In fact, contracts can be oral or written. A **contract** is simply a promise or promises that the courts will enforce. Oral contracts are enforceable, but written contracts are preferable. They reduce the possibility of disagreement and the courts give them great weight in a lawsuit. A written contract can consist of a sales slip, a notation on a check, or any other writing that evidences the promises that the parties made.[30]

Salespeople are sometimes the legal representatives of their company and, therefore, must be careful when signing written contracts. They often oversee contracts with customers, suppliers, and resellers. Salespeople also frequently sign employment contracts at the time they are hired. Most of these agreements include a noncompete clause. One of the most common clauses, a noncompete clause prohibits salespeople from joining a competing firm for a period of time after they leave. Most clauses are legally binding even when an employee's position is cut. Employers see employment contracts as an effective way to protect intellectual property, customer lists, and other resources an employee might take to a competing firm.[31]

Many companies are learning that resolving legal disputes can be very costly and time consuming. Resolving a dispute in the courts can sometimes take several years. A serious effort to prevent unethical activities can prevent costly litigation.

Building Trust with the Transactional, Consultative and Strategic Alliance Buyer

Everyone involved in personal selling must work hard to build relationships based on trust. Customers are more apt to trust salespeople they believe to be ethical, leading to a much more productive partnership.[32] Although trust is an essential element of every sale, the meaning of trust changes with the type of sale.[33]

- *Trust in transactional sales.* The primary customer focus in this type of sale is trust in the product. Is the product reliable? Is the product priced as low as possible? Can the product be delivered in a timely fashion? The transactional buyer may purchase a product from a salesperson they do not feel totally comfortable with if it meets their purchase criteria.
- *Trust in consultative sales.* In a consultative sale, the customer focus shifts from the product to the person who sells the product. The consultative buyer is thinking, "Can I trust this salesperson to identify my problem and offer me one or more solutions?" Customers involved in a consultative sale usually do not separate the product from the person selling it. They want to do business with a salesperson who displays such positive qualities as warmth, empathy, genuineness, competence, and integrity.
- *Trust in strategic alliance sales.* The strategic alliance buyer wants to do business with an institution that can be trusted. This buyer looks beyond the well-qualified salesperson and assesses the entire organization. A strategic alliance customer will not feel comfortable partnering with a company whose values differ greatly from his or her own. Ethical accountability will greatly influence the way an alliance partner is judged and valued.

Trust exists when we strongly believe in the integrity, ability, and character of a person or an organization. Although trust is an intangible, it is at the very core of all meaningful relationships. Trust is quickly lost and slowly won.[34]

Character strength builds as we display loyalty, mutual commitment, and the pursuit of long-term goals. These are the qualities needed to build strong buyer–seller relationships.

Source: Pressmaster/Shutterstock

3.4 Describe how ethical
decisions influence the
building of partnering
relationships in selling

Making Ethical Decisions That Build Selling Relationships

Business ethics comprise principles and standards that guide behavior in the world of business. They help translate values into appropriate and effective foundational behaviors that build and strengthen partnering relationships in day-to-day life. Whether a specific behavior is right or wrong, ethical or unethical, is often determined by company leaders, customers, investors, the legal system, and the community.[35] Of course, the views of various stakeholders may be in conflict. As noted in the examples cited, kickbacks and secret payoffs may be acceptable practices to the vice president of sales and marketing or a supplier, yet may be viewed as unethical by the customer, members of the sales force, the board of directors, investors, and the general public.

There is no one uniform code of ethics for all salespeople as societal and relational norms can vary from person to person.[36] However, a large number of business organizations, professional associations (see Figure 3.5), and certification agencies have established written codes. For example, the National Association of Sales Professionals (NASP) states that members must abide by its Standards of Professional Conduct.[37]

Influence of Character in Ethical Decision Making

Today, we recognize that character and integrity strongly influence building partnering relationships in personal selling. **Character** is composed of personal standards, including honesty, integrity, and moral strength. Your character is based on your internal values and the resulting judgments you make about what is right and what is wrong. The ethical decisions you make reflect your character strength. It is a quality that is highly respected in the field of personal selling.

Integrity is the basic ingredient of character that is exhibited when you achieve congruence between what you know, what you say, and what you do.[38] In a world of uncertainty and rapid change, integrity has become a valuable character trait. Salespeople with integrity can be trusted to do what they say they will do. One way to achieve trustworthiness in personal selling is to refrain from deceiving or misleading the customer.

We are indebted to Stephen Covey, author of *The Seven Habits of Highly Effective People*, for helping us better understand the relationship between character strength and success in personal selling. In his best-selling book, Covey says that there are basic principles that must be integrated into our character. One example is to always do what you say you are going to do. "As we make and keep commitments, even small commitments, we begin to establish an inner integrity that gives us the awareness of self-control and courage and strength to accept more of the responsibility for our own lives."[39] Fulfilling your commitments builds trust, and trust is the most important precondition of partnering relationships that create value.

Colleges and universities are beginning to play a more active role in character development. Courses that focus on ethics are becoming quite common. When a new ethics course was developed at the University of Virginia, the faculty indicated that the purpose of the course is not to point out what is right and what is wrong. The course is designed to help students understand the consequences of their actions when they face an ethical dilemma.[40]

The Erosion of Character on Ethical Decision Making

Despite a growing interest in business ethics, unethical behavior has become all too common. A survey conducted by *Newsweek* suggests that the current generation of workers may be more tolerant of deception. Many of those involved in the survey did not view lying and cheating as unacceptable.[41] Employees who are involved in unethical behavior often report that they were under pressure to act unethically or illegally on the job.

As the past decade unfolded, many large, inflexible corporations were transformed into smaller, more nimble competitors. New economy thinking prevailed as business firms, large and small, worked hard to become lean, innovative, and profitable. We witnessed an almost unrelenting emphasis on earnings that was driven, in some cases, by executive greed. It was during this period that some of America's most respected companies began to cross the ethical divide.[42]

A company cannot build partnering relationships and enjoy long-term success unless its employees are honest, ethical, and uncompromising about values and principles. Yet many employees engage in dishonest practices that erode character. The collapse of Lehman Bros., one

Ethical Norms and Values for Marketers

PREAMBLE

The American Marketing Association commits itself to promoting the highest standard of professional ethical norms and values for its members (practitioners, academics, and students). Norms are established standards of conduct that are expected and maintained by society and/or professional organizations. Values represent the collective conception of what communities find desirable, important and morally proper. Values also serve as the criteria for evaluating our own personal actions and the actions of others. As marketers, we recognize that we not only serve our organizations but also act as stewards of society in creating, facilitating and executing the transactions that are part of the greater economy. In this role, marketers are expected to embrace the highest professional ethical norms and the ethical values implied by our responsibility toward multiple stakeholders (e.g., customers, employees, investors, peers, channel members, regulators and the host community).

ETHICAL NORMS

As Marketers, we must:

1. Do no harm. This means consciously avoiding harmful actions or omissions by embodying high ethical standards and adhering to all applicable laws and regulations in the choices we make.
2. Foster trust in the marketing system. This means striving for good faith and fair dealing so as to contribute toward the efficacy of the exchange process as well as avoiding deception in product design, pricing, communication, and delivery of distribution.
3. Embrace ethical values. This means building relationships and enhancing consumer confidence in the integrity of marketing by affirming these core values: honesty, responsibility, fairness, respect, transparency and citizenship.

ETHICAL VALUES

Honesty – to be forthright in dealings with customers and stakeholders. To this end, we will:
- Strive to be truthful in all situations and at all times.
- Offer products of value that do what we claim in our communications.
- Stand behind our products if they fail to deliver their claimed benefits.
- Honor our explicit and implicit commitments and promises.

Responsibility – to accept the consequences of our marketing decisions and strategies. To this end, we will:
- Strive to serve the needs of customers.
- Avoid using coercion with all stakeholders.
- Acknowledge the social obligations to stakeholders that come with increased marketing and economic power.
- Recognize our special commitments to vulnerable market segments such as children, seniors, the economically impoverished, market illiterates and others who may be substantially disadvantaged.
- Consider environmental stewardship in our decision making.

Fairness – to balance justly the needs of the buyer with the interests of the seller. To this end, we will:
- Represent products in a clear way in selling, advertising and other forms of communication; this includes the avoidance of false, misleading, and deceptive promotion.
- Reject manipulations and sales tactics that harm customer trust. Refuse to engage in price fixing, predatory pricing, price gouging or "bait-and-switch" tactics.
- Avoid knowing participation in conflicts of interest. Seek to protect the private information of customers, employees, and partners.

Respect – to acknowledge the basic human dignity of all stakeholders. To this end, we will:
- Value individual differences and avoid stereotyping customers or depicting demographic groups (e.g., gender, race, sexual orientation) in a negative or dehumanizing way.
- Listen to the needs of customers and make all reasonable efforts to monitor and improve their satisfaction on an ongoing basis.
- Make every effort to understand and respectfully treat buyers, suppliers, intermediaries and distributors from all cultures.
- Acknowledge the contributions of others, such as consultants, employees and coworkers, to marketing endeavors.
- Treat everyone, including our competitors, as we would wish to be treated.

Transparency – to create a spirit of openness in marketing operations. To this end, we will:
- Strive to communicate clearly with all constituencies.
- Accept constructive criticism from customers and other stakeholders.
- Explain and take appropriate action regarding significant product or service risks, component substitutions or other foreseeable eventualities that could affect customers or their perception of the purchase decision.
- Disclose list prices and terms of financing as well as available price deals and adjustments.

Citizenship – to fulfill the economic, legal, philanthropic and societal responsibilities that serve stakeholders. To this end, we will:
- Strive to protect the ecological environment in the execution of marketing campaigns.
- Give back to the community through volunteerism and charitable donations. Contribute to the overall betterment of marketing and its reputation.
- Urge supply chain members to ensure that trade is fair for all participants, including producers in developing countries.

IMPLEMENTATION

We expect AMA members to be courageous and proactive in leading and/or aiding their organizations in the fulfillment of the explicit and implicit promises made to those stakeholders. We recognize that every industry sector and marketing subdiscipline (e.g., marketing research, e-commerce, Internet selling, direct marketing, and advertising) has its own specific ethical issues that require policies and commentary. An array of such codes can be accessed through links on the AMA Web site. Consistent with the principle of subsidiarity (solving issues at the level where the expertise resides), we encourage all such groups to develop and/or refine their industry and discipline-specific codes of ethics to supplement these guiding ethical norms and values.

FIGURE 3.5

This code of ethics serves as a foundation for the members of the American Marketing Association (AMA).

Source: American Marketing Association Code of Ethics. Used by permission of American Marketing Association.

of the largest U.S. corporations ever to file for bankruptcy, can be traced to a culture that emphasized risk taking, personal ambition over teamwork, and earnings growth at any cost. The new economy depends on innovation and aggressive development of markets, but actions that weaken the moral contract with customers, employees, and shareholders can bring serious consequences. Let's examine some "half-truths" that have influenced the erosion of character in ethical decision making.

- *We are in it only for ourselves.* Some critics of today's moral climate feel that the current moral decline began when society's focus shifted from "what is right" to "what is right for me." In personal selling, this point of view can quickly subtract rather than add value to a relationship with the customer. Fortunately, there are many salespeople for whom integrity and self-respect are basic values. Darryl Ashley, a pharmaceutical representative for Eli Lilly Company, suspected that a pharmacist (a customer) was diluting chemotherapy drugs in order to increase profit margins. Ashley shared his suspicions with one of the cancer doctors who was purchasing the drug from the pharmacist. Tests indicated that the drug had been diluted.[43]
- *Corporations exist to maximize shareholder value.* In the past, corporations were more often viewed as *economic* and *social* institutions—organizations that served a balanced group of stakeholders. In recent years, analysts, stock traders, CEOs, and the media have too often focused on a single standard of performance—share price.[44] Marjorie Kelly, former editor of *Business Ethics*, says, "Managing a company solely for maximum share price can destroy both share price and the entire company."[45]

Pressure to increase "numbers" led to sales abuses at WorldCom Incorporated. Some salespeople double-booked accounts in order to make their quota and collect increased commissions. The false reporting was identified by an internal company probe and the guilty sales representatives were fired.[46]

- *It's not wrong because everyone is doing it.* Shoshana Zuboff, contributing columnist for *Fast Company* magazine, sees widespread acceptance of wrong as normal. She points to acceptance in some industries of the belief that "It's not wrong because everyone is doing it."[47] Employees working for prominent companies such as Merck, WorldCom, Putman Investments, Tyco, and Edward D. Jones & Company have been involved in ethical lapses.[48] Most white-collar crime is committed by persons who lack character and integrity, or who had a momentary but disastrous lapse in judgment.
- *Companies need to be lean and mean.*[49] Downsizing has become a common practice even when the economy is strong. After the layoffs, companies must deal with serious problems of low morale and mistrust of management. Those employees who remain after a company reduces its ranks often feel demoralized, overworked, and fearful. The stress of long hours and a faster pace can result in quality losses and bad service that alienate customers. Richard Sennett, author of *The Corrosion of Character*, says that the decline of character strength can be traced to conditions that have grown out of our fast-paced, high-stress, information-driven economy. He states that character strength builds in a climate that encourages loyalty, mutual commitment, and the pursuit of long-term goals.[50] These are the ethical qualities needed to build a foundation for strong partnering style interactions that create value.

Today, many business firms are struggling to align their values, ethics, and principles with the expectations of their salespeople and their customers. The process of negotiating ethical standards and practices must be ongoing. Citigroup Incorporated, one of the world's largest financial services firms, is working hard to move beyond regulatory scandals. Charles Prince, past CEO of Citigroup, wanted the company to better balance its "delivering-the-numbers" culture with a long-term attention to reputation. He readily admitted that "at times, our actions have put at risk our most precious commodity—the trust of our clients, the patience of our employees, and the faith of our shareholders."[51]

Can moral behavior be taught? The National Business Ethics Survey, conducted annually by the Ethics Resource Center (www.ethics.org), found that 90 percent of employees said that ethics training is useful or somewhat useful to them. A growing number of students are completing business ethics courses as part of their undergraduate or graduate programs.[52]

SELLING IN ACTION

When the Competition Uses Negative Practices

Negative selling practices create two problems for companies with integrity. First, the salesperson must use valuable time correcting misinformation presented by the competition. Second, a sale may be delayed until the customer rejects the untruth. Jim Galtan, former director of sales for Schick Technologies, Inc., the leading manufacturer of digital dental X-ray technology, often learns that the competition has said something negative about his product. When this happens, he looks the customer in the eye and says, "Having the best product often frustrates our competition." He also tells customers that if the competition is honest in their assessment, they should be willing to prepare a letter outlining their concerns. Galtan says documentation is the easiest way to cope with negative selling because no one's going to document untruth.[b]

Developing a Personal Code of Ethics That Adds Value

3.5 Discuss guidelines for developing a personal code of ethics that creates value

Too often people confuse their ethical standards with legal standards. They believe that if you are not breaking the law, then you are acting in an ethical manner.[53] A salesperson's personal code of ethics must extend beyond the legal definition of what is right and wrong. To view ethics only in terms of what is legally proper encourages the question, "What can I get by with?" A salesperson must develop a personal code of ethics that extends beyond the letter of the law.

Bruce Weinstein, a professional ethicist who is often introduced as "The Ethics Guy," offers sound advice on living an ethical life. He says we should do the right thing simply because it's the right thing to do. The only way you can build a loyal and growing client base is to demonstrate that you have the customers' own best interests at heart. You are trying to make things better for them. "Here is where ethics differs from the law. It demands more of us," says Weinstein.[54]

Many people considering a career in selling are troubled by the thought that they may be pressured into compromising their personal standards of right and wrong. These fears may be justified. The authors of *The Ethical Edge*, a book that examines organizations that have faced moral crises, contend that business firms have given too little thought to the issue of helping employees to function ethically within organizations.[55] Many salespeople wonder whether their own ethical philosophy can survive in the business world. These are some of their questions:

"Can a profitable business and good ethics coexist?"
"Are there still business firms that value adherence to high ethical standards?"
"Is honesty still a valued personal trait in the business community?"

In the field of athletic competition, the participants rely heavily on a written set of rules. The referee or umpire is ever present to detect rule violations and assess a penalty. In the field of personal selling, there is no universal code of ethics. However, some general guidelines can serve as a foundation for a personal code of business ethics.

1. *Relationship comes first, task second.* Sharon Drew Morgan, author of *Selling with Integrity*, says that you can't sell a product unless there is a level of comfort between you and the prospect. She encourages salespeople to take the time to create a level of comfort, rapport, and collaboration that encourages open communication.[56] Placing task before relationship is based on the belief that the salesperson knows more than the customer. Morgan reminds us, "The buyer has the answers, and the seller has the questions."[57] These answers surface only when the buyer–seller relationship is characterized by rapport and trust.

2. *Be honest with yourself and with others.* To achieve excellence in terms of ethical practices, you have to believe that everything you do counts. Tom Peters in *Thriving on Chaos* said, "Integrity may be about little things as much as or more than big ones."[58] Integrity is about accuracy in completing your expense account. There is always the temptation to inflate the expense report for personal gain. Integrity is also about avoiding the temptation to stretch the truth, to exaggerate, or to withhold information. Paul Ekman, author of *Telling Lies*, says that withholding important information is one of the primary ways of lying.[59] A complete and informative sales presentation may include information concerning the product's

Personal selling must be viewed as an exchange of value. Salespeople who accept this ethical guideline view personal selling as something you do for customers, not something you do to customers.

Source: Kablonk/SuperStock

limitations. If you let your character and integrity be revealed in the little things, others can see you as one who acts ethically in all things. Any violation of honesty, however small, dilutes your ethical strength, leaving you weaker for the big challenges you will face sooner or later.[60]

3. *Personal selling must be viewed as an exchange of value.* Salespeople who maintain a value focus are searching for ways to create value for their prospects or customers. This value may take the form of increased productivity, greater profit, enjoyment, or security. The value focus motivates the salesperson to carefully identify the prospects' wants and needs.[61] Salespeople who accept this ethical guideline view personal selling as something you do *for* customers, not something you do *to* customers. The role of the salesperson is to diagnose buyer needs and determine whether value can be created. Always be prepared to add value.

CHAPTER LEARNING ACTIVITIES

Reviewing Key Concepts

Explain the importance of developing a relationship strategy
The manner in which salespeople establish, build, and maintain relationships is a major key to success in personal selling. Emotional intelligence, defined as the capacity for monitoring our own feelings and those of others, for both motivating ourselves and managing emotions well in ourselves and in our relationships, is critical to the development of a successful selling relationship strategy.

Describe issues that challenge the ethical decision making of salespeople
A selling career, more than most other careers, is frequently subjected to situations that provide short-term gain, resulting in the long-term erosion of integrity and destruction of relationships. Various stakeholders to a sale make requests and offers that are unethical and, in a number of situations, illegal. Salespeople are repeatedly challenged to make ethical decisions. Ethics, therefore, forms the foundation for partnering relationships upon which relationships, product, customer, and presentation strategies exist.

In the field of personal selling, the temptation to maximize short-term gains by some type of unethical conduct is always present and occurs more often than in most other careers. Salespeople are especially vulnerable to *un*ethical decision making, because they are subject to many temptations. These temptations are often motivated by offers from clients, competitors, company personnel and suppliers, and may involve personal gain on the part of the salesperson. While attractive to one or more of the stakeholders associated with the sale in the short run, they serve as the basis for the destruction of long-term, trusted, partnering relationship strategies, as well as product, customer, and presentation strategies.

Describe the factors that influence the ethical conduct of sales personnel
At the international level, ethical and legal issues can be very complex. The global marketplace reflects a great number of cultures, each with its unique qualities. Coping with illegal activities throughout the world is also very challenging. Illegal demands for bribes, kickbacks, or special fees can serve as a barrier to business transactions.

Salespeople can benefit from the stabilizing influence of good role models. Although top management personnel are usually far removed from day-to-day selling activities, they can have a major impact on salespeople's conduct. Dishonesty at the top of an organization can cause an erosion of ethical standards at the lower echelons. Sales managers provide another important role model. They interpret company policies and help establish guidelines for acceptable and unacceptable selling practices.

Describe how ethical decisions influence the building of partnering relationships in selling

Character and integrity strongly influence relationships in personal selling. Unethical sales practices will ultimately destroy relationships with customers. These practices undermine trust, which is at the very core of all meaningful relationships.

Many colleges and universities are playing a more active role in character development. Character education is often integrated into courses that focus on ethics. Character is composed of personal standards of behavior, so all of us can do things that build character. Keeping our commitments to others provides just one example of how character is built.

Discuss guidelines for developing a personal code of ethics that creates value

Salespeople must establish their own standards of personal conduct. They must decide how best to serve their company and build strong partnerships with their customers. The pressure to compromise one's ethical standards surfaces almost daily. The primary deterrent is a strong sense of right and wrong. Three general guidelines can serve as a foundation for a personal code of ethics:

a. Relationship comes first; task, second.
b. Be honest with yourself and with others.
c. Personal selling must be viewed as an exchange of value.

Key Terms

Emotional intelligence, p. 51	Values, p. 59	Business ethics, p. 62
Culture, p. 53	Cooling-off laws, p. 60	Character, p. 62
Reciprocity, p. 56	Contract, p. 60	Integrity, p. 62

MyMarketingLab

To complete the problems with the ⭐ in your MyLab, go to the EOC Discussion Questions.

Review Questions

3-1 List the three prescriptions that serve as the foundation for development of a relationship strategy.

⭐ **3-2** How does business slander differ from business libel?

⭐ **3-3** What major factors help influence salespeople's ethical conduct?

3-4 What is the Uniform Commercial Code? Why is it needed?

⭐ **3-5** Why must a salesperson's ethical sense extend beyond the legal definition of what is right and wrong?

3-6 Explain why the sales manager plays such an important role in influencing the ethical behavior of salespeople.

3-7 A company policy on ethics should cover several major areas. What are they?

3-8 List and describe three guidelines used as a foundation of a self-imposed code of business ethics.

Ethics Application Exercises

Gray Issues–Ethical Decision Making in Selling Today is an assessment designed to help make more informed ethical decisions. Many of the ethical issues included in this assessment will be faced when one applies for and obtains a personal selling position. Completion of this assessment will provide an introduction to a wide range of real-life ethical dilemmas. It will stimulate in-depth thinking about the ethical consequences of one's decisions and actions.

This application exercise is a two-part assessment. Part I includes five mini-cases that introduce ethical dilemmas likely to be faced when applying for a sales position. Part II includes seven ethical dilemmas that will likely be encountered in a typical sales position. Each mini-case poses four solutions. In some cases, only one solution is the correct choice; in others, more than one choice has merit. Keep in mind, however, that one solution will be the best selection from the options listed.

It is important to read the Park Shores Resort and Convention Center Account Executive Position Description on page 427 of Appendix 3 prior to taking the assessment. You can also learn more about Park Shores by accessing the link at www.pearsonhighered.com/manning.

Circle Your Best Choice

Part I—Mini-Case 1—Prior to the interview, T. J. McKee, the Sales Manager, requests a personal resume. Your current grade point average is 2.9, but it will very likely increase to 3.0 or higher at the end of the current semester. What should you do?

a. Indicate that your current grade point average is 3.0.
b. Indicate that your current grade point average is 3.0, but make a mental note to explain (during the interview) that it is currently 2.9 but will likely increase to 3.0 or higher at the end of the semester.
c. Indicate that your current grade point average is 2.9.
d. Omit this information from the resume.

Mini-Case 2—Recently, you received an invitation to become a member of Alpha Phi Omega, a fraternity that honors students who have a record of outstanding service to the community. Very few students are invited to join and the membership committee, which screens applications, occasionally rejects applications. Should you list membership in Alpha Phi Omega on your resume?

a. Do not list this membership on your resume.
b. List this membership on your resume but indicate that approval is pending.
c. Do not list this membership on the resume, but describe your community service activities.
d. List the membership on the resume without any additional information.

Mini-Case 3—During the interview, T. J. McKee requests salary information about your most recent full-time position. You believe this information may influence the starting salary offer, should you be offered the job. The Park Shores uses a commission plan with a guaranteed salary. What should you do?

a. Tactfully tell Mr. McKee that this information is personal and you would rather not discuss past earnings.
b. Provide the information as requested.
c. Provide an inflated figure in hope of receiving a higher initial salary offer.
d. Refuse to provide the information, but do tell him the amount you hope to earn if hired.

Mini-Case 4—Prior to visiting San Diego, California, for the interview, you receive a letter from T. J. McKee that explains that you will be reimbursed for all travel and meal expenses. You will stay in a complimentary room at the Park Shores Resort and Convention Center. The letter states that the daily meal expense (per-diem) is $65. The early morning flight to San Diego includes a complimentary snack. You have lunch with Sara Millen, manager of the hotel, and she pays the bill. That evening you have dinner on your own at a restaurant near the hotel. The bill, including tip, is $36.25. The next morning, you take an early morning flight home and once again enjoy a complimentary snack on the plane. When you turn in your expenses, what amount of meal reimbursement should you request?

a. Request $36.25 for the evening meal.
b. Request $65, which is the amount available for meals.
c. Request $41.50 in order to cover the cost of the evening meal and snacks you purchased at the hotel gift shop.
d. Turn in no meal expenses because the amount spent was quite small.

Mini-Case 5—A large hotel and conference center in Orlando, Florida, has invited you to interview for a sales position. All expenses will be paid. You have no interest in moving to Florida, but you would enjoy visiting Orlando and having an opportunity to visit Disney World. What should you do?

a. Accept the invitation. You need the experience that only a real interview can provide.
b. Do not accept the invitation because you have no interest in relocating to Florida.
c. Accept the invitation because you will have an opportunity to visit Disney World.
d. Accept the invitation and approach the interview with an open mind. Do not close the door on a job opportunity.

Part II—Mini-Case 1—On November 18, a customer requests a price quotation for a conference that will be held on March 22. This customer has scheduled two previous conferences at the Park Shores Convention Center. You know that on December 1 the hotel will announce a special conference "package plan" that will provide this customer with a lower rate. The new rate schedule will extend from December 1 to April 1. What action should you take at this time?

a. Prepare a price quotation for the current rate.
b. Delay preparing the price quotation until December 1.
c. Prepare a price quotation using the rates that will be announced December 1.
d. Prepare a price quotation at the current price, but make a mental note to send the customer a revised quotation on December 1.

Mini-Case 2—Throughout the past several weeks, you have met with a representative of Follett Corporation on several occasions. You are anxious to book a large conference that will involve over 200 Follett employees. Every detail of the proposal has been negotiated, but the prospect seems reluctant to sign the contract. One option available is to tell the customer that room availability is limited, and any additional delays may create scheduling problems during the time period requested. In reality, business is usually very slow during the time period requested, so room availability should not be a problem. What should you do?

a. Stop making contact with the prospect and wait for a decision.
b. Continue to make an effort to close the sale, but do not provide any information that is not accurate.
c. Make another call on the customer and point out that scheduling problems will likely arise if the contract is not signed now.
d. Make another call on the customer and this time offer a significant price reduction.

Mini-Case 3—After closing a sale with a very difficult customer (the "customer from hell"), you indicated that you would follow up on a special room layout request and a minor menu substitution. During negotiations, you developed a strong dislike and distrust for this customer because of the unethical negotiation techniques he used. Because of the demands made during negotiations, and the fact that these requests were talked about after the customer signed the contract, you are thinking about forgetting the special requests and providing only the services specifically outlined in the contract. What should you do?

a. Provide all items specified in the contract and take care of the special requests.
b. Follow up on the special request and add additional fees to the final bill.
c. Provide only those items specified in the contract.
d. Contact the customer a few days before the scheduled meeting and tell him you will be unable to fulfill his special requests.

Mini-Case 4—The Park Shores Resort and Convention Center has offered a special bonus to any salesperson who develops 10 new accounts during the current fiscal year. You need one more account to earn the bonus. Apco Equipment Corporation is considering your hotel and conference center for an upcoming business meeting. Your contact at Apco says the meeting is tentative and may not be scheduled. One option is to offer Apco a contract with major price concessions and a liberal cancellation clause. The signed contract will qualify you for the bonus. What should you do?

a. Make the special offer to Apco, but search for another new account in case the Apco deal falls through.
b. Make the special offer to Apco and make every effort to close the sale.
c. Give up the search for new accounts and enjoy a less stressful life.
d. Pursue the Apco account, and other new accounts, but offer Apco a standard contract and no special concessions.

Mini-Case 5—When you accepted a sales position at the Park Shores Resort and Convention Center, you signed a noncompete agreement. This agreement states that information acquired while representing the Park Shores cannot be taken to a new employer. With the press of a button on your computer keyboard, you can download a profile of all established accounts you were given at the time you started working for the Park Shores, a profile of each new account you have developed, and the name and address of all prospects that you have identified. You have been offered a sales position at a competing hotel and you are tempted to take this information with you. What should you do?

a. Take all of this information home so it will be available when you start the new job.
b. Take only the list of prospects you identified.
c. Do not take any of the information because it would be covered by the noncompete agreement.
d. Request the permission to take this information home.

After completing the assessment, refer to the suggested answer key in Appendix 3 on page 485. A point total and rationale is provided for each solution.

Role-Play Exercise

This morning, you met with a customer who has purchased office supplies from you for almost three years. You are quite surprised when she says, "I am prepared to place a $10,500 order, but you must match an offer I received from a competitor." She then explains that the competitor is offering *new* customers a seven-day trip to Disney World in Orlando if they place an order of more than $10,000. All expenses will be paid. What would you do?

Prepare to role-play your response with another student. Review the material in this chapter, paying special attention to ways you can add value and build long-term relationships with ethical decision making.

Reality Selling Video Case Problem: Edith Botello/Mattress Firm

Mattress Firm (www.mattressfirm.com) is one of the largest and most successful specialty bedding companies in the world. It offers sleep solutions, including conventional and specialty mattresses, as well as bedding-related products. The company has grown to become one of the largest and fastest-growing retailers in the nation. The company operates more than 560 stores in 38 markets nationwide and carries the top mattress brands. From the very beginning, the company, which hires only college graduates, set out to be a different kind of mattress retailer, focused on creating a unique shopping experience.

According to Edith Botello, featured at the beginning of this chapter, the biggest differentiator between Mattress Firm and its competitors is the sales process. As Botello puts it, buying a mattress can be overwhelming: How do you know which one is the best if all you see when you walk into a store are dozens of white rectangles? At Mattress Firm, sales reps make it simple for their customers to pick out their mattress without trying out every single bed. The process invites customers to get fitted for a mattress, just as with suits, shoes, and gowns. This is done through the company's Sleep Diagnostic System, which asks the customer a series of questions about their sleep quality and then measures their weight distribution and postural alignment. The system then recommends a type of support and eliminates 80 percent of the beds in the showroom. Taking the risk out of buying a mattress by letting customers know what mattresses are best for them is something that only Mattress Firm offers.

How can ethical aspects of selling come into play in Botello's job as a retail salesperson? One example would be that sometimes salespeople have the opportunity to write up a sale where they would get credit, but have not earned the right to do so. At times, customers shop around and end up at the same store and want the same product that was offered to them previously. In such a case, the customer may request the particular salesperson who helped him or her previously. If that salesperson is not there, the new salesperson could choose to not give her/him credit. Another example might be a customer who tries to get greater price discounts by making untrue statements about a competitor's price offering or shopping around at different Mattress Firm locations in order to get the lowest possible price. In many cases, however, the salesperson will recognize this behavior and act accordingly.

Being ethical is a core value at Mattress Firm. New hires are made aware of Mattress Firm's expectations from the beginning of their employment to ensure that they are ethical with their customers and other salespeople. Mattress Firm's Code of Conduct is a guide to the general principles that permeate the employees' relationships with customers, business partners, and, last but not least, each other. The Code goes far beyond compliance with laws and regulations. It is also a set of practical instructions to help employees in their day-to-day work. It explains, for example, how to manage potential conflicts of interest and how to report suspected violations of the rules.

At Mattress Firm, several policies and elements in the incentive compensation system exist that also help to safeguard ethical behavior. The Standard Operating Procedure (SOP) dedicates an entire section to commission sales and how to handle different situations such as team selling, ticket trading, SPIFFS, bonuses, and so forth. For example, the commission system encourages sales reps to hold the line on price concessions. National sales contests are also audited to ensure ethical behavior. The SOP and Employee Code of Conduct are housed on the company's intranet and are available to view at any time. (See the chapter opener on page 50 and *Reality Selling Today* Role-Play 3 in Appendix 1 for more information.)

Questions

3-9 Put yourself in Edith Botello's place as a sales representative who is selling mattresses. Can you imagine situations in your job that might challenge your ethical conduct?

3-10 For retailers such as Mattress Firm, what are the major areas that should be covered in a company policy on ethics?

3-11 Revenue-based incentive compensation plans, by their very nature, pressure sales representatives to generate high sales, which might cause unethical sales practices. How could an incentive compensation system be designed that stimulates sales generation, but safeguards ethical sales behavior at the same time?

3-12 Imagine you are a salesperson for Mattress Firm, just like Edith Botello. A customer walks into your store and, after awhile, shows great interest in a specific Tempur-Pedic. When it comes to the price, the customer mentions that your competitor across the street offered him exactly that mattress at a 10 percent lower price than Mattress Firm. You have some doubts that this statement is actually true, but you do not want to disgruntle and compromise the customer. How would you react?

MyMarketingLab

Go to the Assignments section of your MyLab to complete these writing exercises.

3-13 A number of important factors influence ethical decision making. Describe the factors influencing the ethical decision making of salespeople.

3-14 Salespeople must establish their own standards of personal conduct. Discuss the process that is involved in the development of a personal code of ethics that adds value.

4

Creating Value with a Relationship Strategy

Source: Michael Ahearne

Reality Selling Video—Susana Rosas/CB Richard Ellis

Susana Rosas, a real estate broker at CB Richard Ellis (http://www.cbre.us/o/houston /Pages/houston-commercial-real-estate.aspx), places a great deal of emphasis on building rapport during the first contact. She, like most other real estate professionals, knows that rapport with commercial real estate clients is of critical importance. She knows that to build relationships with clients, a good knowledge of the market is necessary but not sufficient. She has to master a multitude of skills, among which keeping an open and empathetic conversation style with her clients is the key; above all, listening closely to everything that prospects say helps a salesperson to accurately identify their wants and needs. Furthermore, she works closely with her team members in the same collaborative manner to make sure all of those identified needs are met. ●

Relationships Add Value

Ron Willingham, author of *Integrity Selling for the 21st Century*, says there is a relationship between the salesperson's achievement drive and his view of personal selling. Salespeople who feel a professional responsibility to create as much value for customers as possible exhibit more energy, a stronger work ethic, and a greater eagerness to ask customers for decisions.[1]

The manner in which salespeople establish, build, and manage relationships is not an incidental aspect of personal selling; in the information age, it is the key to success. In the information economy, business is defined by customer relationships, and sales success depends on adding value. Daniel Pink, author of *To Sell Is Human* and *A Whole New Mind*, says we are moving from the information age to the conceptual age. He predicts that one of the major players in the conceptual age will be the **empathizer**. Empathizers have the ability to imagine themselves in someone else's position and understand what that person is feeling. They are able to understand the subtleties of human interaction.[2]

Daniel Pink, well-known author of the best-selling *To Sell Is Human* and *A Whole New Mind*, predicts that one of the major players in the future will be the empathizer. Empathizers have the ability to imagine themselves in someone else's position and understand what the person is feeling. They are able to understand the subtleties of human interaction.

Source: fototext/Alamy

4.1   Explain how partnering relationships add value

We have defined value-added selling as *a series of creative improvements in the sales process that enhance the customer experience.* Customers perceive that value is added when they feel comfortable with the relationship they have with a salesperson. A good relationship causes customers to feel that, if a problem arises, they will receive a just and fair solution. A good relationship creates a clearer channel of communication about issues that might surface during each step of the sales process. Len Rodman, CEO from 1998 to 2013 at Black & Veatch, a large engineering and construction company, recalled a problem operation on the West Coast. Earnings were minimal and the person in charge could not sell to high-tier clients. Rodman put a salesperson in charge whose strength was building relationships. Within an 18-month period, that region became one of the most profitable.[3]

The salesperson who is honest, accountable, and sincerely concerned about the customer's welfare brings added value to the sale. These characteristics give the salesperson a competitive advantage—an advantage that is becoming increasingly important in a world of "look-alike" products and similar prices.

Partnering—The Highest-Quality Selling Relationship

Salespeople today are encouraged to think of everything they say or do in the context of their relationship with the customer. They should constantly strive to build a long-term partnership. In a marketplace characterized by increased levels of competition and greater product complexity, we see the need to adopt a relationship strategy that emphasizes the "lifetime" customer. High-quality relationships result in repeat business and those important referrals. A growing number of salespeople recognize that the quality of the partnerships they create is as important as the quality of the products they sell. Today's customer wants a quality product *and* a quality relationship. One example of this trend is the J.D. Power and Associates customer satisfaction studies. For example, the North American Hotel Guest Satisfaction Index Study measures guest satisfaction among frequent business travelers. J.D. Power conducts customer satisfaction research in several different industries.[4]

In Chapter 2 we defined "partnering" as a strategically developed, high-quality, long-term relationship that focuses on solving the customer's buying problems.[5] This definition is used in the sales training video titled "Partnering—The Heart of Selling Today." Traditional industrial age sales training programs emphasized the importance of creating a good first impression and then "pushing" your product. Partnering emphasizes building a strong relationship during every aspect of the sale and working hard to maintain a quality relationship with the customer after the sale. Today, personal selling must be viewed as a process, not an event.[6]

PREPARING WRITTEN CUSTOMER COMMUNICATIONS WITH CRM

Exceptional **Customer Relationship Management (CRM)** systems such as Salesforce.com enable you to quickly process written communications with numerous clients. One example is the form letter or e-mail. Preparing a standard letter or template in advance lets you quickly select and send a personalized letter or e-mail. "Personalized" means that the system will automatically add to the document the recipient's name, title, and other contact information you choose, even if the letter is going out to many recipients. Careful thought should be given to each template created so that the language reflects your win-win philosophy, your relationship strategy, and your professionalism. This is where technology can

help in a big way. Personalized letters should reflect prior helpdesk interfaces with the customer. Such knowledge bases can be easily integrated through customer service management application tools offered by firms such as Parature (now owned by Microsoft), Autotask and Freshdesk.

Recipients of your appointment confirmations, information verifications, company or product news, or brief updates recognize and appreciate your effort to keep them informed. The written word conveys consideration and helps avoid misunderstandings and miscommunications. CRM empowers you to easily use the written word to advance your relationship building.

Larry Wilson, noted author and founder of Wilson Learning Worldwide, identified partnering as one of the most important strategic thought processes needed by salespeople. He points out that the salesperson who is selling a "one-shot" solution cannot compete against the one who has developed and nurtured a long-term, mutually beneficial partnership. Wilson believed there are three keys to a partnering relationship:

- The relationship is built on shared values. If your client believes that you both share the same ideas and values, it goes a long way toward creating a powerful relationship.
- Everyone needs to clearly understand the purpose of the partnership and be committed to the vision. Both the salesperson and the client must agree on what they are trying to do together.
- The role of the salesperson must move from selling to supporting. The salesperson in a partnership is actively concerned with the growth, health, and satisfaction of the company to which he or she is selling.[7]

Salespeople willing to abandon short-term thinking and invest the time and energy needed to develop a high-quality, long-term relationship with customers are rewarded with greater earnings and the satisfaction of working with repeat customers. Sales resulting from referrals also increase.

Relationship Strategies Focus on Four Key Groups

Establishing and maintaining a partnering-type relationship internally as well as with the customers is a vital aspect of selling. High-performance sales personnel build strong relationships with four groups (Figure 4.1):

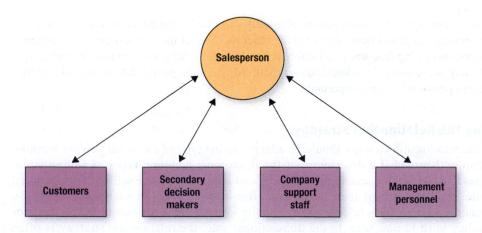

FIGURE 4.1

An effective relationship strategy helps high-performing salespeople build and maintain win-win relationships with a wide range of key groups.

Today's customer wants a quality product and a quality relationship. This means that salespeople can create value with a well-developed relationship strategy.

Source: bikeriderlondon/Shutterstock

1. *Customers.* As noted previously, a major key to success in selling is the ability to establish working relationships with customers in which mutual support, trust, and goals are nurtured over time. Salespeople who maintain regular contact with their customers and develop sound business relationships based on mutual trust are able to drive up sales productivity, according to research conducted by the American Productivity and Quality Center.[8]

   Cisco Systems is one of many companies that now measure themselves by the quality of their relationships with their customers. Salespeople earn their bonuses in large part based on customer satisfaction instead of gross sales or profit.[9]

2. *Secondary decision makers.* High-performance salespeople understand the importance of building relationships with the people who work with customers. In many selling situations, the first person the salesperson meets is a receptionist, a secretary, or an assistant to the primary decision maker. These persons often can facilitate a meeting with the prospect. Also, the prospect may involve other people in making the buying decision. For example, the decision to buy new office furniture may be made by a team of persons including the buyer, the chief financial officer, the facilities manager, and persons who will actually use the furniture.

3. *Company support staff.* The maintenance of relationships internally is a vital aspect of selling. Support staff may include persons working in the areas of needs analysis, demonstrations, market research, product service, credit, training, or shipping. Influencing these people to change their priorities, interrupt their schedules, accept new responsibilities, or fulfill any other request for special attention is a major part of the salesperson's job. At UPS, the drivers are the eyes and ears of the sales force. The most successful UPS salespeople nurture a relationship with the drivers in their sales territory.[10]

4. *Management personnel.* Sales personnel usually work under the direct supervision of a sales manager, a department head, or some other member of the firm's management team. With the increasing frequency and effectiveness of team selling, the company president or CEO may accompany the salesperson on a call. Maintaining good relationships with management personnel is very important.

Adapting the Relationship Strategy

Ideally, the relationship strategy should be adapted to the type of customer you are working with. Chapter 2 provided a description of the three most common types of selling situations: transactional selling, consultative selling, and strategic alliance selling. Transactional buyers are usually aware of their needs and often stay focused on such issues as price, convenience, and delivery schedules. They usually know a great deal about the products or services they wish to purchase. In the transactional sale, the relationship strategy is often secondary.

In the consultative sale, however, the impact of relationships on the sale is quite important. A consultative sale emphasizes need identification, which is achieved through effective communication and a relationship built upon mutual trust and respect. The consultative salesperson must display a keen ability to listen, define the customer's problem, and offer one or more solutions. The opportunity to uncover hidden needs and create custom solutions is greatly enhanced by a well-conceived relationship strategy.[11]

In terms of relationship building, strategic alliance selling is often the most challenging. Very often the salesperson is working with a company team made up of people from such areas as research and development (R&D), finance, and distribution. The salesperson must build a good working relationship with each team member. Forming an alliance with another company involves building relationships with several representatives of that buying organization.

Customers almost never buy products from someone whom they dislike. A salesperson who is not viewed as being helpful and trustworthy will not succeed in any type of selling situation. A quick review of the 20 CRM contact reports found in Appendix 2: The NewNet Systems Regional Accounts Management Case Study illustrates the importance of strong relationships with all four of the Key Selling Groups.

Thought Processes That Enhance Your Selling Relationship Strategy

4.2 Discuss how thought processes can enhance your relationship strategy

Industrial age folklore created the myth of the "born" salesperson—a dynamic, outgoing, highly assertive individual. Experience acquired during the information age has taught us that many other factors determine sales success. Key among these factors is a positive self-concept and the ability to relate to others in effective and productive ways. With the aid of knowledge drawn from the behavioral sciences, we can develop the relationship strategies needed in a wide range of selling situations.

Self-Concept—An Important Dimension of the Relationship Strategy

Your **self-concept** is the bundle of facts, opinions, beliefs, and perceptions about yourself that are present in your life every moment of every day.[12] The self-concept you have today reflects information you have received from others and life events that occurred throughout childhood, adolescence, and adulthood. You are *consciously* aware of some things you have been conditioned to believe about yourself. But many comments and events that have shaped your self-concept are processed at the *unconscious* level and continue to influence your judgments, feelings, and behaviors whether you are aware of them or not.[13]

Phillip McGraw, author of *Self Matters*, says we often sabotage our own success by adopting limiting beliefs. These are the specific things we think about that cause us to conclude that we are not capable of achieving success. These beliefs restrict our thinking and our actions.[14] McGraw, better known as "Dr. Phil," has developed a one-sentence guide to understanding the importance of your self-concept: *The past reaches into the present, and programs the future, by your recollections and your internal rhetoric about what you perceived to have happened in your life.*[15] Past experiences and events, which McGraw describes as "defining moments," can influence your thinking for a lifetime.

How can you develop a more positive self-concept? How can you get rid of self-destructive ways of thinking? Bringing your current self-concept out into the open is the first step in understanding who you are, what you can do, and where you are going. Improving your self-concept does not happen overnight, but it can happen. A few practical approaches are summarized as follows:

1. *Focus on the future and stop being overly concerned with past mistakes or failures.* We should learn from past errors, but they should not immobilize us.
2. *Develop expertise in selected areas.* By developing "expert power," you not only improve your self-image but also increase the value of your contributions to your employer and your customers.
3. *Learn to develop a positive mental attitude.* To develop a more positive outlook, read books and view YouTube videos and DVDs that describe ways to develop a positive mental attitude.

Stephen Covey, author of *The Seven Habits of Highly Effective People*, said the ability to build effective, long-term relationships is based on character strength, not quick-fix techniques.

Source: EPA/Alamy

Consider materials developed by Daniel Pink, Harvey Mackay, Jack Canfield, Stephen Covey, Brian Tracy, Dale Carnegie, and Phillip McGraw.

Later in this chapter, you will learn how to develop and initiate a plan for self-improvement. If you want to improve your self-image, consider adopting this plan.

The Win-Win Philosophy

As noted in Chapter 2, the marketing concept is a philosophy that leaves no doubt in the mind of every employee that customer satisfaction is of primary importance. Salespeople, working closely with customers, are in the best position to monitor customer satisfaction.

Adopting the win-win philosophy is the first step in developing a relationship strategy. Stephen Heiman and Diane Sanchez, authors of *The New Conceptual Selling*, describe the "win-win" approach as follows:

> In Win-Win selling, both the buyer and seller come out of the sale understanding that their respective best interests have been served—in other words, that they've both won. It is our firm conviction, based on thousands of selling situations, that over the long run the only sellers who can count on remaining successful are the ones who are committed to this Win-Win philosophy.[16]

The win-win strategy is based on such irrefutable logic that it is difficult to understand why any other approach would be used. The starting point to the development of a win-win philosophy is to compare the behaviors of persons who have adopted the win-lose approach with the behaviors of persons who have adopted the win-win approach (Figure 4.2).

Empathy and Ego Drive

We have described the growing importance of being able to *empathize,* the ability to imagine yourself in someone else's position, to understand what that person is feeling. A salesperson simply cannot sell well without the invaluable ability to get critical feedback from the client through empathy. When you sense what the customer is feeling, you can change pace and make whatever modifications in your sales presentation are needed.[17] Fortunately, the ability to relate and connect with customers can be learned.

Ego drive is another basic quality that is of critical importance in personal selling. **Ego drive** is an inner force that makes the salesperson want and need to make the sale. Closing the sale provides a powerful means of enhancing the salesperson's ego. Research indicates that top salespeople have the motivation to make the sale, and empathy gives them the connecting tool with which to do it. Therefore, empathy and ego drive reinforce each other.[18]

FIGURE 4.2

The starting point to developing a win-win relationship strategy is to compare behaviors of win-lose salespeople with those of salespeople who have adopted the win-win approach.

Source: Adapted from a list of losers, winners, and double winners in *The Double Win* by Denis Waitley.

Win-Lose People	Win-Win People
• See a problem in every solution	• Help others solve their problems
• Fix the blame	• Fix what caused the problem
• Let life happen to them	• Make life a joyous happening for others and themselves
• Live in the past	• Learn from the past, live in the present, and set goals for the future
• Make promises they never keep	• Make commitments to themselves and to others and keep them both

GLOBAL BUSINESS INSIGHT

Creating Value with Your Relationship Strategy in Japan

Many American businesspeople travel to Japan because it is one of the largest U.S. trading partners. Japan is the world's third-largest economy, so it helps to become familiar with the Japanese business culture.

- Courtesy is a major key to success in Japan. When you address someone, be sure to use titles such as Mr., Ms., or Dr., and wait to be invited before using first names.
- The Japanese are very hierarchical, so the business card is an important source of information regarding the relative status

of the other person. Accept the card with care and then examine it. Do not put it in your pocket or wallet. Place it in a cardholder.

- In Japan, the culture emphasizes the group over the individual. It would not be appropriate to praise one member of a group.
- Decision making in Japan is done very slowly. Be patient as the group reaches a consensus. Aggressive sales methods should be avoided.[a, b]

Verbal and Nonverbal Strategies That Add Value to Your Selling Relationships

4.3 Identify and describe the major nonverbal factors that shape our sales image

The first contact between a salesperson and a prospect is very important. During the first few minutes—or seconds, in most cases—the prospect and the salesperson form impressions of each other that either facilitate or distract from the sales call. Malcolm Gladwell, author of the best-selling book *Blink*, says that when two people meet for the first time, each will make very superficial, rapid judgments about the other person. This decision-making process, he argues, usually happens subconsciously in a split second (in the blink of an eye).[19]

Every salesperson projects an image to prospective customers, and this image influences how a customer feels about the sales representative. The image you project is the sum total of many verbal and nonverbal factors. The quality of your voice, the clothing you wear, your posture, your manners, and your communication style represent some of the factors that contribute to the formation of your image. We discuss several forms of verbal and nonverbal communication in this chapter. Communication style is examined in Chapter 5.

Adding Value with Nonverbal Messages

When we attempt to communicate with another person, we use both verbal and nonverbal communications. **Nonverbal messages** are "messages without words" or "silent messages." These are the messages (other than spoken or written words) that we communicate through facial expressions, voice tone, gestures, appearance, posture, and other nonverbal means.[20]

Research indicates that when two people communicate, *nonverbal messages convey much more impact than verbal messages.* Words play a surprisingly small part in the communication process. Every spoken message has a vocal element, coming not from *what* we say but from *how* we say it. The voice communicates in many ways: through tone, volume, and speed of delivery. A salesperson wishing to communicate enthusiasm needs to use a voice that is charged with energy.

As we attempt to read nonverbal communication, it is important to remember that no *one* signal carries much meaning. If the person you meet for the first time displays a weak grip during the handshake, don't let this one signal shape your first

Malcolm Gladwell, noted author of the best-selling book *Blink*, says that when two people meet for the first time, each in a split second, at a subconscious level, will make very superficial rapid judgments about the other person.

Source: Evan Agostini/Invision/AP Images

impression. Such factors as posture, eye contact, gestures, clothing, and facial expression must all be regarded together.[21]

Nonverbal messages influence your relationships and can reinforce or contradict the spoken word. When your verbal message and body language are consistent, they tend to give others the impression that you can be trusted and that what you say reflects what you truly believe. When there is a discrepancy between your verbal and nonverbal messages, you are less apt to be trusted.[22]

INFLUENCE OF YOUR ENTRANCE AND CARRIAGE As noted earlier, the first impression we make is very important. The moment a salesperson walks into a client's office, the client begins making judgments. Susan Bixler, author of *The Professional Image* and *Professional Presence*, makes this comment:

> All of us make entrances throughout our business day as we enter offices, conference rooms, or meeting halls. And every time we do, someone is watching us, appraising us, sizing us up, and gauging our appearance, even our intelligence, often within the space of a few seconds.[23]

Bixler says that the key to making a successful entrance is simply believing—and projecting—that you have a reason to be there and have something important to offer the client. You can communicate confidence with a strong stride, a good posture, and a friendly smile. A confident manner communicates to the client the message, "This meeting will be beneficial to you."

INFLUENCE OF SHAKING HANDS An inadequate handshake is like dandruff: No one mentions it, but everyone notices it. Today, the handshake is an important symbol of respect and, in most business settings, it is the proper greeting.[24]

In the field of selling, the handshake is usually the *first* and frequently the *only* physical contact one makes during a sales call. The handshake can communicate warmth, genuine concern for the prospect, and an image of strength. It also can communicate aloofness, indifference, and weakness to the customer. The message we communicate with a handshake is determined by a combination of five factors:

1. *Eye contact during the handshake.* Eyes transmit more information than any other part of the body, so maintain eye contact throughout the handshaking process and display a pleasant smile.
2. *Degree of firmness.* Generally speaking, a firm handshake communicates a caring attitude, whereas a weak grip (the "dead-fish" handshake) communicates indifference.
3. *Depth of interlock.* A full, deep grip communicates friendship to the other person.
4. *Duration of grip.* There are no specific guidelines to tell us what the ideal duration of a grip should be. However, by extending the duration of the handshake we can often communicate a greater degree of interest and concern for the other person. Do not pump up and down more than once or twice.

Spending an afternoon with a customer on the golf course is part of the relationship strategy of this salesperson. Many companies support this approach to building and maintaining relationships.

Source: Exactostock/Superstock

SELLING IN ACTION

Remembering Names

In the field of personal selling, remembering a person's name is very important. To improve your ability to recall names, use one or more of these memory aids.

- *Verify the spelling.* After hearing the name ask, "Is that Reece with a 'c' or 's'?" Repetition helps you remember the name.
- *Ask how the person wants to be addressed.* Ask, "Should I call you Thomas or Tom?" This presents another opportunity for repetition.
- *Relate the name to something easy to remember.* If the person's last name is Park, connect this name with "Yosemite" in

your mind. Some aspect of appearance (hairstyle, eyeglasses, etc.) might serve as a connecting reference.

- *Use the name quickly.* Work the person's name into the conversation right away: "Mary, can I ask you a few questions?"
- *Use the name frequently.* During and at the end of the meeting, work the name into the conversation: "Eric, thank you for meeting with me."

Sources: Reprinted with permission of the publisher from "Secrets of Power Persuasion for Salespeople" ©2003. Published by Career Press, Pompton Plains, NJ. All rights reserved. See Roger Dawson, "And Your Name Was Again?" *Value-Added Selling* 21, July 16, 2007, p. 2. Used with permission.

5. *Degree of dryness of the hands.* A moist palm not only is uncomfortable to handle but also can communicate the impression that you are quite nervous. Some people have a physiological problem that causes clammy hands and should keep a handkerchief within reach to remove excess moisture.[25]

    The best time to present your name is when you extend your hand. When you introduce yourself, state your name clearly and then listen carefully to be certain you hear the customer's name. To ensure that you remember the customer's name, repeat it. In some cases you need to check to be sure you are pronouncing it properly. When appropriate, it is a good idea to write the name.

INFLUENCE OF FACIAL EXPRESSIONS If you want to identify the inner feelings of another person, watch facial expressions closely. The face is a remarkable communicator, capable of accurately signaling emotion in a split second and capable of concealing emotion equally well. We can often determine whether the customer's face is registering surprise, pleasure, or skepticism (Figure 4.3). Facial expressions are largely universal, so people around the world tend to "read" faces in a similar way. It is worth noting that the smile is the most recognized facial signal in the world, and it can have a great deal of influence on others. George Rotter, professor emeriti of psychology at Montclair State University, said, "Smiles are an enormous controller of how people perceive you." People tend to trust a smiling face.[26] Get in the habit of offering a sincere smile each time you meet with a prospect.

INFLUENCE OF EYE CONTACT When the customer is talking, eye contact is one of the best ways to say, "I'm listening." If you are looking across the room or at papers in your briefcase, the customer will assume you are not listening. However, prolonged eye contact can send the wrong message. A prolonged, direct stare can be threatening. To avoid the prolonged stare, take fleeting glances at your notes. As the customer speaks, nod occasionally to indicate agreement or interest.[27]

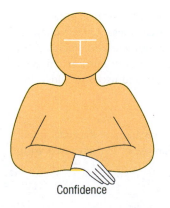

Confidence

Boredom

Evaluation

FIGURE 4.3

Our subtle facial gestures are continuously sending messages to others.

Impact of Appearance on Relationships

We form opinions about people based on a pattern of immediate impressions conveyed by appearance. The clothing we wear, the length and style of our hair, the fragrances we use, and the jewelry we display all combine to make a statement about us to others—a statement of primary importance to anyone involved in selling.

We all have certain views, or **unconscious expectations**, concerning appropriate dress. In sales work, we should try to anticipate the expectations of our clientele. The clothing worn by salespeople does make a difference in terms of customer acceptance because it communicates powerful messages. The clothing we wear can influence our credibility and likability, thereby adding value to our selling relationships.

Most image consultants agree that there is no single "dress for success" look. The appropriate wardrobe varies from one city or region to another and from company to company. However, there are some general guidelines that we should follow in selecting clothing for sales work. Four key words should govern our decisions: simplicity, appropriateness, quality, and visual integrity.[28]

SIMPLICITY The color of clothing, as well as design, communicates a message to the customer. Some colors are showy and convey an air of casualness. In a business setting we want to be taken seriously, so flashy colors should usually be avoided.

APPROPRIATENESS Selecting appropriate clothing for sales work can be a challenge. We must carefully consider the clients we serve and decide what may be acceptable to them. Many salespeople are guided by the type of products they sell and the desired image projected by their employers. Deciding what constitutes appropriate attire in today's business casual world begins with an understanding of what it means to "dress down." **Business casual** is clothing that allows you to feel comfortable but looks neat and professional. Pay close attention to the clothing your clients wear.[29] If a client is wearing a nice sports coat, a collared long-sleeved shirt, and dress slacks, don't wear khaki trousers and a short-sleeve polo shirt. In recent years, the casual dress trend has been reversed at many companies, and workplace dress codes have become more formal.[30]

QUALITY The quality of our wardrobe also influences the image we project to customers. A salesperson's wardrobe should be regarded as an investment, with each item carefully selected to look and fit well. Susan Bixler says, "If you want respect, you have to dress as well as or better than your industry standards."[31]

VISUAL INTEGRITY Visual presence must have a certain amount of integrity and consistency. The images you project are made up of many factors, and lack of attention to important details can negate your effort to create a good impression. Too much jewelry, a shirt that does not fit well, or unshined shoes can detract from the professional look you want to project. People often are extra alert when meeting someone new, and this heightened consciousness makes every detail count.[32]

Keep in mind that customer contact often takes place in several settings. The first meeting with a customer may take place in the office, but the second meeting may be on the golf course. And the third meeting may take place at a nice restaurant. The clothing you wear in each of these settings is important.

Impact of Voice Quality on Relationships

As noted previously, every spoken message has a vocal element. What we hear is greatly influenced by the speaker's tone of voice, vocal clarity, and verbal expressiveness. On the telephone, voice quality is even more important because the other person cannot see your facial expressions, hand gestures, and other body movements. You cannot trade in your current voice for a new one. However, you can make your voice more pleasing to others and use it to add value to your relationships. How?

Consider these suggestions:

1. *Do not talk too fast or too slowly.* Rapid speech often causes customers to become defensive. It raises psychological barriers because a "rapid-fire monologue" is associated with

high-pressure sales methods. Many salespeople could improve their verbal presentation by talking more slowly. The slower presentation allows others to follow, and it allows the speaker time to think ahead—to consider the situation and make judgments. Another good tip is to vary the speed of your speech, leaving spaces between thoughts. Crowding too many thoughts together may confuse the listener.[33]

2. *Avoid a speech pattern that is dull and colorless.* The worst kind of voice has no color and no feeling. Enthusiasm is a critical element of an effective sales presentation. It also is contagious. Your enthusiasm for the product is transmitted to the customer.

3. *Avoid bad speech habits.* Kristy Pinand, a youthful-looking 23-year-old, routinely used "teen speak." For example, she described a recent promotion as "so cool." Her supervisor felt she not only looked young, but she also sounded very young, and this image could potentially hurt her ability to win the respect of clients. She urged Ms. Pinand to select her words more carefully. Ms. Pinand heeded the constructive advice and now rehearses her remarks aloud before she calls a client.[34]

Some speech habits can make us sound poorly educated and inarticulate. At age 22, Mike White learned that his east Tennessee accent and colorful backwoods speech patterns created problems at work. He recognized that his southern drawl was a "turnoff" to some of the image-conscious people he worked with. One day, his sales manager asked him if he had his racquetball equipment with him, and White replied, "Yeah, I brung it." Fortunately, White's supervisor was willing to tactfully correct his grammatical problems and help him communicate with greater clarity. Today, Mike White is CEO of a successful company and a frequent speaker at trade shows.[35]

Impact of Etiquette on Your Relationships

The study of etiquette (sometimes called "manners" or "protocol") reveals a number of ways to enhance your relationship strategy and add value. Salespeople who possess knowledge of the rules of etiquette can perform their daily work with greater poise and confidence. Think of etiquette as a universal passport to positive relationships and respect.

With practice, anyone can develop good etiquette without appearing to be "stiff" and at the same time win the respect and admiration of others. Space does not permit a complete review of this topic, but we cover some of the rules of etiquette that are especially important to salespeople.

1. *Avoid the temptation to address a new prospect by first name.* In a business setting, too much familiarity too quickly can cause irritation.

2. *Avoid offensive comments or stories.* Never assume that the customer's value system is the same as your own. Rough language, off-color stories, or personal views on political issues can do irreparable damage to your image.

3. *Recognize the importance of punctuality.* Ann Marie Sabath, owner of a firm that provides etiquette training for business employees, says "We teach people that if you're early, you're on time, and if you're on time, in reality, you're late." Most clients will view showing up late for an appointment as rudeness.[36]

4. *When you invite a customer to lunch, do not discuss business before the meal is ordered unless the client initiates the subject.* Also, avoid ordering food that is not easily controlled, such as ribs, chicken, or lobster.

5. *When you use voice mail, leave a clear, concise message.* Do not speak too fast or mumble your name and number.

6. *Avoid cell phone contempt.* Turn off the cell phone ringer anytime you are with a client. Never put your phone on the table during a meal. If you must respond to a call, inform your client ahead of time.

It has been said that good manners make other people feel better. This is true because good etiquette requires that we place the other person's comfort ahead of our own. One of the best ways to develop rapport with a customer is to avoid behavior that might be offensive to that person.

Ken Viselman, chairman of Itsy Bitsy Entertainment in New York, provides salespeople with many artifacts to talk about in his office. He states that "behind every object in [my] office is a story and a bit of my life." These items include an 18th-century armoire, a crowded shelf of toys, and a Picasso lithograph, to name only a few.

Source: Arnold Adler

4.4 Describe conversational strategies that help us establish relationships

Conversational Strategies That Enhance Relationships

The foundation for a long-term relationship with the customer is frequently a "get acquainted" type of conversation that takes place before any discussion of business matters. Within a few minutes, it is possible to reduce the relationship tension that is so common when two people meet for the first time. This informal visit with the customer provides the salesperson with an opportunity to apply three guidelines for building strong relationships, featured in *How to Win Friends and Influence People*, the classic book written by Dale Carnegie.

- *Become genuinely interested in other people.* Tim Sanders, former Leadership Coach at Yahoo!, says, "How we are perceived as human beings is becoming increasingly important in the new economy."[37] When you become genuinely interested in the customer, you add value and create an experience that is long remembered.
- *Be a good listener; encourage others to talk about themselves.* Stephen Covey, noted author and consultant, recommends empathic listening. This requires listening with your ears, your eyes, and your heart.[38] We live in a culture where empathic listening is quite rare. Interrupting has become all too common as people rush to fill every gap in the conversation.

SOCIAL MEDIA AND SELLING TODAY

Enhancing Your Relationship Strategy with Social Media

It is likely that your sales contacts and others associated with your accounts are using social media. This means that their postings will appear occasionally on Facebook, LinkedIn, and other similar sites. Most of these online services permit you to be notified by e-mail when such postings occur. Many entries in most social sites are frivolous, so a review of every post may be unnecessary. However, it is wise to monitor these posts carefully enough to detect important relationship information. It is always more efficient to use a social media dashboard to manage multiple profiles simultaneously. Tools such as Hootsuite and Fan Page Robot among others are particularly helpful here.

You may wish to make note of many of these postings in your sales database. A sales contact may mention recent activities such as events attended, hobbies, or notable experiences. Someone might make reference to an alma mater or to a friend who is well known. You can use this kind of information to add value to subsequent conversations with the person who posted. The information may give you a chance to point out interests or friends you have in common. You may also take note of issues to avoid, such as commenting on a recent varsity game your contact's school may have lost.

Your own entries on social websites can also add value to your relationship with sales contacts. Usually, you can directly comment on a sales contact's post instead of waiting until a subsequent conversation. You might comment that you agree with the entry or add helpful—and positive—information that supports the contact's comment.

The length of this conversation depends on your sense of the prospect's reaction to your greeting, how busy the prospect appears to be, and your awareness of topics of mutual interest. Keep any small talk conversation relatively short unless your client wants to expand on it. Even then, it is important to plan a way to move the conversation to the overriding business reason for your call. Never engage in any small talk conversation unless you are genuinely interested in the topics brought up. If your customer shows any indication of noninterest, move immediately to the business you are there to conduct. In developing this conversation, the following three areas should be considered. There will often be other times during the sales call when it may be appropriate to engage in one or more of these three areas of conversation.

Comments on Here and Now Observations

Observant salespeople are aware of the things going on around them. These observations can be as general as unusual developments in the weather or as specific as noticing unique artifacts in the prospect's office. These observations often provide the basis for "small talk," which can break the ice and speed up the building of a relationship.

Compliments

When you offer a *sincere* compliment to your prospect, you are saying, "Something about you is special." Most people react positively to compliments because they appeal to the need for self-esteem. Your admiration should not be expressed, however, in phony superlatives that seem transparent. Jack Canfield, author of *The Success Principles*, reminds us that everything we say to a customer produces an effect: "Know that you are constantly creating something—either positive or negative—with your words."[39]

Search for Mutual Acquaintances or Interests

A frequent mode for establishing rapport with a new prospect is to find friends or interests you have in common. If you know someone with the same last name as your prospect, it may be appropriate to ask whether your friend is a relative. Anything you observe in the prospect's office or home might suggest an interest that you and your prospect share. A strong bond often develops between two persons who share the same interest or hobby. Frances Carlisle, an estate planner in New York, says her love of animals lands her many clients. Some of these clients wish to include provisions for the care of pets in their estate plans. Sometimes an unusual hobby (e.g., sky diving, mountain climbing, or auto racing) is the perfect way to stand out and cultivate relationships with clients.[40]

Self-Improvement Strategies That Add Value

5.5 Explain how to establish a self-improvement plan based on personal development strategies

One of the most highly respected actors in this country once said, "Every actor is very busy getting better or getting worse." To a large extent, salespeople are also "very busy getting better or getting worse." To improve, salespeople must develop a value-adding, ongoing program for

---

self-improvement (see Chapter 16). It is important to keep in mind that all improvement is self-initiated. Each of us controls the switch that allows personal growth and development to take place.

In Chapter 3, we introduced the concept of emotional intelligence. We noted that this form of intelligence can be increased with the aid of self-development activities. Would you like to develop a more positive self-image? Improve your ability to develop win-win relationships? Develop effective nonverbal communication skills? Improve your speaking voice? These relationship-building strategies can be achieved if you are willing to follow these steps:

Step one: Set goals. The goal-setting process begins with a clear, written statement that describes what you want to accomplish. If your goal is too general or vague, progress toward achieving that goal is difficult to observe. Next, you must identify the steps you will take to achieve your goal. Perseverance is the key to goal achievement.

Step two: Use visualization. To **visualize** means to form a mental image of something. The power to visualize (sometimes called "guided imagery") is in a very real sense the power to create. If you really want to succeed at something, picture yourself doing it successfully. For example, spend time developing mental pictures of successful sales presentations or visualize yourself as one of the top salespeople in your organization. Once you have formed a clear mental picture of what you want to accomplish, identify the steps needed to get there and then mentally rehearse them. The visualization process needs to be repeated over and over again.[41]

Step three: Use positive self-talk. People with a strong inner critic will receive frequent negative messages that can erode their self-esteem. It helps to refute and reject those negative messages with positive self-talk. **Self-talk** takes place silently in the privacy of your mind. It is the series of personal conversations you have with yourself almost continually throughout the day. Just like statements from other people, your self-talk can dramatically affect your behavior and self-esteem.[42]

Step four: Reward your progress. When you see yourself making progress toward a goal, or achieving a goal, reward yourself. This type of reinforcement is vital when you are trying to change a behavior. There is nothing wrong with taking pride in your accomplishments.

Self-improvement efforts can result in new abilities or powers, and they give us the motivation to utilize more fully the talents we already have. As a result, our potential for success is greater.

CHAPTER LEARNING ACTIVITIES

Reviewing Key Concepts

Explain how partnering relationships add value

The concept of *partnering* is revisited and discussed in detail. Partnering emphasizes building strong relationships during every aspect of the sale and working hard to maintain a quality relationship with the customer after the sale. Relationship building must also include management personnel, company support staff, and secondary decision makers. Partnerships can be strengthened when salespeople use value-added relationship strategies.

Discuss how thought processes can enhance your relationship strategy

An understanding of the psychology of human behavior provides a foundation for developing relationship strategies. In this chapter, we discuss the link between self-concept and success in selling. Self-imposed fears can prevent salespeople from achieving success. The relationship strategy is built on the win-win philosophy, empathy and ego drive, and character and integrity.

Identify and describe the major nonverbal factors that shape our sales image

We describe several factors that influence the image we project to customers. The image others have of us is shaped to a great extent by nonverbal communication. We may choose the right words to persuade a customer to place an order, but aversive factors communicated by our clothing, handshake, facial expression, voice quality, and etiquette miscues may prejudice the customer against us and our product or service.

Describe conversational strategies that help us establish relationships

The various conversational strategies that enhance relationships are reviewed. These include comments on here and now observations, compliments, and the search for mutual acquaintances. Dale Carnegie's guidelines for building strong relationships are discussed.

Explain how to establish a self-improvement plan based on personal development strategies

We discussed the importance of adopting strategies for self-improvement. A four-step self-improvement plan is the key to relationship building.

Key Terms

Empathizer, p. 73
Self-concept, p. 77
Ego drive, p. 78

Nonverbal messages, p. 79
Unconscious
   expectations, p. 82

Business casual, p. 82
Visualize, p. 86
Self-talk, p. 86

MyMarketingLab

To complete the problems with the ⭐ in your MyLab, go to the EOC Discussion Questions.

Review Questions

⭐ **4-1** How important are establishing, building, and maintaining relationships in the selling process?

4-2 List the four groups of people with whom sales personnel must be able to work effectively.

⭐ **4-3** Why is partnering described as the highest-quality selling relationship? Why has the building of partnerships become more important today?

⭐ **4-4** Describe the win-win approach to selling.

4-5 Describe the four key words that should govern our decision regarding an appropriate set of guidelines to "dress for success" in today's sales environments.

4-6 Identify three conversational methods that can be used to establish relationships.

4-7 Describe the meaning of nonverbal messages. Why should salespeople be concerned about these messages?

4-8 List and describe each step in the four-step self-improvement plan.

Application Exercises

4-9 Select four salespeople you know and ask them if they have a relationship strategy for working with customers, management personnel, secondary decision makers, and company support staff. Ask each salesperson to give you two or three specific examples of steps they have taken to build and maintain a positive relationship with their customers.

4-10 The partnering style of selling is emphasized throughout the book. To gain more insight into the popularity of this concept, use one of your Internet search engines to key in the words "partnering + selling." Notice the large number of documents related to this query. Click on and examine several of these documents to learn more about this approach to selling.

4-11 Complete the following etiquette quiz. Your instructor will provide you with answers so you can check your responses.

    a. On what side should you wear your name tag?

    b. Is it appropriate to drink beer from a bottle at a formal reception or dinner?

    c. When introducing a female salesperson to a male prospect, whose name should be spoken first?

    d. At the table, when should you place your napkin in your lap?

    e. Is it ever proper to comb, smooth, or touch your hair while seated at a restaurant table?

4-12 In October, people of the Hindu religion celebrate Diwali, the festival of lights. The festival of lights is one of the most important and most beautiful Indian festivals. Rick Saulle was a pharmaceutical sales representative employed by Pfizer from 1998 to 2007. He recalls that one of the most important physicians he called on was Indian and celebrated Diwali. He also knew that it is commonplace to provide sweets to Indians who celebrate Diwali. Saulle visited an Indian grocery store and purchased a plate of Indian sweets to celebrate Diwali. When he presented the sweets to the physician, the response was very positive. The doctor grabbed Saulle's hand, shook it forcefully, and sincerely thanked him for honoring this important holiday.[43]

As a nation, we serve as host to a kaleidoscope of the world's cultures, and the trend toward greater diversity will accelerate in the years ahead. Reflect on the gift given by Mr. Saulle and then answer these questions.

    a. Is it appropriate for a salesperson to give a gift to someone who is celebrating a religious holiday?

    b. In addition to giving a gift, what are some other ways to recognize a religious festival or holiday?

    c. List and describe three religious holidays or festivals celebrated by denominations other than Christian.

4-13 Move quickly through the following list of traits. Use a check mark beside those that fit your self-image. Use an *X* to mark those that do not fit. If you are unsure, indicate with a question mark.

    _____ I like myself.

    _____ People trust me.

    _____ I usually say the right thing.

    _____ I dislike myself.

    _____ I waste time.

    _____ I put up a good front.

    _____ I use my talents.

    _____ I feel hemmed in.

    _____ I use time well.

    _____ I enjoy people.

    _____ I usually say the wrong thing.

    _____ I am discouraged about life.

    _____ I have not developed my talents.

    _____ I trust myself.

    _____ I often do the wrong thing.

    _____ People avoid me.

    _____ I enjoy work.

    _____ I control myself.

    _____ I enjoy nature.

    _____ I am dependent on others for ideas.

    _____ I am involved in solving community problems.

    _____ I do not use my talents fully.

    _____ I do not like myself.

    _____ I do not like to be around people.

    _____ People like to be around me.

Now look at the pattern of your self-assessment.

    a. Is there a pattern?

    b. Is there a winner or loser pattern?

    c. What traits would you like to change? (List them.)

    d. Pick the trait you would like to change the most and prepare a plan to achieve this change. Your plan should include specific goal statements.

4-14 It is pointed out in this chapter that clothing communicates strong messages. In this exercise, you become more aware of whether or not your clothes communicate the messages you want them to communicate.

   a. Make a chart like the one that follows:

ITEM OF CLOTHING BEING ANALYZED	WHAT I WANT MY CLOTHES TO SAY ABOUT ME TO OTHERS	WHAT OTHERS THINK MY CLOTHING SAYS

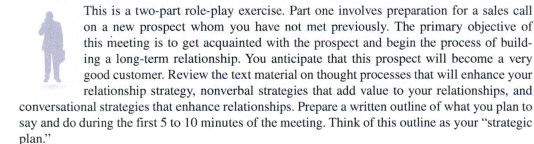

   b. In the first column, list the clothing you are now wearing; for example, dress slacks, dress shoes, and sweater; athletic shoes, jeans, and T-shirt; or suit, tie, and dress shoes.
   c. In the middle column, describe the message you would like the clothes you have chosen to say. For example, "I want to be comfortable," "I want people to trust me," or "I want people to take me seriously."
   d. Have somebody else fill in the third column by describing what your clothes do say about you.
   e. Compare the two columns. Do your clothes communicate what you want them to? Do the same exercise for social dress, casual dress, business attire, and hairstyle.

Note: If you are currently employed, analyze the clothing you wear at work.

Role-Play Exercise

This is a two-part role-play exercise. Part one involves preparation for a sales call on a new prospect whom you have not met previously. The primary objective of this meeting is to get acquainted with the prospect and begin the process of building a long-term relationship. You anticipate that this prospect will become a very good customer. Review the text material on thought processes that will enhance your relationship strategy, nonverbal strategies that add value to your relationships, and conversational strategies that enhance relationships. Prepare a written outline of what you plan to say and do during the first 5 to 10 minutes of the meeting. Think of this outline as your "strategic plan."

Part two involves a role-play with a class member who will play the role of the prospect. Throughout the role-play, try to say and do everything that was part of your plan. At the end of the role-play, give your strategic plan outline to the prospect and request feedback on your performance.

Reality Selling Video Case Problem— Susana Rosas/CB Richard Ellis

The commercial real estate services industry is highly competitive. CBRE, the firm featured at the beginning of this chapter, offers a wide variety of services such as industrial and logistical services, real estate consulting, investment properties services, and global corporate services. When clients want to find an office space, they hold their realtor to high standards. After all, the term of a lease contract is a long-term one, and the stakes are high. CBRE salespeople understand the magnitude and trend of the commercial real estate market. They know that the customers are eager to partner with someone who can be trusted to look after their best interests.

When new salespeople join the CBRE sales force, they usually work under a senior broker. The mentor helps these recruits form a professional image that appeals to the type of clientele served by the company. In the end, there is a direct link between the image projected by the salespeople and the success of the company. CBRE also adopts a team-based selling approach to ensure that the client is in good hands as the relationship between CBRE and the client develops. Susana Rosas, an experienced broker in CBRE's Houston office, believes that working under a mentor to learn how to process a deal with a relationship orientation is invaluable. That mentality is part of CBRE's culture and success. Susana works closely with her team members through several stages of the relationship with CBRE clients, from prospecting to postsales follow-up. When working with new recruits and her team members, she emphasizes the following points:

- Customers notice even the little details, such as the firmness of a handshake or a proper introduction.
- Salespeople at CBRE must be able to build rapport with a variety of personality types. Some customers are quiet, reserved, and somewhat guarded when expressing their views. Others are more impulsive and express their views openly. Salespeople are encouraged to alter their communication style to increase the comfort level of the customer. Susana believes that it is always important for a salesperson to gauge how his or her communication style impacts the prospect. A positive attitude is another important aspect of the relationship-building process at CBRE.
- Susana is a strong believer that salespeople should find out what customers value. Most of the time, a salesperson must come up with innovative solutions to seemingly irreconcilable needs, such as the need to have a large space to accommodate cyclical ups and downs of the customer's industry and the need for efficiency. What is the most important aspect of commercial real estate sales? Most customers do not open up and share important information until they trust the salesperson. (See the vignette on page 73, and Reality Selling Today Video Role-Play 2 in Appendix 1 for more information.)

Questions

4-15 Why should real estate salespeople spend time developing a relationship strategy? What might be some long-term benefits of this strategy?

4-16 Review the four key groups of people that the relationship strategy should encompass. Under each group list the various individuals who would fit into each group.

4-17 Is it ever appropriate to touch your client other than with a handshake? Explain your answer.

4-18 How differently would you behave when dealing with a return client versus a new client?

4-19 What are some precautions to take when preparing a meeting with a foreign-born prospect?

MyMarketingLab

Go to the Assignments section of your MyLab to complete these writing exercises.

4-20 How do relationships add value? Why is the ability to establish, build, and manage relationships a key to sales success?

4-21 Salespersons can use the CARE model as part of his or her self-improvement plan. Explain the CARE model. How can salespersons add value by using the CARE model?

Communication Styles: A Key to Adaptive Selling Today

Learning Objectives

When you finish reading this chapter, you should be able to

5.1 Discuss how communication style influences the relationship process in sales

5.2 Identify the two major dimensions of the communication style model

5.3 Explain the four communication styles in the communication style model

5.4 Learn how to identify your preferred communication style and that of your customer

5.5 Learn to adapt interpersonal versatility and build strong selling relationships with style flexing

Source: Michael Ahearne

Adaptive Selling Training Video Series, Communication Styles—A Key to Adaptive Selling

Communication—or behavior—styles, as they are sometimes called, have been described as one of the most popular training programs in sales and management.

In this two-part Adaptive Selling Training Video, you'll meet Lana, a senior salesperson. While working with Ron (one of her top customers), Sandra (her sales team member), and Raymond (her marketing manager), she shares what she has learned about building selling relationships with different communication styles. We will learn how Lana and her team take a "No, this won't work" response from Ron and, with the adaptive selling "Platinum Rule," attempt to build a mutually rewarding relationship.

Every year, publications such as *BusinessWeek, Fortune,* and *Fast Company* feature profiles of well-known business leaders. These articles often focus on the communication styles of the executives who provide leadership in companies across America. Deborah Hopkins earned the nickname "Hurricane Debby" for the way she conducted business while holding leadership positions at Unisys, GM Europe, Boeing, and Lucent Technologies. Her demanding, ambitious, and sometimes emotional style occasionally created personality clashes. Who can forget Al "Chainsaw" Dunlap, who was described as aggressive, frank, opinionated, and impatient? He earned his nickname by ordering huge layoffs when he was the CEO responsible for restructuring companies such as Scott Paper and Sunbeam Corporation. By contrast, Bill Gates is described as a quiet, reflective person who often seems preoccupied with other matters. And then there is Jeff Bezos, the founder and CEO of Amazon.com, who is often described as the happy extrovert. He seems to enjoy being with other people and often displays spontaneous, uninhibited behavior.[1]

We form impressions of people by observing their behavior. The thoughts, feelings, and actions that characterize someone are generally viewed as their **personality**.[2]

Communication style is an important aspect of our personality. ●

We form impressions of others by observing their behavior. Jeff Bezos, founder of Amazon.com, is often described as the happy extrovert who frequently displays spontaneous, uninhibited laughter. By contrast, Microsoft's Bill Gates is described as a quiet, reflective person who often seems preoccupied with other matters.

Source: Stan Honda/Getty Images

5.1 Discuss how communication style influences the relationship process in sales

Communication Styles—An Introduction to Adaptive Selling

Almost everyone has had the pleasant experience of meeting someone for the first time and developing an instant mutual rapport. There seems to be a quality about some people that makes you like them instantaneously—a basis for a mutual understanding that is difficult to explain. On the other hand, we can all recall meeting people who "turn us off" almost immediately. Why does this happen during the initial contact?

The impressions that others form about us are based on what they observe us saying and doing. They have no way of knowing our innermost thoughts and feelings, so they make decisions about us based on what they see and hear.[3] The patterns of behavior that others observe can be called **communication style**. "Behavior styles" and "social styles" are additional terms frequently used to describe these patterns of behavior.

Adaptive selling, introduced in Chapter 2, is defined as altering sales behaviors in order to improve communication with the customer. It relates to a salesperson's ability to collect information regarding the customer's needs and to respond appropriately. Adaptive selling frequently requires complex behavioral adjustments.[4] Adjusting one's communication style in order to fit individual customer needs and preferences is an important element of adaptive selling.

Communication Style Bias

Bias in various forms is quite common in our society. In fact, local, state, and national governments have passed many laws to curb blatant forms of racial, age, and sex bias. We also observe some degree of regional bias when people from various parts of the country meet.

The most frequently occurring form of bias is not commonly understood in our society. What has been labeled **communication style bias** is a state of mind that almost every one of us experiences from time to time, but we usually find it difficult to explain the symptoms. Communication style bias can develop when we have contact with another person whose communication style is different from our own. For example, an account executive was overheard saying, "I do not know what it is, but I just do not like that purchasing agent." The salesperson was no doubt experiencing communication style bias but could not easily describe the feeling.

Your communication style is the "you" that is on display every day—the outer pattern of behavior that others see. If your style is very different from the other person's, it may be difficult for the two of you to develop a rapport. All of us have had the experience of saying or doing something that was perfectly acceptable to a friend or coworker and being surprised when the same behavior irritated someone else. However, aside from admitting that this happens, most of us are unable to draw meaningful conclusions from these experiences to help us perform more effectively with customers in the future.[5]

In recent years, thousands of sales professionals have learned to manage their selling relationships more effectively through the study of communication styles. Books, such as *I'm Stuck, You're Stuck* by Tom Ritchey, *People Styles at Work* by Robert Bolton and Dorothy Grover Bolton, and *The Versatile Salesperson* by Roger Wenschlag, serve as good references. Many training companies offer seminars that provide enrollees with a practical understanding of communication style theory and practice. Wilson Learning (www.wilsonlearning.com) offers a program titled "The Versatile Salesperson." This program helps salespeople develop the interpersonal skills necessary to work effectively with customers whose communication style is different from their own. More than seven million people worldwide have completed Wilson Learning programs that focus on communication styles.[6]

Communication Style Principles

The theory of behavioral or communication style bias is based on a number of underlying principles. A review of these principles can be beneficial before we examine specific styles.

1. *Individual differences exist and are important.* It is quite obvious that we all differ in terms of physical characteristics such as height, shoe size, facial features, and body build, but the most interesting differences are those patterns of behavior that are unique to each of us. Voice patterns, eye movement, facial expression, and posture are some of the components of our communication style. Additional characteristics are discussed later in this chapter. Research by the Swiss psychoanalyst Carl Jung and others has helped us understand the importance of individual differences.

2. *A communication style is a way of thinking and behaving.* It is not an ability but, instead, a preferred style or way of using abilities one has. This distinction is very important. An *ability* refers to how well someone can do something. A *style* refers to how someone likes to do something.[7]

3. *Individual style differences tend to be stable.* Our communication style is based on a combination of hereditary and environmental factors. Our style is somewhat original at the time of birth; it takes on additional individuality during the first three to five years of life. By the time we enter elementary school, the teacher should be able to identify our preferred communication style. Although an individual's communication style tends to remain fairly constant throughout life, adapting to different communication counterparts or the ability to "flex" can be enhanced and mastered.

4. *There is a finite number of styles.* Most people display one of several clusters of similar behaviors, and this allows us to identify a small number of behavioral categories. By combining a series of descriptors, we can develop a single "label" that describes a person's most preferred communication style.

5. *To create the most productive relationships, it is necessary to get in sync with the communication style of the people you work with.*[8] Differences between people can be a source of friction unless you develop the ability to recognize and respond to the other person's style.

The ability to identify another person's communication style, and to know how and when to adapt your own preferred style to it, can afford you a crucial advantage in dealing with people. Differences between people can be a source of friction. The ability to "speak the other person's language" is an important relationship management skill.[9]

Improving Your Relationship Selling Skills

Anyone who is considering a career in selling can benefit greatly from the study of communication styles. These concepts provide a practical method of classifying people according to communication styles and give the salesperson a distinct advantage in the marketplace. A salesperson who understands communication style classification methods and learns how to adapt them can avoid common mistakes that threaten interpersonal relations with customers. Awareness of these methods greatly reduces the possibility of tension arising during the sales call.

Personal Selling Fills the Seats

Mark Cuban, owner of the NBA Dallas Mavericks, has been described as "probably the most involved owner in day-to-day activities that the pro basketball league has ever seen." When he bought the team, it had not been in the playoffs for 10 years. His mission, of course, was not only to improve the team's on-court performance but also to dramatically increase its revenue from season ticket sales and sponsorships. Within one week, he added 30 new salespeople to the team's five-member sales force. Cuban says, "I think the key to any business is to be able to connect with customers and prove to them that you can give better value than the next guy. We take things into our own hands by selling and talking directly to customers." In one year, paid attendance increased 60 percent, season ticket sales increased 25 percent, sponsorship revenue increased 30 percent, and the Mavericks made the playoffs.[a] Mark Cuban put his Emotive communication style "on stage" with his 2007 appearance on the *Dancing with the Stars* television program.

Mark Cuban, owner of the NBA Dallas Mavericks.

Source: James Devaney/FilmMagic/Getty Images

The first major goal of this chapter is to help you better understand your own most preferred communication style. The second goal is to help you develop greater understanding and appreciation for styles that are different from your own. The third goal is to help you manage your selling relationships more effectively by learning to adapt your style to fit the communication style of the customer. This practice is called "style flexing."

5.2 Identify the two major dimensions of the communication style model

Communication Style Model

This section introduces you to the four basic communication styles. One of these will surface as your most preferred style. The communication style model that defines these styles is based on two important dimensions of human behavior: dominance and sociability. We look at the dominance continuum first.

Dominance Continuum

Dominance can be defined as the tendency to control or prevail over others.[10] Dominant people tend to be quite competitive. They also tend to offer opinions readily and to be decisive, opinionated, self-assertive, and vocal. Each of us falls somewhere on the dominance continuum, which is illustrated in Figure 5.1.

A person classified as being high in dominance is generally a "take charge" type of person who makes his or her position clear to others. A person classified as being low in dominance is usually more reserved, unassertive, and easygoing. Dominance has been recognized as a universal behavioral characteristic. David W. Johnson developed the Interpersonal Pattern Exercise to help people achieve greater interpersonal effectiveness. He believes that people fall into two dominance categories:

FIGURE 5.1

The first step in determining your most preferred communication style is to identify where you are on the dominance continuum.

1. *Lower dominance.* These people have a tendency to be quite cooperative and let others control things. They tend to be lower in assertiveness.

Low  High

TABLE 5.1 Dominance Indicator

Rate yourself on each scale by placing a check mark on the continuum at the point that represents how you perceive yourself.

	I PERCEIVE MYSELF AS SOMEWHAT	
Cooperative		Competitive
Submissive		Authoritarian
Accommodating		Domineering
Hesitant		Decisive
Reserved		Outgoing
Compromising		Insistent
Cautious		Risk taking
Patient		Hurried
Complacent		Influential
Quiet		Talkative
Shy		Bold
Supportive		Demanding
Relaxed		Tense
Restrained		Assertive

2. *Higher dominance.* These people tend to like to control things and frequently initiate demands. They are more aggressive in dealing with others.[11]

The first step in determining your most preferred communication style is to identify where you fall on the dominance continuum. Do you tend to rank low or high on this scale? To answer this question, complete the Dominance Indicator form in Table 5.1. Rate yourself on each scale by placing a check mark on the continuum at the point that represents how you perceive yourself. If most of your check marks fall to the right of center, you are someone who is higher in dominance. If most of your check marks fall to the left of center, you are someone who is lower in dominance. Is there any best place to be on the dominance continuum? The answer is no. Successful salespeople can be found at all points along the continuum.

Sociability Continuum

Sociability reflects the amount of control we exert over our emotional expressiveness.[12] Individuals who are higher in sociability tend to express their feelings freely, while people who are low in this dimension tend to control their feelings. Each of us falls somewhere on the sociability continuum, as illustrated in Figure 5.2.

Sociability is also a universal behavioral characteristic. It can be defined as the tendency to seek and enjoy interaction with others. Therefore, high sociability is an indication of a person's preference to interact with other people. Lower sociability is an indicator of a person's desire to work in an environment where the person has more time alone instead of having to make conversation with others. The person who is classified as being lower in the area of sociability is more reserved and formal in social relationships.

The second step in determining your most preferred communication style is to identify where you fall on the sociability continuum. To answer this question, complete the Sociability Indicator form shown in Table 5.2. Rate yourself on each scale by placing a check mark on the continuum at the point that represents how you perceive yourself. If most of your check marks fall to the

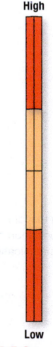

High

Low

FIGURE 5.2

The second step in determining your most preferred communication style is to identify where you are on the sociability continuum.

TABLE 5.2 Sociability Indicator

Rate yourself on each scale by placing a check mark on the continuum at the point that represents how you perceive yourself.

	I PERCEIVE MYSELF AS SOMEWHAT	
Disciplined	/ / / / /	Easygoing
Controlled	/ / / / /	Expressive
Serious	/ / / / /	Lighthearted
Methodical	/ / / / /	Unstructured
Calculating	/ / / / /	Spontaneous
Guarded	/ / / / /	Open
Stalwart	/ / / / /	Humorous
Aloof	/ / / / /	Friendly
Formal	/ / / / /	Casual
Reserved	/ / / / /	Attention seeking
Cautious	/ / / / /	Carefree
Conforming	/ / / / /	Unconventional
Reticent	/ / / / /	Dramatic
Restrained	/ / / / /	Impulsive

right of center, you are someone who is higher in sociability. If most of your check marks fall to the left of center, you are someone who is lower in sociability. Keep in mind that there is no best place to be. Successful salespeople can be found at all points along this continuum.

As you reflect on your dominance and sociability ratings, keep in mind that self-ratings can be misleading. Many people do not see themselves in the same way that others see them. Friends and coworkers who frequently observe your behaviors may be in a better position to identify your communication style.

With the aid of the dominance and sociability continuums, we are now prepared to discuss a relatively simple communication style classification plan that has practical application in the field of selling. We describe the four basic styles: Emotive, Directive, Reflective, and Supportive.

5.3 Explain the four communication styles in the communication style model

Four Styles of Communication

By combining these two dimensions of human behavior, dominance and sociability, we can form a partial outline of the communication style model (Figure 5.3). Dominance is represented by the horizontal axis, and sociability is represented by the vertical axis. Once the two dimensions of human behavior are combined, the framework for communication style classification is established.

EMOTIVE STYLE The upper-right quadrant of Figure 5.4 defines a style that combines higher sociability and higher dominance. We call this the **Emotive style**. Emotive people like New Jersey Governor Chris Christie, Al Roker, and Jimmy Fallon usually stand out in a crowd. They are expressive and willing to spend time maintaining and enjoying a large number of relationships.[13] Vice President Joe Biden, 2016 Presidential Candidate Senator Bernie Sanders,

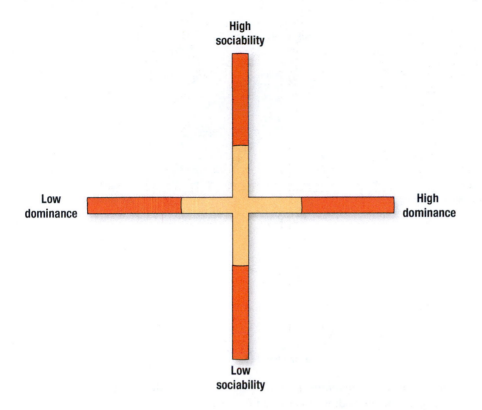

High sociability

Low dominance

High dominance

Low sociability

FIGURE 5.3

When the dominance and sociability dimensions of human behavior are combined, the framework for communication-style classification is established.

Oprah Winfrey, the well-known television personality, and talk show host Steven Colbert provide excellent models of the Emotive communication style. They are outspoken, enthusiastic, and stimulating. Richard Branson, the founder of Virgin Atlantic Airways, also projects the Emotive communication style. The Emotive person wants to create a social relationship quickly and usually feels more comfortable in an informal atmosphere. Some of the verbal and nonverbal clues that identify the Emotive person follow:

1. *Appears quite active.* This person gives the appearance of being busy. A person who combines higher dominance and higher sociability often displays spontaneous, uninhibited behavior. The Emotive person is likely to express feelings with vigorous movements of the hands and a rapid speech pattern.

2. *Takes the social initiative in most cases.* Emotives tend to be extroverts. When two people meet for the first time, the Emotive person is more apt to initiate and maintain the conversation as well as to initiate the handshake. Emotives rate higher in both directness and openness.

3. *Likes to encourage informality.* The Emotive person moves to a "first-name" basis as soon as possible (too soon, in some cases). Even the way this person sits in a chair communicates a preference for a relaxed, informal social setting.

Emotive people, like talk show host Jimmy Fallon and New Jersey Governor Chris Christie are stimulating, excitable, and spontaneous. Emotives generally do not hide their feelings and often express opinions dramatically and impulsively.

Source: Gregorio T. Binuya/Everett Collection/Newscom

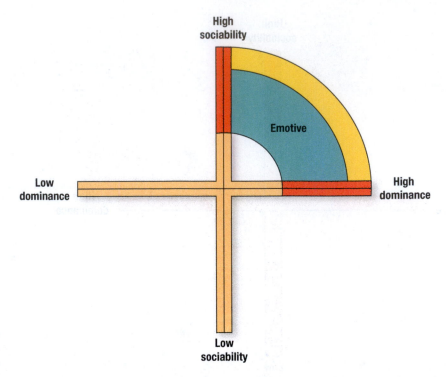

FIGURE 5.4

The Emotive style combines high sociability and high dominance.

4. *Expresses emotional opinions.* Emotive people generally do not hide their feelings. They often express opinions dramatically and impulsively.

Key Words for the Emotive Style

Sociable	Emotional	Personable
Spontaneous	Unstructured	Persuasive
Zestful	Excitable	Dynamic
Stimulating		

DIRECTIVE STYLE The lower-right quadrant defines a style that combines higher dominance and lower sociability. We will call this the **Directive style** (Figure 5.5).

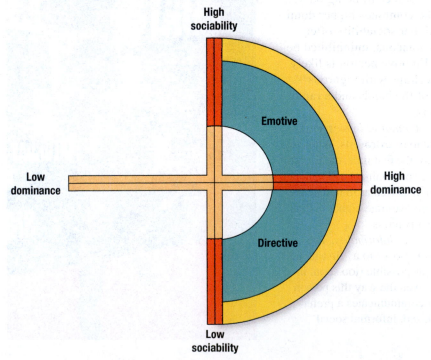

FIGURE 5.5

The Directive style combines high dominance and low sociability.

To understand the nature of people who display the Directive communication style, picture in your mind's eye the director of a Hollywood film. The person you see is giving orders in a firm voice and is generally in charge of every facet of the operation. Everyone on the set knows this person is in charge. 2016 Presidential candidate Ted Cruz displayed these characteristics. Although the common stereotyped image of the Hollywood film director is probably exaggerated, this example is helpful as you attempt to become familiar with the Directive style.

Senator John McCain, Martha Stewart (television personality), former Secretary of State and 2016 Presidential candidate Hillary Clinton, and former Vice President Dick Cheney project the Directive style. These people have been described as frank, demanding, assertive, and determined.

In the field of selling, you will encounter a number of customers who are Directives. How can you identify these people? What verbal and nonverbal cues can we observe? A few of the behaviors displayed by Directives follow:

People who display the Directive style, such as John McCain and Hillary Clinton, like to take charge and maintain control. People who display the Directive style are generally viewed as determined, bold, and serious.

Source: Paul Froggatt/Alamy Stock Photo

1. *Appears to be quite busy.* The Directive generally does not like to waste time and wants to get right to the point. Judy Sheindlin of the *Judge Judy* television show displays this behavior.
2. *May give the impression of not listening.* In most cases, the Directive feels more comfortable talking than listening.
3. *Displays a serious attitude.* A person who is lower in sociability usually communicates a lack of warmth and is apt to be quite businesslike and impersonal. The late Mike Wallace, former star of the popular *60 Minutes* television show, seldom smiled or displayed warmth.
4. *Likes to maintain control.* The person who is higher on the Dominance continuum likes to maintain control. During meetings, the Directive often seeks to control the agenda.[14]

Key Words for the Directive Style

Aggressive	Serious	Opinionated
Intense	Determined	Impatient
Demanding	Frank	Bold
Pushy		

REFLECTIVE STYLE The lower-left quadrant of the communication style model features a combination of lower dominance and lower sociability (Figure 5.6). People who regularly display this behavior are classified as having the **Reflective style**.

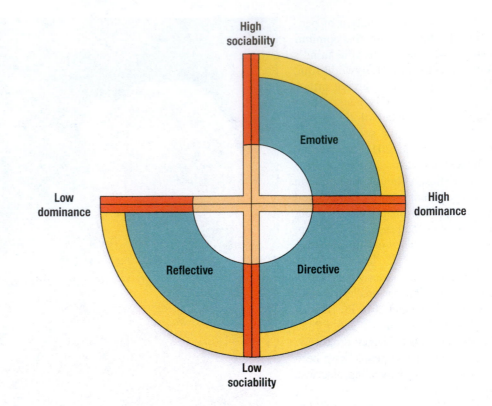

FIGURE 5.6

The Reflective style combines low dominance and low sociability.

The Reflective person tends to examine all the facts carefully before arriving at a decision. Like a cautious scientist, this individual wants to gather all available information and weigh it carefully before taking a position. The Reflective type is usually a stickler for detail.[15] House Speaker Paul Ryan and former Federal Reserve Board Chairman Ben Bernanke fit the description. The late physicist Albert Einstein also displayed the characteristics of the Reflective type.

House Speaker Paul Ryan and former Federal Reserve Director Ben Bernanke display the Reflective style. Persons with the Reflective style are often observed as precise, industrious, and deliberate.

Source: Joshua Roberts/REUTERS/ Alamy

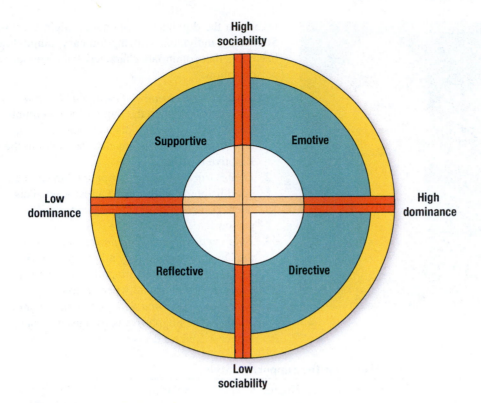

FIGURE 5.7

The Supportive style combines low dominance and high sociability.

The Reflective communication style combines lower dominance and lower sociability; therefore, people with this classification tend to be reserved and cautious. Some additional behaviors that characterize this style follow:

1. *Controls emotional expression.* Reflective people tend to curb emotional expression and are less likely to display warmth openly. Bill Gates displays this personality trait.
2. *Displays a preference for orderliness.* The Reflective person enjoys a highly structured environment and generally feels frustration when confronted with unexpected events.
3. *Tends to express measured opinions.* The Reflective individual usually does not express dramatic opinions. This communication style is characterized by disciplined, businesslike actions.
4. *Seems difficult to get to know.* The Reflective person tends to be somewhat formal in social relationships and therefore can be viewed as aloof by many people.

In a selling situation, the Reflective customer does not want to move too fast. This person wants the facts presented in an orderly and unemotional manner and does not want to waste a lot of time socializing.

Key Words for the Reflective Style

Precise	Aloof	Serious
Deliberate	Scientific	Industrious
Questioning	Preoccupied	Stuffy
Disciplined		

SUPPORTIVE STYLE The upper-left quadrant shows a combination of lower dominance and higher sociability (Figure 5.7). This communication style is called the **Supportive style** because these people find it easy to listen and usually do not express their views in a forceful manner. 2016 Presidential candidate Dr. Ben Carson fit this description. Entertainers Meryl Streep, Kevin Costner, Paul Simon, Julia Roberts, and the late Princess Diana display the characteristics of the Supportive style.

Low visibility generally characterizes the lifestyle of Supportive people. They complete their tasks in a quiet, unassuming manner and seldom draw attention to what they have accomplished. In terms of assertiveness, persons with the Supportive style rank quite low. Someone who ranks

Presidential candidate Dr. Ben Carson, Julia Roberts, and the late Princess Diana display the Supportive style. Persons with the Supportive style are generally observed as warm, patient, and easygoing.

Source: Ron Sachs/dpa picture alliance/ Alamy Stock Photo

higher on the dominance continuum might view the Supportive individual as being too easygoing. Other behaviors that commonly characterize the Supportive person follow:

1. *Gives the appearance of being quiet and reserved.* People with the Supportive communication style can easily display their feelings, but not in the assertive manner common to the Emotive individual.
2. *Listens attentively to other people.* In selling, good listening skills can be a real asset. This talent comes naturally to the Supportive person.
3. *Tends to avoid the use of power.* Whereas the Directive person may rely on power to accomplish tasks, the Supportive person is more likely to rely on friendly persuasion.
4. *Makes decisions in a thoughtful and deliberate manner.* The Supportive person usually takes longer to make a decision.

Key Words for the Supportive Style

Lighthearted	Docile	Relaxed
Reserved	Patient	Compliant
Passive	Sensitive	Softhearted
Warm		

Popularity of the Four-Style Model

We are endlessly fascinated by ourselves, and this helps explain the growing popularity of the four-style model presented in this chapter. To satisfy this insatiable appetite for information, many training and development companies offer training programs that present the four social or communication styles. Figure 5.8 features the approximate equivalents of the four styles presented in this chapter. Although four-style programs were initially created and marketed in the United States, they have become a global phenomenon, according to the staff at Wilson Learning.[16] Inscape Publishing (now known as Everything Disc), the company that developed the DiSC learning instrument more than three decades ago, reports that more than 40 million people worldwide have completed DiSC workshops.[17] The four-style model is one of the most popular training programs used in business.

FIGURE 5.8

The four basic communication styles have been used in a wide range of training programs. For comparison purposes, the approximate equivalents to the four communication styles discussed in this chapter are listed.

Supportive (Manning/Ahearne/Reece)	Emotive (Manning/Ahearne/Reece)
Amiable (Wilson Learning)	Expressive (Wilson Learning)
Supportive-Giving (Stuart Atkins Inc.)	Adapting-Dealing (Stuart Atkins Inc.)
Relater (People Smarts)	Socializer (People Smarts)
Steadiness (Personal Profile System)	Influencing (Personal Profile System)
Supportive (DiSC Behavioral Style)	Influencing (DiSC Behavioral Style)
Reflective (Manning/Ahearne/Reece)	Directive (Manning/Ahearne/Reece)
Analytical (Wilson Learning)	Driver (Wilson Learning)
Conserving-Holding (Stuart Atkins Inc.)	Controlling-Taking (Stuart Atkins Inc.)
Thinker (People Smarts)	Directive (People Smarts)
Cautiousness/Compliance (Personal Profile System)	Dominance (Personal Profile System)
Conscientious (DiSC Behavioral Style)	Dominance (DiSC Behavioral Style)

Determining Your Communication Style

You now have enough information to identify your own communication style. If your location on the dominance continuum is right of center and your position on the sociability continuum is below the center mark, you fall into the Directive quadrant. If your location on the dominance continuum is left of center and your position on the sociability continuum is above the center mark, then your most preferred style is Supportive. Likewise, lower dominance matched with lower sociability forms the Reflective communication style, and higher dominance matched with higher sociability forms the Emotive style.

An Online Assessment of Your Communication Style

You can gain further insight into your communication style by accessing the pearsonhighered .com/manning website and clicking on the Online Assessment of Your Communication Style link. After completing the assessment, you will be supplied with a profile indicating your most preferred communication style. You will also be presented with a profile of your secondary style. See Application Exercises 5-10, 5-11, 5-12, and 5-13 on page 111 for more details on using this online assessment tool.

Of course, all of us display some characteristics of the Emotive, Directive, Reflective, and Supportive styles. However, one of the four styles is usually predominant and readily detectable.[18] This is your preferred style.

Some people who study the communication style model for the first time may initially experience feelings of frustration. They find it hard to believe that one's behavioral style tends to remain quite uniform throughout life. People often say, "I am a different person each day!" It is certainly true that we sometimes feel different from day to day, but our most preferred style tends to remain stable.

The Supportive person might say, "I sometimes get very upset and tell people what I am thinking. I can be a Directive when I want to be!" There is no argument here. Just because you have a preferred communication style does not mean you never display the behavioral characteristics of another style. Some people use different styles in different contexts and in different relationships.[19] Reflective people sometimes display Emotive behavior, and Emotive people sometimes display Reflective behavior. We are saying that each person has one most preferred and habitually used communication style. The online assessment mentioned earlier will help you identify the frequency of you displaying a secondary style.

Minimizing Communication Style Bias

5.4 Learn how to identify your preferred communication style and that of your customer

Salespeople often make the mistake of focusing too much on the content of their sales presentation and not enough on how they deliver their message.[20] Communication style bias is a barrier to success in selling. This form of bias is a common problem in sales work simply because salespeople deal with people from all four quadrants. You cannot select potential customers on the basis of their communication style. You must be able to develop a rapport with people from each of the four quadrants. When people of different styles work together but don't adapt to one another, serious problems can develop.[21]

SELLING IN ACTION

Closing the Sale with Adaptive Selling

Rich Goldberg, President of Warm Thoughts Communications, a New Jersey-based marketing communications company, sensed he was about to lose an important client. He met with his staff, and together they created a profile based on their knowledge of the client's communication style. It soon became apparent that there was a mismatch between the client and the salesperson who called on that person. The customer was low in sociability but high in dominance. The customer was also described as someone who needed facts and figures. The salesperson was working on relationship building, and this approach was agitating the client. Goldberg counseled his staff to keep conversations with this customer brief, use facts and figures frequently, and clearly spell out the company's commitment to the client.[b]

How Communication Style Bias Develops and Erodes Partnering Relationships

To illustrate how communication style bias develops in a sales situation, let us observe a sales call involving two people with different communication styles. Lana Wheeler entered the office of Ron Harrington, one of her large accounts, with a feeling of optimism. She was sure that her proposal would save Ron's company several thousand dollars a month. She was 99 percent certain that, this being her third call on Ron, the sale would be closed. Ten minutes after meeting Ron, she was walking out of his office without the order. What went wrong?

Lana Wheeler is an "engaging" type who is an Emotive in terms of communication style. Her sales calls are typically fast paced. She entered Ron's office and immediately began to close the sale. Ron interrupted and told Lana he couldn't commit to her proposal. Lana appeared to ignore Ron's response, told him she could put some more figures together on pricing, and then used another trial close. Ron finally told Lana, "Look, you don't understand the way I do business. We have bigger issues than additional figures. As I said, this is a 'no go' project."

Ron's communication style is Directive. He feels uncomfortable when someone is making a decision for him. He wants to maintain control and be in charge of making his own decisions. He felt tension when Lana tried to get him to make a decision on her terms. If Lana had spent more time asking questions, listening more closely, and allowing Ron to feel like the decision was his, she may have found out what the "bigger issues" were. The approach she used would be more appropriate for the Supportive or the Emotive communication style.

A salesperson who is highly adaptable can usually build a rapport with customers regardless of their communication style. Style flexibility is a sales strategy that can be learned and is crucial to building partnering relationships.

Adaptive Selling Requires Versatility That Builds Strong Relationships

Personal selling has become more customer-focused than ever before, so every effort should be made to reduce the tension between the salesperson and customer. Dr. David Merrill, one of the early pioneers in the development of communication style instruments and training programs, uses the term **versatility** to describe our ability to minimize communication style bias.[22] Roger Wenschlag, author of *The Versatile Salesperson*, describes versatility as "the degree to which a salesperson is perceived as developing and maintaining buyer comfort throughout the sales process." *Adapting* to the customer's preferred communication style can enhance sales performance.[23]

MATURE AND IMMATURE BEHAVIOR There is a mature and an immature side to each behavioral style. Let us examine the Emotive style to illustrate this point. People with this style are open, personable individuals who seem genuinely friendly. The natural enthusiasm displayed by the mature Emotive is refreshing. On the other hand, an Emotive person who is too talkative and too emotional may have difficulty building rapport with some customers; this is the immature side of the Emotive communication style.

You recall that we use the words "industrious" and "precise" to describe the Reflective style. These are words that apply to the mature side of the Reflective person. We also use the words "aloof" and "stuffy." These words describe the immature side of the Reflective. The good news is that we all have the potential for developing the mature side of our communication style.

STRENGTH–WEAKNESS PARADOX It is a fact of life that your greatest strength can become your greatest weakness. If your most preferred style is Reflective, people are likely to respect your well-disciplined approach to life as one of your strengths. However, this strength can become a weakness if it is exaggerated. The Reflective person can be too serious, too questioning, and too inflexible. Robert Haas, former CEO of Levi Strauss & Company, is known for extraordinary (some say obsessive) attention to detail. Those who work with

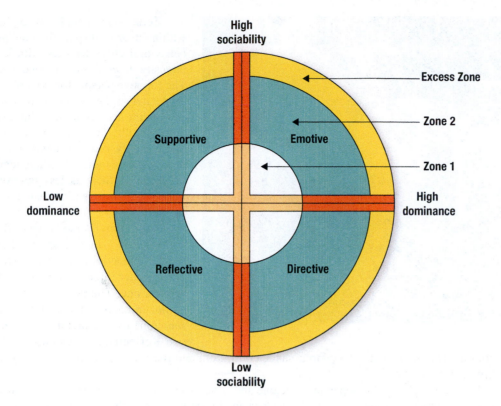

FIGURE 5.9

The completed communication-style model provides important insights needed to manage the relationship process in selling.

him say an offhand conversation can sound like a lecture. This Reflective, however, has the ability to flex his style. Levi's employees were fiercely loyal to Haas and describe him as compassionate to a fault.[24]

People with the Directive style are open and frank. They express their true feelings in a direct manner. In most cases, we appreciate candor, but we do not like to be around people who are too straightforward or too blunt in expressing their views. Steven Ballmer, CEO of Microsoft from 2000 to 2014, was known as a very demanding executive during his early years with the company. His explosive temper was legendary and he often put the fear of God into his staff members. He once needed throat surgery because he yelled so much. Later, he became more diplomatic and less domineering.[25] When people come across as *opinionated*, they tend to antagonize others. We should avoid pushing our strengths to the point of unproductive excess.[26]

To illustrate how strengths become weaknesses in excess, let us add more detail to our communication style model. Note that it now features three zones that radiate out from the center (Figure 5.9). These dimensions might be thought of as intensity zones.

KEEPING TRACK OF COMMUNICATION STYLES WITH CRM

Customer relationship management (CRM) software empowers a salesperson with information essential to continue a relationship. The software can be used to record, retain, and produce personal information including such factors as marital status, names and ages of children, and individual preferences. (An astute sales organization will implement privacy policies for such personal information.) With a large client list, before placing a call, the salesperson could quickly review the database information to refresh her memory about the prospect. This can be especially helpful when preparing to talk with someone with a specific communication style. The former **Regional Account Manager (RAM)** in the Appendix 2: The NewNet Systems Regional Accounts Management Case Study recorded the communication style in the CRM Contact Reports for each of the 20 customers he was working with. This information is invaluable for a new RAM taking over these accounts in building partnering relationships.

In his early years Steve Ballmer, CEO of Microsoft who followed Bill Gates, pushed his Directive strengths to the point of excess. His explosive temper was legendary. In recent years, he has displayed greater adaptability and versatility, and is now observed as being more diplomatic and less domineering.

Source: Armando Arorizo/Pi/ZUMA Press/Newscom

Zone one People who fall within this zone display their unique behavioral characteristics with less intensity than those in zone two. The Emotive person, for example, is moderately high on the dominance continuum and moderately high on the sociability continuum. As you might expect, zone one communication styles are more difficult to identify because there is less intensity in both dimensions (dominance and sociability).

Zone two Persons who fall within this zone display their unique behavioral characteristics with greater intensity than persons in zone one. The people identified earlier in each of the styles represent zone two behaviors. The zone two Reflective, for example, falls within the lowest quartile of the dominance continuum and the lowest quartile of the sociability continuum.

The boundary line that separates zone one and zone two should not be seen as a permanent barrier restricting change in intensity. Under certain circumstances, we should abandon our most preferred style temporarily. A deliberate move from zone one to zone two, or vice versa, is called "style flexing."

Excess zone The excess zone is characterized by a high degree of intensity and rigidity. When people allow themselves to drift into this zone, they become very inflexible, which is often interpreted by others as a form of bias toward their style. In addition, the

The excess zone is characterized by a high degree of intensity and rigidity. We are more apt to move into the excess zone under very stressful conditions.

Source: Blend Images/Superstock

Doing Business in Canada

Canada and the United States share a continent, a border, an auto-racing series (CART), and a hockey league. Yet, it would be a mistake to assume that business practices are the same in both countries. Canada is a more formal country than the United States and businesspeople are less likely to be on a first-name basis. Jan Yager, author of *Business Protocol*, says, "The worst faux pas an American doing business with a Canadian might commit is to say to a Canadian, 'You and I, we Americans . . .'." Canadians are proud of their country and do not think of themselves as Americans. Although Canada is bilingual and most businesspeople speak English, some provinces such as Quebec are French speaking and carry business cards printed in both English and French.[c]

strengths of the inflexible person become weaknesses. Extreme intensity in any quadrant is bound to threaten interpersonal relations and excess zone behavior frequently destroys relationships.

We are apt to move into the excess zone and exaggerate our style characteristics under stressful conditions. Stress tends to bring out the worst in many people. Some of the behaviors that salespeople and customers may display when they are in the excess zone follow:

Emotive style	Expresses highly emotional opinions
	Stops listening to the other person
	Tries too hard to promote own point of view
	Becomes outspoken to the point of being offensive
Directive style	Gets impatient with the other person
	Becomes dictatorial and bossy
	Does not admit being wrong
	Becomes extremely competitive
Reflective style	Becomes stiff and formal
	Is unwilling to make a decision
	Avoids displaying any type of emotion
	Is overly interested in detail
Supportive style	Agrees with everyone
	Is unable to take a strong stand
	Becomes overly anxious to win approval of others
	Tries to comfort everyone

Building Strong Relationships Through Style Flexing

5.5 Learn to adapt interpersonal versatility and build strong selling relationships with style flexing

Style flexing is the deliberate attempt to adapt one's communication style to accommodate the needs of the other person. You are attempting to communicate with the other person on his or her own "channel." Ron Willingham, in his book *Integrity Selling*, reminds us: "People are more apt to buy from you when they perceive you view the world as they view the world."[27] In a selling situation, you should try to determine the customer's most preferred style and flex your own accordingly. If your preferred communication style is Directive, and your customer is a Supportive, try to be more personal and warmer in your presentation. Once you know the customer's style,

BusinessWeek identified Indra Nooyi, when she served as president of PepsiCo, and former CEO Steven Reinemund as the "odd couple." Indra, born and raised in India and now serving as CEO of PepsiCo, is a free-spirited strategist while Steven was a spit-and-polish detail man. Individuals with different communication styles can work well together if they possess communication style flexibility.

Source: Joe Raedle/Getty Images

flexing your style can strengthen the relationship and make the difference between a presentation that falters and one that exceeds your expectations.[28] Style sensitivity and flexing add value to the sales process.

Throughout the preapproach, you should learn as much as possible about the customer and try to determine his or her style. Once you are in the presence of the customer, do not become preoccupied analyzing the person's style. If you are trying hard to analyze the person's style, you may not listen closely enough to what she is trying to tell you. If you are truly tuned into the customer, you can absorb many cues that help you determine her style. After the sales call, analyze the communication and record your findings. Use this information to plan your next contact with the customer.[29] Listen closely to the customer's tone of voice. A Supportive person sounds warm and friendly. The Reflective customer's voice is more likely to be controlled and deliberate. Pay particular attention to gestures. The Emotive individual uses his hands to communicate thoughts and ideas. The Directive also uses gestures to communicate but is more controlled and less spontaneous. The Reflective person appears more relaxed, less intense. The Emotive individual is an open, impulsive communicator, whereas the Reflective person is quite cautious. The Supportive type is personal and friendly, while the Reflective person may seem difficult to get to know. To avoid relationship tension, consider the following suggestions for each of the four styles.

Building Relationships with Emotive Customers

If you are attempting to sell products to an Emotive person, keep in mind the need to move at a pace that holds the attention of the prospect. Be enthusiastic and avoid an approach that is too stiff and formal. Take time to establish goodwill and build relationships. Do not place too much emphasis on the facts and details. To deal effectively with Emotive people, plan actions that provide support for their opinions, ideas, and dreams.[30] Plan to ask questions concerning their opinions and ideas, but be prepared to help them get "back on track" if they move too far away from the topic. Maintain good eye contact and, above all, be a good listener.

Building Relationships with Directive Customers

The key to relating to Directives is to keep the relationship as businesslike as possible. Developing a strong personal relationship is not a high priority for Directives. In other words, friendship is not usually a condition for a good working relationship. Your goal is to be as efficient, time

The Platinum Rule®

The **Platinum Rule**, created by Dr. Tony Alessandra, provides each of us with the motivation we need to treat others the way they want to be treated. This rule is a simple, proven method for building strong relationships with our customers.

"Do Unto Others As They Want Done Unto Them."

The Platinum Rule (www.platinumrule.com) is at the heart of the style-flexing sales strategy. When we take time to determine whether the customer is behaving as an Emotive, Directive, Reflective, or Supportive, we can then treat them the way they want to be treated.[d]

---

disciplined, and well organized as possible and to provide appropriate facts, figures, and success probabilities. Most Directives are goal-oriented people, so try to identify their primary objectives and then determine ways to support and help with these objectives. Early in the sales presentation, ask specific questions and carefully note responses. Look for specific points you can respond to when it is time to present your proposals.

Building Relationships with Reflective Customers

The Reflective person responds in a positive way to a thoughtful, well-organized approach. Arrive at meetings on time and be well prepared. In most cases, it is not necessary to spend a great deal of time building a social relationship. Reflective people appreciate a no-nonsense, business-like approach to personal selling. Use specific questions that show clear direction. Once you have information concerning the prospect's needs, present your proposal in a slow, deliberate way. Provide as much documentation as possible. Do not be in too big a hurry to close the sale. Never pressure the Reflective person to make quick decisions.

Building Relationships with Supportive Customers

Take time to build a social relationship with the Supportive person. Spend time learning about the matters that are important in this individual's life—family, hobbies, and major interests. Listen carefully to personal opinions and feelings. Supportive individuals like to conduct business with sales personnel who are professional but friendly. Therefore, study their feelings and emotional needs as well as their technical and business needs. Throughout the presentation, provide personal assurances and support for their views. If you disagree with a Supportive person, curb the desire to disagree too assertively; Supportive people tend to dislike interpersonal conflict. Give them the time to comprehend your proposal. Patience is important.

As you develop your communication style identification skills and become more adept at style flexing, you become better able to manage the relationship process. With these skills, you should be able to open more accounts, sell more to established customers, and more effectively meet the pressures of competition. Most important, your customers will view you as a person better able to understand and meet their needs.

Word of Caution

It is tempting to put a label on someone and then assume the label tells you everything you need to know about that person. If you want to build an effective partnering type of relationship with a prospect, you must acquire additional information about that person. Stuart Atkins, a respected authority on communication styles and author of *The Name of Your Game*, says we should be careful not to use labels that make people feel boxed in, typecast, or judged. He believes we should not classify *people*; we should classify their *strengths* and *preferences* to act one way or another under certain circumstances.[31] You also must be careful not to let the label you place on yourself become the justification for your own inflexible behavior. Try not to let the label justify or reinforce why you are unable or unwilling to communicate effectively with others.

CHAPTER LEARNING ACTIVITIES

Reviewing Key Concepts

Discuss how communication style influences the relationship process in sales

Many sales are lost because salespeople fail to communicate effectively with the prospect. Communication style bias contributes to this problem. Every salesperson who is willing to develop style sensitivity and engage in appropriate style flexing can minimize one of the most common barriers to success in selling.

Identify the two major dimensions of the communication style model

The communication style model is based on two continuums that assess two major aspects of human behavior: dominance and sociability. By combining them as horizontal and vertical continuums, we create quadrants that define four styles of communication. We have called these the Emotive, Directive, Reflective, and Supportive styles.

Explain the four communications styles in the communication style model

The Emotive style combines high sociability and high dominance, whereas the Directive style combines high dominance and low sociability. The Reflective style combines low dominance and low sociability, whereas the Supportive style combines low dominance and high sociability.

Learn how to identify your preferred communication style and that of your customer

With practice you can learn to identify your preferred communication style. The starting point is to rate yourself on each scale (dominance and sociability) by placing a check mark at a point along the continuum that represents how you perceive yourself. Completion of the dominance and sociability indicator forms will help you achieve greater awareness of your communication style. This same approach can be used to identify the customer's preferred style.

Learn to adapt interpersonal versatility and build strong selling relationships with style flexing

A third dimension of human behavior—versatility—is important in dealing with communication styles that are different from your own. You can adapt your own style to meet the needs of others—a process called "style flexing." Style flexing is an attempt to change or adapt your style to meet the needs of the customer.

Key Terms

Personality, p. 91
Communication style, p. 92
Adaptive selling, p. 92
Communication style bias, p. 92

Dominance, p. 94
Sociability, p. 95
Emotive style, p. 96
Directive style, p. 98
Reflective style, p. 99

Supportive style, p. 101
Versatility, p. 104
Style flexing, p. 107
Platinum Rule, p. 109

MyMarketingLab

To complete the problems with the ⭐ in your MyLab, go to the EOC Discussion Questions.

Review Questions

5-1 What is the meaning of the term *communication style*?

5-2 Describe the five major principles that support communication style theory.

5-3 What are the benefits to the salesperson who understands communication style?

5-4 What two dimensions of human behavior are used to identify communication style?

⭐ **5-5** Describe the person who tends to be high in sociability.

5-6 What are the four communication styles? Develop a brief description of each of the styles.

⭐ **5-7** What is the reaction of most people who study communication styles for the first time? Why does this reaction surface?

⭐ **5-8** Define style flexing. How can style flexing improve sales productivity?

5-9 Explain the statement, "Your greatest strength can become your greatest weakness."

Application Exercises

5-10 Communication or behavior styles are one of the most popular training programs. Worldwide, 47 million people have participated in the Wilson and DiSC programs. An understanding of communication styles assists us in building better personal and business relationships. As indicated in this chapter, the first step in applying what you have learned about communication styles is to identify and understand your own style. Using the Online Communication Style Assessment at the pearsonhighered.com/manning website, assess your communication style.

    a. Do you agree with your assessment of your most preferred style? How about your results on your secondary style?

    b. Referring to the material presented in the chapter, identify the strengths and weaknesses of your style.

    c. Identify the styles you enjoy working with best. Identify the styles you enjoy working with least.

    d. Refer to page 107. Can you identify those behaviors you tend to exhibit when you feel stressed?

    e. Explain why you think so many individuals and companies have participated in this program. From Figure 5.8 on page 102, list the names other training programs have used to identify your most preferred style.

5-11 Self-awareness is important in personal selling. As we get to know ourselves, we can identify barriers to acceptance by others. Once you have identified your most preferred communication style, you have taken a big step in the direction of self-awareness. We have noted that self-ratings can sometimes be misleading because some people lack a high degree of self-awareness. They do not see themselves as others see them. Consider asking four or five people (e.g., coworkers) to assess and print the profile of your communication style using the online assessment. Then compare these ratings with your self-rating.

5-12 Many salespeople, after being introduced to communication style concepts, attempt to categorize each of their customers. They report that their relationships become mutually more enjoyable and productive. Select four people whom you know quite well (supervisor, subordinate, customer, teacher, friend, or members of your sports team). Using the Online Communication Style Assessment at the pearsonhighered.com/manning website, assess the communication style of each of these people. Explain how this information can improve your relationship with each of these people.

5-13 To assess your ability to style flex, assume you are going to make four sales calls on customers displaying each of the four communication styles. For purposes of illustration, consider your first call is on an Emotive customer with a communication style like Jimmy Fallon. The second call is on a Supportive customer with a communication style like Dr. Ben Carson; the third is on a Reflective customer with a communication style like

Bill Gates; and the last is on a Directive customer like Hillary Clinton. For each of these customers, refer to the online communication style assessment and assess the behaviors you would demonstrate as you establish your relationship with them. Print each of the profiles and compare them to one another. Did you flex your style of communication to better interact with the customer representing Jimmy Fallon's style versus the customer representing Ben Carson's style? Did you flex differently for the customer representing Bill Gates, and the one representing Hillary Clinton?

5-14 Myers-Briggs Personality Types and Jungian Personality Types are two very popular descriptions of the concepts found in this chapter. Using your search engine, access the Internet sites that refer to these concepts. Type in "Jungian + personality profiles" to access the Jungian personality types. To access the Myers-Briggs types, type in "Myers-Briggs + personality profiles." Does the number of queries indicate anything about the validity and popularity of these theories? Examine specific queries about both of these theories. Do you see the relationship between these two theories and the material in this chapter? Each year, about 2.5 million Americans complete the Myers-Briggs Type Indicator (MBTI). Why is this psychological-assessment instrument so popular?

Role-Play Exercise

For the purpose of this role-play, assume the role of Ray Perkins, who is described in the following case problem. Ray is described as a quiet, amiable person who displays the Supportive communication style. You will meet with Ms. Maynard, who is also described in the case problem. For the purpose of this role-play, assume that Ms. Maynard displays the characteristics of the Directive communication style. Prior to the role-play, study the chapter material on style flexing and information on how to sell to persons with the Directive communication style.

Adaptive Selling Case Problem—
Ray Perkins/Grant Real Estate

Ray Perkins has been employed at Grant Real Estate for almost two years. Prior to receiving his real estate license, he was a property manager with a large real estate agency in another community. During his first year with Grant, he was assigned to the residential property division and sold properties totaling $825,000. He then requested and received a transfer to the commercial division.

Three months ago, Ray obtained a commercial listing that consisted of 26 acres of land near a growing residential neighborhood. The land is zoned commercial and appears to be ideally suited for a medium-sized shopping center. Ray prepared a detailed prospectus and sent it to Vera Maynard, president of Mondale Growth Corporation, a firm specializing in development of shopping centers. One week later, he received a letter from Ms. Maynard requesting more information. Shortly after receiving Ray's response, Ms. Maynard called to set up an appointment to inspect the property. A time and date were finalized, and Ray agreed to meet her plane and conduct a tour of the property.

Ray is a quiet, amiable person who displays the Supportive communication style. Friends say that they like to spend time with him because he is a good listener.

Questions

5-15 If Ms. Maynard displays the characteristics of the Directive communication style, how should Ray conduct himself during the meeting? Be specific as you describe those behaviors that would be admired by Ms. Maynard.

5-16 If Ms. Maynard wants to build a rapport with Ray Perkins, what behavior should she display?

5-17 It is not a good idea to put a label on someone and then assume the label tells us everything about the person. As Ray attempts to build a rapport with Ms. Maynard, what other personal characteristics should he try to identify?

MyMarketingLab

Go to the Assignments section of your MyLab to complete these writing exercises.

5-18 Many sales are lost because salespeople fail to communicate effectively with the prospect. What key factor(s) contribute to this problem and how may salespeople overcome this barrier?

5-19 There are four communications styles in the communication style model. Explain how the use of the dominance and sociability form helps you identify your preferred communication style. Why would this be helpful to achieve success in sales?

PART 2 ROLE-PLAY EXERCISE

Developing a Relationship Strategy

Scenario

You are an experienced sales representative employed by American Steel Processing, a company that has been in business for more than 25 years. American is an ISO 9002-certified manufacturing company that has earned many accolades, including three consecutive J.D. Power and Associates awards for customer satisfaction. Over the years, the company has invested heavily in automation technology as a means of ensuring consistent manufacturing quality. The American Steel Processing sales force understands that the company will not be the lowest bidder in most sales situations because the highest quality can never be obtained at the lowest price.

Customer Profile

Tyler Hensman has held the position of senior purchasing agent at Regina Steel Fabricators for several years. Throughout this period of time, Tyler has negotiated more than a dozen purchase agreements with Dana Davis, senior account representative with American Steel Processing. Tyler takes pride in purchasing quality steel products at the best price.

Salesperson Profile

Dana Davis began working for American Steel Processing about four years ago. After completion of an extensive sales training program, Dana was assigned to a territory in central Ohio. After three successful years, Dana Davis was promoted to senior account representative.

Product

American Steel Processing sells a wide range of steel products. Many of the orders filled are for high-stress steel beams, stainless steel bolts and nuts, and structural tubing used in commercial building construction. Most orders specify a certain quality of steel.

Instructions

For this role-play, you will assume the role of Dana Davis, senior account representative employed by American Steel Processing. To prepare for the role-play, you should carefully read the case problem at the end of Chapter 3. This information will help you understand the issues that need to be addressed during the role-play. During the early stages of the role-play, you will want to obtain more information from the customer and resolve any misunderstandings. You want to obtain the order for type 316 stainless steel bolts and nuts, and maintain a good relationship with this important customer. Keep in mind that ethical decisions can greatly influence the relationship between a salesperson and the customer. Reflect on the important information covered in Chapter 3 prior to meeting with Tyler Hensman.

Character strength builds as we display loyalty, mutual commitment, and the pursuit of long-term goals. These are the qualities needed to build strong buyer–seller relationships.

PART 3

Source: michaeljung/Shutterstock

DEVELOPING A PRODUCT STRATEGY

Part 3 examines the important role of complete and accurate product, company, and competitive knowledge in personal selling. Lack of knowledge in these areas impairs the salesperson's ability to configure value-added solutions. Part 3 also describes several value-added selling strategies.

Creating Product Solutions

Source: Michael Ahearne

Reality Selling Video Series— Amy Vandaveer/*Texas Monthly*

▶

Since her university graduation Amy Vandaveer, in the photo above, has had a highly successful sales career. Amy was a sales representative for *Texas Monthly* (www.texasmonthly .com), and is now a sales instructor at the University of Houston. *Texas Monthly* is a magazine that focuses largely on leisure activities and events in Texas and their sales staff is responsible for selling the large amount of advertising space available in the magazine. It may sound like a relatively easy job; after all, *Texas Monthly* has a large, loyal reader base and would be an attractive advertising outlet for many businesses. Remember, though, that *Texas Monthly* has many direct and indirect competitors, all of whom are trying to sell their services to the same group of businesses that Amy works with.

Because of the many options available to a prospective advertiser, Amy had to first become an expert on what her customers want, what *Texas Monthly* can offer them, and what *Texas Monthly*'s competitors can offer. By doing so, she was able to improve her ability to answer customers' questions and emphasize the benefits, in the context of her customers' needs, of choosing *Texas Monthly* over other advertising outlets. She realized she was no longer just selling advertising space; instead, she was able to offer her customers her own knowledge and experience at creating solutions that address their needs.[1] ●

Developing Product Solutions That Add Value

As noted in Chapter 2, a product strategy helps salespeople make correct decisions concerning the selection and positioning of products to meet identified customer needs. The **product strategy** is a well-conceived plan that emphasizes becoming a product expert, selling specific benefits, and configuring value-added solutions (Figure 6.1). Configuring value-added solutions is discussed in detail in Chapter 7. A McKinsey survey of more than 1,200 B2B purchasing decision makers revealed that, among the habits that undermine the sales experience, the second "most destructive" was a lack of knowledge about either their products or those of their competitors.[2]

Selling Solutions

A **solution** is a mutually shared answer to a recognized customer problem. In many selling situations, a solution is more encompassing than a specific product. It often provides measurable results such as greater productivity, increased profits, or less employee turnover. Selling a solution, versus selling a specific product, usually requires a greater effort to define and diagnose the customer's problem.[3] Think of **solution selling** as a process by which the salesperson uncovers and clarifies a customer's problem, works with the customer to create a vision of how things could be better, and then develops a plan for implementing the vision.[4]

Most salespeople have adopted a broad definition of the term *product*. It is broadly interpreted to encompass information, services, ideas, tangible products, or some combination of these that satisfy the customer's needs with the right solution.[5] Let's look at the sales process at two firms:

- Trilogy, an Austin, Texas–based company, creates configuration software for large manufacturers such as Boeing and Hewlett-Packard. These two companies sell products with a great many variants. Boeing, for example, can use a wide range of components to assemble a plane that matches the customer's highly specific preferences. With the aid of Trilogy software, Boeing sales representatives, using a laptop computer, can translate a customer's specific needs into a workable specification.[6]
- Sunflower Travel Corporation, based in Wichita, Kansas, creates specialized vacation packages for individuals and groups. A package might include airline tickets, hotel reservations, and accommodations on a cruise line. The sales staff at Sunflower have the knowledge to plan a highly customized trip.[7]

From the customer's point of view, salespeople employed by Trilogy and Sunflower are selling primarily information and expertise. The problem-solving ability these salespeople provide the customer is viewed as the product. When you sell a complex product, it is knowledge and expertise that create value.

A recent Corporate Executive Board study of more than 1,400 B2B customers found that those customers completed much of their decision making—such as researching solutions, ranking options, setting requirements, benchmarking pricing, and so on—before even having a conversation with a supplier.[8] With our information-rich, Internet-driven marketplace, often

Strategic/Consultative Selling Model	
Strategic Step	**Prescription**
Develop a Personal Selling Philosophy	☑ Adopt Marketing Concept ☑ Value Personal Selling ☑ Become a Problem Solver/Partner
Develop a Relationship Strategy	☑ Maintain High Ethical Standards ☑ Project Professional Image ☑ Manage the Relationship Process
Develop a Product Strategy	☐ Become a Product Expert ☐ Sell Specific Benefits ☐ Configure Value-Added Solutions

FIGURE 6.1

Developing a product strategy enables the salesperson to custom-fit products or services to the customer's needs.

salespeople will have to be more insightful into unrecognized needs the customer may not have considered, and sell solutions to these needs. If they don't, they likely will find themselves in a price war with their competitors. Salespeople in this environment will have to master the use of what are called "implication" or "pain" questions to help customers discover their unrealized needs. These questions will be discussed in detail later in Chapter 11.

TAILORING THE PRODUCT STRATEGY A product strategy should be tailored to the customer's buying needs. Transactional buyers are usually well aware of their needs. Most of these customers have conducted their own research and have a good understanding of the product that will meet their needs. The office manager who frequently buys a large amount of copy paper knows that this standard item can be purchased from several vendors. The quality of the paper usually does not vary from one vendor to another.

The consultative buyer may lack a "needs awareness" and will usually welcome "need clarification." This customer will want help evaluating possible solutions and usually needs a customized product solution. The customized solution appeals to the customer's desire for choices that are tailored to his or her needs. Developing a product strategy for the strategic alliance customer usually offers the greatest challenge. Study of the proposed alliance partner can be very time consuming, but the rewards of a successful alliance may be substantial. In some cases, the company that wishes to form an alliance with a new customer must be prepared to make a large investment in capital-intensive technology and additional personnel.[9]

Explosion of Product Options

The domestic and global markets are overflowing with a vast array of goods and services. In some industries, the number of new products introduced each year is mind-boggling. Consumer-product makers, for example, churn out more than 30,000 new products each year. Want to buy a product in the securities and financial services field? In the segment of mutual funds alone, you can choose from more than 7,000 products.[10]

For the customer, this much variety creates a "good news–bad news" situation. The good news is that almost all buyers have a choice when it comes to purchasing a product or service. People like to compare various options. The bad news is that so many choices often complicate the buying process. One of the most important roles of the salesperson is to simplify the customer's study of the product choices. Later in this chapter we discuss how product features (information) can add value when converted into specific benefits (knowledge) that can help the buyer make an intelligent buying decision.

Creating Solutions with Product Configuration

The challenge facing both customers and salespeople in this era of information overload is deciding which product applications, or combination of applications, can solve the buying problem. If the customer has complex buying needs, then the salesperson may have to bring together many parts of the company's product mix to develop a custom-fitted solution. The product selection process is often referred to as **product configuration**. Salespeople representing Cisco Systems are often involved in the sale of new products to new and established customers. They use Cybrant Solutions Architect software to quickly identify solutions. The software helps salespeople ask prospects the right questions to discover their needs and then configures a solution that best meets those needs.[11]

Amy Vandaveer takes pride in her ability to create solutions based on product configuration. In fact, every proposal she prepares is customized to fit the needs of a *Texas Monthly* customer.

Many companies use product configuration software because it develops customized product solutions quickly and accurately. It incorporates product-selection criteria and associates them directly with customer requirements. Members of the sales force can use the sales configurator to identify product options, prices, delivery schedules, and other parts of the product mix while working interactively with the customer. Most of today's product configuration software can be integrated with contact management software programs such as Salesforce.com, ACT!, and NetSuite. In addition to improving the quality of the sales proposal, this software reduces the time-consuming process of manually preparing written proposals.

A major element of product configuration is *quotation management*. Quick and accurate pricing is critical in today's fast-paced sales environment. Leading companies are aggressively automating their quotation management process.[12]

Preparing Written Proposals

Written proposals are frequently part of the salesperson's product strategy. It is only natural that some buyers want the proposed solution put in writing. "Written proposals" can be defined as a specific plan of action based on the facts, assumptions, and supporting documentation included in the sales presentation.[13] A well-written proposal adds value to the product solution and can set you apart from the competition. It offers the buyer reassurance that you will deliver what has been promised. Written proposals, which are often accompanied by a sales letter, vary in terms of format and content. Many government agencies, and some large companies, issue a request for proposal (RFP) that specifies the format of the proposal. Most proposals include the following parts:

Budget and overview. Tell the prospect the cost of the solution you have prescribed. Be specific as you describe the product or service features to be provided and specify the price. When you confirm pricing with a proposal, misunderstandings and mistakes can be avoided.

Objective. The objective should be expressed in terms of benefits. A tangible objective might be to "reduce payroll expense by 10 percent." An intangible objective might be stated as "increased business security offered by a company with a reputation for dependability." Focus on specific benefits that relate directly to the customer's needs.

Strategy. Briefly describe how you will meet your objective. How will you fulfill the obligations you have described in your proposal? In some cases, this section of your proposal includes specific language: "Your account will be assigned to Susan Murray, our senior lease representative."

Schedule. Establish a time frame for meeting your objective. This might involve the confirmation of dates with regard to acquisition, shipping, or installation.

Rationale. With a mixture of logic and emotion, present your rationale for taking action now. Once again, the emphasis should be on benefits, not features.[14]

Some written proposals follow a specific format developed by the company. The length of a proposal can vary from a single page to dozens of pages for a complex product.

The proposal should be printed on quality paper and free of any errors in spelling, grammar, or punctuation. Before completing the proposal, review the content one more time to be sure you have addressed all the customer's concerns. Bob Kantin, author of *Sales Proposals Kit for Dummies* (2001), says the proposal is really the first "product" that the customer receives from you, so be sure it is perfect.[15] Neil Rackham, noted author and sales consultant, says to address your proposal to the "invisible" customer. Very often the proposal will be reviewed by individuals the salesperson has never met. And these are often the people who will make or break the deal.[16]

The remainder of this chapter is divided into five major sections. The first two sections examine the kinds of product information and company information required by the salesperson. The third section describes the type of information about the competition that is helpful to salespeople. Sources of information are covered in the fourth section, and the fifth section describes how product features can be translated into buyer benefits.

Becoming a Product Expert

6.2 Describe the importance of becoming an expert regarding product knowledge

One of the major challenges facing salespeople is winning the customer's trust. A survey reported in *Sales & Marketing Management* ranked product knowledge as the number-one characteristic of salespeople who are able to build trust.[17] Ideally, a salesperson possesses product knowledge that meets and exceeds customer expectations, increasing sales effectiveness and willingness to pay.[18] Noted author and management consultant Tom Peters says that when it comes to product knowledge, remember: "More, more, more. And, more important: Deeper, deeper, deeper." In summary: "He or she who has the largest appetite for Deep Knowledge wins."[19] The recognized expert in any field is the one who is frequently "sought out by others, thereby in selling, significantly shortening the sales cycle and better meeting customer wants and and needs."

This section reviews some of the most common product information categories: (1) product development and quality improvement processes, (2) performance data and specifications, (3) maintenance and service contracts, and (4) price and delivery. Each is important as a potential source of knowledge concerning the product or service.

SELLING IN ACTION

Effective Sales Letter Writing Is a Must

Sales letters are increasingly being used by salespeople to describe features and benefits, position products, build relationships, and provide assurances to customers. Sales letters also are used in conjunction with prospecting plans. Several standard rules apply to all written sales letters. These include the following:

1. Sales letters should follow the standard visual format of a business letter. They should contain (in the following order) a letterhead or the sender's address, date, inside address (the same as on the outside of the envelope), salutation, body of letter, complimentary close, typed name and handwritten signature of sender, and a notation of enclosures (if there are any).

2. Placement of the letter on paper should provide a balanced white-space border area surrounding the entire letter. Three to five blank lines should separate the date and inside address; a single blank line should separate the inside address and the salutation, salutation and opening paragraph of the letter, and each paragraph. A single blank line should separate the last paragraph and the complimentary close. Single spacing should generally be used within the paragraphs.

3. Proper business punctuation includes a colon after the salutation and comma after the complimentary close.

4. Most sales letters include at least three paragraphs. The first paragraph should indicate the objective of your letter; the second should be a summary of the benefits proposed; and the third paragraph should state what the next action step will be for the salesperson, the customer, or both.

5. Proper grammar and spelling must be used throughout the entire letter. Business letters provide an opportunity to build a stronger relationship with the customer and close the sale. Improper placement, punctuation, spelling errors, or weak content convey a negative impression to the reader and may result in a lost sale.

6. The use of the personal pronoun "I" should be minimized in a sales letter. To keep the letter focused on the customer's needs, the pronouns "you" and "your" should appear throughout the body of the letter.

A quick response to a customer's questions about product configurations or pricing can serve as a product strategy improvement within the sales process. This salesperson is adding value by using her notebook computer and cell phone to access and quickly communicate information.

Source: Tetra Images/Alamy Stock Photo

Product Development and Quality Improvement Processes

Companies spend large amounts of money in the development of their products. In **product development**, the original idea for a product or service is tested, modified, and retested several times before it is offered to the customer. Each of the modifications is made with the thought of improving the product. Salespeople should be familiar with product development history. Often this information sets the stage for stronger sales appeals.

Patagonia, a company that makes high-quality sports and outdoor equipment and clothing, uses a unique product development process. Patagonia hires many expert kayakers, skiers, climbers, and fishermen who under actual conditions help develop and test the company's products. In the outdoor recreation market, Patagonia wins high praise for its many product innovations.[20] Quality improvement continues to be an important long-term business strategy for most successful companies.[21] Salespeople need to identify quality improvement processes that provide a competitive advantage and be prepared to discuss this information during the sales presentation. Gulfstream Aircraft Company, Ritz-Carlton Hotels, Toyota, and Sea Ray Boats are examples of companies that have implemented important quality controls. **Quality control**, which involves measuring products and services against established standards, is one dimension of the typical quality improvement process.

Sea Ray Boats, a quality leader in the pleasure boat industry, worked hard to become an ISO 9002 certified builder. This certification, from the International Organization for Standardization (ISO), assures a high level of quality in the manufacturing process. The company is the industry leader in robotic applications, a means of ensuring consistent quality from boat to boat. Sea Ray Boats has also earned two consecutive J.D. Power and Associates awards for customer satisfaction.[22]

Performance Data and Specifications

Most potential buyers are interested in performance data and specifications. Some typical questions that might be raised by prospects are:

> "What is the frequency response for this stereo loudspeaker?"
> "What is the anticipated rate of return on this mutual fund?"
> "What is the energy-consumption rating for this appliance?"
> "Are all your hotel and conference center rooms accessible to persons with physical disabilities?"

A salesperson must be prepared to address these types of questions in the written sales proposal and the sales presentation. Performance data are especially critical in cases in which the customer is attempting to compare the merits of one product with another.

To become familiar with the performance of Whirlpool appliances, salespeople literally "live" the brand. The company rented and redesigned an eight-bedroom farmhouse near corporate headquarters and outfitted it with Whirlpool dishwashers, refrigerators, washers, dryers, and microwaves. Salespeople, in groups of eight, live at the house for two months and use all of the appliances. Whirlpool engineers visit the home and present information on design, performance data, and specifications. A recent graduate of the training program says, "I have a confidence level that's making a difference in my client contacts."[23]

Maintenance and Service Contracts—Servicing the Sale

Prospects often want information concerning maintenance and care requirements for the products they purchase. The salesperson who can quickly and accurately provide this information has the edge. Proper maintenance usually extends the life of the product, so this information should be provided at the time of the sale.

Today, many salespeople are developing customized service agreements that incorporate the customer's special priorities, feelings, and needs. They work hard to acquire a real understanding of the customer's specific service criteria. If call-return expectations are very important to the customer, the frequency and quantity of product-related visits per week or month can be included in the service contract. Customized service agreements add value to the sale and help protect your business from the competition.[24]

Pricing and Delivery

Potential buyers expect salespeople to be well versed in price and delivery policies and be in a position to set prices and plan deliveries. If a salesperson has pricing authority, buyers perceive the person as someone with whom they can really talk business. The ability to set prices puts the salesperson in a stronger position.[25]

Decision-making authority in the area of pricing gives the salesperson *more power and responsibility*. If the salesperson negotiates a price that is too low, the company may lose money on the sale. Price objections represent one of the most common barriers to closing a sale, so salespeople need to be well prepared in this area.

In most situations, the price quotation should be accompanied by information that creates value in the mind of the customer. The process of determining whether or not the proposal adds value is often called **quantifying the solution**. When the purchase represents a major buying decision, such as the purchase of a new computer system, quantifying the solution is important. One way to quantify the solution is to conduct a cost–benefit analysis to determine the actual cost of the purchase and savings the buyer can anticipate from the investment (Table 6.1).

Another way to quantify the solution is to calculate **return on investment (ROI)**. As products and services become more complex and more expensive, customers are more likely to look at the financial reasons for buying. This is especially true in business-to-business selling. Salespeople who can develop a sales proposal that contains specific information on return on

TABLE 6.1 Quantifying the Solution with Cost–Benefit Analysis

Quantifying the solution often involves a carefully prepared cost–benefit analysis. This example compares the higher-priced Phoenix semitruck trailer with the lower-priced FB model, which is a competing product.

Cost Savings of the Phoenix versus FB Model for a 10-Year Period (All Prices Are Approximate)

	COST SAVINGS
• Stainless steel bulkhead (savings on sandblasting and painting)	$ 425.00
• Stainless steel rear door frame (savings on painting)	425.00
• Air ride suspension (better fuel mileage, longer tire life, longer brake life)	3,750.00
• Hardwood or aluminum scuff (savings from freight damages and replacement of scuff)	1,000.00
• LED lights (last longer; approximate savings: $50 per year × 10 years)	500.00
• Light protectors (save $50 per year on replacement × 10 years)	500.00
• Threshold plate (saves damage to entry of trailer)	200.00
• Internal rail reinforcement (saves damage to lower rail and back panels)	500.00
• Stainless steel screws for light attachment (savings on replacement cost)	200.00
• Domestic oak premium floor—1⅜ (should last 10 years under normal conditions)	1,000.00
• Doors—aluminum inner and outer skin, outside white finish, inside mill finish, fastened by five aluminum hinges (savings over life of trailer)	750.00
• Five-year warranty in addition to standard warranty covers bulkhead rust, LED lights, floor, scuff liner, glad hands, rear frame, mudflap assembly, and threshold plate (Phoenix provides a higher trade-in value)	1,500.00
Total approximate savings of Phoenix over 10-year period (all the preceding is standard equipment on a Phoenix; this trailer will sell for $23,500; an FB standard trailer would sell for $19,500)	$10,750.00
Less additional initial cost of Phoenix over FB standard	4,000.00
Overall cost savings of Phoenix over FB trailer	$ 6,750.00

investment are more likely to get a favorable response from key decision makers. Chief financial officers, for example, are more inclined to approve an expensive purchase if it results in a good return on investment.[26]

Performing accurate ROI calculations often requires the collection of detailed financial information. You may need to help the prospect collect information within the company to build a case for the purchase. BAX Global offers customers multimodal shipping solutions. It has the capabilities to employ more than one mode of transportation for a customer. In order to develop a customized solution for the customer, the sales representative must collect a great deal of financial and nonfinancial data from the prospect. Transportation modes (trucks, airplanes, railroads, etc.) vary in terms of cost, speed, dependability, frequency, and other criteria, so preparation of the sales proposal can be a complicated process.[27]

The use of ROI selling appeals requires more work upfront, but it often leads to shorter sales cycles. The salesperson who is not well schooled in financial issues, and cannot compute and supply price information accurately, may be at a serious disadvantage. In Chapter 7, we discuss how to position products according to price.

Knowing, understanding, and being able to clarify information in product literature adds value within the sales process. Customers seek out the "product experts" who can assist them in making intelligent buying decisions.

Source: Goodluz/Shutterstock

Become a Company Expert

We should never underestimate information about the company itself as a strong appeal that can be used during the sales presentation. This is especially true when the customer is considering a strategic alliance. Before teaming up with another company, the strategic alliance buyer will want to learn a great deal about the firm the salesperson represents. In many cases, you are selling your company as much or more as you are selling a product.[28]

Some companies such as Google, Bass Pro Shops, Apple, Four Seasons Hotels, and Ferrari have what might be called "brand power." These companies, and the products offered to consumers, are quite well known. However, if you are selling loudspeakers made by Klipsch or financial services offered by Van Kampen Equity, you may find it necessary to spend considerable time providing information about the company. In this section, we examine the types of information needed in most selling situations.

Company Culture and Organization

Many salespeople take special pride in the company they work for. Salespeople employed by Cisco Systems feel good about the company's high ranking on *Fortune* magazine's list of the 100 best companies to work for. This network-equipment provider survived the dot-com bubble burst and has recorded record sales in recent years.[29]

As noted in Chapter 5, character and integrity are the hallmark of a successful sales organization. Michael L. Eskew, former chairman and CEO of UPS Incorporated, says, "The strategies change and the purpose changes, but the values never change."[30]

Every organization has its own unique culture. **Organizational culture** is a collection of beliefs, behaviors, and work patterns held in common by people employed by a specific firm. Most organizations over a period of time tend to take on distinct norms and practices. At Lexus, employees are guided by a statement of values that communicates what is held important by the company (Figure 6.2). Research indicates that the customer orientation of a firm's salespeople is influenced by the organization's culture. A supportive culture that encourages salespeople to offer tailor-made solutions to buyer problems sets the stage for long-term partnerships.[31]

Many prospects use the past performance of a company to evaluate the quality of the current product offering. If the company has enjoyed success in the past, there is good reason to believe that the future will be bright.

6.3 Describe the importance of becoming an expert regarding company knowledge

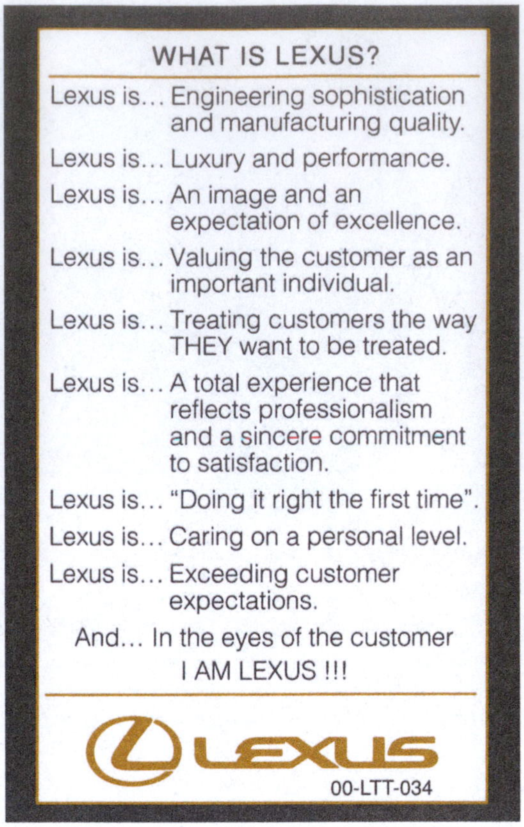

WHAT IS LEXUS?

Lexus is... Engineering sophistication and manufacturing quality.

Lexus is... Luxury and performance.

Lexus is... An image and an expectation of excellence.

Lexus is... Valuing the customer as an important individual.

Lexus is... Treating customers the way THEY want to be treated.

Lexus is... A total experience that reflects professionalism and a sincere commitment to satisfaction.

Lexus is... "Doing it right the first time".

Lexus is... Caring on a personal level.

Lexus is... Exceeding customer expectations.

And... In the eyes of the customer I AM LEXUS !!!

LEXUS

00-LTT-034

FIGURE 6.2

At Lexus, the employees are guided by a statement of values that communicates what is held important by the company. Shared values are especially important when the sales process involves development of strategic partnerships.

Source: COURTES

Company Support for Product

Progressive marketers support the products they sell. In some cases, product support takes the form of sales tools that can be used in preparation for a sales call or during a sales call. Hunter Douglas, a manufacturer of window fashions, has developed a Dealer Merchandising Portfolio. A dealer sales representative can select and order sample books, brochures, videos, in-store display material, and many other items.[32]

Company support after the sale is also very important. Olin Corporation, a major chemical corporation, regularly checks with customers to get their reaction to services and to keep real needs in perspective. Jagemann Stamping Company, a tool-and-die firm in Manitowoc, Wisconsin, often uses a sales team made up of a salesperson, an engineer, and line workers. Line workers can often answer the technical questions raised by a customer. Whenever there is a problem or defect, a small group of line workers is sent out with either a salesperson or an engineer to investigate. This involvement raises the workers' commitment to the customer.[33]

6.4 Describe how expert knowledge of competition and industry trends improves personal selling

Become the Industry Expert—Know Your Competition

Acquiring knowledge of your competition is another important step toward developing complete product knowledge. Salespeople who have knowledge of their competitor's strengths and weaknesses are better able to emphasize the benefits they offer and add value. Prospects often raise specific questions concerning competing firms. If you cannot provide answers or if your answers are vague, the sale may be lost.

Doing Business in Australia

American and Australian businesspeople have a lot in common. Everyone in Australia speaks English and business dress is similar in both countries. However, subtle differences do exist.

- When you greet an Australian businessperson, give your full name and then firmly shake hands.
- Australians tend to be modest people who often root for the underdog. Keep information about your power and wealth to yourself.

- Although Australian businesspeople tend to be informal and friendly, they still expect you to be a good listener and be completely familiar with your product.
- Keep your presentations simple. Most Australians want you to get to the point.[a]

Salespeople need to become experts in the industry they represent. In many cases, this means moving beyond the role of product specialist and becoming a business analyst. Staying current and developing an understanding of business processes takes time and may require additional education.[34] If your clients work in the banking industry, read the appropriate trade journals and become active in professional associations that serve bankers' needs.

Develop and Communicate a Healthy Attitude toward Your Competition

Regardless of how impressive your product is, the customer naturally seeks information about similar products sold by other companies. Therefore, you must acquire facts about competing products before the sales presentation. It has never been easier to obtain information about competing products. Check the competitor's website, annual reports, press releases, and marketing material. Once armed with this information, you are more confident in your ability to handle questions about the competition.

The attitude you display toward your competition is of the utmost importance. Every salesperson should develop a set of basic beliefs about the best way of dealing with competing products. A few helpful guidelines follow:

1. *In most cases, do not refer to the competition during the sales presentation.* This shifts the focus of attention to competing products, which is usually not desirable.
2. *Never discuss the competition unless you have all your facts straight.* Your credibility suffers if you make inaccurate statements. If you do not know the answer to a specific question, simply say, "I do not know."
3. *Never criticize the competition.* You may be called on to make direct comparisons between your product and competing products. In these situations, stick to the facts and avoid emotional comments about apparent or real weaknesses.
4. *Be prepared to add value.* The competition may come to your prospect with a comparative advantage in price, delivery, or some other area. Be prepared to neutralize the competitor's proposal with a value-added approach. If your competitor has slow delivery, encourage the customer to talk about why prompt delivery is important.[35]

Customers appreciate an accurate, fair, and honest presentation of the facts. They generally resent highly critical remarks about the competition. Avoid mudslinging at all costs. Fairness is a virtue that people greatly admire.

Sources of Product, Company and Industry Information

6.5 List major sources of product, competitor, and industry information

Several sources of product information are available to salespeople. Some of the most common include (1) web-based catalogs and other product literature developed by the company, (2) sales training programs, (3) plant tours, (4) internal sales and sales-support team members, (5) customers, (6) product, and (7) publications.

E-learning has become popular because it is inexpensive and fast, and it can be geared to the flexible schedules of salespeople. This regional sales team is receiving sales training from the company's home office.

Source: ONOKY–Photononstop/ Alamy Stock Photo

Web-Based Sources, Catalogs, and Marketing-Related Sales Support Information

Most companies prepare materials that provide a detailed description of their product. This information is usually quite instructional, and salespeople should review it carefully. If the company markets a number of products, a print or web-based sales catalog is usually developed. To save salespeople time, many companies give them computer software that provides a constantly updated, online product catalog. Advertisements, promotional brochures, and audiocassettes also can be a valuable source of marketing-related product information.

Mitsubishi Caterpillar Forklift America presents its basic product information online, so it's available to dealer representatives in the privacy of their homes, hotel rooms, or wherever else they bring their laptops. Each of the seven product information courses takes about an hour. To reinforce basic product knowledge, the company offers advanced instructor-led courses.[36] Some companies are using interactive distance learning (delivered via satellite) to present different types of sales training.

Engage in Plant Tours

Many companies believe that salespeople should visit the manufacturing plant and see the production process firsthand. Such tours not only provide valuable product information but also increase the salesperson's enthusiasm for the product. A new salesperson may spend several days at the plant getting acquainted with the production process. Experienced personnel within the organization also can benefit from plant tours.

Build Strong Relationships with Internal Sales and Sales Support Team Members

Team selling has become popular, in part, because many complex sales require the expertise of several sales and sales support personnel. Expertise in the areas of product design, finance, or transportation may be needed to develop an effective sales proposal. Pooled commissions are sometimes used to encourage team members to share information and work as a team.

Today's Wired Customers Have a Lot of Product, Competitive, and Industry Knowledge

Persons who actually use the product can be an important source of information toward improved sales performance.[37] They have likely researched your products and those of your competitors on the Web, observed its performance under actual working conditions, and can provide an objective assessment of the product's strengths and weaknesses. Some companies collect testimonials from satisfied customers and make this persuasive information available to the sales staff. Patagonia customers include mountain bikers, backcountry skiers, sailors, paddlers, and fly fishermen. The company's success lies in maintaining a close connection to persons who actually use their products.[38]

Salespeople employed by semiconductor manufacturer Intel Corporation are expected to take the company's business customers from the conceptual stage of their purchase all the way to delivery of the finished product. The dialogue with the customer begins very early in the sales

USING CRM TO FIND PRODUCT INFORMATION

New salespeople can be overwhelmed by the amount of information they need to master. This includes information about the company and its people, processes, products, and customers. **Product information management (PIM)** helps manage digital assets such as images. Middleware solutions such as Oracle Product Information Management manage heterogeneous product information at a central location and thereby improve visibility of information across the extended enterprise while lowering data management costs. A sales organization can now make learning easier with information technology. Stored information can now be made available to new salespeople through a variety of delivery channels. Depending on security levels, an employee can access data from nearly anywhere, at any time. Training software can enable new salespeople to learn at their own pace about company information such as product specifications, features, benefits, uses, and selling points.

New people can find electronic copies of previous sales proposals to help determine appropriate solutions. Configuration software can enable a new salesperson to select and price components for a proposal while assembling a custom-tailored solution and be assured that all necessary parts will be included and compatible.

Salesforce.com, as well as most other CRM suppliers, allows approved partners to integrate their product configuration software. One example is Big Machines Express. This software enables users to quickly and easily select and price the best products, and add them to sales quotes and opportunities. Access Big Machines Express website at www.bigmachines.com for more information including demos, videos, case studies, etc. The speed and functionality of CRM assures customers obtain information when needed and adds crucial efficiency to performing many sales-related tasks.

cycle when the customer needs help designing the end product.[39] This approach requires the empowerment of the sales force with greater depth and breadth of product information.

Researching and Using Products

The product itself should not be overlooked as a source of valuable information. Salespeople should closely examine and, if possible, use each item they sell to become familiar with its features. Investigation, use, and careful evaluation of the product provide a salesperson with additional confidence.

Reading and Studying Publications

Trade and technical publications such as *Supermarket Business* and *Advertising Age* provide valuable product information. Popular magazines and the business section of the newspaper also offer salespeople considerable information about their products and their competition. A number of publications such as *Consumer Reports* test products extensively and report the findings in nontechnical language for the benefit of consumers. These reports are a valuable source of information.

Word of Caution

Is it possible to be overly prepared? Can salespeople know too much about the products and services they sell? The answer to both questions is generally no. Communication problems can arise, however, if the salesperson does not accurately gauge the prospect's level of understanding.[40] There is always the danger that a knowledgeable salesperson can overwhelm the potential buyer with facts and figures. This problem can be avoided when salespeople adopt the feature–benefit strategy.

Creating Value with a Feature–Benefit Strategy

6.6 Explain how to add value with a feature–benefit strategy

Frederick W. Smith, founder of Federal Express, first proposed the concept of overnight delivery in a paper that he wrote as an undergraduate at Yale University. The now-famous paper was given a "C" by his professor. Many years later, Smith said, "I don't think that we understood our real goal when we first started Federal Express. We thought that we were selling the transportation of goods; in fact, we were selling peace of mind."[41]

Throughout this chapter, we emphasize the importance of acquiring information on the features of your product, company, and competition. Now it is important to point out that successful sales presentations create value by translating product features into benefits that meet a specific need expressed by the customer. The "peace of mind" that Frederick W. Smith mentioned is a good example of a buyer benefit. When a product feature is converted to a buyer benefit, "you are talking the customer's talk" with solution-oriented statements that make an impact on the customer.

Distinguish between Features and Benefits

To be sure we understand the difference between a product feature and a benefit, let us define these two terms.

A **feature** is data, facts, or characteristics of your product or service. Features often relate to craftsmanship, design, durability, and economy of operation. They may reveal how the product was developed, processed, or manufactured. Product features often are described in the technical section of the written sales proposal and in the literature provided by the manufacturer. Salespeople new to selling and unfamiliar with the importance of benefits have a tendency to throw out information about a product or service without tying that information to the essential needs of the client. In general, a person might do a **feature dump**, talking about all the great things product X or service Y has without enabling a customer to see what it means to him or her. Ultimately, prospects and existing clients consistently want to know, "What's in it for me?"[42]

A **benefit** is whatever provides the customer with a personal advantage or gain. It answers the question, "How will I benefit from owning or using the product?" If you mention to a prospect "We have one of the most extensive fiber networks in the city with direct connection to your office park," you are talking about a product feature. If you go on to point out "This means that your wait time is decreased drastically and your employees will be able to be more productive and 60% faster than by working with your traditional telecommunications provider," you are pointing out benefits.

GENERAL VERSUS SPECIFIC BENEFITS Neil Rackham, author of *The SPIN Selling Fieldbook*, says that a statement can only be a benefit if it meets a specific need expressed by the buyer. When you link a benefit to a buyer's expressed need, you demonstrate that you can help solve a problem that has been described by the customer. A general benefit shows how a feature can be helpful to a buyer, but it does not relate to a specific need expressed by the buyer. Here are two examples of specific benefits:

> "Our water purification system meets the exact specifications you have given us for EPA compliance."

> "Our XP400 model meets the safety criteria you've spelled out."

Rackham says that benefit statements linked to the customer's expressed need (key benefits) are especially effective in large or complex sales.[43]

INCORPORATING ADVANTAGE STATEMENTS Some sales training programs suggest that salespeople need to include advantages in the sales presentation. **Advantages** are characteristics of the product (features) that can be used or will help the buyer. Consider the following statement:

> "Prior to shipping, all of our containers are double wrapped. This means that our product is completely free of contamination when it arrives at your hospital."

Some salespeople develop an advantage statement for each important product feature. Unfortunately, these advantages are often included in the sales presentation even when the buyer has not expressed a need for this information. When this happens, the advantage can be described as a general benefit.

Successful salespeople focus on specific benefits that relate to an explicit need expressed by the customer. Less successful salespeople take the position that the best way to create value is to present as many benefits as possible, also known as a "benefit dump." They use a "shotgun" approach to benefits, assuming that more benefits create higher volume. Today's customer measures value by how well your product's benefits fit their specific needs. High-performance salespeople work hard to discover which benefits the customer really cares about.[44]

Use Bridge Statements

We know that people buy benefits, not features. One of the best ways to present benefits is to use a bridge statement. A **bridge statement** is a transitional phrase that connects a statement of features with a statement of benefits. This method permits customers to connect the features of your product to the benefits they receive. A sales representative of Fleming Companies, Inc., might use bridge statements to introduce a new snack food.

"This product is nationally advertised, *which means* you will benefit from more presold customers."

"You will experience faster turnover and increased profits *because* the first order includes point-of-purchase advertising materials that focus on the Valentine's Day promotion you have planned."

Some companies prefer to state the benefit first and the feature second. When this occurs, the bridge statement may be a word such as "because."

Identify Features and Benefits

A careful analysis of the product helps identify both product features and buyer benefits. Once all the important features are identified, arrange them in logical order. Then write beside each feature the most important benefit the customer can derive from that feature. Finally, prepare a series of bridge statements to connect the appropriate features and benefits. By using this three-step approach, a hotel selling conference and convention services and a manufacturer selling electric motors used to power mining equipment developed feature–benefit worksheets (Tables 6.2 and 6.3). Notice how each feature is translated into a benefit that would be important to someone purchasing these products and services. Table 6.3 reminds us that company features can be converted to benefits.

Avoiding Information Overload

Knowing your product has always been essential to good selling, but concentrating on product alone can be a serious mistake. Salespeople who love their products, and possess vast product knowledge, sometimes overload their customers with product data they neither need nor want. This practice is often described as a "data dump." With the aid of specific types of questions (see Chapter 11), the customer's needs can be identified. Once the customer's needs are known, the salesperson can develop a customized sales presentation that includes selected features that can be converted to specific benefits.

TABLE 6.2 Selling Product Benefits with a Feature–Benefit Worksheet

Salespeople employed by a hotel can enhance the sales presentation by converting features to benefits.

FEATURE	BENEFIT
Facilities	
The hotel conference rooms were recently redecorated.	This means all your meetings will be held in rooms that are attractive as well as comfortable.
All our guest rooms were completely redecorated during the past six months and most were designated as nonsmoking rooms.	This means your people will find the rooms clean and attractive. In addition, they can easily select a nonsmoking room.
Food Services	
We offer four different banquet entrees prepared by Ricardo Guido, who was recently selected Executive Chef of the Year by the National Restaurant Association.	This means your conference will be enhanced by delicious meals served by a well-trained staff.
Our hotel offers 24-hour room service.	This means your people can order food or beverages at their convenience.

TABLE 6.3 Selling Company Benefits with a Feature–Benefit Worksheet
Here we see company features translated into customer benefits.

FEATURE	BENEFIT
Our company has . . .	This means for you . . .
1. The best selection of motors in the area	• Choice of the best models to interface with your current equipment • Equipment operates more efficiently
2. Certified service technicians	• Well-qualified service personnel keep your equipment in top running condition • Less downtime and higher profits

CHAPTER LEARNING ACTIVITIES

Reviewing Key Concepts

Explain the importance of developing product solutions that add value
A product strategy helps salespeople make the right decisions concerning the selection and positioning of product solutions that meet specific customer needs. It is a carefully conceived plan that emphasizes becoming a product expert, selling specific benefits, and configuring value-added solutions.

Describe the importance of becoming an expert regarding product knowledge
Salespeople should become product experts and possess product knowledge that meets and exceeds customer expectations. Some important product information categories include product development and quality improvement processes, performance data and specifications, maintenance and service contracts, and price and delivery.

Describe the importance of becoming an expert regarding company knowledge
Information about the company can be used to develop strong appeals that can enhance the sales presentation, especially in a situation where there are many look-alike competing products. This is especially true when the customer is considering a strategic alliance. Important company information includes an understanding of the firm's culture and organization, and company support for products offered.

Describe how expert knowledge of competition and industry trends improves personal selling
Prospects often raise specific questions concerning competing firms and industry trends. Salespeople who have knowledge of their competitors' strengths and weaknesses and these industry trends are better able to emphasize the benefits they offer and add value. The attitude you display toward your competition is of the utmost importance.

List major sources of product, competitor and industry information
Salespeople gather information from many sources. Company websites, literature, and sales-training programs are among the most important. Other sources include factory tours, customers, competition, industry publications, the Internet, and actual experience with the product itself.

Explain how to add value with a feature–benefit strategy

In the sales presentation and in preparing the written sales proposal, your knowledge of the product's features and your company's strengths must be presented in terms of the resulting benefits to the buyer. We distinguished between general and specific benefits. Specific benefits, linked to a customer's expressed need, are very effective.

Key Terms

Product strategy, p. 117	Product development, p. 120	Feature, p. 128
Solution, p. 117	Quality control, p. 120	Feature dump, p. 128
Solution selling, p. 117	Quantifying the solution,	Benefit, p. 128
Product configuration, p. 118	p. 121	Advantages, p. 128
Written proposals, p. 119	Organizational culture, p. 123	Bridge statement, p. 128

MyMarketingLab

To complete the problems with the ⭐ in your MyLab, go to the EOC Discussion Questions.

Review Questions

6-1 Provide a brief description of the term *product strategy*.

6-2 Distinguish between *product features* and *buyer benefits*.

6-3 What is "product configuration"? Provide an example of how this practice is used in the sale of commercial stereo equipment.

6-4 Review the Lexus statement of values and then identify the two items that you believe contribute the most to a salesperson's career success.

⭐ **6-5** Define the term *organizational culture*. How might this company information enhance a sales presentation?

6-6 Basic beliefs underlie the salesperson's method of handling competition. What are four guidelines a salesperson should follow in developing basic beliefs in this area?

⭐ **6-7** Explain what the customer's expectations are concerning the salesperson's attitude toward competition.

6-8 List and briefly describe the five parts included in most written sales proposals.

⭐ **6-9** What are the most common sources of product information?

Application Exercises

6-10 Secure a copy of a customer-oriented product sales brochure or news release that has been prepared by a marketer. Many salespeople receive such selling tools. Study this information carefully; then develop a feature–benefit analysis sheet.

6-11 Today, many companies are automating their product-configuration and proposal-writing activities. Go to the Internet and find these providers of the following software: www .bigmachines.com/salesforce.php and www.results-online.com. Click on each company's demonstration software and study the design of each product.

6-12 Select a product you are familiar with and know a great deal about. (This may be an item you have shopped for and purchased, such as a compact disc player, laptop computer, or an automobile.) Under each of the categories listed, fill in the required information about the product.

    a. Where did you buy the product? Why?

    b. Did product design influence your decision?

    c. How and where was the product manufactured?

<ol type="a" start="4">
<li value="4">What different applications or uses are there for the product?</li>
<li>How does the product perform? Are there any data on the product's performance? What are they?</li>
<li>What kinds of maintenance and care does the product require? How often?</li>
<li>Could you sell the product you have written about in categories (a) through (f)? Why or why not?</li>
</ol>

Role-Play Exercise

Study the convention center information in Part 1, Developing a Sales-Oriented Product Strategy, in Appendix 3, paying special attention to pricing on the meals and meeting rooms. Access the pearsonhighered.com/manning website. Click on the sales proposal link and configure a sales proposal for your instructor (using your school name and address) who is responsible for setting up a student-awards meeting. The meeting includes a banquet-style meal of Chicken Wellington for 26 attendees from 5:30 P.M. to 8:00 P.M. on the last Wednesday of next month. The meal will be served at 5:45 P.M., and the awards session is scheduled from 6:45 P.M. to 8:00 P.M. in the same room. The seating should be banquet style. Present the completed proposal to another student (acting as your customer) and communicate the features and benefits of your proposal.

Reality Selling Video Case Problem— Amy Vandaveer/*Texas Monthly*

Texas Monthly is a regional magazine covering politics, business, and culture, but focusing largely on leisure activities and events in Texas. The magazine has a large real estate–advertising section, as well as classified sections in which nearly all advertisers are Texas-based businesses appealing to a prospective buyer who is interested in connecting with Texas history and culture. It also has a large, loyal reader base all over Texas, mostly urban, well educated, and affluent; the magazine's salespeople pride themselves on their ability to find creative solutions for their customers.

Today, Amy Vandaveer, a sales representative for *Texas Monthly*, is meeting with the marketing director for the Woodlands Town Center, a major community-development organization. The Woodlands is a planned community outside of Houston, and the recently added Woodlands Town Center includes restaurants, shops, and a hotel and convention center.

The marketing director's goal is to make the Woodlands Town Center a destination for Houston residents, rather than another area serving people who already live in the Woodlands. Up to this point, the Woodlands Town Center has relied mostly on word of mouth and the positive publicity that it received after winning awards to attract visitors; now, the marketing director is interested in using more print advertising and has scheduled this meeting with Amy to learn more about the possibilities of advertising with *Texas Monthly*.

As a rule, Amy uses relatively informal presentations on her sales calls. The most significant part of her presentation is a copy of *Texas Monthly*; showing potential customers a recent issue gives them the opportunity to see the magazine's overall look and feel, as well as to have a good look at the context in which their ads would appear. Over the course of the informal presentation, Amy also shows the customer statistics on the reader base of *Texas Monthly* and the ways in which they respond to ads in the magazine, as well as a price sheet for various types of ads.

After listening to what the Woodlands Town Center needs, Amy proposes a four-page color ad, which can also be printed separately from the magazine for use as a brochure. Although the price depends on the number of stand-alone brochures that are ordered, she estimates that the cost of the ad would be about $50,000. The marketing director and Amy agree on a timeline for a more formal proposal that can be shared with the rest of the Woodlands Town Center board, and Amy moves on to the rest of her day. (See Chapter 6 opener and Reality Selling Today Video Role-Play 3 in Appendix 1 for more information.)

Questions

6-13 Explain how Amy Vandaveer can use the three prescriptions for a product selling strategy in preparing and presenting product solutions.

6-14 What are the major benefits that Amy incorporates into her presentation?

6-15 What are the most likely objections that the marketing director might raise?

6-16 In addition to the actual product strategy, how important will information about *Texas Monthly* (its history, mission, past performance, etc.) be in closing the sale?

Partnership Selling: A Role-Play (see Appendix 3)

Developing a Product Strategy

Read Employment Memorandum 1 in Appendix 3, which introduces you to your new training position with the Hotel Convention Center. You should also study the product strategy materials that follow the memo to become familiar with the company, product, and competitive knowledge you need in your new position.

Read the Customer Service/Sales Memorandum in Part I of Appendix 3 and complete the two-part customer/service assignment provided by your sales manager. In item 1, you are to configure a price/product sales proposal; in item 2, you are to write a sales cover letter for the sales proposal. Note that the information presented in the price/product sales proposal consists of product facts/features, and the information presented in your sales cover letter should present specific benefit statements. These forms should be custom-fitted to meet the specific needs of your customer, B. H. Rivera. All the product information you need is in the product strategy materials provided as enclosures and attachments to Employment Memorandum 1.

Park Shores Resort and Convention Center.
Source: Courtesy of Beach Resort

MyMarketingLab

Go to the Assignments section of your MyLab to complete these writing exercises

6-17 What is a product strategy and how can it assist salespeople in making the right decisions?

6-18 Describe how a salesperson creates value with a feature-benefit strategy. Use an example of a feature-benefit strategy to illustrate.

Learning Objectives

When you finish reading this chapter, you should be able to

7.1 Describe positioning as a product-selling strategy

7.2 Explain the 3D product solutions selling model

7.3 Discuss product-positioning options

7.4 Explain how to sell your product with a price strategy

7.5 Explain how to sell your product with a value-added strategy

Source: Creativa Images/Fotolia

Introduction

You have just finished paying off your college loans and it's time to replace that old rust bucket with a new car. You have looked at the sport-compact cars available, but they all seem so small. Now you are eagerly looking at cars in the sports-sedan category. The cars in this niche offer a good blend of comfort, attractive design, and performance. However, there are almost too many choices. *Road & Track* says there are 11 different automobiles in this group. The list price for these cars ranges from $29,000 to $40,000. Many now, including the Cadillac ATS, Audi A4, Infinity G37, and Volvo S60, offer all-wheel drive. As you learn more about the choices available, it becomes clear that each manufacturer has taken steps to differentiate its product.[1]

Several years ago, automobile manufacturers from around the world began to develop and position cars for the sports-sedan segment. Research indicated that demand for these cars would increase. The result was the introduction of 11 different marques, each with its own unique characteristics. At the dealer level, the process of product differentiation continues. If you want something more than standard equipment, the salesperson can describe a variety of options that can add $7,000 to $10,000 to the price. Each car can be accessorized to meet your personal needs. The dealer can also help position this product with modern facilities, customer-friendly service policies, and a reputation for honesty and integrity.

Some automobile manufacturers see the sports-sedan category as critical to their success. At BMW, the 3 Series sports sedan accounts for nearly half of the company's sales worldwide. Sports sedans can be very profitable because many buyers purchase expensive options such as special wheel and tire packages, antiskid electronics, ground-effects trim, and top-of-the-line audio systems. ●

Source: Audi AG/AP Images

Source: ZUMA Press, Inc./Alamy Stock Photo

Source: Raymond Boyd/Getty Images

Source: Neilson Barnard/Getty Images

Salespeople at the dealer level can play an important role in positioning the automobile for competitive advantage. They can describe the quality control process that ensures the build quality of the Audi A4 or demonstrate the sportscar driving characteristics of the Cadillac CTS. Adding value depends on the salesperson's ability to provide a competitive analysis using knowledge of the manufacturer, the automobile, and the dealership.

Product Positioning—In a Competitive Marketplace

7.1 Describe positioning as a product-selling strategy

Long-term success in today's dynamic global economy requires the continuous positioning and repositioning of products.[2] **Positioning** involves those decisions and activities intended to create and maintain a certain concept of the product in the customer's mind. It requires developing a sales and marketing strategy aimed at influencing how a particular market segment perceives a product in comparison to the competition.[3] In a market that has been flooded with various types of sport-utility vehicles (SUVs), Land Rover has been positioned as a dependable vehicle that can climb a steep, rock-covered hillside with ease. Every effort has been made to create the perception of safety, durability, and security. To give sales representatives increased knowledge to share with clients to effectively position the Land Rover against it competitors, the company has arranged plant tours and the opportunity to observe actual testing of the Land Rover vehicles under extremely demanding conditions.

Good positioning means that the product's name, reputation, and niche are well recognized and respected. However, an effective positioning strategy cannot be accomplished solely by the company. The positioning process must be continually configured and custom fitted by the salesperson to match each customer's specific wants and needs.[4]

Essentials of Product Positioning

Most salespeople use a combination of marketing and sales strategies to position their products, based on the unique needs of each of their customers. Therefore, every salesperson needs a good understanding of the fundamental practices that contribute to product positioning. The chapter begins with a brief introduction to the concept of product differentiation. This is followed by an explanation of how products have been redefined in the age of information. The remainder of the chapter is devoted to three product-selling strategies that can be used to position a product. Emphasis is placed on positioning your product with a value-added strategy. In the age of information, salespeople who cannot add value to the products they sell will diminish in number and influence.

Salesperson's Role in Product Differentiation

With so much publicly available product and competitive information, one of the basic tenets of sales and marketing is the principle of product differentiation. **Differentiation** refers to your ability to separate yourself, your product, and/or your company from that of your competitors. It is the key to building and maintaining a competitive advantage.[5] The competitors in virtually all industries are moving toward differentiating themselves on the basis of quality, price, convenience, economy, or some other factor. Salespeople, who are on the front line interacting with customers, assume one of the most important roles in the product differentiation process.

Differentiating your product helps you stand out from the crowd. It often allows you to distance yourself from the competition. In many cases, the process of differentiation creates barriers that make it difficult for the buyer to choose a competing product simply on the basis of price.[6]

Custom Fitting and Communicating the Value Proposition

A well-informed customer will usually choose the product that offers the most value. Therefore, salespeople need to position their product with a value proposition. A **value proposition** is the set of benefits and values the salesperson configures to meet and exceed their customers' specific needs. The value proposition presented by Porsche promises driving performance and excitement.[7] Kinko's, which is now part of FedEx, is attempting to differentiate itself from Sir Speedy, AlphaGraphics, and print shops found at Office Depot, OfficeMax, and Staples. The new value proposition promises that 1,200 FedEx Kinko's locations offer a breadth of services unparalleled in the industry. These new centers leverage the traditional strengths and brand awareness of FedEx and Kinko's.[8] Salespeople have an important responsibility to custom-fit and then attractively communicate aspects of the value proposition that meet the specific needs of the customer.

QUANTIFYING THE VALUE PROPOSITION In many situations, salespeople must quantify the value proposition. This is especially true in B2B when the customer is a business buyer. (Business buyer behavior will be discussed in Chapter 8.) The value quantification process raises customers' comprehension levels as they discover the merits of buying your product or service.[9] Let's assume you are selling Kenworth trucks and one of your customers is Contract Freighters, Inc., based in Joplin, Missouri. This large company is planning to purchase 700 new trucks. Your Kenworth diesel trucks cost 10 percent more than rivals' trucks. Within your proposal, you will need to quantify the benefits of buying Kenworth trucks, which may include greater reliability, higher trade-in value, lower maintenance costs, and the plush interiors that will help the buyer attract better drivers.[10] Understanding the Three-Dimensional (3-D) Product Solutions Selling Model concept discussed next enables a salesperson to position and differentiate the most valuable parts of the value proposition.

The Three-Dimensional (3-D) Product Solutions Selling Model

Ted Levitt, former editor of the *Harvard Business Review*, says that products are problem-solving tools. People buy products if they fulfill a problem-solving need. Today's better-educated and more demanding customers are seeking a *cluster of satisfactions.* **Satisfactions** arise from the product itself, from the company that makes or distributes the product, and from the salesperson who sells and services the product.[11] As noted in Chapter 6, many companies are attempting to transform themselves from *product selling* to *solution selling.* Figure 7.1 provides a description of the **Three-Dimensional (3-D) Product Solutions Selling Model**. The 3-D Product Solutions Selling Model illustrates the product, company, and salesperson features available to satisfy the customer's potential 3-D cluster of satisfactions. To develop and sell solutions with many competitive "look-alike" products, salespeople must be familiar with the unique satisfactions that meet the needs of each customer.

To illustrate how the 3-D Product Solutions Selling Model works in a business setting, let us examine a complex buying decision. Elaine Parker, a sales representative for Elmore Industries Incorporated, sells metals for manufacturing operations. Over a period of six months, she frequently called on a prospect who had the potential to become a valued customer. During every call, the buyer's receptionist told her they were happy with their current supplier. She refused to give up and finally the buyer agreed to see her. At first, she was greeted with cool silence, so she decided to ask him some questions about his business: "How's the slow economy affecting your sales?" The buyer's answers focused on materials costs. He said his company could not raise prices or cut quality. He wanted to lower costs, but was unsure how it could be done. Parker, offering product developments the buyer wasn't familiar with, suggested he consider trying some new alloys that were less expensive than the standard metals he had been purchasing. As she described the new alloys, which exceeded the buyer's expectations, interest began to build. She offered to bring in two of her company's best product engineers to help make a full presentation to the buyer and his engineers at a follow-up meeting. The second meeting was a success. Soon after that meeting, Parker received her first order from the customer. Within a year, she had become the customer's most trusted advisor on technological developments in the industry and his exclusive supplier.[12]

Elaine Parker used questions to engage the customer and identify his problem. She also provided satisfactory answers to questions raised by the customer:

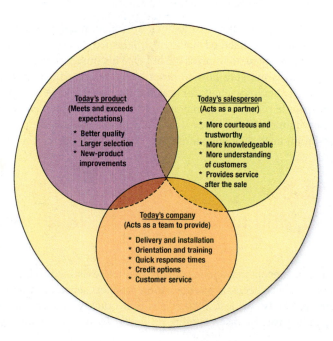

FIGURE 7.1

The Three-Dimensional (3-D) Product Solutions Selling Model

A successful product strategy should include a cluster of satisfactions that meets the needs of today's better-educated and more demanding customers. Drawing from this cluster, with the 3-D Product Solutions Selling Model the salesperson can configure value-added solutions that meet and potentially exceed individual customer's needs.

Questions Related to the Product

What product is best for our type of operation?
Are there new product developments we aren't aware of?
Does the solution meet our quality standards?
Given the cost of this product, will we maintain our competitive position in the marketplace?

Questions Related to the Company

Does this company provide the most advanced technology?
What is the company's reputation for quality products?
What is the company's reputation for standing behind the products it sells?
Is there a technical support team available?

Questions Related to the Salesperson

Does this salesperson possess the knowledge and experience needed to recommend the right product?
Can the salesperson clearly communicate specific buyer benefits?
Can this salesperson serve as a trusted advisor?
Will this salesperson provide support services after the sale?

Understanding the the 3-D Product Solutions Selling Model (or cluster of product-selling satisfactions model, as it is sometimes referred to) enables the salesperson to custom-fit solutions that successfully position, yet differentiate their solutions in today's competitive and often complex situations. Elaine Parker used all three parts of the cluster of satisfactions product-selling model to differentiate and position her selling solution—a product that exceeded the customer's expectations, relationship skills that set her apart as a trusted partner, and technical customer-support personnel. In many of today's selling situations, the products offered by various suppliers are very similar, often referred to as "look-alike" products. In these situations, while being able to meet the product needs of the customer, the competitive advantage may be the knowledge and relationship skills of the salesperson and/or the company's support personnel. For example, salespeople in the competitive automobile-retailing marketplace face this situation. The service departments and the knowledge and relationship-building skills of the salesperson are increasingly becoming the most important parts of successfully meeting customers' needs.

Salespeople who are knowledgeable in all areas of the 3D Product Solutions Selling Model are better able to position their product solution. This knowledge also helps to achieve product differentiation, understand the competition, and prepare an effective value proposition. The competitive analysis worksheet (Table 7.1) can help you discover ways to position and differentiate your product as the superior choice over your competition.

A WORD OF CAUTION Because many of today's information age products are very complex, product differentiation must be handled with care. Salespeople are sometimes tempted to use technical lingo, real and invented, to impress the buyer. This problem often surfaces in a situation in which the salesperson is not sure how to describe the value-added features of the product. Robert Notte, former technology chief for travel outfitter Backroads, says that, during the telecom boom, salespeople representing major suppliers often babbled endlessly, using industry jargon that was often unintelligible. "They wanted you to be impressed," Mr. Notte says. Some customers were so intimidated they were afraid to ask questions or make a buying decision.[13]

7.3 Discuss product-positioning options

Product-Positioning Strategies to Sell New (vs. Mature), and Low-Priced (vs. Value-Added) Products

Product positioning is a concept that applies to both new and existing products. Given the dynamics of most markets, it may be necessary to reposition products several times in their lives because even solid, popular products can lose market position quickly. Salespeople have assumed an important and expanding role in differentiating products. To succeed in our over-communicated

TABLE 7.1 Competitive Analysis Worksheet

A value-added product-selling strategy is enhanced when salespeople analyze product, company, and salesperson attributes of the competition in relation to the benefits they offer. This information helps the salesperson differentiate and create value within the sales process.

	MY COMPANY	COMPETITOR A	COMPETITOR B
Product Attributes			
Quality			
Durability			
Reliability			
Performance			
Packaging flexibility			
Warranty			
Brand			
Company Attributes			
Reputation			
Industry leadership			
Facilities			
Ease of doing business			
Distribution channels			
Ordering convenience			
Returns, credits, etc.			
Salesperson Attributes			
Knowledge/expertise			
Responsiveness			
Pricing authority			
Customer orientation			
Honesty/integrity			
Follow-through			
Presentation skills			

society, marketers must use a direct and personalized form of communication with customers. Advertising directed toward a mass market often fails to position a complex product.

Throughout the remainder of this chapter, we discuss specific ways to use various product-positioning strategies to differentiate your value proposition. We explain how salespeople can (1) position new and emerging products versus well-established products, (2) position products with price strategies, and (3) position products with value-added strategies.

Selling New Products Versus Well-Established Products

In many ways, products are like human beings. They are born, grow up, mature, and grow old. In marketing, this process is known as the **product life cycle**. The product life cycle includes the

Selling a New Product

Gregg Buchbinder is chairman of Emeco Ltd., a small company in Pennsylvania that manufactures modern chairs. One of the company's newest products is a sleek, six-and-a-half-pound aluminum chair called the Superlight. This chair was created by renowned architect Frank Gehry. When Buchbinder acquired Emeco from his father in 1998, he dreamed of becoming a producer of hip home furnishings. The problem was that Emeco was unfamiliar to most of the architects and designers he wanted to do business with. So Buchbinder hit the streets of SoHo, knocking on shop doors with a copy of a magazine that showed his modern aluminum chairs. He also visited trade shows in search of new prospects. Today, revenues have reached about $10 million and Buchbinder is optimistic about the future.[b]

Source: Carol Kaplan

stages a product goes through from the time it is first introduced to the market until it is discontinued. As the product moves through its cycle, the strategies relating to competition, promotion, pricing, and other factors must be evaluated and possibly changed. The nature and extent of each stage in the product life cycle are determined by several factors, including the following:

1. The product's perceived advantage over available substitutes
2. The product's benefits and the importance of the needs it fulfills
3. Competitive activity, including pricing, substitute product development and improvement, and effectiveness of competing advertising and promotion
4. Changes in technology, fashion, or demographics[14]

As we attempt to develop a product-selling strategy, we must consider where the product is positioned in terms of the life cycle. The sales strategy used to sell a new and emerging product is much different from the strategy used to sell a mature, well-established product (Figure 7.2).

SELLING NEW AND EMERGING PRODUCTS Selling strategies used during the new and emerging stage (see Figure 7.2) are designed to develop a new level of expectation, change

Time →

New and emerging products →	Mature and well-established products →

FIGURE 7.2

New Versus Mature Product-Selling Model

Product-selling strategies are significantly different for selling new versus mature products. Selling new products requires successfully providing new insights to add value, while selling mature products requires positioning product and company superiority over competition.

Product-selling strategy	Product-selling strategy
• Develop new levels of expectations	• Emphasize brand superiority
• Change habits	• Emphasize company superiority
• Establish new standards	• Point out unique features
• Build desire for product	• Provide outstanding customer service
• Focus on creating new markets	• Focus on sustaining existing market share

habits, and, in some cases, establish a new standard of quality.[15] The goal is to build desire for the product. Highly talented and resourceful salespeople are needed during the product initiation phase.[16] Salespeople must be resourceful, possess information regarding every aspect of the product, and be able to present a convincing value proposition.[17]

When Brother International Corporation introduced its line of Multi-Function Center (MFC) machines, the goal was to convince buyers that one machine could replace five separate machines. However, before buyers would give up their copy machine, fax machine, laser printer, and other machines, they asked some hard questions. Is a multifunction machine reliable? Does the quality match that of the current machines? Finding the best machine for each customer is challenging because Brother offers more than 10 different MFC models from which to choose.

In some cases, the new product is not a tangible item. Several years ago, IntraLinks closed its first big sale, a $50,000 contract, with J.P. Morgan. The company got its start providing the financial services industry with the secure transmission of highly confidential information across the Internet. Patrick Wack and his business partners convinced J.P. Morgan and other financial firms that they did not need to rely on an army of foot messengers and FedEx trucks to deliver sensitive documents. They were not only selling a new product; they were selling a vision that included new levels of expectations. The value proposition focused on faster, more secure document transfer, which, in the customer's mind, translated into improved customer service and cost savings. Today Patrick Wack is selling this document transfer concept to customers in a variety of business communities.[18]

SELLING MATURE AND WELL-ESTABLISHED PRODUCTS Mature and well-established products are usually characterized by intense competition as new brands enter the market. Customers who currently buy your product will become aware of competing products. With new and emerging products, salespeople may initially have little or no competition and may dominate the market; however, this condition may not last long.

New York Life Insurance Company provides its sales agents with new products almost every year. The product portfolio was recently expanded to include the Asset Preserver, which allows the policy death benefit to be accelerated, on an income tax–free basis, to pay for long-term care services. The company also developed the Universal Life Protector, which offers long-term protection at lower prices. New products offered by a market leader are quickly copied by competing insurance companies. When competing products enter the market, New York Life agents must adopt new strategies. One positioning strategy is to emphasize the company's 150 years of

---

SELLING IN ACTION

Pricing Professional Fees—Creating a Value Proposition

The age of information has created many career opportunities for people who want to sell professional services. Strong demand for professional services has surfaced in such diverse fields as telecommunications, banking, computer technology, training, and healthcare. Dana Martin spent 18 years working in the human resources division of Allstate Insurance Company. His specialty was the design and delivery of training programs. He decided to leave the corporate environment and start his own training firm. Martin, like thousands of other professional service providers, had to develop a value proposition and decide how much to charge for his service. Before he could sell the first training program, he had to decide how much to charge. Should he price his service on an hourly basis or on a project basis? Here are some points to consider when determining fees to quantify a professional services–value proposition:

- *Experience:* In the case of Dana Martin, new clients benefit from what he has learned during many years at Allstate.

- *Exclusivity:* If you are one of only a small number of people with a particular capability, you may be able to charge more. Specialists often charge higher fees than generalists.

- *Target market:* Some markets are very price sensitive. If you are selling your services to large corporations that are used to paying high fees, you may be able to set your fees higher. If you are providing your services to small-business clients, expect resistance to high fees.

- *Value:* How important is your service to the client? In the late 1990s, many companies needed help preparing their computers for transition to the year 2000. This was known as the "Y2K" problem. These firms were willing to pay high fees for this assistance. Some service providers charge higher fees because they add value in one form or another.[c]

outstanding service to policyholders. They can also note that New York Life is a "mutual" company; it is owned by policyholders, not corporate shareholders. The objective is to create in the customer's mind the perception that New York Life is a solid company that will be strong and solvent when it's time to pay premiums.[19]

The relationship strategy is often critical in selling mature and well-established products. To maintain market share and ward off competitors, many salespeople work hard to maintain a strong relationship with the customer. At New York Life, salespeople have found that good service after the sale is one of the best selling strategies because it builds customer loyalty.

7.4 Explain how to sell your product with a price strategy

Selling Products with a Price Strategy

Price, promotion, product, and place are the four elements that make up the marketing mix. Pricing decisions must be made at each stage of the product life cycle. Therefore, setting the price can be a complex process. The first step in establishing price is to determine the firm's pricing objectives. Some firms set their prices to maximize their profits. They aim for a price as high as possible without causing a disproportionate reduction in unit sales. Other firms set a market share objective. Management may decide that the strategic advantage of an increased market share outweighs a temporary reduction in profits. Many of the new companies doing business on the Internet adopt this approach.

Pricing strategies often reflect the product's position in the product life cycle. When large, high-definition, flat-screen TVs were in the new and emerging stage, customers who wanted this innovative product were willing to pay $5,000 or more for a unit.

TRANSACTIONAL SELLING TACTICS THAT EMPHASIZE LOW PRICE Some marketers have established a positioning plan that emphasizes low price and the use of transactional selling tactics. These companies maintain a basic strategy that focuses on meeting competition. If the firm has "meeting competition" as its pricing goal, it makes every effort to charge prices that are identical or close to those of the competition. Once this positioning strategy has been adopted, the sales force is given several price tactics to use. Salespeople can alter (lower) the base price through the use of discounts and allowances. Discounts and allowances can take a variety of forms. A few of the more common ones follow:

Quantity discount. The quantity discount allows the buyer a lower price for purchasing in multiple units or above a specified dollar amount.

Seasonal discount. With seasonal pricing, the salesperson adjusts the price up or down during specific times to spur or acknowledge changes in demand. Off-season travel and lodging prices provide examples.

Promotional allowance. A promotional allowance is a price reduction given to a customer who participates in an advertising or a sales support program. Many salespeople give supermarkets promotional allowances for advertising or displaying a manufacturer's products.

Trade or functional discounts. Channel intermediaries, such as wholesalers, often perform credit, storage, or transportation services. Trade or functional discounts cover the cost of these services.[20]

Another option available to salespeople facing a buyer with a low-price buying strategy is to "unbundle" product features. Let's assume that a price-conscious customer wants to schedule a conference that will be accompanied by a banquet-style meal. To achieve a lower price, the salesperson might suggest a cafeteria-style meal, thereby eliminating the need for servers. This product configuration involves less cost to the seller, and cost savings can be passed on to the buyer. Timken Company, a century-old bearing maker, has adopted bundling as a way to compete with other manufacturers around the world. The company now surrounds its basic products with additional components in order to provide customers with exactly what they need. These components can take the form of electronic sensors, lubrication systems, castings, or installation and maintenance. Giving customers bundling options has given Timken a big advantage over foreign competitors who often focus on the basic product. Salespeople who represent Timken have flexible pricing options.[21]

These examples represent only a small sample of the many discounts and allowances salespeople use to compete on the basis of price. Price discounting is a competitive tool available to large numbers of salespeople. Excessive focus on low prices and generous discounts, however, can have a negative impact on profits and sales commissions.

CONSEQUENCES OF USING LOW-PRICE TACTICS Pricing is a critical factor in the sale of many products and services. In markets where competition is extremely strong, setting a product's price may be a firm's most complicated and important decision.

The authors of *The Discipline of Market Leaders* encourage business firms to pick one of three disciplines—best price, best product, or best service—and then do whatever is necessary to outdistance the competition. However, the authors warn us not to ignore the other two disciplines: "You design your business to excel in one direction, but you also have to strive to hit the minimum in the others."[22] Prior to using low-price tactics, everyone involved in sales and marketing should answer these questions:

- *Are you selling to high- or low-involvement buyers?* Some people are emotionally involved with respected brands such as BMW, Sony, and Apple's Macintosh computers. A part of their identity depends on buying the product they consider the best. Low-involvement buyers care mostly about price.[23]
- *How important is quality in the minds of buyers?* If buyers do not fully understand the price–quality relationship, they may judge the product by its price. For a growing number of customers, long-term value is more important than short-term savings that result from low prices.
- *How important is service?* For many buyers, service is a critical factor. Even online customers, thought to be very interested in price, rate quality of service very highly. This is especially true in business-to-business sales. A survey conducted by Accenture reports that 80 percent of nearly 1,000 corporate buyers rate a strong brand and reliable customer service ahead of low prices when deciding which companies to do business with online.[24]

INFLUENCE OF ELECTRONIC COMMERCE ON PRICING Companies large and small are racing to discover new sales and marketing opportunities on the Internet. Products ranging from personal computers to term insurance can be purchased from various websites. Salespeople who are involved primarily in transactional selling and add little or no value to

The Ritz Carlton Hotel Chain, Yellow Freight Company, and Apple Computer all have a Value-Added Pricing Strategy that allows their salespeople to offer most customers more than they expected.

Source: ZUMA Press, Inc./Alamy

the sales transaction often are not able to compete with online vendors. To illustrate, consider the purchase of insurance. At the present time, it is possible to purchase basic term insurance online from InsureMarket.com, AccuQuote.com, and other websites. A well-informed buyer, willing to visit several websites, can select a policy with a minimum amount of risk. In the case of long-term care insurance, which can pay for healthcare at home or in a nursing home, the buyer needs the help of a well-trained agent. These policies are complex and the premiums are high.

Investors now have more choices than they have had in the past. Persons who need little or no assistance buying stocks can visit the E*Trade website or a similar online discount vendor. The person who wants help selecting a stock can turn to a broker, such as Merrill Lynch or UBS PaineWebber, that offers both full-service and online options. Full-service brokers can survive and may prosper as long as they can add value to the sales transaction. The new economy is reshaping the world of commerce and every buyer has more choices.

7.5 Explain how to sell your product with a value-added strategy

Selling Your Product with the Value-Added Product-Selling Model

Most high-performing salespeople have adopted sales strategies that emphasize *value-added* selling. Salespeople can add value to their product with one or more intangibles: with improved insights and knowledge of customer needs, products benefits, and competitive offerings; stronger relationship and partnership building; better use of sales technologies; more dependable product deliveries; better service after the sale; and innovations that truly improve the product's value in the eyes of the customer. In today's highly competitive marketplace, these value-added benefits give the salesperson a unique niche and a competitive edge. Salespeople who don't make selling and delivering high-value solutions a high priority will consistently lose sales to competitors.[25]

To understand fully the importance of the value-added concept in selling, and how to apply it in a variety of selling situations, it helps to visualize every product as being four-dimensional. The **Value-Added Product-Selling Model** is made up of four "possible" products: the generic product, the expected product, the value-added product, and the potential product (Figure 7.3).[26]

FIGURE 7.3

The Value-Added Product-Selling Model

An understanding of the Value-Added Product-Selling Model is essential when the salesperson is developing a presentation that first must meet, and then be designed to exceed, the customer's expectations. Exceeding a customer's expectations is extremely important in building long-term partnerships.

Potential product

Value-added product

Expected product

Product (generic)

(Customer's perceptions)

(Salesperson's knowledge)

(Mutually discovered possibilities)

GENERIC PRODUCT—THE STARTING POINT The **generic product** is the basic, substantive product you are selling. Generic product describes only the product category; for example, life insurance, rental cars, or personal computers. Every Ritz-Carlton hotel offers guest rooms, one or more full-service restaurants, meeting rooms, guest parking, and other basic services. For Yellow Freight System, a company that provides shipping services, the generic product is the truck and trailer that moves the customer's freight. At the generic level, Nordstrom provides categories of goods traditional to an upscale specialty-clothing retailer. The generic products at a bank are money that can be loaned to customers and basic checking account services.

The capability of delivering a generic product simply gives the marketer the right to play in the game, to compete in the marketplace.[27] Generic products, even the lowest-priced ones, often cannot compete with products that are "expected" by the customer.

EXPECTED PRODUCT—UNDERSTANDING THE CUSTOMER'S PERCEIVED NEED Every customer has minimal purchase expectations that exceed the generic product itself.[28] Ritz-Carlton salespeople must offer not only a comfortable guest room but also a clean one. Some customers expect a "super" clean room. Yellow Freight System salespeople must provide clean, well-maintained trucks *and* well-trained drivers. The **expected product** is everything that represents the customer's minimal expectations. The customer at a Nordstrom store *expects* current fashions and well-informed salespeople.

The minimal purchase conditions vary among customers, so the salesperson must acquire information concerning the expected product that exists in the customer's mind. When the customer expects more than the generic product, the product can be sold *only* if those expectations are met. Every customer perceives the product in individualized terms, which a salesperson cannot anticipate.

Determining each customer's expectations requires the salesperson to make observations, conduct background checks, ask questions, and listen to what the customer is saying. You are attempting to discover both feelings and facts. Top salespeople encourage customers to think more deeply about the problems they face and discover for themselves the value of a solution. They *avoid* offering solutions until the needs are clearly spelled out. If the buyer says, "The average gas mileage for our fleet of delivery trucks is only 17 miles per gallon," the salesperson might respond with this question: "How does this low mileage rate affect your profitability?" To move the customer's attention from the expected product to a value-added product, you need to keep the customer focused on solutions.[29]

Research reported in the *Harvard Business Review* indicates that it is very difficult to build customer loyalty if you are selling only the expected product. Customer satisfaction and loyalty do not always move in tandem.[30] The customer who purchases the services of Ernst & Young Consulting may feel satisfied after the project is completed but never do business with the company again. Customer loyalty is more likely to increase when the purchase involves a value-added product.[31]

VALUE-ADDED PRODUCT—MAXIMIZING YOUR CUSTOMER'S SATISFACTION The **value-added product** exists when salespeople offer customers more than they expect and may not even know exists. Coupling CRM with a differentiation strategy provides one way for a salesperson to add value.[32] When you make a reservation at one of the Ritz-Carlton hotels and request a special amenity such as a tennis lesson, a record of this request is maintained in the computer system. If you make a reservation at another Ritz-Carlton at some future date, the agent informs you of the availability of a tennis court. The guest who buys chocolate chip cookies in the lobby gift shop in New Orleans may find a basket of them waiting in his room in Boston two weeks later. The hotel company uses modern technology to surprise and delight guests.[33]

Several years ago, Yellow Freight System was a troubled, long-haul carrier offering customers a generic product. Bill Zollars was hired to transform the company by adding a variety of services built around unprecedented customer service. The new services positioned the company to satisfy a broader range of transportation needs. For example, the company launched Yellow's Exact Express, its first time-definite, guaranteed service. Exact Express is now Yellow's most expensive and most profitable service. Today, Yellow Freight System salespeople are able to offer its 300,000 customers a value-added product.[34]

Doing Business in India

India is a very large country that is growing in importance in terms of international trade. Indians' customs are often dictated by their religious beliefs. In addition to Hindus and Muslims, there are dozens of other religious groups. Study the Indian culture carefully before your first business trip to this country.

- Customs of food and drink are an important consideration when you do business in India. Avoid eating meat in the presence of Hindus because they are vegetarians and consider the cow a sacred animal. Muslims will not eat pork or drink alcoholic beverages.
- There is a very strict caste system in India, so be aware of the caste of the clients with whom you are dealing and any restrictions that may apply to that caste.
- Most members of the Indian business community speak English.
- Indians tend to be careful buyers who seek quality and durability. They respect a salesperson who is caring and well informed. Personal relationships in business transactions are very important.

Source: Yuri Arcurs/Alamy

Among the most important factors that contribute to the value-added product is the overall quality of employees with whom the customer has contact. Sales and sales support staff who display enthusiasm and commitment to the customer add a great deal of value to the product.[35]

POTENTIAL PRODUCT—BUILDING LONG-TERM PARTNERSHIPS After the value-added product has been developed, the salesperson should begin to conceptualize the **potential product**. The potential product refers to what may remain to be done; that is, what is possible.[36] As the level of competition increases, especially in the case of mature products, salespeople must look to the future and explore new possibilities.

Steelcase's "Think" chair answered their customers wishes for potential products that are more environmentally safe. It is 99 percent recyclable.

Source: UIG via Getty Images

In the highly competitive food services industry, restaurant owners like to do business with a distribution sales representative (DSR) who wants to help make the business profitable. The DSR who assumes this role becomes a true partner and looks beyond the customer's immediate and basic needs. The potential product might be identified after a careful study of the restaurant's current menu and customer base. To deliver the potential product, a salesperson must discover and satisfy new customer needs, which requires imagination and creativity.

Steelcase Incorporated, a leading manufacturer of office furniture, has developed the "Think" chair, which is 99 percent recyclable and can be disassembled with basic hand tools in about five minutes. This $900 chair meets a growing demand for products made of parts that can be recycled several times and manufactured in ways least harmful to the environment. Steelcase developed this "potential product" after learning that customers are increasingly seeking environmentally safe products and are sometimes willing to pay a premium for them.[37]

DISTRIBUTING PRODUCT INFORMATION WITH CRM

Today, salespeople are challenged to manage a steady stream of information about customers (needs) and products (solutions). From this stream of information, the salesperson must select product information that is relevant to a specific customer and deliver the information in a manner that can be understood by the customer. **Customer relationship management (CRM)** assists the busy salesperson by providing tools that can collect information and rapidly link it to those who need it. Most CRM systems can receive and organize information from many sources, within and outside the organization. For example, Salesforce.com is linked to Google AdWords, an online advertising service. Advertisements placed on search engines, including Google, direct users to pages with forms to complete for more information. The data entered on these forms are downloaded directly into Salesforce.com. The statistics generated by the service permits a quick analysis of online advertising. Once information is received from the various sources, sales professionals can add value to this information by summarizing, combining, and tailoring the information to meet a customer's needs.

When new information about a product is received, the customer database can be quickly searched to find those customers who might have an interest. The new product data can be merged into an e-mail, fax, or letter to those customers, along with other information (benefits) that can help the recipients assess its value. Later, the CRM system can display an alert, reminding the sales professional to follow up on the information that was shared with the customer.

The potential product is more likely to be developed by salespeople who are close to their customers. Many high-performing salespeople explore product possibilities with their customers on a regular basis. Potential products are often mutually discovered during these exchanges.

Every indication points toward product-selling strategies that add value becoming more important in the future. New-product life cycles are shrinking, so more companies are searching for ways to add value during the new and emerging stage. Some companies that have experienced low profits selling low-priced products are reinventing those products. They search for product features that provide benefits customers think are worth paying for. Maytag Corporation developed the expensive environment-friendly Neptune washing machine for customers who will pay more for a washer that uses less water. Yellow Freight System created value for customers with the addition of Yellow's Exact Express and other service options.

Value Creation Product Strategies for Transactional, Consultative, and Strategic Alliance Buyers

In most cases, value creation investments during the transactional sale are minimal. Emphasis is usually placed on finding ways to eliminate any unnecessary costs associated with the sale and avoiding delays in processing the order. Technology investments can sometimes play a big role in improving efficiencies.[38] For example, customers may be encouraged to order products online.

A considerable amount of value creation takes place in consultative sales. Higher investments in value creation are permitted because companies need to invest in developing a good understanding of the customer's needs and problems. This is especially true in large, complex sales. The opportunity to create custom-tailored solutions and deliver more real benefits to the customer provides the opportunity for high margins. If your company is selling mobile autonomous robots, for example, the sales cycle will be quite long and investments will be quite high. It may take several weeks to study the applications of this product in a hospital, a manufacturing plant, or a large warehouse facility. The use of these robots may ultimately result in significant cost savings for the customer.[39]

Value creation investments in strategic alliance sales are the highest. As noted in Chapter 2, strategic alliances represent the highest form of partnering. Building an alliance is always preceded by a careful study of the proposed partner. Creating value often requires leveraging the full assets of the company, so investments go well beyond the sales force. Alliances are often developed by a team of specialists from such areas as finance, engineering, and marketing. A proposed alliance may require investments in new technology, manufacturing facilities, and warehouses.[40]

CHAPTER LEARNING ACTIVITIES

Reviewing Key Concepts

Describe positioning as a product-selling strategy

Success in today's dynamic global economy requires the continuous positioning and reposition-ing of products. Product positioning involves those decisions and activities intended to create and maintain a certain concept of the firm's product in the customer's mind. Salespeople can make an important contribution to the process of product positioning.

Explain the 3-D Product Solutions Selling Model

Today's better-educated customers are often seeking a cluster of satisfactions. They seek satisfac-tions that arise from today's new three-dimensional (3-D) Product Solutions Selling Model that includes (1) the product itself, (2) the company that makes or distributes the product, and (3) the salesperson who sells and services the product.

Discuss product-positioning options

We described the major product-positioning strategies available to salespeople: positioning new and emerging products versus mature and well-established products; positioning with a price strategy; and positioning with a value-added strategy.

Explain how to sell your product with a price strategy

Pricing decisions must be made at each stage of the product life cycle. Some companies use transactional selling tactics that emphasize low price. Salespeople are often given permission to alter (lower) the base price through the use of discounts and allowances. Consequences of using low-price tactics are discussed in this chapter.

Explain how to sell your product with a value-added strategy

To understand fully the importance of the value-added concept in selling, it helps to visualize every product as being four dimensional. This range of possibilities includes the generic product, the expected product, the value-added product, and the potential product.

Key Terms

Positioning, p. 135
Differentiation, p. 135
Value proposition, p. 136
Satisfactions, p. 137
3-D Product Solutions Selling
 Model, p. 137
Product life cycle, p. 139

Quantity discount, p. 142
Seasonal discount, p. 142
Promotional allowance,
 p. 142
Trade or functional discount,
 p. 142

Value-Added Product-Selling
 Model, p. 144
Generic product, p. 145
Expected product, p. 145
Value-added product, p. 145
Potential product, p. 146

MyMarketingLab
To complete the problems with the ★ in your MyLab, go to the EOC Discussion Questions.

Review Questions

 7-1 Why has product differentiation become so important in sales and marketing?

7-2 According to Ted Levitt, what is the definition of a product? What satisfactions do customers want?

7-3 Explain what is meant by *positioning* as a product-selling strategy. What is a value proposition?

 7-4 Why have salespeople assumed an important role in positioning products?

7-5 Briefly describe the influence of electronic commerce on pricing. What types of products are likely to be sold on the Internet?

7-6 Read the Selling in Action feature titled "How Do Customers Judge Service Quality?" on page 136. How might this information help a salesperson who wants to adopt the value-added selling strategy?

7-7 What are some of the common ways salespeople add value to the products they sell?

7-8 What are the four possible products that make up the *value-added product-selling* concept?

7-9 Describe the difference between a generic product and a value-added product.

7-10 What is the relationship between value-added selling strategies and the cluster of product-selling satisfactions?

7-11 Is it true that selling products with a low-price strategy largely ignores customer satisfaction? Discuss.

Application Exercises

7-12 Search the Internet for two competing electronic industrial supply catalogs or two competing direct-mail catalog companies. Assume one of the represented businesses is your employer. After studying the catalogs, make a comparative analysis of your company's competitive advantages.

7-13 The Ritz-Carlton hotel chain illustrates the total product concept discussed in this chapter. Research value-added information on the Ritz-Carlton chain by accessing www .ritzcarlton.com. Choose a location and click "Meetings." Click "Quick Facts" and print the information presented. Circle at least five features you consider to be value-added features. Examine the room rates by clicking "Accommodations." On the fact sheet you printed, record the room rate for single- and double-occupancy rooms.

7-14 Call a local financial services representative specializing in stock, bond, or equity fund transactions. Ask what percentage of clients rely on the information given to make complex decisions on their investments. Also ask this person if customers believe that advice on custom-fitting investment programs adds value to their decision making. Find out whether financial products are getting more or less complex and what effect this will have on providing value-added service in the future.

Role-Play Exercise

 Study the Convention Center information in Part 1 of Appendix 3. Analyze this information and determine the value-added product that would appeal to a meeting planner (customer). Prepare a value proposition that summarizes the mix of key benefits on which your product is positioned. The proposition might include, for example, the free limousine service to and from the airport. Present your value proposition to another class member who will assume the role of the customer. Consider using information sheets, pictures, and other materials that will enhance your presentation.

Reality Selling Case Problem:
Selling New Products at Steelcase

Source: UIG via Getty Images

Many of the most profitable companies have discovered that there are "riches in market niches." They have developed products and services that meet the needs of a well-defined or newly created market. Steelcase Incorporated, a leading source of information and expertise on work effectiveness, has been working hard to develop products that meet the needs of people who do most of their work in an office environment. The company's motto is "the office environment company." One of its newest products is the "Think" chair. Steelcase also developed the Personal Harbor Workspaces, a self-contained, fully equipped, and totally private podlike workstation. Steelcase sales literature describes the product as ideal for companies that are tired of waiting for the future:

> They were developed to support the individual within a highly collaborative team environment, and they work best when clustered around common work areas equipped with mobile tables, carts, benches, screens, and other Steelcase Activity Products. These "commons" are meant to be flexible spaces that enhance communication and facilitate interaction.

Steelcase realized that selling this advanced product would not be easy, so a decision was made to develop an advanced sales team to presell the Personal Harbor before its major introduction. Once the team started making sales calls, it became evident that a traditional product-oriented sales presentation would not work. The Personal Harbor was a departure from conventional office design, so many customers were perplexed. Sue Sacks, a team member, said, "People acted like we had fallen from Mars." Team members soon realized that, to explain the features and benefits of the product, they had to begin studying new organizational developments such as team-oriented workforces and corporate reengineering. The advanced sales team was renamed the "advanced solutions team." Sales calls put more emphasis on learning about the customers' problems and identification of possible solutions. Members of the team viewed themselves as consultants who were in a position to discuss solutions to complex business problems.

The consultative approach soon began to pay off in sales. One customer, a hospital, was preparing to build a new office building and needed workstations for 400 employees. The hospital had formed a committee to make decisions concerning the purchase of office equipment. After an initial meeting between the Steelcase sales team and the hospital committee, a visit to Steelcase headquarters in Grand Rapids, Michigan, was arranged. The hospital committee members were able to tour the plant and meet with selected Steelcase experts. With knowledge of the hospital's goals and directions, Sue Sacks was able to arrange meetings with Steelcase technical personnel who could answer specific questions. The hospital ultimately placed an order worth more than a million dollars.

Questions

7-15 To fulfill a problem-solving need, salespeople must often be prepared to communicate effectively with customers who are seeking a cluster of satisfactions (see Figure 7.1). Is it likely that a customer who is considering the Personal Harbor Workspaces will seek information concerning all three dimensions of the Product-Selling Model? Explain your answer.

7-16 What product-selling strategies are most effective when selling a new and emerging product such as the Personal Harbor Workspaces?

7-17 Sue Sacks and other members of her sales team discovered that a traditional product-oriented presentation would not work when selling the Personal Harbor Workspaces. Success came only after the team adopted the consultative style of selling. Why was the product-oriented presentation ineffective?

7-18 Sue Sacks and other members of the advanced solutions team found that the consultative approach resulted in meetings with people higher in the customer's organization. "We get to call on a higher level of buyer," she said. Also, the team was more likely to position the product with a value-added strategy instead of a price strategy. In what ways did the advanced solutions team members add value to their product? Why was less emphasis placed on price during meetings with the customer?

MyMarketingLab

Go to the Assignments section of your MyLab to complete these writing exercises.

7-19 Ted Levitt, former editor of the *Harvard Business Review*, says that products are problem-solving tools. Briefly describe The Three-Dimensional Product Solutions Selling Model. Why must salespeople be familiar with the unique satisfactions that meet the needs of each customer?

7-20 Most high-performing salespeople have adopted sales strategies that emphasize *value-added* selling. How do salespersons sell products with the value-added product-selling model?

PART 3 ROLE-PLAY EXERCISE

Developing a Product Strategy

Scenario

First National Bank is a full-service bank with a reputation for excellent customer service. Personal selling efforts by tellers, loan officers, and financial consultants are considered an integral part of the bank's customer service program.

Customer Profile

At age 45, Gianni Diaz is looking forward to early retirement. To supplement a company-sponsored retirement program, a certificate of deposit (CD) in the amount of $4,000 is purchased each year. The annual percentage yield earned on CDs is currently in the range of 1.75 to 2.00 percent. Diaz is not interested in stocks and bonds because these products represent high-risk investments.

Salesperson Profile

Deaven Ray is a senior investment officer with First National Bank. Ray represents a wide range of financial products such as stock and bond mutual funds, blue chip stocks, diversified mutual funds, fixed annuities, money market funds, and certificates of deposit. Ray feels that Gianni Diaz may be a good candidate for an investment in fixed annuities. Diaz has agreed to meet and discuss investment options.

Product

Electric Capital Assurance Company offers a guaranteed-growth annuity at an annual percentage yield of 2.0 percent for a term of five years. This product gives the customer a guaranteed principal and a fixed rate of return. At the contract maturity date, the customer can select several payout options. This is a tax-deferred annuity, which means you won't pay income taxes on earnings until you choose to withdraw the funds. You can add funds to your account throughout the contract period. You need not close the account at the end of the contract period. You can allow your money to continue to grow at the same interest rate. If funds are withdrawn prior to the end of the contract, a withdrawal charge will be assessed. The minimum single premium purchase is $5,000.

Instructions

For this role-play activity, you will meet with Gianni Diaz and discuss current and future financial plans. You will determine whether Diaz might benefit by investing in a guaranteed-growth annuity. Prior to meeting with the customer, review the following material in Chapter 6:

- Adding value with a feature–benefit strategy
- Use of bridge statements
- General versus specific benefits

Also, think about the implications of the 3D Product-Selling Model (Figure 7.1) introduced in Chapter 7. At the beginning of the role-play, use appropriate questions to acquire information regarding the customer's needs. Be prepared to recommend this product and close the sale if you feel the customer will benefit from this purchase.

PART 4

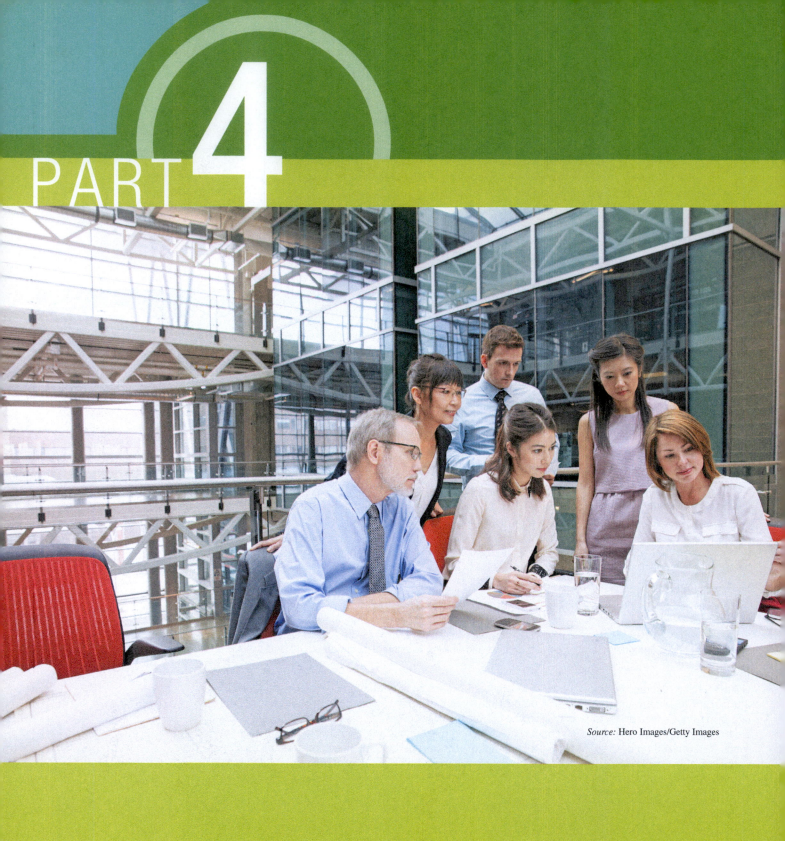

Source: Hero Images/Getty Images

DEVELOPING A CUSTOMER STRATEGY

With increased knowledge of the customer, the salesperson is in a better position to achieve sales goals. This part presents information on understanding the buying process, understanding buyer behavior, and developing a prospect base.

RELATIONSHIP STRATEGY

ETHICS

ETHICS

ETHICS

PRESENTATION STRATEGY

PRODUCT STRATEGY

PARTNERING TO CREATE VALUE

CUSTOMER STRATEGY

The Buying Process and Buyer Behavior

Learning Objectives

When you finish reading this chapter, you should be able to

8.1 Discuss the meaning of a customer strategy

8.2 Explain the difference between consumer and business buyers

8.3 Understand the importance of alignment between the selling process and the customer's buying process

8.4 Understand the buying process of the transactional, consultative, and strategic alliance buyer

8.5 Discuss the various influences that shape customer buying decisions

Source: Michael Ah

▶ Reality Selling Video Series—Ashley Pineda/PulteGroup

Ashley Pineda is a new-home sales representative for PulteGroup (www.pultegroupinc .com). The company offers different product lines: homes for first-time homebuyers, move-up homes, and active adult communities. With three different customer groups, Ashley must have a general understanding of the buying motives of each group. In her work with individual customers in each of these groups, she must develop an in-depth understanding of that customer's buying interests.

Most of Ashley's customers are in the first-time homebuyers group who have lived in an apartment but have developed an interest in purchasing a home. Because she has developed an in-depth understanding of this buying group, a central purpose of Ashley's sales presentations is to educate her prospects on renting versus owning and the benefits of owning a home. She also understands this customer group often knows little about the logistics of owning a home; therefore, she provides her prospects with information and on-site impressions about the neighborhood, the area, the amenities of the community, as well as shopping areas and schools around the neighborhood. All these details help Ashley's customers envision raising their children in one of Pulte's neighborhoods.

Another very important thing Ashley understands about the buying needs of this first-time buying group is the question of the financing of their new home. Ashley typically needs to address the following questions from her customers: What about our credit scores? What qualifies us to buy a new home? Do we need a down payment? What will our monthly payment be? Will it be comfortable with our budget? PulteGroup supplies Ashley with the knowledge to be able to professionally provide and implement that knowledge and make customers feel comfortable with the financial scenario involved in owning their first home.

As is commonly known, buyers tend to buy from people they like and trust. Considering that many customers buy the largest asset they may ever own from sales professionals like Ashley, trust in the seller becomes especially critical. Therefore, building rapport and trust throughout the whole buying process is essential for Ashley to be successful. Furthermore, Ashley describes having a positive mindset, good time management, and multi-tasking abilities as the most important skills to be a successful salesperson in her particular business. In essence, sales reps like Ashley have to be able to run their own business in the communities for which they are responsible. ●

Developing a Customer Strategy

8.1 Discuss the meaning of a customer strategy

The greatest challenge to salespeople in the age of information is to understand realized and unrealized needs and improve responsiveness to customers. In fact, a growing number of sales professionals believe the customer has supplanted the product as the driving force in sales today. This is especially true because many of today's customers no longer care where or from whom they buy. They are a new generation of aggressive, Internet-empowered customers. They are "new experts." They are confident and determined because they are equipped with purchasing firepower unavailable to any previous generation. They employ three power tools to get their way.

1. Instant comprehensive information from the Internet about all products and services sold online and offline.
2. Immense choice in every segment of commerce—a wide variety of options and prices in every local community and from every corner of the world.
3. Real-time price comparison at the moment and location of purchase on increasingly advanced technology.[1]

Jerry Acuff, author of *Stop Acting Like a Seller and Start Thinking Like a Buyer*, encourages salespeople to develop a customer strategy that adds value. Acuff says, "In order to think like a buyer, salespeople must understand the new buying processes and focus on what the customer is looking for."[2]

Jerry Acuff, author of *Stop Acting Like a Seller and Start Thinking Like a Buyer* encourages salespeople to develop a customer strategy that adds value. He says, "In order to think like a buyer, salespeople must understand the buying process and focus on what the customer is looking for.

Source: Jerry Acuff

Adding Value with a Customer Strategy

A **customer strategy** is a carefully conceived plan that results in understanding the customer's perceptions and maximizing customer satisfactions and responsiveness. One major dimension of this strategy is to achieve a better understanding of the customer's buying needs and motives. As noted in Chapter 1, information has become a strategic resource (Figure 1.2). When salespeople take time to discover realized and unrealized needs and motives, they are in a much better position to offer customers a value-added solution to their buying problem.

Every salesperson who wants to develop repeat business should figure out a way to collect and systematize customer information. The authors of *Reengineering the Corporation* discuss the importance of collecting information about the unique and particular needs of each customer:

Customers—consumers and corporations alike—demand products and services designed for their unique and particular needs. There is no longer any such notion as *the* customer; there is only *this* customer, the one with whom a seller is dealing at the moment and who now has the capacity to indulge his or her own personal tastes.[3]

The first prescription for developing a customer strategy focuses on the customer's buying process (see Figure 8.1). Buying procedures and policies can vary greatly from one buyer to another. This is especially true in business-to-business selling. If a salesperson fails to learn how the buyer plans to make the purchase, then there is the danger that the selling process will be

FIGURE 8.1

Today, one of the greatest challenges to salespeople is improving responsiveness to customers. A well-developed customer strategy is designed to meet this challenge.

Strategic/Consultative Selling Model	
Strategic Step	**Prescription**
Develop a Personal Selling Philosophy	☑ Adopt Marketing Concept
	☑ Value Personal Selling
	☑ Become a Problem Solver/Partner
Develop a Relationship Strategy	☑ Maintain High Ethical Standards
	☑ Project Professional Image
	☑ Manage the Relationship Process
Develop a Product Strategy	☑ Become a Product Expert
	☑ Sell Benefits
	☑ Configure Value-Added Solutions
Develop a Customer Strategy	☐ Understand the Buying Process
	☐ Understand Buyer Behavior
	☐ Develop Prospect Base

out of alignment with the customer's buying process. Keith Eades, author of *The New Solution Selling*, says:

> If we haven't defined how our buyers buy, then we make assumptions that throw us out of alignment with our buyers. Misalignment with buyers is one of selling's most critical mistakes.[4]

The second prescription focuses on why customers buy. This topic will be discussed in detail later in this chapter. The third prescription for developing a customer strategy emphasizes building a strong prospect or account base, which is discussed in Chapter 9.

Complex Nature of Customer Behavior

The forces that motivate customers can be complex. Arch McGill, former vice president of IBM, reminds us that "individual customers perceive the product in their own terms and that these terms may be 'unique, idiosyncratic, human, emotional, end-of-the-day, irrational, erratic terms.'" [5] Different people doing the same thing (e.g., purchasing a commercial office building) may have different needs that motivate them, and each buyer may have several motives for a single action.

The proliferation of market research studies, public opinion polls, surveys, and reports of "averages" makes it easy to fall into the trap of thinking of the customer as a number. The customer is a person, not a statistic. Companies that fully accept this basic truth are likely to adopt a one-to-one marketing strategy. The one-to-one strategy is based on a bedrock concept: Treat different customers differently.[6]

8.2 Explain the difference between consumer and business buyers

Consumer Versus Business Buyers

Consumer buyer behavior refers to the buying behavior of individuals and households who buy goods and services for personal consumption. Each year, consumers purchase many trillions of dollars' worth of goods and services. **Business buyer behavior** refers to the organizations that buy goods and services for use in the production of other products and services that are sold, rented, or supplied to others.[7] In many business-buying situations, several people work together to reach a decision. The **buying center** is a cross-functional team of decision makers who often represent several departments. Each team member is likely to have some expertise needed in a particular purchase decision. Salespeople must continually identify which individuals within a firm will be members of the buying center team.[8]

It is not uncommon for salespeople to sell products and services to both consumer and business buyers. A well-established interior decorating firm will likely work with homeowners as well as commercial clients who own hotels, restaurants, or art galleries. A salesperson employed

Consumer Buyers	Organizational Buyers
• Purchases for individual or household consumption	• Purchases made for some purpose other than personal consumption
• Decisions usually made by individuals	• Decisions frequently made by several people
• Purchases often made based on brand reputation or personal recommendations with little or no product expertise	• Purchases made according to precise technical specification based on product expertise
• Purchases based primarily on emotional responses to product or promotions	• Purchases based on primarily rational criteria
• Individual purchasers may make quick decisions	• Purchasers may engage in lengthy decision process
• Products: consumer goods and services for individual use	• Products: often complex; classified based on how organizational customers use them

FIGURE 8.2

Differences Between Consumer and Organizational Buyers

Source: Solomon, Michael R.; Marshal, Greg W.; Stuart, Elnora W., *Marketing: Real People, Real Choices,* 6th ed., © 2009, p. 139. Reprinted and electronically reproduced by permission of Pearson Education, Inc. Upper Saddle River, New Jersey.

by an automobile dealership will often sell to corporate customers who maintain a fleet of cars or trucks as well as consumers who buy vehicles for personal use.

There are some similarities between consumer markets and business markets. Both involve people who assume the role of buyer and make purchase decisions to satisfy needs. These two markets differ, however, in some important areas. Figure 8.2 provides a brief review of some of these differences. A business purchase is likely to involve more decision participants and these participants may be well trained. Most purchasing agents spend time learning how to buy better.[9]

Types of Business Buying Situations

There are three major types of business-to-business buying situations. The amount of time and effort organizational buyers spend on a purchase usually depends on the complexity of the product and how often the decision must be made.[10] At one extreme is the *straight rebuy,* which is a fairly routine decision. At the other extreme is the *new-task buy,* which may require extensive research. In the middle is the *modified rebuy,* which will require some research.[11]

NEW-TASK BUY A first-time purchase of a product or service is a **new-task buy**. Depending on the cost and complexity of this purchase, the buying decision may require several weeks of information gathering and the involvement of numerous decision participants. In some cases, a buying committee is formed to consider the new product's quality, price, and service provided by suppliers. Salespeople who are involved in new-task buying situations must rely heavily on consultative selling skills.

STRAIGHT REBUY A **straight rebuy** is a routine purchase of items needed by a business-to-business customer. Let's assume you have decided to open a new restaurant and need a steady supply of high-quality cooking oil. After talking to several restaurant suppliers and testing several oils, you select one that meets your needs. Your goal now is to simplify the buying process with the use of a straight rebuy plan. As long as the supplier meets your criteria for price, quality, service, and delivery, future purchases will be very routine. Organizations often use the straight rebuy approach for such items as cleaning supplies, copy paper, and cartridges for computer printers. Salespeople must constantly monitor every straight rebuy situation to be sure the customer is completely satisfied. A competing supplier will be quick to exploit any sign of dissatisfaction by the customer.

MODIFIED REBUY The tide of change is a powerful force in the world of business. From time to time, your customers may wish to modify product specifications, change delivery schedules, or renegotiate prices. Several years ago, American automobile manufacturers, faced with greater competitive pressures from China, Korea, Japan, Germany, and other nations, turned to their suppliers and demanded price reductions. Suppliers were required to become involved in a **modified rebuy** situation or risk loss of the account. A modified rebuy often requires the involvement of several participants.

Well-trained professional salespeople work hard to provide outstanding service after the sale and anticipate changes in customer needs. Some salespeople regularly ask their customers what they value most about the existing buying situation and how improvements can be made in this area.

BUILDING STRATEGIC ALLIANCES In Chapter 2, we described strategic alliances as the highest form of partnering. Alliances are often formed by companies that have similar business interests and believe the partnership will help them gain a mutual competitive advantage. Large companies often form several alliances. Some strategic alliances take the form of systems selling. **Systems selling** appeals to buyers who prefer to purchase a packaged solution to a problem from a single seller, thus avoiding all the separate decisions involved in a complex buying situation.[12]

Several years ago, Kinko's reinvented itself as a document solutions provider for business firms of all sizes. Full-service Kinko's stores began offering the buyer networks of computers equipped with popular software, ultrafast color printers, high-speed Internet connections and, of course, a variety of document preparation services. After Kinko's was purchased by FedEx, a network of 1,200 digitally connected FedEx Kinko's locations began offering a wider selection of customized, needs-based document solutions. One large financial institution consolidated the services of 13 vendors by forming an alliance with FedEx Kinko's.[13] Systems selling efforts at FedEx Kinko's have become an important strategy for winning and holding accounts.

Types of Consumer Buying Situations

As noted previously, consumer buying behavior refers to purchases of products for personal or household use. The amount of time consumers devote to a purchase decision can vary greatly depending on the cost of the product, familiarity with the product, and the importance of the item to the consumer. Few buyers invest much effort in selecting a tube of toothpaste, but the purchase of a new automobile or a home will involve extensive decision making. Consumer buying situations can fall into one of three categories depending on the degree of buyer involvement.

HABITUAL BUYING DECISIONS **Habitual buying decisions** usually require very little consumer involvement and brand differences are usually insignificant.[14] For frequently purchased, low-cost items such as shampoo, copy paper, or laundry detergent, consumer involvement in the decision-making process is very low. Supermarket shoppers often display habitual buying behavior as they select items.

VARIETY-SEEKING BUYING DECISIONS **Variety-seeking buying decisions** are characterized by low customer involvement, but important perceived brand differences.[15] Brand switching is not uncommon among these buyers because they can be influenced by advertising appeals, coupons, or lower prices to try a new brand. Brand switching is usually motivated by the desire for variety rather than dissatisfaction.[16]

COMPLEX BUYING DECISIONS **Complex buying decisions** are characterized by a high degree of involvement by the consumer. Consumers are likely to be highly involved when the product is expensive, purchased infrequently, and highly self-expressive.[17] The purchase of a vacation home, a long-term care insurance policy, an expensive boat, or a costly piece of art would require a complex buying decision. The learning process for some purchases can be very lengthy.

8.3 Understand the importance of alignment between the selling process and the customer's buying process

Achieving Alignment with the Customer's Buying Process

The foundation of a successful sales effort comes from knowing how buyers buy. If you don't know what the customer's decision-making process is and you proceed according to your own agenda, you risk losing the sale. If you have not defined how buyers buy, then you make assumptions that throw your sales process out of alignment with the buyer's buying process.[18] Too often salespeople rely on generalizations about the buyer's decision-making process rather than acquiring specific information.

The **buying process** is a systematic series of actions, or a series of defined, repeatable steps intended to achieve a result.[19] Organizational purchasing structures and buying procedures can vary greatly from company to company, so you need to be clear on how decisions are being made within each account. In some cases, the steps in the buying process have been clearly defined by the organization and this information is available to any potential supplier. However, this information may not tell you the whole story. Salespeople need to obtain answers to these types of questions:

- How urgent is my proposal to the buyer? When will a buying decision be made?
- Will any political factors within the organization influence how decisions are made?
- Has the money needed to purchase my product been allocated?
- Which person or persons in the buying organization will actually use or supervise the use of the product I am selling?[20]

Customers make buying decisions in many ways, so understanding each individual buyer's decision-making process is central to success in personal selling. Some buyers will have multiple buying processes. Buying decisions involving a straight rebuy, for example, will likely differ from buying decisions involving a new-task buy.[21]

Steps in the Typical Buying Process

The term "process" brings to mind a set formula that applies to every situation. But buying decisions are made in different ways, so it would be inappropriate to view the buying process as a uniform pattern of decision making. However, there is a model—a form of decision making that buyers usually apply to their unique circumstances. Figure 8.3 shows the typical stages in the buying decision process: needs awareness, evaluation of solutions, resolution of problems, purchase, and implementation. This model is especially helpful in understanding organizational buying decisions and large consumer acquisitions. Consumers who make habitual buying decisions often skip or reverse some of these stages.[22]

NEEDS AWARENESS Needs awareness is the first stage in the buying process. The buyer recognizes that something is imperfect or incomplete. The need for energy conservation technology may surface when oil prices rise to higher levels. The need for a customer service

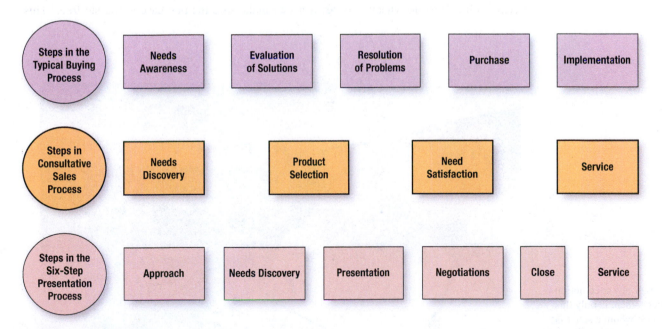

FIGURE 8.3

Typical Buying Process Model

In this figure, for purposes of illustration, the Typical Buying Process Model is aligned with the two most popular Selling Process Models. It is important salespeople understand the customer's unique buying process, where the customer is in that buying process, and then align the sales process to satisfy their customer's needs.

training program may become evident when customer satisfaction survey scores decline. Salespeople can create value at this stage of the buying process if they can help determine the magnitude of the customer's problem and identify a solution. For example, a sales representative may be able to help the buyer estimate the cost of poor customer service and recommend a way to improve service. Customers often need help in determining whether they have a problem large enough to justify the cost of a solution.[23]

EVALUATION OF SOLUTIONS Buyers who experience need awareness usually begin searching for information that will help them evaluate possible problem solutions. They realize, at this point, that the problem they face is amenable to some type of solution. In some cases, there are several solutions that the customer needs to study. Salespeople can add value at this stage by providing useful information that helps the customer make an informed choice. In some cases, the value justification can be presented in terms of cost reduction or increased revenues. In other cases, the value justification may be an intangible such as customer satisfaction, improved security, or reduced stress. In business-to-business selling situations, value justification that can be measured is usually the most powerful.

To establish a true partnership with the customer, you need to be sure that you are offering them information that will help them achieve their objectives. If you possess a good understanding of the customer's buying process, you will know what they are trying to accomplish.[24]

RESOLUTION OF PROBLEMS At this stage of the buying process, the customer is aware of a need and has evaluated one or more solutions. The customer has resolved to do something. However, the customer is likely to have issues and concerns that must be resolved before moving ahead. This is especially true in the case of complex sales.[25]

Some customers will want the proposed solution put in writing. Competitors may be invited to submit written proposals. A well-written proposal is one way to add value (see Chapter 6). Some customers may request specific information that can be provided only by the supplier's engineers or accountants. Other customers may insist on visiting the supplier's manufacturing plant so they can see the production process firsthand. Buyers often need help overcoming obstacles that prevent them from moving to the purchase stage of the buying process.[26]

PURCHASE After all the customer's obstacles and concerns have been overcome, the purchase decision is made. Professional salespeople create value in many ways at this stage of the buying process.[27] First, they do whatever is necessary to make sure the purchase is "hassle free." This

There is no longer any such notion as the customer—there is only this customer, the one whom a seller is dealing with at the moment. Discovering the individual needs of this customer can be challenging.

Source: Javier Larrea/age fotostock/ Alamy Stock Photo

may mean working with the customer to arrange the best financing or supervising the delivery and installation of the product. Salespeople add value by becoming a "customer advocate" within their own organizations. This may mean negotiating with various departments to expedite the order. Buyers want to work with salespeople who are able to quickly solve any order fulfillment problems.[28]

IMPLEMENTATION The first sale is only the beginning of the relationship with the buyer. Repeat sales occur when the supplier has demonstrated the ability to add value in various ways after the sale. Value creation can take the form of timely delivery, superior installation, accurate invoicing, follow-up contacts by the salesperson, or something else that is important to the customer.

Understanding the Buying Process of the Transactional, Consultative, and Strategic Alliance Buyer

8.4 Understand the buying process of the transactional, consultative, and strategic alliance buyer

The next step in understanding the customer's buying process is to discuss three value creation-selling approaches that appeal to certain types of customers. In Chapter 1, we briefly introduced transactional selling, consultative selling, and strategic alliance selling. We will now discuss how to work effectively with each type of buyer.[29]

Transactional Process Buyer

Transactional buyers are well aware of their needs and usually know a great deal about the products or services they intend to purchase. In a true transactional sale, buyers will become frustrated if the salesperson attempts to use needs assessment, problem solving, or relationship building. They are not looking for new information or advice from the salesperson. Most transactional buyers have conducted their own research and, in most cases, have decided which product best meets their needs. They don't want hand-holding and they don't want the salesperson to waste their time.[30]

How can a salesperson add value to a transactional sale? If the buyer is already aware of his needs, has evaluated solutions, and has no issues or concerns that need to be resolved, then the salesperson needs to focus on the purchase stage of the five-part buying process model (see Figure 8.3). Do whatever is necessary to facilitate a convenient and hassle-free purchase. Eliminate any unnecessary costs or delays in processing the order. The transactional buyer may quickly turn to a competitor if they experience unnecessary costs or delays.

Consultative Process Buyer

Consultative selling, a major theme of this text, was described in Chapter 2. The consultative selling approach appeals to buyers who lack needs awareness or need help evaluating possible solutions. Some buying decisions require assistance from a consultative salesperson because the product is very complex and/or the cost of the product is very high. The purchase of a new home provides a good example in the consumer arena. Homebuyers usually seek the assistance of an experienced realtor. The purchase of Internet phone-calling equipment provides a good example in the business-to-business arena. Organizations that are considering the purchase of complex Internet telephone equipment seek answers to several questions: Can we keep a portion of our traditional phone network or must we adopt an all-Internet phone system? Will the new system provide the same voice quality as our traditional system? Internet phone-calling equipment is available from several suppliers, including Avaya Incorporated and Cisco Systems Incorporated. Some customers will need help comparing the technology available from these and other suppliers.[31]

Successful consultative salespeople focus a great deal of attention on needs awareness, which is step one in the buying process model (see Figure 8.3). This is where salespeople can create the most value by helping customers gain an understanding of their problems and create solutions that correct these problems.[32] Many customers seek help defining needs and solutions, but avoid dealing with a sales representative who simply wants to sell a product.

Consultative selling encompasses the concept that salespeople should conduct a systematic assessment of the prospect's situation. This usually involves collecting as much information as possible prior to the sales call and using a series of carefully worded questions to obtain the customer's point of view during the sales call. Two-way communication will provide for a mutual exchange of ideas, feelings, and perceptions.

The consultative salesperson will help the customer evaluate solutions and help resolve any problems that surface prior to the purchase stage. Consultative salespeople also work hard to add value at the implementation stage of the sales process. This may involve supervising product delivery and installation, servicing warranties, and providing other services after the sale.

Strategic Alliance Process Buyer

As noted previously, the goal of strategic alliances is to achieve a marketplace advantage by teaming up with another company. Alliances are often formed by companies that have similar business interests and seek to gain a mutual competitive advantage. Dell Computer, for example, formed a partnership with Microsoft and Intel to provide customized e-business solutions. In the highly competitive global market, going it alone is sometimes more difficult.[33]

Step one in building an alliance is a careful study of the proposed partner. This research is often coordinated by senior management and may involve persons working in the areas of sales, marketing, finance, and distribution. At some point, representatives from both companies will meet and explore the mutual benefits of the alliance. Both parties must be prepared to explain how they will add value once the alliance is formed.

The Buyer Resolution Theory

Several theories explain how customers arrive at a buying decision. One traditional point of view is based on the assumption that a final buying decision is possible only after the prospect has answered five logical questions (see Figure 8.4). This is called the **buyer resolution theory**. One strength of this buying theory is that it focuses the salesperson's attention on five important factors that the customer is likely to consider before making a purchase. Answers to these five questions provide valuable insights about the customer's buying strategy. One important limitation of

FIGURE 8.4

The buyer resolution theory, sometimes referred to as "The 5 W's Theory," focuses attention on questions the customer may need answers to before making a purchase. The absence of an answer to any of these will likely result in a customer's objection.

Buyer Resolution Theory

This view of the buying process recognizes that a purchase is made only after the prospect has made five buying decisions involving specific affirmative responses to the following questions:

Why Should I Buy?
Realistically, it is sometimes difficult to provide prospects with an answer to this question. In many cases, salespeople fail in their attempt to help customers become aware of a need. Thus, large numbers of potential customers are not sufficiently persuaded to purchase products that provide them with genuine buyer benefits.

What Should I Buy?
If a prospect agrees that a need does exist, then you are ready to address the second buying decision. You must convince the prospect that the product being offered can satisfy the need. In most cases, the buyer can choose from several competing products.

Where Should I Buy?
As products become more complex, consumers are giving more attention to "source" decisions. In a major metropolitan area the person who wants to buy a Laserjet 3160 or a competing product can choose from several sources.

What Is a Fair Price?
Today's better educated and better informed consumers are searching for the right balance between price and value (benefits). They are better able to detect prices that are not competitive or do not correspond in their minds with the product's value.

When Should I Buy?
A sale cannot be closed until a customer has decided when to buy. In some selling situations, the customer may want to postpone the purchase because of reluctance to part with the money.

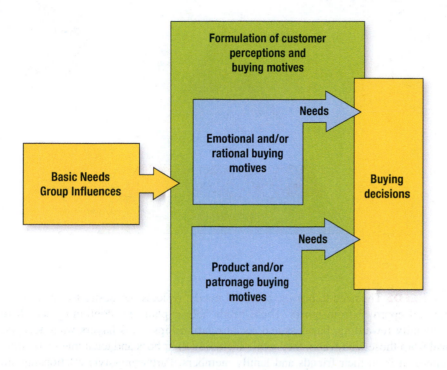

FIGURE 8.5

The Buyer Behavior Model

This model illustrates the many complex psychological and socio-logical forces that influence buyer behavior.

this theory is that it is often not possible to anticipate which of the five buying decisions might be most difficult for the prospect to make. If the selling process does not mesh with the buying process, a sale is less likely. There is no established sequence in which prospects make these five decisions, so a highly inflexible sales presentation would not be effective.

Understanding Buyer Behavior

8.5 Discuss the various influences that shape customer buying decisions

Although every customer is unique, salespeople need an understanding of the important social and psychological influences that tend to shape customers' buying decisions. We will review concepts that come from the fields of psychology, sociology, and anthropology. Figure 8.5 illustrates the many forces that influence buying decisions.

Basic Needs That Affect Buyer Behavior

Basic human needs have changed little throughout our economic history. However, the ways in which needs are fulfilled have changed greatly during the age of information.[34] The starting point for developing an understanding of the forces influencing buying decisions is a review of the individual needs that shape the customer's behavior. To gain insights into customer behavior mo-tivated by both physiological and psychological needs, it is helpful to study the popular hierarchy of needs developed by Abraham Maslow.

MASLOW'S HIERARCHY OF NEEDS According to Abraham Maslow, basic human needs are arranged in a hierarchy according to their strength (Figure 8.6). His theory rests on the assumption that as each lower-level need is satisfied, the need at the next level demands attention.

PHYSIOLOGICAL NEEDS Sometimes called "primary" needs, **physiological needs** include food, water, sleep, and shelter. Maslow placed our physiological needs at the bottom of the pyramid because he believed that these basic needs tended to be strong in the minds of most people.

SECURITY NEEDS After physiological needs have been satisfied, the next need level that tends to dominate is safety and security. **Security needs** represent our desire to be free from danger and uncertainty. The desire to satisfy the need for security and safety can be an important buying motive. Buyers want to feel secure that their salesperson is highly ethical and the products they are considering will perform as they expect. If a customer does not feel secure and safe in a transaction, it will almost always destroy any opportunity for a successful relationship and sale to develop.

FIGURE 8.6

Maslow's Hierarchy of Needs Model

The forces that motivate customers to make specific buying decisions are complex. This model illustrates Maslow's hierarchy of needs.

Source: Maslow, Abraham H., Frager, Robert D., Fadiman, James, *Motivation and Personality*, 3rd ed., © 1987. Adapted and electronically reproduced by permission of Pearson Education, Inc., Upper Saddle River, New Jersey.

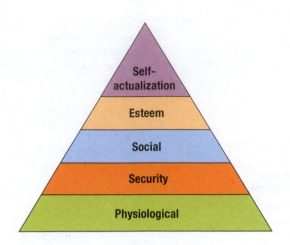

SOCIAL NEEDS The need to belong, or **social needs**, reflects our desire for identification with a group and approval from others. These needs help explain our continuing search for long-term, mutually rewarding, business and social relationships. B2B buyers want acceptance and approval from those with whom they work, including their boss and team members. B2C buyers want approval from their friends and family members. Partnering-style relationship strategies, and value-added product and presentation solutions provide customers and clients an important element of social needs satisfaction.

ESTEEM NEEDS At the fourth level of Maslow's needs priority model appears **esteem needs**. Esteem needs reflect our desire to feel worthy in the eyes of others. We seek a sense of personal worth and adequacy, a feeling of competence.[35] Salespeople who custom-fit a value-added solution that meets and exceeds their clients' needs provide a feeling of competency to buyers in complex buying situations. Assurances and outstanding service after the sale also make the customer feel worthwhile in making correct buying decisions.

SELLING IN ACTION

Selling to the Four Generations

It is important to understand the context in which people from different generational groups live and work. After all, success in personal selling requires the ability to create rapport and develop trust with buyers who may differ from us. Picture yourself as a Millennial (Generation Y), who early studies report were born between 1977 and 2000. Chances are you welcome the latest high-tech communications technology and do not resent the never-ending sea of information that demands your immediate attention and response. Some of the customers you call on are members of the baby boom generation, who were born between 1946 and 1964. These individuals may welcome traditional memos, letters, phone calls, and face-to-face communications, and feel uncomfortable working in today's wireless world. Generation Xers, born between 1965 and 1980, want proof; relationships are less important—be careful with chitchat. Matures, who have an in-built need to conform, prefer a traditional face-to-face sales process.[36] Generational differences shaped by sociological, political, and economic conditions can influence our values. Dave Stein, author of *How Winners Sell,* says, "Before you ever meet that prospect, understand that 'different' in terms of cross-generational selling is neither right nor wrong; it's just different."[a]

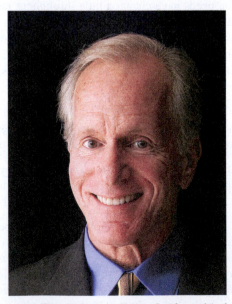

Source: Dave Stein, Sales Expert, Speaker and Author

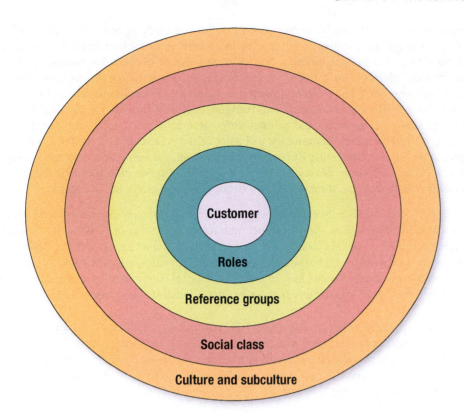

FIGURE 8.7

Group Influences That Influence Buying Decisions Model

To gain additional insights into customers' motivations, it is helpful to study the group influences that affect buying decisions.

SELF-ACTUALIZATION NEEDS Maslow defined the term **self-actualization** as a need for self-fulfillment, a full tapping of one's potential. It is the need to "be all that you can be," to have mastery over what you are doing. Working with customers engaged in the buying decision process to discover the value-added and potential products described in Chapter 7 is an example of them meeting their need for self-fulfillment. Developing a trust-filled problem-solving role with a buyer concerned about finding a long-term, highly ethical, partnering-style salesperson is another example of fulfilling the buyer's need for self-actualization.

The five-level need priority model developed by Maslow is somewhat artificial in certain instances. Many times several of these needs are interacting together during a sale. One example is the business lunch. Not only are you conducting business with a client, but you are also satisfying physiological needs for food and beverages, for engaging in social activities, and perhaps for feeling important in your own eyes and—you hope—in the eyes of your customer. The model also provides salespeople with a practical way of understanding which need is most likely to dominate customer behavior in different buying situations.

Group Influences That Affect Buying Decisions

As noted earlier, the people around us also influence our buying decisions. These **group influences** can be grouped into four major areas: (1) roles, (2) reference groups, (3) social class, and (4) culture and subculture.[37] (See Figure 8.7.) Salespeople who understand these roles and influences can develop the type of insight customers view as being valuable.

ROLE INFLUENCE Throughout our lives, we occupy positions within groups, organizations, and institutions. Closely associated with each position is a **role**: a set of characteristics and expected social behaviors based on the expectations of others. All the roles we assume (student, member of the school board, or position held at work) influence not only our general behavior but also our buying behavior. In today's society, for example, a woman may assume the role of mother at home and purchasing manager at work. In the manager's role, she may feel the need to develop a conservative wardrobe, enroll in a leadership-training course, or join a professional association. These various roles can play an important part in motivating certain buying decisions.

REFERENCE GROUP INFLUENCE A **reference group** consists of the categories of people that you see yourself belonging to, and with which you habitually compare yourself. The popular four-generation model—the matures, baby boomers, generation Xers and millenials—provides an excellent example representing influences of the members of each of these age categories. Not understanding their influences often destroys some aspect of the sales process leading to a successful sale. Members of a reference group tend to influence the values, attitudes, and behaviors of one another.[38] The reference group may act as a point of comparison and a source of information for the individual member.[39] For example, Pi Sigma Epsilon, the national fraternity in marketing, sales management, and selling, may serve as a reference group for a college business major. In the business community, a chapter of the American Society for Training and Development, or Sales & Marketing Executives International, may provide a reference group for its members. As members of a reference group, clients often observe other people in the group to establish their own norms, and these norms can strongly affect purchasing decisions.

SOCIAL CLASS INFLUENCE **Social classes** are society's relatively permanent and ordered divisions whose members share similar values, interests, and behavior.[40] The criteria used to rank people according to social class vary from one society to another. In some societies, land ownership allows entry into a higher social class. In other societies, education is a major key to achieving upper-class status. Social class, in most cases, is not determined by a single factor. It is determined by a combination of factors such as income, education, occupation, and accumulated wealth.

Social class can have a major influence in B2C purchasing situations. The purchase of consumer products such as homes, cars, vacations, and clothing are heavily influenced by social class membership. A home may be purchased as a vacation home or a primary residence depending on the buyer's social class. A new Ferrari will likely be purchased by a different social class member than a Chevrolet Cruze.

CULTURE AND SUBCULTURE INFLUENCE **Culture** can be defined as the accumulation of values, rules of behavior, forms of expression, religious beliefs, transmitted behavior patterns, and the like for a group of people who share a common language and environment. Culture tends to encourage or discourage particular behaviors and mental processes.[41] We maintain and transmit our culture chiefly through language. Culture has considerable influence on buying behavior. Today, culture is getting more attention because of the rapid increases in immigrant groups. As cultural diversity increases, companies must reexamine their sales and marketing strategies.

Within most cultures are groups whose members share value systems based on common life experiences and situations. We call such a group a **subculture**. Some subcultures, such as mature consumers, Hispanic, African American, and generation Y (born between 1977 and 1994), make up important market segments.[42] These subcultures need to be understood by salespeople because they can significantly affect customer-buying behavior.

Perception—How Customer Needs Are Formed

Perception is the process through which sensations are interpreted, using our knowledge and experience. These sensations are received through sight, hearing, touch, taste, and smell. Buyer behavior is often influenced by perception.[43] When Volkswagen announced that it would build an ultraluxury car selling for $70,000, many people questioned the merits of this decision. Could the maker of the Beetle and Thing compete in the market segment dominated by Lexus, Mercedes-Benz, Jaguar, and BMW?

MANAGING MULTIPLE CONTACTS WITH CRM

Salespeople often find that groups of their contacts have common interests and buying motives. Customers and prospects may be segmented into groups by buying influences, by the products they purchase, by the industries they are involved in, or by their size. **Customer relationship management (CRM)** software such as Capsule CRM helps manage contacts by setting up tags for categories, sorting, duplicate contacts management, etc. CRM software can enable the salesperson to easily link contacts together as groups and "mass produce" information that appears custom-fitted to the need of each person in a specific group. For example, each owner of a specific product may receive a telephone call, personalized letter, or report that describes the benefits of a new design feature available from the salesperson.

Sales globally of the Volkswagen Phaeton ended in 2016 even though most automobile journalists viewed it as a true luxury car.[44] Is perception the barrier to sales growth?

We tend to screen out or modify stimuli, a process known as "selective attention," for two reasons. First, we cannot possibly be conscious of all inputs at one time. Just the commercial messages we see and hear each day are enough to cause sensory overload. Second, we are conditioned by our social and cultural backgrounds, and our physical and psychological needs, to use selectivity.

Buyers may screen out or modify information presented by a salesperson if it conflicts with their previously learned attitudes or beliefs. The business buyer who feels the new office furniture designs that combine individual workspace will only encourage impromptu employee chitchat is apt to use selective attention when the salesperson begins discussing product features. Salespeople who can anticipate this problem of selective attention should acquire as much background information as possible before meeting with the prospect. During the first meeting with the customer, the salesperson should make every effort to build a strong relationship so that the person opens up and freely discusses personal perceptions. Salespeople who do this have accepted one of the great truisms in sales and marketing: "Facts are negotiable. Perception is rock solid."

Buying Motives

Every buying decision has a motive behind it. A **buying motive** can be thought of as an aroused need, drive, or desire. This motive acts as a force that stimulates behavior intended to satisfy the aroused need. Our perceptions influence or shape this behavior. An understanding of buying motives provides the salesperson with the reasons why customers buy. Unfortunately, some buyers will not or cannot tell you their buying motives. A company may be planning a new product launch and wants to keep this initiative a secret. In some cases, revealing important information may make the customer feel vulnerable. And, some customers may not be aware of one or more buying motives that will influence the purchase decision.[45]

As you might expect, many buying decisions are influenced by more than one buying motive. The buyer of catering services may want food of exceptional quality served quickly so all her guests can eat together. This customer also may be quite price conscious. In this situation, the caterer should attempt to discover the *dominant buying motive* (DBM). The DBM may have the greatest influence on the buying decision.[46] If the customer is eager to make a good impression on guests who have discriminating food tastes, then food quality may be the dominant buying motive.

Successful salespeople have adopted a product strategy that involves discovery of the buying motives that influence the purchase decision. In Chapter 10, we describe a need identification process that can be used to discover the customer's buying motives.

EMOTIONAL VERSUS RATIONAL BUYING MOTIVES A careful study of buyer behavior reveals that people make buying decisions based on both emotional and rational buying motives. An **emotional buying motive** is one that prompts the prospect to act because of an appeal to some sentiment or passion. When customers buy expensive Harley-Davidson motorcycles, they are paying for much more than a high-flying hog. They are purchasing entry into a community of like-minded enthusiasts who share a passion for all things Harley.[47] Emotions can be powerful and often serve as the foundation of the dominant buying motive.[48] A **rational buying motive** usually appeals to the prospect's reason or judgment based on objective thought processes. Some common rational buying motives include profit potential, quality of service, and availability of technical assistance.

EMOTIONAL BUYING MOTIVES A surprising number of purchases are guided by emotional buying motives. Recent research indicates that buying is a lot more emotional than most marketers thought. Many buyers are guided more by feelings than by logic.[49] Even technology firms sometimes rely on emotional appeals as part of their marketing strategy. Doing business in America, or anyplace else in the world, is never purely a rational or logical process. Recognize that there is an emotional component to every sale and tune in to the emotional cues such as body language, tone of voice, and emotive words. With the power of empathy you can get on the same page, emotionally, as your customer.[50] Consumer buying behavior may be primarily motivated by emotional buying motives; however, in high-dollar purchasing decisions, rational decision making may be a barrier as the buyer considers the cost/benefit of a purchase.

Selling NASCAR in Manhattan

NASCAR is one of America's most popular sports. This form of auto racing, with deep roots in the South, is attracting fans throughout the nation. About 40 million people consider themselves avid fans. Although NASCAR TV ratings are very high and races are frequently sold out, someone still needs to sell this product to team sponsors. Brett Yormark is a corporate sales representative representing NASCAR in New York City. It now costs $10–$14 million to sponsor a top team, so he is a key member of the NASCAR sales and marketing team. Yormark faces major challenges because he is selling stock car racing to an upscale, urban crowd. Many of his prospects are corporate executives who have never seen a NASCAR race.[b]

Source: KRT/Newscom

RATIONAL BUYING MOTIVES A purchase based on rational buying motives is generally the result of an objective review of available information. The buyer closely examines product or service information with an attitude that is relatively free of emotion. Business buyers are most likely to be motivated by rational buying motives such as on-time delivery, financial gain, competent installation, saving of time, increased profits, or durability.

Business buyers representing large firms such as Ford Motor Company, IBM, and General Electric rely on a buying process that is more formalized than the consumer buying process. Purchases made by these companies usually call for detailed product specifications, written purchase orders, and formal approval. The business buyer and the salesperson work closely during all stages of the buying process that begins with a precise definition of the customer's problem. Salespeople who sell to business buyers spend a great deal of time gathering, interpreting, and disseminating customer-specific information.[51] It is important to recognize business buyers also use emotional decision making, deciding in many cases if they like the salesperson with whom they will be working. A value-added relationship strategy is important in these situations.

PATRONAGE VERSUS PRODUCT BUYING MOTIVES Another way to help explain buyer behavior is to distinguish between patronage and product buying motives. Patronage buying motives and product buying motives are learned reasons for buying. These buying motives are important because they can stimulate repeat business and referrals.

Strategic Initiatives Identified	Need Awareness	Evaluation of Solutions	Resolution of Problems	Purchase	Implementation
Present and/or design unique strengths that fit the strategic initiative.	Partner with customers to understand unique needs in new and improved ways.	Configure or adapt superior solutions to unique needs.	Provide assistance and advice to overcome problems and provide solutions.	Adapt and suggest effective methods to purchase and enjoy solutions.	Assist and/or train customers in maximum satisfaction from purchase.

FIGURE 8.8

Creating Value Throughout the Buying Process Model

A sample list of methods for creating value throughout each of the steps in the buying process. Specific methods should be created after arriving at a careful understanding of the unique needs of the individual customer.

Different Business Buying Processes in Different Cultures

Going global? If so, remember that your business customer might have different ways of getting back to you in their buying process, based on the country they come from.

- The Japanese decision-making process is a total group process with all levels involved in the final decision.
- The Chinese one is usually a group process headed by a senior negotiator.
- For Germans, even the most routine decisions are made by the top-level management.

Also, remember that:

- Chinese discussions are long and repetitive and everything should be written down.
- For Latin Americans, socialization and relationship building come before negotiations.
- Germans are very systematic, with great emphasis on details.[c]

PATRONAGE BUYING MOTIVES A **patronage buying motive** is one that causes the prospect to buy products from one particular business. The prospect has had prior direct or indirect contact with the business and has judged this contact to be beneficial. In those situations where there is little or no appreciable difference between two products, patronage motives can be highly important. At a time when look-alike products are very common, these motives take on a new degree of importance. Some typical patronage buying motives are superior service, complete selection of products, competence of sales representatives, and ability to buy online.

PRODUCT BUYING MOTIVES A **product buying motive** is one that leads a prospect to purchase one product in preference to another. Interestingly enough, this decision is sometimes made without direct comparison between competing products. The buyer simply believes that one product is superior to another. There are numerous buying motives that trigger prospects to select one product over another. These include brand preference, quality preference, price preference, and design or engineering preference.

It is hard to imagine how salespeople can create values for customers without first understanding the latter's buying motives. Figure 8.8 provides various examples of how salespeople can put this understanding into creating values at different stages of the buying process.

To fully understand the customer's buying strategy, the salesperson must conduct a careful needs discovery or assessment. This is done by asking appropriate questions, listening to the customer's responses, and making careful observations. Chapter 11 provides in-depth coverage of these important adaptive selling skills.

Source: Goodluz/Shutterstock

CHAPTER LEARNING ACTIVITIES

Reviewing Key Concepts

Discuss the meaning of a customer strategy

The importance of developing a customer strategy was introduced in this chapter. This type of planning is necessary to ensure maximum customer responsiveness. Buying procedures and policies can vary greatly from one buyer to another. If a salesperson does not learn how the buyer plans to make the purchase, then there is the strong possibility that the selling process will be out of alignment with the customer's buying process.

Explain the difference between consumer and business buyers

Business buyer behavior was compared to consumer buyer behavior. Three types of business buying situations were described: straight rebuy, new-task buy, and the modified rebuy. Systems selling, a common business buying strategy, was also described. Three types of consumer buying situations were defined: habitual buying decisions, variety-seeking buying decisions, and complex buying decisions.

Understand the importance of alignment between the selling process and the customer's buying process

Customers make buying decisions in many ways, so it would be inappropriate to view the buying process as a uniform pattern of decision making. However, there is a common decision-making model that most buyers apply to their unique circumstances. The typical stages in the buying decision process are needs awareness, evaluation of solutions, resolution of problems, purchase, and implementation.

Understand the buying process of the transactional, consultative, and strategic alliance buyer

Three value-creation selling approaches that appeal to certain types of customers were discussed: the transactional process buyer, the consultative process buyer, and the strategic alliance process buyer. The consultative process buyer offers the greatest challenge to most salespeople.

Discuss the various influences that shape customer-buying decisions

We noted that buyer behavior is influenced in part by individual (physical and psychological) needs. Maslow's popular model ranks these needs. There is also a number of group influences that shape our psychological needs to various degrees. Buyer behavior is influenced by the roles we assume, reference groups, social class, and culture. "Perception" was defined as the process of selecting, organizing, and interpreting information inputs to produce meaning. We discussed emotional and rational buying motives and compared patronage and product motives.

Key Terms

Customer strategy, p. 155
Consumer buyer
  behavior, p. 156
Business buyer behavior,
  p. 156
Buying center, p. 156
New-task buy, p. 157
Straight rebuy, p. 157
Modified rebuy, p. 158
Systems selling, p. 158
Habitual buying
  decisions, p. 158

Variety-seeking buying
  decisions, p. 158
Complex buying
  decisions, p. 158
Buying process, p. 159
Buyer resolution theory, p. 162
Physiological needs, p. 163
Security needs, p. 163
Social needs, p. 164
Esteem needs, p. 164
Self-actualization, p. 165
Group influences, p. 165

Role, p. 165
Reference group, p. 165
Social classes, p. 166
Culture, p. 166
Subculture, p. 166
Buying motive, p. 167
Emotional buying motive,
  p. 167
Rational buying motive, p. 167
Patronage buying motive,
  p. 169
Product buying motive, p. 169

> ## MyMarketingLab
> To complete the problems with the ⭐ in your MyLab, go to the EOC Discussion Questions.

Review Questions

8-1 According to the Strategic/Consultative–Selling Model, what are the three prescriptions for the development of a successful customer strategy?

8-2 List and describe the three most common types of organizational buying situations.

8-3 Describe the five major stages in the typical buying process.

8-4 List and describe three value-creation selling approaches that appeal to various types of customers.

8-5 According to the buyer resolution theory, a purchase is made only after the prospect has made five buying decisions. What are they?

⭐ **8-6** Explain how Maslow's hierarchy of needs affects buyer behavior.

8-7 Describe the four group influences that affect buyer behavior.

⭐ **8-8** What is meant by the term "perception"?

⭐ **8-9** J. D. Power, founder of J.D. Power and Associates, says, "We define quality as what the customer wants." Do you agree or disagree with his observations? Explain your answer.

Application Exercises

8-10 Select several advertisements from a trade magazine. Analyze each one and determine what rational buying motives the advertiser is appealing to. Do any of these advertisements appeal to emotional buying motives? Then select a magazine that is aimed at a particular consumer group, for example *Architectural Digest*, *Redbook*, or *Better Homes and Gardens*. Study the advertisements and determine what buying motives they appeal to.

8-11 J.D. Power and Associates is a global marketing information services firm that helps businesses and consumers make better decisions through credible, customer-based information. The company provides an unbiased source of marketing information based on opinions of consumers. Visit www.jdpower.com and become familiar with the type of information services offered.

Role-Play Exercise

 In this role-play, you will assume the role of a salesperson working at a Brooks Brothers clothing store. The inventory includes a wide range of business professional clothing such as suits, sport coats, dress shirts, and accessories; the store also offers a full range of business casual clothing. A member of your class will assume the role of a customer who visits your store for the purpose of buying clothing for work. He recently graduated from college and will start work at a new job in about two weeks. In addition to clothing, your store offers complete alteration services and credit plans. During the role-play, you should develop a relationship with the customer using strategies discussed in previous chapters and determine the customer's needs with questions, attentive listening, and observation.

Reality Selling Video Case Problem— Ashley Pineda/PulteGroup

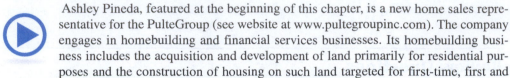

Ashley Pineda, featured at the beginning of this chapter, is a new home sales representative for the PulteGroup (see website at www.pultegroupinc.com). The company engages in homebuilding and financial services businesses. Its homebuilding business includes the acquisition and development of land primarily for residential purposes and the construction of housing on such land targeted for first-time, first and second move-up, and active-adult home buyers. Its homebuilding operations offered homes for sale in 842 communities. The company's financial services business consists of mortgage banking and title operations. It arranges financing through the origination of mortgage loans for its homebuyers, sells such loans and the related servicing rights, provides title insurance policies as an agent, and provides examination and closing services to its home buyers. PulteGroup offers a one-stop shopping experience for prospective customers. Sales reps help clients to finance their homes (with Pulte Mortgage) and to close their homes with PGP Title. One of PulteGroup's key strengths is the ability to provide customers with an exceptional home-buying experience and, ultimately, satisfaction with their homes. Being able to offer everything under one roof and walk the customers through each step of the entire home-buying process makes their experience very comfortable.

Ashley Pineda sells the company's Centex product line, which is primarily geared toward first-time homebuyers by delivering quality homes at an affordable price. Ashley describes a typical selling process as follows: When a customer walks in the door, she engages them by welcoming them and building rapport. The company provides its sales reps with a consultative questioning strategy that allows the reps to smoothly walk the customer through the buying process. For example, the reps may ask the customers about their location preferences or what they consider most important when they buy a home. Ashley asks these types of questions to help her guide first-time home buyers through the variety of different homes available, ranging from one- to two-story homes, from three to five bedrooms, from 1,183 to 2,600 square feet, and a price range from $145,000 to $220,000. Across various options, the customers are asked how well the different options align with their needs and wants.

The customers are also given the opportunity to touch and feel their future homes. This process typically involves a car tour through the neighborhood, where they are shown the different homes' features and colors, and walk-throughs of both completed homes and homes under construction. The latter type helps to demonstrate the quality of Pulte's workmanship, the insulation, and the energy efficiency of a home. Altogether, this allows potential customers to feel comfortable with the construction of the homes and the home-buying process.

In the next step, Ashley typically talks about financing issues with first-time home-buyers such as the amounts of their monthly payments and potential down payments. PulteGroup equips Ashley with the knowledge to be able to professionally provide that information and make customers feel comfortable with the financial scenario involved in owning their first home. Once comfortable with the financial scenario, Ashley and her customers can move forward toward opening the agreement to buy a home. Generally, when you sign a contract, you are opening the agreement to take the next steps. These steps include financing, completing construction, and ultimately closing on the home and moving in. That entire process typically lasts from 45 days to approximately four months. (See the chapter opener and Reality Selling Today Role-Play 6 in Appendix 1 for more information.)

Questions

8-12   Which of the prescriptions of the Strategic/Consultative–Selling Model (see Figure 8.8) does Ashley Pineda follow? Please explain.

8-13   How does Ashley elicit the needs and preferences of the prospective customers? What questions does she ask?

8-14   Outline a typical buying process that a middle-class couple with two young kids goes through in a first-time home buy. What questions and problems might arise at different stages of the buying process?

8-15   What might be key influencing factors for the couple's home-buying decisions? To what extent are rational and emotional buying motives important?

8-16   Put yourself in the position of Ashley Pineda. How can she create value at different stages of the young couple's buying process? Give examples.

8-17   Ashley sells new homes in the company's Centex product line, which is primarily geared toward first-time homebuyers. One of her job responsibilities is to monitor competition. Who might be direct and indirect competitors whom Ashley should watch?

MyMarketingLab

Go to the Assignments section of your MyLab to complete these writing exercises.

8-18   The greatest challenge to salespeople in the age of information is to understand realized and unrealized needs and improve responsiveness to customers. Describe how salespersons add value with a customer strategy. How does a customer strategy benefit both customer and salesperson?

8-19   Discuss the importance of understanding aligning the buying process with the sales process. What are the implications of not understanding this alignment?

Developing and Qualifying Prospects and Accounts

Learning Objectives

When you finish reading this chapter, you should be able to

9.1 Discuss the importance of developing a prospect or account

9.2 Identify and assess important sources of prospects and accounts

9.3 Describe criteria for qualifying prospects and accounts

9.4 Explain common methods of collecting and organizing prospect and account information

9.5 Describe the steps in managing the prospect or account list

Source: Michael Ahearne

▶ Reality Selling Video Series—Dave Levitt/Salesforce.com

Salesforce.com offers hosted applications that manage customer information for sales, marketing, and customer support, providing clients with a rapidly deployable alternative to buying and maintaining enterprise software. The company's applications are used by approximately 80,000 clients for generating sales leads, maintaining customer information, and tracking customer interactions. Dave Levitt (pictured above) joined Salesforce.com as a regional sales manager, leading a team of six sales representatives.

With prior experience as a direct salesperson in the enterprise software industry, Levitt has profound knowledge about how to prospect, approach and qualify prospects in his business. For his sales representatives, there are various ways to build a prospect database: Some prospects will inquire at the company's website, and that will be forwarded directly to the sales representative so that he/she can follow up. Direct-response advertising, trade shows, or customer referrals can also be important sources of new accounts. Besides having the customers reach out to them, salespeople at Salesforce.com also try to utilize the knowledge on the company's 80,000 customers. For example, if the sales representative has a chemical company as one of his prospects, he/she will take a look at the CRM system and ask: What other chemical companies are current customers, and how did they benefit from using our services? Then the representative could use referral selling and thus demonstrate credibility with the prospect.

According to Dave Levitt, the key to successful selling is empathy; that is, the ability to understand the customer's business so that the sales representative can identify areas where he can add value. Levitt points out: "We cannot count on the customer to know what we offer, because our services can be applied in many different ways. The burden is on the sales representative to use his industry and product knowledge to probe and uncover opportunities, and then to qualify and pursue them accordingly." Hence, the salesperson has to be able to look at accounts holistically, understand what the real business drivers are at a company, and then apply Salesforce.com's service solutions in different areas. ●

Account-based software vendors such as Salesforce.com, NetSuite, and Oracle Siebel are helping companies develop effective **customer relationship management (CRM)** systems. These systems are at the heart of every successful one-to-one marketing initiative.

Prospecting and Account Development— an Introduction

Gerhard Gschwandtner, publisher of *Selling Power*, says, "The main purpose of a salesperson is not to make sales, but to create customers."[1] Identifying and developing potential customers is an important aspect of the customer strategy. In the terminology of personal selling, this process is often referred to as **prospecting** in Business-to-Consumer (B2C) selling. In Business-to-Business (B2B), this process is often referred to as **account or business development**. Throughout this chapter, we will use these terms interchangeably. A potential **prospect** or account is an individual or business who meets the qualification criteria established by you or your company.

Some B2B companies employ account or business development representatives (Figure 9.1) whose primary responsibility is to locate and establish account relationships and then turn them over to a strategic account manager or the field sales organization.[2] The account manager or members of the field sales organization then manages the entire sales process through to a successful conclusion, including closing and servicing the sale.

Finding prospects and accounts who can make the purchase is not as easy as it sounds. This is especially true in business-to-business sales. In many situations, the salesperson must make the sales presentation to multiple decision makers. One of these decision makers might be the

---

POSITION DESCRIPTION ACCOUNT DEVELOPMENT REPRESENTATIVE

The **Business Development Representative** (BDR) engages with accounts, targeting key and influential contacts. The BDR will be responsible for qualifying opportunities and staging initial sales meetings for the field sales organization.

Primary Responsibilities
- Drive sales opportunities by staging introductory sales meetings, product demonstrations, and on-site meetings for the field sales organization.
- Work an assigned enterprise account list; proactively identify revenue-generating customers via e-mail campaigns and outbound phone calls.
- Perform pre-call planning including, but not limited to, researching accounts, identifying key influencers and decision makers, formulating initial sales plan of action, etc.
- Maintain and manage the SFDC database, including comprehensive data entry, precise follow-up planning, lead and opportunity tracking, pipeline reporting, etc.
- Collaborate with marketing, support, sales management, product management and account management to maintain an effective level of prospecting activity and pipeline growth.

Required Skills/Experience
- Degree required
- Minimum 2 years B2B enterprise account development experience
- Strong communication skills; ability to establish rapport with customers quickly
- Experience meeting/exceeding prospecting goals and account development metrics
- Microsoft Office and Customer Relationship Management (CRM) skills

FIGURE 9.1

The Account or Business Development Representative (ADR) Position Description

Account or Business Development Representatives in Business-to-Business (B2B) selling are responsible for engaging with key influential contacts and qualifying sales opportunities.

technical expert who wants an answer to the question: "Does the product meet the company's specifications?" Another decision maker may be the person who will actually use the product. The employee who will use the forklift truck you are selling may be involved in the purchase decision. Of course, there is often a "purse-string" decision maker who has the ultimate authority to release funds for the purchase. During periods of economic uncertainty, the decision-making process often moves upward. It is sometimes difficult to make connections with upper-level executives. One solution is to plan a joint sales call involving a higher-level executive from your company.[3]

The goal of prospecting is to build a qualified **prospect base** made up of current customers and potential customers. Building a large prospect base involves the use of CRM software to monitor movement of the customer through the sales process. Many successful companies find that current customers account for a large percentage of their sales. Every effort is made to devise and implement a customer strategy that builds, fosters, nurtures, and extends relationships with established customers. CRM software is critical to building this kind of partnership with a large customer base.[4]

Importance of Prospecting and Account Development

Every salesperson must cope with customer attrition; that is, the inevitable loss of customers over a period of time, which can be attributed to a variety of causes. Unless new prospects are found to replace lost customers, a salesperson eventually faces a reduction in income and possible loss of employment.

To better understand the significance of prospecting, let us examine a few common causes of customer attrition.

The account may have a one-time need or there is an extended period of time between purchases. Because of this, Coldwell Banker Richard Ellis's Susana Rosas realizes new prospects for commercial real estate must be continually added to her prospect base.

The customer may move to a new location outside the salesperson's territory. The American population is very mobile. This cause of attrition is especially common in the retail and service areas and is a major issue experienced by Tom James Company's Alex Homer with many of his successful upwardly mobile clients.

A firm may go out of business or merge with another company. In some areas of business, the failure rate is quite high. In recent years, we have witnessed a record number of mergers that have caused massive changes in purchasing plans.

A loyal buyer or purchasing agent may leave the position because of promotion, retirement, resignation, or serious illness. The replacement may prefer to buy from someone else.

Sales are lost to the competition. In some cases, the competition offers more value. The added value may take the form of better quality, a better price, a stronger relationship, better service, or some combination of these factors.

A company or salespersons want to grow and increase the size of their business. Many companies and individuals want to increase their profits of income. With this objective, they will often develop strategic plans to develop more accounts and prospects.

Some studies reveal that the average company loses 15 to 20 percent of its customers every year. Depending on the type of selling, this figure might be higher or lower. It becomes clear that many customers are lost for reasons beyond the salespersons' control. If salespeople want to keep their earnings at a stable level, they need to develop new customers.

Joe Girard, once recognized by the *Guinness Book of Records* as the world's greatest salesperson, used the "Ferris wheel" concept to illustrate the relationship between prospecting and loss of customers due to attrition.[5] As people get off the Ferris wheel, the operator fills their seats one at a time, moves the wheel a little, and continues this process until all the original riders have left the wheel and new ones come aboard (Figure 9.2). In reality, of course, established customers do not come and go this fast. With the passing of time, however, many customers must be replaced.

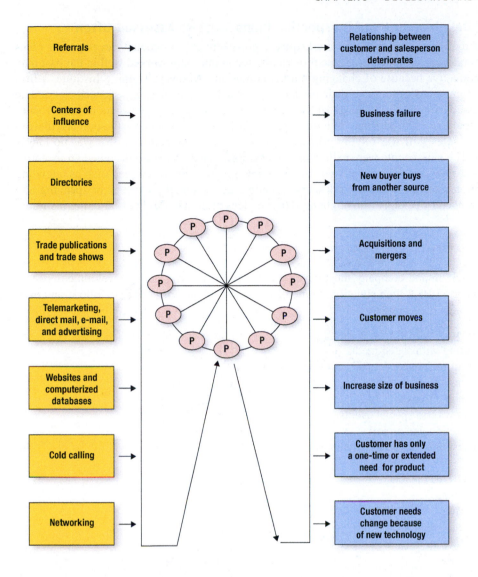

FIGURE 9.2

"Ferris Wheel" Model

The "Ferris wheel" concept, which is aimed at supplying an ongoing list of prospects, is part of world-sales record-holder Joe Girard's customer strategy.

Prospecting and Account Development Requires Planning

9.1 Discuss the importance of developing a prospect or account

Prospecting and account development should be viewed as a systematic process of locating potential customers. Some prospecting efforts can be integrated easily into a regular sales call. Progressive marketers are doing three things to improve the quality of the prospecting effort:

1. *Increase the number of people or accounts who board the Ferris wheel.* You want to see a continuous number of potential prospects board the Ferris wheel because they are the source of sales opportunities. If the number of potential prospects declines sharply, the number of sales closed also declines.

2. *Improve the quality of the prospects who board the Ferris wheel.* Companies often establish quality standards that ensure a steady supply of prospects with high-profit potential. For example, some companies focus their prospecting efforts on consultative process buyers. These are prospects who often lack need awareness and need help evaluating possible solutions.

3. *Shorten the sales cycle by quickly determining which of the new prospects are qualified prospects—qualified as to need, authority to buy, ability to pay, and authority to purchase the product.* Gerhard Gschwandtner says, "Time is the ultimate scorekeeper in the game of selling." He points out that many salespeople do not meet their sales goals because they do not quickly qualify new prospects.[6] Later in this chapter, we examine qualifying practices and discuss how to shorten the sales cycle with sales automation methods.

Account Development and Prospecting Plans Must Be Assessed Often

In today's dynamic, ever-changing marketplace, prospecting and account development plans must be monitored continuously. Some prospecting techniques that worked well in the past may become ineffective because of changing market conditions. Midwest Training Institute, a firm that helps companies to improve their production and sales efficiency, experienced a dramatic sales decline during the first quarter of the year. This decline came after years of steady sales increases. Joel Pecoraro, president of the company, initiated a thorough investigation and discovered that his sales staff was relying primarily on one prospecting approach that was no longer successful: The salespeople were calling established customers. Pecoraro designed an incentive program that rewarded salespeople who adopted new prospecting techniques such as attending an association meeting where the salesperson could meet potential prospects, or speaking at a meeting attended by persons who might need the services offered by Midwest Training Institute.[7]

9.2 Identify and assess important sources of prospects and accounts

Sources of Prospects and Accounts

Every salesperson and company must develop a prospecting and account development system suited to a particular selling situation. Some of the many sources of prospects follow, and each should be carefully examined:

Referrals
Prospecting with social media
Centers of influence, friends, and family members
Directories
Trade publications
Trade shows and special events
Telemarketing and e-mail
Direct-response advertising and sales letters
Website
Computerized database
Cold calling
Networking
Educational seminars
Prospecting by nonsales employees

Your request for referrals is more likely to receive a positive response if made after you have built a strong trusting relationship. In most cases referral leads result in higher close rates, larger sales, and shorter sales cycles.

Source: suhendri/Shutterstock

Referrals

The use of referrals as an account development approach has been used successfully in a wide range of selling situations. In most cases, referral leads result in higher close rates, larger sales, and shorter sales cycles. A **referral** is a prospect that has been recommended by a current customer or by someone who is familiar with the product. Satisfied customers, business acquaintances, and even prospects who do not buy often can recommend the names of persons who might benefit from purchasing the product.

When you build value into your sales process, you increase the odds that the customer will give you a referral. Steve Lewis, managing partner of New England Financial, says, "Our attitude is that we can't ask for referrals until clients have perceived value in the process."[8]

ENDLESS CHAIN REFERRALS The endless chain approach to obtaining referrals is easy to use because it fits naturally into most sales presentations. A salesperson selling long-term healthcare insurance might say, "Miss Remano, whom do you know who might be interested in our insurance plan?" This open-ended question gives the person the freedom to recommend several prospects and is less likely to be answered with a no response. Be sure to use your reference's name when you contact the new prospect—"Mary Remano suggested that I call you…."

REFERRAL LETTERS AND CARDS The referral letter method is a variation of the endless chain technique. In addition to requesting the names of prospects, the salesperson asks the customer to prepare a note or letter of introduction that can be delivered to the potential customer. The correspondence is an actual testimonial prepared by a satisfied customer. Some companies use a referral card to introduce the salesperson. The preprinted card features a place for your customer to sign the new prospect's name and his own name, and can be used as part of the sales presentation.

Within the field of personal selling, there is no complete agreement regarding the timing of the referral request. Some sales training programs encourage salespeople to request the referral immediately after closing the sale. Others point out that if you are working with a new customer, it takes time to earn the customer's trust. The customer may feel there is a risk involved in giving you referrals. Once you have built a strong, trusting relationship with the customer, referral requests are more likely to receive a positive response.[9]

REFERRAL ORGANIZATIONS Some salespeople have found that membership in a referral organization is an effective way to obtain good leads. BNI (Business Network International) is one of the largest business networking organizations with more than 3,600 chapters worldwide (www.bni.com). BNI offers members the opportunity to share ideas, contacts, and referrals.[10] In addition, some local organizations such as breakfast clubs offer referrals as a member benefit.

Centers of Influence, Friends, and Family Members

The center-of-influence method involves establishing a relationship with a well-connected, influential person who is willing to provide prospecting information. This person may not make buying decisions but has influence with other people who do. To illustrate, consider the challenge facing Gary Schneider, creator of a powerful software product that would help small farmers optimize their crop selection. After spending several years developing the product, Schneider and his wife began selling the product one copy at a time. During one cold call on a major crop insurer, American Agrisurance, he met a senior researcher who immediately saw the benefits of the software product. This respected researcher is in a position to influence buying decisions at his company and to provide prospect information for other crop insurers.[12]

SOCIAL MEDIA AND SELLING TODAY

Prospecting with Social Media

Social media provide an excellent opportunity for finding prospects and reaching out to them. For example, LinkedIn offers an advanced search tool which you can use to narrow down your search and find people by company, job function, organizational position, etc. In Twitter, you can use tools such as FollowerWonk, TweetDeck, HootSuite, or SproutSocial to identify users based on the words they use in their bios and their tweets. These tools make it easy to find those users who are tweeting about your products or services or their company. Creating a business page on Facebook is maybe the most straightforward way to get on the radar of your potential customers.

Once you've found prospects on social media, it's extremely important to remember the nature of these media: they are personal networks. Sending cold messages like "we offer shipping solutions that are tailor-made for your particular needs…" is very likely to end up where all unsolicited e-mails and cold prospecting efforts end up, the recycle bin. Instead of spamming people with unwanted messages, focus on building relationships with relevant customers, since relationships are what social media are all about. Joining those circles, groups, and pages that your customers are members of and are relevant to you and your business is one way of starting new relationships. Also a wise use of social media is monitoring what people are saying about your products and joining those conversations. In all of your social media presence, you should always follow the rules of participation in mind: your messages should be relevant, targeted, reasonably expected, and timely.[11]

A person who is new in the field of selling often uses friends and family members as sources of information about potential customers. It is only natural to contact people we know. In many cases, these people have contacts with a wide range of potential buyers.

Directories

Directories can help salespeople search out new accounts and determine their buying potential. A list of some of the more popular national directories is provided next:

Middle Market Directory lists 14,000 firms worth between $500,000 and $1 million (available from Dun & Bradstreet, www.dnb.com).

Standard & Poor's Corporation Records Service provides details on more than 11,000 companies (www.spglobal.com).

Thomas Register of American Manufacturers provides a listing of 60,000 manufacturers by product classifications, addresses, and capital ratings (www.thomasregister.com).

Polk City Directory provides detailed information on the citizens of a specific community. Polk, in business for more than 125 years, publishes about 1,100 directories covering 6,500 communities in the United States and Canada (www.citydirectory.com).

The Encyclopedia of Associations lists more than 23,000 U.S. associations and more than 20,000 international organizations with details on membership, publications, and conferences (www.gale.com).

These are just a few of the better-known directories. There are hundreds of additional directories covering business and industrial firms on the regional, state, and local levels. Some directories are free, whereas others must be purchased at a nominal fee. One of the most useful free sources of information is the telephone directory. Most telephone directories have a classified (yellow pages) section that groups businesses and professions by category. Web Yellow Pages (www.bigyellow.com) provides more than 11 million U.S. business listings.

Trade Publications

Trade publications provide a status report on every major industry. If you are a sales representative employed by SuperValu Stores, Fleming Companies Inc., Sysco Corporation, or one of the other huge, food-wholesaling houses that supply supermarkets, then you can benefit from a monthly review of *Progressive Grocer* magazine. Each month, this trade publication reports on trends in the retail food industry, new products, problems, innovations, and related information. Trade journals such as *Institutional Distribution, Home Furnishings, Hardware Retailer, Modern Tire Dealer,* and *Progressive Architecture* are examples of publications that might help salespeople identify prospects.

Trade Shows and Special Events

A trade show is a large exhibit of products that are, in most cases, common to one industry, such as electronics or office equipment. The prospects walk into the booth or exhibit and talk with those who represent the exhibitor. In some cases, sales personnel invite existing customers and prospects to attend trade shows so they can have an opportunity to demonstrate their newest products.

SELLING IN ACTION

Account Development with Your Partners

When Megan Michael sees a new office building going up, she stops her car and makes inquiries about who is to occupy the building. As a sales representative for BKM OfficeWorks, an office furniture supplier in San Diego, she needs to be aware of new office space. However, this approach is not her most important prospecting method. She has found the telephone to be her most effective prospecting tool. Michael speaks regularly with her customers to find out if they know companies that might need BKM's products. Architects, designers, and builders who have previously worked with Michael have proved to be good sources of referrals. The key to her prospecting success is maintaining a strong relationship with her customers. She realizes that you must be an effective partner before you can ask for help.[a]

Bentley Motor Cars invited a number of potential clients to the famous Le Mans 24-hour endurance race. This special event helped the company develop its prospect base.

Source: WENN Ltd/Alamy Stock Photo

Research studies indicate that it is much easier to identify good prospects and actually close sales at a trade show. In most cases, fewer sales calls are needed to close a sale if the prospect was qualified at a trade show. Once a trade show contact is identified and judged to be a qualified lead, information regarding the lead should be carefully recorded. When a prospect enters a Xerox Corporation booth, a salesperson uses a few questions to qualify the lead and types the answers into an on-screen form. Xerox uses software developed by NewLeads on record and process data obtained from prospects who have been qualified by a salesperson working in the booth.[13]

A special event can be a baseball game, golf tournament, reception for a dignitary, or charity event. Bentley Motor Cars invited a number of potential clients to the famous Le Mans 24-hour endurance race. Prospects watched the Bentley race car compete while sipping champagne. Back in America, charity events serve as a venue for cultivating wealthy clientele who can afford a Bentley automobile.[14]

Telemarketing and E-Mail

Telemarketing is the practice of marketing goods and services through telephone contact. It is an integral part of many modern sales and marketing campaigns. One use of telemarketing is to identify prospects. A financial services company used telemarketing to identify prospects for its customized equipment–leasing packages. Leads were given to salespeople for consideration. Telemarketing also can be used to quickly and inexpensively qualify prospects for follow-up. Some marketers use the telephone to verify sales leads generated by direct mail, advertisements, or some other method.

Although the response rate for sales e-mails is quite low, they have proven to be a source of leads for many salespeople. Ideally, sales e-mails should be sent only to existing

Research shows that it is much easier to identify good prospects and actually close sales at a trade show.

Source: George Doyle/Thinkstock/Stockbyte/Getty Images

customers or others who have "opted in" to receive them. When you use *broadcast* e-mails, there is the risk that you will be blocked and end up on a spammer blacklist. Online sales specialist Mac MacIntosh says those who use broadcast e-mails should stay within antispam laws by giving recipients the right to opt out of future e-mails.[15]

Putting your company name in the subject line can help get e-mails opened by prospects who are familiar with it. Some salespeople send newsletters to current and prospective customers. Lee Levitt, director of sales for software consultant IDC, sends a monthly newsletter to current IDC clients and professionals at large technology companies. He wants to expose them to services his company can provide. Levitt says, "The key is to offer something of value they can quickly digest and use in day-to-day work."[16]

Direct-Response Advertising and Sales Letters

Many advertisements invite the reader to send for a free booklet or brochure that provides detailed information about the product or service. In the category of business-to-business marketing, advertising has strong inquiry-generating power. Some firms distribute postage-free response cards (also known as "bingo cards") to potential buyers. Recipients are encouraged to complete and mail the cards if they desire additional information. In some cases, the name of the person making the inquiry is given to a local sales representative for further action.

Sales letters, sent via e-mail or the U.S. postal service, can be incorporated easily into a prospecting plan. The prospecting sales letter is sent to persons who are in a position to make a buying decision. Shortly after mailing the letter (three or four days), the prospect is called and asked for an appointment. The call begins with a reference to the sales letter. To make the letter stand out, some salespeople include product information. As noted in Chapter 6, all sales letters must be written with care. To get results, sales letters must quickly get the reader's attention.

Website

Thousands of companies and businesspeople have established websites on the World Wide Web. A **website** is a collection of Web pages maintained by a single person or organization. It is accessible to anyone with a computer and a modem. Large firms, such as Century 21, maintain websites that feature numerous Web pages. Websites frequently offer prospects the opportunity to acquire product information that can help them make a buying decision. Financial services companies describe home financing and refinancing options. Salesforce.com's website provides detailed descriptions of Salesforce.com products and solutions. When someone clicks on a Web page and requests information, they will likely become a prospect. Some websites offer an incentive to leave contact information.

Computerized Database

With the aid of electronic data processing, it is often possible to match product features with the needs of potential customers quickly and accurately. In many situations, a firm can develop its own computerized database. In other cases, it is more economical to purchase the database from a company that specializes in the collection of such information. One example, Salesgenie, is offered by infoUSA. With the aid of this software, you can easily obtain lead generation and account

---

CISCO SYSTEM'S GLOBAL CRM SOFTWARE APPLICATION

Cisco has committed to deploying the Salesforce.com CRM solution to 25,000 global users. Salesforce.com provides Cisco with effective prospect management tools, such as dashboards, account planning tools, and reports regarding partner relationships.

- Dashboards track metrics such as opportunities, lead conversion rates, number of account plans, and top accounts for sales representatives and managers. Salespeople can create their own reports to chart their progress.

- Account planning, which had previously been difficult to manage on a worldwide basis, is increasingly leveraged with Salesforce.com.
- Partners are part of Cisco's customer "eco system." Overall productivity and effectiveness are improved by extending leads to partners, such as resellers, and tracking their conversion to opportunities and ultimately to sales.

selection information for different market segments. Gary Hand, president of USAlarms, LLC needs to keep his sales team supplied with plenty of leads. Salesgenie provides him with a list of prospects by geographical location and by the value of each house. Salesgenie handles these two classifications easily and has therefore become a major time saver.[17] Salesgenie can provide salespeople with leads in such diverse market segments as medical services, engineering, architecture, agriculture, and education.

Another product available from infoUSA, OneSource, provides in-depth prospect information needed by sales personnel involved in complex, long-cycle sales. Let's assume you are part of a sales team that wants to do business with a group of companies that appear to be highly qualified. OneSource will provide data needed to make sales projections for a specific geographic area and industry type. The real strength of OneSource comes in high-value sales where a thorough understanding of prospects is needed for the first sales call.[18]

Most salespeople use CRM software in the development of their prospecting and sales forecasting plan. This software allows the convenient preparation and management of prospect lists.

Source: Fancy Collection/Superstock

With the aid of a personal computer and smartphones, salespeople can develop their own detailed customer files. This means that salespeople can accumulate a great deal of information about individual customers and use this information to personalize the selling process. For example, a PC can help an independent insurance agent maintain a comprehensive record of each policyholder. As the status of each client changes (marriage, birth of children, etc.), the record can be easily updated. With the aid of an up-to-date database, the agent can quickly identify prospects for the various existing and new policy options.

Cold Calling

With products such as Alex Homer's custom clothing line offered by Tom James Company, cold call prospecting is an effective approach to prospect identification. In **cold calling**, salespeople select a group of people they anticipate may become actual prospects and then call (by phone or personal visit) on each one. The sales representative for a wholesale medical supply firm might call on every hospital in a given community, assuming that each one is a potential customer. Many new salespeople must rely on the cold call method because they are less likely to get appointments through referrals.

Edward Jones Corporation, a financial services company, is a strong supporter of cold calling. Sales representatives knock on doors and introduce themselves with a friendly, professional message:

> Hi, my name is Brad Ledwith. I represent the Edward Jones Corporation, and we sell financial services. We're a unique firm because we try to do all of our business face-to-face. I just wanted to stop by and let you know that I've opened up a Jones office in the area and to find out if it's OK to contact you when I have an investment idea.[19]

Sales representatives such as Brad Ledwith connect personally with members of their communities. This kind of cold call opener is often referred to as an **"elevator presentation."** This is a 30-second message that summarizes what you want people to know about you, your company, and your product line. Practicing the elevator speech in front of a mirror can significantly improve its effectiveness.

Successful cold calls do not happen spontaneously. Some strategic thinking and planning must precede personal visits and telephone calls. Whom do you contact? What do you say during the first few seconds?

In order to appear confident and competent, carefully develop your opening remarks. If you appear to be nervous or unprepared, the prospect will assume you lack experience. Many salespeople who make cold call phone calls prepare a well-polished script. The script helps keep you on message and guarantees you will not leave out important information.[20]

Samantha Ettus, CEO of Ettus Media Management, a New York City public relations agency, says cold calls helped her firm land some of its biggest accounts. Ettus does plenty of research before she reaches for the phone. She collects all the pertinent information she can find—memberships and professional affiliations, career history, awards received, and, of course, information regarding the prospect's business. Then she makes the call, which is as brief and precise as possible. Immediately after the call, she sends the prospect a personalized e-mail that summarizes what her firm has to offer. Ettus views the cold call as nothing more than a way to introduce herself and her company to an account.[21]

Networking

One of the most complete books on networking is *Dig Your Well Before You're Thirsty* by Harvey Mackay. He says, "If I had to name the single characteristic shared by all the truly successful people I've met over a lifetime, I'd say it's the ability to create and nurture a network of contacts."[22] Networking skills are of special importance to new salespeople who cannot turn to a large group of satisfied customers for referrals and leads. Professionals (accountants, lawyers, consultants, etc.), entrepreneurs, managerial personnel, and customer service representatives also must develop networking skills. Networking skills are also of critical importance to job seekers because, at any given time, about 80 percent of all available jobs are not posted in the classifieds or on Internet job boards.[23]

In simple terms, **networking** is the art of making and using contacts, or people meeting people and profiting from the connections. Although networking is one of the premier prospecting methods, some salespeople are reluctant to seek referrals in this manner. In addition, many salespeople do not use effective networking practices. Skilled networkers suggest the following guidelines for identifying good referrals:

1. *Meet as many people as you can.* Networking can take place on an airplane, at a Rotary Club meeting, at a trade show, or at a professional association meeting. Don't make the mistake of limiting your networking activities to business contacts. The term **social network** refers to your set of *direct and indirect contacts*. An indirect contact might be the brother of a close friend. The brother works for a large company and can help you see more clearly into the operation of this firm.[24]
2. *When you meet someone, tell the person what you do.* Give your name and describe your position in a way that explains what you do and invites conversation. Instead of saying, "I am in stocks and bonds," say, "I am a financial counselor who helps people make investment decisions." Listen more than you talk. Developing and perfecting an elevator presentation, mentioned earlier, can be very effective when networking.
3. *Do not do business while networking.* It usually is not practical to conduct business while networking. Make a date to call or meet with the new contact later.
4. *Offer your business card.* The business card is especially useful when the contact attempts to tell others about your products or services.
5. *Edit your contacts and follow-up.* You cannot be involved with all your contacts, so separate the productive from the nonproductive. Send a short e-mail message to contacts you deem productive and include business information, brochures—anything that increases visibility.[25] Make sure your materials are professional. Use inexpensive contact management software, such as Salesforce.com, to organize your contact information.

There are three types of networks salespeople should grow and nurture (Figure 9.3). Every salesperson can be well served by networking within his or her organization. You never know when someone in finance, technical support, or shipping may be needed to help solve a problem or provide you with important information. A second form of networking involves establishing contacts inside your industry. Make contact with experts in your field, top performers, leaders, successful company representatives, and even competitors. The third form of networking involves business contacts with people outside of your industry such as bankers, government officials, developers, and other people in your community. The local golf course is frequently a good place to make these contacts.[26]

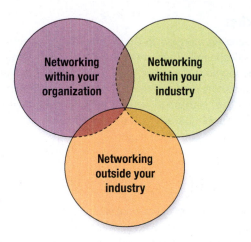

FIGURE 9.3

Networking Model

Top-performing salespeople recognize that networking can take place in three areas.

Educational Seminars

Many salespeople are using educational seminars as a method of identifying prospects. Seminars provide an opportunity to showcase your product without pressuring prospects to buy. Many banks, accounting firms, wine merchants, and consulting companies use seminars to generate new prospects. Previously we mentioned that Edward Jones's sales representatives often make cold calls on prospects. They also schedule seminars that provide prospects with an opportunity to acquire information regarding the potential benefits of investing in a mutual fund. Another popular seminar topic is the benefits of tax-free investing. A complimentary lunch is usually served before the informative presentation. When inviting prospects, be clear about the seminar's content and always deliver what you promise.

Prospecting and Account Development by Nonsales Employees

Should service technicians, receptionists, bank tellers, and other nonsales personnel be involved in prospecting? In a growing number of organizations, the answer is yes. Prospecting does not need to be the exclusive responsibility of the sales force. Janet Dixon, a UPS sales representative, needed help making contact with an important prospect. This person wouldn't take her calls. She talked to the UPS service provider (driver) who called on this account and requested his help. He had serviced this company for years and was like part of the family. He knew the prospect personally and persuaded her to accept a call from the salesperson.[27]

SELLING IN ACTION

Account Development with Seminars

The use of educational seminars has become an important account development method. You can educate prospective customers with brochures, news releases, catalogs, or your website, but educational seminars offer the advantage of face-to-face contact. Barbara Siskind, in her book *Seminars to Build Your Business*, identifies 15 objectives for hosting seminars. A few of the most important ones follow:

Obtain sales leads. This is one of the most common objectives for seminars. You can obtain the names of attendees and arrange appointments for future sales calls. Seminars also may help identify actual product users, technical support people, or engineers who, although they may not be the decision maker, may influence the purchase decision.

Promote your place of business. Your place of business can become a destination for people who might otherwise not consider visiting it. You have an opportunity to create awareness of your company and develop a positive image for your entire operation and its capabilities.

Showcase and demonstrate your expertise. Seminars allow you to show a carefully targeted group of people that you really know your stuff. Salespeople can be supported by technical experts and others in the organization who can address clients' specific concerns.

Polaroid Canada advertised educational seminars across Canada where imaging specialists assisted prospective clients in exploring imaging solutions. Toronto-based Charon Systems, Incorporated, a systems integrator that deploys networks for organizations, regularly organizes seminars for 80 to 100 technology people from midsized firms. President David Fung estimates that 25 percent of prospects become clients.[b]

Combination Approaches

In recent years, we have seen an increase in the number of prospecting and account development approaches used by salespeople. In many cases, success in selling depends on your ability to use a combination of the methods described in this chapter. For example, the large number of prospects identified at a trade show might be used to develop an effective telemarketing program. Prospects are called and an effort is made to set up a personal call. Prospects identified at a trade show or educational seminar might be sent a sales-oriented newsletter, a sales letter, or an e-mail message inviting prospects to visit your Web page.

9.3 Describe criteria for qualifying prospects and accounts

Qualifying Prospects and Accounts

One of the most important keys to success in personal selling is the ability to qualify prospects. **Qualifying** is the process of identifying prospects who appear to have a need for your product and should be contacted. Top salespeople use good research and analysis skills to qualify leads effectively.[28]

The qualifying process is also the first opportunity to consider what the needs of the buyer might be, and how those needs match with the product characteristics being sold.[29] Some sales organizations link the qualifying process with the need discovery step in the consultative sales process. In most cases, this linkage will depend on the nature and complexity of the prospect's buying process. The more complex the buying process, the more likely these two sales functions will be separate steps in the sales process. We will explore fully the need discovery step in Chapter 11.

Every salesperson needs to establish qualifying criteria. The process involves finding answers to several basic questions.

1. *Does the prospect or account have a need for my product?* If you sell imaging or copy products, it might appear that every business firm is a prospect. However, a firm that is outsourcing its copy work to FedEx Kinko's may not be a legitimate prospect.

   Qualifying involves probing for real needs. Let's assume you sell real estate for a large agency. You receive a call from someone who believes that owning a home is a good tax benefit. At this point, it's important to find out what else makes owning a home important for that person. Get permission to ask questions and then determine the person's real needs. In the final analysis, you may decide it would be a waste of your time and the prospect's time to visit several homes that are on the market.[30]

2. *Does the prospect or account have the authority to buy my product?* Ideally, you should talk to an individual who has the authority to buy or can influence the buying decision. Talking to the right person within a large organization may involve collecting information from several sources. Some buying decisions are made by individuals and others are made by a committee. In B2B selling, high-cost products often require the approval of a decision maker higher up in the organization.

3. *Does the account or prospect have the financial resources to buy my product?* It is usually not difficult to obtain credit information for consumer and business buyers. If you are selling products to a business, the *Dun & Bradstreet Reference Book* is an excellent source of credit information. A local credit bureau can provide credit information for a consumer buyer.

   Although the collection of credit information is not difficult, detecting financial instability can be much more complicated. In recent years, we have seen a steady stream of corporate scandals involving accounting irregularities, inflated balance sheets, and outright fraud.[31] Salespeople must be aware of the possibility that a customer may provide incorrect or misleading information.

4. *Does the prospect or account have the willingness to buy my product?* Rick Page, author of *Hope Is Not a Strategy*, reminds us that many prospects evaluate products but do not buy. When an evaluation stalls, the prospect may have determined that the problem is not of great enough magnitude or urgency to make the purchase. Also, in some cases there is not enough support within the company to reach closure. Rather than walk away from this situation, some salespeople move higher in the organization to determine the level of support for the purchase.[32]

A large number of senior executives say they get involved in the sale early in the decision process, yet salespeople have difficulty meeting with high-level decision makers. Most senior executives will not meet with salespeople who are making cold calls. When appointments are granted, the time allocated may be very short; 5 to 10 minutes is not uncommon. How do you establish credibility for yourself and your company in a short time period? Be sure you know a great deal about the company before the appointment and be prepared to demonstrate your knowledge of the company and the industry it serves. Do not propose solutions until you fully understand the buyer's problems. Be sure to communicate value.[33]

This list of questions can be revised to meet the needs of many different types of salespeople. A sales representative for an industrial equipment dealer may see the qualifying process differently from the person who sells commercial real estate. The main consideration is providing accurate answers to each question.

Collecting and Organizing Account and Prospect Information

9.4 Explain common methods of collecting and organizing prospect and account information

The Internet and information revolution continue to make acquiring and managing sales leads much easier.[34] When it comes to collecting and organizing prospect information, salespeople have a large assortment of computer-based systems available. Companies such as Salesforce .com, Oracle, NetSuite, Sage, and Microsoft all offer software applications designed to collect and organize prospect information. Most of these sales force automation (SFA) systems or customer relationship management (CRM) systems, as they are now known, have preset categories or fields that contain sales data on the prospect. This **sales data** is the information seen in most CRM systems, including the contact name, title, address, phone number, e-mail, and so forth. It may also include information about what products have been purchased, what sales opportunities exist in the future, who the various members or influencers are in the buying center, what their preferred communication styles are, past sales and forecasted sales, volume, and percentage change and date of closing the sale. All of the sales data information about a prospect in a CRM system is presented in the account screen report. Figure 9.4 shows an account screen report for Aeroflot Airlines. The information in this report, including any notes about previous sales calls, is accessed and studied before the salesperson makes a sales call.

When bringing new prospects into the database, it is expected that the salesperson will acquire this sales data and enter it into the records kept on the prospect. In most CRM systems, this information goes into a shared database that allows other members of the sales team to access the information and make additions as they work with prospects. In the event a new salesperson takes over an existing prospect database, all of this information can be accessed quickly and used to plan sales strategies to work effectively with prospects.

Sales Intelligence

In addition to collecting sales data, the collection of **sales intelligence** is necessary when the sale is complex and requires a long closing cycle. Sales intelligence goes beyond data, giving salespeople access to insights into the prospects' marketplace, their firm, their competitors, even about the prospects themselves. Sales intelligence is needed today over and above sales data because prospects are looking for insights and knowledge from salespeople above and beyond the product features and benefits. In many buying situations today, prospects using advanced search engines have already learned about features and benefits. In terms of sales intelligence, prospects and accounts expect salespeople to know answers to many of the following questions. Answers to these questions create much of the value that results in successfully turning prospects and accounts into long-term customers:

Do You Know Me? You need to know more than my name and title. Do you know my role, my goals, how I am evaluated, and how long I have been with the organization? Do you know the projects I am working on, my style of doing business, and what the requirements are for me to meet my objectives? Do you know about previous dealings I have had with your company? Do I have a favorable opinion of your company and do you know my role and the role of other influencers in the decision-making process?

Do You Know My Company and My Marketplace? Do you know our company mission statement, culture, and vision for the future? Do you know clearly what we are doing, how

FIGURE 9.4

The CRM Account Report

This account report shows purchasing data for Aeroflot Airlines. Information in both the Contact Screen and Notes Screen, from previous sales calls, was entered by Account Manager Lee Bizon, of NewNet Systems. (For more information on NewNet Systems, see Regional Accounts Management Case Study on p. 395.)

Contact Screen

Account 2: Aeroflot Airlines
Contact: Mr. John Poltava
Phone: 214-555-6113
Fax: 214-555-2856
Title: V.P. Purchasing
Dear: John

Address: 499 Park Avenue
Suite 213
Email: jpolt21@aeroflot.com
City: Dallas
State: TX
ZIP Code: 75201

Last Results: Qualified
ID/Status: Prospect
Firm Size: 3,500 People
Network Now: 10 Novell Systems
Workstations: 2,750
Account Code: Airline

Network Need: WAN
Likelihood: 0.80
Dollar Amount: $75,000
Date Close: 1/31

Notes Screen

11/09: John wants to meet soon. Will have his key people at meeting, including their CFO and CEO. John said new network expenditures should cut costs and enhance their bottom line by 4%. Need Joe to do a needs analysis. Maybe need Charlene also as she is best at the numbers when she does the configuration.

11/02: John is an emotive. Very interested in new network to improve productivity and bottom line. They have a very ambitious company-wide 5-year projection of 12% bottom line after taxes. They need a WAN system that connects their offices in 20 airports and 12 warehouses. Lots of problems including a lack of centralized file sharing and document control, inability for their remote employees to efficiently access and share files with the corporate office and a number of website issues that were causing security concerns. John has been with Aeroflot since '97. He will decide on vendor after his management information systems director chooses a system. John said to call a Mr. Ortega at Southern Motors in Ennis. Ortega, it seems, is in the market now. Sent him a thank you for the Ortega information.

we are performing in the marketplace, what issues keep us up all night, and who and what our competitors are doing? Do you know where we fit into the existing competitive landscape? Are we the leader or are we in the position of having to play catch-up to survive? Can you relate what you sell directly to what we need to accomplish our goals? Do you know who our partners are? What is the effect the current economy has on our business? *Do You Have Any Special Value-Add?* You have a product or service you think we need, but what else can you bring to the table? Are there additional resources you can bring to bear to solve my problems or improve my internal business processes? Can you educate me on how you are truly different from the other players in your area of expertise so I can support my recommendation to work with you? Can you help me build a case for **return on investment (ROI)**?[35]

Answers to these questions come from many sources. CRM suppliers like Salesforce.com, info USA.com, Sales-i.com, and Vecta.net have programs that supply this kind of sales intelligence to companies and salespeople. Salesforce's Radian6, used by more than one-half of the Fortune 500 companies, tracks social media for pertinent information on prospects.[36] Their Data.com product tracks B2B account information and supplies prospect and account information to their subscribers.[37] infoUSA's OneSource is one example of a supplier of sales intelligence. OneSource supplies sales intelligence to Cardinal Logistics Management, a major provider of logistics, transportation, and supply-chain solutions to large retailers, manufacturers, and distribution companies. Cardinal's salespeople must know each account inside and out in order to sell logistics solutions effectively to their 5,000 customers. OneSource supplies 24/7, anywhere access to detailed customer profiles, executive contact data and biographies, financial statements, news trade articles, and analyst reports. A special feature keeps salespeople up-to-date on any and all developments within their customer's company and their industry, including both their customer's customer and their competitors.[38]

Most importantly, this information must be entered into the company's CRM system to get a 360-degree view of the prospect. This information will also be used to move the prospect through the steps in the sales process.

Managing the Account and Prospect Base

9.5 Describe the steps in managing the prospect or account list

High-performing salespeople today are focused on effectively managing sales activities for all prospects in their database (Figure 9.5). This means the size and number of prospects are more carefully considered. Too few prospects in various stages of the sales cycle can quickly signal problems. Alternatively, too many customers can drain a salesperson's resources so that too little effort is focused on prospects with the best opportunities. This is a particular problem when salespeople spend too much effort on prospects that have limited potential. CRM software can help organize customer data into meaningful and easy-to-interpret information.

To effectively and efficiently manage the prospect or account base, sales managers and salespeople often conduct an **account analysis** to estimate the sales potential for each prospect. It is a necessary step before deciding how to allocate sales calls across accounts. The portfolio model and the sales process model are two popular models salespeople use for performing account analysis and deciding how much time and effort, and what sale strategies to use with the contacts in their database.

Portfolio Models

Portfolio models involve the use of multiple factors when classifying accounts. Figure 9.6 illustrates a typical four-cell model based on two factors: overall account opportunity for the seller and the seller's competitive position, that is, the ability to capitalize on these opportunities.[39]

The portfolio model provides an excellent framework to facilitate communication between salespeople and the various sales support personnel. Teamwork at this stage in the sales cycle can develop improved strategies for working successfully with difference accounts and contacts in the account base. Portfolio models are most effective where salespeople must understand individual customer needs and where relationship strength is important to sales success.

NewNet Systems, San Jose Market Prospect/Account/Contact List

Lee Bizon, Account Executive   Casey Arnold, Sales Manager

Account	Contact	Phone	E-Mail
Able Technologies, Inc.	Mr. Bradley J. Able	254-555-1000	bja@able.com
Aeroflot Airlines	Mr. John Poltava	214-555-6113	jpolt21@aeroflot
Southern Motors	Mr. Dwayne Ortega	972-555-4094	d_ortega@btas.com
Bryan Enterprises	Mr. Bill Bryan	214-555-4567	bbryan@bryan.com
Computer Products	Ms. Joanna Barkley	713-555-2345	j_b@yahoo.com
Computerized Labs	Mr. Sam Pearlman	713-555-5454	spman@complabs.com
Designers Associates	Dr. Simon Sayers	972-555-6866	sisa@designers.net
Ellis Enterprises	Mr. Timothy P. Ellis	214-555-1234	tpellis75@mchsi.com
Engineering Software Inc.	Mr. Ian Cortez	214-555-8979	ian@exso.com
General Contractors	Mr. Brian Allan	214-555-2947	brian@gentors.com
International Studios	Mr. Robert G. Kelly	214-555-3456	rgk@internstudio.com
Johnson and Associates	Mr. Ralph Johnson	817-555-3212	rjohnson13@mchsi.com
Lakeside Clinic	Dr. Jeff Gray	214-555-6600	jgray@lakeside.com
Landers Engineering	Ms. Colleen Landers	817-555-6121	clanders@aol.com
Media Conglomerate	Mr. Joe Romera	214-555-9090	Joro@media.com
Mercy Hospital	Ms. Kerri Mathers	214-555-1880	kmathers@mercy.com
Modern Designs	Ms. Cheryl Castro	214-555-1098	ccastro@modes.com
Murray D'Zines	Ms. Karen Murray	817-555-1111	kmuray@dzines.com
Piccadilly Studio	Ms. Judith Albright	214-555-3084	jalbright@Pic.com
Quality Builders	Ms. Sherry Britton	817-555-6886	sherry@qbuild.com

FIGURE 9.5

The Account Base

This CRM record presents a list of accounts for NewNet Systems Account Manager Lee Bizon. Note this list includes the Account Name, Contact Person, Phone Number, and E-Mail Address.

Source: Courtesy of Salesforce.com.

FIGURE 9.6

The Portfolio Model

This portfolio model uses account opportunity (forecasted sales) and competitive position (the ability to capitalize on the opportunity) to classify how much sales effort should be made on individual accounts in the prospect database. Those prospects listed in the strategic accounts cell (high sales forecast and strong position for closing the sale) will receive the largest amount of sales effort, while those in the drag accounts cell will receive little, if any, attention.

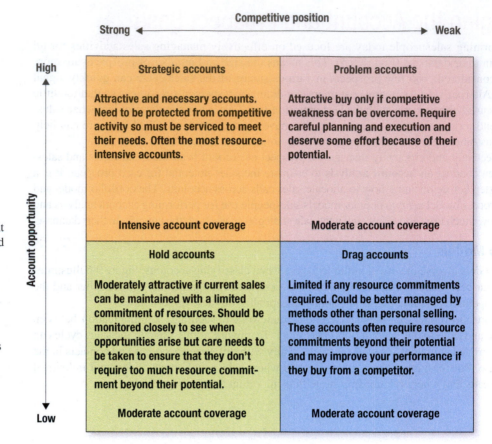

Sales Process Models

Sales process models, also referred to as "sales funnel models," classify prospects based on where they are in the sales process. The **sales process model** is the total set of accounts being pursued at any given time. The sales process model is illustrated in Figure 9.7. This six-step model includes Prospect, Qualified, Needs Analysis, Presentation, Negotiations, and Closed/Service. An account might be simply a prospect who has potential but has not been contacted, a qualified prospect ready for a needs analysis, or in serious negotiations with the salesperson. In sales process model reports like Figure 9.7, clicking on any part of any funnel graph will drill down into and report all the supporting data on prospects in each stage of the sales process. Where an account is in the sales process has implications for "if and when" the salesperson will be able to close the sale.

The sales cycle for complex technical sales such as networking installations might be several months in duration. The number of prospects in the sales process or funnel for selling networking installations may be small compared to the number for an insurance or real estate salesperson. Insurance salespeople know they need to contact a larger number of people to gain permission to make a smaller number of presentations, to make an even small number of sales. In any selling situation, it is important that salespeople balance their portfolio of prospects that are at various stages of the selling process.[40] A **balanced funnel** enables salespeople to know how many prospects and how much revenue are needed at each stage in the sales process to meet sales projections and quotas.[41] As indicated earlier with Joe Girard's "Ferris wheel" concept, this means that salespeople must ensure that sufficient prospects are regularly added to the funnel, so it does not become empty. In addition to the number of prospects, the quality of the prospects added to the funnel and the ability of the salesperson to manage the sales process will affect the number of sales opportunities that are successfully closed.

Salespeople need to ensure that they "work" the whole funnel so that it is always in balance. They should work on sales opportunities in the negotiation and close stages first; that is, close those that are near the end of the sales process. Then they should work on adding new prospects, and those that are in the earlier stages of the sales process. Prospecting

Total Potential Sale Analysis

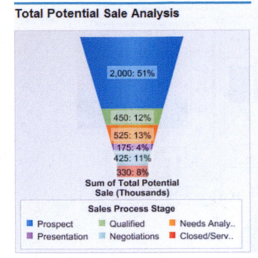

Forecast Analysis

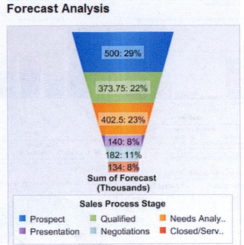

FIGURE 9.7

The CRM Sales Funnel (or Sales Process) Dashboard

The sales funnel, or "sales process dashboard" as it is frequently called, classifies prospects according to where they are in the sales process. In this figure, both the total sales potential funnel and the forecasted funnel are presented. The forecasted funnel amounts are arrived at by multiplying the total sale by the forecast amount or likelihood the salesperson projected for successfully closing the sale. The sales forecast needs to be accurate because it is the amount most firms use to project future operating results for the company. You can click any stage on these two charts and drill down to find the underlying data.

Source: Courtesy of Salesforce.com.

is an activity that some salespeople dislike, but, if it is not given sufficient attention, there is a real danger that the funnel or pipeline will empty. Finally, salespeople should work on those opportunities that are in the sales process, moving them along through the funnel and ensuring there are regular, predictable sales over time.[42]

Pipeline Management, Pipeline Analytics, and Pipeline Dashboards

This process of managing all the prospects in the salesperson's sales funnel to ensure that sales objectives are being met is called **pipeline management**. CRM software provides an efficient and effective tool for forecasting and managing pipelines. Using sales data entered into the contact screens and notes applications, sales forecasts can be continually updated as prospects move through the stages in the sales process. Prospects in the database who are no longer qualified, for whatever reason, can be quickly dropped from the sales funnel.

   Pipeline analytics, defined as the ability to conduct sophisticated data analysis and modeling, are found in most CRM systems. Using pipeline analytics, new reports can be generated regarding the movement of the prospects through the sales pipeline. These reports can be more clearly presented with the use of dashboards. **Pipeline dashboards** (Figure 9.8) are at-a-glance visualizations that define, monitor, and analyze the relationships existing in the pipeline. Sales team members including the sales manager working together from a shared CRM database can collaborate to create value and enhance the sales strategies to help the salesperson move prospects through the pipeline to a successful sale. CRM pipeline dashboards allow the user to quickly and easily drill down into the reports and records supporting them. This provides for quick updates as prospects move through the sales funnel. Dashboards can also provide insight into the need to add new prospects, as existing ones are moved through the stages of the sales process.

GLOBAL BUSINESS INSIGHT

Doing Business in Germany

Germany represents the world's fourth-largest economy and is America's largest European trading partner. If you are a salesperson planning a business trip to Germany, keep in mind that there is greater formality in the German business community.

- Germany has been described as a "low-context" culture in which words carry most of the information. Messages tend to be explicit and direct. In this culture, negotiations (verbal or written) tend to be explicit in defining terms of the agreement. By comparison, China is a high-context culture in which exact phrasing and the verbal part of the messages tend to be less significant than your relationship with the other person.

- There is a strong emphasis on punctuality, so avoid being late for appointments. Germans tend to make appointments far in advance.

- Lunch is the most common meal for business meetings. Dining etiquette in Germany involves eating continental style—holding the fork in the left hand continually and the knife in the right hand.

- The sales presentation should include data and empirical evidence that support your proposal. Brochures and other printed information should be serious and detailed, not flashy.[c]

FIGURE 9.8

Pipeline Dashboards

These additional pipeline dashboards are at-a-glance visualizations that define, monitor, and analyze the relationships existing in the pipeline or funnel. Pipeline analytics exist in most modern CRM systems and are used to produce these important prospect movement reports. The salesperson can quickly and easily access detailed information on specific prospects, and then use this information to plan strategies for moving the prospect to the next stage of the sales process.

Source: Courtesy of Salesforce.com.

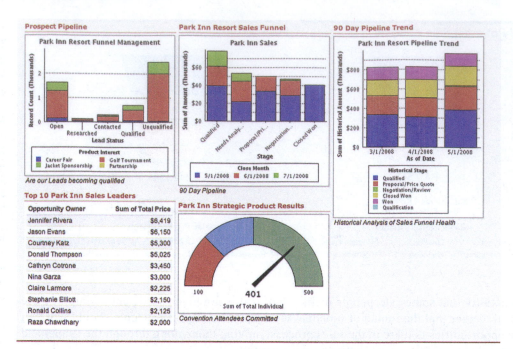

CHAPTER LEARNING ACTIVITIES

Reviewing Key Concepts

Discuss the importance of developing a prospect or account

Prospect identification has been called the lifeblood of selling. A continuous supply of new customers must be found to replace those lost for various reasons. "Prospecting" is the systematic process of locating potential customers. Prospecting requires careful planning.

Identify and assess important sources of prospects and accounts

Analysis of both your product and your existing customers can help to identify, locate, and profile your prospects. Important sources of new customers include referrals (endless chain referrals and referral letters and cards), centers of influence, friends and family members, directories, trade publications, trade shows and special events, telemarketing and e-mail, direct-response advertising and sales letters, websites, computer databases, cold calling, education seminars, networking, and prospecting by nonsales employees. The use of social media to secure new prospects is also discussed.

Describe criteria for qualifying prospects and accounts

Prospecting techniques produce a list of names that must be evaluated using criteria developed by each salesperson. The process of prospect evaluation is called "qualifying."

The qualifying process involves finding answers to several basic questions: Does the prospect have a need for my product? Can the prospect make the buying decision? Can the prospect pay for the purchase? Does the prospect have the willingness to buy my product? An estimate of the amount of sales that could be generated from this prospect and the prospect's credit rating should also be determined.

Explain common methods of collecting and organizing prospect and account information

Most companies rely on customer relationship management (CRM) systems to keep track of sales data. The collection of sales intelligence beyond sales data enables salespeople to impress their knowledgeable customers with insights that are above and beyond the product and/or service features and benefits.

Describe the steps in managing the prospect or account list

Salespeople need to allocate their resources wisely to make the most of the prospect base. They do so by conducting account analysis, using either the portfolio model or the sales funnel model.

Key Terms

Prospecting, p. 175	Website, p. 182	Sales intelligence, p. 187
Account or business development, p. 175	Cold calling, p. 183	Account analysis, p. 189
	Elevator presentation, p. 183	Sales process model, p. 190
Prospect, p. 175	Networking, p. 184	Balanced funnel, p. 190
Prospect base, p. 176	Social network, p. 184	Pipeline management, p. 191
Referral, p. 178	Qualifying, p. 186	Pipeline analytics, p. 191
Telemarketing, p. 181	Sales data, p. 187	Pipeline dashboards, p. 191

MyMarketingLab

To complete the problems with the ⭐ in your MyLab, go to the EOC Discussion Questions.

Review Questions

9-1 List and briefly explain the common causes of customer attrition.

9-2 Describe three steps progressive marketers are taking to improve the quality of the prospecting and account development effort.

9-3 List the major sources of prospects.

9-4 Explain how the endless chain referral prospecting and account development method works.

9-5 What is "networking"? How might a real estate salesperson use networking to identify prospects?

9-6 What does the term "qualifying" mean? What are the four basic questions that should be answered during the qualifying process?

9-7 What are the most common methods of organizing prospect information?

⭐ 9-8 When is sales intelligence important? What are the three most important pieces of sales intelligence a salesperson needs to know?

⭐ 9-9 Describe two popular models for performing the account analysis.

Application Exercises

9-10 Prior to getting involved in networking, it's a good idea to prepare an elevator presentation. This is a 30-second pitch that summarizes what you want people to know about you. You might think of yourself as a "product" to be sold to an employer who has a job opening. Make your presentation upbeat and brief. Who are you? What are you currently doing? What type of work are you looking for? Practice the presentation alone in front of a mirror and then present it to one or two class members.

9-11 You are a sales representative for Xerox Corporation. Assuming Xerox has just designed a new, less expensive, and better-quality copying machine, make a list of 15 prospects you would plan to contact. From the material in this chapter, identify the sources you would use in developing your prospect list.

9-12 You are in the process of interviewing for a sales position with CIGNA Insurance Company. In addition to filling out an application form and taking an aptitude test, one of the items the agency manager requests of you is to develop a list of prospects with whom you are acquainted. He informs you that this list includes the prospects you will be working with during the first few weeks of employment. The agency manager recommends that you list at least 50 names. Prepare a list of 10 acquaintances you have that would qualify as prospects.

9-13   Sales automation software is most commonly used in the prospecting phase of selling. New-product releases are continually being developed that provide additional features and benefits to salespeople. The software used in this book is marketed by a leader in the field. Access www.salesforce.com and research the latest additions to Salesforce.com such as Radian6 and Data.com. View the introductory videos on their new products.

9-14   Locating companies to work for is a form of prospecting. Assuming you are interested in changing careers, develop a list of 10 companies for which you would like to work. Assign each company a priority according to your interest, from the most desirable (1) to the least (10). Organize your list in six columns showing the company name, telephone number, address, and person in charge of hiring, prospect information, and priority. What sources did you use to get this information?

Role-Play Exercise

For this role-play, you will assume a sales position at a Lexus dealership. You have just completed a successful sale by signing the papers for the second new Lexus this customer has purchased in

the past four years. Because you know your prospect has had a very successful experience with his first Lexus, you have decided to use the referral methods described in this chapter. Review the material on referrals and plan what you will say to your customer to build your prospect base. Pair off with another student who will assume the role of your customer. Explain that satisfied customers often know other people who would consider purchasing a Lexus. You might say, "Considering the positive experience you have had as a Lexus owner, you probably know others who appreciate fine automobiles. Is there anyone who comes to mind?" If, after probing, your customer doesn't recall someone immediately, ask permission to call him later to see if anyone has come to mind. Ask this person for actual names, addresses, and other qualifying information about prospective customers whom he knows. Also, ask the customer if he would write a referral note or letter that you could use.

Reality Selling Video Case Problem–Dave Levitt/Salesforce.com

 Dave Levitt, featured at the beginning of this chapter, is a regional sales manager for Salesforce.com. The CRM solution provider is exclusively a cloud-computing vendor offering hosted applications. This model sets the company apart from competitors such as SAP, Oracle, or Microsoft, who are predominantly on-premise providers. Cloud-computing systems have a high degree of flexibility as they can be customized for each individual account and implemented within a very short time frame. Salesforce .com's unique selling proposition is therefore closely linked to the speed with which a client can gain the benefit: Cloud-computing implementation times are typically weeks or months, whereas competitive on-premise solutions can take years to be implemented. Therefore, the total cost of ownership is much lower, and the ROI is much higher and comes in faster.

Before getting in touch with a prospect, Levitt's sales representatives typically spend a substantial amount of time preparing for a sales call and keeping up with news releases. Such upfront investigative work is necessary to uncover such things as changes in top management or factors that are driving a company to change a business model. Working for a CRM company, Salesforce .com's salespeople have comprehensive access to additional news and information directly about each of their customers and prospects. Hence, by the time representatives have decided to pick up the phone to prospect, they already have a sense for why they are calling and what the value proposition is going to be specifically for that account.

For providers of enterprise software solutions, it is important to have contacts and relationships with three different types of individuals within the prospective customer company: (1) executive financial influencers who have ultimate responsibility for the budget and the project itself, (2) a coach who can give guidance on a day-to-day basis, and (3) IT specialists who can facilitate the process and who would be the custodians after the implementation of the solution. Therefore the sales representative has to be an orchestrator of resources within Salesforce.com for different buying influencers in the prospect's organization at different points in the sales cycle. For example, the salesperson would include a technical employee from Salesforce.com as part of the sales team that could apply the customer's needs to the product itself and perform demonstrations of software. One would also need to incorporate an internal sales executive who aligns with the customer's executive. Furthermore, the internal services organization or a third-party implementation partner is needed to explain and execute the implementation of the product. There could also be a wide variety of other specialists depending on which specific tasks have to be accomplished.

Typically, the sales representative would start to qualify the opportunity through conversations with the coach. Using various questioning techniques during the initial discovery process, the sales representative has to understand the following: What is the prospect's business model? Why might the prospect be interested in our offerings? What is the prospect's problem, and how big is it? What is the complexity of the problem the prospect is trying to address? Will there be a good fit? Is it worth investing the time and money it takes to win the account? What is the prospect's time frame? How is the prospect going to measure success?

If the initial discovery shows that the problem can be addressed, the sales representative would then ask for access to the ultimate decision maker and all the other key stakeholders. Then he/she would perform a similar discovery as was done with the first person (i.e., the coach), constantly trying to qualify the value of the service solution offering and making sure that it is worth pursuing the opportunity (as for large opportunities, it could be a one-year investment to win it). So the sales representative has to make sure and qualify that (1) it is a legitimate opportunity, (2) it can be won, and (3) it is worth winning the opportunity. As Levitt emphasizes, it has to be a win-win perspective: "We do not sell a commodity, but a specialty. We do not compete on price alone, but on quality and value." (See the chapter opener and *Reality Selling Today* Role-Play 7 in Appendix 1 for more information.)

Questions

9-15 Imagine you were in the position of Dave Levitt, selling CRM services to different business clients. What would be the most promising sources of prospects for you?

9-16 What criteria does Dave Levitt use for qualifying the prospect?

9-17 What questions does Dave Levitt ask to understand the needs of the customer?

9-18 What product features does Dave Levitt highlight that will help a user of Salesforce.com improve his business?

9-19 Does it appear that Dave Levitt is utilizing previously collected sales intelligence to impress the potential buyer with insights that are above and beyond the product features and benefits? Please specify.

Regional Accounts Management Case Study
Chapters 9–15 Real-World Sales Assignments!

Your Value Adding Systems Partner

Regional Account Management Case Study

Developing and Qualifying the Account Database (Refer to Appendix 2)

Introducing Your New Regional Account Management (RAM) Sales Responsibilities.
Casey Arnold has hired you as a regional account manager to sell for NewNet beginning December 1. Casey has given you the customer files of Lee Bizon, the former account manager who has just been promoted to another NewNet territory. Lee projected the possibility of over $1.8 million in sales for your new territory, with the actual forecast reduced by the likelihood of closing each account. Your responsibilities include carefully studying the Contact Screens and analyzing where each customer is in the NewNet sales/buying process. The steps include Qualifying, Needs Analysis, Presenting, Demonstrating; Negotiating; Closing; and Servicing the Sale. Lee has indicated the last step each of your accounts has completed in the sales process. Additional information to analyze on each contact screen includes: projected date to close, likelihood of closing, size of forecasted sale—in addition to other contact information presented.

The Notes Screens includes notes Lee prepared after making a sales call. You should analyze this information carefully and become very familiar with it. In this process, you will discover you are working with large purchases significantly impacting your customer's business. Lee has worked with teams of high-level personnel on the customer/buying side of the sale, as well as sales support team members from NewNet. In the Notes Screens, you will learn about the outstanding technical sales support team members you will have working with you on the technical side of your work with your accounts.

Your clients have been notified that Lee is leaving and a new regional account manager, you, will be contacting them. The following exercises in this chapter and at the end of Chapters 10–15 simulate this important activity by requesting that you extract, from an existing database, the information needed to take effective strategic sales action. You will find a printout of all your accounts in Appendix 2. Casey has asked you to review the status of your 20 accounts including where they are in the sales cycle, and what is the next strategic action you will have to take to move the sale process forward and close the forecasted sales.

You are to meet with Casey next Monday and to be prepared to answer the following questions. The questions below relate to the account development concepts presented in this chapter. Additional questions will appear at the end of the next five chapters. They will relate to the selling and account management concepts presented in each of those chapters. The questions in this Regional Account Management Case Study relate to successfully moving your accounts through the stages in the sales process. Answering these questions all relate to the sales process, and do not require you to have technical networking product knowledge. Your technical sales support team members, Camila, Joe, and Charlene, will be working on the technical side of the sales process. It will be your responsibility to bring them into the sales process at the appropriate time to meet and exceed the needs of your accounts.

Questions

9-20 Using the following headings, prepare a regional account metrics report for your meeting on the current status of your 20 new accounts found in an appendix. Keep a copy for future reference.

Newnet Systems Account Management

Name   Regional Accounts Manager, NEWNET SYSTEMS

Date	Account Name	Dollar					
Close	Contact Name	Sales Amt.					

9-21 Which contact can you ignore immediately for making a potential purchase?

9-22 Referring only to the *date close* category in the contact screens, which four accounts would you contact immediately?

9-23 Referring only to the *dollar amount* of sales forecasted category in the contact screens, which four accounts would you call first? Does the likelihood of closing percentage category have any influence on decisions concerning which accounts to call first? Why? Total the dollar amount of sales for each account and record the total projected sales.

9-24 According to information in the notes screens, which account development method did Lee Bizon appear to use the most? Give examples.

9-25 Identify any accounts where there may be ethical or legal issues to be considered. Describe what these issues may be.

MyMarketingLab

Go to the Assignments section of your MyLab to complete these writing exercises.

9-26 Identifying and developing potential customers is an important aspect of the customer strategy. Discuss the significance of the identification and development of potential customers as they relate to customer attrition. What are some of the common causes of customer attrition?

9-27 One of the most important keys to success in personal selling is the ability to qualify prospects. What are the basic questions savvy salespersons use as qualifying criteria? Why is this process important?

PART 4 ROLE-PLAY EXERCISE

Developing a Customer Strategy

Scenario

You are a sales representative employed by the Park Shores Resort and Convention Center. One of your primary responsibilities is to identify prospects and make sales calls that result in the development of new accounts. During each of these calls, you plan to build a relationship with the customer and describe selected value-added guest services and amenities offered by the Park Shores. You also try to learn as much as possible about the customer's buying process.

Customer Profile

Shannon Fordham is the founder and chief executive officer of USA Technologies, a growing, high-tech firm with more than 300 employees. The company manufactures and sells security systems that can be used in residential homes, retail stores, and other commercial buildings. According to a recent article in the *Wall Street Journal*, USA Technologies is poised to grow very rapidly in the next year. The article described Shannon Fordham as a workaholic who usually puts in an 80-hour workweek. Delegation does not come easy to this personable, hard-charging entrepreneur.

Salesperson Profile

You have just completed the Park Shores sales training program and now want to develop some new accounts. In addition to taking care of established customers, you plan to call on at least four new prospects every week.

Product

Park Shores International is a full-service hotel and convention center located in Mission Beach, California. The hotel recently completed a $4.8 million renovation of its meeting and banquet rooms.

Instructions

For this role-play activity, you will meet with Shannon Fordham, who appears to be a good prospect. During the first sales call, plan to learn more about the prospect as an individual and acquire more information about USA Technologies. This meeting will provide you with the opportunity to begin building a long-term partnership.

During the first meeting with a prospect, you like to present a limited amount of important product information. In this case, the length of the appointment is 15 minutes, so you should not try to cover too much information. To prepare for the first sales call, read Employment Memorandum 1 in Appendix 3. This memo describes the value-added guest services and amenities offered by the Park Inn. For the purpose of this role-play, Shannon Fordham should be considered a consultative process buyer. You can assume that the prospect will need help identifying and evaluating possible solutions. As you prepare for the first call, think about what may take place during future calls. Review the steps in the typical buying process (see Figure 8.3). Keep in mind that today's more demanding customers are seeking a cluster of satisfactions. Study the Product-Selling Model (Figure 7.1) prior to meeting with the prospect.

Your request for referrals is more likely to receive a positive response if made after you have built a strong trusting relationship. In most cases, referral leads result in higher close rates, larger sales, and shorter sales cycles.

PART 5

DEVELOPING A PRESENTATION STRATEGY

The chapters included in Part 5 review the basic principles used in the strategic/consultative sales presentation. This information is used as you prepare presentation objectives, develop a presentation plan that adds value, and identify ways to provide outstanding service after the sale.

10 Approaching the Customer with Adaptive Selling

Learning Objectives

When you finish reading this chapter, you should be able to

10.1 Describe the three prescriptions that are included in the presentation strategy

10.2 Discuss the two-part preapproach process

10.3 Describe team presentation strategies

10.4 Explain how adaptive selling builds on four broad strategic areas of personal selling

10.5 Describe the six main parts of the presentation plan

10.6 Explain how to effectively approach the customer

10.7 Describe seven ways to convert the prospect's attention and arouse interest

Source: Michael Ahearne

▶ Reality Selling Video—Alim Hirani/Hilti Corporation

The worldwide Hilti Corporation (www.hilti.com) specializes in providing leading-edge technology to the global construction industry. With some 20,000 employees in more than 120 countries around the world, Hilti actively pursues a value-added orientation in all of its activities.

As part of this orientation, Hilti puts its new salespeople through a rigorous training curriculum that includes one-month pretraining on Hilti products and services, a three-week intensive training in product and services sales, and a two-week training on software applications. In addition, these salespeople also ride along with experienced sales managers to get hands-on experience. Furthermore, the company offers refresher courses to keep its salespeople updated on Hilti's products and services, the construction market, and corporate strategy. Equipped with this in-depth knowledge and the value orientation that is deeply rooted in the corporate culture, salespeople like Alim Hirani, on the right in the photo above, are always well prepared to approach customers to make sales presentations, demonstrate and explain Hilti's products and services, and show the customers both the tangible and intangible benefits that Hilti can offer.

With a direct sales model, Hilti relies heavily on its salespeople to make the connection and deliver its values to its global customers. Alim is a strong believer that he and his sales team are the face of the company. His credibility is embedded in Hilti's credibility and vice versa. He always makes sure that his sales presentations are well prepared in advance. More importantly, he builds and maintains rapport with his customers from the very beginning of the business relationship because such partnership mentality motivates the customers to disclose their actual concerns. In the end, customers value only solutions that address their actual needs, and Alim as a Hilti salesperson knows that by heart. ●

Developing The Presentation Strategy

The presentation strategy combines elements of the relationship, product, and customer strategies. Each of the other three strategies must be developed before a salesperson can create an effective presentation strategy.

The **presentation strategy** is a well-conceived plan that includes three prescriptions: (1) establishing objectives for the sales presentation, (2) developing the presale presentation plan needed to meet these objectives, and (3) renewing one's commitment to providing outstanding customer service (Figure 10.1).

The first prescription reminds us that we need to establish one or more objectives for each sales call. High-performance salespeople like Alim Hirani understand that it is often possible to accomplish several goals during a single call. A common objective of sales calls is to collect information about the prospect's needs. Another common objective is to develop, build, or sustain a relationship with those who make the buying decision.

A carefully prepared presentation plan ensures that salespeople are well organized during the sales presentation and prepared to achieve their objectives. A six-step presentation plan is introduced later in this chapter.

Establishment of objectives for the sales presentation and preparation of the presentation plan must be guided by a strong desire to offer outstanding customer service. Achieving excellence is the result of careful needs analysis, correct product selection, clear presentations, informative demonstrations, win-win negotiations, and flawless service after the sale. Salespeople who are committed to doing their best in each of these areas are richly rewarded.

10.1 Describe the three prescriptions that are included in the presentation strategy

Strategic/Consultative Selling Model*	
Strategic Step	**Prescription**
Develop a Personal Selling Philosophy	✔ Adopt Marketing Concept ✔ Value Personal Selling ✔ Become a Problem Solver/Partner
Develop a Relationship Strategy	✔ Maintain High Ethical Standards ✔ Project Professional Image ✔ Manage the Relationship Process
Develop a Product Strategy	✔ Become a Product Expert ✔ Sell Benefits ✔ Configure Value-Added Solutions
Develop a Customer Strategy	✔ Understand the Buying Process ✔ Understand Buyer Behavior ✔ Develop Prospect Base
Develop a Presentation Strategy	✔ Prepare Objectives ✔ Develop Presentation Plan ✔ Provide Outstanding Service

*Strategic/consultative selling evolved in response to increased competition, more complex products, increased emphasis on customer needs, and growing importance of long-term relationships.

FIGURE 10.1

The Strategic/Consultative Selling Model provides the foundation for a value-added consultative presentation strategy.

Presentation Strategy Adds Value

How does precall planning add value? Value is added when you position yourself as a resource—not just a vendor. You must prove that you have important ideas and advice to offer.[1] A well-planned presentation adds value when it is based on carefully developed sales call objectives and a presentation plan needed to meet these objectives. Good planning ensures that the presentation is customized and adapted to meet the needs and time constraints of the prospect. Increasingly, customers' time is very limited and they want a concise and thoughtful presentation. Careful planning is the key to delivering more value and increasing your sales productivity.[2]

Salespeople need to be aware of the changing needs of their customers or risk losing out to the competition. Some salespeople do not pay enough attention to how they conduct business with their established customers. Without a precall plan, it's easy to miss opportunities to increase your knowledge of the customer's business, sell new products, or discover ways to improve service.[3]

10.2 Discuss the two-part preapproach process

Planning The Preapproach

Preparation for the actual sales presentation is a two-part process. Part one is referred to as the **preapproach**. The preapproach involves preparing presale objectives and developing a presale presentation plan. Part two is called the **approach** and involves making a favorable first impression, securing the prospect's attention, and transitioning to need identification (Figure 10.2). The preapproach and approach, when handled correctly, establish a foundation for an effective sales presentation.

The preapproach should be viewed as a key step in preparing for each sales presentation. Professional salespeople complete the preapproach for every presentation whether it involves a new account or an established customer. Top salespeople often spend two or three hours planning for a 25-minute sales call. The preapproach includes the first two prescriptions for developing a presentation strategy: establishing objectives and creating a presale presentation plan.

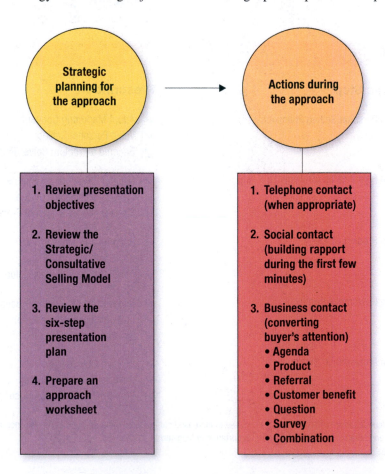

FIGURE 10.2

Preparing for the presentation involves planning for the activities that occur before meeting the prospect and for the first few minutes of actual contact with the prospect.

Establishing Presentation Objectives

Preparation for a sales call is part research, part planning, and part critical thinking. Sales representatives employed by Nalco Chemical Company prepare for each sales call by filling out a 13-point precall planner. One section of this form requires the salesperson to identify the objectives of the call. Nalco is a company that emphasizes professionalism, long-term partnerships, and staying focused on customer needs.[4]

In Chapter 8, we introduced the five stages of the typical buying process (see Figure 8.3). When you are calling on a *consultative* or *strategic alliance* buyer, you will usually not cover all of these stages during a single sales call.

Multi-call sales presentations are especially common in complex sales. Therefore, it's best to develop presentation objectives suitable for each stage of the buying process. During the first stage—need awareness—customers may or may not be aware of their needs and problems. The need awareness stage is the "investigation" stage. Uncovering and clarifying needs will require the use of appropriate questions (covered in detail in Chapter 11). The following presentation objectives would be appropriate during the first call on a new prospect:

- Establish rapport and begin building a relationship with the customer.
- Obtain permission to ask need identification questions.
- Obtain personal and business information to establish the customer's file.

During stage two of the buying process—evaluation of solutions—the customer is ready to consider possible problem solutions. In some cases, there may be several solutions that must be evaluated. Presentation objectives for stage two might include the following:

- Involve the customer in a product demonstration.
- Provide value justification in terms of cost reduction and increased revenues.
- Compare and contrast the features of, for example, a truck fleet lease plan with a fleet purchase plan.

Every sales call should have an **action objective**. An action objective is something that you want the customer to do during the sales presentation: provide specific financial information, schedule a visit to your manufacturing plant, agree to a trial use of your product, agree to a follow-up meeting, or place an order. An action objective brings a sharp focus to the sales presentation.[5]

Once you have an appointment with the prospect and the presentation objectives have been established, consider sending a fax or e-mail message that outlines the agenda for the meeting. This will confirm the appointment and clarify the topics to be discussed.[6]

Multi-call sales presentations are common in many areas, including the retail field. The sale of expensive recreational vehicles, leased automobiles, boats, and quality sound systems for the home or business often requires more than one sales call. High-ended clothing companies, retail stores and independent tailors make office calls to sell tailored clothing. One example is Tom James Clothing introduced in Chapter 1. Another is Mitchells/Richards, with stores in Westport and Greenwich, Connecticut. This progressive retailer, with a reputation for superior customer service, makes office calls upon request. Working with a customer at his office usually requires more than one sales call.[7]

Team Selling Presentation Strategies

10.3 Describe team presentation strategies

In today's ever-changing business environment, team selling has surfaced as a major development. Team selling is ideally suited to organizations that sell complex or customized products and services that require direct communication between customers and technical experts. Sales teams can often uncover problems, solutions, and sales opportunities that no individual salesperson could discover working alone.[8] In some situations, the involvement of technical experts can shorten the selling cycle. The team approach often results in more precise need identification, improved selection of the product, and more informative sales presentations.

Team sales presentations require a more detailed precall plan than individual sales calls. Each team member must have a clear understanding of the role he or she will play during the sales call. Sales presentation objectives should be clearly stated. Team members should be given

A survey of 19,000 salespeople and sales managers found that about one-fourth of the people contacted use sales teams. A carefully conceived presentation strategy, with each participant having a clear understanding of the role and value he or she will add during the sales call, is essential.

Source: Monkey Business Images/Shutterstock

detailed information about the customer, understand the basics of a consultative sales presentation, and be prepared to add value.[9]

Companies that have moved to team sales have discovered that this approach is not easily executed. At Hickok Cole Architects in Washington, D.C., team selling is the primary approach used to obtain new accounts. However, staff members did not easily master the team selling process. Determining who would communicate when, and determining how presentations would fall into place seamlessly, took months of practice among the company's teams, which often consisted of six or more people. Without sufficient practice, the staff at Hickok Cole discovered that team presentations were sometimes disorganized.[10]

Some marketers use a variation of the team approach to selling. Salespeople are trained to seek the assistance of another salesperson or actually turn the customer over to another

---

 SOCIAL MEDIA AND SELLING TODAY

Team Selling, Buying Committees, and "Chatter"

Sales of complex or customized products and services invariably involve two teams of people—the selling team and the buying committee or team. Important communications occur between and among members of the two teams. Information about technical and financial matters, information technology, facilities management, and other sales-related issues is exchanged throughout the sales process. Salesforce.com has introduced a system called "Chatter" to facilitate collaborative communication throughout the sales process.

Chatter is linked to the Salesforce.com CRM system and incorporates the benefits of social media. Chatter is a secure, cloud-based, online service similar to most social media systems. Members of both teams may create personal profiles similar to those on Facebook. This personalizes the people working together and makes it easy for anyone with access in both companies to get acquainted with everyone involved in the sales transaction. Users can follow selected personnel in either company, sort the profiles by expertise, and form networks of specialists. Messages are easily transmitted among all participants and recorded for reviewing later. Although it appears to be social media, wise users should retain a "casual business" writing style and avoid too much informality.

Chatter conversations can pertain to specific subjects so users receive real-time news feeds and participate in the development of each part of the solution. This creates value for the total transaction in that anyone in the buying company not involved in the solution development, such as a board of directors, can review the exchanges to understand the results achieved. Sections of the Chatter system are for people within the selling company to confidentially comment and exchange ideas on how to best solve problems and move the sale ahead. When it is time for the sales presentation, everyone following Chatter's continuous collaboration will be well prepared to confirm that the proposed solution is a good fit. The presentation contributions by sales team members can be better organized and coordinated. For more information, go to www.Salesforce.com/chatter.

salesperson when problems surface. The other salesperson may bring to the selling situation greater ability to identify the customer's needs or select the appropriate product. Salespeople who have well-prepared presale objectives know when to seek assistance from another professional.

Strategies for Selling to a Buying Committee

In some cases, salespeople must address and satisfy both the individual and collective concerns of each participant in a multi-buyer situation. The decision makers may be members of a well-trained buying committee, or a board of directors.

As in any type of selling situation, the salesperson should attempt to determine the various buying influences. When possible, the role of each decision maker, the amount of influence he or she exerts, and each decision maker's needs should be determined before the presentation. Careful observation during the presentation can reveal who may use the product (user influencer), who controls the finances (financial influencer), and who can provide the expertise necessary to make the correct buying decision (technical influencer).

When you make a presentation to a buying committee, make sure all parties feel involved. Any member of the group who feels ignored could prevent you from closing the sale. Be sure to direct questions and comments to all potential decision makers in the group. As early as possible, identify the most powerful influences.

Find out if there are any silent team or committee members. A "silent member" is one who can influence the buying decision but does not attend the presentation. Silent members are usually senior managers who have a major influence on the buying decision. If a silent member does exist, you must find a way to communicate, directly or indirectly, with this person.[11]

Adaptive Selling: Builds on Four Strategic Areas of Personal Selling

10.4 Explain how adaptive selling builds on four broad strategic areas of personal selling

At the very heart of *adaptive selling* is the belief that every sales call must be tailored to the unique needs, wants, and concerns of the customer. As noted in Chapter 5, adaptive selling involves altering sales behaviors in order to improve communication with the customer. Identifying and responding to the customer's needs frequently requires complex behavioral adjustments before and during the sales call. These adjustments are based on the relationship needs and product needs of the customer. Salespeople today must develop a broader repertoire of selling strategies and apply more effective information-acquisition skills.[12]

The strategic planning that takes place during the preapproach can greatly enhance the adaptive selling process. This plan includes *strategies* that you use to position yourself with the customers and *tactics* you will use when you are face-to-face with a customer. Planning the approach involves consideration of how the *relationship, product,* and *customer* and *presentation* (described earlier in this chapter) *strategies* can enhance the sales presentation.

REVIEW THE RELATIONSHIP STRATEGY As noted in Chapter 3, salespeople need to think of everything they say or do in the context of their relationship with the customer. Customers want a quality product and a quality relationship. Building and nourishing a long-term partnership with the customer often begins with attention to many small details. Confirming the appointment with a brief e-mail message and arriving for the appointment a few minutes early send a positive message to the customer before the first face-to-face meeting.

The first contact between a salesperson and a prospect is very important. A positive or negative first impression can be formed in a matter of seconds. The customer is receiving a variety of verbal and nonverbal messages that can either facilitate or distract from the sales call. Your behaviors and appearance create an image that others observe and remember. Identification of the customer's preferred communication style should be given a high priority during the initial contact. Once you are in the presence of the customer, absorb the many clues that will help you with style identification. Then use *style flexing* to accommodate the needs of that person.

REVIEW THE PRODUCT STRATEGY During the preapproach, you will learn some new things about the potential customer. You will no doubt acquire information that did not surface during the prospecting stage. If this is the case, it pays to take another look at your product. Now it will

The strategic planning and preparation that take place during the preapproach can greatly enhance the adaptive selling process. This planning includes a clear understanding of the relationship, product, and customer strategies. This planning and preparation enabled Lana and her sales team to create a presentation strategy that met the relationship and product needs of Ron, one of her largest customers.

Source: Michael Ahearne

be easier to identify features with special appeal to the person you are calling on. In addition, you can more accurately identify questions that the prospect might raise.

Product knowledge, combined with knowledge of the customer, builds confidence. Salespeople who are confident in their ability to alter the sales approach as needed are much better prepared to engage in adaptive selling.[13] Customers today are eager to do business with salespeople who have developed "expert power."

REVIEW THE CUSTOMER STRATEGY Personal selling provides us with the opportunity to apply the marketing concept during every contact with the customer. All energies can be directed toward an individual who is likely to think and act differently from anyone else. Customers today have become increasingly sophisticated in their buying strategies. They have higher expectations for value-added products and long-term commitments. A customer strategy focuses on understanding the customer's needs, wants, and buying conditions. A careful review of information contained in the prospect database is an essential part of reviewing the customer strategy. With this understanding, adaptive selling strategies are formulated to meet both the relationship and product needs of the customer.

10.5 Describe the six main parts of the presentation plan

Developing the Six-Step Presentation Plan

Once you have established objectives for the sales presentation, the next step (prescription) involves developing the presentation plan. This plan helps you achieve your objectives.

SELLING IN ACTION

No Tech to High Tech

Account planning by the 70 sales representatives at Sebastiani Winery used to be a time-consuming process. Without the aid of modern technology, salespeople were forced to manually analyze two monthly reports that were inches thick. Preparing for a sales call was burdensome. Some salespeople said that they spent almost half their time analyzing reports. A major sales force automation (SFA) initiative was started. The project had these four objectives:

• Improve communication through the use of e-mail, file sharing, and intranet technology.

• Support needed development of multimedia presentations.
• Provide data analysis capabilities.
• Ease the administrative burden.

Each member of the Sebastiani sales force received a laptop loaded with Windows, PowerPoint, e-mail, and Business Objects—the software needed for analyzing data. The new technology was introduced during a three-day training program. Today, salespeople have the ability to do account planning that is much more effective than in the past.[a]

Today, with increased time constraints, fierce competition, and rising travel costs, the opportunity for a face-to-face meeting with customers may occur less frequently. The few minutes you have with your customers may be your only opportunity to win their business, so careful planning is more critical than ever.

Planning the Presentation

Once you have collected background information, you are ready to develop a "customized" presale presentation plan. Preparing a customized sales presentation can take a great deal of time and energy. Nevertheless, this attention to detail gives you added confidence and helps you avoid delivering unconvincing hit-or-miss sales talks. The plan is developed after a careful study of the **six-step presentation plan** (Figure 10.3). In most cases, the sales process includes the following activities:

1. *Approach.* Preparation for the approach involves making decisions concerning effective ways to make a favorable first impression during the initial contact, securing the prospect's attention, and developing the prospect's interest in the product. The approach should set the stage for an effective sales presentation.

2. *Need discovery.* The need discovery, also commonly referred to as "needs assessment" or "needs analysis process," is one of the most critical parts of the selling process. If the salesperson is unable to discover the prospect's buying needs and select a product solution that meets those needs, the sale will likely be lost. Chapter 11 covers all aspects of the need discovery process and selecting products that meet individual needs.

3. *Presentation.* Three types of need-satisfaction presentation strategies are available to adapt the sales presentation to the needs of the prospect. After deciding which strategy to use, the salesperson carefully prepares the presentations following the guidelines presented. Selling tools or proof devices are used to demonstrate and document the benefits presented. Chapter 12 is devoted exclusively to adapting presentations to meet customer needs.

The Six-Step Presentation Plan

Step One: Approach	☐ Review Strategic/Consultative Selling Model ☐ Initiate customer contact
Step Two: Need Discovery	☐ Ask strategic questions ☐ Determine customer needs ☐ Select Product Solution
Step Three: Presentation	☐ Select presentation strategy ☐ Create presentation plan ☐ Initiate presentation
Step Four: Negotiation	☐ Anticipate buyer concerns ☐ Plan negotiating methods ☐ Initiate win-win negotiations
Step Five: Close	☐ Plan appropriate closing methods ☐ Recognize closing clues ☐ Initiate closing methods
Step Six: Servicing the Sale	☐ Follow through ☐ Follow-up calls ☐ Expansion selling

Service, retail, wholesale, and manufacturer selling

FIGURE 10.3

The Six-Step Presentation Plan

A presale plan is a logical and orderly outline that features a salesperson's thoughts from one step to the next in the presentation. Each step in this plan is explained in Chapters 10 to 15.

Doing Business in England

Linda Phillips, codirector of Executive Etiquette Company, says, "First and foremost is the British attention to detail." English businesspeople also tend to be more formal in terms of dress and person-to-person communication. It's helpful to study English business customs before visiting that country.

- Introductions in England tend to be very formal. The British look for whose name is spoken first. If you are calling on a client named Robert Timmons, the introduction of your sales manager would be, "Mr. Timmons, I would like you to meet Raymond Hill, my sales manager." In this case the client's name

is first because he is the more important person. Never address someone by his or her first name unless you are invited to do so.

- Making decisions is often a time-consuming process, so don't expect a quick close.
- Do not use aggressive sales techniques, such as the hard sell, and avoid criticism of competing products. Focus on objective facts and evidence during the presentation.
- It would be poor manners to discuss business after the business day in England. This is true even when you have drinks or a meal with a businessperson.[b]

---

4. *Negotiation.* Buyer resistance is a natural part of the selling/buying process. An objection, however, does present a barrier to closing the sale. For this reason, all salespeople should become skillful at negotiating resistance. Chapter 13 covers this topic.

5. *Close.* As the sales presentation progresses, there may be several opportunities to confirm and close the sale. Salespeople must learn to spot closing clues. Chapter 14 provides suggestions on how to close sales.

6. *Servicing the sale.* The importance of developing a long-term value-adding relationship with the prospect has been noted in previous chapters. This rapport is often the outgrowth of postsale service. Learning to service the sale is an important aspect of selling. Chapter 15 deals with activities that build value-adding partnerships.

Adapting the Presentation Plan to the Customer's Buying Process

A truly valuable idea or concept is timeless. The six parts of the presale presentation plan checklist have been discussed in the sales training literature for many years; therefore, they might be described as fundamentals of personal selling. These steps are basic elements of most sales and frequently occur in the same sequence. However, the activities included in the six-step presentation plan must be selected with care. Prior to developing the sales call plan, the salesperson must answer one very important question: Do these activities relate to the customer's *buying process*? As noted in Chapter 8, purchasing structures and buying procedures can vary greatly from company to company. In some cases, the steps in the buying process have been clearly defined by the organization and this information is available to vendors. Selling steps are of little value *unless* they are firmly rooted in your customer's buying process.[14]

10.6 Explain how to effectively approach the customer

The Approach

After a great deal of preparation, it is time to communicate with the prospect, either by face-to-face contact, by telephone, or some other appropriate method of communication. We refer to the initial contact with the customer as the "approach." A high-quality and professional approach is a powerful way to add value and differentiate yourself from your competitors.[15] All the effort you have put into developing relationship, product, and customer strategies can now be applied to the presentation strategy. If the approach is effective, you may be given the opportunity to make the sales presentation. If, however, the approach is not effective, the chance to present your sales story may be lost. You can be the best-prepared salesperson in the business, but, without a good approach, there may be little chance for a sale.

The approach has three important objectives. First, you want to build rapport with the prospect. This will be accomplished with your *telephone and/or social contact*. Second, you want to capture the person's full attention with your *business contact*. These first two steps are extremely important in establishing how much *influence* you will have throughout the rest of the sales process. Never begin your sales story if the prospect seems preoccupied and is not paying attention. Third, you want to *transition to the next stage of the sales process.* In the early part of the sales process, this will likely be the need discovery; in multi-call presentations, it may be one of the other stages in the sales process such as the presentation, negotiations, or closing the sale. In some selling situations, the first contact with the customer is a telephone call. The call is made to schedule a meeting or, in some cases, conduct the sales presentation. The face-to-face sales call starts with the social contact and is followed by the business contact. The telephone contact, social contact, and business contact are discussed in this section.

ESTABLISH YOUR CREDIBILITY EARLY During your approach, everything you do affects the amount of credibility and influence you will have throughout the sales process. Your actions will either increase your perceived value or detract from it.[16] Thomas A. Freese (www.qbsresearch. com/), author of *Secrets of Question-Based Selling*, says credibility is critical to your success in sales. Credibility is an impression that people often form about you very early in the sales process.[17] Sometimes, little things can erode your credibility and influence before you have a chance to prove yourself. Strategic communications consultant and executive coach Mark Jeffries (www.markjeffries. com), in a training video on "*The Art of Networking,*" provides examples regarding how misspelled words or grammatical errors in an e-mail, arriving late for an appointment, answering a cell phone or reading an e-mail while with a customer, failing to maintain good eye contact, acknowledging only certain members of a buying group, or failing to send the prospect information that was promised can quickly weaken the amount of influence you have in a relationship. Failure to be well prepared for the sales call will also undermine your credibility. Credibility and influence grow when the customer realizes you are a competent sales representative who can add value throughout the sales process.

The Telephone Contact

A telephone call provides a quick and inexpensive method of scheduling an appointment. Appointments are important because many busy prospects may not meet with a salesperson who drops in unannounced. When you schedule an appointment, the prospect knows about the sales call in advance and can, therefore, make the necessary advance preparation.

Some salespeople use the telephone exclusively to establish and maintain contact with the customer. As noted in Chapter 1, inside salespeople rely almost totally on the telephone for sales. **Telesales**, not to be confused with telemarketing, include many of the same elements as traditional sales: gathering customer information, determining needs, prescribing solutions, negotiating objections, and closing sales. Telesales usually are not scripted, a practice widely used in telemarketing. In some situations, telesales are as dynamic and unpredictable as a face-to-face sales call.

Capturing the customer's full attention is a major objective of the approach. Attention has become a very scarce resource in today's fast-paced world.

Source: Goodluz/Shutterstock

In Chapter 4, we examined some of the factors that influence the meaning we attach to an oral message from another person. With the aid of this information, we can see that communication via telephone is challenging. The person who receives the call cannot see our facial expressions, gestures, or posture, and, therefore, must rely totally on the sound of our voice and the words used. The telephone caller has a definite handicap.

The telephone has some additional limitations. A salesperson accustomed to meeting prospects in person may find telephone contact impersonal. Some salespeople try to avoid using the telephone because they believe it is too easy for the prospect to say no. It should be noted that these drawbacks are more imagined than real. With proper training, a salesperson can use the telephone effectively to schedule appointments. When you make an appointment by telephone, use the following practices:

> *Plan in advance what you will say.* It helps to use a written presentation plan as a guide during the first few seconds of the conversation. What you say is determined by the objectives of the sales call. Have a calendar available to suggest and confirm a date, time, and place for the appointment. Be sure to write it down.
>
> *Politely identify yourself and the company you represent.* Set yourself apart from other callers by using a friendly tone and impeccable phone manners. This approach helps you avoid being shut out by a wary gatekeeper (secretary or receptionist).
>
> *State the purpose of your call and explain how the prospect can benefit from a meeting.* In some cases, it is helpful to use a powerful benefits statement that gets the prospect's attention and whets the person's appetite for more information. Present only enough information to stimulate interest.
>
> *Show respect for the prospect's time by telling the person how much time the appointment may take.* Once the prospect agrees to meet with you, say, "Do you have your appointment calendar handy?" Be prepared to suggest a specific time: "Is Monday at 9:00 a.m. okay?"
>
> *Confirm the appointment with a brief note, e-mail message, or letter with the date, time, and place of your appointment.* Enclose your business card and any printed information that can be of interest to the prospect.[18]

You should anticipate resistance from some prospects. After all, most decision makers are very busy. Be persistent and persuasive if you genuinely believe a meeting with the prospect can be mutually beneficial.

EFFECTIVE USE OF VOICE MAIL The growing popularity of voice mail presents a challenge to salespeople. What type of message sets the stage for a second call or stimulates a return call? It's important to anticipate voice mail and know exactly what to say if you reach a recording. The prospect's perception of you is based on what you say and voice quality. The following message almost guarantees that you will be ignored:

> Ms. Simpson, I am Paul Watson and I am with Elliott Property Management Services. I would like to visit with you about our services. Please call me at 555–1500.[19]

Note that this message provides no compelling reason for the prospect to call back. It offers no valid item that would stimulate interest. The voice mail message should be similar to the opening statement you would make if you had a face-to-face contact with the prospect:

> Miss Simpson, my name is Paul Watson and I represent Elliott Property Management Services. We specialize in working with property managers. We can help you reduce the paperwork associated with maintenance jobs and provide an easy way to track the progress of each job. I would like the opportunity to visit with you and will call back in the morning.[20]

Note that this message is brief and describes benefits that customers can receive. If Paul Watson wants a call back, then he needs to give the best time to reach him. He should give his phone number slowly and completely. It's usually best to repeat the number. If you are acting on a referral, be sure to say who referred you and why.

EFFECTIVE USE OF E-MAIL Many prospects and established customers like the convenience of e-mail correspondence and prefer it as an alternative to telephone contact. Your challenge is to make it easy for your correspondents to read and handle your e-mail. Always use a meaningful, specific subject line. People who receive large amounts of e-mail may selectively choose which ones to read by scanning the subject lines and deleting those of no interest. An e-mail with a subject line titled "Action Steps from Our 9/28 Meeting" is more likely to be read than a subject line like "Meeting Notes."[21]

The e-mail message should tell the reader what you want and then encourage a response. Identify the main point of your e-mail within the first or second paragraphs. Format the e-mail so it's easy to read. This may require the use of headings (with capitals or boldface print) to identify the main elements of the memo. Proofread all e-mails for proper grammar, punctuation, and spelling.[22] Always use the grammar and spell-check tools. Messages that contain errors may misrepresent your competence. Finally, use a signature file—a small block of text that automatically follows each e-mail you send. A typical signature file includes full name, title, affiliation, phone number, and in some cases a slogan.

EFFECTIVE USE OF TEXT MESSAGING Connecting with your customer is more important than ever and in certain situations text messaging can be a highly effective technique. There are two trends that make text messaging more important than ever. First is the total integration of mobile devices as the primary communication device in our lives, and second, most people feel compelled to read and/or respond to text messages immediately.

It is important that you identify yourself and your company early in your message so your customer doesn't delete an unfamiliar message. Text messages should be very focused and to the point; however, avoid abbreviations, acronyms and slang, as these can appear unprofessional. Keep the message to 1-4 sentences and less than 250 characters when possible. It is critical that nothing in your text message might seem slick and promotional. Before clicking "send," as is the case with emails, be sure to read your message a second time.

The Social Contact—Building Rapport

According to many image consultants, "First impressions are lasting impressions." This statement is essentially true, and some profitable business relationships never crystallize because some trait or characteristic of the salesperson repels the prospective customer. Sales personnel have only a few minutes to create a positive first impression. Susan Bixler, author of *The New Professional Image*, describes the importance of the first impression this way:

> Books are judged by their covers, houses are appraised by their curb appeal, and people are initially evaluated on how they choose to dress and behave. In a perfect world this is not fair, moral, or just. What's inside should count a great deal more. And eventually it usually does, but not right away. In the meantime, a lot of opportunities can be lost.[23]

Building rapport should lead to credibility, which leads to trust. Once trust is established, the customer is likely to open up and share information. This information will provide clues regarding ways to create value. To be certain your first impression is appropriate, review the material in Chapters 3, 4, and 5. The information in those chapters is timeless and can serve you well today and in the future.

The goal of good social contact is to build rapport. Building rapport leads to credibility, which leads to trust. Once trust is established, the customer is likely to open up and share information.

Source: StockLite/Shutterstock

PLANNING PERSONAL VISITS USING CRM

Personally visiting prospects and customers helps build strong relationships, yet traveling is expensive and time consuming. A salesperson is challenged to plan visits that optimize the investment represented by each trip. Access to customer relationship management (CRM) contact records helps salespeople quickly identify all the accounts in a given geographic area that can be visited during one trip. CRM tools such as Portatour® help plan personal sales routes as sales people visit more customers even while driving fewer miles.

CRM empowers salespeople to rapidly review and compare an area's contacts on the basis of their stage in the sales process, the potential size of the account or purchase, the likelihood of a sale, and the contribution the visit could make to information gathering and relationship building. A well-managed CRM database provides salespeople with appropriate business and social topics to discuss when calling selected prospects for an appointment.

The brief, general conversation that often occurs during the social contact should hold the prospect's attention and establish a relaxed and friendly atmosphere for the business contact that is to follow. As mentioned in Chapter 4, there are three areas of conversation that should be considered in developing a social contact.

Comments on here-and-now observations. These comments may include general observations about an article in the *Wall Street Journal*, the victory of a local athletic team, or specific comments about awards on display in the prospect's office. Janis Taylor, sales representative with Trugreen Chemlawn, likes to start each new appointment by seeking "common ground" with her prospects. She looks for such items as a picture of the prospect's children or a trophy.[24]

Compliments. Most customers react positively to sincere compliments. Personal items in the prospect's office, achievements, or efficient operation of the prospect's business provide examples of what can be praised. A salesperson might say, "I learned recently that your company is ranked number one in customer satisfaction by J.D. Power and Associates."

Search for mutual acquaintances or interests. The discovering of mutual friends or interests can serve as the foundation for a strong social contact. Most people enjoy talking about themselves, their hobbies, and their achievements. Debra Fine, author of *The Fine Art of Small Talk*, says, "Small talk isn't stupid. It's the appetizer for all relationships."[25]

GUIDELINES FOR GOOD SOCIAL CONTACT The social contact should be viewed as rapport-building communication on a personal basis. This brief conversation establishes the foundation for the business contact, so it should never be viewed as an insignificant part of the presentation strategy. The following guidelines can help you develop the skills needed to make a good social contact.

1. *Prepare for the social contact.* Conduct a background check on topics of interest to the person you are contacting. This includes reviewing information in the prospect database, reading

SELLING IN ACTION

Effective Design and Use of the Business Card

The business card continues to be a powerful tool for salespeople. It provides a personal touch in our high-tech world. The business card is a convenient way to communicate important information to customers and others involved in the sales process. When you develop your business card, keep these tips in mind.

- Use eye-catching items such as your company logo, raised letters, and textured paper. The card should be tasteful and pleasing to the eye. Do use a white background.
- The card should feature all current contact information such as your e-mail address, telephone numbers, and mailing address. List a home phone number only if there's a second line for business calls.

- Consider using both sides of the card. You might print your customer service philosophy on the back of the card or list the products you sell.

Give your cards generously to anyone who might need to contact you later. Always offer your business card when networking. The card is useful when the contact tells others about your products or services.

How you respond to someone else's business card is important also. According to communications trainer Mark Jeffries, mentioned earlier, when someone hands you their business card, find something about it you can comment on before putting it away. You can comment on things such as the design, the company, or the individual's title. He contends people will have a favorable memory of you, if done successfully.[c]

industry reports, and searching the Internet. Once you arrive at the customer's office, you will discover additional information about the person's interests. Most people communicate what is important to them in the way they personalize their work environment.

2. *Initiate social contact.* The most effective opening comments should be expressed in the form of an open-ended question, such as, "I understand you have just been elected president of the United Way?" You can improve the possibility of a good response to your verbal question by applying nonverbal communication skills. Appropriate eye contact, voice inflections that communicate enthusiasm, and a warm smile will increase the customer's receptivity to your opening comments.

3. *Respond to the customer's conversations.* When the customer responds, it is imperative that you acknowledge the message both verbally and nonverbally. The verbal response might be "That is really interesting" or any other appropriate comment. Nonverbally, you let the customer know you are listening by taking notes, maintaining good eye contact, and occasionally nodding of your head. These gestures communicate you want her to continue talking.

4. *Keep the social contact focused on the customer.* Because you cannot control where a conversation might go, you may be tempted to focus the conversation on topics with which you are familiar. A response such as, "Several years ago I was in charge of our company's United Way campaign and we had a difficult time meeting our goal," shifts the focus of the conversation back to you. While an occasional short personal reference may be appropriate, it is best to keep the conversation focused on topics that are of interest to the customer. Dale Carnegie said that one of the best ways to build a relationship is to encourage others to talk about themselves.

Communication on a personal basis is often the first step in discovering a common language that can improve communication between the salesperson and the prospect. How much time should be devoted to the social contact? There is no easy answer to this question. The length of the conversation depends on the type of product or service sold, how busy the prospect appears to be, and your awareness of topics of mutual interest.

In many cases, the rapport-building conversation will take place over lunch or dinner. Some sales professionals contend that social conversation should occur before the meal is served, reserving business conversation until later. In some cases, it may be during a sporting event, such as a golf outing. It may also occur during a social event, such as a Broadway play that is offered in appreciation of prior or future business. Many successful sales have been closed during or after a social event. This explains why some companies enroll their sales staff and other customer contact personnel in dining etiquette classes.

The Business Contact

Converting the prospect's attention from the social contact to the business proposal is an important part of the approach. When you convert and hold your prospect's attention, you have fulfilled an important step in the selling process. Furthermore, without this step, the door has been closed on completing the remaining steps of the sale.

Some salespeople use a carefully planned opening statement or a question to convert the customer's attention to the sales presentation. A statement or question that focuses on the prospect's dominant buying motive is, of course, more likely to achieve the desired results. Buyers must like what they see and hear and must be made to feel that it is worthwhile to hear more.

Converting the Prospect's Attention and Arousing Interest

10.7 Describe seven ways to capture the prospect's attention and arouse interest

Throughout the years, salespeople have identified and used a number of effective methods to capture the prospect's attention, arouse interest, and transition into the next step of the presentation. Seven of the most common are explained in the following material:

Agenda approach
Product demonstration approach
Referral approach
Customer benefit approach

Question approach
Survey approach
Premium approach

We also discuss combining two or more of these approaches.

Agenda Approach

One of the most effective methods to transition from the social contact to the business contact is to thank the customer for taking time to meet with you and then review the call objectives you have prepared for the meeting. You might say, "Thank you for meeting with me this morning. I would like to accomplish three things during the time you have given me." This statement shows you value the person's time and you have preplanned a specific agenda. Always be open to changing the agenda based on input from the customer.[26] This approach is welcomed by buyers in multi-call situations.

Product Demonstration Approach

This straightforward method of getting the prospect's attention can be achieved by showing the actual product, a sample, a mock-up, a video, or a well-prepared brochure either in print form or on a computer screen. It is a popular approach used by sales representatives who sell convention services, technical products, pharmaceuticals, photographic equipment, automobiles, construction equipment, office furniture, and many other products. In many multi-call situations, salespeople leave samples for the customer to examine and try out at a later date. Trish Ormsby, a sales representative for Wells Fargo Alarm Services, uses her laptop computer to create a visual image of security systems that meet the customer's security needs.[27]

Referral Approach

Research indicates that another person is far more impressed with your good points if these points are presented by a third party rather than by you. The referral approach is quite effective because a third party (a satisfied customer) believes the prospect can benefit from your product. This type of opening statement has universal appeal among salespeople from nearly every field.

When you use the referral approach, your opening statement should include a direct reference to the third party. Here is an example: "Mrs. Follett, my name is Kurt Wheeler, and I represent the Cross Printing Company. We specialize in printing all types of business forms. Mr. Ameno—buyer for Raybale Products, Incorporated—is a regular customer of ours, and he suggested I mention his name to you."

Customer Benefit Approach

One of the most effective ways to gain a prospect's attention is to immediately point out benefits of purchasing your solution or value proposition. As noted in Chapter 7, the benefit could focus on either the product, company, or salesperson. Begin with the most important issue (or problem) facing the client. When using this approach, the most important buyer's benefit is included in the initial statement. For example, the salesperson selling a portable Sony projector might open with this product benefit statement:

> The Sony VPL-CS4 lightweight projector strikes a balance between cost, size, brightness, and convenience. It's a good choice for a quick business trip or for a work-at-home presentation.

A *company benefit* example taken from the financial services field is:

> When you meet with a Charles Schwab investment specialist, you can obtain advice on over 1,200 no-load, no-transaction-fee mutual funds.

The customer benefit approach is also used with what is sometimes referred to as the "elevator speech." The **elevator speech** focuses on the *benefit of working with the salesperson* and is used to open the door and establish credibility to meet a need. It is about offering to take excellent care of the prospect. The elevator speech should be short, prepared well in advance, and extensively rehearsed before it is used. It is used most appropriately in the initial call on a prospect where the prequalifying research indicates the buyer is more interested in the benefits of working with a highly qualified salesperson than finding a new product solution or supplier.

Here is an employment services example of a salesperson benefit statement using the elevator speech approach:

> Hello, I'm Chad Leffler. I partner with companies like yours that need to find talented people to help their business grow and become more profitable.

As noted, the key to achieving success with the customer benefit approach is advance preparation. Customers are annoyed when a salesperson cannot quickly communicate the benefits of meeting with them. Bruce Klassen, sales manager for Do All Industrial Supply, says, "Our salespeople begin the sales process by researching the prospect and the company. We need to be sure that our sales calls are going to benefit that prospect before we make even an initial sales approach."[28]

Question Approach

The question approach has two positive features. First, an appropriate question almost always triggers prospect involvement. Very few people avoid answering a direct question. Second, a question gets the prospect thinking about a problem that the salesperson may be prepared to solve.

Molly Hoover, a sales training consultant, conducts training classes for sales managers and car dealers who want to better understand the subtleties of selling to female car buyers. She suggests an approach that includes a few basic questions such as:

> "Is the vehicle for business or pleasure?"
> "Will you be buying within the next week or so?"[29]

These opening need-related questions will be discussed in detail in the next chapter and are generally not difficult to answer, yet they get the customer mentally involved. Some of the best opening questions are carefully phrased to arouse attention. The authors of *The Sales Question Book* offer some good examples:

> "Are you aware that we just added three new services to our payroll and accounting package? Could I tell you about them?"
> "We are now offering all our customers a special auditing service that used to be reserved for our largest accounts. Would you be interested in hearing about it?"[30]

Once you ask the question, listen carefully to the response. If the answer is yes, proceed with an enthusiastic presentation of your product. If the answer is no, then you may have to gracefully try another approach or thank the prospect for his or her time and depart. The use of questions will be discussed in detail in the next chapter and will provide information on the specific types of questions to use to approach your customer.

Survey Approach

Robert Hewitt, a Monterey, California, financial planner, has new clients fill out a detailed questionnaire before the first appointment. This procedure is part of his customer strategy. He studies the completed questionnaire and other documents before making any effort to find a solution

The survey approach offers many advantages. It is generally a nonthreatening way to open a sales call. You simply ask permission to acquire information that can be used to determine the buyer's need for the product.

Source: carlosseller/Shutterstock

to any of the customer's financial planning needs. The survey or "needs discovery," as it is also called, is an important part of the problem-solving philosophy of selling. It often is used in selling products where the need cannot be established without careful study.

The survey approach offers many advantages. It is generally a nonthreatening way to open a sales call. You simply are asking permission to acquire information that can be used to determine the buyer's need for your product. Because the survey is tailor-made for a specific business, the buyer is given individual treatment. Finally, the survey approach helps avoid an early discussion of price. Price cannot be discussed until the survey is completed. We will discuss the survey or needs discovery in detail in Chapter 11.

Premium Approach

The premium approach involves giving the customer a free sample or an inexpensive item. A financial services representative might give the customer a booklet that can be used to record expenses. Sales representatives for a large U.S. textbook publisher give faculty members a monthly planner. Product samples are frequently used by persons who sell cosmetics. Creative use of premiums is an effective way to get the customer's attention.

The agenda, product, referral, customer benefit, question, survey, and premium approaches offer the salesperson a variety of ways to set the stage for the presentation strategy. With experience, salespeople learn to select the most effective approach for each selling situation. Table 10.1 provides examples of how these approaches can be applied in real-world situations.

TABLE 10.1 Business Contact Worksheet

This illustrates how to prepare effective real-world approaches that capture the customer's attention.

METHOD OF APPROACH	WHAT WILL YOU SAY?
1. Agenda	**1.** (Office supply) "Thank you for meeting with me. During the next 45 minutes, I plan to accomplish three things."
2. Product	**2a.** (Retail clothing) "We have just received a shipment of new fall sweaters from Braemar International."
	2b. (Business forms manufacturer) "Our plant has just purchased a $300,000 Harris Graphics composer, Mr. Reichart; I would like to show you a copy of your sales invoice with your logo printed on it."
3. Customer benefit	**3.** (Real estate) "Mr. and Mrs. Stuart, my company lists and sells more homes than any other company in the area where your home is located. Our past performance would lead me to believe we can sell your home within two weeks."
4. Referral	**4.** (Food wholesaler) "Paula Doeman, procurement manager for Mercy Medical Center, suggested that I provide you with information about our computerized 'Order It' system."
5. Question	**5.** (Hotel convention services) "Mrs. McClaughin, will your Annual Franchisee Meeting be held in April?"
6. Survey	**6a.** (Custom-designed computer software) "Mr. Vasquez, I would like the opportunity to learn about your accounts receivable and accounts payable procedures. We may be able to develop a customized program that will significantly improve your cash flow."
	6b. (Retail menswear) "May I ask you a few questions about your wardrobe? The information will help me better understand your clothing needs."
7. Premium	**7.** (Financial services) "I would like to give you a publication titled *Guaranteed Growth Annuity*."

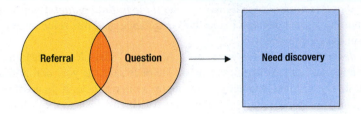

FIGURE 10.4

Combination approaches provide a smooth transition to the need discovery part of the consultative presentation.

Combination Approaches

A hallmark of adaptive selling is flexibility. Therefore, a combination of approaches sometimes provides the best avenue to need identification. Sales personnel who have adopted the consultative style, of course, use the question and survey approaches most frequently. Some selling situations, however, require that one of the other approaches be used, either alone or in combination with the question and survey approaches (Figure 10.4). An example of how a salesperson might use a referral and question approach combination follows:

Salesperson: Carl Hamilton at Simmons Modern Furniture suggested that I visit with you about our new line of compact furniture designed for smaller homes. He believes this line might complement the furniture you currently feature.

Customer: Yes, Carl called me yesterday and mentioned your name and company.

Salesperson: Before showing you our product lines, I would like to ask you some questions about your current product mix. First, what do you currently carry in the area of bedroom furniture?

Suggesting the use of a combination approach, noted sales authority Linda Richardson of Richardson Learning Systems advised to "go in armed to the gills with a full portfolio of knowledge, insights, data, and ideas. Use that portfolio to engage customers by sharing insights and asking business challenge questions that show that you know what you are talking about and that *lead* into your value. Intelligent questions provide as much insight as answers. They give you insights into the customer's thinking and jumpstart the collaborative process. They also help you validate that your insight is relevant."[31]

Coping with Sales Call Reluctance

The transition from the preapproach to the approach is sometimes blocked by sales call reluctance. Fear of making the initial contact with the prospect is one of the biggest obstacles to sales success. For new salespeople, the problem can be career threatening. **Sales call reluctance** includes the thoughts, feelings, and behavioral patterns that conspire to limit what a salesperson is able to accomplish. It is an internal, often emotional, barrier to sales success. Sales call reluctance can be caused by several different thought patterns:[32]

- Fear of taking risks
- Fear of group presentations
- Lack of self-confidence
- Fear of rejection

Regardless of the reasons for sales call reluctance, you can learn to deal with it. These are some suggestions:

- *Be optimistic about the outcome of the initial contact.* It is better to visualize and anticipate success than to anticipate failure. Martin Seligman, professor of psychology at the University of Pennsylvania and author of the best-selling book *Learned Optimism*, says that success in selling requires a healthy dose of optimism.[33] It is important to frequently recommit yourself to the double-win value-adding approach to working with customers discussed earlier. The anticipation of failure is a major barrier to making the initial contact.
- *Practice your approach before making the initial contact.* A well-rehearsed effort to make the initial contact increases your self-confidence and reduces the possibility that you may handle the situation badly.

- *Recognize that it is normal to feel anxious about the initial contact.* Even veteran salespeople experience some degree of sales call reluctance, and this reluctance can surface anywhere in the sales process.
- *Develop a deeper commitment to your goals.* Abraham Zaleznik was a leading professor of psychodynamics at Harvard Business School. He once said, "If your commitment is only in your mind, then you'll lose it when you encounter a big obstacle. If your commitment is in your heart *and* your mind, you'll create the power to break through the toughest obstacles."[34]

Selling to the Gatekeeper

Many decision makers have an assistant or secretary who manages their daily schedule. This person is often referred to as the "gatekeeper." If you want to reach the decision maker, work hard to align yourself with the person who schedules this person's appointments. Rule number one is to treat the gatekeeper with respect. Learn their names and what they do. Keep in mind this person can be an important source of information. For example, the gatekeeper can tell you how the buying process works and provide information regarding new developments in the company. This person may be able to help you make a preliminary qualification before you reach the decision maker. When you treat the person as an expert by soliciting their views, you establish a relationship that can pay big dividends today and in the future.[35]

When possible, use personal referrals from someone the prospect knows. If you have met the prospect previously, describe the meeting and tell the gatekeeper why you feel a second meeting would be beneficial.

CHAPTER LEARNING ACTIVITIES

Reviewing Key Concepts

Describe the three prescriptions that are included in the presentation strategy

Developing a presentation strategy involves preparing presale objectives, developing a presale presentation plan, and providing outstanding customer service. The presentation strategy combines elements of the relationship, product, and customer strategies.

Discuss the two-part preapproach process

Preparation for the sales presentation is a two-part process. Part one is referred to as the *preapproach* and involves preparing presale objectives and developing a presale presentation plan. It's best to develop presentation objectives for each stage of the buying process. Part two is called the *approach* and involves making a good first impression, securing the prospect's attention, and transitioning to need identification.

Describe team presentation strategies

In recent years, team selling has surfaced as a major development. Sales teams can often uncover problems, solutions, and sales opportunities that no individual salesperson could discover working alone. Team sales presentations require a more detailed precall plan than individual sales calls. Without careful planning and extensive practice (rehearsal), team presentations are likely to be delivered in a disorganized manner.

Explain how adaptive selling builds on four broad strategic areas of personal selling

Adaptive selling involves altering sales behaviors in order to improve communication with the customer. Salespeople today are challenged to develop a broader repertoire of selling strategies. Salespeople skilled in adaptive selling consider how the relationship, product, and customer strategies can enhance the sales presentation.

Describe the six main parts of the presentation plan

After collecting background information, salespeople need to create a customized presale presentation plan. The plan is developed after careful study of the six-step presentation plan, which includes approach, need discovery, presentation, negotiation, close, and servicing the sale.

Explain how to effectively approach the customer

The approach may involve face-to-face contact, telephone contact, or some other appropriate method of communication. If the approach is effective, the salesperson will be given an opportunity to make the sales presentation. A major goal of the *social contact* is to make a good first impression, build rapport, and establish credibility. The *business contact* involves converting the prospect's attention from the social contact to the sales presentation.

Describe seven ways to convert the prospect's attention and arouse interest

Over the years, salespeople have identified several ways to convert the prospect's attention and arouse interest in the presentation. Some of the most common ways include the agenda approach, product demonstration approach, referral approach, customer benefit approach, question approach, survey approach, and premium approach.

Key Terms

Presentation strategy, p. 201	Action objective, p. 203	Telesales, p. 209
Preapproach, p. 202	Six-step presentation	Elevator speech, p. 214
Approach, p. 202	plan, p. 207	Sales call reluctance, p. 217

MyMarketingLab

To complete the problems with the ⭐ in your MyLab, go to the EOC Discussion Questions.

Review Questions

10-1 What is the purpose of the preapproach? What are the two prescriptions included in the preapproach?

⭐ **10-2** Explain the role of objectives in developing the presale presentation plan.

10-3 Why should salespeople establish multiple-objective sales presentations? List four possible objectives that would be appropriate for stage one and stage two of the buying process.

10-4 Compare and contrast team sales presentations and individual sales calls.

⭐ **10-5** Describe the major steps in the presentation plan. Briefly discuss the role of adaptive selling in implementing the presentation plan.

10-6 What are the major objectives of the approach?

10-7 Briefly describe the four guidelines that can help you make a good social contact.

10-8 What are some rules to follow when leaving a message on voice mail? On e-mail?

⭐ **10-9** What methods can the salesperson use to convert the prospect's attention to the sales presentation?

Application Exercises

10-10 Assume that you are a salesperson who calls on retailers. For some time you have been attempting to get an appointment with one of the best retailers in the city to carry your line. You have an appointment to see the head buyer in one and one-half hours. You are sitting in your office. It will take you about 30 minutes to drive to your appointment. Outline what you should be doing between now and the time you leave to meet your prospect.

10-11 Tom Nelson has just graduated from Aspen College with a major in marketing. He has three years of experience in the retail grocery business and has decided he would like to go to work as a salesperson for the district office of Procter & Gamble. Tom has decided to telephone and set up an appointment for an interview. Write out exactly what Tom should *plan* to say during his telephone call.

10-12 Concepts from Dale Carnegie's *How to Win Friends and Influence People* can help you prepare for the social contact. Access the Dale Carnegie Training home page (www.dalecarnegie.com) and examine the courses offered. Search for the sales advantage course. Read the course description and review the two main things you will learn in this program. View the online sales action plan demo video to learn how Dale Carnegie's Web-based coaching program enhances what is learned in the course.

Role-Play Exercise

Research the type of computer that you would like to purchase in the future or one that you have just purchased. Strategically prepare to meet a potential customer who has been referred to you by a friend and who would like to purchase a similar computer. Using Table 10.1 on page 216, prepare four different business contact statements or questions you could use to approach your prospect. Review the material in this chapter and then pair off with another student who will assume the role of your customer. First, role-play the telephone contact and set up an appointment to get your customer into your store to meet with you and look at the computer. Second, role-play the approach you will use when the customer actually comes into the store. Review how well you made the approach.

Reality Selling Video Case Problem—Alim Hirani/Hilti Corporation

The global construction industry is a lucrative market, with customer needs ranging from measuring products to sophisticated construction solutions. Hilti Corporation, the company featured at the beginning of this chapter, provides its customers around the world with leading-edge construction products and services with outstanding added value. Hilti prides itself for its direct sales model, which allows its salespeople and service teams to work directly *with* and *for* the customers.

Alim Hirani, an account manager for Hilti, adopts the relationship marketing approach in his selling strategy. He often starts his sales calls, which have been carefully preplanned, with icebreakers such as asking about the customer's family rather than making the sales immediately. His sales presentations may take place in the client's office or even at the construction site. Consequently, he must always plan well in advance the best way to make his sales presentations for specific sales calls. At all times, he must attempt to establish his own and his company's credibility by demonstrating the premium value that Hilti's products and services can offer his clients. Whenever possible, he tries to get the customer involved in product demonstration because seeing is believing. Once the customers see for themselves the benefits of Hilti's product features, moving the customers from the investigation and evaluation stages to the action stage is just a procedure.

Alim sells not only individually but also as part of a team. For major clients who require a complete package of building/construction, mechanical/electrical, telecom, and interior finishing products and services, Alim works closely with his team members to make sure the information he acquires from the customer during initial contacts is made available to other salespeople and technical personnel of the team. In the construction industry, closing the sale is—most of the time—just the beginning. Well-trained product application specialists join Alim to offer the customers after-sales services, technical support, and training. (See the chapter opener and Reality Selling Today Role-Play 6 in Appendix 1 for more information.)

Questions

10-13 Why should Alim Hirani adopt the three prescriptions for the presentation strategy?

10-14 Salespeople are encouraged to establish multiple-objective sales presentations. What are some objectives Alim Hirani should consider when he calls on construction managers at the construction site?

10-15 What are some special challenges Alim Hirani faces when he makes his sales presentations in a nonoffice setting?

10-16 Put yourself in the position of a construction salesperson. Can you envision a situation when you might combine different ways to convert the prospect's attention and interests into action? Explain.

Regional Account Management Case Study (refer to Appendix 2)

NewNet Systems®

Your Value Adding Systems Partner

Establishing Your Approach

Casey Arnold, your sales manager at NewNet Systems, has notified Lee Bizon's former accounts by letter that you will be calling on them soon. She wants to meet with you tomorrow to discuss your preapproach to your new accounts.

Questions

10-17 As a part of your preapproach preparation for your meeting, you would like to have information on the communication styles of each of your accounts. Using the table you prepared for Chapter 9, add a column as noted below and list the communication style of each of your customers.

NewNet Systems Account Management

Name   Regional Account Manager, NEWNET SYSTEMS

Date	Account Name/	Dollar	**Comm.**				
Close	Contact Name	Sales Amt.	**Style**				

10-18 Casey wants you to call on Robert Kelly. Describe what your call objectives would be with Mr. Kelly. Describe how you will strategically use Mr. Kelly's communication style in your approach.

10-19 Your call on Aeroflot Airlines involves both team selling and selling to a buying committee. Who are the members of the Aeroflot buying committee and what kind of preapproach planning will be needed? Who will you be teaming with from NewNet and what kind of pre-approach planning will be needed?

10-20 Reviewing the social contact information in this chapter, what topics might be appropriate when meeting with Dwayne Ortega, Robert Kelly, Bradley Able, Sherry Britton, and Karen Murray?

10-21 In analyzing Lee Bizon's notes, each of the four communications styles are represented. If you haven't done so, Casey would like you to complete the online Communication Style assessment presented in Chapter 5 (see also communication style assessment at www .pearsonhighered.com/manning) and assess your preferred and secondary styles. With this information, summarize how you will use the platinum rule described in Chapter 5 to flex your style to work collaboratively with the four styles exemplified by your new contacts.

10-22 Casey has given you a reprint of a new article about using networks for warehouse applications. Which of your accounts might have a strong interest in this kind of article? How would you use this article to make an approach to that account?

10-23 It is not uncommon for new account managers to experience some call reluctance when taking on a new set of accounts. Referring to the section on "Coping with Sales Call Reluctance," describe how, if this might happen with you in taking over Lee Bizon's accounts, you might overcome this potential problem. Build your answer around the four suggestions in this chapter.

Partnership Selling: A Role-Play (see Appendix 3)

Developing a Relationship Strategy

Park Shores Resort and Convention Center.

Source: Courtesy of Beach Resort

Read Employment Memorandum 2, which announces your promotion to account executive. In your new position, you will be assigned by your instructor to one of the two major account categories in the convention center market. You will be assigned to either the *association accounts market* or the *corporate accounts market*. The association accounts market includes customers who have the responsibility for planning meetings for their association or group. The corporate accounts market includes customers who have the responsibility for planning meetings for the company they represent. (You will remain in the account category for the rest of the role-plays.)

Note the challenges you may have in your new position. Each of these challenges is represented in the future sales memoranda you receive from your sales manager.

Read Sales Memorandum 1 for the account category you are assigned. (Note that the "A" means association and your customer is Erin Adkins, and "B" means corporate and your customer is Leigh Combs.) Follow the instructions in the sales memorandum and strategically prepare to approach your new customer. Your call objectives are to establish a relationship (social contact), share an appealing benefit, and find out if your customer is planning any future conventions (business contact).

You may be asked to assume the role of a customer in the account category to which you are not assigned as a salesperson. Your instructor will provide you with detailed instructions for correctly assuming this role.

MyMarketingtLab

Go to the Assignments section of your MyLab to complete these writing exercises.

10-24 What does the development of the presentation strategy involve and what are its components?

10-25 Adaptive selling builds on four strategic areas of personal selling. What is adaptive selling? What are the factors at the heart of adaptive selling and why are these important?

11 Determining Customer Needs with a Consultative Questioning Strategy

Source: Michael Ahearne

Adaptive Selling Video—Questions, Questions, Questions

The effective use of questions is the starting point of the consultative sales process. Questions are used to build adaptive style selling relationships, discover customer needs, and adapt and present product solutions that meet those needs. Questions span the entire sales process and are also used to successfully negotiate, close, and service a sale.

"Questions, Questions, Questions," the second video in our Adaptive Selling Today Training Video Series, introduces and shows how to use the four adaptive selling questions described in this chapter. An Internet telephone systems sales representative featured in the video learns one of his largest accounts may be going with another supplier. The salesperson's company brought in a new sales training program on how to use questions effectively, and the salesperson is the first to learn the system. With his newly acquired knowledge and skills, the salesperson schedules another call to see if he can, with the use of questions, reestablish his relationship and salvage the sale.

In this follow-up call, we find out how well he has learned to adapt and use questions to discover and better understand the customer's needs, create value, solve the customer's buying problem, and retain the account. Throughout the three-part video, our salesperson learns about the following four-part multiple-questioning strategy and what these questions will reveal during the consultative sales presentation.

Survey Questions	*Reveal*	Problems and situation
Probing Questions	*Reveal*	Pain and implications
Need-Satisfaction Questions	*Reveal*	Pleasure and need satisfaction
Confirmation Questions	*Reveal*	Mutual understanding

The use of an effective questioning strategy, so important to the consultative sales process, is one of the greatest challenges facing salespeople. Need discovery and questioning will be explored in this chapter (Figure 11.1), and the sales presentation and demonstration will be presented in the next chapter. ●

223

Extensive research regarding the use of questions in the sales process reveals the importance of developing and perfecting a multiple questioning strategy to understand and solve customer needs. The Adaptive Questions video dramatically presents how these questions are used in the sales process.

Source: Michael Ahearne

The Six-Step Presentation Plan

Step One: Approach	☑ **Review Strategic/Consultative Selling Model** ☑ **Initiate customer contact**
Step Two: Need Discovery	☐ **Ask strategic questions** ☐ **Determine customer needs** ☐ **Select Product Solution**
Step Three: Presentation	☐ **Select presentation strategy** ☐ **Create presentation plan** ☐ **Initiate presentation**
Step Four: Negotiation	☐ **Anticipate buyer concerns** ☐ **Plan negotiating methods** ☐ **Initiate win-win negotiations**
Step Five: Close	☐ **Plan appropriate closing methods** ☐ **Recognize closing clues** ☐ **Initiate closing methods**
Step Six: Servicing the Sale	☐ **Follow through** ☐ **Follow-up calls** ☐ **Expansion selling**

Service, retail, wholesale, and manufacturer selling

FIGURE 11.1

Creating the Sales Presentation

The consultative sales process involves adding value by accurately determining the prospect's needs and selecting an appropriate product or service.

11.1 Outline the benefits of the consultative sales process

The Consultative Sales Process Adds Value

A growing number of salespeople, like the Internet telephone system salesperson pictured above, have adopted the consultative sales process. New competitive structures and customer demands have forced companies to continuously adapt and redefine their value-adding processes.[1] Consultative selling, as introduced in Chapter 2, is a value-adding process. Consultative selling involves meeting customer needs by asking strategic questions, listening to customers, understanding—and caring about—their problems, selecting the appropriate solution, creating the sales presentation, and following through after the sale. Consultative selling is a very customer-centric form of selling that creates value for the customer and, in the process, creates value for the firm.[2] This approach is very different from product-oriented selling. As one author noted, "Product-oriented selling can easily lapse into product evangelism." Product-oriented selling is usually inefficient and ineffective.[3,4]

New entrants in the field of personal selling sometimes wonder why some people excel in selling products or services, while others, who seem to work just as hard, fall short of meeting company or personal selling goals. The answer can be found by reviewing the behaviors displayed by top sales performers from *Fortune 500* and smaller entrepreneurial-based companies. High-performance sales personnel have learned how to skillfully diagnose and solve problems better than their competitors.[5] This consultative problem-solving capability translates into the following:

INCREASED CUSTOMER SATISFACTION Customers prefer to purchase solutions that truly meet their needs. The solution that is "just right" for the customer adds value, maximizes satisfaction, and sets the stage for a partnership relationship and repeat business. In some cases, the right solution will cost more than the customer planned to pay, but the added value will usually compensate for the higher price.

Jeff Thull, author of *Mastering the Complex Sale* and *The Prime Solution,* states, "In too many buyer–seller relationships, there is a value gap where the customer is not getting the satisfaction they believe was promised."[6] Consultative salespeople with the ability to diagnose and solve customer problems are able to close this value gap.

MORE SALES CLOSED The extra time taken to carefully solve the customer's buying problem will set the stage for closing more sales. A certain amount of buyer resistance surfaces in nearly every selling situation. Understanding your customer's needs and configuring the most suitable solution from available options add value to both your customer and your company. It will help you avoid unnecessary objections from the customer.

FEWER ORDER CANCELLATIONS AND FEWER RETURNS It is always disappointing to have a customer cancel an order a few days after the sale was closed. The frequency of order cancellations can be reduced with consultative style selling. Returned merchandise is another serious problem. Whether the product is returned or needs to be reconfigured, the expense will often wipe out the profit earned on several sales.

INCREASED REPEAT BUSINESS AND REFERRALS Many business firms do not make a profit on the first sale. In fact, some firms do not earn a profit until the customer has placed the third or fourth order. The same is true for the salesperson. Without repeat business and a steady list of referrals, the salesperson will generally not experience the financial and psychic rewards described in Chapter 1. If at any point the customer does not feel the treatment was fair, the time and cost invested in partnership building and obtaining the initial order, as well as future sales, may be lost. Repeat business also builds a sense of pride within everyone associated with the business.

Satisfied customers represent a potent form of sales promotion. A group of satisfied customer forms what might be called an "auxiliary" sales force. Through word-of-mouth advertising, especially with the availability of social media and blogging, these people are referring potential customers and building new business for both the salesperson and the firm. Most of us can't resist sharing positive experiences with friends and business acquaintances.

The sales environment is changing. In competitive markets, success increasingly hinges on developing and maintaining mutually rewarding customer relationships.[7] Salespeople using the consultative sales presentation model are able to create more value and gain competitive advantage in their markets.

The Four-Part Need-Satisfaction Model

11.2 Describe the four parts of the need-satisfaction model

To be most effective, the salesperson should think of the sales process as a four-part model. The Consultative Sales Process Guide features these four parts (Figure 11.2).

Part One—Need Discovery

Since the emergence of the marketing concept discussed in Chapter 2, where the activities of a firm revolve around the needs of the customer, need discovery forms the essence of salespeople being able to create value, meet the needs of their customers, and execute the firm's commitment to the

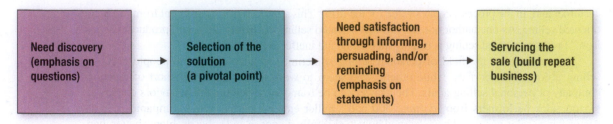

FIGURE 11.2

The Consultative Sales Process Guide

To be most successful, the salesperson should think of the sales presentation as a four-part process.

marketing concept. A review of the behaviors displayed by high-performance salespeople helps us understand the importance of precise need discovery. They have learned how to skillfully diagnose and solve the customer's problems better than their competitors. This problem-solving capability translates into more repeat business and referrals and fewer order cancellations and returns.[8]

Unless the selling situation requires mere order taking (customers know exactly what they want), need discovery in the information economy is a critically important part of the sales presentation. It may begin during the qualifying stage of building the prospect database or during the approach if the salesperson uses questions or a survey during the initial contact with the customer. Need discovery generally begins after you transition from the approach. In multi-call situations, need discovery may be the primary call objective during the first or second call. In most multi-call settings, it is wise to reconfirm the needs discovered in earlier calls.

The pace, scope, depth, and time allocated to inquiry depend on a variety of factors. Some of these include the sophistication of the product, the selling price, the customer's knowledge of the product, the product applications, and, of course, the time available for dialogue between the salesperson and the prospect. Each selling situation is different, so a standard set of guidelines for need discovery is not practical. Additional information on need discovery is presented later in the chapter.

Part Two—Selection of the Solution

The emphasis in sales and marketing today is on determining customer needs and then selecting or configuring custom-fitted solutions to satisfy these needs. Therefore, an important function of the salesperson is product selection, also often referred to as "product configuration." Product recommendations in complex sales generally involve writing a detailed product proposal. The salesperson must choose the product or service that can provide maximum satisfaction. When making this decision, the salesperson must be aware of all product options, including those offered by the competition.

Salespeople who have the ability to conduct an effective, value-added needs analysis achieve the status of trusted adviser. Mary Langston, personal shopper at Nordstrom's Michigan Avenue store in Chicago, helps customers update their wardrobes. When asked what her days are like, she says, "It starts and ends with being a good listener." She promises her customers that she will never let them walk out of the store with clothing that does not look right.[9]

Part Three—Need Satisfaction Through Informing, Persuading, or Reminding

The third part of the consultative sales process consists of creating a need-satisfaction sales presentation and communicating to the customer, both verbally and nonverbally, the satisfaction that the product or service can provide. The salesperson places less emphasis on the use of questions and begins making value-adding statements. These value-adding statements are organized into a presentation that informs, persuades, or reminds the customer of the most suitable product or service. In several of the remaining chapters, we discuss specific strategies used in conjunction with the sales presentation/demonstration, negotiating buyer resistance, and closing and servicing the sale.

Part Four—Servicing the Sale

Servicing the sale is a major way to create value. These activities, which occur after closing the sale, ensure maximum customer satisfaction and set the stage for a long-term relationship.

Pharmaceutical salespeople generally have only a short time to present their product. In some situations, the doctor may immediately indicate a willingness to prescribe. However, in other situations the salesperson may be asked to make an informative need-satisfaction presentation to several members of the practice.

Source: Custom Medical Stock Photo/Alamy

Service activities include expansion selling, making credit arrangements, following through on assurances and promises, and dealing effectively with complaints. This topic is covered in detail in Chapter 15.

In those cases where a sale is normally closed during a single sales call, the salesperson should be prepared to go through all four parts of the Consultative Sales Process Guide. However, when a salesperson uses a multi-call approach, preparing for all the parts is usually not practical. The person selling networking systems or investments, for example, almost always uses a multi-call sales process. Need discovery (part one) is the focus of the first call.

Creating Value with Need Discovery

11.3 Discuss the use of questions to discover customer needs

A lawyer does not give the client advice until the legal problem has been carefully studied and confirmed. A doctor does not prescribe medication until the patient's symptoms have been identified. In like manner, the salesperson should not recommend the purchase of a product without thorough need identification. You start with the assumption that the client's problem is not known. The only way to determine and confirm the problem is to get the other person talking. Effective relationship builders are willing to listen to better understand customer challenges. They ask questions that lead to consultative conversations, which open doors to greater opportunities.[10] You must obtain information to properly clarify the need, propose a single solution, or offer a range of solutions.

Customers may not realize that they actually have a problem. Even when they are aware of their need, as noted earlier by Salesforce.com's Dave Levitt, given the wide range of solutions and new products available today, they may not realize that an actual solution to their problem exists. Bringing new insights regarding both their buying problem and enhanced solutions creates value for your customer.

Need discovery (sometimes called "need analysis" or "needs assessment") begins with pre-call preparation when the salesperson is acquiring background information on the prospect. As noted in Chapter 9, this part of need discovery is also referred to as "qualifying the prospect." Need discovery, and in some cases the qualification process, continues once the salesperson and the customer are engaged in a real dialogue. Through the process of need discovery, the salesperson establishes two-way communication by asking appropriate questions and listening carefully

ADAPTIVE SELLING TODAY TRAINING VIDEO SERIES

Neil Rackham Interview on *Selling Today*

Neil Rackham is one of the most recognized sales educators and sales authors of all time. Celebrated for his pioneering book titled *SPIN Selling*, Neil is a sought-after expert who consults with global organizations on improving and streamlining their sales functions. We partnered with Neil and interviewed him on his insights and passion for selling. In this new, exclusive to *Selling Today* video, Neil shares with us his insights and updates about the concept of SPIN Selling, the impact of the Internet and technology on salespeople, and the future of careers in selling.

Source: Michael Ahearne

- **Insights and Passion for Selling** Personal selling to customers, outside the company as well as at all levels within a company, is the thing that makes business prosper because it releases value that creates the business. However, even though companies are moderately well run today, the way companies work together is not as good. Therefore, the job of sales is to enable a company to collaborate and partner with other companies and individuals who are their customers.
- **SPIN Selling** In successful sales calls, it is the customer who does most of the talking, not the salesperson. In high-level selling that requires multiple calls, questioning skills are critical. Salespeople in high-level selling do not present their solutions until very late in the sales process following the SPIN path: Situation, Problem, Implication, Need-payoff.
- **The Internet** The Internet and sophisticated websites have made purchasing of many mature and standard products convenient. However, new and sophisticated products require high-level salespeople who can systematically solve

complex buying problems through their pattern of questions and sophisticated need discovery.
- **Creating Value** Selling has moved from communicating value to creating unique value that appeals to the customer. A successful sales career will be accomplished through a shift in sales training that focuses on Sales Education. This shift will focus on understanding finance, quality improvement, and customer decision making—important value considerations for the customer.
- **Careers in Selling** Through automation, technology will eliminate lower-end selling jobs that still focus on explaining the product. Higher-end selling positions that require *creativity and listening skills* are unlikely to be automated in the next fifty years, therefore providing excellent long-term career opportunities.

to the customer's responses. These responses usually provide clues concerning the customer's dominant buying motives (Figure 11.3).

Need Discovery—Asking Questions

The effective use of questions to achieve need identification and need satisfaction is one of the greatest challenges facing most professional salespeople. The types of questions you ask, the timing of those questions, and how you pose them greatly impact your ability to create customer value. In many situations, asking high–value-added questions that enlighten your prospect both about their needs and possible solutions results in an immediate sale.

The strategic approach to asking questions has been the focus of two major studies. These studies were conducted in response to the emergence of the marketing concept and evolution of the consultative and strategic selling eras discussed in Chapter 2. Neil Rackham conducted this research for his book *SPIN Selling* and SPIN Selling Sales Training programs, and Xerox Learning Systems for their successful Personal Selling Skills (PSS) course.

THE SPIN SELLING MODEL According to research conducted during the strategic selling era (see Chapter 2, Table 2.1 Evolution of Personal Selling) on more than 35,000 salespeople by Neil Rackham, mastering the use of questions can increase one's success in sales by 17 percent.[11] Questions help clarify the exact dimensions of the problem, help the customer evaluate a range of solutions, and assist the customer in evaluating the potential outcome of the solution that is implemented.[12] Rackham's research focused on strategies for making large-ticket sales and is based on a close examination of successful salespeople. Rackham found the investigative or need-discovery stage of the sales process has the most impact on the buyer's decision to purchase a product. He recommends a multiple-question approach that involves using four types of questions in a specific sequence (see Selling in Action on p. 234). Spin sales training programs are presented by the Miller Heiman Group (www.millerheimangroup.com/sales-ready/).

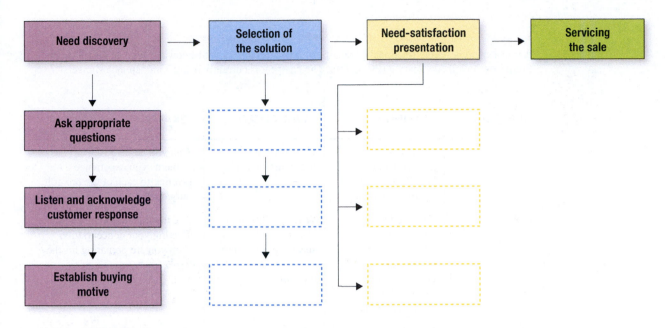

FIGURE 11.3

Three Dimensions of Need Discovery

PERSONAL SELLING SKILLS MODEL The importance of questioning to establish two-way communication was revealed in another study conducted during the consultative selling era. Research conducted by Xerox Learning Systems was used to develop the original Xerox Personal Selling Skills training program. Sales personnel were interviewed to identify the characteristics of a successful sales call. The results were quite surprising. A successful sales call lasts an average of 30 minutes. During this period, the salesperson asks an average of 13.6 questions, discusses an average of 7.7 product features, and describes approximately six product benefits. During the successful sales call, the customer asks approximately eight questions.[13] This 18-month study of behavioral differences among high-, average-, and low-performance salespeople illustrates that a successful sales call is a model of good two-way communication. Regarding the specific use of questions, the results revealed high performers do the following:

- Use effective questions to gather information and build a clear, complete, mutual understanding of customer needs.
- Guide the direction of a sales call by striking an appropriate balance between open and closed questions.
- Use their questioning strategy to facilitate an open exchange of information.[14]

This study has been used to create and update the very successful Personal Selling Skills training program, now also presented by Miller Heiman Group (www.millerheimangroup.com/achieveglobal/).

SOCRATIC SELLING MODEL The art and science of using questions was also discussed by Socrates more than 2,500 years ago. He noted, among other things, that questions tend to make people think. It's nearly impossible to remain passive when confronted with a direct question. Today, there are sales training programs such as Michael Hargrove's "Using the Socratic Selling Methods" and books such as Kevin Daley's *Socratic Selling: How to Ask the Questions That Get the Sale* that include many of the observations of Socrates.[15]

In every selling situation, you want the prospect to be actively thinking, sharing thoughts, and asking questions. Appropriate questions reduce tension and build trust in a selling situation because they communicate interest in the other person's welfare. Until the person begins to talk freely, the salesperson will have difficulty diagnosing and solving the customer's problems.

The Four-Part Consultative Questioning Strategy

Table 11.1 illustrates the use of a multiple-questioning strategy to discover customer needs. This strategy is based upon the research studies discussed earlier, as well as that conducted for the

TABLE 11.1 Types of Questions Used in Conjunction with Consultative Selling

A salesperson is selling fractional ownership of a jet aircraft to a well-known golf professional on the Professional Golf Association (PGA) Tour. The prospect is currently using commercial air travel.

TYPE OF QUESTION	DEFINITION	WHEN USED	EXAMPLES
Survey	*Discovers basic facts about the buyer's problem and existing situation*	Usually at the beginning of a sale	"Can you describe the problems you experience traveling to each of the pro golf tournaments?"
Probing	*Designed to uncover pain, and clarify the circumstances and implications surrounding the customer's problem*	When you feel the need to obtain more specific information to fully understand the *problem*	"Are the travel problems affecting your concentration when you are preparing for the event?"
Confirmation	*Used throughout the sales process to verify the accuracy and assure a mutual understanding of information exchanged by the salesperson and the buyer*	After important information has been exchanged	"So you think the uncertainty associated with commercial air travel is having some effect on your game?"
Need Satisfaction	*Designed to move the sales process toward commitment and action; focuses on the pleasure or payoff achieved from the proposed solution*	When you change the focus from the problem to a discussion of the solution	"With fractional ownership of your own jet, what personal benefits would this bring to your performance in the 30 tournaments you play each year?"

"Questions, Questions, Questions" sales training video described in the opening material for this chapter. The four types of questions are situation questions, probing questions, confirmation questions, and need-satisfaction questions. Developing skill in the use of these questions will work best if the consultative salesperson develops the mind-set that it is more important to understand the customer than it is to persuade the customer. You will note similarities to the SPIN Selling and personal selling skills questioning strategies, as well as those found in other popular selling books.

SURVEY QUESTIONS REVEAL CUSTOMER'S PROBLEMS At the beginning of most sales presentations, there is a need to collect basic facts about the buyer's existing situation and problem. **Survey questions**, or "information-gathering questions," as they are sometimes called, are designed to obtain this knowledge. To accomplish this, there are two types of survey questions.

General survey questions help the salesperson discover facts about the buyer's problem and existing situation and are often the first step in the partnership-building process. Rackham refers to these as *Situation Questions*. Here is a sampling of general survey questions that can be used in selected selling fields:

> "I understand that your regional facilities don't necessarily use the same delivery carriers, is that correct?" (Shipping Service)
> "Tell me about the new challenges you are facing in the area of data storage." (File Server)

"What is your current rate of employee turnover?" (Customer Service Training)

"Can you provide me with information on the kinds of meetings and conventions you plan for your clients and employees?" (Hotel Convention Services)

"Can you describe the style of home furnishings you prefer?" (Retail Home Furnishings)

In most selling situations, general survey questions are followed by specific survey questions. **Specific survey questions** are designed to give prospects a chance to describe in more detail the problem, issue, or dissatisfaction they are experiencing from their point of view. These specific survey questions (see Selling in Action on p. 234), or "*problem* questions" as they are referred to in the SPIN Selling sequence, are designed to delve more deeply into the customer's buying situation. Five examples of specific survey questions are:

"Has it occurred to you that by not consolidating your shipping with one carrier, you're likely spending more than is really necessary?" (Shipping Service)

"How do you feel about installing another server to your system?" (File Server)

"To what extent is employee turnover affecting your customer service?" (Customer Service Training)

"What meal function features are most important to your guests?" (Hotel Convention Services)

"Are you looking for an entertainment center that blends in with your existing furniture?" (Retail Home Furnishings)

Survey questions, general or specific, should not be used to collect factual information that can be acquired from other sources, such as your Customer Relationship Management (CRM) prospect database prior to the sales call. The preapproach prospect qualification effort is especially important when the salesperson is involved in a large or complex sale. These buyers expect the salesperson to do their homework and not waste the buyer's time asking general survey questions and discussing basic factual information that is available from other sources. Rackham's research revealed that more experienced salespeople tended to ask more specific survey or problem questions, and ask them sooner.

Although survey questions are most often used at the beginning of the sales process, they can be used at other times. Gaining a better understanding of the customer's situation or buying problem may be necessary at any time during the sales presentation. We present the four types of questions in a sequence that has proven to be effective in most selling situations. However, it would be a mistake to view this sequence as a *rigid* plan for every sales presentation. High-performing salespeople spend time strategically preparing tentative questions before they make the sales call. Table 11.2 provides some examples. Note that both open and closed questions are listed. **Open questions** require the prospect to go beyond a simple yes/no response. **Closed questions** can be answered with a yes or no, or a brief response.

Open questions are very effective in certain selling situations because they provoke thoughtful and insightful answers. The specific survey question "What are the biggest challenges you face in the area of plant security?" focuses the prospect's attention on problems that need solutions. Closed questions, however, can be equally effective when the sales conversation needs to be narrowed or focused on a specific issue.

PROBING QUESTIONS REVEAL CUSTOMER'S PAIN Early in the sales process, the salesperson should make every effort to fully understand the buying *problem* and the pain, implications, or consequences surrounding the problem. This is especially important when the problem is difficult to describe, the solution is complex, and the potential impact of a wrong decision is enormous.[16]

Probing questions help you uncover and clarify the pain, implications, and circumstances surrounding the customer's buying problem. They are used more frequently in large, complex sales. These questions often uncover the current level of customer concern, fear, or frustration related to the problem. The following probing questions, also referred to as "*implication*" questions in Rackham's *SPIN Selling,* are more focused than the survey questions presented earlier.

"But, doesn't every incorrect label cost you to ship to an incorrect address, then cost you again to have it shipped back to you?" (Shipping Service)

"What would be the consequences if you choose to do nothing about your current server situation?" (File Server)

TABLE 11.2 Need Discovery Worksheet

Preplanned questions (sometimes used in conjunction with company-supplied forms) are often used in service, retail, wholesale, and manufacturer selling. Salespeople, such as Johnny in the Questions, Questions, Questions video, who use the consultative approach frequently record answers to their questions and use this information to correctly select and recommend solutions in subsequent calls in their multi-call sales situations. Open and closed questions used in the area of financial services appear in the following list.

PREPLANNED QUESTIONS TO DISCOVER BUYING MOTIVES	CUSTOMER RESPONSE
1. "Now, as I understand it, you're currently pursuing an Internet phone system to offset your high cellular costs?" (Closed/General Survey/Situational)	
2. "Are you aware that with the system you are currently using, your brokers may have to keep their laptop 'on' in order to make and receive Internet calls?" (Closed/Specific Survey/Problem)	
3. "So what happens if, say, your broker is waiting for an important return call and then inadvertently logs off their laptop without a way to roll over the client's return call into a centralized system?" (Open/Probing/Pain/Implication)	
4. "Let's see if WE understand this—the brokers won't support the system you're considering because it doesn't include instant messaging? And, since the brokers would be the primary users of the new system, you're concerned that the system will fail without their support, is that correct?" (Closed/Summary Confirmation)	
5. "What if we could develop a communications system for you that included I.M. and met the SEC requirements? What positive impact could that have on your situation?" (Open/Need Satisfaction/Pleasure)	
6.	
7.	
8.	

"How does senior management feel about employee turnover and the related customer service problem?" (Customer Service Training)

"Is poor service at the meal function negatively affecting the number of people returning to your seminar?" (Hotel Convention Services)

"Is it important that you have easy access for connecting your DVD, TIVO, and your wireless LAN network?" (Retail Home Furnishings)

Probing or implication questions help the salesperson and customer gain a mutual understanding of *why* a problem is important. Asking effective probing questions requires extensive knowledge of your company's capabilities, much insight into your customer's buying problem, and a great deal of practice.

The best sales presentations are characterized by active dialogue. As the sales process progresses, the customer becomes more open and shares perceptions, ideas, and feelings freely. A series of appropriate probing questions stimulates the prospect to discover things not considered before.

CONFIRMATION QUESTIONS REVEAL MUTUAL UNDERSTANDING Confirmation questions are used throughout the sales process to verify the accuracy and assure a mutual understanding of information exchanged by the salesperson and the buyer (see Table 11.1). They are also used to gain commitment, a critically important part of achieving success in larger complex sales. Without commitment throughout the sales process, the chances of a successful sale evaporate rapidly.

These questions, which are an important update to the research on the use of questioning strategies, help determine whether there is mutual understanding of the problems and circumstances the customer is experiencing, as well as the possibilities for a solution. Throughout the sales process, there is always the potential for a breakdown in communication. Perhaps the language used by the salesperson is too technical. Information and initial needs discovered during the qualifying stage of the need discovery may have changed. Maybe the customer is preoccupied and has not listened closely to what has been said. Many confirmation questions are simple and to the point.

"If I understand you correctly, the monitoring system we are looking at for data storage must be set up for both your corporate headquarters and the manufacturing operation. Is that correct?" (File Server)

"I want to be sure I am clear that you feel there is a direct relationship between employee turnover and the problems that exist in customer service." (Customer Service Training)

"Did you say that your seminar attendance dropped 12 percent last year?" (Hotel Convention Services)

"So you want a new entertainment center that blends with your current, light-colored oak furniture?" (Retail Home Furnishings)

The length of the sales process can vary from a few minutes during a single-call presentation to weeks or even months in a complex multi-call sales presentation. As the sales process progresses, the amount of information available to the salesperson and the customer increases. As the need discovery progresses, the customer's buying criteria or buying conditions surface. **Buying conditions** are those qualifications that must be available or fulfilled before the sale can be closed. The customer may buy only if the product is available in a certain configuration or can be delivered by a certain date. In some selling situations, product installation or service after the sale is considered an important buying condition by the customer. In a large, complex sale, several buying conditions may surface. The salesperson has the responsibility of clarifying, confirming, and gaining commitment on each condition. The same is true for gaining commitment of each of the specific benefits presented to the customer.

One of the best ways to clarify, confirm, and gain commitment on several buying conditions is with a **summary-confirmation question**. To illustrate, let us consider a situation in which Alexis Rodriguez, sales manager at a major hotel, has interviewed a prospect who wants to schedule a large awards banquet. After a series of survey, probing, and confirmation questions, Alexis feels confident that the information collected is complete to prepare a proposal. However, to be sure all the facts have been collected, Alexis asks the following summary-confirmation question to gain commitment on the important buying conditions:

> "Let me summarize the major items you have mentioned. You want all banquet attendees served within an eight-minute time frame after the opening speaker has finished his speech. And you need a room that will comfortably seat 60 people banquet style and 10 of these people will be seated at the head table. Is this correct?"

Once all the buying conditions are confirmed, Alexis can prepare a proposal that reflects the specific needs of her customer. The result is a win-win situation for the customer and the salesperson. The chances of closing the sale greatly improve. In multi-call sales processes, it is wise to begin subsequent calls with summary-confirmation questions that reestablish what was discussed in the previous call(s):

> (Re-qualifying the new prospect) "I would like to revisit the information we have in our database about your company's purchasing procedures. You prefer limiting your suppliers and developing long-term partnerships where they are committed to your profitability and your customers' total customer satisfaction. You also require e-commerce linkages that allow your people to review the status of their order, delivery dates, and the projected costs including transportation and financing. Is that correct?"

> (The second call in a multi-call sale situation) "Let me begin by going over what we discussed in our last visit. Your current shipper gives you a 50 percent discount and provides its own custom label printer?" If the customer responds in the affirmative, the salesperson continues with another summary-confirmation question. "You also have to buy fairly expensive custom labels and, at around $90 a pack, you're spending over $20,000 just on labels; is that still correct?"

This enables the salesperson to verify that the previously discovered buying conditions have remained the same and not changed since the last meeting. Summary-confirmation questions are also used to effectively clarify, confirm, and gain commitment to several product benefits after they have been presented, generally one at a time. Commitment to the value of the benefits usually results in transitioning the presentation to the closing and servicing of the sale.

NEED-SATISFACTION QUESTIONS REVEAL PLEASURE The fourth type of question used in the sales process is fundamentally different from the other three. **Need-satisfaction questions** are designed to focus on the solution and the benefits of the solution. Spin Selling refers to these questions as Need-Payoff questions. These are helpful questions that move the sales process toward commitment and action. The chances of closing the sale greatly improve because need-satisfaction questions, or, as they are sometimes called "solution" or "pleasure questions," focus on specific benefits and build desire for a solution.

Survey, probing, and confirmation questions focus on understanding and clarifying the customer's problem. Need-satisfaction questions help the prospect see how your product or service provides a solution to the problem you have uncovered. The opportunity to close the sale greatly improves because you have cast the solution in a pleasurable light.

In most cases, these questions are used after the salesperson has created awareness of the seriousness of the buyer's problem. The need-satisfaction questions you ask will replace their current levels of concern, pain, or frustration with pleasurable thoughts about a solution. The following examples provide insight into the use of need satisfaction, or as SPIN Selling refers to them, "need-payoff" questions:

> "And if I told you that I can offer you cost savings of at least 5 percent over your current shipping expenses, would that be meaningful?" (Shipping Service)
>
> "Tests on similar applications show a new file server can increase data storage by 30 to 40 percent. How much of an increase do you feel you would achieve?" (File Server)

In many selling situations, a product demonstration is an essential stage in the sales process. In this case, the salesperson might use the following need-satisfaction question:

> "What benefits do you see if we provided a demonstration of one of the training modules to senior management so they can understand what you and I have discovered about reducing employee turnover?" (Customer Service Training)

Once the prospect needs are clearly identified, need-satisfaction questions can be valuable closing tools. Consider this example:

> "Considering the benefits we have summarized and agreed on, and noting the fact that our staff will deliver an outstanding meal function, would you like to sign this confirmation so we can reserve the rooms and schedule the meals that you need?" (Hotel Convention Services)

Need-satisfaction questions such as these are very powerful because they build desire for the solution and give ownership of the solution to the customer. When the prospect understands which parts of the problem(s) your solution can solve, you are less likely to invite objections. In some cases, you may identify problems that still need to be clarified. When this happens, you can use survey, probing, or confirmation questions to obtain more information.

At this point, you have received an introduction to the four most common types of questions used during the selling process. (For more insight into the application of questions to the sales process, view the three videos in the "Questions, Questions, Questions" series referred to in this chapter's opening vignette. Also refer to the Role-Play Application Exercises on pages 243–244.) We will revisit these important sales tools later in this chapter and in Chapters 12, 13, 14, and 15.

SELLING IN ACTION

Asking Questions, Not Telling at CARQUEST

CARQUEST Auto Parts promises to deliver what customers need. To achieve this lofty goal, the company enrolled its 1,200 outside sale force members in *Action Selling*. A major objective of this sales training program is to help salespeople become trusted business consultants. They learned that asking—not telling—is the key to sales success. Emphasis throughout the course is placed on asking more and better questions. Duane Sparks, who developed *Action Selling*, says "The success rate of sales calls rises significantly when more than two specific customer needs are uncovered by questioning."[a,b]

SELLING IN ACTION

Selling in Action

The use of questions to discover needs and present solutions is discussed in several popular personal selling books. For comparison purposes, the approximate equivalents to the four types of questions described in this chapter are listed.

Selling Today by Manning, Ahearne, and Reece	The SPIN Selling Fieldbook by Rackham	The New Solution Selling by Eades	The New Conceptual Selling by Heiman, Sanchez, with Tuleja	Secrets of Question-Based Selling by Freese
SURVEY	SITUATION	OPEN ENDED	CONFIRMATION	STATUS
PROBING	PROBLEM	CLOSED ENDED	NEW INFORMATION	ISSUE
CONFIRMATION	IMPLICATION	CONFIRMING	ATTITUDE	IMPLICATION
NEED SATISFACTION	NEED PAYOFF		COMMITMENT	SOLUTION
			BASIC ISSUE	

The questions above are listed in the sequence presented by the authors. To determine the exact definition of each type of question, check the source.

Qualifying to Eliminate Unnecessary Questions

It is important to avoid the use of unnecessary questions during a sales call. Prequalifying the prospect, as described in Chapter 9, is especially important when the prospect is a business buyer. Successful salespeople acquire as much information as possible about the prospect before the first meeting. They use sources such as the prospect's website, LinkedIn, previous phone calls or e-mails, and information recorded in the salesperson's CRM system. This prior understanding of the prospect allows the salesperson to direct the qualifying conversation using effective confirmation questions like: "Your website mentions your company has recently expanded into a new product market. Can you tell me more about that?" Buyers expect the salesperson to be well informed about their operation and not waste time asking a large number of basic survey questions. Confirmation questions communicate this prior knowledge and allow the salesperson and customer to move ahead in the consultative sales process with more important probing and need-satisfaction questions.

Robert Jolles, author of *Customer-Centered Selling*,[17] suggests that salespeople be careful when determining whether the person with whom they are meeting has the authority to make the purchase decision. According to Jolles, asking a survey question like "Are you the one who will be making the decision on this purchase?" encourages prospects without decision-making authority to lie in order to maintain their pride in the situation. Instead, Jolles recommends the question, "Who, besides yourself, will be responsible for this purchase decision?" This subtle, yet strategic rephrasing to a confirmation/survey question, allows the prospect to tell the truth and maintain his or her dignity.

Need Discovery—Listening and Acknowledging the Customer's Response

11.4 Describe the importance of active listening and the use of confirmation questions

To fully understand the customer, we must listen closely and acknowledge every response. The authors of *First Impressions* offer these words of advice to salespeople who use questions as part of the need identification process:

> What you do after you ask a question can reveal even more about you than the questions you ask. You reveal your true level of interest in the way you listen.[18]

Most of us are born with the ability to hear, but we have to learn how to listen. The starting point is developing a listening attitude. Always regard the customer as worthy of your respect and full attention.[19] Salespeople with high levels of customer orientation truly care about customers, and thus engage in actions that customers value such as listening to customer feedback and solving customer problems. Once you have made a commitment to becoming a better listener, develop active-listening skills.

DEVELOPING ACTIVE-LISTENING SKILLS **Active listening** is the process of sending back to the prospect what you as a listener think the person meant, both in terms of content and in terms of feelings. Active listening requires intense involvement as you concentrate on what you are hearing, exhibit your listening attitude through your nonverbal messages (see Chapter 3), and give feedback to the prospect on what you think he or she meant.[20]

Developing active-listening skills involves three practices that can be learned by any salesperson willing to make the commitment.

FOCUS YOUR FULL ATTENTION This is not easy because the delivery of the messages we hear is often much slower than our capacity to listen. Thus, we have plenty of time to let our minds roam, to think ahead, and to plan what we are going to say next. Our senses are constantly feeding us new information while someone is trying to tell us something. Staying focused is often difficult and involves use of both verbal and nonverbal messages.[21] To show that you are paying attention, lean toward the prospect while saying "uh-huh," "okay," or "I understand" and nodding in agreement when appropriate. Avoid nodding rapidly or saying "uh-huh" rapidly because this will communicate impatience or a desire to turn the conversation back to you.[22]

It is important to listen to the emotion involved in your customer's comments. A poor listener listens to facts; a good listener listens to emotions. Theoretically, 20 percent of communications is strictly facts and 80 percent is emotion—the emotion we all have and put into every thought. Listening for the emotions in your client's conversation enables you to receive the entire message.[23] Emotional-buying motives were discussed in detail in Chapter 8.

Within every sales presentation there will be times when silence should be welcomed. Use silence to control the flow of information and draw out the customer. Customers are often inclined to fill silence by talking. Throughout an effective sales presentation, the customer should be talking more than the salesperson.[24]

PARAPHRASE THE CUSTOMER'S MEANING After the customer stops talking, pause for two or three seconds and then state in your own words, with a confirmation question, what you think the person meant. This technique not only helps ensure understanding, but also is an effective customer relations strategy. The customer feels good knowing that, not only are you listening to what has been said, but you are also making an effort to ensure accuracy.

In addition to paraphrasing the content, use questions to dig for full understanding of the customer's perceptions.[25] The use of survey or probing questions is appropriate anytime you need to clarify what is being said by the prospect.

TAKE NOTES Although note taking is not necessary in every sales presentation, it is important in complex sales in which the information obtained from the customer is critical to the development of a buying solution. Taking accurate notes is a good way to demonstrate to the customer that you are actively listening. When you take notes, you increase your memory of what you heard. Your notes should be brief and to the point.[26] If the information you receive from the customer is too technical or unfamiliar, do not hesitate to ask for clarification of information you don't understand.

CRM—REVIEWING ACCOUNT STATUS

Salespeople regularly review the status of their prospects' records in their customer relationship management (CRM) databases. In some cases, this is done on the computer screen. In other situations, a printed copy of the records can enhance the process.

Salespeople review their files to ascertain at what phase each prospect is in the Consultative Sales Presentation Guide sales cycle. Then they decide which action to take to help move the prospect to the next phase. Sales managers can be helpful with this process,

especially for new salespeople. Managers can help salespeople evaluate the available information and suggest strategies designed to move to the next phase.

Even experienced salespeople count on their sales managers to help plan presentations. Managers can help salespeople evaluate their contacts' needs, select the best solution, and plan a presentation most likely to succeed.

Need Discovery—Establishing Buying Motives

The primary goal of questioning, listening, and acknowledging is to uncover prospect needs and establish buying motives. Our efforts to discover prospect needs can be more effective if we focus our questioning on determining the prospect's primary reasons for buying. When a customer has a definite need, it is usually supported by specific buying motives.

The greatest time investment in personal selling is on the front end of the sales process. First, you must plan the sales call and then, once you are face-to-face with the customer, you can begin the need-discovery stage. It is during the early stage of the sales process that you can create the greatest value for the customer.[27]

Selecting Solutions that Create Value

11.5 Select solutions that match customer needs

Salespeople are no longer selling just a "product"; instead, they are providing a valuable "solution" to customer problems.[28] Consultative salespeople act as product experts and generally provide a customized solution. The second part of the consultative sales process consists of selecting or configuring a solution that satisfies the prospect's buying motives.

As we have noted, most salespeople bring to the selling situation a variety of products and/or services. In today's information economy, salespeople are increasingly selling related services as a part of their product solution. This is especially true in the Western industrialized countries where profit margins on B2B goods-related solutions are declining. In Germany, for example, six of the 30 largest firms have established specific organization units to offer services.[29] The challenge to select the correct solution is growing. Digesting relevant information, perceiving patterns, and determining the unique solution that will work in each unique selling situation requires a considerable amount of time and effort.[30] This process, done correctly, can create significant value for the customer and build a long-term partnership of repeats and/or referrals.

After identifying the buying motives, the salesperson carefully reviews the available product options. At this point, the salesperson is searching for a customized solution to satisfy the prospect's buying motives. Once the solution or product configuration has been selected, the salesperson makes a recommendation or proposal to the prospect (Figure 11.4). The following

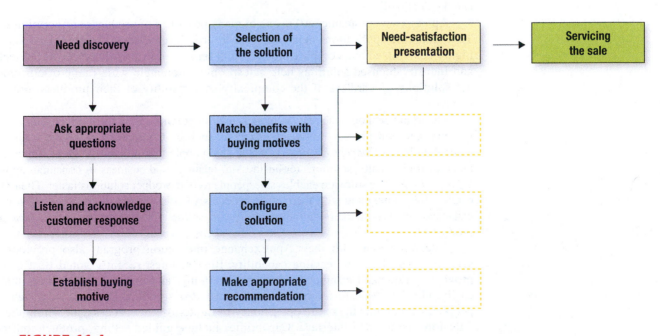

FIGURE 11.4

Three Dimensions of Product Selection

customer response to this process illustrates the value created when this process is done correctly: "She listened to and worked with the ideas that I had concerning my desires and preferences, as well as made recommendations that complemented and enhanced the vision that I had for my home."[31]

Selecting Solutions—Match Specific Benefits with Buying Motives

As we noted in Chapter 7, products and services represent problem-solving tools. People buy products when they perceive that they fulfill a need. We also note that today's more demanding customers seek a cluster of satisfactions that arise from the product itself, from the company that makes or distributes the product, and from the salesperson who sells and services the product (see Figure 7.1). Tom Reilly, author of *Value-Added Selling*, says, "Value-added salespeople sell three things: the product, the company, and themselves."[32] This is the Three Dimensional (3D) Product Solutions Selling Model discussed in Chapter 7. When possible, the salesperson should focus on benefits related to each dimension of value. Of course, it is a mistake to make benefit statements that do not relate to the specific needs of the customer. High-performance salespeople present benefits that are precisely tailored to the customer's needs. Benefits that are not relevant to the customer's needs waste time and may invite objections.[33]

Selecting Solutions—Product Configuration

Most salespeople bring to the sale a variety of products or services. Salespeople who represent food distributors can offer customers a mix of several hundred items. Most pharmaceutical sales representatives can offer the medical community a wide range of products. Best Buy, a large retailer of electronics, offers customers a wide range of audio and visual entertainment options. The customer who wants to purchase an entertainment system, for example, can choose from many combinations of receivers, speakers, and so on. Selecting the right solution is referred to by many sales organizations as "product configuration."

If the sale involves several needs and the satisfaction of multiple-buying motives, selection of the solution may take several days or even weeks and may involve the preparation of a detailed sales proposal. In addition, research conducted by Neil Rackham revealed that top-performing salespeople tend to introduce their solutions later in the sale—after several problems were uncovered.

A company considering the purchase of automated production equipment would likely present this type of challenge to the salesperson. The problem needs careful analysis before a solution can be identified.

Aptean (www.aptean.com/) is one of many providers of product configuration solutions. Their software applications help configure-to-order organizations to quote, market, and sell highly customized and complex products and service offerings. Their advanced technology and industry-focused solutions help salespeople automate a wide range of customer product solutions—regardless of the complexity or variability of their products, processes, or services.[34]

Electronic catalogs also play an increasingly important role in the product selection or product configuration process. Software programs such as Configure One's (www.configureone.com) Web-based *Concept E-Catalog* enable salespeople to rapidly implement and easily maintain electronic catalog solutions for business-to-business and business-to-consumer applications. *Concept E-Catalog* software enables salespeople to find product solutions faster. Their electronic catalog fully integrates with their other products (e-commerce and configurator software) or can stand alone. With their e-commerce software, salespeople and customers can have access to product solutions 24/7.

Salesforce.com with their AppExchange integration program also provides product selection and electronic catalog capability. BigMachines, recently voted Best Quote App, provides on-demand product configuration, pricing, and proposal capabilities that can be easily added to Salesforce.com's on-demand CRM solution. BigMachines enables salespeople to streamline the entire opportunity-to-quote-to-order process, all within the familiar Salesforce.com CRM interface. Capabilities include guided selling, product configuration, complex pricing and discounting, approval workflow, and proposal generation.[35] Electronic product configurators, product catalogs and e-commerce enable salespeople to create value for the customer by providing time-sensitive, professionally prepared, information-rich alternatives in selecting solutions that meet the unique needs established during the need discovery. For many salespeople, the use of sales force technology has changed their methods of selling.[36]

In some selling situations, the salesperson will solely create the solution based on the needs analysis. In more complex selling situations, however,[37] both the salesperson and the customer often play an active role and together co-create the solution. This co-creation process takes place through conversations between the customer and the salesperson. Research reveals this process often helps customers better understand their own needs and conceive of possible solutions that fit those needs. This application of the Value-Added Product-Selling Model discussed in Chapter 7 creates value and, as a consequence, customers make smarter buying choices that conform to the salesperson's solutions and sales propositions.

Selecting Solutions—Make Appropriate Recommendations

The recommendation strategies available to salespeople are similar to those used by a doctor who must recommend a solution to a patient's medical problem. In the medical field, three possibilities for providing patient satisfaction exist. In situations in which the patient easily understands the medical problem and the appropriate treatment, the doctor can make a recommendation, and the patient can proceed immediately toward a cure. If the patient does not easily understand the medical problem or solution, the doctor may need to discuss thoroughly with the patient the benefits of the recommended treatment. If the medical problem is not within his/her medical specialty, the doctor may recommend a specialist to provide the treatment. In consultative selling, the salesperson has these same three counseling alternatives.

RECOMMEND SOLUTION—CUSTOMER BUYS IMMEDIATELY The selection and recommendation of products to meet customer needs may occur at the beginning of the sales call, such as in the product approach; during the presentation just after the need discovery; or near the end, when minor resistance has been negotiated. At any of these three times, the presentation of products that are well matched to the prospect's needs may result in an immediate purchase.

RECOMMEND SOLUTION—SALESPERSON MAKES NEED-SATISFACTION PRESENTATION This alternative requires a presentation of product benefits including demonstrations and negotiating objections before the sale is closed. In this situation, the customer may not be totally aware of a buying problem, and the solution may not be easily understood or apparent. Because of this, the salesperson needs to carefully define the problem and communicate a solution to the customer. The need-satisfaction presentation will be discussed later in the book.

RECOMMEND ANOTHER SOURCE Earlier, we indicated that professional salespeople may recommend that a prospect buy a product or service from another source, maybe even a competitor. If, after a careful needs assessment, the salesperson concludes that the products represented do not satisfy the customer's needs, the consultative salesperson should recommend another source.

Paul Roos, a sales representative for Hewlett-Packard (HP), once met with a customer who wanted to buy a newly introduced HP product for an application that would not work. He explained why the application would not work and then took time to configure a competing product to meet the customer's needs. He lost that sale to a competitor, but the assistance provided confirmed his integrity and made a lasting impression on the customer. That customer later became a high-value account.[38] In situations like Paul Roos's, where the unique needs of a customer cannot be solved and an alternative recommendation is made to buy from another supplier, long-term partnerships are often created that result in future sales and/or referred business. This creates value for the customer who is looking for a unique solution.

Need Discovery and the Transactional Buyer

Throughout this chapter, you have been given a comprehensive introduction to the consultative-sales process. It is important to keep in mind that the fundamentals of consultative selling must be customized to meet the individual needs of the customer. For example, some of the guidelines for developing an effective consultative presentation must be abandoned or greatly altered when you are working with a transactional buyer. In most cases, transactional buyers understand what product they need and when they need it. The Internet has armed many transactional buyers with a great deal of information, so the salesperson who spends time asking survey questions or making a detailed informative presentation may be wasting the customer's time. Most of these buyers want the salesperson to configure a product solution that focuses on pricing and delivery issues.[39]

When working with the transactional buyer, it is important to understand the difference between a transaction and a consultative relationship. Transactions create one-time value; consultative relationships create long-term value and a stable business foundation.[40]

Involving the Prospect in the Need Discovery

In most selling situations, there is a certain amount of time pressure. Rarely does a salesperson have an unlimited amount of time to spend with the customer. As noted earlier, the salesperson is often allotted only 30 minutes for the sales call. Some buyers limit all their appointments to 30 minutes or less.

Figure 11.5 illustrates an ideal breakdown of time allocation between the salesperson and the prospect during three parts of the sales process. In terms of involvement, the prospect assumes a greater role during the need-discovery stage. As the salesperson begins the product-selection process, the prospect's involvement decreases. During the need-satisfaction stage, the salesperson is doing more of the talking, but note that the prospect is never excluded totally.

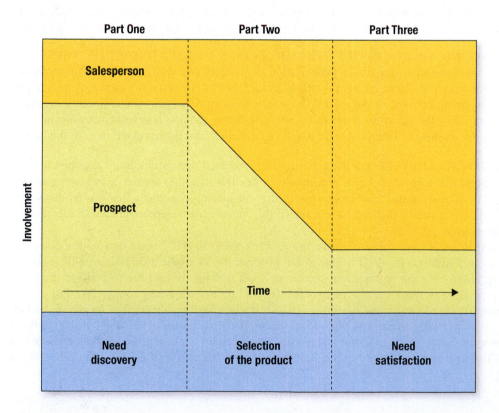

FIGURE 11.5

Time Used by Salesperson and Customer During Each Part of the Consultative Sales Presentation

Transitioning to the Presentation

As we note in Chapter 10, there is a need to make an effective transition from the approach to the need-discovery stage. There is the same need to transition from the need-discovery/product-selection stage to the need-satisfaction presentation stage. As noted earlier, if your customer buys immediately, you will transition to the close and conduct those activities associated with servicing the sale. Those activities will be discussed in Chapters 14 and 15. If you and your customer decide another supplier might better meet their needs, you might transition directly to servicing the sale to achieve a future sale or a referral.

If it is decided a need-satisfaction presentation is needed to communicate specific features and benefits, a statement such as "I would like to point out some of the specific benefits of the solution we have agreed upon." If the need-satisfaction presentation is made during a separate call of a multi-call presentation, the transition should include a summary-confirmation question covering the buying conditions discussed. The summary-confirmation question would be used in closing the existing call and opening the next call. Creating and involving the prospect in the need-satisfaction presentation stage will be discussed in detail in Chapter 12.

Planning and Execution—Final Thoughts

The importance of strategic planning and execution of the need discovery and product selection parts of the consultative-sales presentation model is explained in this chapter. Figure 11.6 summarizes the key concepts that must be addressed during the planning and execution process. These planning and execution activities will impact your ability to create customer value and build a partnering relationship. This approach can be used in the three major employment settings: service, B2B, and B2C.

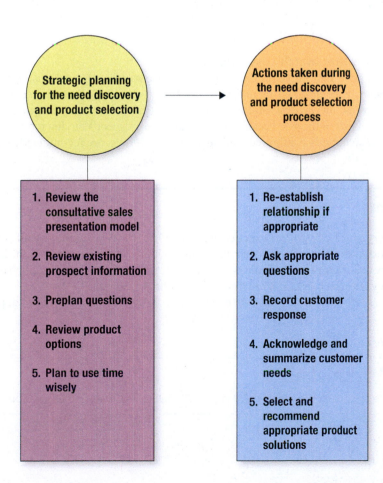

FIGURE 11.6

Need discovery and product selection activities are the first step in creating value and building a partnering relationship with your customer.

CHAPTER LEARNING ACTIVITIES

Reviewing Key Concepts

Outline the benefits of the consultative sales process

Salespeople use the consultative sales presentation because this customer-focused selling model results in increased customer satisfaction, more closed sales, and more repeat and referred business. Research indicates high-performance salespeople have learned how to skillfully use the consultative model to diagnose and solve their customers' buying problems better than their competitors.

Describe the four parts of the need-satisfaction model

A well-planned and well-executed consultative sales process is an important key to success in personal selling. To be most effective, the presentation should be viewed as a four-part process: need discovery; selection of the solution; need satisfaction through informing, persuading, or reminding; and servicing the sale.

Discuss the use of questions to discover customer needs

The most effective sales process is characterized by two-way communication. It should be encouraged with survey, probing, confirmation, summary confirmation, and need-satisfaction questions.

Describe the importance of active listening and the use of confirmation questions

Beware of assuming information about the prospect, and be sure the language of your presentation is clearly understood. Listen attentively as the prospect responds to your questions or volunteers information. The effective use of confirmation questions to enhance active listening assures a mutual understanding of buying motives.

Select solutions that match customer needs

After making a good first impression during the approach and getting the customer's full attention, the salesperson begins. During the process of (or shortly after) determining and/or confirming customer needs, the process of configuring a solution begins. The salesperson's ability is tested during this part of the sale because this is where the prospect's buying motives are matched with benefits, a solution is configured, and appropriate solutions are recommended.

Key Terms

Need discovery, p. 227

Survey questions, p. 230

General survey questions, p. 230

Specific survey questions, p. 231

Open questions, p. 231

Closed questions, p. 231

Probing questions, p. 231

Confirmation questions, p. 232

Buying conditions, p. 233

Summary-confirmation questions, p. 233

Need-satisfaction questions, p. 234

Active listening, p. 236

MyMarketingLab

To complete the problems with the ⭐ in your MyLab, go to the EOC Discussion Questions.

Review Questions

11-1 List and describe the four parts of the Consultative Sales Process Guide.

11-2 Describe the findings of the two major research projects on the strategic use of questions in selling.

11-3 List and describe the four types of questions commonly used in the selling field.

11-4 Define the term "buying conditions." What are some common buying conditions?

 11-5 Discuss the three dimensions of need discovery.

11-6 Describe the three dimensions of selecting a product solution.

11-7 Describe the ideal time allocation for each part of the consultative sales presentation between the salesperson and the prospect.

11-8 Describe the nature of the need discovery process when working with a transactional buyer.

11-9 Describe how to transition to the presentation part of the consultative sales presentation model.

Role-Play Application Exercises for "Questioning" Video Series

Most sales skill development exercises used in the classroom are product-oriented. As noted on page 225, "Product-oriented selling can easily lapse into product evangelism." This three-part video series on questioning focuses on the customer's buying process, consultative selling, and building high-quality partnerships.

Source: Michael Ahearne

The goal of this series is the identification and clarification of the customer's problem and finding a solution. The first video focuses on the appropriate use of survey and confirmation questions to identify the customer's problem. The second video introduces the use of probing and need-satisfaction questions. Probing questions examine and clarify the potential issues surrounding the customer's problem, while need-satisfaction questions focus the sales process on the appropriate solution. The third video demonstrates the use of these questions in a challenging yet typical contemporary sales setting.

The role-play exercises presented here challenge the participant to understand, apply, and integrate questioning skills presented in this chapter and in the video series. Product information needed for these exercises is found in Appendix 3 on pages 429–457. Customer information will be found in the B. H. Rivera Contact Report presented on page 459 (disregard any other information on this page). You will assume the role of a newly hired salesperson as described in the Position Description on page 427. Refer to the questioning material and examples presented on pages 228–235. Use a Need Discovery Worksheet like the one on page 231 for developing your questions.

After viewing the video "Questions—Discovering and Confirming Customer Problems," study the information presented in Appendix 3, pages 424–462. Refer to the Contact Report on page 459 (as noted, disregard any other information on this page). Assume you were assigned to this account and you are meeting B. H. Rivera to inquire about additional information regarding dates when the meeting will be held, and what audiovisual equipment might be needed. Prepare a list of general survey and specific survey questions that reveal when, during the next month, the meeting will be held and what, if any, audiovisual equipment (see page 451) might be needed. Plan to use a summary-confirmation question to verify the existing four items on the contact sheet. Using the questions you have created, role-play this part of the need discovery process.

After viewing the video "Questions—Discovering Pain and Pleasure," and reviewing the information you prepared in the previous role-play, prepare three probing questions. These questions should clarify and reveal a mutual understanding of issues and consequences regarding food service, facility design, and audiovisual equipment. Also, using the information on pages 424–462, prepare five need-satisfaction questions that reveal how the features of your convention center provide a solution to the buying situation. Select appropriate proof devices to demonstrate these specific benefits. Using these questions, meet again with B. H. Rivera, and role-play this part of the questioning process. Prepare and use confirmation questions as the need arises.

After viewing the video "Questions—Getting It Right," and using the information in the first two role-plays, prepare a need-satisfaction presentation to Cameron Rivera, a new meeting planner just hired at Graphic Forms. Cameron, a cousin of B. H., had been previously employed as a training coordinator at West College. Due to extensive growth in the company, B. H. has turned all meeting planning over to Cameron. Cameron will make the final selection of a facility for the meeting described on page 459, plus 11 more identical meetings to be scheduled in the next 12 months. You have also been informed that the Marriott and Sheraton Hotels will be making presentations (note the comparative room, parking, and transportation rates). You will travel to Graphic Forms to make your presentation. Prepare appropriate survey, probing, confirmation, and need-satisfaction questions and presentation strategies that will help secure this important account—then role-play this presentation.

Reality Selling Case Problem—Debora Karish/Amgen

When Deborah Karish wakes up in the morning, she does not have to worry about a long commute to work. Her office is in her home. As an Amgen (www.amgen.com) pharmaceutical sales representative, Deborah spends most of her day visiting hospitals, medical clinics, and doctors' offices. She spends a large part of each day serving as a consultant to doctors, head nurses, pharmacists, and others who need information and advice about the complex medical products available from her company. As might be expected, she also spends a considerable amount of time conducting informative presentations designed to achieve a variety of objectives. In some situations, she is introducing a new product; in other cases, she is providing up-to-date information on an existing product. Some of her presentations are given to individual healthcare professionals; others are given to a group. Each of these presentations must be carefully planned.

Deborah uses informative and reminder presentations almost daily in her work. Informative presentations are given to doctors who are in a position to prescribe her products. The verbal presentation often is supplemented with audiovisual aids and printed materials. Reprints of articles from leading medical journals are often used to explain the success of her products in treating patients. These articles give added credibility to her presentations. Some of her informative presentations are designed to give customers updates on the prescription drugs she sells. Reminder presentations are frequently given to pharmacists who must maintain an inventory of her products. She has found that it is necessary to periodically remind pharmacists of product delivery procedures and policies and special services available from Amgen. She knows that without an occasional reminder, a customer can forget information that is beneficial.

In some cases, a careful needs analysis is needed to determine whether her products can solve a specific medical problem. Every patient is different, so generalizations concerning the use of her products can be dangerous. When doctors talk about their patients, Deborah must listen carefully and take good notes. In some cases, she must get additional information from company support staff. If a customer needs immediate help with a problem, she gives the person a toll-free 800 number to call for expert advice. This line is an important part of the Amgen customer service program.

Deborah's career in pharmaceutical sales has required continuous learning. In the beginning, she had to learn the meaning of dozens of medical terms and become familiar with a large number of medical problems. If a doctor asks, "What is the bioavailability of Neutogen?" she must know the meaning of the medical term and be knowledgeable about this Amgen product.

Deborah also spends time learning about the people with whom she works. She recently said, "If I get along with the people I work with, it makes my job a lot easier." When meeting someone for the first time, she takes time to assess his communication style and then adjusts her own style to meet his needs. She points out that, in some cases, the competition offers a similar product at a similar price. In these situations, a good relationship with the customer can influence the purchase decision.

Questions

11-10 Would need discovery be an important part of Deborah Karish's sales process with a new medical practice? Explain.

11-11 Would Deborah use the same questioning strategy with medical personnel (e.g., the office manager or receptionist) that she would with medical professionals (e.g., nurses or doctors)?

11-12 Describe the nature of the multi-call sales process that Deborah might use.

11-13 Describe what Deborah might plan to do in the first call, in the second call, and in a third call on the same medical practice.

Regional Account Management Case Study (refer to Appendix 2)

NewNet Systems®

Your Value Adding Systems Partner

Conducting Needs Assessments

Casey Arnold, your sales manager at NewNet Systems, wants to meet with you this afternoon to discuss the status of your accounts. It is common for accounts to have several contacts with NewNet before ordering a network system. These multi-call contacts, or sales cycle phases, usually include getting acquainted and qualifying, need discovery, proposal presentation, closing, and account maintenance. Casey wants to know what phase each account is in and, particularly, which accounts may be ready for a presentation.

Questions

11-14 For your meeting with Casey, using the table you prepared in the last chapter, add another column titled "Sales Process Stages" as indicated below. Review the metrics on your 20 accounts and indicate the last stage of the sales process each account has gone through. This information will be used as you prepare your future calls.

Newnet Systems Account Management

Name					Regional Accounts Manager, NEWNET SYSTEMS		
Date	Account Name/	Dollar	Comm.	**Sales Process**			
Close	Contact Name	Sales Amt.	Style	**Stage**			

11-15 Which four accounts already have had a needs analysis? Which two accounts are scheduled for a needs analysis? When do you need to enter them on your calendar?

11-16 Reviewing the notes and the likelihood of buying, which six accounts are likely to buy but have not yet had a needs analysis?

11-17 Which two accounts have had a needs analysis and now need a product solution configured? What two accounts appear to want to buy but have not yet had any needs analysis, or product configurations? What threats does this pose?

11-18 Reviewing the Network Now entry, which three accounts do not now have a network, but appear to be ready for moving the sales process to the next stage, and what will be your next stage?

11-19 Which accounts appear to be planning to buy without a need discovery or product-configuration proposal? What risks does this pose?

Partnership Selling: A Role-Play (see Appendix 3, page 419)

Understanding Your Customer's Buying Strategy

Read Sales Memorandum 2 ("A" or "B," depending on the account category you were assigned in Chapter 10). Your customer has called you back because you made such a good approach in call 1 and wants to visit with you about a convention recently assigned. In this call, you are to use the information gathered in sales call 1 to reestablish a good relationship, discover your customer's convention needs, and set an appointment to return and make a presentation.

Follow the instructions carefully and prepare survey questions prior to your appointment. Keep your survey questions general and attempt to get your customer to openly share information. Use specific survey questions later during the appointment to gain more insight. Be careful about doing too much of the talking. In the need

Park Shores Resort and Convention Center.
Source: Courtesy of Beach Resort

discovery, your customer should do most of the talking, with you taking notes and using them to ask confirmation and summary-confirmation questions to check the accuracy of your perceptions concerning what the customer wants. After this meeting, you will be asked to prepare a sales proposal from the information you have gathered.

Your instructor may again ask you to assume the role of a customer in the account category that you are not assigned to as a salesperson. If so, you will receive detailed customer instructions that you should follow closely. This will provide you with an opportunity to experience the strategic/consultative/partnering style of selling from a customer's perspective.

Extensive research regarding the use of questions in the sales process reveals the importance of developing and perfecting a multiple-questioning strategy to understand and solve customer needs. The Adaptive Questions video dramatically presents how these questions are used in the sales process.

MyMarketingLab

Go to the Assignments section of your MyLab to complete these writing exercises.

11-20 Why would a salesperson use the consultative sales presentation?

11-21 How does a salesperson avoid selling "just a product", but rather provide valuable solutions?

12

Creating Value with the Consultative Presentation

Learning Objectives

When you finish reading this chapter, you should be able to

12.1 List and describe three types of need-satisfaction presentation strategies

12.2 Present guidelines for creating consultative presentations that add value

12.3 Describe the elements of a persuasive presentation strategy

12.4 Describe elements of an effective group presentation

12.5 Develop selling tools that add value to your sales demonstrations

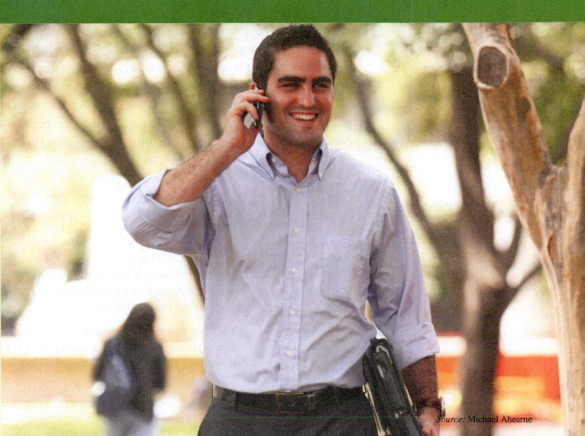

Source: Michael Ahearne

▶ Reality Selling Video—Chris Wylie/Ecolab

Chris Wylie (pictured above) is a sales representative for Ecolab. With more than $6 billion in global sales, Ecolab is the world leader in cleaning, sanitizing, food safety, and infection control products and services. Headquartered in St. Paul, Minnesota, the company has more than 26,000 employees worldwide. Ecolab serves customers in more than 160 countries across North America, Europe, Asia Pacific, Latin America, the Middle East, and Africa. The company delivers comprehensive programs and services to various industries, including food service, food and beverage processing, hospitality, healthcare, government and education, retail, and others.

Chris Wylie is a territory manager in Ecolab's Institutional Business unit, which is the core of Ecolab. In his territory, Chris serves approximately 80 customers throughout the month. Most of his customers are restaurants, but he also calls on some hotels and a few hospitals. When visiting a customer, he first meets with his contact, who would typically be the general manager, procurement manager, or executive chef. He asks them a series of questions about their business and operations (e.g., how busy they have recently been, whether they had any problems or repairs, or whether a big event like a banquet is coming up). Through these questions, Chris gains insight into his customer's operations, which will later help him create his solutions and sales presentation.

As a part of his call, Chris also has to take care of servicing Ecolab's products by making sure that the dispensers for the products and the dishwashers are working properly, that the calibrations are set correctly, and so forth. Throughout his presentation, Chris constantly tries to discover different needs such as determining needed repairs, identifying up-selling or cross-selling opportunities, and expanding the business with that customer by showing him new products.

Besides serving his existing customer base, Chris also engages in new business selling. In a typical prospecting type of sales call, Chris would meet with the general manager or the executive chef, introduce himself and Ecolab, and eventually ask them whether he can conduct a need discovery survey of their kitchen to see what their operation looks like and assess whether he can create additional value with some of Ecolab's products and services. Then Chris would typically do a series of tests on the current chemicals and equipment that the prospect is using to see if they are functioning effectively and efficiently. Based on these tests, Chris creates a value proposition in terms of cost savings or results improvements (e.g., improved glassware or dishware results). Since Ecolab products are not sold on price, Chris, using a combination of presentation strategies, carefully and persuasively presents those improved results to demonstrate to the -prospect the Ecolab value of excellent service and quality products. ●

12.1 List and describe three types of need-satisfaction presentation strategies

Need Satisfaction—Selecting a Consultative Presentation Strategy

Conducting business in the 21st-century information economy, which is based on the assets of knowledge and information, requires that we think about ways to improve the sales presentation. This is how one author described this challenge:[1]

> As we move from the rutted byways of the Industrial Age to the electronic thoroughfares of the Information Age, business presentations become a measure of our ability to adapt to new surroundings. The most successful and forward-thinking companies already have assigned presentations a new, fundamental, and strategic importance.

After you have configured a solution that matches the customer's needs, you must select which presentation strategy or combination of strategies to emphasize (Figure 12.1). Need satisfaction can be achieved through selecting an informative, persuasive, or reminder presentation strategy, creating the presentation plan, and initiating the presentation. Salespeople, such as Ecolab's Chris Wylie, often will use a combination of the three presentation strategies.

Need Satisfaction—The Informative Presentation Strategy

To be informative, a message must be clearly understood by the customer. Of course, clarity is important in any presentation, but it needs special attention in a presentation whose primary purpose is to inform. The **informative presentation** emphasizes factual information often taken from technical reports, company-prepared sales literature, or written testimonials from persons who have used the product.

This type of presentation is commonly used to introduce new products, highly complex products, and services of a technical nature. Salespeople, such as Ecolab's Chris Wylie and Hilti's Alim Hirani, play a key role in the ultimate success of a firm's new-product innovations.[2] Pharmaceutical sales representatives frequently use the informative presentation strategy to describe the details of their products to physicians who may be engaged in an educated search for a prescription drug best suited to meet their patients' medical needs.[3] This strategy emphasizes clarity, simplicity, and directness, and in many cases is welcomed by the reflective and directive communication style customers presented in Chapter 5. Salespeople need to keep in mind the "less is more" concept. Too often the prospect is given far too much information and detail.[4]

It is important to keep in mind the partner/problem-solver role of the salesperson when making an informative presentation. Today, information is not just plentiful, but also available directly to customers in overwhelming amounts. As a result, customers no longer value sales professionals as just information providers. To use the informative presentation strategy effectively, the salesperson must transition from an information conveyer to the role of a trusted business advisor.[5]

The Six-Step Presentation Plan

Step One:
Approach

☑ Review Strategic/Consultative
  Selling Model
☑ Initiate customer contact

Step Two:
Need Discovery

☑ Ask strategic questions
☑ Determine customer needs
☑ Select product solution

Step Three:
Presentation

☐ Select presentation strategy
☐ Create presentation plan
☐ Initiate presentation

Step Four:
Negotiation

☐ Anticipate buyer concerns
☐ Plan negotiating methods
☐ Initiate win-win negotiations

Step Five:
Close

☐ Plan appropriate closing methods
☐ Recognize closing clues
☐ Initiate closing methods

Step Six:
Servicing the Sale

☐ Follow through
☐ Follow-up calls
☐ Expansion selling

Service, retail, wholesale, and manufacturer selling

FIGURE 12.1

Creating value with the presentation.

Need Satisfaction—The Persuasive Presentation Strategy

Many salespeople believe that, when a real need for their product exists, the stage is set for a persuasive presentation. **Persuasion** is a communication process by which you motivate someone else to voluntarily do something you'd like him or her to. The key word is "voluntary." Persuasion is not compelling or manipulating others to do what you want. You must present your audience with a legitimate choice of options. True persuasion occurs when someone not only chooses your preferred option but also feels good about it afterwards.[6] The major goal of the **persuasive presentation** strategy is to influence the prospect's beliefs, attitudes, or behavior and to encourage buyer action. Persuasive sales presentations include a subtle transition stage where the dialogue shifts from an intellectual emphasis to an emotional appeal. This situation may occur when Ecolab's Chris Wylie discovers a safety issue that needs immediate attention. Every buying decision is influenced by both reason and emotion, but the amount of weight given to each of these elements during the decision-making process can vary greatly depending on the prospect.[7]

In the field of personal selling, persuasion is an acceptable strategy once a need has been identified and a suitable product has been selected. When it is clear that the buyer can benefit from ownership of the product or service, an enthusiastic and persuasive sales presentation is usually appropriate.

The persuasive presentation strategy requires a high level of training and experience to be effective because a poorly planned and delivered persuasive presentation may raise the prospect's anxiety level. The persuasive presentation, when handled improperly, can trigger fear or distrust.

Need Satisfaction—The Reminder Presentation Strategy

Studies show that awareness of a company's products and services declines as promotion is stopped. This problem represents one of the reasons many companies employ missionary salespeople to maintain an ongoing awareness and familiarity with their product lines. Other types

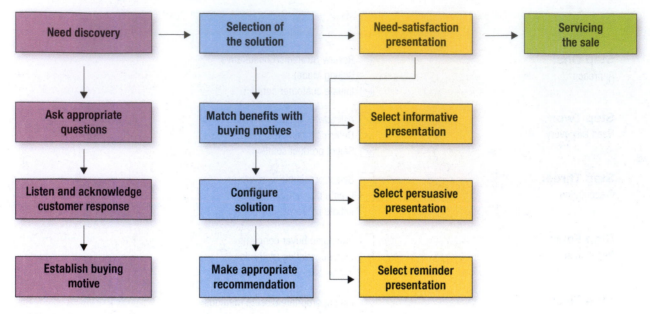

FIGURE 12.2

The three strategies to use in developing an effective need-satisfaction presentation.

of salespeople also use this presentation strategy. Route salespeople rely heavily on **reminder presentations** (sometimes called "reinforcement presentations") to maintain their market share. Salespeople, such as the Tom James Company's Alex Homer introduced in Chapter 1, know that if they do not make frequent calls and remind customers of their products, the competition is likely to capture some customers (Figure 12.2).

The reminder presentation is sometimes a dimension of service after the sale (see Chapter 15). Sales personnel, such as the B2B detail salesperson described in Chapter 1, working with repeat customers are in a good position to remind them of products or services they offer. In B2C selling situations, retail sales personnel can remind their regular customers of additional products in their own department or another department located in some other area of the business. Some products require special care and maintenance. Busy customers may need to be reminded of the maintenance services offered by your company. In some cases, the service department is a major profit generator, so reminder calls need to be given a high priority.

Reminder presentations are often used by salespeople who may have been unsuccessful in a previous call. Sometimes, when the buyer has a strong relationship with a competing supplier, the best you can hope is that the current relationship weakens. You want to be top-of-mind when that happens, and a reminder presentation can often achieve that result. There are also some customers who, after they understand you are truly committed to getting their business, will eventually give you a trial order.

Some customers get used to the great quality and service you provide and begin to view your product as a commodity. Once this happens, the customer may ask for a price reduction. To keep customers focused on value rather than price, remind them (from time to time) of the value-added services you provide.[8]

12.2 Present guidelines for creating consultative presentations that add value

Guidelines for Creating a Presentation That Adds Value

It is important to distinguish between a planned consultative presentation and a **canned presentation**. In most cases, the canned presentation, also referred to as the "memorized or scripted presentation,"[9] is built around a standard set of steps, ignores the unique needs of each customer, and is presented in the form of a repetitive speech given to all customers interested in a particular

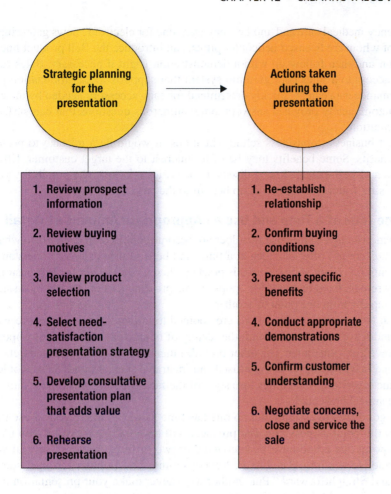

FIGURE 12.3

Salespeople who truly represent value to their customers plan ahead strategically for the actions taken during the consultative sales presentation.

item. Although an effective planned presentation will generally add value from the customer's perspective, a canned presentation today will likely be discounted by the customer and may take away from the value a product has to offer. With the planned consultative presentation, the salesperson is considered a strategic resource and partner for the customer, rather than just a provider of a product or service.[10]

In some group selling situations, a variation of the canned presentation has to be presented because the audience has such a wide variety of needs. In any case, every effort should be made to understand those needs and adapt the group presentation as much as possible to meet the needs of the audience. More will be presented later in this chapter on group presentations.

Strategic planning, of course, sets the stage for an effective consultative presentation that adds value to the sale (Figure 12.3). Some of the most important ways to create value with the presentation are discussed next.

Adapt the Presentation to Meet Unique Needs of the Customer

Salespeople who have mastered adaptive selling skills adjust their sales strategies in ways that better fit customer needs and preferences.[11] In consultative selling, each presentation is custom tailored because, as we found in Chapter 11 on need discovery, individual client problems and priorities are unique. In other words, every aspect of the sales presentation should be adapted to the needs or problems mutually identified by the prospect and the salesperson.

It is possible to develop a sales presentation so structured and so mechanical that the prospect feels like a number. We must try to avoid what some veteran marketing people refer to as the "depersonalization" of the selling/buying process. If the presentation is overly structured, it cannot be personalized to meet specific customer wants and needs.

Bell Helicopter (www.bellhelicopter.com) sells several models with countless custom options, and each option changes its price and performance. One customer may want a helicopter for emergency medical care and another may want one for electronic news gathering. Bell's sales force, all of whom are licensed helicopter pilots, can introduce the Bell product line with a video presentation and then follow up with a demonstration flight if necessary. Sales representatives also have access to a sales configuration system that supports the customization process. Price and performance data can be quickly determined for each accessory needed by the customer. The software automatically provides answers to the numerous questions that can surface during the sales presentation.[12]

In most business-to-business selling situations, it would be a mistake to present all of the product benefits. Some benefits may be of no interest to the target customer. Effective precall preparation and well-executed need-discovery activities minimize the possibility you will spend time discussing features that provide no benefit to the customer.

Cover One Idea at a Time and Use an Appropriate Amount of Detail

Pace the demonstration so the customer does not become confused. In response to what was learned in the need discovery, offer one idea at a time, and be sure the customer understands each point before moving on. When you neglect this practice, there is the danger that the customer's concentration may remain fixed on a previous point. Some presentations are ruined by a salesperson who moves too rapidly from one point to another.

At least two types of presentations are doomed to failure. One is a sales presentation that is too basic and leaves the prospect with the feeling of being "patronized." It is important to avoid "talking down" to a customer. The other provides the prospect with too much detail. It is overly technical and leaves the buyer in a confused and frustrated state of mind. Salespeople who sell the same product every day sometimes lose sight of the fact that some customers cannot understand a highly technical presentation.

It is a good idea to assume that no one has time to waste. Make your presentation as concise and to the point as possible. The prospect will be greatly annoyed if you use 10 minutes to make a point that could have been covered in two or three minutes. Several years ago, the "KISS" principle was introduced to the field of selling. This popular acronym stands for "Keep It Simple and Straightforward." Put another way, never make your presentation more complex than it needs to be. Make sure the terms you use and ideas you present are familiar to your customers.

Use Proof Devices to Demonstrate Buyer Benefits

A well-planned and well-executed sales demonstration is one of the most convincing forms of proof. This is especially true if your product has dramatic points of superiority.

Business-to-business salespeople representing Epson, Canon, Hewlett-Packard, and other manufacturers can offer the customer a wide range of printers. What is the real difference between a $2,000 printer and an $8,000 printer? The most effective way to provide proof of this buyer benefit is to show the customer material that has been printed on both printers. By letting the prospect compare the examples, the salesperson is converting product features to a buyer benefit. Be prepared to prove with tests, findings, and performance records every claim you make.

In a complex sale, it is imperative to check every part of your demonstration prior to the presentation. During the presentation, you should cover one idea at a time and secure agreement before moving on.

Source: Image Source/Fotolia

PROOF DEVICES We have noted that when trust is present, customers are more open to the sales presentation. One way to build trust is to use proof devices that enhance your credibility. **Proof devices** can take the form of a statement, a report, a testimonial, customer data, or a photograph. A salesperson selling conference services for a large hotel/conference center might use the following proof statement: "We were selected by *Training* magazine as one of the nation's top 10 conference centers."

Later the salesperson shows the customer photographs of the conference facilities and guest rooms. Then the customer is given a copy of a testimonial letter from a satisfied customer. The statement, photos, and letter help build the customer's confidence in the product. Later in this chapter, we will examine proof devices in more detail. More on proof devices will be presented in the "Selling Tools" section of this chapter.

Appeal to as Many Senses as Appropriate

In conducting an effective value-added sales presentation, it is a good idea to appeal to all appropriate senses. Each of the five senses—sight, hearing, smell, touch, and taste—represents an avenue by which the salesperson can attract the prospect's attention and build desire.

Although sight is considered the most powerful attention-attracting sense, it may not be the most important motivating force in every selling situation. When presenting a food product, the taste and aroma may be critical. Designers and decorators tell us that most furniture buyers still want to touch and feel the product before they buy it.

Gary Beetle, owner of Beetle Winery located in San Luis Obispo County, California, understands the importance of reaching the prospect through as many senses as possible. He spends considerable time each year selling his wines to retailers and restaurant owners.[13] The sales presentation for a quality wine usually highlights four areas:

Consumer demand. The wine's sales potential is described in realistic terms.
Marketing strategies. Suggested ways to merchandise the wine are discussed.
Bouquet. The distinctive fragrance of the wine is introduced.
Taste. A sample of the wine is given to the prospect in a quality wineglass.

Note that a sales presentation featuring these appeals can reach the prospect through four of the five senses. Collectively, these appeals add value. When you involve more than one sense, the sales presentation is more informative and more persuasive.

Balance Telling, Showing, and Involvement

A Chinese proverb says, "Tell me, I'll forget; show me, I may remember; but involve me, and I'll understand."[14] Some of the most effective sales demonstrations combine telling, showing, and involvement of the prospect. To plan an effective demonstration, consider developing a presentation worksheet. Simply divide a sheet of paper into four columns. Head the first column, "Feature to Be Presented." Head the second column, "Proof Device to Be Used." Head the third column, "What I Will Say." Head the fourth column, "What I or the Customer Will Do." List the major features you plan to present in proper sequence in the first column. In the second column, describe the proof devices you will use. In the third column, describe what you will say about the feature, converting the feature to a customer benefit. In the fourth column, describe what you (or the customer) will do at the time this benefit is discussed. A sample presentation worksheet appears in Figure 12.4.

When appropriate and possible, try to involve the customer in the sales presentation. The best way to highlight the style, fit, and comfort of a high-end men's suit is to have the customer try it on. The Rumination Station office chair offers rich, soft leather; cushy arms and headrest; a spacious, first-class seat; and a footrest for reclining. To fully appreciate this expensive chair, the customer must try it out.

If it is not possible for the prospect to participate in the demonstration or handle the product, place sales literature, pictures, or brochures in the person's hands. After the sales call, these items remind the prospect of not only who called but also why.

Develop Creative Presentations

Presenting product features and buyer benefits in an interesting and appealing way requires some amount of creativity. Creativity is needed to adapt a sales presentation that can gain attention, increase desire, and add value. The ability to come up with problem-solving answers or different ways of looking at situations is greatly valued in today's fast-changing business environment. Creativity is enhanced by expertise in the field of endeavor. For salespeople, this means knowledge of the sales process, product knowledge, and an understanding of human behavior. Creativity is also enhanced by the capacity for divergent thinking and a willingness to take risks.[15]

Demonstration Worksheet			
Feature to Be Demonstrated	Proof Device to Be Used	What I Will Say (Include Benefit)	What I or the Customer Will Do
Special computer circuit board to accelerate drawing graphics on a color monitor screen.	Monitor and software	"This monitor is large enough to display multiple windows. You can easily compare several graphics."	Have the customer bring up several windows using the computer keyboard.
Meeting room setup at a hotel and conference center.	Floor plan	"This setup will provide 3 feet of elbow space for each participant. For long meetings, the added space provides more comfort."	Give the customer a tour of the room and invite her to sit in a chair at one of the conference tables.

FIGURE 12.4

The Demonstration Worksheet

The demonstration worksheet enables the salesperson to strategically plan and then rehearse demonstrations that strengthen the presentation.

Consider the Use of Humor—in Moderation

According to Burt Teplitzky, author of *Sell It with Humor*, humor, if used in moderation and used appropriately, can work wonders to break down barriers, build rapport, and foster long-term and mutually beneficial customer relationships. If used improperly, it can distance you from your customer. Teplitzky suggests one should never tell jokes off the cuff when speaking to customers. He suggests your use of humor should be preplanned and communicate that you don't take yourself too seriously.

One part of the sales process in which he likes to use humor is the transition to the presentation. He might open his presentation with a line such as, "Before we get started, I promise not to bore you with a *long* presentation. . . . I'm sure I can do it with a *short* one." As he says, this would never go over in a comedy club, but in an environment where people are glad for any release, they appreciate the humor. Humor should never be used to attack anybody, nor should it be used during your transition to the close.[16]

Choose the Right Setting

The location of the sales presentation can make a difference. Some companies routinely rent space at a hotel, motel, or conference center so that the presentation can be conducted in a controlled environment free of noise and other interruptions.

However, in these busy times, prospects are often unwilling or unable to participate in a presentation held off premises. In these situations, many organizations do have conference rooms that can be reserved with advanced preparation and notice.

Document the Value Proposition

In Chapter 7 we defined "value proposition" as a set of key benefits and values the salesperson promises to deliver to satisfy the customer's needs. Salespeople must be prepared to substantiate the points presented during the sales presentation. Recent research indicates that salespeople often make claims of savings and benefits to the customer but fail to back them up. Failure to demonstrate and document claims is a common barrier to closing the sale.[17]

In many cases, the most effective value proposition is one that focuses on favorable points of difference between your product and *the next best alternative*. The salesperson recognizes that the customer can purchase the product from one or more competitors. Once the customer's requirements and preferences are clearly understood, and knowledge of the competitor's product is acquired, the salesperson can focus on key points of difference.

The most effective value proposition describes the few elements that matter most to your customer. This approach recognizes that today's buyers are extremely busy and want to do business with salespeople who fully grasp the critical issues in their business and are able to deliver a value proposition that is simple yet powerfully captivating. So, focus on favorable points of difference between your product and the *next best alternative*.[18]

Quantify the Solution

In Chapter 6, we explained that the process of determining whether or not a sales proposal adds value is called "quantifying the solution." If the cost of the proposal is offset by added value, closing the sale will be much easier. In business-to-business selling, quantifying the solution is very common. Let's assume you represent a manufacturing company that sells robots—a reprogrammable machine capable of performing a variety of tasks. The two primary benefits are (1) payroll cost savings and (2) vastly improved quality. One way to quantify the solution in this case is to use a simple **cost–benefit analysis** (see Table 6.1). This involves listing the costs to the buyer and the savings to be achieved from the purchase of the robots.

Another way to quantify the solution is to calculate the net profits or savings, expressed as a percentage of the original investment. This is called **return on investment (ROI)**. Using the following formula, you can determine the net profits or savings from a given investment.

$$ROI = Net\ Profits\ (or\ Savings)/Investment \times 100$$

If the robotic system costs $16,000 but saves the firm $4,000, the ROI is 25 percent ($4,000/$16,000 $\times$ 100 = 25 percent). Some companies set a minimum ROI for new products or cost-saving programs. Salespeople often acquire this information at the need-assessment stage and then include it in the written proposal.

Space does not permit a review of the many methods of quantifying the solution. Some of the additional ways include payback period, opportunity cost, net present value, after-tax cash flow, turnover, and contribution margin.

Check Sales Tools

Be sure to check every item to be used in conjunction with the sales presentation. If you are using audiovisual equipment, be certain that it is in good working condition. Always carry an extension cord and a spare bulb. If you are making a laptop presentation, be sure you can go online in front of the customer. If you plan to demonstrate a website, save it on a thumb drive instead of going online. Be prepared for technological snags and have the customary multiple backups. Always carry extra batteries for your laptop.[19]

Summarize Major Points

The allotted time for a presentation usually provides the opportunity to present a significant amount of information. Most people talk at a speed of about 125 words per minute. In a short time span of just 15 minutes, the customer may be bombarded with approximately 1,900 words. For this reason, the salesperson should occasionally use a summary-confirmation question to summarize and confirm major points. The customer needs this form of value-added assistance.

Guidelines for a Persuasive Presentation Strategy That Adds Value

12.3 Describe the elements of a persuasive presentation strategy

Earlier in this chapter, we introduced you to the persuasive presentation strategy as one of the three strategies you could choose from in creating a need-satisfaction presentation. A study on persuasion in the *Journal for Management in Engineering,* published by the American Society of Civil Engineers, reported that effective communicators recognize that conviction (emotion) is more vital to persuasion than position (logic). People make decisions based primarily on what they feel and then test or rationalize their choice with logic. Table 12.1 illustrates the contrast between traditional technical communication and persuasive communication.[20]

Technical communication, illustrated in the first column of Table 12.1, would be more appropriate for the *informative presentation strategy* introduced in Chapter 11. Persuasive communication, appropriately used, will enhance the success of the *persuasive presentation strategy*.

There are many ways to incorporate persuasion into a presentation strategy and most, if used appropriately, will create value for the customer. In this section, we review a series of guidelines that should be followed during preparation of a persuasive presentation.

TABLE 12.1 Technical Vs. Persuasive Communication

TECHNICAL COMMUNICATION	PERSUASIVE COMMUNICATION
Impersonal, objective	Personal, subjective
Intellectual response	Emotional response
Emphasizes features	Emphasizes benefits
Information-driven	Influence-driven

Place Special Emphasis on the Relationship

Relationships are enhanced by the salesperson's ability to communicate in compelling and creative ways.[21] Throughout this book, we emphasize the importance of the relationship strategy in selling. Good rapport between the salesperson and the prospect establishes a foundation for an open exchange of information. Robert Cialdini, writing in the *Harvard Business Review*, says the science of persuasion is built on the principle of liking: *People like those who like them.*

Salespeople, acting as relationship managers, play a key role in the development and management of partnering relationships.[22] Establish a bond with the customer early by uncovering areas of common interest, using praise when it's appropriate, and being completely trustworthy.[23] Don't forget to adjust your communication style to accommodate the needs of the customer (see Chapter 5). Also, remember that good salespeople today use smart social-media strategies to enhance customer relationships. They make it their business to stay connected to their customers through Twitter, Facebook, and LinkedIn.[24] When building important partnering relationships, it is well to remember, most people don't care how much you know until they know how much you care.

Target Emotional Links and Use a Persuasive Vocabulary

Emotional links are the connectors between your messages and the internal emotions of the prospect.[25] Some common emotional links in the business community are quality improvement, on-time delivery, increased market share, innovation, customer service, and reduction of operating expenses. Targeting just a few emotional links can increase your chances of closing the sale.

*you	*advantage
save	guarantee
money	security
health	discovery
easy	*new
now	*benefits
safety	positive
results	proven

*Many marketing people agree that the words with asterisks are probably the most important of all in selling and advertising.

When you target emotional links, use persuasive words. Research conducted on persuasion suggests the following list of words to use in persuasive communication. Consider the appropriate use of these words when planning a persuasive presentation strategy.

Sell Specific Benefits and Obtain Customer Reactions

People do not buy things; they buy what the things can do for them. At Mattress Firm, Edith Botello realizes her customers do not buy a mattress; they buy a relaxing, comfortable, uninterrupted physically healthy evening of rest. Chief information officers do not buy computers or programming services, they buy timely, easy to access, easy to understand, economically priced information. Every product or service offers the customer certain benefits. The benefit might be ease of operation, greater comfort, security, feelings of confidence, or economy.

If you are selling Allstate insurance, for example, you should become familiar with the service features. One feature is well-trained employees and the convenient locations of Allstate offices across the nation. The benefit to customers is greater peace of mind in knowing that they can receive good service at a nearby location. Allstate salespeople understand the importance of selling the company, the product, and themselves.

After you state the feature and convert it into a buyer benefit, obtain a reaction from the customer by using confirmation or need-satisfaction questions (refer to Table 11.1). You should always check to see if you are on the right track and your prospect is following the logic of your presentation. Some examples follow:

Feature	Benefit	Question
Seven-hour battery life*	Fewer work interruptions when traveling	"Battery life is important to you, isn't it?" (confirmation question)
Automatic climate control system for automobile	Temperature in car not varying after initial setting	"Would you like the luxury of setting the temperature and then not worrying about it?" (need-satisfaction question)

*Feature of Fujitsu Lifebook laptop.

The feature–benefit–reaction or, as IBM salespeople call it, the "FBR approach," is used by many high-performance salespeople. Involving the customer with appropriate questions helps you maintain two-way communication.

Use of Showmanship

Showmanship is defined as an interesting and attractive way of communicating an idea to others. If done tastefully and appropriately, it can do a lot to improve the persuasiveness and effectiveness of a sales presentation. Showmanship in selling need not be equated with sensational or bizarre events. It may be a very subtle act such as the furnishing and accessorizing, or "staging" as it is sometimes called, of a home being shown by PulteGroup's Ashley Pineda, introduced in Chapter 8. Another example of showmanship would be carefully placing a fine diamond on a piece of black velvet before showing the jewel to the customer.

Some good examples of showmanship can be seen at trade shows, where new products are displayed. One company demonstrated the fireproof quality of their insulation by holding a piece in front of a blowtorch. In simplest terms, showmanship is the act of presenting product features and benefits in a manner that will gain attention and increase desire. It is never a substitute for thorough preparation and knowledge of your customer, company, and your product. And effective showmanship is never based on deceit or trickery. It should not be gaudy or insincere. When showmanship detracts from the image or the product or the salesperson, it is counterproductive.

Minimize the Negative Impact of Change

As noted earlier, salespeople are constantly threatening the status quo. They sell people the new, the different, and the untried. In nearly all selling situations, the customer is being asked to consider change of some sort, and in some cases it is only natural for the person to resist change. Whenever possible, we should try to help the customer view change in a positive and realistic way. Change is more acceptable to people who understand the benefits of it and do not see it as a threat. Always anticipate the one question (spoken or unspoken) that every buyer asks: "How will this product benefit me?" To minimize the impact of change, be sure to personalize the benefit with a specific reference to the customer's need.

Place the Strongest Appeal at the Beginning or End

Research indicates that appeals made at the beginning or end of a presentation are more effective than those given in the middle. A strong appeal at the beginning of a presentation, of course, gets the prospect's attention and possibly develops interest. Made near the end of the presentation, the appeal sets the stage for closing the sale.

Use the Power of Association with Metaphors, Stories, and Testimonials

Research reveals salespeople who use the power of association through sharing information they previously experienced with other clients help their customers better understand their own needs and make smarter buying choices.[26] Metaphors, sometimes referred to as "figurative language," are highly persuasive sales tools. Metaphors are words or phrases that suggest pictorial relationships between objects or ideas. With the aid of metaphors, you can paint vivid, visual pictures for prospects that command their attention and keep their interest. The success of the metaphor rests on finding common ground (shared or well-known experiences) so that your message gets a free boost from a fact already known or believed to be true. A salesperson representing Cobalt boats, a line of high-quality runabouts selling for $30,000 to $300,000, might refer to his products as "the Steinways of the runabout class."[27]

Stories not only help you sell more products but also help you enrich relationships with your customers. Salespeople, such as Liberty Mutual's Marcus Smith, often use stories about a timely settlement for a large loss to explain the benefits of adequate insurance protection. A good story focuses the customer's attention and can effectively communicate the value of a product or a service as well. The story should be appropriate to the customer's situation, short, and told with enthusiasm.[28]

Many salespeople find it beneficial to quote a specific third party. Third-party testimonials from satisfied clients can help a prospect feel confident about using your product.

12.4 Describe elements of an effective group presentation

Guidelines for a Group Sales Presentation

Preparing a sales presentation for a group is more demanding than one-on-one sales calls. Meeting the diverse needs of the audience can be very challenging. Therefore, *Rule One* is to identify the titles and roles of the people who will attend. Among those attending,

Preparing a sales presentation for a group is more demanding than one-on-one sales calls. Too much reliance on technical devices during a demonstration can affect the relationship, so important to partnering effectively with prospects.

Source: Vitchanan Photography/ Shutterstock

who is most likely to influence the buying decision? If you learn that the audience will include the prospect's CEO, your CEO should be there. Anticipate that the audience will include demanding, high-level decision makers who will likely ask some difficult questions. Be prepared![29]

Rule Two is to check out the meeting room in advance. What are the room configurations, audiovisual capabilities, seating options, lighting, and heating or air conditioning? Always arrive at the meeting room about 60 minutes before the meeting begins. Use the first 40 minutes to check and double-check presentation tools, seating arrangements, lighting, and so forth. Use the other 20 minutes for rapport building with attendees as they arrive.

Rule Three is to be sure your presentation is characterized by clarity and simplicity. Minimize the number of features and benefits you present. Focus on the few benefits that appeal to your prospect. Don't use jargon or technical terms that might confuse persons in attendance. If you are part of a team sales presentation (see Chapter 10), then be sure all team members understand their responsibilities and the time they will be given for their presentation. Give the team time for rehearsal before the group presentation.

Rule Four is to anticipate the diversity of questions such as finance, delivery, competition, and service, in addition to traditional product issues you are likely to be asked. You must be prepared with answers that are concise and persuasive. Questions should be welcomed because they help you understand what is truly important to the customer.

Enhancing the Group Presentation with Mental Imagery

Mental imagery is the ability to visualize an object, concept, or action not actually present. A sales demonstration can be greatly enhanced with the use of auditory and visual imagery. Today, there is no shortage of compact, lightweight, portable presentation devices. Sony Electronics, Hitachi Software, and NEC offer sales professionals projectors that weigh only a few pounds and project a clear, bright image. These presentation tools also offer quick and easy setup.[30]

Impatica, a company that specializes in the delivery and viewing of PowerPoint presentations over the Internet and wireless networks, has developed a small, lightweight device that enables salespeople to project presentations wirelessly from a BlackBerry handheld. Users need only hook the ShowMate to the VGA port projector, LCD, or plasma screen and the BlackBerry will deliver the PowerPoint presentation using Bluetooth technology.[31] Of course, salespeople should never rely on presentation tools to sell products. Dianne Durkin, president of the consulting firm Loyalty Factor, offers this advice:

> When a salesperson is tied to the technical device and the presentation, they miss the opportunity to build the personal relationship by asking questions and listening to the customer. A questioning and listening strategy is the secret weapon for the salesperson.[32]

Video or Media Enhanced Presentation Fundamentals

Many companies provide their salespeople with audiovisual or media tools such as DVDs or computer-based presentations. YouTube has also become an important tool to consider. Unfortunately, they sometimes fail to explain how to use these tools in the most effective way. Here are some suggestions on how to use audiovisual presentations to achieve maximum impact:

1. Do not rely too heavily on "bells and whistles" to sell your products. Video provides support for the major points in your presentation, but it does not replace an interactive sales demonstration.
2. Be sure the prospect knows the purpose of the presentation. Preview the material and describe a few highlights. Always try to build interest in advance of the audiovisual presentation.
3. Be prepared to stop the presentation to clarify a point or to allow the prospect to ask questions. Do not permit the audiovisual presentation to become a barrier to good two-way communication.
4. At the conclusion of the audiovisual presentation, review key points and allow the prospect an opportunity to ask questions.

12.5 Develop selling tools that add value to your sales demonstrations

Selling Tools for Effective Demonstrations

Nearly every sales organization provides its staff with proof devices and sales tools of one kind or another to use in the demonstration part of the consultative presentation. Some companies refer to these as "marketing tools." Many proof devices and sales tools, when used correctly, add value to the sales effort. If the company does not provide these items, the creative salesperson secures or develops sales tools independently. In addition to technology-based presentations, sales personnel can utilize a wide range of other selling tools. Creative salespeople are continually developing new types of sales tools. The following section summarizes some of the most common proof devices and selling tools used today.

Many firms, like Engineered Machine Products that produces high-efficiency thermal management systems for cooling engines, have learned one of the keys to closing a large complex sale is to conduct a plant tour.

Source: Tyler Olson/Shutterstock

Product and Plant Tours

Without a doubt, the best-selling tool is often the product itself. As noted previously, Bell Helicopter uses an effective video to describe various products. However, some customers do not buy without a demonstration ride. In the growing market for ergonomic office chairs, ranging in price from $700 to $1,500, furniture makers know the best way to close the sale is to provide an opportunity for the customer to sit in the chair. With growing awareness of the hazards of poor sitting posture and bad ergonomics, more people are searching for a comfortable work chair.[33]

Doug Adams was the first salesperson hired by a major manufacturer of high-quality optical equipment.

Although he was not a technician or an engineer, he quickly realized that the equipment had product superiority that physicians would recognize if they saw it demonstrated. During the first year, he sold 28 machines, far surpassing the expectations of his employer.[34]

As noted in a previous chapter, plant tours provide an excellent source of product information. Engineered Machine Products (EMP) makes high-efficiency thermal management systems for cooling engines. Products are made at a state-of-the art manufacturing facility in Escanaba, Michigan. The company has learned that the key to closing many large, complex sales is a facility tour.[35]

Models

In some cases, it is not practical to demonstrate the product itself because it is too big or immobile. It is easier to demonstrate a small-scale model or cross-section of the original equipment. A working model, like the actual product, can give the prospect a clear picture of how a piece of equipment operates.

With the aid of modern technology, it's possible to create a model in picture form. ClosetMaid (www.closetmaid.com), a manufacturer of ventilated wire for commercial closets and other storage products, uses desktop visualization software to create a three-dimensional presentation that allows customers to see exactly what the finished facility will look like. Sales representatives can print out a hard copy so the customer has a picture of the custom-designed model for future reference. With the aid of this visualization technology, ClosetMaid salespeople can modify closet layouts on-screen and produce a detailed bill of materials for each project.[36]

Photos, Illustrations, and Brochures

The old proverb "One picture is worth a thousand words" can be put into practical application by a creative salesperson. A great deal of valuable information can be given to the prospect with the aid of photos and illustrations. Chris Roberts, area manager for Downing Displays (www.downingretail.com), a manufacturer of trade show displays, says that the photo presentation book is the most important item he takes on a first sales call. He says, "Because what we sell is very visual, it's important for the client to *see* the displays."[37]

Many companies develop brochures that visually reinforce specific need/benefit areas. Brochures can be effective during the initial discussion of needs when the salesperson wants to provide a brief overview of possible solutions. Someone planning to remodel a kitchen might be given a "Colors of Corian" brochure that features color photos of numerous countertop materials and kitchen design examples.[38]

Portfolios

A **portfolio** is a portable case or loose-leaf binder containing a wide variety of sales-supporting materials. The portfolio is used to add visual life to the sales message and to prove claims. Advertising salespeople such as *Texas Monthly*'s Amy Vandaveer, introduced in Chapter 6, customizes portfolios to appeal to the unique interests and needs of individual clients. She carefully selects sales tools to include such as the following:

Sample advertisements used in conjunction with other successful campaigns
Selected illustrations that can be incorporated into advertisements
A selection of testimonial letters
Rate cards
Market research studies and results on readership and buying habits
Case histories of specific clients who have used the media with success

The portfolio has been used as a sales tool by people who sell interior design services, insurance, real estate, securities, and convention services. It is a very adaptable proof device that can be revised at any time to meet the needs of each customer.

Reprints

Leading magazines and journals sometimes feature articles that directly or indirectly support the salesperson's product. A reprint of the article can be a forceful selling tool. It is also an inexpensive selling tool. Pharmaceutical and medical sales representatives often use reprints from journals that report on research in the field of medicine. A few years ago, Closure Medical Corporation received approval to sell Dermabond (www.dermabond.com), a surgical glue used to close cuts. This innovative product received national attention when the prestigious *Journal of the American Medical Association* concluded that gluing a wound could be just as effective as sewing it shut. Salespeople representing Dermabond used the article to help educate doctors on the product's merits and applications.[39]

In many cases, prospects are far more impressed with the good points of your product if they are presented by a third party rather than you. A reprint from a respected journal can be very persuasive.

Catalogs

A well-designed catalog shows the range and comprehensiveness of your product line. It may include specifications needed for installation and current price information. If you plan to give customers a copy of your catalog, review the important features, such as a comprehensive index or important appendix material.[40]

Graphs, Charts, and Test Results

Graphs and charts can be used to illustrate the change of some variable such as payroll expense, fuel consumption, or return on investment. For example, a bar graph might be used to illustrate the increase in fuel costs over a 10-year period.

Although graphs are usually quite descriptive, the layperson may misunderstand them. It is best to interpret the graph for the prospect. Do not move too fast because the full impact of the message may be lost.

Test results from a reliable agency often can be convincing. This is especially true when the test results are published by a respected independent agency such as J.D. Power and Associates.

Bound Paper Presentations

Although many salespeople are using some type of presentation technology in conjunction with the sales demonstration, paper is still widely used. For many sales and marketing organizations, bound paper presentations continue to be a very popular medium.[41] With the aid of computer-generated graphics, it is easy to print attractive graphs, charts, and other proof information. Product guarantees and warranties are sometimes included in a bound paper presentation. Some marketers use guarantees and warranties to differentiate their products from competing products. Customer testimonials represent another common element of bound paper presentations. A testimonial letter from a prominent satisfied customer provides persuasive evidence that the product has support in the industry. Prospects like bound paper presentations because the document is readily available for future reference.

GLOBAL BUSINESS INSIGHT

Doing Business in Italy

The majority of Italian Americans have roots in Sicily or southern Italy. American businesspeople tend to think that all Italians are like the Italian Americans whom they have had contact with in America. In reality, Italy is a very varied country where you will find all types of physical characteristics—fair, dark, short, tall, and varied accents and customs.

- Italian businesspeople tend to be quite formal in terms of introductions and dress. When you introduce yourself, say your last name only and then shake hands. Wait until invited

to use your first name. Personal and professional titles are used almost all the time in business dealings.

- Entertaining clients is typically done in restaurants and not in the home.
- Most Italian businesspeople are not in a hurry, so be patient and do not try to rush the sale.
- The practice of gift giving will vary. A nominal gift such as a bottle of wine at Christmas is quite common.[b,c,d]

Tablets, Laptop Computers and Demonstration Software

A survey conducted by *Selling Power* magazine found that 87 percent of salespeople use laptops during their sales presentations.[42] Many salespeople will tell you that their tablet or laptop computer is the single most powerful sales tool they use. Many of the things needed during the demonstration can be stored in the computer. If the customer is interested in a specific product, pull up the appropriate brochure or video on your laptop screen. If the client wants a copy of printed material, you can either print the pages or send them via e-mail. If the customer raises a question regarding product availability, use your laptop to access the information. You can place an order and in some cases print an invoice.[43]

Thanks to modern computer technology, it's possible to conduct impressive multiple, simultaneous product demonstrations without leaving your office. Let's assume you are presenting a new employee disability insurance plan to members of the BMW of North America human resources staff. One key decision maker is based in Germany and the other in the United States. With the aid of Pixion PictureTalk software, or a similar product, you can use the Internet to conduct the demonstration for both persons in real time. Sales managers might use this same approach to train members of their sales team in remote offices.

Personal computers (laptop) with the support of online presentation technologies and presentation software have played an important role in increasing sales force productivity. Salespeople have instant access to customer data, so it is often easier to customize the sales presentation. Many salespeople report that PC-based presentations, using graphics software, are very effective. Today's personal computer or laptop can produce striking visuals and attractive printed material that can be given to the customer for future reference.

ENHANCING DEMONSTRATIONS WITH POWERPOINT The PowerPoint software program from Microsoft has been available to salespeople for 20 years. PowerPoint is so common that many prospects find the standard presentation graphics very familiar, even dull. Salespeople who want their demonstration to look unique and different can create their own corporate template, animate their logo, or put video clips of their own company information into the PowerPoint presentation. When developing a PowerPoint presentation, use bold, simple, and large fonts (such as Arial and Veranda) and put graphics on several slides. Limit the number of words to 15 or fewer per slide. Keep in mind that two quality alternatives to PowerPoint are Apple's Keynote and Corel's Presentations.[44]

CREATING ELECTRONIC SPREADSHEETS For many years, salespeople have been using electronic spreadsheets to prepare sales proposals. The electronic spreadsheet is an excellent tool to organize the numbers involved in preparing quotes, such as quantities, costs, and prices. CB

SOCIAL MEDIA AND SELLING TODAY

Using YouTube for Presentations/Demonstrations

A sales presentation video posted on YouTube can add value to the sales process. Once reserved for large corporations that could afford professional sales presentation productions, now individual salespeople and small companies have easy access to the Internet and can make their presentations to larger groups of prospective customers.

YouTube and other sites are making it possible for salespeople to easily post a sales presentation on the Internet. YouTube presentations enable salespeople to focus on the key issues involving their customers' needs and their solutions. Different video presentations can be posted that meet the unique needs of individual customers. Various decision makers such as the user and the financial and technical influencers may view a video of a salesperson's presentation at any time during the sales process.

Lack of funds is not a barrier. Small investments are offset by creativity to communicate value. Inexpensive stock pictures,

footage, music, and other sounds are available to enhance and add value to your videotaped sales presentation.

To post a sales presentation video on YouTube, follow these steps:

1. Register and sign in to YouTube.com.
2. On the home page, click "Upload." You will be prompted to browse your computer for the video file of your sales presentation.
3. Select the file and complete the video information and privacy settings form.
4. Copy the Web address for your video.
5. Press "Save changes."

Richard Ellis's Susana Rosas, introduced in Chapter 4, frequently uses electronic spreadsheets to justify the purchase or rental of commercial properties. The electronic spreadsheet allows the user to answer "what if" questions about the effects of lowering costs or raising prices. Once the preparation work is finished, the electronic spreadsheet itself can be printed and used to serve as the proposal or to accompany the proposal.[45] The spreadsheet data can also be converted to a chart or graph that can enhance the proposal. When presenting the spreadsheet on a laptop computer, with minor adjustments, client questions regarding alternative proposals can be quickly generated.

Many computers sold today include an electronic spreadsheet program. The leading electronic spreadsheet, Excel, is part of Microsoft's Office Suite of products. If you have access to Excel, or any other electronic spreadsheet software, you can explore the power of this tool for preparing proposals.

WEB-BASED PRESENTATIONS Salespeople who want to avoid long airport security lines, lengthy terminal wait times, high-priced hotels, and expensive rental car rates are turning to Web-conferencing solutions. Popular alternatives to in-person sales presentations include GoToMeeting, Cisco WebEx Sales Center, Raindance Meeting Edition, Adobe's Macromedia Breeze 5, and Microsoft Office Live Meeting. Some salespeople create computerized demonstrations that are stored in a central library and accessed on demand. With a few clicks of a mouse, presenters can call up the information they wish to showcase using a Web browser. The salesperson can show PowerPoint presentations, present product features, and conduct question-and-answer sessions in real time. Prior to scheduling an online meeting, be sure to find out if the customer's firewall restricts the usage of your Web-conferencing software.[46]

Rehearse the Presentation

While you are actually putting on the presentation, you need to be concentrating on a variety of details. The movements you make and what you say and do should be so familiar to you that each response is nearly automatic. To achieve this level of skill, you need to rehearse the presentation.

Rehearse both what you are going to say and what you are going to do. Say the words aloud exactly as if the prospect were present. It is surprising how often a concept that seems quite clear as you think it over becomes hopelessly mixed up when you try to discuss it with a customer. Rehearsal is the best way to avoid this embarrassing situation. Whenever possible, have your presentation/demonstration recorded before you give it.

Play it back and watch for these things:[47]

- Do you frequently use words that take away from your professional image? Examples include "you know" and "like."
- Check your pace—are you talking too rapidly or too slowly?
- Do you present information with clarity? Are you convincing?

Plan for the Dynamic Nature of the Consultative Sales Presentation

The sales presentation is a dynamic activity. From the moment the salesperson and the customer meet, the sales presentation is being altered and fine-tuned to reflect the new information available. The salesperson must be able to execute strategy instantaneously. In the movie *Top Gun*, Kelly McGillis asks Tom Cruise, "What were you thinking up there?" His reply was, "You don't have time to think. You take time to think up there, you're dead." By that, he meant the response must be habit and reflex.[48]

During a typical presentation, the salesperson asks numerous questions, discusses several product features, and demonstrates the appropriate product benefits. The customer also is asking questions and, in many cases, voicing concerns. The successful sales presentation is a good model of two-way communication. Because of the dynamic nature of the sales presentation, the salesperson must be prepared to apply several different selling skills to meet the variety of buyer responses. Figure 12.5, The Selling Dynamics Matrix, illustrates how the various selling skills can be applied during all parts of the sales presentation. In creating effective presentations, the salesperson should be prepared to meet a wide range of buyer responses with effective questions, benefit statements, demonstrations, negotiating methods, and closing methods. Methods for negotiating, closing and confirming, and servicing the sale will be described in the next three chapters.

Consultative selling skills	Parts of the Sales Presentation			
	Need discovery	**Selecting solution**	**Need-satisfaction presentation**	**Servicing the sale**
Questioning skills	• As a question approach • To find needs and buying motives • To probe for buying motives • To confirm needs and buying motives	• To confirm selection	• To confirm benefits • To confirm mutual understanding • To increase desire for a solution	• To make suggestions • To confirm delivery and installation • To resolve complaints • To build goodwill • To secure credit arrangements
Presenting benefits	• As a benefit approach • To discover specific benefits	• To match up with buying motives	• To build support for the solution	• To make suggestions • To use credit as a close
Demonstrating skills	• As a product approach • To clarify need	• To clarify selection	• To strengthen product claims	• When making effective suggestions
Negotiating skills	• To overcome initial resistance to sales interview • To overcome need objection	• To overcome product objection	• To overcome source, price, and time objections	• In handling complaints • To overcome financing objection
Closing skills	• When customer has made buying decision	• When buyer immediately recognizes solutions	• Whenever buyer presents closing signals	• After suggestion • To secure repeats and referrals

FIGURE 12.5

The Selling Dynamics Matrix

In creating effective presentations, the salesperson should prepare to meet a wide range of buyer responses with effective questions, benefit statements, demonstrations, negotiating methods, and closing methods.

Source: Based on Philip Kotler and Gary Armstrong, *Principles of Marketing*, 12th ed. (Upper Saddle River, NJ: Prentice Hall, 2008), p. 467.

CHAPTER LEARNING ACTIVITIES

Reviewing Key Concepts

List and describe three types of need-satisfaction presentation strategies

Once you have selected a solution that matches the customer's needs, you must decide which presentation strategy to emphasize. Need satisfaction can be achieved through informing, persuading, or reminding. The salesperson can, of course, use a combination of these presentation strategies in some cases.

Present guidelines for creating consultative presentations that add value

The perception of value is enhanced with a well-developed consultative presentation, whether it be the informative, persuasive, or reminder need-satisfaction presentation strategy. A sales presentation that adds value is the result of both planning and practice with the guidelines described in this chapter. An effective, well-organized demonstration helps to uncomplicate the buying process.

Describe the elements of a persuasive presentation strategy

There are many ways to incorporate persuasion into a sales presentation and most will—if used appropriately—create value for the customer. Seven specific methods are presented.

Describe elements of an effective group presentation

Group presentations are almost always more challenging than one-on-one sales calls. Be sure you identify the titles and roles of the persons who will attend. Check out the meeting room in advance to assess audiovisual capabilities and seating options. As you prepare your presentation, take into consideration the needs of the audience. In many cases, audiovisual tools can be used to enhance the group presentation.

Develop selling tools that add value to your sales demonstrations

Selling tools, also called "proof devices," used to demonstrate the benefits of your solution will add value to the sale presentation. Be prepared to use one or more of the 10 tools discussed in this chapter.

Key Terms

Informative
  presentation, p. 248
Persuasion, p. 249
Persuasive
  presentation, p. 249
Reminder
  presentations, p. 250

Canned
  presentation, p. 250
Proof devices, p. 252
Cost–benefit analysis,
  p. 255

Return on investment, p. 255
Emotional links, p. 256
Showmanship, p. 257
Mental imagery, p. 259
Portfolio, p. 261

MyMarketingLab

To complete the problems with the ⭐ in your MyLab, go to the EOC Discussion Questions.

Review Questions

12-1 Distinguish among the three types of need-satisfaction presentations: informative, persuasive, and reminder.

12-2 List the guidelines to follow in planning an effective consultative presentation.

 12-3 Discuss the advantages of using the presentation worksheet.

12-4 Explain why a salesperson should organize the sales presentation so that it appeals to as many of the five senses as possible.

12-5 What are the guidelines to be followed when developing a persuasive sales presentation?

 12-6 Describe the merits of a bound paper presentation. What can be done to strengthen the persuasive power of a bound paper presentation?

12-7 Explain how magazine and trade journal reprints can be used to assist the salesperson in a persuasive sales presentation.

 12-8 Describe the audiovisual presentation fundamentals.

12-9 What are some of the common sales functions performed by small laptop computers and demonstration software?

Application Exercises

12-10 In many selling situations, it is difficult, if not impossible, to demonstrate the product itself. List means other than the product itself that can be used to demonstrate the product features and benefits.

12-11 Develop a list of sales tools you could use in a job interview situation. What tools could you use to demonstrate your skills and capabilities?

12-12 As noted in this chapter, presentation software is becoming increasingly popular. Real estate salespeople are using this software to showcase homes to prospective buyers. Assume you are a salesperson for Iowa Realty, and you have a customer who wants a $250,000 to $300,000 condo/townhome in the suburb of West Des Moines. Go to www.IowaRealty.com, input the data you have from your customer, and request a search for homes in this category. From your search, select a listing with a Virtual Tour button. Click on the various views and examine the features of this home.

Role-Play Exercise

Study the product-selling strategy memo and proof devices found in Appendix 3 on pages 419. In this role-play, you will be selling to a human resource manager who is interested in controlling costs for a regional meeting of company employees. All 75 of the attendees will be staying at the hotel—50 of them will be driving to the hotel, whereas the other 25 will be flying. Prepare a comparative cost–benefit graph to show the total amount this meeting planner can expect to save by selecting your hotel. Use the proof devices you have prepared to demonstrate the cost savings to the meeting planner. Plan also to use the map on page 431 to demonstrate the ease of finding the hotel and local attractions.

Reality Selling Case Problem—Chris Wylie/Ecolab

Ecolab (www.ecolab.com) is the global leader in cleaning, sanitizing, food safety, and infection prevention products and services. With more than 14,000 sales and service experts, Ecolab employs the industry's largest and best-trained direct sales and service force, which advises and assists customers in meeting a full range of cleaning, sanitation, and service needs. Chris Wylie, the Ecolab sales representative featured at the beginning of this chapter, is continually prospecting for new accounts, servicing existing accounts, and introducing new products and services. He primarily calls on restaurants and hotels to sell and service a wide array of cleaning and sanitizing products like bathroom air

Source: Michael Ahearne

fresheners, bathroom cleaners, dispensers, floor cleaners, glass cleaners, dish machines, detergents, dish racks, and safety equipment.

In his sales demonstrations, Chris follows certain guidelines and tries to add value in various ways. Sales reps at Ecolab utilize the HELP sales process and move toward a survey solution they can sell their customers. The sales rep's goal is to determine the decision-making team, uncover the relevant facts, identify the problem/opportunity, and present the implications of the problem such that the customer decides to accept the solution that is presented by Ecolab. One central element of the HELP sales process is a so-called three-minute demo in which Chris can show the prospect deficiencies in his kitchen that he might not be aware of. To that end, he possesses a series of measurement tools to test the chemicals and certain concentration ratios. After conducting the whole series of tests and analyzing the results, Chris goes back to his customer and asks him for a few minutes of his time to show him that same survey on his piece of restaurant equipment (e.g., a dish machine). Through specific guidelines, Chris can show the prospect certain machine deficiencies that he has with the current provider. He can then demonstrate the features and benefits that Ecolab can offer to overcome these deficiencies.

In his sales demonstrations, Chris tries to interact with his customers to get them involved and to fully capture their attention. He even engages customers in the survey process by asking them to execute parts of the tests with him. In addition, Chris involves his customers by asking them questions like: "What do you think this result means? Let's think about this together for a second." Then he would lead the customer into developing a good solution for the result they got. In this way, Chris helps customers to paint their own picture of the problem. Chris knows that this kind of customer engagement is much more effective and eye-opening than just telling the customer about the deficiencies.

In some situations, it might be difficult or even impossible for Chris to demonstrate a product itself. An example could be a dishwasher that is too large and heavy to be taken to the customer's or prospect's location. If Chris makes claims about how efficient Ecolab's machine is compared to others, it appears that his customers would have to take his word on that. Another way to demonstrate the effectiveness and efficiency of a dishwasher that he is trying to pitch would be to bring the prospect into an existing account that already uses the dishwasher. This would enable Chris to show how the dishwasher operates while somebody is actually working on it. (See this chapter's opener, and *Reality Selling Today* Role-Play 9 in Appendix 1 for more information).

Questions

12-13 If you were in the position of Chris Wylie and found a potential serious health problem in one of your customers' kitchens, which presentation strategy or combination described in this chapter would you use? List and describe five guidelines you would use in creating your presentation. What demonstration tools would you use?

12-14 Make a list of buyer concerns and objections that a salesperson like Chris Wylie would typically expect from new prospects. How could different elements of a sales demonstration be used to overcome these concerns and objections? Think about it as a two-step sales call: In the first step, Chris would ask for permission to conduct a survey of the kitchen and/or bathroom. In the second step, he would ask the prospect to buy from him.

12-15 In the video case, which of the six actions (as listed on the right-hand side of Figure 12.3) does Chris Wylie take during his demonstration?

12-16 In some situations, it might be difficult or even impossible for Chris Wylie to specifically demonstrate a product or service. What other means can Chris use to demonstrate the features and benefits of, for example, large products or intangible services?

NewNet Systems®

Your Value Adding Systems Partner

Regional Account Management Case Study (refer to Appendix 2)

Custom Fitting Presentations/Demonstrations

Your NewNet Systems sales manager, Casey Arnold, has asked you to meet with her to discuss demonstrations. As you prepare to make your demonstrations, she would like you to review the likelihood of closing each sale. Lee recorded this in percentage form. She also wants you to review the notes windows of your accounts and tell her if any of your accounts need a demonstration and, if so, what type of demonstration.

Questions

12-17 Using the table you prepared for Chapter 11, add another column to record the metrics regarding the likelihood of closing each account. Lee Bizon recorded this information in the Contact Screen.

NewNet Systems Account Management

Name				Regional Account Manager, NEWNET SYSTEMS			
Date	Account Name/	Dollar	Comm.	Sales Process	**Likeli-**		
Close	Contact Name	Sales Amt.	Style	Stage	**hood**		

12-18 Which two medium-sized accounts with a high likelihood of purchase need a demonstration of the speed and power capabilities of the recommended network? What is the likelihood of closing each of them? Based on projected date to close, which should you work on first?

12-19 Which account wants a very specific network and information-management system and needs to be shown that the recommended network product configuration and demonstration will meet their exacting specifications? Is this something to work on immediately?

12-20 Which account with many sites needs a demonstration of NewNet's ability to put together a complex solution? With many sites, will this be an account you need to spend a lot of time on soon? Explain.

12-21 Which medium-sized account seeking a low price needs a testimonial of NewNet's value-added ability to help customers maximize the power of their network? What is the likelihood of closing this sale and how large could it be? What is the close date?

12-22 Which medium-sized account with a fairly short close date needs a demonstration of NewNet's financial stability?

Partnership Selling: A Role-Play (see Appendix 3, page 419)

Developing a Sales Presentation Strategy—The Presentation

Read Sales Memorandum 3 ("A" or "B," depending on the category you were assigned in sales call 1). In this role-play, your call objectives are to make a persuasive presentation, negotiate any customer concerns, and close and service the sale.

At this time, you should complete item 1 of the presentation plan and prepare and price a product solution. This should include completing the sales proposal form. Also, you should obtain a three-ring binder with pockets in the front and back for the development of a portfolio presentation. In this binder, you should prepare your presentation and demonstration, following the instructions in items 2a, 2b, 2c, and 2d under the presentation plan. The presentation and demonstration materials (use the product strategy materials, i.e., photos, price lists, menus, awards, etc., provided to you with Employment Memorandum 1) should be placed in the three-ring binder as a part of your portfolio or your PowerPoint presentation.

Using PowerPoint and Excel software, you may want to produce computer-generated presentation graphics to enhance your demonstrations. You should also

Park Shores Resort and Convention Center.
Source: Courtesy of Beach Resort

consider using presentation paper and sheet protectors. You may want to select a person as your customer and rehearse the use of these materials.

When salespeople use effective visual proof devices in their presentations, research indicates that retention increases from 14 to 38 percent and the time needed to present a concept is reduced by up to 40 percent.

MyMarketingLab

Go to the Assignments section of your MyLab to complete these writing exercises.

12-23 Once you have selected a solution that matches the customer's needs, you must decide which presentation strategy to emphasize. Discuss the three types of need-satisfaction presentation strategies.

12-24 What are the guidelines for creating a presentation that adds value? Also, distinguish between the canned presentation and the planned consultative presentation.

Learning Objectives

When you finish reading this chapter, you should be able to

13.1 Describe the principles of formal negotiations as part of the win-win strategy

13.2 Describe common types of buyer concerns

13.3 Discuss specific methods of negotiating buyer concerns

13.4 Outline methods for creating value in formal negotiations

13.5 Work with buyers who are trained in negotiation

Source: Michael Ahearne

Reality Selling Video—Heather Ramsey/Marriott International

▶

Marriott International, Inc. (www.marriott.com) is a world-renowned company with approximately 8,500 salespeople and 3,000 lodging properties around the world. One of its properties is the Marriott Houston Hobby, which is located within a mile of the Hobby Airport in Houston, Texas. Apart from accommodation, the hotel offers comprehensive meeting facilities complemented by expert catering and audiovisual resources.

Corporate catering manager, Heather Ramsey, in the photo above, is in charge of convention and meeting sales at the Marriott Houston Hobby Airport. She always has a ready win-win response when customers raise buyer concerns about prices and the tranquility of an airport hotel. She emphasizes the value to the customers by describing superior benefits including the state-of-the-art meeting and conference facilities offered by the hotel, its convenience to travelers, as well as other unique features not offered by the competition. Sometimes, customers do not communicate openly about their needs and concerns to Heather. She must often work hard with a series of consultative questions to identify their actual needs to offer them the best value and bring benefits to the hotel as well. Her negotiation process with new customers will normally involve identifying their actual needs and then listening to, clarifying, and negotiating concerns that the customers express. ●

The Six-Step Presentation Plan

Step One:
Approach
- ☑ Review Strategic/Consultative Selling Model
- ☑ Initiate customer contact

Step Two:
Need Discovery
- ☑ Ask strategic questions
- ☑ Determine customer needs
- ☑ Select product solution

Step Three:
Presentation
- ☑ Select presentation strategy
- ☑ Create presentation plan
- ☑ Initiate presentation

Step Four:
Negotiation
- ☐ Anticipate buyer concerns
- ☐ Plan negotiating methods
- ☐ Initiate win-win negotiations

Step Five:
Close
- ☐ Plan appropriate closing methods
- ☐ Recognize closing clues
- ☐ Initiate closing methods

Step Six:
Servicing the Sale
- ☐ Follow through
- ☐ Follow-up calls
- ☐ Expansion selling

Service, retail, wholesale, and manufacturer selling

FIGURE 13.1

Negotiating Customer Concerns and Problems

Many sales professionals are very proficient in need discovery and selecting the right solution, but are weak in the area of negotiating win-win agreements that create value for the customer and the salesperson's firm. Many buyers with responsibility for purchasing have formal training in how to negotiate favorable terms. Most customers are studying competitive offers and increasingly attempting to secure the best deal possible. These market conditions require that salespeople anticipate buyer concerns and plan collaborative win-win negotiated solutions, prior to meeting with their customers (see Figure 13.1). A recent poll reports that as many as 83 percent of sales executives from 25 industries said they generally enter negotiations with no formal strategy![1] Another common mistake is making last-minute concessions in order to close the sale.[2] In this chapter, we describe effective strategies for anticipating and negotiating buyer concerns.

We have noted previously that the heaviest time investment in value-added selling is on the front end of the sale. This is especially true for large, complex sales that require a long sales cycle. Identifying the customer's needs and developing the best solution can be very time consuming. However, when you do these things effectively, you are creating value in the eyes of the customer. When you build value on the front end of the sale, price becomes less of an issue on the back end of the sale.[3]

13.1 Describe the principles of formal negotiations as part of the win-win strategy

Formal Integrative Negotiation—Part of the Win-Win Relationship Strategy

Frank Acuff, negotiations trainer and author of *How to Negotiate Anything with Anyone, Anywhere Around the Globe*, says, "Life is a negotiation."[4] Negotiating skills have applications almost daily in our personal and professional lives. Some traditional personal selling books discuss how to "handle" buyer objections. The message communicated to the reader is that personal selling is a "we versus they" process resulting from distributive negotiations: Somebody wins, and somebody loses. The win-win solution, where both sides win, is not offered as an option. In this chapter, we focus on integrative negotiations, which are built on joint problem solving, trust,

Negotiations, Solving the Tough Problems

One of the biggest challenges to the Adaptive Selling and Partnering Strategy is evident as one deals with the tough problems that often come up during the negotiation stage of the sales process. In this new Adaptive Selling Today Negotiations Video, Lana, a medical equipment representative, is faced with the following tough problems: dealing with an angry customer about pricing issues, dealing with skepticism about sourcing and timing issues, dealing with how to be understood about product issues, and dealing with how to walk away yet keep the door open to salvage the order. The customer, Dr. Arroyo, director of a hospital radiology department, has a huge responsibility to make the right selection at the right price, and he therefore has concerns requiring an adaptive negotiations strategy. Hopefully, Lana's negotiations skills result in a win-win solution. Refer to the Application Exercises at the end of the chapter on page 288 for more information.

Dr. Arroyo is a tough negotiator who uses all he knows with Lana to get the right solution.
Source: Michael Ahearne

and rapport to achieve win-win situations.[5] Ron Willingham, author of two books on integrity selling, says:

> When trust and rapport are strong, negotiation becomes a partnership to work through customer concerns. But when trust and rapport are weak, almost any negotiation becomes too combative.[6]

Trust and rapport must be established on the front end of the sale and maintained throughout the sales process. High-performance salespeople, like Heather Ramsey, take time to discover the customer's needs and try to recommend the best possible solution. Always keep in mind that any agreement that leaves one party dissatisfied will come back to hurt the other party later, sometimes in ways that cannot be predicted.[7]

What is **negotiation**? One definition is "working to reach an agreement that is mutually satisfactory to both buyer and seller." It involves resolving the problems or concerns that prevent people from buying.[8] As we noted in Chapter 2, the salesperson increasingly serves as a consultant or resource and provides solutions to buyers' problems. The consultant seeks to establish and maintain long-term relationships with customers. The ability to negotiate problems or objections is one of the most effective ways to create value for the customer. Figure 13.2 outlines the steps a salesperson can take to anticipate and negotiate problems.

Negotiation Is a Process

By definition, negotiations seek to move polarized parties into the realm of common interests.[9] Negotiations can take place before the sales call or at any time during the sales presentation. Early negotiations may involve the meeting location, who will attend the sales presentation, or the amount of time available for the first meeting. Salespeople sometimes make early concessions to improve the relationship. This approach may set a costly precedent for later in the sale.[10] Some concessions can have a negative influence on the sales presentation.

In most cases, you can anticipate that the most important negotiations will take place during stage three of the buying process (refer to Figure 8.3). Resolution of problems can sometimes be very time consuming. Establishing a strategic alliance, described in Chapter 2 as the highest form of partnering, requires lengthy negotiations. These negotiations may extend over several months. Once the alliance is finalized, negotiations continue when concerns voiced by one party or the other surface.

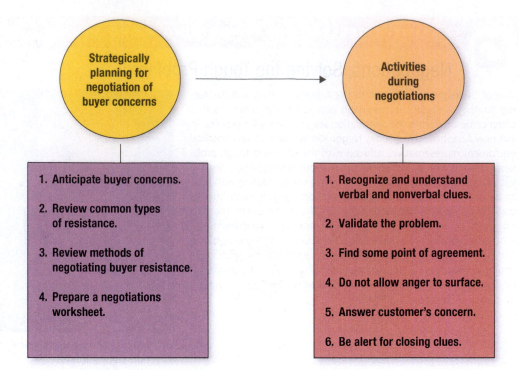

FIGURE 13.2

Today, salespeople must be prepared to anticipate and negotiate buyer concerns and problems.

Planning for Formal Negotiations

Professional buyers are well-trained negotiators. To negotiate with them effectively, salespeople first need to engage in detailed planning. Ironically, one of the most common mistakes negotiators commit is not doing their homework in advance.[11]

GATHER INFORMATION BEFORE THE NEGOTIATION Exhaustive preparation is more important than aggressive argument.[12] Robert H. Schuller offers invaluable advice in this crucial step.[13] First, a salesperson should prepare from both counterparts' points of view by identifying the similarities and differences of the goals and objectives of both sides. Then, information sources are tapped. The information might be from business associates, buyers' websites, or even previous vendors for the same buyers. The salesperson should bear in mind that negotiation is an information game: the more, the better.[14]

Negotiation is defined as "working to reach an agreement that is mutually satisfactory to both buyer and seller." It involves building relationships instead of making one-time deals.

Source: Zurijeta/Shutterstock

DECIDE TEAM VERSUS INDIVIDUAL NEGOTIATIONS FOR BOTH SELLER AND BUYER The next logical step in this preparatory process is to decide who will be in the negotiations. For Susana Rosas at CB Richard Ellis working in a business-to-business selling context, it is not unusual to create a cross-functional team consisting of individuals from finance, construction, and zoning to bring to a meeting with the buying center at the buyer's premises. Other situations might call for her to bring senior managers from her firm. If teams are involved, make sure there is a leader and establish guidelines for information exchange among the team members. Creating a cohesive negotiation team can pay off with higher ending profits after the conclusion of negotiations.[15]

UNDERSTAND THE VALUE OF WHAT YOU ARE OFFERING It is important for Salesforce .com's Dave Levitt to know what is of real value to the customer and not consider value only in terms of purchase price. The real value of what you are offering may be a value-added intangible such as expert product knowledge, superior configuration programming, seamless integration with other vendors, short set-up times, effective training, product support, or a reputation for honest dealings. An important aspect of the negotiation process is discovering what is of utmost importance to the buyer (see Table 13.1). The focus of personal selling today should be the mutual search for value. Some salespeople make the mistake of offering a lower price the moment buyer concerns surface. In the customer's mind, price may be of secondary importance compared with the quality of service after the sale. Detailed tactics for creating values in formal negotiations appear at the end of the chapter.

DETERMINE YOUR GOALS AND FINANCIAL OBJECTIVES Two important concepts warrant mentioning. First is **BATNA** (Best Alternative to Negotiated Agreement), defined as "what alternative(s) will be acceptable to you if your negotiation does not succeed."[16] You will likely make concessions in formal negotiations; therefore, you must assess both your and your customer's BATNA. The second important planning tool is **ZOPA** (Zone of Possible Agreement), defined as the space between the seller's walk-away point and the buyer's highest willingness to pay.[17] The walk-away point represents the lowest offer a party would be willing to accept and is also called the "reservation value." For example, if your walk-away point is $42.65M and the highest price the buyer is willing to pay is $48M, your ZOPA is any offer that falls within this range, or a zone of $5.35M (= $48M – $42.65M).[18]

Ed Brodow (www.brodow.com), popular speaker, international consultant, and author of *Negotiating Bootcamp*, contends it is best to *aim high* when configuring your solution. In his new training video, "Six Principles of Negotiation," he suggests *doing your homework* and preparing a range of terms that include the maximum you could expect to receive, what you would hope to receive, and your bottom line or the minimum you could accept before having to walk away from the sale. In many buying situations today, buyers expect there to be alternative solutions with alternative pricing.

PREPARE AN AGENDA An agenda outlines what will and will not be discussed and in what sequence. As the seller, you want to achieve "small wins" to create goodwill before dealing with tough issues. Therefore, you want to prioritize these items on your proposed agenda. Sometimes items should be discussed simultaneously, rather than sequentially.[19] Experienced buyers, however, also come to the meeting table with a detailed agenda. Negotiations might start with a discussion about the agenda itself.

REVIEW ADAPTIVE SELLING STYLES The successful negotiation of buyer concerns is based in large part on understanding human behavior. This knowledge, coupled with a good measure of common sense, helps us overcome most buyer concerns. In one-on-one negotiations, adaptive-selling styles are useful (review Chapter 5). The Platinum Rule of negotiating is, "Do unto others as they want to be done unto."[20] When negotiations are conducted in teams, the situation gets more complicated. The role of the negotiation leader is to maintain smooth information exchange and foster strong relationships despite various communication styles.[21]

PREPARE A NEGOTIATIONS WORKSHEET Your planning must be systematically organized. It helps to predict and classify possible resistance with the aid of a negotiations worksheet. To illustrate how this form works, let us review an example from the food industry. Mary Turner is a salesperson for Durkee Famous Foods. She represents more than 350 products. Mary calls on

> **TABLE 13.1 Handling Objections**
> Objections are often requests for more information to justify the buying decision. Objections can tell us a lot about the real source of hesitation and what type of information the customer is seeking.

OBJECTION	SOURCE OF HESITATION	REQUEST FOR . . .
"Price too high"	Perceived cost versus benefit	Value articulation
"Think about it"	Afraid to make a bad decision	Create comfort, provide proof
"Talk to boss"	Unable to justify decision	Risk reduction, benefit review
"Need more quotes"	Unsure you're their best option	Targeted solutions, value
"Set with current provider"	Doesn't see benefit of change	Differentiation
"Bad history"	Past experience is affecting current view	Offer proof of change

Source: Adapted from "Hide-and-Seek," a table from Nancy J. Martini (formerly Stephens), President & CEO, PI Worldwide, Wellesley Hills, MA, "Objections Are a 'Yes' About to Happen," *Selling*, November 1998, p. 3. Printed with permission of Nancy J. Martini.

supermarkets daily and offers assistance in the areas of ordering and merchandising. Recently, her company decided to offer retail food stores an allowance of $1 per case of olives if the store purchased 15 or more cases. Prior to talking with her customers about this offer, Mary sat down and developed a negotiations worksheet, shown in Figure 13.3. We cannot anticipate every possible problem, but it is possible to identify the most common problems that are likely to arise. The negotiations worksheet can be a useful tool.

Conducting the Negotiation Session

During the formal negotiation session, it is beneficial to master the skills presented throughout the book that is, establishing a good social contact, asking good questions, listening actively, using proof devices, and applying methods of negotiating objections. A salesperson should internalize a number of golden rules to be successful in formal negotiations. These include understanding the problem, creating alternative solutions, periodically recapitulating what has been agreed upon, and making wise concessions in a timely manner.

UNDERSTAND THE PROBLEM David Stiebel, author of *When Talking Makes Things Worse!*, says we need to understand the difference between a misunderstanding and a true disagreement. A "misunderstanding" is a failure to accurately understand the other person's point. For example, the salesperson believes the customer is primarily interested in price, but the customer's primary need is on-time delivery. A "disagreement," in contrast, is a failure to agree that would persist despite the most accurate understanding.[22] Be certain that both you and the prospect are clear on the true nature of what each party's needs are regarding the issues to be negotiated (see Table 13.1). When the prospect begins talking, listen carefully and then listen some more. With *probing questions*, you can fine-tune your understanding of the problem.

CREATE ALTERNATIVE SOLUTIONS THAT CAN ADD VALUE When the prospect finishes talking, it is a good practice to validate the problem, using a *confirmation question*. This helps to isolate the true problem and reduce the chance of misunderstanding. The confirmation question might sound like this: "I think I understand your concern. You feel the warranty

Negotiations Worksheet

Customer's concern	Type of concern	Possible response
"Fifteen cases of olives will take up valuable space in my receiving room. It is already crowded."	Need	**Combination direct denial/Superior benefit** "You will not have to face that problem. With the aid of our merchandising plan you can display 10 cases immediately on the sales floor. Only five cases will become reserve stock. You should move all 15 cases in about two weeks."
"This is a poor time of the year to buy a large order of olives. People are not buying olives at this time."	Time	**Combination indirect denial/Third-party testimony** "I agree that it has been a problem in the past, but consumer attitudes seem to be changing. We have found that olives sell well all year long if displayed properly. More people are using olives in the preparation of omelets, pizza, and other dishes. Of course, most relish trays feature olives. We will supply you with point-of-purchase material that provides kitchen-tested ways to use this high-profit item."
"I have to stay within my budget."	Price	**Superior benefit** "As you know, olives represent a high-profit item. The average margin is 26 percent. With the addition of our $1.00 per case allowance the margin will rise to about 30 percent. This order will give you a good return on your investment."
"I am very satisfied with my present supplier."	Source	**Combination question/Trial order** "What can I do to get you to take just a trial order?"

FIGURE 13.3

The Negotiations Worksheet

Before the presentation, it is important to prepare a negotiations worksheet. Note how combination methods are frequently used to effectively respond to customer concerns.

GLOBAL BUSINESS INSIGHT

Negotiating Across Cultures

Negotiations in the international area vary from one country to another because of cultural differences. German buyers are more apt to look you in the eye and tell you what they do not like about your product. Japanese buyers, on the other hand, do not want to embarrass you and, therefore, bury their concerns beneath several layers of courtesy. In China, negotiations are more straightforward. People who have been doing business in China for many years suggest a very direct approach to negotiations. However, do not become antagonistic or discourteous. Do get involved in native business rituals that are intended to create a friendly atmosphere.

When you enter into negotiations in foreign countries, it is important to understand and accommodate the customer's culture. You may not get every detail exactly right, but you win respect by trying.

Selling in certain cultures often requires more time in bonding and building a rapport. Several meetings may be needed to lay the groundwork for the actual sale.[a]

does not provide you with sufficient protection. Is this correct?" By taking time to ask this question, you accomplish two important objectives. First, you are giving personal attention to the problem, which pleases the customer. Second, you gain time to think about the best possible response.

The best possible response is very often an alternative solution. In formal negotiations, this is often referred to as **logrolling**.[23] Many of today's customers do not want to hear that there is only one way or a single solution. In the age of information, people have less time to manage their work and their lives, so they expect new levels of flexibility. For Marriott's Heather Ramsey there are many issues such as group pricing, alternative menus, complimentary rooms, and so forth that can be introduced into the negotiations for convention services. In many cases, these additional issues take the focus off price, and can actually create value for the customer and possibly for the seller. Here are additional issues that can be introduced into negotiations when a buyer is focused on price: delivery dates, financing, contract length, quality, exclusivity clauses, levels of service support, and warranties.

PERIODICALLY REVIEW ACKNOWLEDGED POINTS OF AGREEMENT Negotiating buying problems is a little like the art of diplomacy. It helps to know what points of agreement exist. This saves time and helps establish a closer bond between you and the prospect. At some point during the presentation, you might summarize by using a *summary-confirmation question*: "Let us see if I fully understand your position. You think our product is well constructed and will provide the reliability you are looking for. Also, you believe our price is fair. Am I correct on these two points?"

Once all the areas of agreement have been identified, there may be surprisingly few points of disagreement. The prospect suddenly sees that the advantages of ownership far outweigh the disadvantages. Now that the air is cleared, both the salesperson and the customer can give their full attention to any remaining points of disagreement.

The business environment is sometimes turbulent. Hence, it might be advisable in negotiations to "pack a reserve parachute." To avoid buyers' frustration when things do not go as agreed upon, lay the groundwork for the unexpected and be open about backup plans with the buyers.[24]

DO NOT MAKE CONCESSIONS TOO QUICKLY Give away concessions methodically and reluctantly, and always try to get something in return. Negotiations consultant Ed Brodow suggests when preparing to make a concession we should prepare to get something in return by asking "if we do this for you, will you do this for us?" A concession given too freely can diminish the value of your product.[25] Also, giving a concession too easily may send the signal you are negotiating from a position of weakness. Neil Rackham, author of several books on SPIN selling, says, "Negotiate late, negotiate little, and never let negotiation become a substitute for good selling."[26]

TIMING AND THE PARETO LAW Time plays a critical role in negotiations. Most often, negotiations will conclude in the final 20 percent of the time allowed. In negotiations, experience with the Pareto Law reveals that 80 percent of your results are generally agreed upon in the last 20 percent of your time. Since influence tactics are more likely to exert an effect when their target is under time pressure, negotiators should use time as a strategic weapon by buying more time to fully consider concessions or giving a deadline to speed up agreement.[27]

Know When to Walk Away

For many reasons, salespeople must sometimes walk away from a potential sale. If the customer's budget doesn't allow the purchase of your product, don't press the issue. If the customer's best offer is not favorable for your company, don't continue to waste your time. If the buyer is interested only in the lowest possible price, and you represent a marketer committed to a value-added sales strategy, consider withdrawing from negotiations. If you discover that the prospect is dishonest or fails to keep his or her word, discontinue negotiations. Be aware of how much flexibility (your BATNA and ZOPA) you have in terms of price, specifications, delivery schedules, and so forth, and know when you have reached your walk-away point.[28] The lyrics to the popular song, "you got to know when to hold them, when to fold them, when to walk away and when to run" applies to many of the issues above.

Finally, when appropriate, document negotiated settlements in writing. These will be helpful when formal contracts are drawn up. Negotiation minutes will also serve as a control tool for follow-up actions.

Common Types of Buyer Concerns

13.2 Describe common types of buyer concerns

Salespeople learn that patterns of buyer resistance exist and, therefore, they can anticipate that certain concerns may arise during the sales call. With this information, it is possible to be better prepared for each meeting with a customer. The great majority of buyer concerns fall into five categories: need, product, source, time, and price.

Concerns Related to Need for the Product

If you have carefully completed your precall planning, then the prospect will likely have a need for your product. You still can expect, however, that the initial response may be, "I do not need your product." This might be a conditioned response that arises nearly every time the prospect meets with a sales representative. It also may be a cover-up for the real reason for not buying, which might be lack of funds, lack of time to examine your proposal carefully, or some other reason.

Sincere need resistance is one of the great challenges that face a salesperson during the early part of the sales process. Think about it for a moment. Why would any customer want to purchase a product that does not seem to provide any real benefits? Unless we can create need awareness in the prospect's mind, there is no possible way to close the sale.

If you are calling on business prospects, the best way to overcome need resistance is to prove that your product is a good investment. Every business hopes to make a profit. Therefore, you must demonstrate how your product or service can contribute to that goal. Can your product increase sales volume? Can it reduce operating expenses? If the owner of a hardware store says, "I already carry a line of high-quality tools," point out how a second line of less expensive tools can appeal to another large segment of the buying public. With the addition of the new line, the store can be in a better position to compete with other stores (discount merchandise stores and supermarkets) that sell inexpensive tools.

Concerns About the Product or Services

You will recall from Chapter 8 that consultative-process buyers may lack needs awareness or need help evaluating possible solutions. Therefore, the product (solution) often becomes the focal point of buyer resistance. When this happens, try to discover specific reasons why the prospect has doubts about your product or services. Often you may find that one of the following factors has influenced the buyer's attitude:

1. *The product or service is not well established.* This is a common buyer concern if you are selling a new or relatively new product. People do not like to take risks. They need plenty of assurance that the product is dependable. Use laboratory test results, third-party testimonials from satisfied users, or an effective demonstration to create value.
2. *The current product or service is satisfactory.* Change does not come easily to many people. Purchasing a new product may mean adopting new procedures or retraining employees. In the prospect's mind, the advantages may not outweigh the disadvantages, so buyer resistance surfaces. To overcome this concern, you must build a greater amount of desire in the prospect's mind. Concentrate on a value proposition that gives your product or service a major advantage over the existing one, or reconfigure the product and offer customized services to better meet the customer's needs.

Concerns Related to Source

Concerns related to source can be especially challenging when the prospect is a strategic alliance buyer. The buyer may already have well-established partnerships with other companies. If the prospect feels genuine loyalty to its current supplier, you will have to work harder to establish a relationship and begin the need discovery process.

When dealing with the loyalty problem, it is usually best to avoid direct criticism of the competing firm. Negative comments are apt to backfire because they damage your professional image. It is best to keep the sales presentation focused on the customer's problems and your solutions. There are positive ways to cope with the loyalty objection. Some suggestions follow:

1. *Work harder to identify problems your company can solve with its products or services.* With the help of good questions, you may be able to understand the prospect's problems better than your competitors.
2. *Point out the superior benefits of your product and your company.* By doing this, you hope the logic of your presentation can overcome the emotional ties that may exist between the prospect and the present supplier.
3. *Work on recruiting internal champions to build more support for your message.* Use referrals whenever possible.[29]
4. *Try to stay visible and connected.* Every contact with the prospect is one more step in building a relationship. Anthony Tringale, owner of Insurance Consulting Group in Fairfax, Virginia, says that he is involved with many potential clients in social and charitable events.[30]

Concerns Related to Time

If a prospect says, "I want time to think it over," you may be encountering concerns related to time. Resistance related to time is often referred to as the **stall**. A stall usually means the customer does not yet perceive the benefits of buying now. In most cases, the stall indicates that the prospect has both positive and negative feelings about your product. Consider using *probing questions* to determine the negative feelings: "Is it my company that concerns you?" "Do you have any concerns about our warranty program?"

It is all right to be persuasive if the prospect can truly benefit from buying now. If the price may soon rise, or if the item may not be available in the future, then you should provide this information. You must, however, present this information sincerely and accurately. It is never proper to distort the truth in the hope of getting the order.

Renewing a contract also calls for renegotiations. In these cases, be upfront and explain the benefits in precise terms concerning what additional values the new price will bring to the client. Sometimes it is advisable to offer a break in the payment schedule to overcome the client's adverse feelings about the price hike.[31] To enhance the relationship with long-term business partners, the seller sometimes has to look at the market to reevaluate what is really fair pricing and voluntarily renegotiate with the buyer to lower the price before the buyer asks for it.[32]

Concerns Related to Price

Price objections are one of the biggest obstacles salespeople have to conquer.[33] There are two important points to keep in mind concerning price resistance. First, it is one of the most *common* buyer concerns in the field of selling. Therefore, you must learn to negotiate skillfully in this area. Second, price objections may be nothing more than an excuse. If you are selling a product or service to a transactional buyer, price may be the primary barrier to closing the sale. When people say "Your

SELLING IN ACTION

You Don't Get What You Deserve, You Get What You Negotiate

Chester L. Karrass, creator of the Effective Negotiating seminar, says, "In business, you don't get what you deserve, you get what you negotiate." This is good advice for the job seeker. Most employers do not propose the highest wage possible at the beginning of the offer. If you want a higher starting wage, you must ask for it. Employers often have a predetermined range for each position and the highest salary is reserved for the applicant who brings something extra to the job. To prepare for a productive negotiation, you must know your own needs and you must know something about the worth of the position. Many employers tell you the salary range prior to the interview. The Internet can be a good source of salary information for certain types of jobs. In terms of your needs, try to determine what you care about the most: interesting work, future promotion, or flexible work schedule. If you are willing to negotiate, you can increase your pay by hundreds or even thousands of dollars. Be prepared to sell yourself, negotiate the salary you believe is appropriate, and achieve a win-win solution in the process.[b]

price is too high," they probably mean "You have not sold me yet." In the eyes of most customers, value is more important than price. Always try to position your product with a convincing value proposition. Customers who perceive added value are less likely to choose a competing product simply on the basis of price. We will present specific tactics to deal with this issue shortly.

Specific Methods of Negotiating Buyer Concerns

13.3 Discuss specific methods of negotiating buyer concerns

There are eight specific methods of negotiating buyer concerns. In analyzing each buyer concern, we should try to determine which method could be most effective. In most cases, we can use a combination of the following methods to negotiate buyer concerns.

Direct Denial

Direct denial involves refuting the opinion or belief of a prospect. The direct denial of a problem is considered a high-risk method of negotiating buyer concerns. Therefore, you should use it with care. People do not like to be told they are wrong. Even when the facts prove the prospect is wrong, resentment can build if we fail to handle the situation properly.

When a prospect offers buyer resistance that is not valid, we sometimes have no option other than to openly disagree. If the person is misinformed, we must provide accurate information. For example, if the customer questions the product's quality, meet the concern head-on with whatever proof seems appropriate. It is almost never proper to ignore misinformation. High-performance salespeople counter inaccurate responses from the prospect promptly and directly.

The manner in which you state the denial is of major importance. Use a win-win approach. Be firm and sincere in stating your beliefs, but do not be offensive. Above all, do not patronize the prospect. A "know-it-all" attitude can be irritating.

Indirect Denial

Sometimes the prospect's concern is completely valid or at least accurate to a large degree. This method is referred to as the **indirect denial**. The best approach is to bend a little and acknowledge that the prospect is at least partially correct. After all, if you offered a product that is objection proof, you would likely have no competitors. Every product has a shortcoming or limitation.[34] The success of this method is based in part on the need most people have to feel that their views are worthwhile. For this reason, the indirect denial method is widely used. An exchange that features the use of this approach follows. The salesperson is a key account sales representative for Pacific Bell Directory.[35]

Salesperson: The total cost of placing your 6 × 8-inch ad in the yellow pages of five different Pacific Bell directories is $32,000.

Prospect: As a builder, I want to reach people who are planning to build a home. I am afraid my ad will be lost among the hundreds of ads featured in your directories.

Salesperson: Yes, I agree the yellow pages in our directories do feature hundreds of ads, but the section for general contractors features fewer than 30 ads. Our design staff can prepare an ad that can be highly visible and can set your company apart from ads placed by other contractors. In addition, we will do the same with your website.

$ SELLING IS EVERYONE'S BUSINESS

Selling Saves Factory Jobs

The workers at the Parker Hannifin Corporation factory in Irwin, Pennsylvania, count on Ken Sweet to save their jobs. He is the general manager. When sales at this automation-equipment plant drop, there is pressure to cut the payroll. The pressure to cut costs through layoffs builds during a recession when sales typically decline. Fortunately, Mr. Sweet has an ace up his sleeve. As general manager, he is responsible for sales as well as getting the product out the door.

When manufacturing operations slow down, Mr. Sweet redoubles his sales efforts. He urges his equipment-development teams to focus on potential customers who offer the best chance for big contracts. Some production workers are recruited to help with the sales effort. When work is scarce at the plant, Jim Manion, an assembler, calls prospects who have visited the company's website. These sales efforts help save jobs.[c]

Note that the salesperson used the words "Yes, I agree . . ." to reduce the impact of denial. The prospect is less likely to feel her point of view has been totally disproved. One note of caution: Avoid the "Yes . . . but" response. When you use the word "but," it invalidates anything preceding it. A more effective response would be, "I understand your concerns, Ms. Thomas; however, there is another way to view this issue."[36]

FEEL–FELT–FOUND Successful salespeople are sensitive to clues that indicate the client feels something is wrong. One way to empathize with the client's concerns is to use the "feel–felt–found" strategy. Here is how it works. Assume the customer is concerned about the complexity of the new computer software, and says, "I do not think I will ever understand the process." Your response might be, "I understand how you *feel*, Mr. Pearson. Many of my customers *felt* the same way, until they started using the software and *found* it quite easy to master."

Questions

Throughout this chapter, we have described several situations where probing or confirmation questions can enhance the negotiation process. We must also keep in mind the important role of need-satisfaction questions. In Chapter 11, we noted that *need-satisfaction questions* are designed to move the sales process forward toward commitment and action. These questions focus on the solution.[37] Consider the following exchange that involves a price concern:

Buyer: It would be difficult for our Human Resources Department to absorb the cost of your psychological tests.

Seller: What would a 10 percent reduction in employee turnover save your company? (Need-Satisfaction Question)

In these examples, the questions are designed to get the customer's attention focused on the solution. These questions also give ownership of the solution to the prospect. See Chapter 11 for more examples of the need-satisfaction question.

Superior Benefit

Sometimes the customer raises a problem that cannot be answered with a denial. For example: "Your television commercial proposal does not include payroll costs for actors who will be used during the shoot. This means we must cover this expense." You should acknowledge the valid objection and then discuss one or more superior benefits: "Yes, you are correct. We do conduct the talent search and coach the actors throughout the development of the commercial. In addition, if you are not happy with the performance of the actors, we will conduct a second search for new actors and remake the commercial at no additional cost to you." A **superior benefit** is a benefit that in most cases outweighs the customer's specific concern.

Demonstration

If you are familiar with your product as well as that of your competition, this method of negotiating buyer resistance is easy to use. You know the competitive advantages of your product and can discuss these features with confidence.

At Mattress Firm, Edith Botello realizes the product demonstration is one of the most convincing ways to overcome any skepticism her customers might have. With the aid of an effective demonstration, you can overcome specific concerns. Sometimes a second demonstration is needed to overcome buyer skepticism. This demonstration can provide additional proof. High-achieving sales personnel know when and how to use proof devices to overcome buyer resistance.

Trial Offer

A **trial offer** involves giving the prospect an opportunity to try the product without making a purchase commitment. The trial offer (especially with new products) is popular with customers because they can get fully acquainted with your product without making a major commitment. Assume that a buyer for a large restaurant chain says, "I am sure you have a good cooking oil, but we are happy with our current brand. We have had no complaints from our managers." In response to this comment, you might say, "I can understand your reluctance to try our product. However, I do believe our oil is the finest on the market. With your permission, I would like to ship you 30 gallons of our oil at no cost. You can use our product at selected restaurants and

The product demonstration is one of the most convincing ways to overcome buyer skepticism.

Source: Deklofenak/Shutterstock

evaluate the results. If our oil does not provide you with superior results, you are under no obligation to place an order."

Third-Party Testimony

Studies indicate that the favorable testimony of a neutral third party can be an effective method of responding to buyer resistance. Let us assume that the owner of a small business states that he can get along without the services of a professional landscaping service. The salesperson might respond in this manner: "Some business owners feel the way you do. However, once they contract for our service, they do not regret the decision. Mark Williams, owner of Williams Hardware, says our service completely changed the image his business projects to the public." Third-party testimony provides a positive way to solve certain types of buying problems. The positive experiences of a neutral third party almost never trigger an argument with the prospect.

Postpone Method

Today's customers are well informed and may want to engage in negotiations early in the sales process. The customer may raise concerns that you would prefer to respond to later in the presentation. Let's assume you are calling on an office manager who is interested in well-equipped cubicles for eight employees. Soon after you present some product information, the customer says, "How much will eight well-equipped cubicles cost us?" Using the **postpone method**, your response might be, "I would prefer to answer that question in a few minutes. Once I learn what features you prefer, I can calculate a cost estimate." Every customer concern should be taken seriously. Always try to explain why you want to postpone the response.

COMBINATION METHODS As noted previously, consultative selling is characterized by flexibility. A combination of methods sometimes proves to be the best way to deal with buyer resistance. For example, an indirect denial might be followed by a need-satisfaction question: "The cost of our business security system is a little higher than the competition. The price I have quoted reflects the high-quality materials used to develop our system. Wouldn't you feel better entrusting your security needs to a firm with more than 25 years of experience in the business security field?" In this situation, the salesperson might also consider combining the indirect denial with an offer to arrange a demonstration of the security system.

A salesperson might attempt to turn the objection into a **trial close** by concluding the sale without prejudicing the opportunity to continue the selling process with the buyer should they refuse to commit themselves. This might take the form of "If I can address this final concern of yours, would you buy it?"[38] See Figure 13.3 on page 277 for more examples of combination methods.

13.4 Outline methods for creating value in formal negotiations

Creating Value During Formal Negotiations

The challenge a salesperson faces in almost every negotiation is to sell products and services based on fair and unique value propositions, not on price.[39] If salespeople rely on price only to capture and retain business, they reduce whaxtever they're selling to a commodity. Once that happens, there is no customer loyalty.[40] In this section, we focus on how the salesperson can tactfully create value for buyers during formal negotiations without compromising profits.

How to Deal with Price Concerns

As we have noted, price resistance is common, so we must prepare for it. There are some important "do's and don'ts" to keep in mind when the price concern surfaces.

DO CLARIFY PRICE CONCERNS WITH QUESTIONS When you are confronted with a price objection, determine what the customer is really saying. You will recall from Chapter 11 that *specific survey questions* encourage the customer to give you more details. The following questions might be used when price concerns surface:

> "When you say we are higher, could you be more specific, please?"
> "What did you anticipate the price to be?"

When the customer says budget is the primary reason for delaying the purchase, you might ask, "If you had the budget, would you buy?" Questions can help you determine what the customer is really thinking.[41]

DO ADD VALUE WITH A CLUSTER OF SATISFACTIONS As noted in Chapter 7, a growing number of customers are seeking a cluster of satisfactions that includes a good product, a salesperson who is truly a partner, and a company that stands behind its products (see Figure 7.1). Many business firms are at a competitive disadvantage when the price alone is considered. When you look beyond price, however, it may become obvious that your company offers more value for the dollar.

Stephen Smith, senior account manager for Bell Atlantic, says that price is like the tip of the iceberg—it is often the only feature the customer sees. Salespeople need to direct the customer's attention to the value-added features that make up the bulk of the iceberg that is below the surface (Figure 13.4).[42] Do not forget to sell yourself as a high-value element of the sales proposal. Emphasize your commitment to customer service after the sale. Also, listen carefully to identify and reconfirm what intangibles in addition to the product or service the customers *actually* value.[43]

DO NOT MAKE PRICE THE FOCAL POINT OF YOUR SALES PRESENTATION You may need to discuss price, but do not bring it up too early. The best time to deal with price is after you have reviewed product features and discussed buyer benefits. You increase the chances for a win-win outcome by increasing the number of issues you can resolve. If you negotiate price along with delivery date, support services, or volume purchases, you increase the opportunities for a trade-off so you and the customer both win something of value.[44]

DO NOT APOLOGIZE FOR THE PRICE When you do mention price, do so in a confident and straightforward manner. Do not have even a hint of apology in your voice. Convey to the prospect that you believe your price is fair and make every effort to relate price to value. Many people fear paying too much for a product or service. If your company has adopted a value-added strategy, point this fact out to the prospect. Then discuss how you and your company add value.

DO POINT OUT THE RELATIONSHIP BETWEEN PRICE AND QUALITY In our highly competitive, free enterprise economy, there are forces at work that tend to promote fair pricing. The highest quality can never be obtained at the lowest price. Quality comes from that Latin word *qualitas*, meaning "What is the worth?" When you sell quality, price is more likely to be secondary in the prospect's mind. Always point out the value-added features that create the difference in price. Keep in mind that cheap products are built down to a price rather than up to a standard.[45]

Price

Assistance from salesperson after the sale

Favorable credit terms

Excellent technical assistance

Quick delivery

Comprehensive warranty

FIGURE 13.4

A sales proposal is sometimes like an iceberg. The customer sees the tip of the iceberg (price) but does not see the value-added features below the surface.

DO EXPLAIN AND DEMONSTRATE THE DIFFERENCE BETWEEN PRICE AND COST Price represents the initial amount the buyer pays for the product. Cost represents the amount the buyer pays for a product as it is used over a period of time. The price–cost comparison is particularly relevant with a product or service that lasts a long time or is particularly reliable. Today, airlines are comparing the price and operating cost of small regional jets manufactured by Bombardier of Canada with large jets sold by Boeing and Airbus. Sales representatives at Bombardier compare their smaller $21 million cost of the 50 passenger CRJ200 with the larger $150 million cost of the 150 passenger A320 offered by Airbus, and point out the fast speed (534 MPH) and low fuel consumption of the CRJ200.

The Pitfalls of Paying Too Little

It's unwise to pay too much. But it's worse to pay too little.

When you pay too much, you lose a little money, that is all.

When you pay too little you sometimes lose everything, because the thing you bought was incapable of doing the thing it was bought to do.

The common law of business balances prohibits paying a little and getting a lot. It can't be done.

If you deal with the lowest bidder, it is well to add something for the risk you run.

John Ruskin, British Writer

Negotiating Price with a Low-Price Strategy

As noted in Chapter 7, some marketers have positioned their products with a price strategy. The goal is to earn a small profit margin on a large sales volume. Many of these companies have empowered their salespeople to use various low-price strategies such as quantity discounts, trade discounts, seasonal discounts, and promotional discounts. Some salespeople are given permission to match the price of any competitor. Many *transactional buyers* are primarily interested in price and convenience during negotiations, so consider eliminating features that contribute to a higher selling price.

13.5 Work with buyers who are trained in negotiation

Working with Buyers Trained in Formal Negotiation

In recent years, as noted earlier, we have seen an increase in the number of training programs developed for professional buyers. One such course is Fundamentals of Purchasing for the Newly Appointed Buyer, offered by the American Management Association. Enrollees learn how to negotiate with salespeople. Some salespeople also are returning to the classroom to learn negotiation skills. Learning how to negotiate is one of the linchpins of effective selling.[46] Acclivus Corporation (www.acclivus.com), a Dallas-based training company, offers the Acclivus Sales Negotiation System for salespeople who work in the business-to-business selling arena. Karrass Limited (www.karrass.com) offers the Effective Sales Negotiating seminar.

Professional buyers often learn to use specific tactics in dealing with salespeople. Homer Smith, author of *Selling Through Negotiation*, provides the following examples.

Budget Limitation Tactic[47]

The buyer may say, "We like your proposal, but our budget for the convention is only $8,500." Is the buyer telling the truth, or is the person testing your price? The best approach in this instance is to take the budget limitation seriously and use appropriate negotiation strategies. One strategy is to reduce the price by eliminating some items, sometimes described as **unbundling**. In the case of a fleet truck sale, the salesperson might say, "We can deliver the trucks with a less powerful engine and, thus, meet your budget figure. Would you be willing to purchase trucks with less powerful engines?"

Take-It-or-Leave-It Tactic[48]

How do you respond to a buyer who says, "My final offer is $3,300, take it or leave it"? A price concession is, of course, one option. However, this is likely to reduce profits for the company and lower your commission. An alternative strategy is to confidently review the superior benefits of your product and make another closing attempt. Appealing to the other person's sense of fairness also may move the discussion forward. If the final offer is totally without merit, consider calling a halt to the negotiation to allow the other party to back down from his position without losing face.[49]

Let-Us-Split-the-Difference Tactic[50]

In some cases, the salesperson may find this price concession acceptable. If the buyer's suggestion is not acceptable, then the salesperson might make a counteroffer.

"If . . . Then" Tactic

This approach involves the buyer saying something like, "Unless you agree immediately to a price reduction of 20 percent, we'll have to look elsewhere for a supplier." In this setting, the consequence could be serious. The correct response depends upon the outcome of the assessment of the balance of power conducted during the preparation. If the buyer does have a number of options, all of which offer the same kind of benefits as yours, then you may have to concede. If your product offers clear advantages over the competition, then you may be able to resist the challenge.

"Sell Low Now, Make Profits Later" Tactic

In this situation, also referred to as the "Reward in Heaven Tactic," the buyer may say something like, "If you can reduce the price another $500 on this job, I will give you all my future work." This may be a genuine statement and, in fact, may meet your own objective of gaining a foothold in your buyer's business. You might respond with, "Because of the price I have quoted, I am unable to discount this job. However, if you do give me this job and your future jobs, I will discount your future work." This negotiation approach can actually create value for both you and your customer.

These tactics represent only a sample of those used by professional buyers. To prepare for these and other tactics, salespeople need to plan their negotiating strategies in advance and have clear goals. Decide in advance on the terms you can (and cannot) accept. It is important that you have the authority to set prices. Buyers want to do business with someone who has decision-making authority.

CHAPTER LEARNING ACTIVITIES

Reviewing Key Concepts

Describe the principles of formal negotiations as part of the win-win strategy

Negotiations play a central role in the selling profession. Generic principles of formal integrative negotiations include preparing for negotiations, knowing the value of what you are offering, understanding the problem, creating alternate solutions, finding some point of agreement, and knowing when to walk away. If a salesperson uses a negotiations worksheet, then it can be much easier to plan systematically.

Describe common types of buyer concerns

Sales resistance is natural and should be welcomed as an opportunity to learn more about how to satisfy the prospect's needs. Buyers' concerns often provide salespeople with precisely the information they need to close a sale. These concerns fall into five broad categories: buyers' needs, the product, the source, time, and price. Whatever the reasons, the salesperson should *negotiate* sales resistance with the proper attitude, never making too much or too little of the prospect's concerns.

Discuss specific methods of negotiating buyer concerns

We describe eight specific methods of negotiating buyer concerns: direct denial, indirect denial, need-satisfaction questions, superior benefits, demonstration, trial offer, testimony, and postpone method. The use of these methods and combinations thereof varies depending on the particular combination of salesperson, product, services, and prospect.

Outline methods for creating value in formal negotiations

We have described several specific methods for creating value in formal negotiations, but you should remember that practice in applying them is essential and that there is room for a great deal of creative imagination in developing variations or additional methods. With careful preparation and practice, negotiating buyer concerns about price should become a stimulating challenge to each salesperson's professional growth.

Work with buyers who are trained in negotiation

Buyers who are trained in negotiations resort to a number of tactics that a salesperson should be prepared for. In any case, the ultimate goal of formal integrative negotiations is to achieve win-win solutions by offering buyers the value they appreciate without compromising the sellers' benefits.

Key Terms

Negotiation, p. 273
BATNA, p. 275
ZOPA, p. 275
Logrolling, p. 278

Stall, p. 280
Direct denial, p. 281
Indirect denial, p. 281
Superior benefit, p. 282

Trial offer, p. 282
Postpone method, p. 283
Trial close, p. 283
Unbundling, p. 286

MyMarketingLab

To complete the problems with the ⭐ in your MyLab, go to the EOC Discussion Questions.

Review Questions

13-1 Explain why a salesperson should welcome buyer concerns.

13-2 List the common types of buyer resistance that might surface in a presentation.

13-3 How does the negotiations worksheet form help the salesperson prepare to negotiate buyer concerns?

⭐**13-4** Explain the value of using *probing* and *confirmation* questions when negotiating buyer concerns.

13-5 List eight specific strategies for negotiating buyer resistance.

⭐**13-6** John Ruskin says that it is unwise to pay too much when making a purchase, but it is worse to pay too little. Do you agree or disagree with this statement? Explain.

13-7 What is the most common reason that prospects give for not buying? How can salespeople deal effectively with this type of concern?

13-8 Professional buyers often learn to use specific negotiation tactics in dealing with salespeople. List and describe two tactics that are commonly used today.

⭐**13-9** Discuss the merits of using need-satisfaction questions to negotiate buyer concerns.

"Negotiations: Solving the Tough Problems" Video Application Exercises

13-10 Research for this Adaptive Selling Today Training Video revealed that anger does surface during the sales presentation and can be very challenging to negotiate. Anger can be something the other party experiences outside of the sale itself, or it can be caused by some aspect of the sale. Lana, the medical equipment salesperson, received an angry call from the doctor she was working with and had to prepare for solving both the anger problem and the reason for it. What three actions did she learn to use in negotiating with an angry customer? Describe how she adapted these actions during the sale to move the doctor's apparent position of "I am going to win, I don't care if you win;" to an "I want to win and I want you to win also."

13-11 As was shared by the doctor, it is not unusual for a customer to experience skepticism and doubt about the pricing, timing, supplier, need, and/or the product solution during the sales process. Skepticism creates an "I may not win" customer reaction and can prevent the other party from making a good and correct decision, resulting in a no sale. What three actions did Lana use to help her customer overcome the skepticism he was experiencing?

13-12 Research also reveals the most common problem in negotiations is the price problem. Customers often want to be sure they are getting the best price possible, as well as the best product solution. What three actions did Lana use to attempt to achieve a win-win solution with the doctor's concern about staying within a budget? Describe them in detail.

13-13 The action of "walking away" from a potential sale is often considered a high-risk negotiations strategy. What three actions did Lana employ before she walked away from this sale?

Role-Play Exercise

You work for the sales department of an apparel manufacturing company. Company XYZ, with which you have met during a recent trade fair, is going to visit your facilities next week. You understand that this company wants to "buy low" but normally places large orders. However, you want to "sell high." Your company might not be able to deliver very large orders unless you invest in new facilities. Company XYZ says it will send over a team of three people: the vice president of marketing, the purchasing manager, and a designer. They are interested in developing a collection for the next season and going over a "price exercise" with you. In addition, they are interested in placing a trial order at the price of a bulk order (i.e., large order). Delivery of the order is to be made in two weeks. Unfortunately, this trial order is well below the minimum quantity you're willing to accept, and your company normally needs one month to fill a new order.

13-14   How do you convey this information to the other departments within your company to prepare for this meeting? Will you invite your boss to the meeting? Why?

13-15   Using a negotiations worksheet, plan your responses to the following statements made by the purchasing manager: (a) We are concerned that you will not be able to meet our quality requirements; (b) Your price is too high; (c) Either take this trial order or we will look for another vendor. Decide at what point in the negotiations on price and delivery date you will decide to turn down the offer or accept the offer. Role-play your response to each of these statements.

Reality Selling Video Case Problem—Heather Ramsey/Marriott International

Each year, public and private organizations send thousands of employees to meetings held at hotels, motels, convention centers, conference centers, and resorts. These meetings represent a multimillion-dollar business in the United States. Airport hotels such as the Marriott Houston Hobby, introduced at the beginning of this chapter, are a good example of such a destination. The Marriott Houston Hobby is located at a convenient location, only one mile from the Hobby Airport in Houston, Texas. It also has a competitive edge because it lies outside of the flight path. In addition to convenience and tranquility, the goal of the hotel is to provide guests outstanding meeting and conferences services. The hotel offers 235 deluxe guest rooms, 52 suites, 13 soundproof meeting rooms with state-of-the-art audiovisual technology, and continuous break service that can accommodate any agenda. Lavish customized meal events from a wide variety of international cuisines are a specialty of the Marriott Houston Hobby.

In an ideal situation, Heather Ramsey, corporate catering manager at the hotel, tries to get the prospects out for a site inspection of the property. Prospects might also sample hors d'oeuvres or lunch meals during this site tour. This tour, in some ways, fulfills the function of a sales demonstration. Throughout the tour, she describes special amenities and services offered by the hotel. She also uses this time to get better acquainted with the needs of the prospect. Once the tour is completed, she escorts the prospect back to her office and completes the needs assessment. Next, she prepares a detailed sales proposal or, in some cases, contracts. The proposal needs to contain accurate and complete facts because, when signed, it becomes a legally enforceable sales contract.

For big events, the sales proposal is rarely accepted without modification. Professional meeting planners are experienced negotiators and press hard for concessions. Some have completed training programs developed for professional buyers. The concessions requested may include a lower guest-room rate, lower meal costs, complimentary suites, or a complimentary event such as a wine and cheese reception. It might take as long as two months to reach an agreement with sophisticated buyers.

Of course, some buyer resistance is not easily identified. Heather Ramsey says that she follows four steps in dealing with buyer concerns:

1. *Identify the actual needs of the prospects.* To achieve win-win deals, Heather spends time asking specific questions about the customer's needs such as the audience of the event, the size and timing of the event, or the customer's budget. The prospects normally focus on negotiating details of food menu choice, group rates for room rental, and audiovisual facilities.
2. *Locate the resistance.* Some prospects are reluctant to accept the offer, but the reason may be unclear. Heather has discovered in some cases that asking open-ended questions goes a long way in understanding the actual resistance. Once this perception is uncovered, Heather knows how to deal with it.
3. *Clarify the resistance.* If a prospect says, "I like your facilities, but your prices are a little high," then the salesperson must clarify the meaning of this objection. Is the prospect seeking a major price concession or a small price concession?
4. *Overcome the objection.* Heather says, "You must be prepared for negotiations by understanding both your flexibility and the customers' needs." The hotel must earn a profit or publicity, so concessions can be made only after careful consideration of the bottom line and other intangible benefits.

Heather has discovered that the best way to negotiate buyer concerns is to make sure both the prospect and the resort feel like winners once the negotiations are finalized. If either party feels like a loser, a long-term relationship will not be possible. During peak seasons, Heather might also need to negotiate the schedule of events with prospects to minimize opportunity costs for the hotel while keeping the customers happy by offering off-season concessions. Refer to the opening paragraph of this chapter for more information. (See chapter opener on page 271, and *Reality Selling Today* Role-Play 7 in Appendix 1 for more information.)

Questions

13-16 If you were selling convention services for a hotel located in a large city, what types of buyer concerns would you expect from a new prospect?

13-17 Let us assume that you are representing the Marriott Houston Hobby Airport and you are meeting with a new prospect at the hotel for a site tour. This prospect is planning to host an important event at your hotel for 200 guests. List the questions that you might ask the prospect in order to identify her actual needs. In doing so, be specific about the alternatives (e.g., high-end, medium, regular packages) that you can offer the prospect and the order of presenting those to the prospect.

13-18 If you meet with a professional buyer who is trained in negotiation, what tactics can you expect the person to use? How would you respond to each of these tactics?

13-19 What subtle questions will you ask to validate that the negotiator is the decision maker without hurting her feelings? What actions will you take if you find out she is not the decision maker?

Your Value Adding Systems Partner

Regional Account Management Case Study (refer to Appendix 2)

Negotiating Buyer Concerns

Casey Arnold has asked you to review Lee Bizon's former accounts. Casey wants to review the likelihood of close and forecast the sales volume that can be expected. She wants you to research the notes for each account that Lee Bizon entered and look for accounts with which you might anticipate objections during a presentation.

Questions

13-20 Using the report you prepared for Chapter 12, add another column titled Forecasted Sales as shown below. In this column, multiply the Dollar Sales Amount times the Likelihood percentage of closing the sale and record the metrics for a forecasted sale for each account.

NewNet Systems Account Management

Name   Regional Account Manager, NEWNET SYSTEMS

Date Close	Account Name/ Contact Name	Dollar Sales Amt.	Comm. Style	Sales Process Stage	Likeli- hood	**Forecasted Sales**	

13-21 Reviewing the account and notes screens, which fairly small account might voice a time objection and say, "We want to put off our decision for now," and how would you propose dealing with this objection? What is the closing date, likelihood, and forecasted sales for this account?

13-22 Reviewing the notes screens, which very large account has voiced a price objection, citing budget issues, and how should you respond? What is the closing date, likelihood, and forecasted sales for this account? Reviewing the "Creating Value During Formal Negotiations" unit in this chapter, which of the "do's and don'ts" will likely be most effective in negotiating the price problem?

13-23 Reviewing the notes screens, which medium-sized account with 100 workstations may be citing the price objection because they don't need all your value-added features or it may be a cover for credit problems? What is the closing date, likelihood, and forecasted sales of this account? Reviewing this chapter's section on "Specific Methods of Negotiating Buyer Concerns," what specific method should you use to negotiate effectively with your contact?

13-24 Reviewing the notes screens, which medium-sized account do you anticipate might voice the source concern "We want to shop around for a good solid supplier"? Reviewing the section in this chapter on "Common Types of Buyer Concerns," which of the four ways to deal with the loyalty or source objection might be most effective? What other strategies could you combine with this method? What is the closing date, likelihood, and forecasted sales of this account?

13-25 Describe how the closing date, likelihood, and forecasted sales might affect your plans for negotiating customer objections and concerns.

Partnership Selling: A Role-Play
(See Appendix 3, page 419)

Developing a Presentation Strategy—Negotiating

Refer to Sales Memorandum 3 and strategically plan to anticipate and negotiate any objections or concerns your customer may have to your presentation. You should prepare a negotiations worksheet to organize this part of your presentation.

The instructions for item 2e direct you to prepare negotiations for the time, price, source, and product objections. You note that your price is approximately $200 more than your customer budgeted for this meeting. You have to be very effective in negotiating a value-added strategy because your convention center is not a low-price supplier (see Chapter 6 on value-added product strategies).

During the presentation, you should use proof devices from the product strategy materials provided in Employment Memorandum 1 to negotiate concerns you anticipate. You may want to use a calculator to negotiate any financial arrangements such as savings on parking, airport transportation, and so on. Using spreadsheet software, you may want to prepare graphs to illustrate competitive pricing. Place these materials in the front pocket of your three-ring binder (portfolio) so that you can easily access them during your presentation. You may want to secure another person to be your customer, instructing him or her to voice the objections you have anticipated, and then respond with your negotiation strategies. This experience can provide you with the opportunity to rehearse your negotiation strategies.

Park Shores Resort and Convention Center.
Source: Courtesy of Beach Resort

<MyMarketingLab>

MyMarketingLab

Go to the Assignments section of your MyLab to complete these writing exercises.

13-26 Negotiations play a central role in the selling profession. What factors of the formal negotiation process are involved in a negotiation strategy that is "win-win?"

13-27 Creating value is an essential part of consultative sales process. Describe and discuss some of the methods a salesperson can use to add value during a formal negotiation process.

Learning Objectives

When you finish reading this chapter, you should be able to

14.1 Describe the proper attitude to display toward closing the sale

14.2 List and discuss selected guidelines for closing the sale

14.3 Explain how to recognize closing clues

14.4 Discuss specific methods of closing the sale

14.5 Explain what to do when the buyer says yes and what to do when the buyer says no

Source: Michael Ahearne

▶ Adaptive Selling Video Series—"Ask for the Order (AFTO)"

"Ask for the Order," or "AFTO," as it is also called, is the third training video in the Adaptive Selling Today Training Video Series. The video begins with a salesperson who has a fear of closing the sale. Research shows that many sales are lost because salespeople fear asking for the order, and that even when they do, it is not unusual to have to ask three or four times. Along with many successful examples of how to ask for the order, AFTO presents a three-dimensional approach to overcome any fear one may have of asking for the order.

AFTO presents many closing methods, described in this chapter, that illustrate the importance of adapting your closing questions to the customer's particular buying situation. Specific methods of asking for the order are clearly presented in dramatic sequences, representing a wide variety of selling situations.

AFTO presents a system to use throughout the sales process to gain a better understanding of your customer's needs, and ultimately help your customers make sound buying decisions. ●

Adapting the Close—an Attitude that Adds Value

Heather Ramsey, Corporate Catering Manager at Marriott Houston Hobby featured in Chapter 13, looks at closing from the prospect's point of view. Although the special event plan she prepared may seem perfect, she realizes that the customer may have a different point of view. A special event in her department may be a corporate reception, a wedding, a bar mitzvah, or a class reunion. She must try to see the actual event through the eyes of the customer and, from this insight, use adaptive closing questions to confirm the sale and a long-term partnership. Heather believes that relationship-building skills must be applied at every step of the sales process. If she is continually

14.1 Describe the proper attitude to display toward closing the sale

adding value throughout the sales presentation, closing is much easier. This is especially true in those cases in which price might be a barrier to closing.[1]

Throughout the evolution of personal selling, we have seen major changes in the way closing is perceived. Prior to the introduction of consultative selling and the partnering era, closing was often presented as the most important aspect of the sales process. The early sales training literature also presented closing methods that encouraged the manipulation of the customer. Use of any closing method that is perceived by the customer as pushy or manipulative will damage your chances of building a long-term partnership, even if you do get the sale.[2]

Closing should not be viewed as a strategy to win at the expense of the customer. The proper attitude should be: "If this is the best solution for the customer, I should help her make the correct decision."[3] Once the best solution is determined, *asking for the order* is the next logical step.

We take the position that in many selling situations the salesperson needs to assume responsibility for obtaining commitment from the customer. Some closing methods can move the customer from indecision to commitment. When these methods are used effectively, the prospect will not feel pressured. In some cases, we need to simply replace defense-arousing language, such as, "This is the lowest price available anywhere," with a positive *need-satisfaction question*, such as, "Wouldn't this new software help you achieve more efficient inventory control?"

Asking for the order is less difficult if the salesperson is strategically prepared for the close. Preparation for the close involves understanding customer needs, custom fitting solutions, and planning appropriate closing methods. Throughout the sales presentation, the salesperson should recognize closing clues and be prepared to use effective adaptive closing methods (Figure 14.1).[4]

Review the Value Proposition From the Prospect's Point of View

Closing the sale is usually easier if you look at the *value proposition* from the prospect's point of view. Have you effectively summarized the mix of key benefits? Will your proposal provide a solution that solves the customer's problem? Is your proposal strong enough to win over a customer who is experiencing buying anxieties?

The Six-Step Presentation Plan	
Step One: Approach	✔ Review Strategic/Consultative Selling Model ✔ Initiate customer contact
Step Two: Need Discovery	✔ Ask strategic questions ✔ Determine customer needs ✔ Select product solution
Step Three: Presentation	✔ Select presentation strategy ✔ Create presentation plan ✔ Initiate presentation
Step Four: Negotiation	✔ Anticipate buyer concerns ✔ Plan negotiating methods ✔ Initiate win-win negotiations
Step Five: Close	☐ Plan appropriate closing methods ☐ Recognize closing clues ☐ Initiate closing methods
Step Six: Servicing the Sale	☐ Follow through ☐ Follow-up calls ☐ Expansion selling

Service, retail, wholesale, and manufacturer selling

FIGURE 14.1

Effective closing methods require careful planning.

Closing should be viewed as part of the selling process—the logical outcome of a well-planned presentation strategy.

Source: wavebreakmedia/Shutterstock

Gene Bedell, author of *3 Steps to Yes*, reminds us that buying often causes emotional stress, sometimes referred to as "buyer's remorse." The following buying anxieties help explain why some customers are reluctant to make a commitment to your proposal.[5]

Loss of options. If the customer agrees to purchase a $5,000 design proposal, then that money will not be available for other purchases or investments. Agreeing to purchase a product or service often means that some other purchase must be postponed. Anxiety and stress build as we think about allocating limited resources.

Fear of making a mistake. If the customer believes that agreeing with a closing request may be the wrong thing to do, he may back away just when the decision seems imminent. Fear of making a mistake can be caused by lack of trust in the salesperson.

Social or peer pressures. Some customers make buying decisions with an eye on the opinions and reactions of others. A business buyer may have to justify a purchase to her boss or employees who will actually use the product. Be prepared to deal with these anxieties as you get closer to closing the sale. Sometimes, just a little gentle persuasion will help the anxious customer make a decision.

Closing the Sale—The Beginning of the Partnership

Tom Reilly, in his book *Value-Added Selling*, says ". . . you don't close sales; you build commitment to a course of action that brings value to the customer and profit to the seller."[6] There is a building process that begins with an interesting approach and need discovery. It continues with effective product selection and presentation of benefits that build desire for the product. After a well-planned demonstration and after negotiating sales resistance, it is time to obtain commitment. Closing should be thought of as the beginning of a long-term partnership.

Guidelines for Closing the Sale

14.2 List and discuss selected guidelines for closing the sale

A number of factors increase the odds that you will close the sale (Figure 14.2). These guidelines for closing the sale have universal application in the field of selling.

Focus on Dominant Buying Motives

Most salespeople incorporate the outstanding benefits of their product into the sales presentation. This is only natural. However, be alert to the *one* specific benefit that generates the most

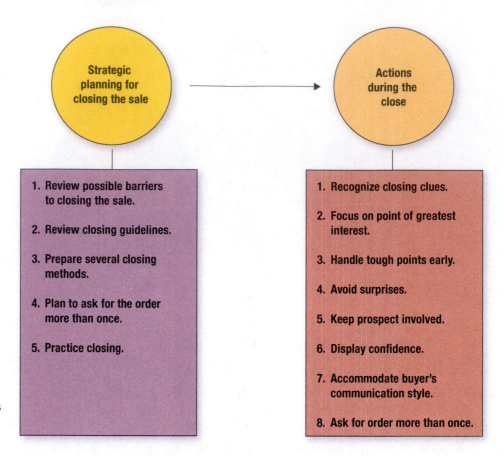

FIGURE 14.2

The presentation strategy should include reviewing these guidelines for closing and confirming the sale.

excitement. The buying motive that is of greatest interest deserves special attention. Vince Peters, director of sales training and development for Wyeth-Ayerst International, tells his 8,000 pharmaceutical salespeople that the key to closing "is to find out exactly what a prospect is looking for."[7]

Throughout the need discovery stage, pay close attention to the buyer's interests. Focus your closing efforts on the point of greatest interest and give the prospect a reason for buying.

Longer Selling Cycles and Incremental Commitments

Longer selling cycles have become a fact of life in many industries. One reason for this change is that more decision makers are involved in purchasing some products. A survey of 1,300 companies by sales analysis firm CSO Insights indicates that increased competition, more complex buying processes, and higher buyer workloads are also adding time to the sales cycle. The buying cycle for many products can be measured in months and some buying cycles can be measured in years.[8]

When you are working on a large, complex sale, you should try to achieve **incremental commitment** throughout the sales process. Some form of commitment should be obtained during each step in a multi-call sales presentation. At the conclusion of the first sales call, you may obtain commitment to an agenda for the second call. At the second call, you might obtain commitment for the prospect to tour your company facilities. Each commitment should move the sale forward toward a signed order.

In some cases, the best way to shorten a sales cycle is to create an entirely new way to locate and approach customers. The customer base for Telegraph Hill Robes (www.telegraphhill.com) is upscale hotels and spas. When Maria Spurlock assumed the duties of CEO, the typical sales cycle was six months to two years. Most Telegraph Hill clients were large, established hotels, and decisions regarding the purchase of robes often involved the general manager and the head of housekeeping. Spurlock decided to focus more sales efforts on hotels still under construction. The key decision maker for a hotel under construction was often just one person, the interior designer. By working with designers, she reduced the sales cycle to three months or less.[9]

Negotiating the Tough Points Before Attempting the Close

Many products have what might be thought of as an Achilles heel. In other words, the product is vulnerable, or appears to be vulnerable, in one or more areas. Negotiate a win-win solution to the tough points before you attempt to close the sale. Such factors can lose the sale if you ignore them. The close should be a positive phase of the sales presentation. This is not the time to deal with a controversial issue or problem.

In the case of Guardsmark security systems, Hickey-Freeman hand-tailored suits, Lexus automobiles, or Ritz-Carlton conference facilities, the Achilles heel may be price. Each of these products may seem expensive in comparison with competing ones. People who sell them find ways to establish the value of their product before attempting the close.

Avoid Surprises at the Close

Some salespeople make the mistake of waiting until the close to reveal information that may come as a surprise to the prospect. For example, the salesperson quotes a price but is not specific concerning what the price includes. Let us assume that the price of a central air-conditioning unit is $6,000. The prospect believes that the price is competitive in relation to similar units on the market and is ready to sign the order form. Then the salesperson mentions casually that the installation charge is an extra $825. The prospect had assumed that the $6,000 fee included installation. Suddenly, the extra fee looms as a major obstacle to closing the sale.

The surprise might come in the form of an accessory that costs extra, terms of the warranty, customer service limitations, or some other issue. Do not let a last-minute surprise damage the relationship and threaten the completion of a sale.

"Tough-Mindedness"—Displaying a High Degree of Self-Confidence at the Close

Do you believe in your product? Do you believe in your company? Do you believe in yourself? Have you identified a solution to the customer's problem? If you can answer yes to each of these questions, then there is no need to display timidity. Look the prospect in the eye and ask for the order. Do not be apologetic at this important point in the sales presentation. The salesperson who confidently asks for the sale is displaying the tough-mindedness that often is needed in personal selling.

Ask for the Order More Than Once

As noted in the adaptive selling film "AFTO," too many salespeople make the mistake of not asking for the order or asking just once. If the prospect says no, they give up. Michael LeBoeuf, author of *How to Win Customers and Keep Them for Life*, reports that almost two-thirds of all sales calls conclude without the salesperson asking for the order. He also says that a majority of all customers say no several times before saying yes.[10] Some of the most productive salespeople ask for the order three, four, or even five times. A surprising number of yes responses come on the fourth or fifth attempt. Of course, not all these closing attempts necessarily came during one call. Determination is a virtue if your product solution solves the customer's problem.

Recognize Closing Clues

14.3 Explain how to recognize closing clues

As the sales presentation progresses, you need to be alert to closing clues (sometimes called "buying signals"). A **closing clue** is an indication, either verbal or nonverbal, that the prospect is preparing to make a buying decision. It is a form of feedback, which is so important in selling. When you detect a closing clue, it may be time to attempt a close.

Many closing clues are quite subtle and may be missed if you are not alert. This is especially true in the case of nonverbal buying signals. If you pay careful attention—with your eyes and your ears—many prospects will signal their degree of commitment.[11] As we have noted earlier in this text, one of the most important personality traits salespeople need is empathy, the ability to sense what the other person is feeling. Recognizing situational clues allows you to modify your self-behavior to use the appropriate strategy for the close.[12] In this section, we review some of the most common verbal and nonverbal clues.

VERBAL CLUES Closing clues come in many forms. Spoken words (verbal clues) are usually the easiest to perceive. These clues can be divided into three categories: (1) questions, (2) recognitions, and (3) requirements.

Questions. One of the least subtle buying signals is the question. You might attempt a trial close after responding to one of the following questions:

> "Do you have a credit plan to cover this purchase?"
> "What type of warranty do you provide?"
> "How soon can our company get delivery?"

Recognitions. A recognition is any positive statement concerning your product or some factor related to the sale, such as credit terms or delivery date. Some examples follow:

> "How long will it take to get delivery?"
> "Will this plane do all the things you say it will?"
> "I have always wanted to own a boat like this."

Requirements. Sometimes, customers outline a condition that must be met before they can buy. If you are able to meet this requirement, it may be a good time to try a trial close. Some requirements that the prospect might voice are:

> "We will need shipment within two weeks."
> "Our staff will need to be trained in how to use this equipment."
> "All our equipment must be certified by the plant safety officer."

In some cases, verbal buying clues do not jump out at you. Important buying signals may be interwoven into normal conversation. Listen closely whenever the prospect is talking.

NONVERBAL CLUES Nonverbal buying clues are even more difficult to detect. Once detected, this type of signal is not easy to interpret. Nevertheless, you should be alert to body movement, facial expression, and tone of voice. Some actions follow that suggest the prospect may be prepared to purchase the product.[13]

> The prospect's facial expression changes. Suddenly, the person's eyes widen, and genuine interest is clear in the facial expression.
> The prospect begins showing agreement by nodding.
> The prospect leans forward and appears to be intent on hearing your message.
> The prospect begins to examine the product or study the sales literature intently.

When you observe or sense one of these nonverbal buying clues, do not hesitate to ask for commitment. There may be several opportunities to close throughout the sales presentation. Important buying signals may surface at any time. Do not miss them.

SELLING IS EVERYONE'S BUSINESS

Brand Development Starts with Personal Selling

Building a brand name for a line of "unmentionables" (bras, underwear, and camisoles) can be a challenge. Alka and Mona Srivastava, sisters and business partners, readily agree that they didn't know what they were getting themselves into when they started Florentyna Intima, a lingerie company. The two economics majors knew very little about design, manufacturing, and marketing. Once they had a business plan and some money borrowed from their parents, Alka and Mona began the search for a designer and manufacturer.

They needed prototypes to show to customers. Once the prototypes were completed by a firm in Bangkok, they tried to hire a sales representative to present the new line. Unfortunately, no one was willing to represent a line sold by an inexperienced manufacturer. That's when they decided to become salespeople. They hit the road, calling on owners of lingerie boutiques coast to coast and visiting trade shows. Soon buyers were calling with orders. Sales have grown about 30 percent each year.[a]

Specific Methods for Closing the Sale

14.4 Discuss specific methods of closing the sale

The sales presentation is a process, not a single action. Each step during the process should create another layer of trust and move the customer closer to making the purchase. Throughout the sales process, you are moving closer to the close by positioning yourself as a valued resource.[14]

There is no *best* closing method. Your best bet is to preplan several closing methods and adapt the ones that seem appropriate to each customer (Figure 14.3). Given the complex nature of many sales, it is often a good idea to be prepared to use a combination of closing methods that fit the customer.[15] Do keep in mind that your goal is not only to close the sale but also to develop a long-term partnership.

Trial Close

A **trial close** is a closing attempt made at an opportune time during the sales presentation to encourage the customer to reveal readiness or unwillingness to buy. It is also known as the **minor point close**. When you are reasonably sure that the prospect is about to make a decision but is being held back by natural caution, the trial close may be appropriate. It is a good way to test the buyer's attitude toward the actual purchase. The trial close can also be effectively adapted to achieving incremental commitment in more complex multi-call sales. A trial close often is presented in the form of a confirmation question. Here are some examples:

"We can arrange an August first shipment. Would this date be satisfactory?"
"Is the timing right to do a presentation to the executive committee?"
"Would you rather begin this plan on July first or July fifteenth?"
"Will a $2,000 down payment be possible at this time?"

Some salespeople use the trial close more than once during the sales presentation. After the salesperson presents a feature, converts that feature to a buyer benefit, and confirms the prospect's agreement that the benefit is important, it would be appropriate to use a trial close.

Closing Worksheet		
Closing clue (prospect)	Closing method	Closing statement (salesperson)
"That sounds fine." (Verbal recognition)	Direct appeal close	"Good, may I get your signature on this order form?"
"What kind of financing do you offer?" (Verbal question)	Multiple options close	"We have two financing methods available: 90-day open credit or two-year long-term financing. Which of these do you prefer?"
"Well, we don't have large amounts of cash available at this time." (Verbal requirement)	Assumptive close	"Based on your cash position, I would recommend you consider our lease–purchase plan. This plan allows you to pay a very small initial amount at this time and keep the cash you now have for your everyday business expenses. I will be happy to write up your order on the lease–purchase plan."
The prospect completes a careful reading of the proposal and communicates (nonverbal clue) a look of satisfaction. (Nonverbal message)	Combination summary-of-benefits/direct appeal close	"That solution surpasses your quality requirements, meets your time deadlines, and provides your accounting department with the details it requested. Can you get your chief financial officer's signature on the order?"

FIGURE 14.3

Preparing for the close requires the preplanning of several closing methods. Research indicates that in many selling situations several closing attempts may be necessary.

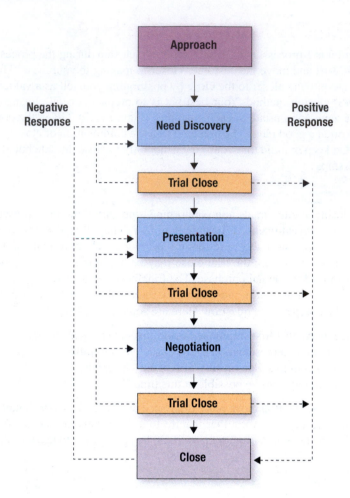

FIGURE 14.4

The trial close should be attempted at an opportune time during the sales presentation. It is appropriate to initiate a trial close after steps two, three, or four of the six-step presentation plan.

In broader terms, it would be appropriate to attempt a trial close after steps two, three, or four of the six-step presentation plan (Figure 14.4).

Direct Appeal Close

The **direct appeal close** has the advantages of clarity and simplicity. This close involves simply asking for the order in a straightforward manner. It is the most direct closing approach, and many buyers find it attractive. Realistically, most customers expect salespeople to ask for the sale.

The direct appeal should not, of course, come too early. It should not be used until the prospect has displayed a definite interest in the product or service. The salesperson must also gain the prospect's respect before initiating this appeal. Once you make the direct appeal, stop talking. John Livesay, West Coast ad director for *W* magazine, says being patient at the close is his "secret weapon." After asking the customer to buy, he stays silent. He avoids asking more questions or making additional statements. This approach gives the customer time to think about the proposal.[16]

A variation of the direct appeal close involves use of a question to determine how close the customer is to making a buying decision. The question might be, "How close are we to closing the sale?" This direct question calls for a direct answer. The customer is encouraged to reflect on the progress of the sale.[17]

Assumptive Close

The **assumptive close** or, as it is sometimes called, the **take-it-for-granted close**, asks for a minor decision, assuming that the customer has already decided to buy.[18] This closing approach comes near the end of the planned presentation. If you have identified a genuine need, presented your solutions in terms of buyer benefits, presented an effective sales demonstration, and

The assumptive close asks for a minor decision, assuming that the customer has decided to buy.

Source: Pressmaster/Shutterstock

negotiated buyer concerns satisfactorily, it may be natural to assume the person is ready to buy. Jeffrey Gitomer (www.gitomer.com), noted sales consultant, says the assumptive close is appropriate when the salesperson has removed perceived risks and the prospect has confidence in the salesperson.[19] The assumptive close usually takes the form of a question that focuses on a minor point. Some examples may include:

> "If you feel the Model 211 gives you the major benefits you are looking for, let's schedule delivery for next Tuesday."
> "Since our production system provides you with the order fulfillment flexibility you require, let's go ahead and place your order."

Most customers will view these statements as the natural conclusion of the events that preceded it. Assumptive closes often include a benefit with your request for action.[20]

This closing method provides a subtle way to ask for a decision when you are quite certain the customer has already decided to buy. You are only bringing the selling/buying process to a close.

Summary-of-Benefits Close

Let us assume that you have discussed and demonstrated the major benefits of your product and you detect considerable buyer interest. However, you have covered a great deal of material. There is a chance that the prospect is not able to put the entire picture together without your help. At this point, you should provide a concise summary of the most important buyer benefits. Your goal in the **summary-of-benefits close** is to reemphasize the value-added benefits that can help bring about a favorable decision. Because of this, this tactic is also referred to as the **step-by-step close**. This closing statement gives you the opportunity to restate how the benefits will outweigh the costs.[21]

Let us see how this closing method works in the hospitality industry. Terry Hall, sales manager of the Emory Hotel, recently called on Mr. Ray Busch, director of marketing for a large corporation. Near the end of the sales presentation, Terry summarized the major benefits and buying conditions in this manner: "Mr. Busch, we can provide you with a conference room that will seat 200 people comfortably and four smaller rooms for the workshops you have planned. Our staff will serve a noon lunch, and the cost will be less than $11 per person. Finally, we will see that each of your employees receives a pad of paper, a pen, and a copy of the conference program. Today, I can reserve these facilities for November 24, which is your first preference for a meeting date. Can I go ahead and enter your reservation into our computer?" Notice that the salesperson has reviewed all the important elements of the value proposition and then asked a *need-satisfaction question.* This question is designed to move the sales process toward commitment and action.

Special Concession Close

The **special concession close** offers the buyer an extra incentive for acting immediately. A special inducement is offered if the prospect agrees to sign the order. The concession may be part of a low-price strategy, such as a sale price, a quantity discount, a more liberal credit plan, or an added feature that the prospect did not anticipate.

You should use this closing approach with care, because some customers are skeptical of concessions. This is especially true when the concession comes after the salesperson has made what appears to be the final offer.

Nicholas Graham, founder and chairman of Joe Boxer Corporation, spends considerable time presenting his novelty underwear line to retailers. Graham recalls that one of his most difficult sales involved Saks Fifth Avenue, the prestigious department store company. He wanted the company to carry Joe Boxer underwear and suggested a Daniel Boone–inspired boxer with a detachable raccoon tail. Graham says, "They had never seen anything so absurd in their life." To close the sale, he let the store take 24 pairs on consignment. "They sold out in one hour," Graham says. Saks has been a committed customer ever since.[22]

Multiple Options Close

In many selling situations, it is a good idea to provide the prospect with options regarding product configuration, delivery options, and price. This is especially true when you are dealing with the price-conscious *transactional* buyer. As noted in the previous chapter, today's customer expects new levels of flexibility. In the **multiple options close**, allow the person to examine several different options, and try to assess the degree of interest in each one. As you near the point at which a close seems appropriate, remove some of the options. This reduces confusion and indecision.

You often see the multiple options close used in office equipment sales. If a small business owner wants to purchase a copy machine, most vendors offer several models for consideration. Let us assume that the prospect has examined four models and seems to be uncertain about which one would be the best choice. The salesperson might determine which copier is least appealing and eliminate it as an option. Now the prospect can choose between three copiers. If the prospect seems to favor one copier, it would be appropriate to ask for the order.

When using the multiple options close, follow these simple steps:

1. Configure more than one product solution.
2. Cease presenting product options when it appears that the prospect has been given ample selection. Too many choices can result in confusion and indecision.
3. Remove products (or features) that the prospect does not seem genuinely interested in and concentrate on the options the prospect seems to be interested in.

Balance Sheet Close

The **balance sheet close** appeals to customers who are having difficulty making a decision even though they have been given plenty of information. Let's assume that the customer feels she has a choice: buy now or buy later. The salesperson draws a T on a sheet of paper and places the captions on each side of the crossbar.

To get the process moving, the salesperson might say, "Let's see how many reasons we can list for buying now." On the left side of the T, the salesperson lists some reasons for buying now. These should be benefits that the customer has already expressed an interest in. On the right side, reasons for not buying now are listed. Throughout the listing process, the salesperson and the customer must engage in a dialogue. This closing method will not be effective if the salesperson is doing all the talking.

Reasons for Buying Now	Reasons for Not Buying Now
1.	1.
2.	2.
3.	3.
4.	4.

Management Close

In previous chapters, we have discussed the merits of involving the sales manager or senior executives in sales calls. To close a major account, salespeople sometimes use the **management close** which calls on top management for help. Ryan Hegman, who works for Hegman Machine Tool Inc. (www.hegmanmachinery.com), recalls a sale that involved a $1.5 million automated manufacturing system. During the sales process, he brought in the president of the company, the vice president of sales, and the lead engineer. "Each added value in a separate way," Hegman explains. One important reason to involve management is to make prospects feel your whole company's resources will be available to support the customer.[23]

Impending Event Close

The **impending event close**, also known as the **positive/negative technique**, involves making positive use of a negative point. This technique of closing requires that you know the needs of the prospects well enough to turn their objections into your selling points. More often than not, you will need to have a good relationship with your prospects to make the method work.

For example, the salesperson might say, "As you have agreed, our product does have several advantages over the competing offerings. I also want to share with you that we cannot make delivery before the middle of next month (the negative point) due to high demand (the positive point). However, I believe you're not looking for delivery until the end of next month (make sure you know this as a fact), so if you place this order today, delivery will not be a problem."

Combination Closes

In some cases, the most effective close is one that combines two or more of the closing methods we have discussed. To illustrate, let us observe Colleen White as she attempts to close a sale in the office of a buyer for a large department store. Colleen represents a firm that manufactures a wide range of leather clothing and accessories. Near the end of her planned presentation, she senses that the prospect is quite interested in her products but seems reluctant to make a decision.

This is how Colleen handles the close: "Ms. Taylor, we have discussed several benefits that seem especially important to you. First, you agree that this line will be popular with the fashion-conscious shoppers your store caters to. Second, you indicated that the prices I quoted will allow you excellent profit margins, and third, if we process your order now, you will have the merchandise in time for the preholiday buying period. With this in mind, let's go ahead and process your order today." Notice that this starts with a summary of benefits and ends with an assumptive close.

Adapting to the Customer's Communication Style

In Chapter 5, we examined the concept of communication styles and achieving versatility through style flexing, otherwise known as the platinum rule. We noted that people with different behavior styles will make their decisions in very distinct ways. We need to take the prospect's style into consideration when deciding how to adapt the close.[24]

DIRECTIVE Most directors are goal-oriented persons who are ready to make quick decisions once they believe your solution meets their needs. They like doing business with salespeople who display confidence that they can give the customer the benefits they want. The director may reject your trial close just to test your confidence level. The highly assertive director will respect persistence and determination.

EMOTIVE The emotive needs social acceptance, so provide support for their opinions and ideas. Maintain good eye contact and be a good listener. Don't let this buyer's emotional statements throw you off balance. Spontaneous statements, spoken dramatically and impulsively, should be expected.

SUPPORTIVE You can expect the supportive customer to be slow in making the buying decision. They are more apt to worry about change or taking risks. It's important to understand their perceived risks so you can reassure them before asking for a buying decision. Curb the desire to put pressure on the supportive customer. Pressure may make this buyer more indecisive. Patience is important.

Applying the Platinum Rule—*Do unto others as they would have you do unto them.*

People with different behavior styles will make their buying decisions in very distinct ways. Therefore, the prospect's communication style must be taken into consideration when deciding how to adapt the close.

Source: Michael Ahearne

REFLECTIVE Before you ask the reflective customer for a buying decision, make sure you review important factual information. These buyers are less likely to be influenced by emotion. Ask reflectives, "Is there any other information I can provide before you make a decision?" Never pressure the reflective customer to make a quick decision.

Practice Closing

Your success in selling can depend in large part on learning how to make these closing methods work for you. Gaining experience using adaptive selling techniques can result in increased recognition of opportunities and greater effectiveness.[25] You may not master these approaches in a few days or a few weeks, but you can speed up the learning process with preparation and practice. Role-playing is one of the best ways to experience the feelings that accompany closing and to practice the skills needed to close sales. To prepare the role-play, anticipate various closing scenarios and then prepare a written script of the drama.[26] Find someone (your sales manager, friend, or spouse) to play the role of the customer and give that person a script to act out. Practice the role-plays in front of a video recorder, and then sit back and observe your performance. The video monitor provides excellent feedback. Use the closing worksheet (see Figure 14.3) to prepare for practice sessions.

14.5 Explain what to do when the buyer says yes and what to do when the buyer says no

Confirming the Partnership When the Buyer Says Yes

Congratulations! You have closed the sale and have established the beginning of what you hope will be a long and satisfying partnership with the customer. Before preparing to leave, be sure that all the details related to the purchase agreement are completed. Check all particulars with the buyer, and then ask for a signature if necessary.

Once the sale has been closed, it is important to take time to reassure the customer. This is the **confirmation step** in closing the sale. Before you leave, reassure the customer by pointing out that she has made the correct decision, and describe the satisfaction that will come with ownership of the product. The reason for doing this is to resell the buyer and to prevent buyer's remorse. **Buyer's remorse** is an emotional response that can take various forms such as feelings of regret, fear, or anxiety.[27] It's common to wonder whether or not we have made the right decision. Compliment the person for making a wise decision. Once the sale is closed, the customer may be required to justify the purchase to others. Your words of reassurance can be helpful.

Before leaving, thank the customer for the order. This is very important. Everyone likes to think that a purchase is appreciated.

Source: Kurhan/Fotolia

Before leaving, thank the customer for the order. This is very important. Everyone likes to think that a purchase is appreciated. No one should believe that a purchase is taken for granted. Even a small order deserves words of appreciation. In many cases a follow-up thank-you letter is appropriate.

In several previous chapters, we note that a satisfied customer is one of the best sources of new prospects. Never hesitate to ask, "Do you know anyone else who might benefit from owning this product?" or a similar question. Some customers may even agree to write an introductory letter on your behalf.

What to Do When the Buyer Says No

High-performance salespeople learn to manage disappointment. A strong display of disappointment or resentment is likely to close the door to future sales. Losing a sale may be painful, but it can also be a valuable learning opportunity. Doing some analysis of what went wrong can help you change the outcome of future sales. Here are some things you should do after a lost sale.[28]

1. *Make sure the deal is really dead.* There is always a chance that the customer's decision can be changed. You might want to mount a last-ditch effort to reopen the presentation.
2. *Review the chain of events.* When you experience a no-sale call, try to benefit from the experience. If you were part of a sales team, get input from each member. Soon after the prospect says no, schedule a debriefing session. If you worked alone, engage in honest self-analysis. Look carefully at your performance during every aspect of the sales process; you may be able to identify weaknesses that can be corrected.
3. *Interview the client.* Obtaining feedback requires a delicate approach. If you probe too aggressively, you may appear argumentative. If your approach is too passive, and the client's comments are general, you will not know how to improve. The key is to couch your questions in neutral terms. Rather than asking, "Why didn't we get the order?" try this approach: "Thank you for considering our company. We hope to do business with you at some time in the future. Would you mind helping me understand any shortcomings in our sales proposal?"

Always keep the door open for future sales. Tell the prospect you would love to work with her at some time in the future. Then, put this person back on your prospect list, record any new information you have learned about the prospect, and continue to keep in touch. Marvin Gottlieb, president of The Communication Project, recalls the loss of a very large piece of business from a large IT firm. This company decided to begin doing its own training rather than outsource it to

Doing Business in South America

Although specific customs vary in the countries of South America, some generalizations can be made. For example, residents of Brazil and America have a different view of appropriate personal space. Brazilians tend to stand closer to you during conversations. To step back may be viewed as being impolite. You should expect more physical contact such as pats on the back and hugs. Lunch is the main meal of the day and it's not uncommon for a business meal to last several hours. Latin Americans often arrive late for appointments. Be patient with decision makers and do not use the hard-sell approach. Be aware of language preferences. Brazilians speak Portuguese; addressing them in Spanish would be insulting. Business associates in Argentina will likely speak English and Spanish. However, your business card should be translated into Spanish.[b]

Gottlieb's company. Rather then give up hope, Gottlieb continued to maintain relationships with key people at the IT firm. After four years, he was invited to present information on a needed service. He closed a $50,000 sale in less than a month.[29]

PREPARE THE PROSPECT FOR CONTACT WITH THE COMPETITION Some prospects refuse to buy because they want to take a close look at the competing products. This response is not unusual in the field of selling. You should do everything possible to help the customer make an intelligent comparison.

It is always a good practice to review your product's strong points one more time. Give special emphasis to areas in which your product has a superior advantage over the competition. Make it easy for the person to buy your product at some future date.

CHAPTER LEARNING ACTIVITIES

Reviewing Key Concepts

Describe the proper attitude to display toward closing the sale

Some of the early closing methods encouraged manipulation of the customer. Use of any closing method that is perceived by the customer as pushy or manipulative will damage your chances of building a long-term partnership. Closing should not be viewed as a strategy to win at the expense of the customer. Once the customer's need has been confirmed, salespeople should determine the most ethical and effective method to move the buyer from indecision to commitment.

List and discuss selected guidelines for closing the sale

Long sales cycles require multiple commitments. These commitments need to be obtained from the prospect throughout a multi-call sales presentation. The buying motive that is of greatest interest deserves special attention at the close. Always negotiate tough points before attempting the close, display a high degree of confidence, and ask for the order more than once.

Explain how to recognize closing clues

The salesperson must be alert to *closing clues* from the prospect. These clues fall into two categories: verbal and nonverbal. Verbal clues are the easiest to recognize, but they may be subtle as well. Again, it is important to be an attentive listener. The recognition of nonverbal clues is more difficult, but careful observation helps in detecting them.

Discuss specific methods of closing the sale

Several closing methods may be necessary to get the prospect to make a buying decision; therefore, it is wise for the salesperson to preplan several closes. These closing methods should be chosen from the list provided in this chapter and then customized to fit the product and the type of buyer with whom the salesperson is dealing. In some selling situations, the use of combination closes is very effective. Flexing to the customer's communication style is important.

Explain what to do when the buyer says yes and what to do when the buyer says no

The professional salesperson is not discouraged or offended if the sale is not closed. Every effort should be made to be of further assistance to the prospect—the sale might be closed on another call. Continue to keep in touch. Even if the sale is lost, the experience may be valuable if analyzed to learn from it.

Key Terms

Incremental commitment, p. 296

Closing clue, p. 297

Trial close (Minor point close), p. 299

Direct appeal close, p. 300

Assumptive close (Take-it-for-granted close), p. 300

Summary-of-benefits close (Step-by-step close), p. 301

Special concession close p. 302

Multiple options close p. 302

Balance sheet close, p. 302

Management close, p. 303

Impending event close (Positive/negative technique), p. 303

Confirmation step, p. 304

Buyer's remorse, p. 304

MyMarketingLab

To complete the problems with the ⭐ in your MyLab, go to the EOC Discussion Questions.

Review Questions

⭐ **14-1**   List some aspects of the sales presentation that can make closing and confirming the sale difficult to achieve.

14-2   Describe three buying anxieties that sometimes serve as barriers to closing the sale.

14-3   What guidelines should a salesperson follow for closing the sale?

⭐ **14-4**   Why is it important to review the value proposition from the prospect's point of view?

14-5   Define the term "incremental commitment." Why is it important to achieve incremental commitments throughout the sale?

14-6   Is there a best method to use in closing the sale? Explain.

14-7   What is meant by a trial close (the minor point close)? When should a salesperson attempt a trial close?

14-8   Explain the summary-of-benefits close (step-by-step close).

⭐ **14-9**   What confirming steps should a salesperson follow when the customer says yes? What should be done when the customer says no?

Application Exercises

14-10 Which of the following statements, often made by prospects, would you interpret as buying signals?
  a. "How much would the payments be?"
  b. "Tell me about your service department."
  c. "The company already has an older model that seems good enough."
  d. "We do not have enough cash flow right now."

e. "How much would you allow me for my old model?"

f. "I do not need one."

g. "How does that switch work?"

h. "When would I have to pay for it?"

14-11 You are an accountant who owns and operates an accounting service. You have been contacted by the president of an advertising agency about the possibility of your auditing his business on a regular basis. The president has indicated that he investigated other accounting firms and thinks they price their services too high. With the knowledge you have about the other firms, you know you are in a strong competitive position. Also, you realize his account would be profitable for your firm. You really would like to capture this account. How will you close the deal? List and describe two closing methods you might use in this situation.

14-12 Zig Ziglar, Brian Tracy, and Tom Reilly are all well-known authors and speakers on the subject of closing the sale. Access each of their websites—www.zigziglar.com, www.briantracy.com, and www.tomreillytraining.com—and research the books, courses, and videos they have available for companies and individuals to purchase, and learn more about closing the sale. Prepare a summary of what you find available. Does the material in this chapter parallel the kind of information these individuals present?

Role-Play Exercise

Examine the superior benefits of the convention center identified in Appendix 3. Specifically research the qualities of the "five-star" executive chef, award-winning renovation of the facility, the cost of parking and transportation to and from the airport, and the easy access on and off the location relative to the freeway. You should assume the role of director of sales and with this information prepare a closing worksheet on the combination summary-of-benefits/direct appeal close for a prospective customer. Also using information from the audiovisual presentation guide, prepare a special concession close, allowing free use of the laser pointer and wireless microphone (a $107.50 value) for a group presentation to the 23 people who will be staying in single rooms at the hotel. Role-play the close of a sale using these closing methods to a prospect who is also seriously considering using one of your competitors.

Reality Selling Video Case Problem—Heather Ramsey/Marriott International

The Corporate Catering Department at Marriott Houston Hobby can make your dreams come true. The staff can help you plan a wedding reception that guests will be talking about for years. If you want to show appreciation to your chief executive officer who is retiring, the staff will make sure the party is truly special. The staff can also help you plan a bar mitzvah, a class reunion, or any other special event.

Heather Ramsey, Corporate Catering Manager, enjoys working with customers. Her customers vary greatly in terms of age, education, income, and social class. The key to working effectively with all of these people is relationship building. Once she builds rapport with clients and establishes a foundation built on trust, they are more likely to open up and discuss their needs. Event planners have at their disposal a wide range of props, facilities, and production expertise, but customer needs guide the use of these resources.

Heather finds that if the sales presentation is well planned and delivered, closing the sale is easier. She believes that good listening skills and careful probing can help uncover dominant buying motives. For example, the client who wants a wedding reception with a special theme may have difficulty expressing her thoughts. Heather must probe and listen closely in order to understand the customer's desires. She must also create value throughout the presentation in order to set the stage for the close. A special event can cost several thousand dollars, so price can be a barrier to closing.

Questions

14-13 What closing clues should Heather Ramsey look for?

14-14 What trial closes would be appropriate?

14-15 What tough points should be negotiated before attempting to close?

14-16 Can you visualize a situation in which Heather Ramsey might use a multiple options close? Explain.

14-17 Assume that a large corporation wants to schedule a recognition party for 40 people. This event will begin with cocktails and appetizers and end with a served meal. Special entertainment will precede the meal. What items might be included in a summary-of-benefits close?

Regional Account Management (RAM) Case Study (refer to Appendix 2)

NewNet Systems®
Your Value Adding Systems Partner

Closing the Sale

You are interested in discovering what your commissions may be for the next few months, just from Lee Bizon's former accounts. To do this, you review the information on each contact. You can estimate each month's likely sales by multiplying the Dollar Amount field number times the Likelihood field percentage number. An 80 percent chance of a $100,000 sale is a forecast of $80,000 in sales. If the Date Close field for several accounts is 12/31, you can calculate the sales for that month (December) by totaling the forecasts for each account. For an estimate of your commission income, multiply each month's forecast by 10 percent.

Lee did not show that any forecasted sales were 100 percent. Lee recognized that the sales might not close, the amount anticipated (Dollar Amount) might not be achieved, and the close might not take place during the month projected. Lee knew that these prospects would not close themselves; certain steps would have to be taken to increase the possibility that the prospect would place an order. To collect your commissions, you have to discover the steps most likely to close these sales.

Questions

14-18 Using the following report format, prepare a metrics report showing what your potential commission income would be for each of Lee Bizon's accounts with a 10 percent commission if you closed them as Lee forecasted. Be sure to figure in the likelihood percentage that was in the forecasted projections. Show what your commissions would be for each of the months shown in Lee's forecast and the total commission you can expect.

NewNet Systems Account Management

Name						Regional Account Manager, NEWNET SYSTEMS	
Date	Account Name/	Dollar	Comm.	Last	Likeli-	Forecasted	**Commission**
Close	Contact Name	Sales Amt	Style	Results	hood	Sales	**(10% Forecast)**

14-19 What kind of special concession might be necessary to close the sale with Quality Builders? What is the closing date, likelihood of closing, and forecasted sales for this account?

14-20 What kind of close seems appropriate to get an order from Computerized Labs? What is the closing date, likelihood, and forecasted sales for this account?

14-21 Should you anticipate a closing problem with Lakeside Clinic's manager, Dr. Jeff Gray's lack of knowledge about networks? What kind of close should you prepare to overcome this problem, if it occurs?

14-22 Refer to this chapter's section titled "Adapting to the Customer's Communication Style." With this information, describe your closing strategy with each of the contacts for: A. Quality Builders, B. Computerized Labs, and C. Lakeside Clinic.

Partnership Selling: A Role-Play (see Appendix 3, page 419)

Developing a Presentation Strategy—Closing the Sale

Park Shores Resort and
Convention Center.
Source: Courtesy of Beach Resort

Refer to Sales Memorandum 3 and strategically plan to close the sale with your customer. To consider the sale closed, you need to secure the signature of your customer on the sales proposal form. This guarantees your customer the accommodations listed on the form. These accommodations may change depending on the final number of people attending your customer's convention. This is an important point to keep in mind when closing the sale; however, you still must get the signature to guarantee the accommodations.

Follow the instructions carefully, and prepare a closing worksheet (see Strategic Planning Form C) listing at least four closes using the methods outlined in this chapter. Two of these methods should be the summary of benefits and the direct appeal. Remember, it is not the policy of your convention center to cut prices, so your methods should include value-added strategies.

Use proof devices to make your closes more convincing and place them in the front pocket of your three-ring binder/portfolio for easy access during your presentation. You may want to secure another person to be your customer, and practice the closing strategies you have developed.

MyMarketingLab

Go to the Assignments section of your MyLab to complete these writing exercises.

14-23 Closing should be viewed as part of the selling process and a number of factors increase the odds a salesperson will close the sale. Describe the factors that increase the salesperson's odds of closing the sale.

14-24 Why is the sales presentation considered a process, not a single action?

Servicing the Sale and Building the Partnership

Learning Objectives

When you finish reading this chapter, you should be able to

15.1 Explain how to build long-term partnerships with customer service

15.2 Describe current developments in customer service

15.3 List and describe the major customer service methods that strengthen the partnership

15.4 Explain how to add value with expansion selling

15.5 Explain how to deal effectively with complaints

Source: Michael Ahearne

▶ Reality Selling Video—Khalid Naziruddin/Sewell Auto

Khalid Naziruddin is an accomplished sales agent at Sewell Automotive, among the largest car dealerships in the country (www.sewell.com). Naziruddin uses partnership based solution selling that focuses on building a relationship with the customer. As an Audi brand specialist, he sells both new and pre owned vehicles.

Mindful of the competition that surrounds luxury product sales and unique needs of high profile clients, Naziruddin's selling approach is to build as much value as possible for his customers. Naziruddin believes that outstanding selling starts by understanding customer's needs and then attempting to create life time value for the both the customer and the seller. He engages the customer by teaming with them through the product selection process.

"Obsessed with Service since 1911", Sewell Auto today sells both luxury marquees such as Audi, Lexus etc. and mainstream brands such as GMC among others. Sewell's annual vehicle sales top 36,000 cars annually sold through more than 2,400 associates across 13 stores, 14 franchises and six cities. As a multi-brand cars sales dealership, Sewell Auto personalizes the car buying experience with well groomed, friendly, highly trained associates, such as Naziruddin, who greet clients by name in an attractive dealership setting of fresh flowers, original art and an ultra clean shop floor. Naziruddin and his colleagues help the firm keep the focus on customer inspired service as it wins numerous awards, delegation visits and returning customers. A graduate of Texas Tech University, Naziruddin epitomizes the company's business strategy that rests on creating the right kind of competitive atmosphere of people tested for intelligence and aptitude during the hiring process. Naziruddin believes that high-performers with high standards of service are uniquely aligned to partner with Sewell Auto's elite customers. Naziruddin's business philosophy is to make customers for life while taking care of them at virtually all costs.

As an Audi brand specialist, Naziruddin must deal with a mature market and focus not just on competition with other luxury brands but also on aspirations of new customers coming from different socio-economic categories who are looking to upgrade themselves to the magnificence of the high-end Audi brand. To build the relationship and create value he often drives customer's attention to car leases—a win-win for both the buyer and seller. Naziruddin often leverages lease agreements (against car loans) to show value to customers who seek lower monthly payments, easier qualifications and lower taxes. To maximize the value proposition of an Audi automobile, Naziruddin's selling approach is to stay well-groomed, in sync with the dealership's luxury décor; and greet every customer with a smile while being genuinely interested in the customer's needs. He starts by finding out what is important for the client (not what is important for him). Next, he partners with the client as he presents the customer with the product and offer suited to the customer's need. Naziruddin's goal is to be seen as fair in negotiation with the customer. He builds relationships by not just making the sale a one-time event. Finally, after negotiations, Naziruddin aims to make the process through finance as efficient as possible. His selling strategy: Build as much value in the product and Sewell Auto and keep in contact with the customer. ●

15.1 Explain how to build long-term partner-ships with customer service

Building Long-Term Partnerships with Customer Service

In a world of increased global competition and narrowing profit margins, customer retention through value-based initiatives can mean the difference between increasing or eroding market share. Progressive marketers are searching for ways to differentiate their service from competitors and to build emotional loyalty through value.[1]

A sales organization that can develop a reputation for servicing each sale (Figure 15.1) is sought out by customers who want a long-term partner to help them with their buying needs. Satisfied customers represent an "auxiliary" sales force—a group of people who recommend customer-driven organizations to others. If customers are pleased with the service that they receive after the sale, be assured that they will tell other people. Research shows that when someone has a good **customer service** experience, he tells an average of six people; when he has an outstanding experience, he tells twice as many.[2]

Achieving Successive Sales

In Chapter 2, we described "partnering" as a strategically developed, long-term relationship that solves the customer's problem. A successful partnering effort results in successive sales and referrals.

Many of today's large companies want to partner with suppliers who sell and deliver quality products and services that continually improve their processes and profits. The first sale is only the beginning of the relationship—an opportunity to earn a repeat sale. Repeat sales come after the supplier demonstrates the ability to add value in various ways.[3] This value may take the form of timely delivery, superior installation, accurate invoicing, technical know-how, social contacts, or something else that is important to the customer. In business-to-business sales, the relationship should intensify as the supplier delivers extensive postsale support. Taking the customer's point of view and acting in the customer's interest, often described as "customer advocacy," is a major factor underlying repeat business.[4]

The Six-Step Presentation Plan	
Step One: Approach	✔ Review Strategic/Consultative Selling Model ✔ Initiate customer contact
Step Two: Need Discovery	✔ Ask strategic questions ✔ Determine customer needs ✔ Select product solution
Step Three: Presentation	✔ Select presentation strategy ✔ Create presentation plan ✔ Initiate presentation
Step Four: Negotiation	✔ Anticipate buyer concerns ✔ Plan negotiating methods ✔ Initiate win-win negotiations
Step Five: Close	✔ Plan appropriate closing methods ✔ Recognize closing clues ✔ Initiate closing methods
Step Six: Servicing the Sale	☐ Follow through ☐ Follow-up calls ☐ Expansion selling
Service, retail, wholesale, and manufacturer selling	

FIGURE 15.1

Servicing the sale involves three steps: follow-through, follow-up calls, and expansion selling.

Responding to Increased Postsale Customer Expectations

People buy expectations, not products, according to Ted Levitt, author of *The Marketing Imagination*. They buy the expectations of benefits you promised. Once the customer buys your product, expectations increase. Levitt points out that after the sale is closed, the buyer's attitude changes. The customer expects the salesperson to remember the purchase as a favor bestowed on him by the buyer.

Nitin Nohria, Harvard Business School professor and coauthor of *What Really Works: The 4 + 2 Formula for Sustained Business Success*, says, "Customers are enormously punishing when companies don't meet their expectations."[5]

Increased customer expectations, after the sale is closed, require a strategic plan for servicing the sale. Certain aspects of the relationship, product, and customer strategies can have a positive influence on the customer's heightened expectations.[6] In most business-to-business sales, the salesperson cannot service the sale alone. To properly manage the account, the salesperson will need assistance from the shipping department, technical support, engineering, and other areas. Customer service is increasingly a team effort.[7]

How do we respond to a customer who has increased expectations? First, we should be certain our customer strategy is on target. We must fully understand the needs and wants of the customer. What is the customer trying to accomplish and how can you help the person do it better?

Second, we should focus like a laser beam on follow-through and follow-up activities. Throughout every sales presentation, the salesperson will offer assurances and make some promises. The salesperson's credibility will be tarnished if any of these commitments are ignored.

This salesperson is preparing a thank-you note that will strengthen the relationship with the customer.

Source: micro10x/Shutterstock

Third, we should reexamine our product strategy. In some cases, we can enhance customer satisfaction by suggesting related products or services. If the product is expensive, we can follow through and offer assistance in making credit arrangements. If the product is complex, we can make suggestions concerning use and maintenance. Each of these forms of assistance may add value to the sale.

High Cost of Customer Attrition

Financial institutions, public utilities, airlines, retail stores, restaurants, manufacturers, and wholesalers face the problem of gaining and retaining the patronage of clients and customers. These companies realize that keeping a customer happy is a winning strategy. To regain a lost customer can be four to five times more expensive than keeping a current customer satisfied.[8]

SELLING IS EVERYONE'S BUSINESS

Job Searches Require Widening the Net

You have a good education, but you don't have a job. This scenario is being played out in the lives of thousands of people across the nation. Before you send out another 1,000 résumés via the Internet or spend more time searching the Net for employment opportunities, consider the results of a study conducted by Drake Beam Morin (DBM) at www.dbm.com, a workplace-consulting firm. Networking is the top tactic for landing a job, outpacing other strategies such as the Internet and newspaper ads. The report indicates that 66 percent of DBM clients found new jobs via networking, whereas just 6 percent found employment through the Internet. Don't overlook the value of personal contact that gives you an opportunity to sell yourself.[a]

Bill Gates, author of *Business @ the Speed of Thought*, predicted that in the new economy customer service may become the primary value-added function.

Source: REUTERS/Mike Segar/ Alamy Stock Photo

There is no longer any doubt that poor service is the primary cause of customer attrition. A surprisingly small number of customers (12 to 15 percent) are lost due to product dissatisfaction. No more than 10 to 15 percent of lost customers leave due to price considerations. Some studies have found that from 50 to 70 percent of customer attrition is due to poor service.[9] A carefully developed strategic plan to reduce customer defection pays big dividends.

Carl Sewell, chairman of Sewell Automotive Companies with dealerships in Dallas, Fort Worth, and San Antonio, has, as noted earlier, fully embraced the customer-for-life philosophy of doing business. He lives, sleeps, eats, and breathes his obsession with customer service and the result is a family of dealerships that are the envy of almost everyone in the automobile business.[10]

Current Developments in Customer Service

Bill Gates, in his book *Business @ the Speed of Thought*, predicted that in the new millennium customer service may become the primary value-added function.[11] He recognized that customer service is the primary method of building and extending the partnership. Customer service, in its many forms, nourishes the partnership and keeps it alive.

Salespeople are in a unique position to enhance *customer satisfaction* and *trust*, the two major contributors to relationship quality.[12] With adequate orientation and training, members of the sales force can build long-term, profitable, customer relationships. Recent research indicates that the building process involves five important service behaviors that are especially important in the context of business-to-business selling.[13]

- *Diligence.* Diligence combines two types of service behaviors: responsiveness and reliability. In today's highly competitive, time-starved business environment, salespeople must provide service in a timely manner. Service behaviors that demonstrate both reliability and responsiveness include following up on commitments, returning phone calls, fulfilling customer requests, and being available when needed. There is a growing trend in which companies rely on their customers' needs, concerns, and future plans.
- *Information communication.* This service behavior involves regularly relaying product information to the customer in a clear and concise manner. Communicating information must encompass the entire sales process. Early in the sales process, this may

15.2 Describe current developments in customer service

involve drawing objective comparisons between your product and competitive offerings, and continually reiterating a clear case for your product. After the sale is closed, information communication often involves providing updated information on product usage.

- *Inducements.* This service behavior is aimed at personalizing the relationship with the customer. In Chapter 4, we noted that the manner in which salespeople establish, build, and maintain relationships is not an incidental aspect of personal selling. Some service behaviors provide the customer with an incentive, or an inducement, for maintaining the relationship with the salesperson. Becoming genuinely interested in the customer, talking in terms of the customer's interests, and doing special favors can strengthen the relationship with the customer.

- *Empathy.* As the information age unfolded and the global economy heated up, we learned that it takes more than quick and accurate information communicated through advanced technology to retain customers. Empathy is one of those high-touch abilities that mark the fault line between salespeople who are highly productive and those who are average or below average in terms of productivity.[14] Salespeople who display a strong willingness to help customers and make an effort to understand them are demonstrating empathetic behavior.

- *Sportsmanship.* This service behavior can be defined as a salesperson's willingness to tolerate setbacks and disappointments without displaying negativism. It means demonstrating good social judgment and professionalism during all customer interactions. If you have a 10:00 A.M. appointment with a customer, but you are required to wait until 10:30 A.M. for the meeting to begin, how will you handle this disappointment?

Computer-Based Systems

Customer-friendly, computer-based systems frequently are used to enhance customer service, loyalty, and sales growth.[15] Computers give both the salesperson and the customer ready access to information and problem-solving alternatives. Nantucket Nectars provides a good example of a company that has enhanced customer service with computer-based systems. The 150 distributors can log on to **www.juiceguys.com** to place and check orders. Nantucket Nectars' 85 field salespeople can log onto NectarNet, a dedicated company website, from their homes to check on the status of customer orders and determine inventory levels.[16]

The sales staff at Mitchells/Richards, the highly successful clothing stores introduced in a previous chapter, uses technology to establish a more personal relationship with the customer. In a matter of seconds, salespeople can review a customer's complete buying history and personal information such as birthday and anniversary, clothing sizes, favorite colors, names of the children, and even the name of the family pet. With this information, salespeople are better able to bond with their customers.[17]

15.3 List and describe the major customer service methods that strengthen the partnership

Customer Service Methods that Strengthen the Partnership

Customer service encompasses all activities that enhance or facilitate the sale and use of one's product or service. The skills required to service a sale are different from those required prior to the sale (Figure 15.2). High-performance sales personnel do not abdicate responsibility for delivery, installation, warranty interpretation, or other customer service responsibilities. They continue to strengthen the partnership with follow-through, follow-up, and expansion selling.

Adding Value with Follow-Through

A major key to an effective customer service strategy is follow-through on assurances and promises that were part of the sales presentation. Properly managing customer relationships enhances the value creation during and after the selling process.[18] Did your sales presentation include

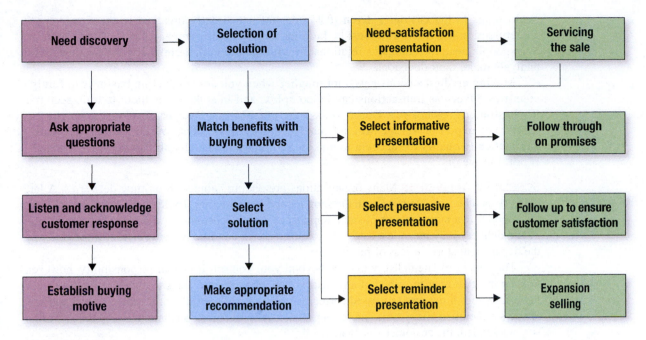

FIGURE 15.2

The completed Consultative Sales Presentation Guide illustrates the ways in which high-performance salespeople use value-added strategies to service the sale and build repeat business and referrals. Customer service provides many opportunities to strengthen the partnership.

claims for superior performance; promises of speedy delivery; assistance with credit arrangements; and guaranteed factory assistance with installation, training, and service?

Most sales presentations are made up of claims and promises that the company can fulfill. However, fulfillment of these claims depends to a large degree on after-sale action. Postsale follow-through is the key to holding that customer you worked so hard to develop. The first sale can be the beginning of a long-term partnership or it can be the last sale. The following services can help ensure a second sale and successive sales.

MAKE CREDIT ARRANGEMENTS Credit has become a common way to finance purchases. This is true of industrial products, real estate, automobiles, home appliances, and many other products. Closing the sale often depends on your ability to develop and present attractive

---

SELLING IN ACTION

The Moment of Magic in the Sales Process

Tony Alessandra (www.alessandra.com), a well-known sales trainer and consultant, says that there are three possible outcomes when a customer does business with an organization.

The moment of truth. In these selling situations, the customer's expectations were met. Nothing happened to disappoint the customer, and the salesperson did not do anything to surpass the customer's expectations. The customer is apt to have somewhat neutral feelings about her relationship with the salesperson. The moment of truth usually does not build customer loyalty.

The moment of misery. This is the outcome of a selling situation in which the customer's expectations were not met. The customer may feel a sense of disappointment or even anger. Many customers who experience the moment of misery may share their feelings with others and often make a decision to "fire" the salesperson.

The moment of magic. This is the outcome of a sale in which the customer received more than he expected. The salesperson surpassed the customer's expectations by going the extra mile and providing a level of service that added value to the customer–salesperson relationship. This extra effort is likely to establish a foundation for increased customer loyalty.[b]

credit plans to the customer. Even if you do not get directly involved in the firm's credit and collection activities, you must be familiar with how the company handles these matters. Salespeople need to establish a relationship with the credit department and learn how credit analysts make their decisions.[19]

Making credit decisions gets a lot tougher when you are conducting business in foreign countries. Overseas transactions can be complex, and in some cases there is little recourse if a customer does not pay. Doron Weissman, president of Overseas Brokers, a freight forwarder and export brokerage firm in Great Neck, New York, says, "When I sell my services, I automatically qualify the account to make sure they're financially able to meet my demands. If not, I move on."[20]

SCHEDULE DELIVERIES Many organizations are adding value with on-time deliveries. A late delivery ca n be a problem for both the supplier and the customer. To illustrate, let us assume that the supplier is a manufacturer of small appliances and the customer is a department store chain. A late delivery may mean lost sales due to out-of-stock conditions, cancellation of the order by the department store, or loss of future sales.

The causes of late delivery may be beyond your control. It is your responsibility, however, to keep the customer informed of any delays. You also can take steps to prevent a delay. Check to be sure your order was processed correctly. Follow up to see if the order was shipped on time. Always remember: Every time an order is handled, the customer is handled. Every time an order sits unattended, the customer sits unattended.[21]

BE PRESENT DURING DELIVERY When the first delivery is made, be there to be sure the customer is comfortable with the purchase. Check to determine whether the order is complete and be available to offer assistance.[22]

MONITOR INSTALLATION Buyer satisfaction is often related to proper installation of the product. This is true of consumer products such as security systems, central air-conditioning, solar heating systems, and carpeting. It also is true of industrial products such as electronic data-processing equipment and air quality control systems. Some salespeople believe it is to their advantage to supervise product installation. They then are able to spot installation problems. Others make it a practice to follow up on the installation to be sure no problems exist.

OFFER TRAINING IN THE USE OR CARE OF THE PRODUCT For certain industries, it is essential that users be skilled in how to use the new product. This is true of factory equipment, electronic cash registers, farm implements, German luxury cars, and many other products. Technology has become so complex that many suppliers must provide training as part of the follow-up to ensure customer satisfaction. Most organizations that sell computers and other types of electronic equipment for office use now schedule training classes to ensure that customers can properly use and care for the products. These companies believe that users must be skilled in handling their equipment.

GLOBAL BUSINESS INSIGHT

Doing Business in Russia

Russia has become an important American trading partner. In recent years, Russia has changed politically, socially, and economically. Prior to doing business in the new Russia, get acquainted with the business etiquette and ethics of this important market for American products and services.

- Meetings may not start on time, but it's still a good idea to be punctual.

- The first meeting with your Russian counterparts may be just a formality. They will attempt to assess your credibility and relationship skills, so be warm and approachable.
- Cultivate relationships with government agencies at all levels. Politicians and government agencies continue to have arbitrary power.
- Most Russians enjoy having a drink and a good meal. Take this opportunity to establish goodwill. Some restaurants and bars do not accept credit cards, so bring cash.[c, d]

PROVIDE PRICE CHANGE INFORMATION Price changes do not need to be a serious problem if they are handled correctly. The salesperson is responsible for maintaining an up-to-date price list. As your company issues price changes, record them accurately. Customers expect you to quote the correct price the first time.

Preventing Postsale Problems

There are ways to prevent postsale problems. The key is conscientious follow-up to be sure everything has been handled properly. Get to know the people who operate your shipping and installation department. They are responsible for getting the right products shipped and installed on time, and it is important that they understand your customers' needs.

Become acquainted with people in the credit department. Be sure that they maintain a good, business-like relationship with your customers. This is a delicate area; even small mistakes (e.g., a "pay now" notice sent too early) can cause hurt feelings. If your company uses a customer support staff to resolve postsale problems, be sure to get acquainted with people who provide this service.

Schedule regular account reviews to determine the level of customer satisfaction. The focus of these reviews should be key decision makers. Are there lingering service-type issues that make you vulnerable to the competition? You want to be certain there are no open doors

---

CREATING THE LIFETIME CUSTOMER

When we build a plant or purchase a computer—when we acquire just about any new asset—by accounting conventions, it begins to depreciate on day one. But there is one asset that can appreciate over the years. That asset is the well-served customer, who becomes the most significant sustainer of the business, the **lifetime customer** (www.tompeters.com).

Tom Peters

Tom Peters believes there is one asset that can appreciate over the years. That asset is the well-served customer, who becomes the most significant sustainer of the business, the lifetime customer.

Source: Toby Talbot/AP Photos

for your competitors. If you discover a problem, act quickly to resolve it. In some cases, these formal account reviews will uncover opportunities to improve customer service. You will also become more of a consultant in the eyes of the customer.[23]

Adding Value with Customer Follow-Up

Customer follow-up methods usually have two major objectives. One is to express appreciation for the purchase and, thus, enhance the relationship established during the sales presentation. You no doubt thanked the customer at the time the sale was closed, but appreciation should be expressed again a few days later. The second purpose of the follow-up is to determine whether the customer is satisfied with the purchase. Both of these methods can strengthen the buyer–seller relationship and build a partnership that results in additional sales.[24]

In survey after survey, poor service and lack of follow-up after the sale are given as primary reasons people stop buying from us. Most customers are sensitive to indifferent treatment by salespeople and sales support personnel. With this fact in mind, you should approach follow-up in a systematic and businesslike way. There are five follow-up methods.

PERSONAL VISIT This is usually the most costly follow-up method, but it may produce the best results. It is the only strategy that allows face-to-face, two-way communication. When you take time to make a personal visit, the customer knows that you really care.

Use the personal follow-up to keep the customer informed of new developments, new products, or new applications. This information may pave the way for additional sales. Use the personal visit to reassess where you stand with the account. The reassessment process should involve something more than a "How's it going?" question. If you want the customer to see you as a partner, ask the tough questions: "Are there any problems that I need to address?" "Can you suggest any ways we can better serve your business?" Tom Reilly, author and sales trainer, says, "Your perception of your performance is meaningless. It's the customer's perceptions that count."[25]

Personal visits provide a wonderful opportunity to engage in value reinforcement. **Value reinforcement** means getting credit for the value you create for the customer. You might review all of your follow-through activities so the customer realizes the many ways you have added

Follow-up calls allow for a two-way exchange of information. In many cases, once an account is well established, you may be able to obtain repeat sales by telephone.

Source: Nathan Michaels/ SuperStock, Inc.

CONFIRMING IMMEDIATELY WITH CRM

Close-up and personal-information sharing creates a core on which successful relationships may be built and sustained. Friends have long supplemented their personal visits with notes, letters, e-mails, telephone calls, and now Facebook posts.

CRM (customer relationship management) technology offers new ways to save time in addition to enhancing and extending relationship-rich communications. Enlightened salespeople use Chatter, instant messaging, and e-mail in addition to faxes and phone calls as fast, and thus effective, methods to give information to their customers. E-mail (and texting and tweeting) can be particularly useful to quickly convey temporary messages such as those that confirm, affirm, or verify.

value. Whenever possible, document your value-added services and point out any benefits that the customer has received. In some cases, positive bragging is an effective value reinforcement technique.[26]

TELEPHONE CALL The telephone provides a quick and efficient way to follow up a sale. A salesperson can easily make 10 or 12 phone calls in a single hour, and the cost can be minimal. If you plan to send a thank-you card or letter, follow it up with a thank-you call. The personal appeal of the phone call increases the effectiveness of the written correspondence. The telephone call has one major advantage over written correspondence. It allows for a two-way exchange of information. Once an account is well established, you may be able to obtain repeat sales by telephone.

E-MAIL OR TEXT MESSAGE In many cases it is a lot quicker to send an e-mail or text message than to make a phone call. Salespeople report that they waste a lot of time playing "phone tag." Some customers prefer e-mail or text messages and may become irritated if you do not adhere to their wishes. If you know that a customer is not in the habit of checking her e-mail or text messages all that often, use the telephone as a back-up method. When in doubt, use parallel channels of communication.

LETTER OR CARD Written correspondence is an inexpensive and personal form of customer follow-up. Letters and cards can be used to thank the customer for the order and to promise continued service. Some companies encourage their salespeople to use a formal letter written on company stationery. Other companies have designed special thank-you cards, which are signed and sent routinely after a sale is closed. The salesperson may enclose a business card. These thank-you cards do have one major limitation: They are mass-produced and, therefore, lack the personal touch of handwritten cards and envelopes. Personalized notes, birthday cards, and anniversary cards can make a positive impression.

CALL REPORT The **call report** is a form that serves as a communications link with people who can assist with customer service. The format varies, but generally it is a simple form with only four or five spaces. Salesforce's Chatter mentioned earlier is an excellent example of a call report. With Chatter, all stakeholders in a sale are copied with the latest information and action regarding the sale. A call report is an important solution to the problem of communication between the company personnel and the customer. It is a method of follow-through that triggers the desired action. It is simple, yet business-like.

Follow-up programs can be as creative or as ingenious as you wish. Every sales organization competes on value, so you must continually think of new ways to add value. Creative use of your interpersonal communication skills can keep your messages fresh and personalized. Keep in mind that people buy both from the head and the heart. Let customers know how much you care about their business.[27] You can use these five methods independently or in combination. Your main consideration should be some type of appropriate follow-up that (1) tells customers you appreciate their business and (2) determines whether they are satisfied with the purchase.

15.4 Explain how to add value with expansion selling

Adding Value with Expansion Selling

Personal selling is the process of identifying and filling the customer's needs. As the salesperson learns more about the customer and establishes a relationship based on trust and mutual respect, opportunities for expansion selling will arise. Expansion selling can take three forms: full-line selling, cross-selling, and upselling.

FULL-LINE SELLING **Full-line selling**, sometimes called "**Suggestion Selling**," is the process of recommending products or services that are related to the main item sold to the customer. The recommendation is made when, in the salesperson's judgment, the product or service can provide additional satisfaction.

To illustrate, let us look at the sale of new homes by KB Home (www.kbhome.com), a builder of large, planned communities. Customers who want to differentiate their home from those down the block are offered an array of options such as marble in the entryway, granite countertops, gourmet kitchen appliances, or Jacuzzi-like tubs for the bathroom. Customization has proven to be a popular, value-added service to customers.[28]

Full-line selling is no less important when selling services. For example, a travel agent has many opportunities to suggest related products. Let us assume that a customer purchases a two-week vacation in Germany. The agent can offer to book hotel reservations or schedule a guided tour. Another related product would be a rental car. Sometimes a new product is simply not "right" without related merchandise. A new business suit may not look right without a new shirt and tie. An executive training program held at a fine hotel can be enhanced with a refreshment break featuring a variety of soft drinks, fresh coffee, and freshly baked pastries.

Customers may view full-line selling as a form of value-added service when it is presented correctly. There is a right way and a wrong way to make recommendations. Some guidelines to follow include:

1. *Plan for full-line selling during the preapproach step.* Before meeting with the customer, develop a general plan that includes your objectives for this important dimension of selling. Full-line selling is easier when you are prepared.
2. *Make recommendations after you have first satisfied the customer's primary need.* Although there are some exceptions to this rule, it's usually best to meet the primary need first. In the case of a new home purchase from KB Home, the customer should first select the model home and then make decisions regarding the upgrades.
3. *Make your suggestions thoughtful and positive.* "We will deliver your new copy machine on Monday. Would you like us to deliver some quality copy paper?" Avoid questions such as, "Can we ship anything else?" This question invites a negative response.
4. *When appropriate, demonstrate the suggested item or use sales tools to build interest.* If you have suggested a shirt to go with a new suit, allow the customer to see it next to the suit. If you are calling on a commercial account, show the customer a sample or at least a picture if the actual product is not available.

Full-line selling is a means of providing value-added service. When you use it correctly, customers thank you for your thoughtfulness and extra service. It is also a proven sales-building strategy.

CROSS-SELLING We have seen an increase in the use of cross-selling to grow sales volume. **Cross-selling** involves selling products that are not directly associated with products that you have sold to an established customer.[29]

A growing number of companies are using cross-selling to discover additional sources of business within established accounts. Buyers often welcome cross-selling efforts because they are searching for ways to consolidate purchases. They like the convenience of buying several items from the same source.[30] Cross-selling is most effective in those situations in which the salesperson and the customer enjoy a true partnership.

Salespeople who have a good understanding of the customer's needs and have earned the customer's respect will face less resistance when recommending a product or service.

To achieve success with cross-selling, you need to use *survey questions* and *probing questions* (see Chapter 11). A general survey question such as "Can you tell me more about your expansion plans?" may uncover information needed to position your cross-selling sales strategy. However, you will likely need to use probing questions to uncover and clarify a buying problem that may open the door to a cross-selling opportunity. Keep in mind that cross-selling has to be a well-thought-out part of your strategy and process.[31]

UPSELLING The effort to sell better-quality products is known as **upselling**. It is an important selling method that often adds customer value. Mike Weber, sales manager at Young Electric Sign Company, offers us two important tips on upselling. First, you need a well-established relationship with the customer—a relationship built on trust. Second, you need to continuously qualify the prospect throughout the buying process. As customers tell you more about their needs, you may see an opportunity to upsell. Weber says his salespeople often engage in upselling at the design stage. The customer is shown a rough sketch of the desired sign and another rendition of something better. The added value of the more expensive option will often become obvious to the customer.[32] In many selling situations, such factors as durability, comfort, or economy help justify the higher-quality product. A professional salesperson explains to the customer why it is in his or her best interest to spend "just a little more" and get the best value for the dollar. Most customers are more concerned with making the right purchase than they are with making the least expensive purchase.[33]

Preplan Your Service Strategy

Servicing the sale is a very important dimension of personal selling, so a certain amount of preplanning is essential. It helps to preplan your service strategy for each of the three areas we have discussed: follow-through, follow-up, and expansion selling. You cannot anticipate every aspect of the service, but you can preplan important ways to add value once the sale is implemented. Develop a servicing-the-sale worksheet, shown in Figure 15.3, prior to each sales presentation.

Partnership-Building Strategies Should Encompass All Key People

Some salespeople do a great job of communicating with the prospect but ignore other key people involved in the sale. To illustrate how serious this problem can be, let us look at the approach used by Jill Bisignano, a sales representative for a major restaurant supply firm. Jill had called on Bellino's Italian Restaurant for several years. Although she was always very friendly to Nick Bellino, she treated the other employees with nearly total indifference. One day she called on Nick and was surprised to learn that he was retiring and had decided to sell his restaurant to two longtime employees.

As you might expect, it did not take the new owners long to find another supplier. Jill lost a large account because she failed to develop a good personal relationship with other key employees. It pays to be nice to everyone. Here is a partial list of people in your company and in the prospect's company who can influence both initial and repeat sales.

1. *Receptionist.* Some salespeople simply do not use common sense when dealing with the receptionist. This person has daily contact with your customer and may schedule most or all calls. To repeatedly forget this individual's name or display indifference in other ways may cost you dearly.
2. *Technical personnel.* Some products must be cleaned, lubricated, or adjusted on a regular basis. Take time to get acquainted with the people who perform these duties. Answer their questions, share technical information with them if necessary, and show appreciation for the work they are doing.
3. *Stock clerks or receiving clerks.* People working in the receiving room are often responsible for pricing incoming merchandise and making sure that these items are stored properly. They also may be responsible for stock rotation and processing damage claims.

Servicing-the-Sale Worksheet

Method of Adding Value	What You Will Say or Do
Follow-Through	
Set up a secure website or extranet so client can track the production and delivery of the custom-engineered research equipment.	Set up the secure website in a timely manner and then contact the customer when it is operational. Explain how to access the website and review the benefits of using this source of assistance.
Schedule training for persons who will be using the new technology.	Send training schedule to customer and confirm the dates with a follow-up call.
Follow-Up	
Send a thank-you letter to each member of the team that made the purchase decision.	Express sincere appreciation for the purchase and explain the steps you will take to ensure a long-term partnership.
Check to be certain that the training was effective.	Visit the customer's research facility and talk with the employees who completed the training. Answer questions and provide additional assistance as needed.
Expansion Selling	
Suggest the purchase of global positioning system (GPS) technology to enhance use of seed research equipment.	"GPS technology will enable you to track all your research and plot the findings on your computer screen."

FIGURE 15.3

Servicing-the-Sale Worksheet

Follow-through on assurances and promises, customer follow-up, and expansion selling must be carefully planned. Use of this worksheet can help you preplan ways to add value.

4. *Management personnel.* Although you may be working closely with someone at the departmental or division level, do not forget the person who has the final authority and responsibility for this area. Spend time with management personnel occasionally and be alert to any concerns they may have.

This is not a complete list of the people you may need to depend on for support. There may well be other key people who influence sales. Always look beyond the customer to see who else might influence the sale as partnerships can be built upon different levels of the organization.[34]

Partnering with an Unhappy Customer

15.5 Explain how to deal effectively with complaints

We have learned that unhappy customers often do not initiate a verbal or written complaint. This means that postsale problems may not come to the attention of salespeople or other personnel within the organization. We also know that unhappy customers do share their negative experiences with other people. A dissatisfied customer often tells 8 to 10 people about his problem.[35] A double loss occurs when the customer stops buying our products and takes steps to discourage other people from buying our products. When complaints do surface, we should view the problem as an opportunity to strengthen the business relationship. Conflict resolution is another aspect of problem solving important to the customer–salesperson relationship.[36] To achieve this goal, follow these suggestions.

1. *Give customers every opportunity to disclose their feelings.* Companies noted for outstanding customer service rely heavily on phone systems—like toll-free "hot lines"—to ensure easy access. At Federal Express, Cadillac Division of General Motors, and IBM, to name a few companies, specially trained advisors answer the calls and offer assistance. When a customer purchases a Ford vehicle, the salesperson introduces the customer to service staff who play a key role in providing postsale service. The goal is to personalize the relationship with another member of the service team. Ford has discovered that after-sale contact builds a perception of value.[37] When customers do complain, by phone or in person, encourage them to express all their anger and frustration. Do not interrupt. Do not become defensive. Do not make any judgments until you have heard all the facts as the customer sees them. If the customer stops speaking, try to get him or her to talk some more. How you deal with anger is very important. Encourage the angry customer to vent his or her feelings. By asking questions and listening carefully to the response, you can encourage the person to discuss the cause of the anger openly. After venting feelings and discussing specific details, the angry customer will expect a response. Briefly paraphrase what seems to be the major concern and express a sincere desire to find ways to solve the problem.[38]

2. *Keep in mind that it does not really matter whether a complaint is real or perceived.* If the customer is upset, you should be polite and sympathetic. Do not yield to the temptation to say, "You do not really have a problem." Remember, problems exist when customers perceive they exist.[39]

3. *Do not alibi.* Avoid the temptation to blame the shipping department, the installation crew, or anyone else associated with your company. Never tear down the company you work for. The problem has been placed in your hands, and you must accept responsibility for handling it. "Passing the buck" only leaves the customer with a feeling of helplessness.

4. *Politely share with the customer your point of view concerning the problem's cause.* At least explain what you think happened. The customer deserves an explanation. At this point a sincere apology is usually appropriate.

5. *Decide what action must be taken to remedy the problem.* Take action quickly and offer a value-added atonement. Don't just do what is expected, but delight the customer by exceeding his expectations. Winning customer loyalty today means going beyond making it right.[40]

The value of customer complaints can emerge in two forms. First, complaints can be a source of important information that may be difficult to obtain by other means. Second, customer complaints provide unique opportunities for companies to *prove* their commitment to service. Loyalty builds in the customer's mind if you do a good job of solving her problem.[41]

A WORD OF CAUTION When you are dealing with major or minor customer service problems and an apology is necessary, do not use e-mail. When a minor problem surfaces, call the customer personally. Do not delegate this task to someone else in your organization. If you need to apologize for a major problem that has occurred, meet with the customer in person. Schedule the meeting as soon as possible.[42]

CHAPTER LEARNING ACTIVITIES

Reviewing Key Concepts

Explain how to build long-term partnerships with customer service

Servicing the sale is a major dimension of the selling process, with the objectives of providing maximum customer satisfaction and establishing a long-term partnership. Servicing the sale encompasses a variety of activities that take place during and after the buying process. In this chapter, we present servicing the sale as a three-part process: follow-through on assurances and promises, follow-up with ongoing communication after the sale, and expansion selling.

Describe current developments in customer service

In the new millennium, customer service has become a primary value-added function. Salespeople are in a unique position to enhance customer satisfaction and trust by displaying five important service behaviors: diligence, information communication, inducements, empathy, and sportsmanship.

List and describe the major customer service methods that strengthen the partnership

A major key to an effective customer service strategy is follow-through on assurances and promises that were part of the sales presentation. Follow-through services may involve making credit arrangements, scheduling deliveries, monitoring installation, training in the use or care of the product, and providing product updates and similar services. Salespeople can also add value with a sincere expression of appreciation. Follow-up methods include personal visits, phone calls, e-mail messages, letters, or call reports.

A salesperson depends on the support of many other people in servicing a sale. Maintaining good relationships with support-staff members who help service your accounts is well worth the time and energy required.

Explain how to add value with expansion selling

As the salesperson learns more about the customer, opportunities for expansion selling will arise. Expansion selling can take three forms: full-line selling, cross-selling, and upselling.

Explain how to deal effectively with complaints

Dealing effectively with unhappy customers should be thought of as an opportunity to strengthen the business relationship. Always give customers every opportunity to disclose their feelings. Encourage angry customers to vent their feelings and listen closely to what is said. Briefly summarize what seems to be the major concern and express a sincere desire to find ways to solve the problem.

Key Terms

Customer service, p. 312
Lifetime customer, p. 319
Value reinforcement, p. 320

Call report, p. 321
Full-line selling, p. 322
Cross-selling, p. 322

Upselling, p. 323
Suggestion Selling, p. 322

MyMarketingLab

To complete the problems with the ⭐ in your MyLab, go to the EOC Discussion Questions.

Review Questions

 15-1   You are currently a sales manager employed by a company that sells long-term care insurance. Tomorrow you will meet with five new sales trainees. Your major goal is to explain why it is important to service the sale. What important points will you cover?

15-2   Define customer service. List the three major activities associated with this phase of personal selling.

15-3   List and describe three current developments in customer service.

15-4   Adding value with follow-through can involve several postsale services. List five possible services.

 15-5   How does credit become a part of servicing the sale?

15-6   This chapter describes the value of the lifetime customer. Is it realistic to believe that people will become lifetime customers in our very competitive marketplace?

15-7   Define upselling and explain how it can add value.

 15-8   What types of customer service problems might be prevented with the use of a call report?

15-9   Describe the steps for partnering with an unhappy customer.

Application Exercises

15-10   You work as a wholesale salesperson for a plumbing supply company. One of your customers, a contractor, has an open line of credit with your company for $10,000 worth of products. He is currently at his limit; however, he is not overdue. He has just received word that he has been awarded a $40,000 plumbing contract at the local airport. The contract requires that he supply $9,000 worth of plumbing products. Your customer does not have the cash to pay for the additional products. He tells you that unless you can provide him with some type of financing, he may lose the contract. He says that he can pay you when he finishes his next job in 60 days. Explain what you will do.

15-11   You have just interviewed for a job that you really would like to have. You have heard it is a good idea to follow up an interview with a thank-you note or letter and an indication of your enthusiasm for the position. Select the strategy you will use for your follow-up, and explain why you chose it.

15-12   Using your search engine, examine the Internet for information on customer satisfaction. Type: "customer satisfaction" + "selling". Are you surprised by the number of queries on this subject? Examine some of the queries related to what customers have said about a specific company's customer service program.

Role-Play Exercise

 An important aspect of personal selling is the need to add value with follow-up and follow-through. Both of these account management activities can be time consuming, especially if the salesperson is not skilled at setting up appointments that fit into a busy schedule. In this role-play, you are to set up three follow-through meetings with a customer who has just purchased convention services from the convention center you represent (see Appendix 3). First, you must contact your client three days from today to confirm the availability of the Revolving Platform Room (see pages 422 and 445) for a meeting of 300 people. Second, you must contact this same client a week from today to get approval on the number of servings of Chicken

Wellington Banquet Style Dinners needed (see page 437 and Guarantees on page 455). And, third, because your client isn't sure about the need for a microphone (see page 449), you need to call your client the day before the meeting (the meeting is scheduled for four weeks from today) to verify whether you or your client will supply a microphone.

Equipped with a calendar, you should establish dates and times when your client will be available to talk or meet with you. Before you meet with your client, plan to recommend at least two times of day that fit into your schedule for each of your meetings. If your client cannot meet at either of these times, ask your client to recommend a time. Do not start out by asking when your client is available because this could conflict with your busy schedule. Write the times and dates in your calendar, suggesting your client do the same, so there will be no misunderstandings. Because these dates are deadlines, suggest that your client call you back if for some reason the schedule changes. Tell your client that you will plan to be at the hotel when the client's meeting starts and that you will be available to make sure everything is properly scheduled. Tell your client to contact you (give your client your phone number and e-mail address) if there are any questions between now and the meeting date.

Reality Selling Video Case Problem—Khalid Naziruddin/ Sewell Auto

Source: Michael Ahearne

The luxury car market is fierce. Sewell Auto, among the largest car dealerships in Texas, sells luxury marquees such as Audi and Lexus and mass brands such as GMC. Sewell has 13 stores selling 14 franchises that are located in 6 cities. Sewell sells to over 36,000 customers annually, supported by 2,400 associates in their sales, finance, service, and support departments. When customers are looking for a new car, they frequently seek out professional leasing agents such as Naziruddin who helps them acquire a product of choice for a fixed period at an agreed price.

Popular with both individual customers and corporations, car leasing is an efficient mechanism that minimizes outright cash requirements while keeping the option to return the vehicle to Sewell Auto either during or at the end of the primary term. Consumers are often attracted by the option to select a new model both during and after the end of lease without fretting over the future value of their car or post warranty repair costs.

While dealing with high-end brand conscious customers of products such as Audi, sales agents at Sewell Auto understand that the stakes are high. Naziruddin and his colleagues closely follw the trends in the luxury car market. They know customers are eager to work with partnership salespeople who understand new product offerings and advanced technologies. Frontline staff such as Khalid Naziruddin are tapping into this shift in the market place, resulting in better margins and newer loyalties.

Sewell Auto's sales agents ensure that they keep the following checklist in order:

- Customers focus on the minutiae, "the 10-second rule" for one.
- Relationship building must be geared to accommodate different personality types—while some customers have already experienced luxury products and lifestyles others may be still be aspiring to experience such life. Communication styles must be cognizant of different customer types.

Questions

15-13 As noted earlier in this chapter, Sewell and their sales representatives, such as Khalid, have been "Obsessed with Service Since 1911." Identify and prioritize those customer service activities listed in this chapter where Khalid can "add value with good follow-through."

15-14 Describe three servicing the sale situations Khalid may find himself in and how he may be responsible for the situation: 1) A Moment of Misery, 2) A Moment of Truth, and 3) A Moment of Magic.

15-15 Provide three examples of how Expansion Selling can provide the customer with a Moment of Magic: 1) full line selling, 2) cross selling, and 3) upselling.

15-16 Describe the procedure Khalid should use in partnering with an unhappy customer.

15-17 Describe Bill Gates's predictions regarding customer service.

Regional Account Management Case Study (refer to Appendix 2)

Your Value Adding Systems Partner

Servicing the Sale

You have taken over a number of accounts of another salesperson, Lee Bizon. Most of these accounts are prospects, which means that they have not yet purchased from NewNet. Two accounts did purchase networks from Lee: Ms. Karen Murray of Murray D'Zines, and Ms. Judith Albright, owner of Piccadilly Studios. You now want to be sure that these sales are well serviced.

Questions

15-18 With whom should you speak, within NewNet, before following through and contacting Karen Murray and Judith Albright? What would you need to discover?

15-19 What will be your follow-up strategy for each of these customers?

15-20 Does the fact that these customers initiated their orders (they were not sold the products, they bought them) influence your follow-up strategy?

15-21 Might other customers or prospects be affected by your service activities? How would this influence your activities? Could customer service be your competitive edge?

15-22 Do you see any expansion selling opportunities with Murray D'Zines and Piccadilly Studios? Which expansion selling methods should you consider?

Partnership Selling: A Role-Play (see Appendix 3, page 419)

Developing a Presentation Strategy—Servicing the Sale

Refer to Sales Memorandum 3 and strategically plan to service the sale with your customer. After closing the sale (getting the customer's signature), there are several steps to add value and build customer confidence and satisfaction. These steps are important to providing total quality customer service and should provide for repeat sales and a list of referred customers.

Follow the instructions in item 2g of your presentation plan. You need to schedule a future appointment to telephone or personally call and confirm the number of people attending the convention and final room and menu needs (see convention center policies). Also, during this conversation, you may suggest beverages for breaks, audiovisual needs, and any other items that can make this an outstanding convention for your customer.

You should have your calendar available to suggest and write down dates and times for this future contact. Any special materials such as a calendar can be placed in the back pocket of your portfolio. You may want to secure another person to be your customer and practice the customer service strategies you have prepared.

At this point, you should be strategically prepared to make the presentation outlined in Sales Memorandum 3 to your customer. Your instructor will provide you with further instructions.

Park Shores Resort and Convention Center.
Source: Courtesy of Beach Resort

PART 5   ROLE-PLAY EXERCISE

Developing a Presentation Strategy

Scenario

This role-play is a continuation of the Part 4 Role-Play Exercise. You recently met with Shannon Fordham, founder and chief executive officer of USA Technologies. The purpose of the first sales call was to begin the relationship-building process and present selected value-added guest services and amenities offered by the Park Shores. You also obtained some information regarding the customer's buying process.

Customer Profile

Prior to starting USA Technologies, Shannon Fordham spent 12 years working in sales and sales management at General Electric Corporation. Working for General Electric (GE), described by *Fortune* magazine as America's most admired company, was a great learning experience. Fordham is trying to apply the GE success formula to USA Technologies. Shannon Fordham is the classic extrovert, a person who combines high sociability and high dominance.

Salesperson Profile

You are new to the field of selling, but you are a quick learner. The first visit with Shannon Fordham went well, and now it is time to prepare for the second sales call. Fordham is planning a large employee recognition banquet, but has not yet selected a location for this event. While working for GE, Fordham had attended more than 25 business conferences and many of these meetings were a big disappointment. Too often, according to Fordham, the meetings were held at look-alike hotels that served bland food. The food was often served by poorly trained waiters who displayed little enthusiasm for their work. Jamie took notes throughout the meeting and will address these concerns during the second sales call.

Product

Park Shores Resort is a full-service hotel and convention center. After completion of a recent $4.8 million renovation, the Park Shores received the "Excellence in Renovation Design" award from the San Diego Architects Association.

Instructions

The first sales call was basically an informative presentation. Near the end of the visit, Shannon Fordham did disclose plans for a large recognition banquet to be held on October 25. This date marks the company's second anniversary. No other information was provided, but Fordham did agree to a second meeting to be held the following week. Based on the information collected during the first call, you are now planning a persuasive presentation that will involve the first three steps of the six-step presentation plan (see Figure 15.1). Upon arrival in Shannon Fordham's office, reestablish the relationship and then initiate the agenda approach (see Chapter 10). Begin the presentation with appropriate survey, probing, and confirmation questions. These questions should be preplanned using information found in Chapter 11. As the need-discovery phase of the presentation progresses, the customer's buying criteria or buying conditions should surface. Prior to the second sales call, you should also select and be prepared to demonstrate appropriate selling tools (proof devices). A variety of selling tools suitable for reproduction can be found in Appendix 3. Also, preplan feature/benefit selling statements that appeal to Shannon Fordham's needs. The importance of selling specific benefits and obtaining customer reactions cannot be overemphasized (see Chapter 11).

A major objective of the second sales call is to move the sale forward by convincing Shannon Fordham that the Park Shores Resort offers an outstanding combination of value-added guest services and amenities, and is prepared to meet the customer's needs. The sale will not be closed during the second call, bur Jamie Julian will try to obtain a commitment to prepare a formal sales proposal that will be presented to Fordham within 48 hours. See page for a sample sales proposal form.

PART 6

Source: Digital Vision/Getty Images

MANAGEMENT OF SELF AND OTHERS

Personal selling requires a great deal of self-discipline and self-direction. Chapter 16 examines the four dimensions of opportunity management. The final chapter examines the fundamentals of sales force management.

Learning Objectives

When you finish reading this chapter, you should be able to

16.1 Discuss the four dimensions of opportunity management

16.2 List and describe time management strategies

16.3 Explain factors that contribute to improved territory management

16.4 Identify and discuss common elements of a records management system

16.5 Discuss stress management practices

Source: Julio Melara

▶ Reality Opportunity Management—Julio Melara, President, Baton Rouge Business Report

Julio Melara (pictured above), born to Honduran immigrant parents, made work the centerpiece of his life at an early age. Throughout high school he cut grass, worked as a busboy, delivered newspapers, and sold newspaper subscriptions. While attending college, he worked as a courier with *New Orleans CityBusiness*, a local business newspaper. By age 23, he was top producer and head of national sales. Later he left the newspaper and went into radio-advertising sales. By age 28, Melara had broken all sales records at radio station WWL and had become the radio's first million-dollar producer. He is a self-motivated person who says that he has learned a great deal from such books as *The Power of Positive Thinking* by Norman Vincent Peale. He is also someone who believes in management of self. Goal setting is the central theme of Melara's sales philosophy (www.juliomelara.com). He believes that written goals (personal and professional) facilitate growth and success.[1]

Today, Julio Melara is sharing his no-nonsense steps for achieving success with audiences throughout America. *Selling Power* magazine has named him one of America's top motivational speakers. He has shared the platform with such distinguished Americans as Secretary of State Colin Powell, Brian Tracy, and numerous business leaders.[2]

A salesperson is much like the individual who owns and operates a business. The successful sales representative, like the successful entrepreneur, depends on good self-management. Both of them must keep their own records, use self-discipline in scheduling their time, and analyze their own performance. ●

Opportunity Management—A Four-Dimensional Process

What makes a salesperson successful? Some people believe the most important factor is hard work. This is only partly true. Some people work hard but do not accomplish much. They lack purpose and direction. This lack of organization results in wasted time and energy. Hard work must be preceded by careful planning. Every moment spent planning, according to some experts in self-management, saves three or four moments in execution.[3]

Wasting time and energy is the key to failure in the age of information. Many salespeople are drowning in information, and the flood of messages each day leaves little time to think and reflect. Sales and sales support personnel, like most other knowledge workers, are working under tighter deadlines. The response time to customer inquiries has been shortened and customers are less tolerant of delays. Thus, prioritizing different sales-force decisions becomes important to managing productivity.[4]

As pressures build, it's easy to overlook opportunities to identify prospects, make sales, and improve service to customers. The ability to perceive opportunities and seize them is an important characteristic of high-achieving salespeople.[5] **Opportunity management** should be viewed as a four-dimensional process consisting of the following components:

1. *Time management.* There are only about 250 business days per year. Within each day, there is only so much time to devote to selling. Selling hours are extremely valuable. When salespeople are asked to evaluate the major challenges they face in their work, "Not enough time" is often rated number one. Dealing with information overload and achieving balance in their lives are also major challenges.
2. *Territory management.* A sales territory is a group of customers and prospective customers assigned to a single salesperson. Every territory is unique. Some territories consist of one or two counties, whereas others encompass several states. The number of accounts within each territory also varies. Today, territory management is becoming less of an art and more of a science.
3. *Records management.* Every salesperson must maintain a certain number of records. These records help to "systematize" data collection and storage. A wise salesperson never relies on memory. Some of the most common records include planning calendars, prospect forms, call reports, summary reports, and expense reports.

Most people who achieve success in selling have a strong work ethic. They are "self-starters" who are committed to achieving their personal and professional goals.

Source: baranq/Shutterstock

Bill Blass Connected with His Customers

The late Bill Blass, American fashion designer, understood the power of personal contact. He also understood that he was working for his customers, not the other way around. Growing up in Fort Wayne, Indiana, during the Depression, he often went to the movies to see Carole Lombard and other stars. He sold his first fashion drawings to New York manufacturers when he was 14. By 17, he had moved to New York and started to build relationships among the city's social elite. Although New York City became his home, he frequently traveled to places like St. Louis, Houston, and Detroit for trunk shows. Bill Blass was one of the first designers to travel with his collections and was generally regarded as the king of the trunk show. He felt it was important to connect with women who were willing to spend $3,500 for a suit. Thus, he built his global reputation one woman at a time.[a]

Source: Richard Drew/AP Images

4. *Stress management.* A certain amount of stress comes with many selling positions. Some salespeople have learned how to take stressful situations in stride. Others allow stress to trigger anger and frustration. Learning to cope with various stressors that surface in the daily life of a salesperson is an important part of the self-management process.

16.2 List and describe time management strategies

Time Management

A salesperson can increase sales volume in two major ways. One is to improve selling effectiveness, and the other is to spend more time in face-to-face selling situations. The latter objective can be achieved best through improved time and territory management.

Improving the management of both time and territory is a high-priority concern in the field of selling. These two closely related functions represent major challenges for salespeople.

Let us first look closely at the area of time management. There is definitely a close relationship between sales volume and the number of customer contacts made by the salesperson. You have to make calls to get results.

Time-Consuming Activities

Some salespeople who have kept careful records of how they spend their time each day are surprised to learn how little is spent in face-to-face selling situations. A national survey of 1,500 salespeople from 13 industries found that, on average, salespeople spend 60 percent of their time on administrative duties or travel.[6] Administrative duties can include such things as completion of sales records and time spent on customer follow-through and follow-up. Salespeople need to carefully examine all of their activities and determine whether too much or too little time is spent in any area. One way to assess time use is to keep a time log. This involves recording, at the end of every hour, the activities in which you were engaged during that time.[7] At the end of the week, add up the number of minutes spent on the various activities and ask yourself, "Is this the best use of my time?"

Once you have tabulated the results of your time log, it should be easy to identify the "time wasters." Pick one or two of the most wasteful areas, and then make plans to correct the problem. Set realistic goals that can be achieved. Keep in mind that wasting time is usually a habit. To manage your time more effectively, you need to form new habits. Changing habits is hard work, but it can be done.[8]

Time Management Methods

Sound time management methods can pave the way to greater sales productivity. The starting point is forming a new attitude toward time conservation. You must view time as a scarce resource not to be wasted.[9] The time-saving strategies presented here are not new, nor are they unique. They are being used by time-conscious people in all walks of life.

DEVELOP A SERIES OF PERSONAL GOALS According to Alan Lakein, author of *How to Get Control of Your Time and Your Life*, the most important aspect of time management is knowing what your goals are. He is referring to all goals—career goals, family goals, and life goals. People who cannot or do not sit down and write out exactly what they want from life lack direction. Brian Tracy, who developed the "Law of Direction," says, "Your ability to set clear, specific goals will do more to guarantee you higher levels of success and achievement than any other single skill or quality."[10]

The goal-setting process requires that you be clear about what you want to accomplish. If your goal is too general or vague, progress toward achieving that goal is difficult to observe. Goals such as "I want to be a success" or "I desire good health" are much too general. The major principles that encompass goal setting are outlined in Table 16.1.

Goals have a great deal of psychological value to people in selling. Sales goals, for example, can serve as a strong motivational force. To illustrate, let us assume that Maria Paulson, sales representative for a cosmetics manufacturer, decides to increase her sales by 15 percent over the previous year. She now has a clear goal to aim for and can begin identifying specific steps to achieve the new goal.

Maria Paulson has established a long-term goal as part of a yearly plan. Some goals require considerable time and should be part of a one-year plan. Next, Maria should set aside an hour or so at the end of each month to decide what she wants to accomplish during the coming month. Weekly planning is also important. Once a week—Friday is a good time—set goals for the next week and develop a plan for reaching them. Finally, Maria should develop a daily plan.[11]

PREPARE A DAILY "TO DO" LIST Sales professionals who complete the time management course offered by Franklin Covey are encouraged to engage in event control. This involves planning and prioritizing events every day.[12] Start each day by thinking about what you want to accomplish. Then write down the activities (Figure 16.1). Putting your thoughts on paper

---

TABLE 16.1 Goal-Setting Principles
The following goal-setting principles give you the power to take control of the present and the future.

1. *Reflect on the things you want to change in your life.* Then prepare written goals that are specific, measurable, and realistic.

2. *Develop a written goal-setting plan that includes the steps necessary to achieve the goal.* Review your plan daily—repetition increases the probability of success.

3. *Modify your environment by changing the stimuli around you.* This may involve finding a mentor or spending less time with persons who are negative.

4. *Monitor your behavior, and reward your progress.* Reinforcement from yourself and/or others is necessary for change.

Source: Based on Personal Development Seminars presented by Barry L. Reece.

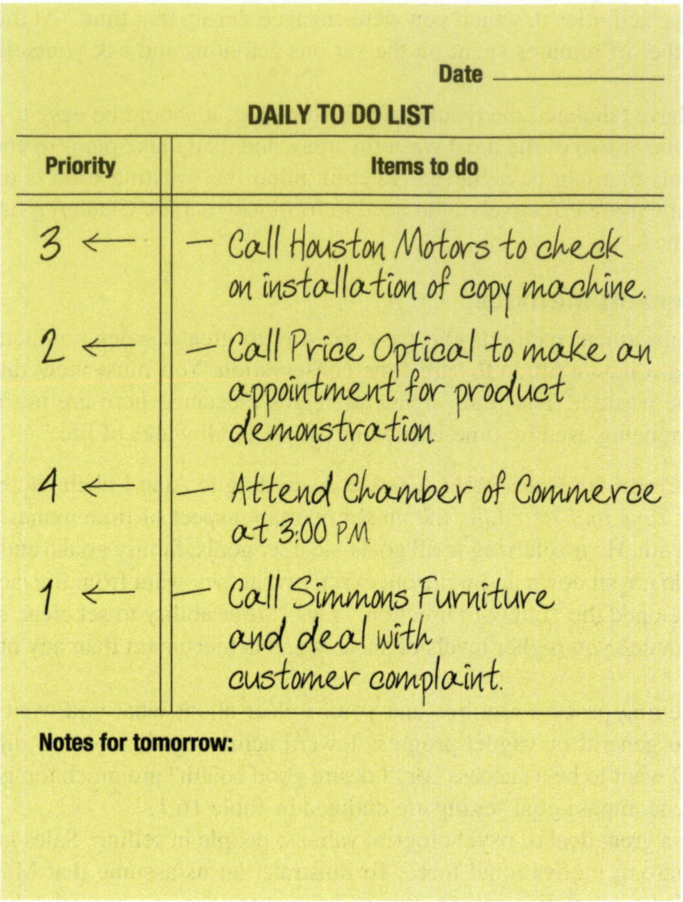

	Date _____
	DAILY TO DO LIST

Priority	Items to do
3 ←	— Call Houston Motors to check on installation of copy machine.
2 ←	— Call Price Optical to make an appointment for product demonstration.
4 ←	— Attend Chamber of Commerce at 3:00 PM
1 ←	— Call Simmons Furniture and deal with customer complaint.

Notes for tomorrow:

FIGURE 16.1

A daily list of activities can help us set priorities and save time. Today, this list is recorded electronically in most CRM systems. The list is one of the first things salespeople see when they access the software each day.

(or in your computer) forces you to clarify your thinking. Heather Gardner, a regional director with the Chicago investment firm William Blair & Company, records her daily planned activities in her BlackBerry and Microsoft Outlook calendar. On a typical day, the BlackBerry will show entries for every half hour. Gardner works through her detailed "to do" list by adhering to one unshakable rule: Avoid nonpaying activities during working hours.[13]

Now you should prioritize your "to do" list and do not let outside distractions interfere with your plan. Begin each day with the highest-priority task.

MAINTAIN A PLANNING CALENDAR Ideally, a salesperson needs a single place to record daily appointments (personal and business), deadlines, and tasks. Unfortunately, many salespeople write daily tasks on any slip of paper they can find—backs of envelopes, three-by-five cards, napkins, or Post-it notes. Hyrum W. Smith, author of *The 10 Natural Laws of Successful Time and Life Management*, calls these pieces of paper "floaters." They just float around until you either follow through on them or lose them. It's a terribly disorganized method for someone who wants to gain greater control of his or her life.[14]

The use of floaters often leads to the loss of critical information, missed appointments, and lack of focus. Select a planning calendar design (the Franklin Covey Day Planner is one option) that can bring efficiency to your daily planning efforts. You should be able to determine at a glance what is coming up in the days and weeks ahead (Figure 16.2).

Many salespeople are using **personal digital assistants** (PDAs) to organize information. Small PDAs available from Apple or BlackBerry offer many of the features common to laptop computers. The salesperson can send and receive e-mails or text messages and download important customer information. Salespeople can also input their customer notes immediately after a sales call. The PDA also serves as an electronic memo pad, calendar, expense log, address book, and more. These organizers can be used to keep track of appointments and serve as a perpetual calendar.

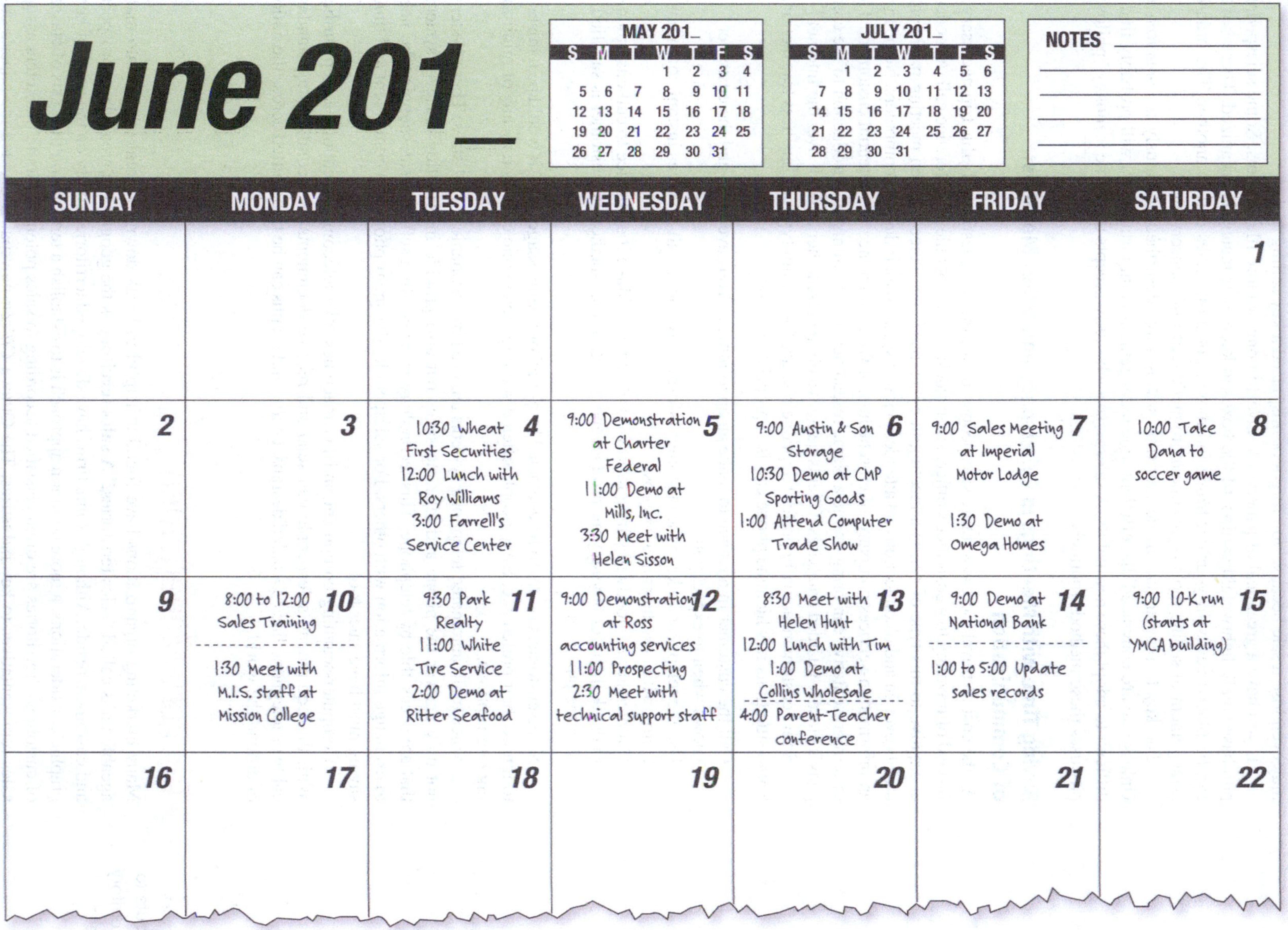

June 201_

SUNDAY	MONDAY	TUESDAY	WEDNESDAY	THURSDAY	FRIDAY	SATURDAY
						1
2	**3**	**4** 10:30 Wheat First Securities 12:00 Lunch with Roy Williams 3:00 Farrell's Service Center	**5** 9:00 Demonstration at Charter Federal 11:00 Demo at Mills, Inc. 3:30 Meet with Helen Sisson	**6** 9:00 Austin & Son Storage 10:30 Demo at CMP Sporting Goods 1:00 Attend Computer Trade Show	**7** 9:00 Sales Meeting at Imperial Motor Lodge 1:30 Demo at Omega Homes	**8** 10:00 Take Dana to soccer game
9 8:00 to 12:00 Sales Training 1:30 Meet with M.I.S. staff at Mission College	**10**	**11** 9:30 Park Realty 11:00 White Tire Service 2:00 Demo at Ritter Seafood	**12** 9:00 Demonstration at Ross accounting services 11:00 Prospecting 2:30 Meet with technical support staff	**13** 8:30 Meet with Helen Hunt 12:00 Lunch with Tim 1:00 Demo at Collins Wholesale 4:00 Parent-Teacher conference	**14** 9:00 Demo at National Bank 1:00 to 5:00 Update sales records	**15** 9:00 10-k run (starts at YMCA building)
16	**17**	**18**	**19**	**20**	**21**	**22**

NOTES

MAY 201_						
S	M	T	W	T	F	S
			1	2	3	4
5	6	7	8	9	10	11
12	13	14	15	16	17	18
19	20	21	22	23	24	25
26	27	28	29	30	31	

JULY 201_						
S	M	T	W	T	F	S
	1	2	3	4	5	6
7	8	9	10	11	12	13
14	15	16	17	18	19	20
21	22	23	24	25	26	27
28	29	30	31			

FIGURE 16.2

Monthly Planning Calendar Sample

Shown are 11 days of a monthly planning calendar for a computer-service sales representative. Monthly planning calendars such as this one are now a key function of most CRM systems.

ORGANIZE YOUR SELLING TOOLS You can save valuable time by finding ways to organize sales literature, business cards, order blanks, samples, and other items needed during a sales call. You may waste time on a callback because some item was not available during your first call. You may even lose a sale because you forgot or misplaced a key selling tool.

If you have a great deal of paperwork, invest in one or more file systems. Some salespeople purchase small, lightweight cardboard file boxes to keep their materials organized. These boxes can be placed easily in your car trunk and moved from one sales call to another. The orderly arrangement of selling tools is just one more method of time conservation.

The key to regular use of the four time-saving tools described previously is *commitment*. Unless you are convinced that efficient time management is important, you will probably find it difficult to adopt these new habits. A salesperson who fully accepts the "time is money" philosophy uses these methods routinely.

Saving Time with Meetings in Cyberspace and Other Methods of Communication

As the cost of travel increases, more salespeople are asking the question, "Is this trip necessary?" Instead of traveling to a customer's office, some salespeople schedule a conference call. A modern alternative to this type of call is a meeting in cyberspace. The voice of each meeting participant travels over an audio connection and attendees view visuals on their desktop computers. Nerac Inc., an information-services company, often schedules a Web conference for potential customers. The sales representative can bring online a Nerac researcher who presents an introduction to the company's closely guarded databases. Clients get to watch the researcher at work over the Internet.[15]

Some customers actually prefer telephone contact for certain types of business transactions. Some situations in which the phone call is appropriate follow:

> Call the customer in advance to make an appointment. You save time, and the customer knows when to expect you.
>
> Use the telephone to keep the customer informed. A phone call provides instant communication with customers at a low cost.
>
> Build customer goodwill with a follow-up phone call. Make it a practice to call customers to thank them for buying your product and to determine whether the customer is satisfied with the purchase.

Some customers prefer to be contacted by e-mail or text messages, and it would be a mistake to ignore their preference. Busy people often discourage telephone calls as a means of minimizing interruptions.

Voice mail–automated telephone systems are used by companies of all sizes. These systems not only answer the phone and take messages but also provide information-retrieval systems that are accessible by telephone. This technology is especially useful for salespeople who need to exchange information with others. For salespeople, the smart phone is a convenient and time-saving must have sales tool.

Computer-scanning equipment and fax machines take telecommunications a step further. With this equipment, salespeople can send and receive documents in seconds, using standard cable or telephone lines. Detailed designs, charts, and graphs can be transmitted across the nation or around the world.

16.3 Explain factors that contribute to improved territory management

Territory Management

Many marketing organizations have found it helpful to break down the total market into manageable units called "sales territories." A **sales territory** is the geographic area where prospects and customers reside. Although some firms have developed territories solely on the basis of geographic considerations, a more common approach is to establish a territory on the basis of classes of customers. Territories are often classified according to sales potential. Some marketers assign sales representatives to key industries. The Ottawa *Citizen* newspaper divided the paper's customer base into major business lines such as real estate and automotive.[16] Regardless of how the sales territory is established, it is essentially a specific number of current and potential accounts that can be called on conveniently and economically. Although uncontrollable by the salesperson, it is acknowledged by managers and researchers as an important factor enabling salespeople to perform well.[17]

What Does Territory Management Involve?

To appreciate fully the many facets of territory management, it is helpful to examine a typical selling situation. Put yourself in the shoes of a salesperson who has just accepted a position with a firm that manufactures a line of high-quality tools. You are responsible for a territory that covers six counties. The territory includes 88 auto supply firms that carry your line of tools. It also includes 38 stores that do not carry your tools. On the basis of this limited information, how would you carry out your selling duties? To answer this question, it is necessary to follow these steps.

STEP 1—CLASSIFY ALL CUSTOMERS Salespeople often divide their territory by area code, by industry, by product, or projected sales volume. Always divide your territory in a way that makes sense.[18] If you classify customers according to potential sales volume, then you must answer two questions: What is the dollar amount of the firm's current purchases? What amount of additional sales might be developed with greater selling effort? Business A may be purchasing $3,000 worth of tools each year, but potential sales for this firm amount to $5,000. Business B currently purchases $2,000 worth of tools a year, and potential sales amount to $2,500. In this example, business A clearly deserves more time than business B.

It is important to realize that a small number of accounts may provide a majority of the sales volume.[19] Many companies get 75 to 80 percent of their sales volume from 20 to 25 percent of their total number of customers. The problem lies in accurately identifying which accounts and prospects fall into the top 20 to 25 percent category. Once this information is available, you can develop customer classification data that can be used to establish the frequency of calls and the level of resources to be allocated to these customers.[20] Jennifer Kline, a pharmaceutical salesperson employed by Schering-Plough's animal care division, gives a high priority to loyal customers.[21]

The typical sales territory is constantly changing, so the realignment of territories from time to time is necessary. A division of AT&T based in Albany, New York, uses MapInfo ProAlign software to realign its sales territories. Accounts are segmented based on industry, size, dollar volume, and complexity. The sales manager enters a variety of account information and then produces maps that show accounts in different configurations.[22]

STEP 2—DEVELOP A ROUTING AND SCHEDULING PLAN Many salespeople have found that travel is one of their most time-consuming, nonselling activities. A great deal of time can also be wasted just waiting to see a customer. The primary objective of a sales routing and scheduling

With the aid of fax machines and computer-scanning equipment, salespeople can send and receive documents in seconds. Hard-copy documents are often needed to move the sales process to a successful outcome.

Source: Andrey Popov/Fotolia

Balancing Career and Family

Women today know that they will probably be working for pay for part or all of their adult lives. Most will also perform multiple roles that can be stressful and tiring. Many women who work full time in sales also assume the responsibilities of wife and mother. Ellyn Foltz, vice president of sales and marketing for Dataline Incorporated, maintains a fully equipped personal computer and Internet hookup at her home. She gets up early and usually spends about 90 minutes on her work while family members are eating breakfast. In the evening, she logs on and completes two or three hours of work after her son is in bed. Foltz has structured her life so that she does not have to make "impossible choices" between work and family. She turned down a high-profile job that would have required constant travel.

Jill Doran, former director of national accounts for National Car Rental, says that her employer gave her the tools and support she needs to maintain balance in her life. She received 10 weeks of maternity leave for each of her children and had the freedom to work from her home part of each week. When at home, Doran checked her voice mail and e-mail frequently to be sure she was responsive to each of her national accounts. She recorded everything in her daytimer to avoid work–family conflicts.

As women struggle to balance career and family choices, many employers are doing more to help. Women, as well as men, who work in sales often have the option of spending part of every week working at home.[b]

plan is to increase actual selling by reducing time spent traveling between accounts and time spent waiting to see customers.

If a salesperson called only on established accounts and spent the same amount of time with each customer, routing and scheduling would not be difficult. In most cases, however, you need to consider other variables. For example, you may be expected to develop new accounts on a regular basis. In this case, you must adjust your schedule to accommodate calls on prospects. Another variable involves customer service. Some salespeople devote considerable time to adjusting warranty claims, solving customer problems, and paying goodwill visits.

There are no precise rules to observe in establishing a sales routing and scheduling plan, but the following guiding principles apply to nearly all selling situations:

1. Obtain or create a map of your territory, and mark the location of current accounts with pins or a marking pen. Each account might be color-coded according to sales potential. This gives you a picture of the entire territory. Many companies are using mapping software to create a territory picture that can be viewed on the computer screen. With the aid of TerrAlign (www.terralign.com) mapping software, salespeople can align sales territories by account size or geography, analyze sales information, generate maps and reports, and produce territory recommendations.[23]

2. If your territory is quite large, consider organizing it into smaller zones. Zip code zones provide one option. You can then plan work in terms of several zones that make up the entire territory.

3. Develop a routing plan for a specific period of time. This might be a one- or two-week period. Once the plan is firm, notify customers by phone, letter, or e-mail of your anticipated arrival time.

4. Develop a schedule that accommodates your customers' needs. Some customers appreciate getting calls on a certain day of the week or at a certain hour of the day. Try to schedule your calls in accordance with their wishes.

5. Think ahead, and establish one or more tentative calls in case you have some extra time. If your sales calls take less time than expected or if there is an unexpected cancellation, you need optional calls to fill in the void.

6. Decide how frequently to call on the basis of sales potential. Give the greatest attention to the most profitable customers. Many salespeople use the 80/20 rule. They spend 80 percent of their time calling on the most productive customers and 20 percent calling on smaller accounts and prospects.[24]

Sales Call Plans

You can use information from the routing and scheduling plan to develop a **sales call plan**. This proposal is a weekly action plan, often initiated by the sales manager. Its primary purpose is to ensure efficient and effective account coverage.

Sales Call Plan

Salesperson_____   For week ending _____

Territory _____   Days worked _____

Planned Calls	**Total Completed Calls**

Number of planned calls _____   Number of calls only _____

Number of planned
presentations _____   Number of presentations _____

Number of planned
telephone calls _____   Number of telephone calls _____

Account Category Planning   Number of orders _____

A. Account calls _____   Total miles traveled _____

B. Account calls _____   A. Account calls _____

C. Account calls _____   B. Account calls _____

C. Account calls _____

Companies called on	Address	Date	Customer rating	Comments about call

FIGURE 16.3

The sales call plan is part of most CRM systems and is sent electronically.

The electronic format most sales managers use is similar to Figure 16.3. One section of the form is used to record planned calls. A parallel section is for completed calls. Additional space is provided for the names of firms called on.

The sales manager usually presents or e-mails the sales call plan to individual members of the sales staff. The plan's success depends on how realistic the goals are in the eyes of the sales staff, how persuasive the sales manager is, and what type of training accompanies the plan's introduction. It is not unusual for members of the sales force to respond with comments such as, "My territory is different," "Do not put me in a procedural straitjacket," or "My territory cannot be organized." The sales manager must not only present the plan in a convincing manner but also provide training that helps each salesperson implement the plan successfully.

Records Management

16.4 Identify and discuss common elements of a records management system

Although some salespeople complain that paperwork is too time consuming and reduces the amount of time available for actual selling, others recognize that accurate, up-to-date records are important. Their work is better organized, and quick accessibility to information often makes it possible to close more sales and improve customer service.[25]

A good computer-generated record-keeping system gives salespeople useful information with which to check their own progress. For instance, an examination of sales call plans at the end of the day provides a review of who was called on and what was accomplished. The company also benefits from complete and accurate records. Reports from the field help management make important decisions. A company with a large sales force operating throughout a wide geographic area relies heavily on information sent to the home office.

Common Records Kept by Salespeople

A good policy is never to require a record that is not absolutely necessary. The only records worth keeping are those that provide positive benefits to the customer, the salesperson, or the personnel who work in sales-supporting areas of the company. Each record should be brief, easy to complete, and free of requests for useless detail. Where possible, the format should provide for the use of check marks as a substitute for written responses. Completing sales record forms should not be a major burden.

What records should you keep? The answer to this question varies depending on the type of selling position. Some of the most common records salespeople keep are described in this section.

CUSTOMER AND PROSPECT FILES Most salespeople find it helpful to keep records of customers and prospects. As noted earlier in the Salesforce.com download exercise, each of the customer files has space for name, address, and phone number. Other information recorded might be the buyer's personal characteristics including their communication style, the names of people who might influence the purchase, or appropriate times to make calls. Most salespeople have replaced card files with computerized record systems.

CALL REPORTS The call report (also called "activity report") is a variation of the sales call plan described earlier in this chapter. It is used to record information about the people you have called on and about what took place. The call report is one of the most basic records used in the field of selling. It provides a summary of what happened during the call and an indication of what future action is required. The call report (daily and weekly) featured in Figure 16.4 is typical of those found in most Customer Relationship Management (CRM) systems and used in the field.

We are seeing less emphasis on call reports that require only numbers (calls made each day, number of proposals written, etc.). Companies that emphasize consultative selling are requesting more personal information on the customer (information that expands the customer profile) and more information on the customer's short- and long-range buying plans.

EXPENSE RECORDS Both your company and the government agencies that monitor business expenses require a record of selling expenses. These usually include such items as meals, lodging, travel, and in some cases entertainment expenses. Several expense-reporting software packages are now available to streamline the expense-reporting process. Automated expense reports save salespeople a great deal of time and allow them to get reimbursed while still on the road.

SALES RECORDS The records used to report sales vary greatly in design. Some companies require daily reports; others, weekly ones. As you would expect, one primary use of the sales report is to analyze salespeople's performance.

GLOBAL BUSINESS INSIGHT

Doing Business in Belgium

Belgium is a country in northwestern Europe on the North Sea. It has long been a strategic crossroads of Europe. The country is culturally divided into Dutch-speaking Flanders to the north of Brussels and French-speaking Wallonia to the south. A small population of German speakers is in the south. Avoid confusing the different languages and cultures. This mistake could come across as insulting. Be sure your business cards are printed in the appropriate language for the area you are visiting. Do not expect one selling strategy to work within its borders given the cultural differences.[c]

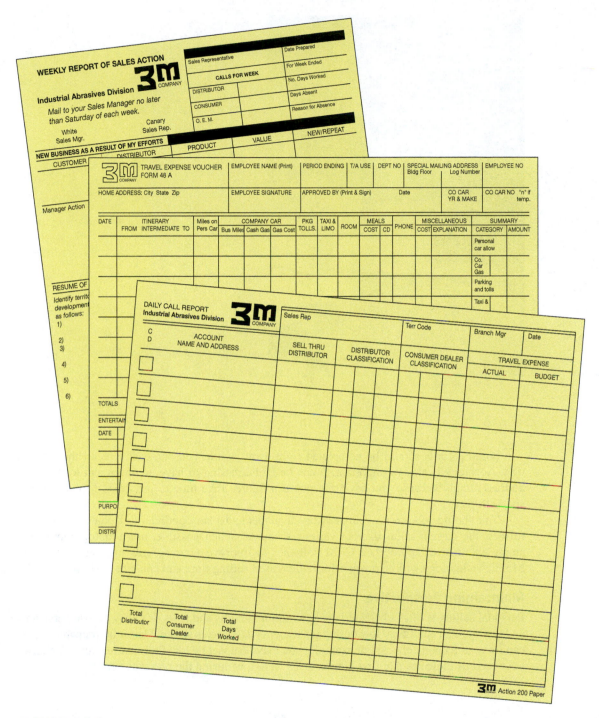

FIGURE 16.4

Call Report, Expense Voucher, and Weekly Sales Report

These are three of the most common records kept by 3M salespeople. Many salespeople process these forms via e-mail.

You can take certain steps to improve a reporting system. Charley Cohon, president of Prime Devices, wanted his salespeople to turn in sales call reports each Monday. However, sales representatives often delayed writing these reports until well after the calls were made. His salespeople were eager to call on prospects, but not eager to write reports. To improve his reporting system, Cohon offered his salespeople a dedicated phone number just to receive and retrieve voice mail. Sales reps could call in their reports, which would be transcribed into their CRM system by a clerk in the office.[26]

Salespeople often use CRM systems to record handwritten notes taken during meetings with the customer.

Source: PhotoAlto/Superstock

Some records should be completed right away, while you can easily recall the information. Accuracy is always important. It can be embarrassing to have an order sent to the wrong address simply because you have transposed a figure. Take time to proofread forms and use a spell checker.

You should reexamine your territory management plan continually. Update it often so it reflects the current status of your various accounts. When possible, use a laptop computer or smart phone with appropriate CRM software to improve your records management system. Mobile technology will help you achieve increased selling time and enhance customer service.

Maintaining Perspective

Personal selling is often characterized by emotional highs and lows. It's easy to lose perspective and drift into an emotional low during what seems like a sales slump. Carefully prepared records can serve as a reality check. For example, you may be upset by low first-quarter sales. A check of your records indicates that first-quarter sales were low during the previous year.[27]

16.5 Discuss stress management practices

Stress Management

Personal selling produces a certain amount of stress. This is due in part to the nonroutine nature of sales work. Each day brings a variety of new experiences, some of which may cause stress. Prospecting, for example, can be threatening to some salespeople. Long hours on the job, the loss of leisure time, and too little time for family members can also be stressful and cause burnout if not coped with properly.[28]

Although "variety is the spice of life," there is a limit to how much diversity one can cope with. One of the keys to success in selling is learning how to bring order to the many facets of the job. We must also be physically and mentally prepared to handle work-related stress.

Stress refers to two simultaneous events: an external stimulus (called a "stressor") and the physical and emotional responses to that stimulus (anxiety, fear, muscle tension, surging heart rate, etc.). Negative, threatening, or worrisome situations accumulated over time can cause depression and burnout, and make us sick.[29] In personal selling, too much negative stress hurts relationships and productivity. Some stress is beneficial because it helps keep us motivated, but too much stress can be unhealthy if left unchecked.

Stress might be caused by trying to figure out ways to meet a sales quota or schedule travel throughout a sales territory. Missed appointments, presentations before large groups, and lack of feedback concerning your performance also can create stress. Ironically, some of the time-saving tools used by salespeople (cell phones, pagers, and e-mail) make it difficult for them to escape the pressures of their job. Many salespeople feel they are "on call" 24 hours a day.

As noted in Chapter 1, information surplus has replaced information scarcity as an important new problem in the age of information. A growing number of knowledge workers report tension with colleagues, loss of job satisfaction, and strained personal relationships as a result of information overload. Too much information also crowds out quiet moments needed to restore balance in our lives.[30]

It is not possible to eliminate stress from your life, but you can adopt stress management strategies that can help you cope with the stress in your life. Four stress management strategies are discussed next.

Develop a Stress-Free Home Office

Many salespeople maintain a home office. With a little effort, it's possible to create a less stressful home office environment. Have a phone or fax that rings only in the office. It's not professional for other family members to answer business calls. If your office is not an appropriate meeting space, meet with clients at their office or at a restaurant. Establish set hours. Try not to let work hours extend into evenings and weekends. Let your neighbors and friends know you keep office hours and cannot be disturbed during "working" hours.[31]

Maintain an Optimistic Outlook

Optimistic thoughts give rise to positive attitudes and effective relationships with customers. According to Martin Seligman, professor of psychology at the University of Pennsylvania and author of *Learned Optimism*, optimists are more likely to view problems as merely temporary setbacks. They focus on their potential success rather than on their failures. Pessimists, in contrast, tend to believe bad events will last a long time and tend to give up more easily when faced with a challenge.[32]

Seligman reminds us that optimism is a learned behavior. For example, you can spend more time visualizing yourself succeeding. If you want to succeed at something, picture yourself doing it successfully. The visualization process needs to be repeated over and over again.[33]

Practice Healthy Emotional Expression

When stress occurs, you may undergo physiological and psychological changes. The heartbeat quickens, the blood pressure rises, and tension builds. To relieve the pressure, you may choose a *fight* or *flight* response. Fighting the problem may mean unleashing an avalanche of harsh words or ignoring the other person. These reactions, of course, are not recommended. This behavior may damage relationships with team members, customers, or customer-support personnel.

Flight is the act of running away from the problem. Instead of facing the issue squarely, you decide to turn your back on it. The flight response is usually not satisfactory; the problem seldom goes away by itself. If you feel stress from an impractical quota, talk to your sales manager and try to get the quota reduced. Don't just give in to the feeling of being overwhelmed. Diminished personal accomplishment can add to further burnout and stress.[34] If you are spending too much time away from family and friends, take a close look at your territory management plan and try to develop a more efficient way to make sales calls. It is not possible to eliminate those elements that cause us stress, but we can find ways to cope with daily stressors. There are stress management activities that can be used during brief pauses in your day (Table 16.2).

Maintain a Healthy Lifestyle

An effective exercise program—jogging, tennis, golf, racquetball, walking, or some other favorite exercise—can "burn off" the harmful chemicals that build up in your bloodstream after a prolonged period of stress. Salespeople at Owens Corning in Toledo, Ohio, formed a sales

TABLE 16.2 Five-Minute Stress Busters

- Take five minutes to identify and challenge unreasonable or distorted ideas that precipitated your stress. Replace them with ideas that are more realistic and positive.
- Take a five-minute stress-release walk outdoors: Contact with nature is especially beneficial.
- Enjoy stress relief with a gentle five-minute neck and shoulder massage.
- Spend five minutes visualizing yourself relaxing at your favorite vacation spot.
- Take a five-minute nap after lunch.
- Spend five minutes listening to a recording featuring your favorite comedian.

Source: From Reece, *Effective Human Relations*, 13E. © 2015 South-Western, a part of Cengage Learning, Inc.

wellness advisory team (SWAT). The team organized a health screening for Owens's 600 salespeople and instituted an incentive program that rewarded those who reached exercise goals.[35] The food you eat can play a critical role in helping you manage stress. Health experts agree that the typical American diet—high in saturated fats, refined sugar, additives, caffeine, and too much sodium—is the wrong menu for coping with stress. Leisure time can also provide you with the opportunity to relax and get rid of work-related stress. Mike McGinnity, director of sales and marketing at the Excelsior Hotel in Little Rock, Arkansas, encourages his salespeople to take full advantage of vacations. He helps them organize their workload so they are able to fully enjoy their vacations.[36]

One additional way to handle stress is to come to work rested and relaxed. One of the most effective strategies for managing the negative aspects of stress is getting enough quality sleep. The number of hours of sleep required for good health varies from person to person, but seven or eight hours seem to be about right for most people. The critical test is whether you feel rested in the morning and prepared to deal with the day's activities.

In many respects, salespeople must possess the same self-discipline as a professional athlete. Sales work can be physically demanding. Lack of proper rest, poor eating habits, excessive drinking, and failure to exercise properly can reduce one's ability to deal with stress and strain.

Increasingly, in the age of information, physical exercise is a very important part of a stress management program. Exercise also helps us maintain peak mental performance.

Source: Monkey Business Images/ Shutterstock

CHAPTER LEARNING ACTIVITIES

Reviewing Key Concepts

Discuss the four dimensions of opportunity management
All salespeople can learn more about their products and improve their selling skills. However, there is no way to expand time. Our only option is to find ways to improve in the four dimensions of opportunity management discussed in this chapter: time management, territory management, records management, and stress management.

List and describe time management strategies
Effective time management methods can pave the way to greater sales productivity. To achieve greater time conservation, salespeople should adopt the following time-saving strategies: develop a series of personal goals; prepare a daily "to do" list; maintain a planning calendar; organize selling tools; and save time with meetings in cyberspace and other methods of communication.

Explain factors that contribute to improved territory management
The first step in territory management is the classification of all customers according to sales volume or some other appropriate criteria. Salespeople normally should spend the most time with accounts that have the greatest sales potential. The second step requires developing a routing and scheduling plan. This plan should reduce time spent traveling between accounts. Salespeople are often guided by a *sales call plan*.

Identify and discuss common elements of a records management system
A good record-keeping system provides many advantages. Accurate, up-to-date records can actually save time because work is better organized. The company also benefits because sales reports provide an important communication link with members of the sales force. Computers are used to develop more efficient record-keeping systems. Common records kept by salespeople include customer and prospect files, call reports, expense records, and sales records.

Discuss stress management practices
There is a certain amount of stress associated with sales work. This is due in part to the nonroutine nature of personal selling. Salespeople must learn to cope with factors that upset their equilibrium. Stress management strategies include developing a stress-free home office, maintaining an optimistic outlook, practicing healthy emotional expression, and maintaining a healthy lifestyle.

Key Terms

Opportunity management, p. 335   Sales territory, p. 340   Stress, p. 346
Personal digital assistants, p. 338   Sales call plan, p. 342

MyMarketingLab
To complete the problems with the ⭐ in your MyLab, go to the EOC Discussion Questions.

Review Questions

⭐ **16-1** Describe how a salesperson is much like the individual who owns and operates a business.

16-2 Opportunity management has been described as a four-dimensional process. Describe each dimension.

16-3 List and briefly describe the four goal-setting principles.

16-4 List four techniques the salesperson should use to make better use of valuable selling time.

16-5 Effective territory management involves two major steps. What are they?

⭐ **16-6** What is a *sales call plan?* Explain how it is used.

16-7 Describe the most common records kept by salespeople.

⭐ **16-8** What is the definition of "stress"? What are some indicators of stress?

16-9 Table 16.2 (on page 348) describes six "five-minute stress busters" to reduce stress. Which of these do you think are most important for persons employed in the sales field? Explain.

Application Exercises

16-10 The key to successful time management lies in thinking and planning ahead. You must become conscious of yourself and decide what you want from your time. You can manage your time only when you have a clear picture of what is going on within and around you. To assess the quality of your working time, it is helpful to keep a careful record for a certain amount of time showing exactly how you have used your day. Over this period of time, write down everything you have done and how long it took. Next, you can appraise your use of time and decide whether or not your time was put to good use. Some pertinent questions you might ask yourself in appraising your use of time are suggested by the following "time analysis questions":

a. What items am I spending too much time on?

b. What items am I spending too little time on?

c. What items offer the most important opportunities for saving time?

d. What am I doing that does not need to be done at all?

e. How can I avoid overusing the time of others?

f. What are some other suggestions?

16-11 Deciding on a goal can be the most crucial decision of your life. It is more damaging not to have a goal than it is not to reach a goal. It is generally agreed that the major cause of failure is the lack of a well-defined direction. A successful life results not from chance but from a succession of successful days. Prepare a list for the following categories:

Career goals
  1.
  2.
  3.
Family goals
  1.
  2.
  3.
Educational goals
  1.
  2.
  3.
Interpersonal relationship goals
  1.
  2.
  3.

16-12 Interview someone you know who uses a planning calendar. What kind is it—computer based, pocket, desk, or some other type? How long has the person been using it? How important is the calendar to daily, weekly, monthly, and yearly planning? Has the person ever considered discontinuing its use? What are the person's suggestions for someone who does not use one? Write your answers.

16-13 Time management is an important part of a successful salesperson's job. Using your search engine, search the Internet for information on time management. Type: "time management" and "selling." Examine the training products and services available on this topic.

Role-Play Exercise

Using the information in the Chapter 15 role-play exercise (see page 327), develop a contact plan regarding the future contacts you set up. Your sales manager has scheduled a status report meeting to go over your activities with this account. With this information and with the information written into your calendar, plan to meet with your sales manager to talk about the account management meetings you have scheduled. Plan to cover how this schedule enhances both your time and territory management and adds value to the sale.

Reality Case Problem—Jose Melara

Julio Melara, introduced at the beginning of this chapter, has achieved success in several different sales and marketing positions in the fields of radio broadcasting and publishing. Today, he is president and co-owner of the *Greater Baton Rouge Business Report* and is one of America's top motivational speakers. He is convinced that success comes to those who have the right attitude and the will to win. Now that he has proved himself in several competitive fields, Melara is ready to share the beliefs and success principles that made a difference in his own career. His success formula is made up of five elements.

Source: Julio Melara

1. You have to believe you can achieve your dreams and desires. He likes to quote a verse from the book of Proverbs that says, "As a man thinketh, so he is." Put another way, "If you believe, you will achieve." Salespeople tend to behave in a way that supports their own ideas of how successful or unsuccessful they will be. Those who have serious doubts about their capabilities tend to reduce their efforts or give up altogether when faced with major challenges.

2. Put all your goals in writing. A written goal, reviewed daily, is much more likely to be achieved. Melara says that a written goal keeps the vision in front of you. Many salespeople avoid setting goals because they do not understand the importance of this self-improvement method. As we make and keep commitments to ourselves, we begin to establish a greater sense of self-confidence and self-control. For many salespeople, goals become an integral part of their plan to break old habits or form new ones.

3. Get all the education and information that you can. Melara is fond of saying, "You'll never earn more unless you learn more." In recent years, most salespeople have had to develop expertise in the area of customer relationship management. Knowledge of the customer's business is not an option if you want to build a strong partnership. Developing expertise in appropriate areas can result in increased self-confidence.

4. Commit to excellence in everything that you do. There is an interconnection among the many areas of work and family. Melara believes that salespeople must fulfill both work and family responsibilities. Many sales and marketing organizations have found that family problems are linked to employee problems such as tardiness, absenteeism, and low productivity. Of course, problems at work often have a negative influence on one's personal life.

5. Protect your enthusiasm. Melara says, "Watch the friends you hang out with, the people you associate with, and the television programs you watch." Enthusiasm for work and work-related activities is often fragile. The negative views of a coworker or a friend can erode our enthusiasm. One of the best defenses against loss of enthusiasm is to maintain positive expectations about the future.

Questions

16-14 Which of these elements can make the most important contribution to a career in personal selling? Explain.

16-15 Reflect on your own approach to accomplishing tasks and select two of Melara's elements you would find easy to adopt. Then select two elements that you would find difficult to adopt. Explain your choices.

16-16 How might goal setting be used in conjunction with time management?

16-17 How might a commitment to excellence improve the processes of territory management and records management?

16-18 Do you agree or disagree that the people you associate with can influence your motivation?

MyMarketingLab

Go to the Assignments section of your MyLab to complete these writing exercises.

16-19 Opportunity management is often described as a four-dimensional process. Discuss opportunity management, its four dimensions, and give a brief explanation of each dimension.

16-20 Many marketing organizations find it helpful to break down the total market into manageable units called "sales territories." What two important activities can a salesperson perform that improves territory management? Briefly describe how each helps improve management of sales territories.

17 Management of the Sales Force

Source: Michael Ahearne

Reality Selling Video Series—Jamie Barouh/McKesson Pharmaceutical

Jamie Barouh (pictured above), district sales manager for McKesson Pharmaceutical (www.mckesson.com), started her career at this largest North American pharmaceutical distributor company as a salesperson calling on retail independent pharmacies. She attributes her success to the training she received from the company and her previous managers. In a highly competitive and ever-changing pharmaceutical industry, continuing training about new products and services is critical. McKesson adopts a multilayer training program. This includes a comprehensive online curriculum covering all products and services the company is offering, hands-on training with current managers, and frequent updates. The company also runs regional and national sales conferences where managers can network with peers and receive updated information. All new recruits also spend two weeks in the corporate distribution center working as an actual distribution staff to familiarize themselves with an extensive line of products.

An avid learner, Jamie Barouh was soon promoted to district sales manager of McKesson's distribution hub in Houston. Working under her supervision are five account managers who are responsible for some $750 million worth of business in Texas and Louisiana. As a sales manager, she makes sure that her subordinates are empowered to fulfill their responsibilities. At the same time, she sets a good example for her subordinates by her strong work ethic. She subscribes to the principle that a good leader should keep regular and open communication with followers without micromanaging. Micromanagement is the enemy of creativity and motivation. She is also actively involved in recruiting and training new staff because she believes that such early involvement in the process will help build a strong sales team. ●

Describe how leadership skills can be applied to sales management

Applying Leadership Skills to Sales Management

If you enter the field of personal selling and experience success, like Jamie Barouh, you may be given the opportunity to manage a sales force. Some salespeople are asked to accept the promotion but decline the offer. They do not want to give up a job they thoroughly enjoy. Many of the salespeople who do rise to management positions become exemplary leaders and advance to positions that offer even greater challenges.

Thanks to the efforts of James Kouzes and Barry Posner, we know a great deal about the practices of exemplary leaders. Many years of research on this topic have been summarized and reported in *The Leadership Challenge*, a best-selling book written by Kouzes and Posner. The book is based on countless interviews and observations conducted around the world.

Lindsay Levin, managing director of Whites Limited, was one of many exceptional leaders cited by the authors of *The Leadership Challenge*. Whites Limited, based in London, is an auto dealership built around three departments—sales, service, and parts. Soon after assuming her new management position, she began searching for answers to one important question: "What do our customers really think of us?" She visualized Whites as a company where every customer would say, "My experience at Whites was amazing." With input from customer focus groups, she was able to identify some areas that needed improvement. She then asked employees to talk about changes they would like to implement and to form small, voluntary teams to work on them.

Lindsay Levin also visualized a company where everyone is treated with respect, and feels involved and valued. She took the position that leaders can never have enough communication with their people. She never hesitated to let the employees know what she was thinking and what she believed. She talked about her values often and listened attentively when employees expressed their views. Levin also recognized employee accomplishments with personal thanks and formal awards.

People who rise to the position of sales manager must understand the difference between leadership and management. Managers who lack certain leadership skills can actually deteriorate salesperson performance.[1] Leadership is the process of inspiring, influencing, and guiding employees to participate in a common effort.[2] Stephen Covey, author of *The Eighth Habit*, says, "Leadership is communicating people's worth and potential so clearly that they come to see it in themselves."[3] Leaders are made, not born. Leadership is a series of skills that can be acquired through study and practice.

Samuel Palmisano, former CEO of IBM, began his career in sales at IBM. After achieving success in sales, he quickly rose through the ranks.

Source: dpa picture alliance archive/ Alamy Stock Photo

Sales management is the process of planning, implementing, and controlling the personal-selling function.[4] The sales manager typically performs such management functions as planning, recruiting, training, budgeting, development of compensation plans, and assessing sales force productivity. Managing the sales force is an external management function, focused on bringing in orders and revenue from outside the company. However, it also requires coordination and cooperation with almost every internal department including marketing, finance, and distribution.[5]

The true essence of sales management has been captured by Lisa Gschwandtner, editorial director of *Selling Power* magazine. She described the sales manager as a leader, coach, mentor, facilitator, goal setter, motivator, number cruncher, and communicator.[6] Figure 17.1 describes the most popular topics covered in training programs designed for sales managers. Needless to say, it's a job that requires many qualities and skills. Today's sales manager is more likely to function in a virtual office environment. Sales force automation permits salespeople to receive data on their laptops or their home computers. The use of other technology—videoconferencing, teleconferencing, e-mail, and voice mail—reduces the need for frequent face-to-face contact with members of the sales team.[7]

Sales managers can have a dramatic influence on the salespeople they supervise. Depending on the leadership qualities adopted, sales managers can have an advantageous, neutral, or even detrimental effect on the performance of sales subordinates.[8]

Effective leadership has been discussed in hundreds of books and articles. A careful review of this material indicates that most successful supervisory management personnel have certain behaviors in common. Two of the most important dimensions of leadership—consideration and structure—have been identified in studies conducted by Ohio State University researchers.[9] By making a matrix out of these two independent dimensions of leadership, the researchers identified four styles of leadership (see Figure 17.2).

Structure

Sales managers who display **structure** clearly define their own duties and those of the sales staff. They assume an active role in directing their subordinates' work. Policies and procedures are

CRITICALLY IMPORTANT AREAS FOR PRIORITIZED SALES TRAINING
MOST IMPORTANT SALES TRAINING TOPICS—IN ORDER OF IMPORTANCE
1. Motivating salespeople
2. Goal setting
3. Providing leadership
4. Orientation and training
5. Assessment and evaluation
6. Territory management
7. Time management
8. Developing sales strategies
9. Recruitment and selection
10. Effective use of CRM software and systemsa
11. Sales forecasting

FIGURE 17.1

Most Popular Topics Covered in Training Programs for Sales Managers

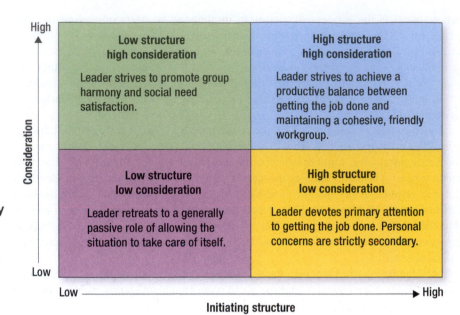

FIGURE 17.2

Basic Leadership Styles From the Ohio State Study

The Leadership Grid is based on two leadership style dimensions: consideration for people and concern for structure.

Source: Based on Edwin A. Fleishman's Ohio State Study.

clearly defined, and subordinates know what is expected of them. Salespeople also know how well they are doing because the structured supervisor evaluates their productivity and provides feedback. Structure is the set of written and unspoken policies, practices, and expectations that surround the job of the salesperson. It can include job descriptions, territory definitions, call reports, and sales process definitions.[10]

The following behaviors provide evidence of structure:

1. *Planning takes place on a regular basis.* The effective sales manager thinks ahead and decides what to do in the future. Strategic planning is the process of determining the company's current position in the market, determining where you want to be and when, and making decisions on how to secure the position you want. Strategic planning gives meaning and direction to the sales force.

2. *Expectations are clearly communicated.* The law of expectations, according to Brian Tracy, states, "Whatever you expect, with confidence, becomes your own self-fulfilling

Besides supervising the sales force, sales managers often are involved in establishing sales quotas, developing long- and short-term forecasts, and seeing that goals are achieved.

Source: Olive/Superstock

prophecy."[11] There is a strong connection between what you expect to accomplish and what you actually achieve. Sales managers must effectively formulate their expectations and then communicate them with conviction to the sales force.

3. *Decisions are made promptly and firmly.* An effective sales manager is willing and able to make decisions in a timely way. An ineffective manager often postpones important decisions, hoping the problem will go away. Of course, most decisions cannot be made until all the facts are available. A good sales manager keeps the lines of communication open and involves salespeople in making the important decisions.

4. *Performance of salespeople is appraised regularly.* All employees want to know "where they stand" with the manager. An effective sales manager provides regular feedback. When a salesperson is not performing up to established standards, the sales manager takes immediate action.

Although structure is an important aspect of sales management, too much structure can create problems. In an effort to become better organized and more systematized, some sales organizations have developed detailed policies and procedures that rob salespeople of time, energy, and creativity. Filling out endless reports and forms, for example, can cause unnecessary frustration and may reduce productivity. Overcontrolling sales managers aren't just annoying; they are also inefficient.[12]

Consideration

A sales manager who displays the dimension of **consideration** is more likely to have relationships with salespeople that are characterized by mutual trust, respect for salespeople's ideas, and consideration for their feelings. A climate of good two-way communication usually exists between the manager and members of the sales team. The following behaviors provide evidence of consideration:

1. *Regular and effective communication receives a high priority.* Whenever possible, the sales manager engages in face-to-face communication with salespeople. They do not rely entirely on e-mail, letters, or sales reports for information sharing but arrange face-to-face meetings. John Morrone, former vice president of sales for Pitney Bowes Management Services (recently rebranded as Novitex Enterprise Solutions), frequently traveled with his salespeople. He says, "My claim to fame is reaching out and touching people."[13] The effective sales manager is a good listener and creates an atmosphere of cooperation and understanding.

2. *Each salesperson is treated as an individual.* The sales manager takes a personal interest in each member of the sales force. No one is treated like a "number." The interest is genuine, not artificial. The effective sales manager does not endanger effectiveness by showing favoritism to anyone.

3. *Good performance is rewarded often.* Positive reinforcement is one of the strongest morale-building factors in the work environment. Ken Blanchard, coauthor of *The One-Minute Manager*, says, "The key to developing people will always be to concentrate on catching them doing something right instead of blaming them for doing something wrong."[14] Recognition for a job well done is always appreciated.

Situational Leadership

Mastery of consideration and structure skills is an important first step toward achieving success in sales management. The next step is to match your leadership style to the various situations that surface among members of your sales force. Paul Hersey is credited with the development of **situational leadership**. This leadership approach is based on the theory that the most successful leadership occurs when the leader's style matches the situation.[15]

Let's assume that a member of your sales team has almost totally abandoned customer service and follow-up activities. She is devoting nearly all of her attention to calls on new customers. Many of her regular customers have complained about poor service, and a crisis situation is developing. At this point, the leadership dimension of *structure* will require the most time and attention. This situation must be corrected immediately.

THE CHARACTER TEST Sales managers who develop consideration and structure skills and the flexibility needed to be a situational leader must pass one additional test. If you fail the character test, you fail as a sales manager. Character is composed of your personal standards of behavior, including your honesty, integrity, and moral strength (also see Chapter 4 on character as an important part of your relationship strategy). It is the major ingredient we seek in our leaders. If you are seen as an honest broker of advice and assistance, as someone who always tells the truth, trust and respect will build. But building trust is a slow process and it can be irreparably destroyed by a single lie or deception.[16]

17.2 List and discuss the qualities of an effective sales manager

Coaching for Peak Performance

Sales managers who develop a leadership style that combines structure and consideration behaviors possess the skills needed to be an effective coach. **Coaching** is an interpersonal process between the sales manager and the salesperson in which the manager helps the salesperson improve performance in a specific area. The coaching process has two primary areas of focus: helping the salesperson recognize the need to improve his or her performance and developing the salesperson's commitment to improve performance.[17]

Coaching is often used to correct a specific performance problem such as ineffective prospecting, poorly developed sales presentations, or failure to create value for the customer. An outline for a coaching strategy involves four steps. Step one in the coaching process involves

---

SELLING IN ACTION

Valuable Advice for Those Who Would Be Leader

Tom Gunter has spent most of his life in sales: Scott Paper, Frito-Lay Canada, Molson Canada, and as vice president of sales for ConAgra Foods in Toronto. Tom had eight directors of sales who reported to him, and each of them was responsible for four to six account managers. Tom has lots of good advice for aspiring sales leaders. The following are some of Tom's comments:

- *Managing change.* When you must change a culture, you have to create stability and put the appropriate structures and processes in place to succeed. The biggest challenge is getting some people to understand the importance of change, and then training them so they can make the change. The ones who can't get to where you want them may have to go elsewhere.

- *Plateaued salespeople.* Every company has a number of people who don't want to move up in the organization, and you need those steady performers as long as they are open to new concepts and ideas. But if they have lost their motivation, you must have an open and honest talk with them about where they fit and let them decide whether they want to stay or not. Some may become remotivated and get excited about helping someone else develop into the company's next senior executive.

- *Sales meetings.* Attendees must be aware of the preparation required and the decisions to be made at the meeting. In addition, the facilitator, timekeeper, and note-taker should be briefed on their roles and responsibilities. If a meeting room is unfamiliar or there are materials to set up, the manager should arrive early to prepare. This ensures that the meeting starts on time, as starting late shows disrespect to the participants.

- *Coaching.* You should involve the salesperson when delivering feedback. You must offer praise where due, but rather than spout criticism, you are better to ask questions that create a dialogue about possible ways to improve the result of what was seen or experienced.

- *Alcohol and drug abuse.* If a salesperson has identified the problem and is seeking help to deal with it, you are required to provide employee assistance to help him or her overcome the problem. If the person fails to acknowledge the problem and continues with the abuse, in spite of your efforts to offer assistance, you should move to termination. It's always advisable to seek legal counsel and involve human resource professionals in these situations as they are delicate and can put your organization in jeopardy if handled poorly.

- *Harassment.* Personalities and outcomes of harassment are very diverse and each situation requires a different course of action. If a salesperson reports harassment, a sales manager must reserve judgment, listen actively, take many notes, and begin an investigative process. The outcome could include third-party counseling, a meeting with the two individuals, a written apology, suspension of duties, or termination.

- *Termination.* Termination should be the last step after all other options are exhausted, but sometimes it is inevitable. If the employee leaves and feels as though he was treated fairly and respectfully, even if he does not agree with the assessment, it reflects well on the company and manager. It will be recognized internally, by other staff, and externally by potential hires. Your organization will be known for its good practices.

- *Final thoughts.* A great employee is focused on his or her own development, whereas a great leader is focused on the development of others. Some final words of wisdom: Be clear and consistent, be honest, maintain a sense of humor, and most important, never ask someone to do something that you wouldn't do yourself.[a]

documentation of performance problems. In some cases, the best approach is to observe and assess performance during actual sales calls. Make note of things the salesperson is neglecting to do. Step two involves getting the salesperson to recognize and agree that there is a need to improve performance in a specific area. Sales managers should never assume the salesperson sees the problem in the same way they do. Step three involves exploring solutions. At this point, it's often best to let the salesperson suggest ways to improve performance. Step four involves getting a commitment from the salesperson to take action. This step may involve development of a contract (written or verbal) that clarifies the coaching goals, approaches, and outcomes. A major goal of coaching meetings is to improve performance while enabling sales managers and salespeople to maintain a relationship based on mutual respect and trust. Most salespeople welcome coaching, even when it involves constructive criticism.[18]

Recruitment and Selection of Salespeople

17.3 Discuss recruitment and selection of salespeople

Careful recruitment and selection of salespeople is very important. This is one of the most difficult tasks sales managers perform because sales organizations have been forced to become more sophisticated. The authors of *How to Hire and Develop Your Next Top Performer: The Five Qualities That Make Salespeople Great* say that about half of the people working in sales should be doing something else. In addition, they say that about 20 to 25 percent of the salespeople currently employed are selling products or services not suited to their personality.[19] If the research reported by these authors is accurate, then it appears that sales managers are frequently hiring the wrong people.

Successful salespeople are often difficult to identify. The selection of sales personnel today is, however, more of a "science" and less of an "art." Sales managers no longer need to rely on "gut feelings." The ability to identify sales aptitude accurately can be acquired. Many progressive sales organizations recognize the need to help sales managers develop the interviewing skills necessary to make profitable hiring decisions. It is impossible to avoid occasionally hiring a poor performer, but sales managers can improve their average by using some established recruitment and selection guidelines.

Determine Actual Job Requirements

To decide what type of applicant is needed, the manager should first outline the duties the person should perform. The sales manager must have a clear picture of the job requirements before beginning the recruitment process.

Ken Blanchard, co author of *The One-Minute Manager*, says the key to developing people is to concentrate on catching them doing something right. Here we see a salesperson receiving recognition.

Source: Digital Vision/Getty Images

Some sales managers make every effort to discover the success factors that contribute to the achievements of their high-performance salespeople. Success factors are the skills, knowledge, abilities, and behaviors considered critical for successful performance. This information may be collected by use of interviews with salespeople or customers, by observing the salesperson during sales calls, or by some other method.

After a careful study of the duties the salesperson should perform and identification of the success factors, a job description should be prepared. A "job description" is an explanation of what the salesperson will do and under what conditions the work will be performed. It is a good idea to spell out in as much detail as possible the abilities and qualities that the applicant needs to be successful. This can be accomplished by answering a few basic questions about the position.

1. Will the person be developing a new sales territory or assuming responsibility for an established territory?
2. Is the product or service well established, or is it new to the marketplace?
3. Will the salesperson work under the sales manager's close supervision or independently?
4. What amount of travel is required? What are the likelihoods of eventual transfer and promotion?

Once the job description is prepared, the foundation has been established to determine the type of person to be hired. There is no substitute for knowing what the job requires.

Search Out Applicants from Several Sources

To identify the best possible person, it is usually best to seek applicants from more than one source. As a rule of thumb, try to interview three or more applicants for each opening. Some suggested sources of new employees follow:

1. *Candidates within the company.* One of the first places to look is within your own company. Is there someone in accounting, engineering, customer service, or some other area who aspires to a sales position? These people have the advantage of being familiar with the company's product offering, policies, operations, and what it takes to please the customer.
2. *College and university students.* Many business firms are turning to college and university campuses to recruit salespeople. As noted in Chapter 1, several colleges and universities have developed personal selling certificate and degree programs. Placement offices are usually cooperative and often publicize openings.
3. *Trade and newspaper advertisements.* A carefully prepared newspaper advertisement often attracts well-qualified job applicants. A well-written ad should describe the job requirements *and* spell out the opportunities. All information should be accurate. The ad should "sell" the position, but it should not exaggerate its benefits.
4. *Employment agencies and listings.* Nearly 2,000 public employment offices are located throughout the United States. These offices recruit applicants and screen them according to your specifications. There is no charge for this service. There are also many private employment recruitment agencies. These firms specialize in matching applicants to the job and usually do some initial screening for employers. A fee is assessed for the services these agencies provide.
5. *Internet.* Many companies are using the Internet to recruit for sales positions. Two popular websites are www.Monster.com and www.JobBankUSA.com.

Select the Best-Qualified Applicant

Once you have identified qualified applicants, the next step is to select the best person. This is becoming more difficult as products become more complex, customers become more sophisticated, and competitors become more aggressive. Selecting the best-qualified applicant is never easy, but there are some qualifications and characteristics that all sales managers should look for. Along with general mental ability, one of the most important qualities is a high level of interest and enthusiasm for the job and high degree of self-motivation.[20] Salespeople have to be self-starters.

Another very important quality is integrity. Dana Telford and Adrian Gostick, authors of *Integrity Works*, say that managers spend about 90 percent of their time on capability-related questions and almost no time on character-based questions. They suggest checking backgrounds and interviewing for character by asking ethics-based questions. Here are a few examples:[21]

> "What are your three core values?"
> "What does integrity mean to you?"
> "Who are your role models and why?"
> "What would your past manager say about you?"
> "Tell me about a time when you were asked to compromise your integrity."

Bruce Diamond, vice president of sales for a large office equipment company, says, "Our salespeople now need to be much more professional, much more educated about the market, customers, products, and business in general."[22] His strategy for finding good salespeople includes discussions of business trends and developments. During the interview, he poses business situations and asks the candidate to come up with solutions. Diamond says he is impressed when a candidate displays an understanding of profitable revenues and finding the right customers to do business with.

Personality and Skills Testing

To increase the quality of new hires, many companies are placing more emphasis on personality and skills testing. The Chally Group has developed the *Chally Talent Audit*, an instrument that can be used to predict performance in a variety of sales positions. The audit provides a skill profile that helps determine strengths and weaknesses in several roles. For example, a candidate may possess the skills needed to develop new accounts, but lack the skills needed for strategic account management. Chally assessment instruments are fully compliant with equal opportunity regulations and are nondiscriminatory.[23]

Western Psychological Services has developed the *Sales Achievement Predictor.* This instrument assesses self-confidence, personal diplomacy, competitiveness, and other qualities that are equally importantly in sales.[24] Caliper Corporation, a testing service with more than 40 years of experience, has developed the *Caliper Profile*, an instrument for personality assessment. Caliper's basic personality profile can be taken online.[25] Online testing has become more popular in recent years. John Wood, former vice president of business development at Chally Group, recommends that firms rely 30 percent on its predictive assessment instruments, 30 percent on a structured interview, 30 percent on references and background checks, and 10 percent on personal reactions to the applicant.[26] Test results always should be used *in conjunction with* information obtained from the interview with the candidate and the findings of reference checks.

Orientation and Training

17.4 Describe effective orientation and training practices

Once you have selected the best-qualified salesperson, two steps should be taken to ensure that this person becomes a productive member of your staff. First, give the new employee a thorough orientation to your business operation. Provide the orientation *before* the person begins working. This should include a review of your company's history, philosophy of doing business, mission statement, business policies, compensation plan, and other important information.

Second, initiate a training program to help the person achieve success. Sales training that is carefully planned and executed can make a major contribution to the performance of every salesperson.[27] Nabisco Corporation developed a two-day professional selling program that helps sales reps plan for and deliver professional presentations. The cost of the training was about $1,000 per enrollee. A careful evaluation of the program indicates that the training resulted in additional sales of more than $122,000 per salesperson and yielded almost $21,000 of additional profit per rep.[28] Study results indicate that salespeople have a more positive view about their job situation, greater commitment, and improved performance when their sales managers clarify their job role, how to execute their tasks, and how their needs can be satisfied with successful job performance.[29] Figure 17.3 provides a framework for developing an effective sales training program.

Even salespeople with great potential are handicapped when the company fails to provide adequate training. Keep in mind that, in the absence of formal training, employees develop their own approaches to performing tasks.

A STRATEGY FOR ESTABLISHING AND CONDUCTING SALES TRAINING PROGRAMS
CONDUCT SALES TRAINING ASSESSMENT
FORMULATE TRAINING OBJECTIVES
DETERMINE SALES TRAINING BUDGETS
DETERMINE WHO WILL DO TRAINING
SET DATES AND LOCATION FOR TRAINING
CONDUCT TRAINING PROGRAMS
EVALUATE RESULTS

FIGURE 17.3

A Framework for Training Salespeople

The size of the firm should not dictate the scope or format of the training program. Even the smallest marketing organization should have a formal sales training program. Online training often reduces training costs. A program should have three dimensions:

1. Knowledge of the product line, company marketing strategies, territory information, and business trends
2. Attitude toward the company, the company's products and services, and the customers to be served
3. Skill in applying personal selling principles and practices—the "doing" part of the sales training program[30]

An important part of the sales training program is foundation-level instruction. This aspect of sales training focuses on the *basics*. If salespeople are to plan and execute a sales call successfully, they must first master certain fundamental selling skills—the skills that form the foundation for everything salespeople do in their careers. The steps that make up the six-step presentation plan (approach, need discovery, presentation, negotiation, close, and servicing the sale) represent fundamental selling skills.

SELLING IN ACTION

Are You Ready for the Sales Interview?

The personal interview is an important part of the selection process when filling sales positions. When companies use a series of interviews, the first one often is used to eliminate unacceptable candidates—those who lack maturity, lack enthusiasm, or display poor appearance. Subsequent interviews are used to match people to job qualifications. At Hewlett-Packard, candidates may have as many as six interviews with various people. At Smith Kline, a team approach is used so candidates do not learn the "right" answers from one interview to the next.

Although interviews vary from one company or interviewer to another, there are some popular questions and requests that you should be prepared to handle:

- Tell me about yourself.
- Describe the sales process as you understand it.

- What books have you read recently on selling or for personal development?
- What is your greatest weakness? Strength?
- What was the most boring job you ever had, and how did you handle it?
- How do you feel about your current (or previous) employer?
- What was the biggest contribution you made to your last employer?
- Sell me this pen (laptop computer, lamp).
- Why should we hire you?

Some employers also ask you to complete a test to demonstrate your written communication skills, or your ability to handle "the numbers." These are both important skills for a sales professional.[b]

Sales Force Motivation

It is helpful to note the difference between internal and external motivation. An **internal motivation** is an intrinsic reward that occurs when a duty or task is performed. If a salesperson enjoys calling on customers and solving their problems, this activity is in itself rewarding, and the salesperson is likely to be self-motivated.[31] Internal motivation is likely to be triggered when sales positions provide an opportunity for achievement and individual growth. **External motivation** is an action taken by another person that involves rewards or other forms of reinforcement that cause the worker to behave in ways to ensure receipt of the award.[32] A cash bonus given to salespeople who achieve a sales goal provides an example of external motivation. Experts on motivation agree that organizations should attempt to provide a mix of external rewards and internal satisfaction.

A basic contention among many sales managers and researchers has been that sales productivity can be improved by staging more elaborate sales contests, giving more expensive recognition awards, having the right number of prize winners, or picking truly exotic meeting locations.[33] This point of view ignores two things we know for sure about the characteristics of motives. First, motives are individualistic. The desire for social standing (status) may be very strong for one salesperson, but not very important to another salesperson. What satisfies one person's needs may not be important to someone else. Second, motives change throughout our lives. What motivates us early in our career may not motivate us later in life.

Because people bring different interests, drives, and values to the workplace, they react differently to attempts at motivation. The owner of an incentive consulting company in Chicago rewarded one of his highly productive employees with an attractive mink coat. She thanked him sincerely, took the coat home, but never wore it. When he asked her why, she explained that she didn't wear fur.[34]

Very often, intrinsic motivators (achievement, challenge, responsibility, advancement, growth, enjoyment of work itself, and involvement) have a longer-term effect on employees' attitudes and behaviors than extrinsic motivators (contests, prizes, quotas, and money). In many cases, sales performance is linked directly to the appreciation the sales manager shows for a job well done. The importance of one-on-one communications cannot be overstated. Everyone likes to be treated as an individual. Taking a personal interest means learning the names of spouses and children, finding out what employees do during their leisure time, and acknowledging birthdays.[35]

Effective Use of External Rewards

Although criticisms of external rewards have a great deal of merit, the fact remains that large numbers of organizations continue to achieve positive results with carefully developed incentive

Sales training that is carefully planned and executed can make a major contribution to the performance of salespeople.

Source: Digital Vision/Photodisc/ Getty Images

Compensating Your Sales Force in China

There has been much written about the importance of *guanxi* (/ gua-nxi), networks of personal connections and relationships, in business transactions in China and countries with Chinese influence such as Hong Kong. In *guanxi* systems, strong social relationships are necessary for building close business relationships and everyday business takes on solid social elements. In *guanxi* systems it is necessary to recognize mutual social obligations. People with this type of culture assume that all social or work-related favors they make will ultimately be repaid.[c]

A famous study of more than a 100 companies operating in foreign countries (either through joint ventures or subsidiaries) has shown that firms operating in Chinese cultures are more likely to include *guanxi* considerations into their sales force management policies than those operating in non-Chinese cultures. In particular, findings show that those firms that recognize the importance of *guanxi* in their business environment are less eager to compensate their sales force merely by commissions. These firms apply systems that rely on salespeople's daily activities and efforts rather than systems which emphasize the amount sold or the number of deals closed as the basis of paying salespeople.[d]

programs. It is possible to design programs that have long-range benefits for both the organization and the individual employee if you follow these guidelines:

1. Design reward programs that focus on several important aspects of the salesperson's job such as developing new accounts, expanding sales of existing accounts, and improving customer service after the sale. Keep contest time frames short so more salespeople have an opportunity to win. However, don't use short-term motivation contests too often and don't use the same incentive plan over and over again.
2. Evaluate your incentive program often to determine what plan has the most impact.[36] Is it cash bonuses? Travel? Merchandise? Bill Grassie, former manager of compensation and business planning for Sprint, likes to use noncash incentives because he believes Sprint salespeople have a solid compensation package. He feels noncash incentives provide a lasting memory, whereas a cash bonus is just one more way to earn money.[37] Of course, a salesperson who is not earning a lot of money in salary and commission might favor a cash incentive.
3. Avoid setting goals that are unrealistic. Some companies are under enormous pressure to meet sales and profit targets. In many cases, sales targets increase while resources decline. A salesperson working for a company in Texas made the President's Club for being 220 percent above quota, and her whole team did well and was recognized as tops in the company. Her boss, the vice president for sales, immediately raised their overall quota by 65 percent for the next year. This was an impossible target and team morale plummeted.

Pressure to reach unrealistic sales goals can produce negative results. Employee loyalty and teamwork erode quickly and, in some cases, so do business ethics. Salespeople who fear loss of their job if they do not meet established targets are more inclined to engage in unethical behavior.[38]

Should sales managers encourage their salespeople to *compete* or encourage them to *cooperate*? This is one of the dilemmas facing managers who want highly motivated salespeople, but they also want members of the sales team to share important information and become resources to each other. One answer is to develop a plan that rewards sales collaboration and the achievement of specific sales goals, whether individual goals, team goals, or both.[39]

17.6 Develop an understanding of selected compensation plans

Compensation Plans

Compensation plans for salespeople combine direct monetary payments (salary and commissions) and indirect monetary payments such as paid vacations, pensions, and insurance plans. Compensation practices vary greatly throughout the field of selling. Furthermore, sales managers are constantly searching for the "perfect" sales force compensation plan.[40] Of course, the perfect plan does not exist. Each plan must be chosen to suit the specific type of selling job, the objectives of the firm's marketing program, and the type of customer served.

As noted in Chapter 1, the highest amount of total compensation is earned by salespeople who are involved in value-added selling. Salespeople who use this approach realize that the solution to the customer's buying problem is more important than price. They are frequently involved in team selling and in some cases they are rewarded with a team compensation plan.

A growing number of companies are abandoning compensation plans that are linked to a single target such as a sales quota. At Siebel Systems, an e-business software provider, 40 percent of each salesperson's incentive compensation is based on the customers' reported satisfaction with service and implementation of the products they have purchased. This plan encourages continuous customer follow-up, which generates repeat business.[41]

In the field of selling, there are five basic compensation plans. Here is a description of each:

- *Straight commission plan.* The only direct monetary compensation comes from sales. No sales, no income. Salespeople under this plan are very conscious of their sales. Lack of job security can be a strong inducement to produce results. However, these people may also concentrate more on immediate sales than on long-term customer development.
- *Commission plan with a draw provision or guaranteed salary.* This plan has about the same impact on salespeople as the straight commission plan. However, it gives them more financial security.
- *Commission with a draw or guaranteed salary plus a bonus.* This plan offers more direct financial security than the first two plans. Therefore, salespeople may adhere more to the company's objectives. The bonus may be based on sales or profits.
- *Fixed salary plus bonus.* Salespeople functioning under this compensation plan tend to be more company centered and to have a fairly high degree of financial security if their salary is competitive. The bonus incentive helps motivate people under this plan.
- *Straight salary.* Salespeople who work under this compensation plan are usually more company centered and have financial security.

According to the *Sales & Marketing Management* research study, most companies participating in the survey used some form of compensation plan that combined base salary and incentive.[42] The salary-plus-bonus and salary-plus-commission plans are both quite popular, while determining the right proportion of these plans depends on many factors.[43]

Strategic Compensation Planning

Many sales managers admit that their current compensation plan does not drive behaviors needed to achieve specific sales objectives. The purpose of strategic compensation planning is to guide salespeople in the right direction. Compensation plans can be designed to achieve a variety of sales objectives:

Specific product movement. Bonus points can be given for the sale of certain items during specified "push" selling periods.

Percentage sales increase. Sales levels can be established with points that are given only when those levels are reached.

Establish new accounts. A block of points can be awarded for opening a new account or for introducing new products through the existing outlets.

Increase sales activity. For each salesperson, points can be awarded based on the number of calls.[44]

There is no easy way to develop an effective compensation plan. There are, however, some important guidelines for your efforts to develop an effective plan. First, be sure that your sales and marketing objectives are defined in detail. The plan should complement these objectives. If sales and marketing objectives are in conflict with the compensation plan, problems surely arise.

Second, the compensation plan should be field-tested before full implementation. Several questions should be answered: Is the new plan easy to administer? How does the proposed plan differ in terms of payout compared with the existing plan?

Third, explain the compensation plan carefully to the sales force. Misunderstanding may generate distrust of the plan. Keep in mind that some salespeople may see change as a threat.

Fourth, change the compensation plan when conditions in the marketplace warrant change. One reason for the poor showing of many plans is that firms fail to revise their plan as the business grows and market conditions change. Review the compensation plan at least annually to ensure that it's aligned with conditions in the marketplace and the company's overall marketing strategy.

17.7 List and discuss criteria for evaluating sales performance

Assessing Sales Force Productivity

As the cost of maintaining a sales force increases, sales managers must give more attention to measuring productivity. The goal is to analyze the profitability of each salesperson's sales volume. This task is complicated because sales territories, customers, and business conditions vary.

The problem of measuring sales force productivity is more complicated than it might appear at first glance. In most cases, sales volume alone does not tell you how much profit or loss you are making on the sales of each member of the sales force. A small manufacturer was losing money until he analyzed the profitability of sales generated by each person. He found that one salesperson created a loss on almost every order. This salesperson was concentrating on a market that had become so competitive that she had to reduce the markup to make sales.

Some sales managers view the frequency of calls as an indicator of success. This information is helpful only when compared with the profit earned on each account. The number of calls made on an account should bear some relationship to the sales and profit potential of that account. In some cases, it is possible to maintain small accounts without making frequent personal calls.

To compare a salesperson's current productivity with the past also can be misleading. Changes in products, prices, competition, and assignments can make comparisons with the past unfair—sometimes to the salesperson, sometimes to the company. It is better to measure cumulative quarterly, semiannual, or annual results in relation to established goals.

Some sales managers use performance evaluation criteria that communicate to the sales force which elements of their jobs are most important and how they are doing in each area. Evaluating salespeople involves defining the bases on which they are to be evaluated, developing performance standards to determine the acceptable level of performance desired on each base, monitoring actual performance, and giving salespeople feedback on their performance.[45] Two of the most common criteria for assessing the productivity of salespeople are **quantitative criteria** and **qualitative criteria**.

> **Quantitative Criteria**
> Sales volume in dollars
> Sales volume compared with previous year's sales
> Sales volume by product or product line
> Number of new accounts opened
> Amount of new account sales
> Net profit on each account
> Number of customer calls
>
> **Qualitative Criteria**
> Attitude
> Product knowledge
> Communication skill
> Personal appearance
> Customer goodwill generated
> Selling skills
> Initiative
> Team collaboration

In most cases, it is best to emphasize assessment criteria that can be expressed in numbers (quantitative). The preceding quantitative items are especially significant when accompanied by target dates. For example, you might assess the number of new accounts opened during a six-month period. Of course, a sales manager should not ignore the other criteria listed here. The other items can affect a salesperson's productivity, and you do have to make judgments in these areas.

Some sales managers ask their salespeople to complete a self-evaluation as part of the overall evaluation process. Many salespeople believe that self-evaluation contributes to their personal development.[46]

CHAPTER LEARNING ACTIVITIES

Reviewing Key Concepts

Describe how leadership skills can be applied to sales management

Many capable salespeople have advanced to the position of *sales manager*. This job involves such diverse duties as recruiting, selecting, training, and supervising salespeople. The sales manager is part of the management team and therefore must be a strong leader. Those who rise to the position of sales manager must understand the difference between leadership and management.

List and discuss the qualities of an effective sales manager

Effective sales managers help members of their sales force feel confident, strong, and capable of fulfilling their duties. Although the qualities of effective leaders are subject to debate, most research tells us that such people display two dimensions: *structure* and *consideration*. Sales managers who develop a leadership style that combines structure and consideration possess the skills needed to be an effective *coach*.

Discuss recruitment and selection of salespeople

Most sales managers are involved directly or indirectly in recruiting and selecting salespeople. This is an important responsibility because mistakes can be costly. A portion of the company's profit picture and the firm's image can be influenced positively or negatively by each member of the sales force. To increase the quality of new hires, many companies are placing more emphasis on personality and skills testing.

Describe effective orientation and training practices

Orientation and training salespeople are almost daily concerns of the sales manager. These duties should always be viewed as an investment in human resources. They help members of the sales force reach their fullest potential. Figure 17.3 provides a comprehensive framework for training salespeople.

Explain effective sales force motivation practices

We discuss the difference between *internal* and *external motivation*. In many cases intrinsic motivators (achievement, challenge, responsibility, involvement, and enjoyment of work itself) have a longer-term effect on employee attitudes and behavior than extrinsic motivators (contests, prizes, and money). Sales managers need to discover the individual differences between salespeople to select the most effective motivation strategies.

Develop an understanding of selected compensation plans

Compensation plans for salespeople combine direct monetary payments (salary and commissions) and indirect monetary payments (e.g., paid vacations, pensions, and insurance plans). Compensation practices vary greatly throughout the field of selling. Strategic compensation planning can be used to guide salespeople in the right direction.

List and discuss criteria for evaluating sales performance

Assessing sales force productivity is a major responsibility of the sales manager. Sales managers use both quantitative and qualitative criteria. In most cases, it is best to emphasize assessment criteria that can be expressed in numbers (quantitative).

Key Terms

Sales management, p. 355	Coaching, p. 358	Quantitative criteria, p. 366
Structure, p. 355	Internal motivation, p. 363	Qualitative criteria, p. 366
Consideration, p. 357	External motivation, p. 363	
Situational leadership, p. 357	Compensation plans, p. 364	

MyMarketingLab

To complete the problems with the ⭐ in your MyLab, go to the EOC Discussion Questions.

Review Questions

17-1 What is the difference between leadership and management?

⭐ **17-2** Are all sales managers' duties the same? Explain.

17-3 What are the two main leadership qualities displayed by most successful sales managers? Define and explain each of these qualities.

17-4 List and describe the four basic steps involved in coaching.

17-5 What is a job description? Explain the importance of job descriptions in selecting salespeople.

17-6 What are four sources of recruiting new salespeople?

⭐ **17-7** What should sales managers look for in selecting new salespeople? Describe at least three important qualities.

17-8 List and describe three guidelines that should be followed when you design a sales motivation program based on external rewards.

⭐ **17-9** List and describe the five basic compensation plans for salespeople.

Application Exercises

17-10 Assume that you are a manager of a wholesale electrical supply business. Sales have increased to a level where you need to hire another salesperson. What sources can you use in recruiting a good professional salesperson? What criteria can you use in selecting the person you hire?

17-11 Carefully analyze the following types of selling positions:
   a. A territory selling position for a national manufacturer that requires the salesperson to provide customer service to a large number of accounts plus open up several new accounts each month
   b. A retail sales position in the cosmetics department of a department store
   c. An automobile salesperson who sells and leases new and used cars
   d. A real estate salesperson who sells residential real estate
   Assuming that each of the preceding positions is full time, identify the type of compensation plan you think is best for each. Supply an explanation for each of your answers.

17-12 Schedule an appointment with two sales managers. Interview each of them, using the following questions as a guide:
   a. What are your functions as a sales manager?
   b. How do the functions of a sales manager differ from those of a salesperson?
   c. What criteria do you use in selecting salespeople?
   d. What kinds of training programs do you have for new salespeople?
   e. What method of compensation do you use for your salespeople?
   f. How do you evaluate the performance of your salespeople?
   g. What personal qualities are important for becoming a sales manager?
   Write the answers to these questions. Summarize the similarities and differences of the sales managers' responses.

17-13 The Internet lists many sources of training in the field of sales management. Using your search engine, type: "sales management" and "training." How many queries did you find? Examine one or more of the training programs and list the topics that are covered. Compare this list of topics with the material presented in this chapter.

Role-Play Exercise

For the purpose of this role-play, assume the role of a sales manager who is currently supervising a sales team made up of 22 salespeople. Your employer manufactures and sells radio equipment for private aircraft. You plan to open a new sales territory in a western state and need a self-motivated salesperson to assume the position. You have identified a person who seems to be a qualified applicant and you have scheduled a meeting to discuss the position. Using information in this chapter, prepare a list of questions you will ask during the role-play. Use these questions to interview another class member who will assume the role of the applicant. After the role-play, review the interview process.

Reality Sales Managment Case Problem— Assessing Productivity

One of the more interesting developments in sales force management is the use of customer feedback to improve the performance of salespeople. These programs go by a variety of names such as "360-degree feedback," "customer-conscious compensation," and "customer satisfaction rewards." Organizations that have adopted this assessment strategy believe salespeople can benefit from feedback collected from the customers they serve. Also, the information collected can be used by the company to improve customer service.

The use of customer-driven evaluation programs is on the increase because of the rising regard for the role of sales at many companies. Tom Mott, a consultant with Hewitt Associates, says, "Salespeople who were volume pushers are now becoming the manager of their company's relationship with the customer." Mott points out that customer feedback is likely to reflect on the performance of the salesperson and the performance of the company. If problems surface in either area, customer dissatisfaction may need attention.

Data collection methodology is not uniform at this point. Some companies use telephone surveys while others use mailed questionnaires. IBM has experimented with a series of in-person meetings that bring together corporate customers, their IBM sales representatives, and the salesperson's boss.

Some salespeople have not welcomed the use of customer evaluations. Maryann Cirenza, senior account executive at Teleport Communications Group (TCG) of New York, said that she felt betrayed when she saw the questionnaire the company was sending to her customers. One of the questions asked was "Does your sales rep know your industry?" Cirenza said, "I thought the company was checking up on me." Later her anger subsided when she learned the survey was not simply a monitoring system but a trial run for a new compensation plan. After field-testing the surveys, TCG used customer feedback to set bonuses. Cirenza was actually rewarded for good customer service by earning a bonus of about 20 percent of her base pay. Greg Buseman, formerly a Chicago-based IBM salesman, believes the shift to compensation through customer feedback has improved personal selling at his company. He now spends more time understanding the customer's business and learning to be a problem solver for his clients.[49]

Questions

17-14 Should the customer be given a major voice in determining how salespeople are performing? Explain.

17-15 Should sales force compensation be linked to customer feedback? What are the advantages and disadvantages of this approach?

17-16 Assume you are a sales manager preparing to develop and implement a customer feedback system. How might you gain support for this system from your salespeople? What data collection method would you use?

17-17 Research indicates that customers rank "understanding of our business" as an important criterion used to evaluate salespeople. Why is this criterion ranked so high?

MyMarketingLab

Go to the Assignments section of your MyLab to complete these writing exercises.

17-18   Effective sales managers help members of their sales force feel confident, strong, and capable of fulfilling their duties. Describe the factors and qualities that contribute to the effective leadership style of these sales managers.

17-19   Assessing sales force productivity is a major responsibility of the sales manager. Why is the problem of assessing productivity and performance more complicated than at first glance? Describe some of the quantitative and qualitative criteria used to assess salespersons.

Appendix 1 REALITY *SELLING TODAY* ROLE PLAYS AND VIDEO SCENARIOS

Table of Contents
Selling Today: Partnering to Create Value—Training Videos

Reality *Selling Today* Role-Play Scenarios

 The 12 role-play scenarios in this appendix are all extensions of the Reality *Selling Today* Videos presented throughout the text. Using the information presented in the chapter opening vignettes, case problems, and videos, and in this section, you will have available the most detailed and realistic setting for selecting, preparing, and presenting a mock role-play.

As you discovered in the videos and related material, these are real salespeople in real selling situations, enjoying successful and rewarding careers in the profession of selling. In these Reality *Selling Today* role-play scenarios, you also assume these same responsibilities by selecting a similar position in the same office as the sales professionals presented in the videos. Just like the evolution of their careers, you will need to learn about your new company, its products, and specifically the customer you will be calling on.

Detailed information is presented in each of the scenarios. Websites are presented to acquire more information about the company, its products, and the industry. Reference is made to reviewing the chapter opening vignettes and corresponding case problems for learning more about your new company and selling responsibility.

The role-plays presented in this appendix are also specifically designed to prepare for professional-selling role-play competition at the annual college and university competitive event conventions (refer to www.coles.kennesaw.edu/ncsc and http://www.deca.org/college -programs/college-competitive-events/ for more information).

The following companies, sales positions, and customer types are presented:

- The Tom James Company, Alex Homer, www.tomjames.com, Custom Clothing—See Chapter 1.
- Independent Owner/Agent, Ryan Guillory, www.twfg.com, Insurance Sales—See Chapter 2.
- Mattress Firm, Edith Botello, www.mattressfirm.com, Mattress Retailing—See Chapter 3.
- CB Richard Ellis, Susana Rosas, www.cbre.com, Commercial, Real Estate Services—See Chapter 4.
- *Texas Monthly*, Amy Vandaveer, www.texasmonthly.com, Advertising and Sales Promotion—See Chapter 6.
- PulteGroup, Ashley Pineda, www.pultegroupinc.com, Home Building—See Chapter 8.
- Salesforce.com, Dave Levitt, www.Salesforce.com, CRM Software—See Chapter 9.
- Hilti Corporation, Alim Hirani, www.hilti.com, Construction Products and Services—See Chapter 10.
- Ecolab, Chris Wylie, www.ecolab.com, Cleaning and Sanitizing Products and Services—See Chapter 12.
- Marriott International, Heather Ramsey, www.marriott.com, Meeting and Convention Services—See Chapter 13.
- Sewell Automotive Company, Khalid Naziruddin, www.sewell.com, Automotive Service and Sales—See Chapter 15.
- McKesson Pharmaceutical, Jamie Barouh, www.mckesson.com, Pharmaceutical Sales—See Chapter 17.

Using the sales information you have learned throughout the book and the sales worksheets presented, prepare to make your sales call.

Reality *Selling Today* Role-Play 1, Tom James Company

Alex Homer
Tom James
Source: Michael Ahearne

(This mock sales call role-play scenario is created exclusively for use with the *Selling Today: Partnering to Create Value* textbook.)

Your Role at Tom James

You will be a sales representative (professional clothier) for the Tom James Company (www.tomjames.com), working out of the same office as Alex Homer, featured in the Chapter 1 opening and Reality *Selling Today* Video. Tom James specializes in offering complete lines of custom, made-to-measure, and ready-made executive apparel. Clients have the opportunity to create a personality for their wardrobe by selecting from the company's more than 500 suit and 250 shirt fabric options. In addition, the company carries an assortment of accessories such as ties, scarves, belts, and shoes to assist in the completion of the client's wardrobe. In business since 1965, Tom James serves more than 300,000 clients through its 107 offices. Each Tom James client purchases directly from one of the company's professional clothiers, who always come to their clients, as appointments are conducted at the client's location of choice. (Refer to the Chapter 1 opening vignette and case problem, and review the Chapter 1 Reality *Selling Today* Video for more information.)

Your Customer: John Leonard

You are calling on John Leonard, a partner at Leonard & Franklin, a small marketing consulting company in Chicago. John, who has been in the consulting business for the last 10 years, has built a reputable name for himself and his company after several years of experience with McKinsey & Company. He is a graduate of the Kellogg School of Management at Northwestern University in Evanston, where he graduated with honors. John has a wife and two kids, ages six and eight. John enjoys outdoor activities near Lake Michigan with his family and is a huge fan of the Chicago Cubs.

You were referred to John by one of his former coworkers at McKinsey by the name of Mike Kerbanian, who is one of your repeat customers. Mike had mentioned John's hobbies, his current professional success, and that he runs a very busy consulting firm.

When you called John on the phone, he was extremely busy, but mildly receptive. He said that because you came well referred he'd be glad to give you 15 minutes, as he does not have a lot of time to sacrifice. John expresses that he is very protective of his personal time with his family and, though interested in refreshing his wardrobe, is reluctant to spend time clothes shopping at local boutiques or department stores. You agree to honor his time and he agrees to the appointment.

Quick Facts about John Leonard's Needs

- In the short phone conversation, John said he is not sure what he might need, but that it has been a while since he last freshened up a suit.
- He wears primarily dark gray, black, and navy—both in solids and stripes. His black solid suit is still in workable condition, though his gray and navy suits have become a little threadbare. He was not sure about the condition of his black and navy pinstripe suits.
- He had mentioned in passing that, for the time being, his off-work attire is in good shape, though he has some older shirts and sweaters that could need replacing.
- John typically wears a combination of shirts and either jeans or slacks to the office on casual Fridays, when he is not with a client. When he is with a client, he prefers to wear dark-colored suits.

Your Call Objectives

You hope to turn John Leonard from a prospect into a first-time customer. This is not an easy job, as John will raise two major objections during the sales call:

- He will perceive your price as being too expensive, and he will ask you for a 20 percent discount for this first-time purchase of the whole bundle that you will offer him.
- He will mention that he once had a suit tailored when he was in Bangkok. And when he received it in the mail a few weeks later, he was disappointed. The suit just did not fit him properly, and the cloth did not feel as comfortable as the swatches. So, he will wonder what his options are if he does not get the quality that he expects.

If his questions are sufficiently answered, he will agree to a sale to try things out.

Reality *Selling Today* Role-Play 2, Independent Owner/Agent

Ryan Guillory
Independent Owner/Agent
Source: Michael Ahearne

(This mock sales call role-play scenario is created exclusively for use with the *Selling Today: Partnering to Create Value* textbook.)

Your Role as an Independent Insurance Owner/Agent

You will be an independent insurance broker for TWFG (see website at www.twfg.com), working in conditions similar to those of Ryan Guillory, featured in Chapter 2 Reality Selling Today Video.

Guillory writes about 75 different personal and commercial lines insurance carriers focused on home, auto, life, and commercial insurance. The Woodlands Financial Group (TWFG) (www.twfg.com), a privately held national firm that works through more than 300 TWFG retail branches and 3,000 independent agents in 38 states across the United States. Guillory's business philosophy is to get his customers the very best coverage available at the best rate available, and to this end he goes over the quote and policies with customers in detail. For Guillory the goal is always to get a commitment which will lead to the sell.

Your Customer: Johnathan Broussard

Johnathan Broussard, 58, is a Houston-based doctor. With a stay-at-home wife, two children, one 17 and the other 23, Broussard has a regular life and accompanying insurance needs. He has a primary home, a lake house that he sometimes rents out to others, four vehicles, a boat, two jet skis and an ATV (four-wheeler).

Johnathan Broussard is among customers who generally trust the insurance agent. While Broussard generally understands insurance needs and what the family needs from insurance firms and agents, you have found him to be a passive buyer at times, especially when it comes to new product offers. Broussard normally does not engage in actively researching the product, unlike some customers who are more independent in using third-party sources to extract maximum value. While such customers open a window of opportunity for agents such as Guillory and you, they also present a challenge—without interaction, the odds of an insurance sale are low.

Quick Facts about Johnathan Broussard's Needs

- The Broussards currently use insurance from Harris Insurance for home insurance and Sasser Insurance for auto insurance.
- Both firms have firmly been with the customer for about half a decade.
- You met Jonathan at a recent wine-tasting session. You learn that the Broussards are probably now looking to shop for new home and auto insurance. You are still not sure whether the family is looking at cross-selling.
- You are keen to engage Johnathan Broussard in an interaction, but before doing so you send the customer an email listing various product offerings. You hope that such action should facilitate more questions, greater simplicity and transparency.

Your Call Objectives

Your key challenge is that even if Johnathan Broussard is open to targeted cross-selling, he is now used to loyalty rewards from both Harris Insurance and Sasser Insurance. Your offer must not only match product expectations but should also create financial incentives for Broussard to switch.

Reality *Selling Today* Role-Play 3, Mattress Firm

Edith Botello
Mattress Firm
Source: Michael Ahearne

(This mock sales call role-play scenario is created exclusively for use with the *Selling Today: Partnering to Create Value* textbook.)

Your Role at Mattress Firm

You will be a sales representative for Mattress Firm (see website at www.mattressfirm.com), working in the same store as Edith Botello, featured in the Chapter 3 opener and Reality *Selling Today* Video. Your company offers sleep solutions, including conventional and specialty mattresses, as well as bedding-related products. Mattress Firm carries the top mattress brands like Sealy, Stearns & Foster, Tempur-Pedic, Simmons, Serta, Sleep to Live, and more. From the very beginning, the company set out to be a different kind of mattress retailer, focused on creating a unique shopping experience.

One aspect that sets Mattress Firm apart from competition is the buying process. Customers are invited to get fitted for a mattress, just as they would do with suits, shoes, and gowns. This is accomplished through the company's Sleep Diagnostic System, which asks customers a series of questions about their sleep quality and then measures their weight distribution and postural alignment. After this is done, it recommends a type of support and eliminates 80 percent of the beds in the showroom, thus making it simpler for customers to find the right mattress without trying out every single bed. Taking the risk out of buying a mattress by letting customers know what mattresses are best for them is something that only the Mattress Firm offers. (Refer to the Chapter 3 opening vignette, and review the end-of-chapter Reality *Selling Today* Video Case for more information.)

Your Customer: Mark Boomershine

Mark and Kelly Boomershine have been married for eight years. They have two kids, Lisa and Marcus, ages three and five. The Boomershines are a typical middle-class family, living in a residential area on the outskirts of Nashville, Tennessee. They have an Airedale Terrier that Kelly loves and that occupies their bed quite frequently. Mark works as a motor mechanic, and Kelly is a nurse at the Nashville General Hospital, where she is primarily on night duty. Mark is into sports, but he has had some severe problems with his back recently due to a slipped disk. He went into the hospital just a week ago and is now recovering at home from the surgery. For the last couple of days, he has been waking up stiff and hurting. Mark and Kelly have had a relatively inexpensive queen-size mattress for the last six years. They were not planning to replace that mattress, but Mark's back problems have forced them to find a supportive mattress for his recovery as soon as possible. Kelly dislikes sleeping on firm mattresses. That is why their current mattress is fairly soft. However, the couple has doubts that a soft mattress would be the ideal solution for Mark, as friends have been telling them that Mark would need a very firm mattress to support his recovery. Today, Mark enters your store to try out some mattresses that would fit his needs. He needs a supportive mattress quite urgently, but wonders whether Kelly and he would actually need two separate mattresses to fit both of their needs.

Your Call Objectives

In your sales call with Mark Boomershine, you hope to build rapport with him, identify his sleeping needs, and sell him a sleeping solution based on these needs. You have to overcome two major objections raised by Mark: (1) What if his back pain persists over a longer time—even on the new mattress that you recommend? Can he simply exchange the mattress at your store for a new one? (2) Since the mattresses that you offer him as possible solutions would mean a fairly high expenditure for the couple, he asks you for a substantial rebate of around 20 percent in case of a purchase. However, the particular mattresses that come into consideration are price-regulated (i.e., the contract with the manufacturer dictates that price negotiation is not allowed). If you manage to overcome these objections and present a good solution, Mark would be ready to buy. Since he needs a supportive mattress urgently, Mark would bring Kelly into your store tomorrow to get her blessings and just make the final choice among the options under consideration.

Reality *Selling Today* Role-Play 4, CB Richard Ellis

Susana Rosas
CB Richard Ellis
Source: Michael Ahearne

(This mock sales call role-play scenario is created exclusively for use with the *Selling Today: Partnering to Create Value* textbook.)

Your Role at CB Richard Ellis

You will be a sales representative for CB Richard Ellis (see website at www.cbre.com), working out of the same office as Susana Rosas, featured in the Chapter 4 Reality *Selling Today* Video. The company offers a variety of premium real estate services, both commercial and industrial. Headquartered in Los Angeles, California, the company has a network of more than 400 branch offices worldwide, with some 30,000 well-trained employees. (Refer to the Chapter 4 opening vignette and case problem, and review the Chapter 4 Reality *Selling Today* Video for more information.)

Your Customer: Norman Flooring Company

You will meet with Kerry Nelson, the owner of Norman Flooring Company. The company was established in 1996, specializing in flooring solutions for both residential and industrial markets in Texas. Despite the slowdown of the U.S. economy, Norman Flooring has been enjoying a healthy annual growth rate in revenue of 10 percent in the last few years. In its headquarters in Houston, Texas, the company has two warehouses that are rented on a short term of six months to a year. Each warehouse also has an office where administrative staff control inventory, deliver flooring materials to subcontractors, and handle other clerical issues. The company realizes that with the current growth rate, it will soon see itself constrained by its somewhat limited warehousing facilities. As a result, it is actively looking for larger industrial properties at locations that are not only easily accessible from highways and ports but also close to major developing residential areas.

The Industrial Property Market

Surprisingly, the U.S. industrial property market has not been strongly influenced by the recent U.S. economic slowdown. The three major industrial property markets include distribution hubs, port facilities, and high-tech centers. Last year, rent growth was greatest in the latter two markets, standing at roughly 3 percent, and the lowest in the former market, at about 0.5 percent. The industrial property market is no exception to the supply and demand rule. Net absorption, defined as the balance between increasing demand and new supply, has been very healthy in markets such as Houston, where availability has been falling. Warehousing represents the largest segment of the industrial property sector. About 25 percent of this warehousing segment was new supply. The industrial market outlook is optimistic, with rent growth expected to remain positive over the next few years.

Quick Facts about Norman Flooring Company's Needs

- The company is looking for industrial warehousing facilities that are in very good condition, with little to no deferred maintenance. The area should be at least 16,000 square feet.
- The location should be easily accessible from the Houston port, in an area that is known to be free from flooding risks.
- The initial lease term will be one year, with the possibility of rent-to-own.

- Preferably, the property site should offer available space for expansion.
- The office building is preferably attached to the warehouse.
- The property should have digital surveillance and perimeter fencing with computer-controlled keypad entry access.

Your Call Objectives

In your meeting with Kerry Nelson, you hope to identify the company's warehousing needs. In addition, you hope to convince Kerry that your company can offer outstanding value-added services, such as nationwide property maintenance consulting.

Reality *Selling Today* Role-Play 5, *Texas Monthly*

Amy Vandaveer
Texas Monthly
Source: Michael Ahearne

(This mock sales call role-play scenario is created exclusively for use with the *Selling Today: Partnering to Create Value* textbook.)

Your Role at *Texas Monthly*

You are a sales representative for *Texas Monthly* magazine (see website at www.texasmonthly.com), working out of the same office as Amy Vandaveer featured in the Chapter 6 Reality *Selling Today* Video. Your magazine covers politics, business, and culture, but focuses largely on leisure activities and events in Texas; it has a large real estate advertising section, as well as classified sections in which nearly all advertisers are Texas-based businesses appealing to a prospective buyer who is interested in connecting with Texas history and culture. Through you, your potential customers have access to a large, loyal reader base all over Texas, mostly urban, well educated, and affluent. (Refer to the Chapter 6 opening vignette and case problem, and review the Chapter 6 Reality *Selling Today* Video for more information.)

Your Customer: Roger Linville Properties

You will meet with Kim Pratt, the marketing director at Roger Linville Properties, a property management company. Kim was referred to you by a family friend, who told you that, although Roger Linville Properties has reached most of its residents through simple word-of-mouth publicity, they are now considering increasing their magazine advertising. According to your friend, who met Kim through their daughters' Girl Scout troop, Kim's career began at an advertising agency specializing in real estate, and then moved to the client side. In all, Kim has 15 years of experience in the marketing of high-end real estate.

Roger Linville Properties started selling units in its first condo building in 1987 and now has 12 upscale high-rise condo buildings in Houston and Galveston. Each property has a sales manager and a marketing manager, and the individual properties do some advertising controlled by those managers, but Kim is ultimately in control of the company's marketing and advertising strategy.

Your supervisor at *Texas Monthly* has some connections to Roger Linville Properties, and he was able to tell you more about their current advertising situation. According to him, Roger Linville Properties does the majority of its advertising in magazines available for free in the Houston area. You've seen these glossy magazines in the waiting areas of restaurants and hotels; they cater to an affluent readership with society pages, event news, and ads for upscale products and services. The company also uses some billboards, and individual properties use direct mail and well-publicized open houses to attract prospective residents.

The majority of the Roger Linville buildings are within the city of Houston. You've learned from their website that there are several buildings in the Galleria area, surrounded by luxury shopping and restaurants, and one near the Rice Village shopping arcade in West University. They also have buildings in the downtown theater district, which has recently become an increasingly popular location for luxury lofts and condos. In Galveston, they have one building in the historic Strand area and several resort-like condos on the beachfront. Judging by the prices and the amenities they offer, such as concierge service and in-building spas, you can tell that their prime market is affluent people looking for a low-maintenance home that they will rarely have to leave. Most of the properties are advertised as second homes, particularly the Galveston condos, which are promoted as the perfect local vacation home.

While on the website, you noticed that the company is currently in the process of building two new properties: one in the River Oaks area, Houston's most exclusive residential neighborhood, and one in the Woodlands, an affluent master-planned community north of Houston. They will begin preselling units in these two properties in the next few months. In addition, your supervisor has heard rumors recently that Roger Linville has been negotiating to acquire land in the Dallas area, suggesting that they may be planning expansion there as well.

Your Call Objectives

In your meeting, you hope to convince Kim Pratt that magazine advertising can be more successful than it has been so far, and that *Texas Monthly* is the magazine to use. Hopefully, you will close a deal by the end of the meeting.

Reality *Selling Today* Role-Play 6, PulteGroup

Ashley Pineda
PulteGroup
Source: Michael Ahearne

(This mock sales call role-play scenario is created exclusively for use with the *Selling Today: Partnering to Create Value* textbook.)

Your Role at PulteGroup

You will be a sales representative for PulteGroup (www.pulte-groupinc.com), working in a similar community as Ashley Pineda, featured in the Chapter 8 Reality *Selling Today* Video Case. PulteGroup offers a one-stop shopping experience for prospective customers. Sales reps help clients to finance their homes (with Pulte Mortgage) and to close their homes with PGP Title. Being able to offer everything under one roof and walk the customers through each step of the entire home-buying process makes their home-buying experience very comfortable. PulteGroup offers different product lines: homes for first-time homebuyers, move-up homes, and active adult communities. Just like Ashley Pineda, you will sell the company's Centex product line (see www.centex.com), which is primarily geared towards first-time homebuyers. One central purpose of your sales presentations is to educate your prospects on renting versus owning and the benefits of owning a home. You also give prospects information about the neighborhood, the area, the schools zoned to the neighborhood, and the amenities of the community, describing the pools and the shopping areas in and around the neighborhood in order to help your customers envision raising their children in one of Pulte's communities. (Refer to the Chapter 8 opening vignette and case problem, and review the Chapter 8 Reality *Selling Today* Video for more information.)

Your Customer: Mary Bartone

Mary Bartone is 37 years old. She is a single mother and has two little children, Laura and Fred, ages four and two. Mary had been married to Tom Bartone for almost seven years. The first years of their marriage were happy ones. The Bartones lived in a nice, large apartment in Chicago's Uptown neighborhood. They really enjoyed living in this trendy and vibrant part of the city. Both Mary and Tom liked going out to restaurants, cafes, and bars together with their friends, many of whom also lived in or close to the Uptown area. In their leisure time, Mary and Tom enjoyed horse riding and going to all kinds of cultural events. Money was never a big issue, since Tom made good money as a design engineer for Honeywell Building Solutions, and Mary earned a decent salary as a senior contact representative for the U.S. Social Security Administration. After some years, however, things started to become worse in their relationship, and about one year ago Tom and Mary eventually decided to split up. They went through a painful divorce. After a tedious court battle, custody of the two children was awarded to Mary, with Tom seeing his children every other weekend.

For almost a year now, Mary and her two children have been living in a 790-square-foot, two-bedroom apartment close to the Uptown area, just about three miles away from their old apartment, where Tom still lives. Mary feels that the apartment is just too small and that the area is not really perfect to raise children. Knowing that the apartment would be only an interim solution, Mary has been dreaming about a new home for quite a while now.

Quick Facts about Mary Bartone's Needs

- Mary is looking for a house with at least 1,200 square feet and three bedrooms.
- Like all parents with young children, Mary is very concerned about her children growing up in a safe and sheltered environment with decent daycare facilities and schools in the neighborhood.
- As a single mother who wants to raise her children in the new home, Mary is very much interested in the warranties that PulteGroup can offer as a builder.

- Mary pays great attention to the warmth and feel of a home and having a large backyard for the children.
- Mary has bank savings of approximately $60,000. Her annual income (including some alimony) is currently around $55,000. Therefore, a solid financing solution that is comfortable with her budget is needed.
- Mary is a true family person. Her parents and her younger sister Susan, who live in Indianapolis, come to visit her in Chicago quite frequently. Before signing a contract for a new home, she would always make sure to have her father's blessings for that.
- Mary is of two minds concerning the location of the house. On the one hand, she knows that having more square footage, a large backyard, and so forth would require her to move further out of the city. On the other hand, she does not want to move too far away from the Uptown area of Chicago where her office is located, and where Tom and many of her friends still live.

Your Call Objectives

In your meeting with Mary, you hope to build rapport with her and identify her needs and requirements for owning a home. You also hope to convince Mary that you can offer her an excellent home in which to raise her children.

Reality *Selling Today* Role-Play 7, Salesforce.com

Dave Levitt
Salesforce.com
Source: Michael Ahearne

(This mock sales call role-play scenario is created exclusively for use with the *Selling Today: Partnering to Create Value* textbook.)

Your Role at Salesforce.com

You are a sales representative for Salesforce.com (see website at www.Salesforce.com), just like Dave Levitt in the Chapter 9 Reality *Selling Today* Video. Your company is the world leader in on-demand customer relationship management (CRM) services. Unlike most CRM applications, companies who use your services store customer and sales data on Salesforce.com. One of the benefits of on-demand CRM services is that customers neither incur upfront capital investment nor on-site administration. Your company also offers solutions that are customized to specific customer needs, such as creating different interfaces for different departments and work groups, and providing limited access to data for specific, authorized work groups. (Refer to the Chapter 9 opening vignette and case problem, and review the Chapter 9 Reality *Selling Today* Video for more information.)

Your Customer: Rename Clothing Company

You will meet with Jesse Golden, the marketing director at Rename Clothing Company. A family-owned business in Garden Grove, California, the company is expanding at a fast pace not only in the United States, but also in Latin American markets that the company entered into two years ago. The company currently has a sales force of 20 people, and outsources its selling activities for overseas operations to local firms. Each salesperson is responsible for three to four customers. Although outsourcing has the advantage of capitalizing on market knowledge of local partners, the company realizes that it does not have full control over its selling efforts. Domestically, the company has strong relationships with its buyers, but there have been signs of work overload among the sales force. While Rename has three in-house brands that it distributes using its own channel, it does provide sourcing solutions to mid- and high-end department stores under their private labels. Rename works closely with its suppliers in more than five countries, mainly in Europe and Asia. It also has a small manufacturing facility in California for sample development and small-batch order production.

Quick Facts about Rename Clothing Company's Needs

The apparel industry is a sophisticated, fast-moving industry with several designs launched every season, and repeat orders must be met as fast as possible before end-users change their tastes. As a company that operates in middle- to high-end markets, Rename positions itself as a sourcing company with a fast turnaround for its customers. The nature of the industry requires salespeople to be highly diligent in market-information gathering, processing, and dissemination across geographic areas and departments.

At present, the in-house salespeople use spreadsheets for almost all of their selling activities such as recording sales calls, reporting to sales managers, and tracking delivery of orders, to name just a few. Jesse joined the company two months ago and realized the current system showed clear signs of overload. Mistakes have started to occur more often, and the company has received quite a few complaints about shipment delays, wrong labeling on products, and wrong packaging. As marketing director, Jesse spent several days making sense of disparate information about Rename's domestic sales and has mixed reports about its overseas operation. Jesse's secretary lamented that the spreadsheets provided by the sales force are not in a uniform format, making it difficult to consolidate the database. Meanwhile, salespeople claim that their customers are not the same, and they need to customize their spreadsheets so that they can keep track of things more easily.

With high pressure for growth, Rename is looking for an efficient way to consolidate and manage its customer database. Jesse is also in the process of establishing a branch office in Mexico and will staff three local salespeople to manage Rename's business in this growing market. In overseas markets, the focus is more on customer acquisition and lead management, while in domestic markets, Jesse is more concerned with keeping Rename's existing customers happy.

Your Call Objectives

In your meeting with Jesse Golden, you hope to convince him that Salesforce.com is the right CRM solution for Rename. You can do this by providing him with interesting facts and benefits Salesforce.com can offer (see more information at www.Salesforce.com). Hopefully, you will close a deal by the end of the meeting.

Reality *Selling Today* Role-Play 8, Hilti Corporation

Alim Hirani
Hilti Corporation
Source: Michael Ahearne

(This mock sales call role-play scenario is created exclusively for use with the *Selling Today: Partnering to Create Value* textbook.)

Your Role at Hilti Corporation

You will be a sales representative for Hilti (see website at www.hilti.com), working out of the same office as Alim Hirani, featured in the Chapter 10 Reality *Selling Today* Video. The company provides the global construction industry with innovative products and services. In addition to a wide variety of high-end products such as measuring systems, drilling and demolition, installation systems, foam systems, and screw-fastening systems, the company also offers its customers customized training programs and consulting services. Hilti sales representatives work directly with customers rather than through intermediary parties. (Refer to the Chapter 10 opening vignette and case problem, and review the Chapter 10 Reality *Selling Today* Video for more information.)

Your Customer: Ellis Exhibition Inc.

You will meet with Casey Smith, procurement manager for Ellis Exhibition Inc. The company owns a 100,000-square-foot exhibition center that hosts several local and regional events in Atlanta, Georgia. Some of these events have become a must-see for the local business community. Depending on the theme and the products being showcased, Ellis Exhibition offers exhibitors outstanding display services that include floor plans, display solutions, display installation, and booth dismantlement. After an event, the installation systems are reused, while installation accessories are generally discarded. Casey Smith believes that by buying the right type of installation accessories, Ellis can save a lot of money, and therefore offer their exhibitor customers more competitive prices.

Quick Facts about the Ellis Exhibition Inc.'s Needs

- Ellis Exhibition Inc. spends about $500,000 a year on installation accessories. These accessories are galvanized, but they can also be painted to match the color theme stipulated by exhibitors.
- Ellis uses a wide variety of installation accessories, from hexagon nuts and head screws to distance holders.
- Ellis does not want to stock these accessories. Exhibitors who want to use Ellis display services are required to place their order three months in advance. Then, an Ellis accountant will calculate the necessary accessories needed for each event.
- Ellis is extremely concerned with the quality of all of its installation systems and accessories.

Your Call Objectives

In your meeting with Casey Smith, you hope to identify the specific types and the expected quantity of installation accessories. You also want to know about delivery requirements. In addition, you might be able to cross-sell other Hilti products and services, such as sprinkler systems.

Reality *Selling Today* Role-Play 9, Ecolab

Chris Wylie
Ecolab
Source: Michael Ahearne

(This mock sales call role-play scenario is created exclusively for use with the *Selling Today: Partnering to Create Value* textbook.)

Your Role at Ecolab

You are a sales representative for Ecolab (see website at www.ecolab.com), working in a territory similar to that of Chris Wylie who is featured in the Chapter 12 Reality *Selling Today* Video. With sales of $6 billion and more than 26,000 associates, your company is the global leader in cleaning, sanitizing, food safety, and infection prevention products and services. Ecolab delivers comprehensive programs and services to food service, food and beverage processing, health care, and hospitality markets in more than 160 countries. You work in the institutional business unit, which is the core of Ecolab—and the world leader in providing cleaning and sanitation products, programs, and services to customers in a variety of industries. Specifically, you serve the food service market, calling on restaurants, cafeterias, and so forth. Today, you will try to get access to the kitchen facilities of one of the largest prospects in your territory, Angelo's Restaurant. (Refer to the Chapter 12 opening vignette and case problem, and review the Chapter 12 Reality *Selling Today* Video for more information.)

Your Customer: Francesco Manchini, Owner of Angelo's Restaurant

The owner of the restaurant is Francesco Manchini (known as "Frankie" by his restaurant friends and patrons). Angelo's is located north of Downtown Seattle in the Fremont neighborhood, a trendy bohemian district. Manchini had a great deal of insight in the potential in the Fremont neighborhood and actually has three restaurants located within a three-block radius. The other two restaurants located here are Pasta e Basta and LaTorre. Based on some initial inspection and speculation, you can assume that each of these three restaurants could possibly purchase $10,000 worth of your product. Angelo's currently uses Swisher, a North American competitor. Swisher was started back in 1986 with the conviction that businesspeople would welcome the opportunity to have their facilities maintained by a true hygiene specialist. You are familiar with the competition and are aware of Swisher's strategy. Typically they gain the bathroom hygiene business and then grow and look for opportunities in the back of the house. This is exactly what happened here. Francesco Manchini has three primary concerns that reflect his problems with Swisher. First, product performance is not to his standards. The Swisher Program is not getting the dishes clean, and spotty dishes are unacceptable for fine dining. Second, the people at Swisher know a lot about bathroom care and maintenance, but they lack a great deal of experience and knowledge about back-of-the-house operations. Third, product service is lacking. Swisher was always front-and-center when they were trying to get the business, but now never show up and seldom return service calls in a timely manner.

Francesco has an expressive personality style. He is talkative and very low on self-monitoring. He is a very emotional person and quick to get red-faced when someone angers him or to slap them on the back when they please him. He never leaves a conversation without getting in the last word and saying whatever he feels. He is quick to tell someone that they are wrong, particularly salespeople, if he thinks they are giving him a load of garbage. Francesco realizes that the bathroom hygiene part of Swisher is good, but the decision to move them into the back of the house may not have been such a great idea. He is quick to tell everyone within earshot why he is unhappy with Swisher. Even though there are some problems, he is not sure what the solution is.

You have a 9:30 A.M. meeting scheduled and realize that you probably have about 20 minutes before the lunch push begins.

Quick Facts about Francesco Manchini's Needs

Thanks to the approval of Francesco's executive chef, Nino Trappatoni, you have already completed a survey of the kitchen prior to your initial meeting with Francesco Manchini. You uncovered several areas of concern and issues that can be leveraged as opportunities. These may be latent and the prospect didn't realize that there are problems or potential problems.

- Floors are covered in grease by the fryer. Floors are slippery, and there are no mats or protective coverings down.
- Limited drying racks. Dishes are stacked on each other, including glasses.
- Poor results: Food soil left on dishes was found by doing a Mikroklene test.
- Some dishes on racks are spotty and covered with soap residue.
- There are no safety devices or equipment such as eyewash stations and first-aid.
- No product dispensers are in place. It looks as if everything is being poured or used in a sprayer bottle.

Your Call Objectives

Since this is your first meeting with Francesco Manchini, you have to introduce yourself and Ecolab to him and try to build rapport. Based on the survey of the kitchen, you then try to convince Francesco to buy from you. To that end, you will have to overcome the following objections:

- We used Ecolab at one of our other properties a few years back. The service was terrible.
- I am sure that if I sign up with Ecolab, you will forget about me once I commit to the change. What guarantees do I have with you that you will be there when I need you?
- I heard that Ecolab uses more soap than necessary to inflate their sales and rip off the customer.
- We cannot afford downtime. I am sure that switching over to Ecolab would put the kitchen out of commission for too long. We can't afford to shut our kitchen down to make the change to Ecolab.

Reality *Selling Today* Role-Play 10, Marriott International Inc.

Heather Ramsey
Marriott International Inc.
Source: Michael Ahearne

(This mock sales call role-play scenario is created exclusively for use with the *Selling Today: Partnering to Create Value* textbook.)

Your Role at Marriott

You will be a sales representative for Marriott International Inc. (www.marriott.com), working out of the same hotel as Heather Ramsey, featured in the Chapter 13 Reality *Selling Today* Video. Founded in 1927 by J. Willard and Alice S. Marriott, Marriott has grown from a root beer stand to a multinational company with more than 3,000 lodging properties located in some 70 countries around the world. Apart from luxurious hotel accommodations under several well-managed brands, the company also offers outstanding services for meetings and events. From weddings to corporate meetings, Marriott's clients know that they are always in good hands. (Refer to the Chapter 13 opening vignette and case problem, and review the Chapter 13 Reality *Selling Today* Video for more information.)

Your Customer: Hiroshi Watanabe/Chris Scott

You will meet with Chris Scott, personal secretary to Mr. Hiroshi Watanabe, the owner of high-end tailor chain stores in California. Mr. Watanabe got married 25 years ago in a simple wedding ceremony. The couple immigrated to the United States with only $5 in their pocket. The young couple worked very hard to make ends meet, and their fate took a turn when both were hired full time for the first time by a small tailor shop, Mr. Watanabe as a deliveryman and his wife as a helper.

With strong entrepreneurial spirit and incessant learning, they soon opened their own business using their own meager savings. Initial clients were mainly friends, but they soon found a niche in the market by combining traditional Japanese garment making with American contemporary fashion. Before they knew it, celebrities started knocking on their door, asking for custom-made evening gowns and suits. A couple of years later, they opened their first concept store under the name Watanabe, and positioned it as a high-end custom-made tailor house. They also provided customers with a full range of custom-designed accessories.

Their two sons soon joined the team, managing stores and franchises in prime locations in Los Angeles and San Francisco, California. As their silver wedding anniversary is approaching, Mr. Watanabe asks Chris to organize something very special for his wife to make up for the hard-working years the couple has been through.

Event Planning

More information on event planning is available at www.marriott.com. You should also be able to get more information on anniversary party ideas from the Internet.

Quick Facts about the Clients' Needs

- The anniversary has to be formal because many celebrities will be invited.
- The menu has to be as bountiful and sumptuous as possible.
- Costs are not a major concern. However, Chris should be shopping for the best offer.

- Chris is in charge of information gathering and screening offers from three major hotels.
- Chris already has an offer from a Marriott competitor.
- The goal is not only to impress the guests but also Mrs. Watanabe.
- The highlight of the anniversary is a recounting of the couple's happy marriage.

Your Call Objectives

In your meeting with Chris Scott, you hope to identify Mr. Watanabe's needs. In addition, you hope to convince him that you provide the best event-planning services that your competitor cannot offer. In doing so, you should be prepared to offer Chris a number of creative ideas to make the event both formal and memorable.

Reality Selling Today Role-Play 11—Sales Agent (Sewell Automotive Company)

Khalid Naziruddin
Sewell Automotive Company
Source: Michael Ahearne

(This mock sales call role-play scenario is created exclusively for use with the *Selling Today: Partnering to Create Value* textbook.)

Your Role as a Sales Agent at Sewell Automotive Company

You will be a sales agent working for Sewell Automotive Company (see website at www.sewell.com), working in conditions similar to those of Khalid Naziruddin, featured in the Chapter 15 Reality *Selling Today* Video.

Naziruddin's partnership-based solution selling is directed at relationship building with the customer. While selling both new and pre-owned cars Naziruddin is aware of the demographics and psychographics of the brand-conscious buyers driven towards the appeal of Audi's luxury image. Sewell Automotive Company is a 105-year-old enterprise selling both high-end brands such as Audi, Lexus etc. and mass products such as GMC, among others. Sewell sells over 36,000 cars annually through its 2,400 associates in six cities. Enabled by Sewell's environment of high performance delivered at high standards of service, Naziruddin's goal is to make customers for life—often by reaching out to the young.

Your Customer: Breanna Wright

Breanna Wright, 25, a freshly minted MBA, is an Austin-based new finance professional looking to upgrade to her first luxury car. Wright's boyfriend, Marc Jensen, a New York-based hedge fund manager, owns a Mercedes-AMG SL63 Roadster. She's thrilled by the 5.5L AMG V8 biturbo machine. Driven towards Jensen's fast-paced lifestyle, Wright aspires to get into the club of luxury car owners but does not know where to start—should she buy a Mercedes or should she shop for something else? Maybe an Audi, known for its *Vorsprung durch Technik*, loosely translated as "Advancement through Technology." Keen to dip into the image of a luxury car and bask in her newfound status and prestige, Wright's looking for not just better quality but also higher performance.

Wright has been invited by Sewell Automotive Company to a product launch party targeting hearts of new generation buyers—many of them Audi *hipsters* who are not only experiencing the brand for the first time but are also indie music and craft-beer lovers of Austin. Naziruddin and colleagues are reaching out to a group that is young and successful but also into fitness, minimalism, yoga, organic foods and Instagram. They are excited by the fact that competitor Mercedes-Benz CLA's recent launch targeted at a new demographic had over two-thirds first-time Mercedes brand buyers.

Quick Facts about Breanna Wright's Needs

- Wright currently drives a 1.8 T Volkswagen Jetta, so she gets the German engineering.
- Her Jetta is on a lease; however, she's open to swapping her lease to get more out of less money per month.
- Wright likes the idea of driving a new car every few years. That works well for Naziruddin who's got an offer on an Audi A4 trim.
- Its bigger and more powerful 2.0 TFSI 220-hp engine can be a draw for Wright. Other features such as the multiple airbags, eight-speed Tiptronic transmission and rear view camera can appeal to Wright's senses.
- Lease options from Sewell Auto can also help Breanna Wright initiate a new lease at a lower payment.
- With almost negligible maintenance worries, and $479/MO lease, Wright might just settle for a black automatic transmission Audi A4.

Your Call Objectives

Now that Wright's at the launch party at Sewell's dealership, you're looking to turn her into a first-time Audi buyer.

But the key challenge is that even if Breanna Wright is open to leasing a new Audi, she will perceive the monthly lease payment as too high, and may even ask you for a 15% discount. Your limitation, following Audi's strict guidelines, is that you're only able to offer a 5% discount, but you can throw in a few new features such as an entertainment system with an LCD monitor in the front (you should remember that Wright's demographic loves indie music!).

The other test for you has to do with product ergonomics. Since Volkswagen and Audi are manufactured on similar product platforms, Wright might not really sense much of a change as she switches from her 1.8 T Volkswagen Jetta to 2.0 TFSI 220-hp Audi A4. Remember she was enthused by her boyfriend's Mercedes-AMG SL63 Roadster.

Can you convince her?

Reality *Selling Today* Role-Play 12, Pharma Supply

Jamie Barouh
McKesson Pharmaceutical
Source: Michael Ahearne

(This mock sales call role-play scenario is created exclusively for use with the *Selling Today: Partnering to Create Value* textbook.)

Your Role at Pharma Supply

You will be a pharmaceutical sales representative for Pharma Supply, a respected pharmaceutical wholesaler that sells medical supplies and drugs to medical clinics, hospitals, other healthcare institutions, and to retail pharmacies, which include many small independent retail pharmacies, large pharmacy chains, and pharmacies that are part of large retail operations such as Walmart, Costco, or various supermarket chains. Your company has recently signed an agreement to represent a generic-drug manufacturer. You will be introducing a new, generic, antidepressant drug, fluoxetine (see websites at www.drugs.com/fluoxetine and www.fluoxetine.com), for Pharma Supply. Competing branded drugs include Ely Lilly's Prozac (see www.prozac.com/index.jsp).

You will start by contacting walk-in clinics and multi-doctor family health practices to get acceptance of your generic drug, so that doctors will be comfortable writing prescriptions for a generic alternative. (Refer to the Chapter 17 opening vignette, and review the Chapter 17 Reality *Selling Today* Video for more information on the nature of a respected pharmaceutical wholesaler. McKesson Pharmaceutical (www.mckesson.com), the featured company in the Chapter 17 Reality *Selling Today* Video, is a wholesale pharmaceutical distribution business similar to Pharma Supply featured in this role-play scenario.)

Your Customer: Family Health Services Clinic

Family Health Services is a downtown clinic. Many of its regular patients live in the immediate area and would be described as lower to lower-middle income patients. You will meet with Payton Diaz, the clinic manager. Payton has been recently hired at this clinic, but you have met Payton a number of times previously at another clinic. Payton always seems quiet and polite, and although you have a friendly relationship, you believe Payton would have a friendly relationship with all salespeople.

Family Health Services has four doctors and two registered nurses:

- Dr. Tom Brown is 36 years old and has been at the clinic for less than a year. He is one of two doctors who begins work at 8:00 A.M. He works each day until 5:00 P.M., but stays on Monday nights until the clinic closes at 8:00 P.M.
- Dr. Lu Bingyu is just a bit younger than Tom. She works the same hours as Tom, but she works late on Friday rather than Monday evenings.
- Dr. Antonio Banderas is the senior doctor at the clinic and is likely going to retire within the next five years. He visits hospital patients each morning and seldom gets to the clinic before noon. He works until 8:00 P.M. Tuesdays through Thursdays.
- Dr. Jane Blenko works each day from noon until 8:00 P.M. Jane's husband is a doctor at one of the local hospitals.
- Nurse Connie Small comes to the clinic each morning when it opens and works until 5:00 P.M. Ben Brothers, the second nurse, comes to work at noon and works each night until 8:00 P.M.

Quick Facts about Selling to Health Clinics and Medical Practices

- Doctors usually resist seeing salespeople and, when they do, the average duration of a sales call is limited to usually just one or two minutes.
- Doctors will sometimes meet with salespeople in a group situation, but only when there are very important reasons to do so. Even then, it is common to arrange somewhat of a social meeting as well—perhaps lunch or a small, catered meal.

- A typical sales call by a pharmaceutical wholesaler salesperson to a health clinic would normally involve talking to the clinic manager to check inventory, take orders, and to ensure there are no service issues or other problems. Rarely would a wholesaler salesperson have to see the medical practitioners.
- When drugs are involved, the amount of product knowledge required is usually beyond what a wholesaler salesperson would be expected to have, so a product specialist would also be involved in the sales call. When such calls are made, it is important to get to see as many members of the medical staff as possible during a single sales call. This requires working with the clinic manager to coordinate a meeting when everyone can attend.
- Doctors are sometimes reluctant to prescribe generic drugs, unless they are certain the drug will be as effective as its branded competitor, even though the cost for a generic alternative can be half the cost of a known brand. However, for patients who must pay for their own prescriptions, doctors will often consider prescribing generic drugs.

Your Call Objectives

During your initial contact, you have developed three call objectives. The first is to re-establish your relationship with Payton. The second is to establish who would be the important people at the clinic who should attend a meeting. Your third objective is to arrange a meeting with the clinic staff, within approximately two weeks, so the product expert who will accompany you on the subsequent sales call can make a presentation and answer questions for attendees. Your product expert is a widely known medical researcher and is widely published in medical journals on the efficacy of the generic antidepressant you distribute.

You are concerned that Payton has been employed with this clinic for only a short time. Payton may not be comfortable trying to arrange a meeting on your behalf, unless you can be convincing that the meeting will be worth everyone's time.

Appendix 2

Table of Contents
Regional Accounts Management Case Study

Part 1
Introduction to the Regional Account Management Case Study

Introduction to Multiple Account Management Selling

Salespeople and new account managers routinely take over a set of existing accounts (see pp. 398–417). Taking over a set of accounts and managing the sales process for all these accounts provide a learning experience different from making a single sale to a single customer. While it is important for a salesperson to be able to make an effective sales presentation, equally important to sales success is developing the skills to move a large number of accounts through various stages of the sales process. This is definitely a "multitasking" process. You will be surprised at how this sales process of moving accounts successfully is very similar to the entrepreneur who is starting a business: working closely with clients to achieve those extremely important sales that provide the company capital to survive and become successful. This success is the basic motivating force behind a growing domestic economy, providing employment to millions of job seekers.

Today, it is common for the new account manager to take over the previous salesperson's electronic database of prospects and customers. Regional account planning, which means learning to evaluate this data and to plan effective value-adding sales efforts for each step in the sales process, is a key factor in growing the expertise of regional account managers. Regional account management is often referred to simply as "RAM." We will be using this reference throughout this case study.

The exercises in this Regional Account Management Case Study simulate this important activity by requesting that a "new account manager" extract, from an existing database, the information needed to take strategic actions to move the accounts through the sales process. The salesperson is asked to review the account data and create value-added regional plans designed to guide the salesperson toward capturing the potential orders that are found within the database.

Introduction to Your New Employer— NewNet Systems

Casey Arnold is the sales manager in the San Jose, California, office of NewNet Systems, which partners and sells B2B network products and services. NewNet is a certified supplier and has access to the latest technologies to connect clients with the right network solution. The productivity and the critical mission of NewNet's customers can be considerably enhanced by selecting and using the correct file and print servers, wide-area network (WAN), virtual private network (VPN), or cabling systems. NewNet is called a value-added reseller (VAR) because its regional account managers and technical sales support teams help customers maximize the value of the products bought through NewNet.

Managing a successful sales process efficiently to solve customer needs and enhance partnering relationships are the primary value-adding activities of the regional account manager. Senior NewNet management personnel are frequently brought into the sales process to add value. The technical needs analysis, product configurations, demonstrations and installations, while managed and overseen by the regional account managers, are the primary responsibility of the technical sales support team members. Because networking is a critical function of the customer's business, financial and technical influencers and user influencers are often a part of the customer buying team.

Introduction to Your New Account Management Position

NewNet's sales and technical support people may spend several months in the sales process (sales cycle). Regional account managers telephone and call on prospects to determine if they qualify for NewNet's attention. Considerable time is taken to study the customer's needs (needs discovery). The expert opinion of NewNet's technical people is incorporated into a product configuration and sales proposal that is presented to the prospective customer. The sales presentation is often made to a number of decision makers in the prospect's firm, including senior management, because of the effect new networking configurations can have on the client's business. Demonstrations are usually required and often include technical NewNet team members. The final decision to purchase may follow after weeks of consideration within the firm and negotiations with NewNet.

Once a decision is made (closing the sale) by a customer to purchase, NewNet's technical and support teams begin the process of acquiring, assembling, and installing the network system and then following through with appropriate training, integration, and support services. (Note: The previous account manager and the company's technical support staff have supplied all the product information needed in these assignments. Your responsibility will be to analyze the buying process of each account, plan sales strategies to move the sales process forward, ultimately forming long-term partnerships and achieving the sales forecast.)

NewNet Regional Account Managers must carefully prospect for customers. NewNet may invest a significant amount of time helping a potential customer configure the right combination of products and services. After careful qualification, only the most serious accounts are cultivated. Further, Casey's regional account managers must ascertain whether, if the investment of time is made in a prospective customer, the account will follow through with purchases from NewNet.

Casey is responsible for assuring that prospect information is collected and used effectively. The regional account salespeople use CRM software designed specifically for value-added resellers, such as NewNet Systems, to manage their prospect information. The system allows salespeople to document and manage their sales process with each prospect.

Refer to Chapter 9, Developing and Qualifying Prospects and Accounts, on p. 196, for your first sales meeting with your new sales manager on the status of your account list. Casey has several account development items for you to review. Additional meetings on moving your accounts successfully through the sales process will be presented at the end of Chapters 10–15.

INTRODUCTION TO YOUR NEWNET SYSTEMS ACCOUNT REPORTS

Lee Bison, NEWNET Senior Accounts Manager   Casey Arnold, NEWNET Sales Manager

Contact Screen

Account 1:	Able Technologies Inc.	Address:	5000 N. Cooper Blvd.
Contact:	Mr. Bradley J. Able		Suite 2000
Phone:	916-555-1000	E-mail:	bja@able.com
Fax:	916-555-1500	City:	Palo Alto
Title:	President	State:	CA
Dear:	Brad	ZIP Code:	94302
User:	Bill Franklin, Chief Engineer	E-mail:	bf@able.com
Phone:	254-555-1254 Cell		

Sales Process Stage–Last Results: Needs Analysis

ID/Status:	Prospect		
Firm Size:	520 People	Network Need:	LAN
Network Now:	None	Likelihood:	70
Workstations:	100	Dollar Amount:	$250,000
Account Code:	Manufacturing	Date Close:	1/31

Notes Screen

11/28: Joe and I met. Joe's report on the needs discovery shows how the 100-user network that they need can be phased in with staggered implementation. Phasing it in can spread the cost over two annual budgets. I think Brad and our CEO will really hit it off.

11/19: Nice meeting this morning. Joe and I spent most of the time with Bill Franklin. Bill's son, Jim, is a junior in engineering at Stanford. Jim is interested in part-time computer-related work. I will mention this to our president; maybe we could help Jim. Bill's chief network concern is work interruptions. Talked a moment about Sam Pearlman. I mentioned Sam's sister, Peggy, and Bill seemed impressed that I knew Peggy is married to Brad. He laughed when I said Joanna was busy. Also, Brad couldn't have been more appreciative of sitting in our reserved seats on the 55th yard line and watching the 49ers in a close call with the NY Jets. We both enjoyed the evening; may want to do this again—I think it is good for business.

11/09: Will meet. I need Joe, our best technical specialist, to team with me on this one—too technical for me—they need a WAN, VPN, and a lot of new cabling. Brad says his BOD wants a two-year 20 percent return on any networking upgrades. Wow, that is $50,000. Thanked Brad for referrals he provided. Joe's great on enhancing our trusted advisor partnering status with clients. Told Brad we had reserved seats at Candlestick. Asked him if he wanted to take in Friday's game with me. Boy, he sure liked that idea and we will meet at the stadium a couple of hours before the game.

11/02: Good guy. Very cooperative. A supportive. Great fan of the SF 49ers. Likes to tailgate before their parties. Has big production facility. Builds vending machines—sold over the globe. Large engineering dept. Bill Franklin is chief engineer but Mr. Able "Call me Brad" wants to stay on top of the new network and workstation decision process. He is really concerned about viruses and spyware taking over their interaction with the computer for commercial gain. He says it's a war they are engaged in every day. Brad may be reluctant to budget for entire network and all workstation needs at one time. "He has a boss too, you know," his board of directors. He wants a future presentation made to them. I think I will bring in our CEO and Casey for that one. Sounds like he wants to negotiate a lower price—going to be a big issue.

Brad suggested we call on Sam Pearlman at 408-555-4545 and Joanna Barkley over in Santa Cruz, at Computer Products.

Contact Screen

Account 2:	Aeroflot Airlines	Address:	499 Park Avenue
Contact:	Mr. John Poltava		Suite 213
Phone:	408-555-6113	E-mail:	jpolt21@aeroflot.com
Fax:	408-555-2856	City:	Sunnyvale
Title:	V.P. Purchasing	State:	CA
Dear:	John	ZIP Code:	94086

Sales Process Stage–Last Results: Qualified

ID/Status:	Prospect		
Firm Size:	3,500 People	Network Need:	WAN
Network Now:	10 Novell Systems	Likelihood:	0.80
Workstations:	2,750	Dollar Amount:	$75,000
Account Code:	Airline	Date Close:	1/31

Notes Screen

11/09:   John wants to meet soon. Will have his key people at meeting, including their CFO and CEO. John said new network expenditures should cut costs and enhance their bottom line by 4 percent. Need Joe to do a needs analysis. Maybe need Charlene also as she is best at the numbers when she does the configuration.

11/02:   John is an emotive. Very interested in new network to improve productivity and bottom line. They have a very ambitious five-year company-wide projection of 12 percent bottom line after taxes. They need a WAN system that connects their offices in 20 airports and 12 warehouses. Lots of problems including a lack of centralized file sharing and document control, inability for their remote employees to efficiently access and share files with the corporate office and a number of website issues that were causing security concerns. John has been with Aeroflot since '97. He will decide on vendor after his management information systems director chooses a system. John said to call a Mr. Ortega at Southern Motors in San Jose. Ortega, it seems, is in the market now. Says Sam spends a lot of time out on the links. Follows the PGA as much as possible. Sent him a thank you for the Ortega information.

Contact Screen

Account 3:	Southern Motors	Address:	717 Main Street
Contact:	Mr. Dwayne Ortega	E-mail:	d_ortega@btas.com
Phone:	415-555-4094	City:	San Jose
Fax:	415-555-4095	State:	CA
Title:	President	ZIP Code:	95124
Dear:	Dwayne		

Sales Process Stage–Last Results: Needs Analysis

ID/Status:	Prospect		
Firm Size:	400 People	Network Need:	WAN, Intranet
Network Now:	5 Novell	Likelihood:	0.90
Workstations:	300	Dollar Amount:	$125,000
Account Code:	Automotive	Date Close:	1/31

Notes Screen

11/10: Met with Dwayne this a.m. Very upscale business. Large facility. Good people work with Dwayne, good team. Dwayne reminded me he wants to see our financials—still concerned about that supplier that went "belly up" costing him a lot of time and money. Mentioned he asked this same info from the other network suppliers he is considering. Joe and Camila met with Dwayne's information systems committee and did the needs analysis while Dwayne and I talked. Dwayne enjoys talking about Central America (C.A.), seems to know what's going on across the region. He's committed to serving his C.A. partners. His offices, shop, etc., reflect a commitment to excellence. We need to get a product configuration and proposal together, and set up another meeting first thing in December. Haven't heard back from Casey about those Pebble Beach PGA tickets—got to check that out.

Talked with Camila and Joe on return. They said there was good "chemistry" between them and their Info Systems Group—I emphasized how important trusted advisor partnering relationships are in this competitive market. They believe the comprehensive network and virtual private network system that they'll configure will meet all of Dwayne's stated needs—speed, power, budget. We really need a "how-to" demo emphasizing these points. Big account and we again will need a good demo showing speed and power and return on investment.

11/02: Dwayne is supportive. Loves to play golf—follows the PGA. Need to talk with Casey about tickets to the February PGA at Pebble Beach. With an account this large, we should be able to do something.

Described his firm as biggest supplier of autos to Central America. He has 400 people. They have old equipment patched together by nothing more than a part-time computer handyman. They are going to need a strong demo of what a new system can do for them. They are having major connectivity issues, problems with data access, file sharing and backup, along with virus and security concerns. Dwayne wants to check us out then do biz with us. One of his former network providers went belly up. We will need to prove that we are a financially secure partner/supplier.

Contact Screen

Account 4:	Bryan Enterprises	Address:	100 Commerce Avenue
Contact:	Mr. Bill Bryan		14th Floor
Phone:	408-555-4567	E-mail:	bbryan@bryan.com
Fax:	408-555-4847	City:	Redwood City
Title:	President	State:	CA
Dear:	Bill	ZIP Code:	94064
User:	Jeremy Miller, Computer Engineer	E-mail:	Jeremy@bryan.com
Phone:	415-556-3124 Cell		

Sales Process Stage–Last Results: Qualified

ID/Status:	Prospect		
Firm Size:	25 People	Network Need:	LAN
Network Now:	1 Peer to Peer	Likelihood:	0.99
Workstations:	25	Dollar Amount:	$75,000
Account Code:	Architectural	Date Close:	11/30

Notes Screen

11/24: We have to be careful with this account. Other notes in this database suggest that this account is having debt problems. Casey, before investing more time in this account, please ask our credit manager to review this account's credit. Also need to make sure what Bill wants will meet his needs.

11/18: Nice talk again. Bill is ready to order just as soon as he gets his computer engineer to agree? I remember meeting Jeremy Miller, his computer engineer, during my visit, but I don't remember anything about Jeremy's role in this. Is he only using Jeremy as an excuse?

11/13: Bill just laughed when I repeated what some of his referrals said about him. He is well liked.
   Bill got our info. Nice meeting. He is sure that, after our visit, they'll be able to order soon. They need a company-wide network, a lot. Too much time spent with paper processing in the company's departments. With a shared system, everyone can have immediate access to all files. Trying to get productivity up and a new network should improve that by 5 percent.

11/08: Bill is certainly an emotive! Very glad we called. Wants a new network. Right Now! Bill is the champion of a shared system with Internet access, has everyone in shop ready. Was looking for someone near. Wants to see us immediately.
   Bill and I really hit it off. Bill referred me to a whole list of people to call. Says there are a number of his professional friends who need updates.

Contact Screen

Account 5:	Computer Products	Address:	789 West 56th Street
Contact:	Ms. Joanna Barkley	E-mail:	j_b@yahoo.com
Phone:	775-555-2345	City:	Santa Cruz
Fax:	775-555-2352	State:	CA
Title:	Purchasing Agent	ZIP Code:	95063
Dear:	Joanna		

Sales Process Stage–Last Results: Qualified

ID/Status:	Prospect		
Firm Size:	30 People	Network Need:	WAN
Network Now:	1 Novell	Likelihood:	0.30
Workstations:	30	Dollar Amount:	$50,000
Account Code:	Engineering	Date Close:	6/30

Notes Screen

11/12: Joanna Barkley had a moment to talk today. She's from Los Angeles. She knew Brad Able there while he was in Navy at San Diego. Says Brad played some semi-pro baseball. They've known each other professionally for years. Joanna had a lot of questions about our firm. She is very goal directed. She wants a specific network and information management system for her company and she'll work with her management team to get it. Our configuration and demo had better meet her exacting specifications. Need to get a needs analysis set up.

11/02: Busy. A Director. To the point. Wants the benefits of a wide-area network. Knows much about it. Told me to call her in a week, send her info about us. Good-bye!

Contact Screen

Account 6:	Computerized Labs	Address:	450980 Wilshire Blvd.
Contact:	Mr. Sam Pearlman		Suite C
Phone:	408-555-5454	E-mail:	spman@complabs.com
Fax:	408-555-5464	City:	Cupertino
Title:	Office Manager	State:	CA
Dear:	Sam	ZIP Code:	95014

Sales Process Stage–Last Results: Presentation

ID/Status:	Prospect		
Firm Size:	30 People	Network Need:	WAN
Network Now:	None	Likelihood:	0.60
Workstations:	30	Dollar Amount:	$75,000
Account Code:	Medical	Date Close:	2/28

Notes Screen

11/20: Talked to Sam. He seems to want to order, but he asked me about a couple of things that I thought we covered well in the presentation. I asked for the order but he was hesitant. He needs a new network—our needs discovery and presentation showed that. He should get started building it immediately. Why hesitate? It's not money—he's budgeted and we're under it. He's not merely negotiating. He seems convinced but confused! I think that he needs a good clear summary of all the benefits that we are proposing. If this goes right, we should be able to directly ask for the order.

11/13: Presentation went well. Charlene worked on the configuration report and proposal for nearly 24 hours straight. The presentation had lots of facts and appealing illustrations. I watched Sam during it and he seemed pleased. Good nods. Call in a week, he said, positively!

11/12: Good meeting. Teamed up with Camila and Charlene, who helped with needs discovery. Those two work together well and are a great technical team. And Charlene is really good at configuring great solutions and proposals. Sam coordinated a series of meetings with his top people. He'd be in and out of them, stroking his beard a lot. Sam is well disciplined—our proposal had better be precise.

11/02: Smooth guy. Reflective. Seemed to be studying my statements. I think we really clicked and that he sees me as someone he can trust. He is interested in a network and a private virtual network, with very fast Internet connections, and is aware of the benefits. Wants all the info we can send. He suggested we call Bryan Enterprises—he's heard they are actively seeking to consolidate and expand their networks. He's okay with appointment after he can read our materials. Sam speaks highly of Brad Able. They take in some baseball games together at Candlestick. Seems Brad is Sam's brother-in-law.

Contact Screen

Account 7:	Designers Associates	Address:	Suite 303	
Contact:	Dr. Simon Sayers		10001 Airport Rd.	
Phone:	415-555-6866	E-mail:	sisa@designers.net	
Fax:	415-555-6874	City:	San Jose	
Title:	Director	State:	CA	
Dear:	Dr. Sayers	ZIP Code:	95121	

Sales Process Stage–Last Results:

ID/Status:	Referral Network		
Firm Size:	3 People	Network Need:	
Network Now:		Likelihood:	0.00
Workstations:		Dollar Amount:	$0.00
Account Code:	Association		
Date Close:			

Notes Screen

11/09: Dr. Sayers is a supportive, easy person with whom to talk. He has been director of Designer Associates for 18 years. His organization serves professional designers in California. They provide educational services and represent designers in government activities.

Dr. Sayers has a staff of three people, none of whom share any files or computer system resources. Dr. Sayers mentioned that he studied architecture but never practiced it. He seems to know just about everyone who owns architectural or engineering firms in California. He said Timothy Ellis probably needs a new network as much as anyone he knows. He said to tell Timothy that one of his biggest competitors, the Billingsly Group, has just come online with a new, private virtual network, and Internet system. Even though Dr. Sayers trusts me, I still have to be a little careful with sharing this information. With such a close-knit marketplace, ethical issues could destroy one's relationships. I think trust will be the bedrock of our ability to succeed.

Contact Screen

Account 8:	Ellis Enterprises	Address:	212 Wacker Drive
Contact:	Mr. Timothy P. Ellis		11th Floor, Suite 9
Phone:	209-555-1234	E-mail:	tpellis75@mchsi.com
Fax:	209-555-5678	City:	Mountain View
Title:	President and Senior Architect	State:	CA
Dear:	Timothy	ZIP Code:	95202

Sales Process Stage–Last Results: Qualified

ID/Status:	Prospect		
Firm Size:	80 People	Network Need:	LAN
Network Now:	2 Peer to Peer	Likelihood:	0.90
Workstations:	80	Dollar Amount:	$175,000
Account Code:	Architectural	Date Close:	1/31

Notes Screen

11/13: Call attempt went badly. Tim seemed to be in a bad mood. This isn't one of my best days either. Tim was preoccupied with something. He mentioned something about an expense budget–cutting meeting he had to go to. Better call back. Got to get this back on track. This will be a great account for us. Maybe need to get Casey and our CEO together and do some strategic thinking.

11/02: Tim. Polished voice. Seems like a reflective. Analytical. Had time to talk. Wanted to know about our firm, me. Knows Bill Bryan from college. Bill was a campus leader. Student body pres. for a while. Bill liked to party. Was President of Stanford ATOs.

Tim is a pilot. Enjoys gliding. Family is large—six children, some adopted. Judy is spouse.

Ellis Enterprises designs and supervises the construction of assisted-living homes. Tim started as an architect in the design department and he is still their network guru. Ellis needs a new network. They have 10 architects on one system, and 30 people on another. They are both the old peer-to-peer networks! He almost apologizes.

Contact Screen

Account 9:	Engineering Software, Inc.	Address:	234 Best Place
Contact:	Mr. Ian Cortez	E-mail:	ian@exso.com
Phone:	775-555-8979	City:	Santa Cruz
Fax:	775-555-8915	State:	CA
Title:	President	ZIP Code:	95061
Dear:	Ian		

Sales Process Stage–Last Results: Qualified–Needs Analysis Scheduled

ID/Status:	Prospect		
Firm Size:	250 People	Network Need:	WAN
Network Now:	Novell	Likelihood:	0.30
Workstations:	35	Dollar Amount:	$75,000
Account Code:	Engineering	Date Close:	6/30

Notes Screen

11/19: Ian received our info. He has already talked with Joe. They will meet the second Thursday in December along with his information systems team for a needs discovery. I need to talk with Joe about my being in that meeting. Got to remember to plan a configuration and demonstration around their need for high-speed connections.

Told Ian about my visit with Kerri—impressive—he was pleased. Told me to be careful while talking to Kerri; don't make any claims that can't be supported. I promised.

Ian is fun to listen to. He's from Canada and his accent is still heavy, almost French. He visits Canada annually; usually fishes while there.

11/12: Ian is definitely a supportive. He wanted to know how he could help. He's been at the company for 2 years. They are one of leading engineering software developers—250 people! They need a new network with high-speed Internet connections for their group of engineers. They exchange large graphics files with other firms. I don't understand what he's saying about compression technology. I've got to get Joe in tech services to visit with Ian. Mention in letter that Joe will call.

Ian said to call Kerri Mathers at Mercy in San Jose re: new network. Kerri is his sister. Kerri heads up MIS there and is only 25.

NewNet Systems
Your Value Adding Systems Partner

Contact Screen

Account 10:	General Contractors	Address:	6748 Mockingbird Ln.
Contact:	Mr. Brian Allan	E-mail:	brian@gentors.com
Phone:	408-555-2947	City:	Cupertino
Fax:	408-555-2922	State:	CA
Title:	Owner	ZIP Code:	95014
Dear:	Mr. Allan		

Sales Process Stage–Last Results: Qualified/Needs Analysis Scheduled

ID/Status:	Prospect		
Firm Size:	90 People	Network Need:	LAN, Upgrade
Network Now:	NT	Likelihood:	0.90
Workstations:	45	Dollar Amount:	$100,000
Account Code:	Engineering	Date Close:	2/28

Notes Screen

11/19: Needs analysis set for second Monday in December. Need to do some thinking about whether to have Joe, or the Charlene and Camila team with me on the needs analysis. Mr. Allan wants enhancements in their network to better serve their clients. Mr. Allan is especially interested in his people using the network in a way that allows clients to look at their engineering drawings from anywhere at any time. This will change the way they do business. Mentioned an extranet and he was interested, but he knew little about it. Our demo, which will be made to all of his department heads, must show how he can accomplish his drawing-sharing objective—he says this is a key to his growth.

11/09: Mr. Allan is a director. Told me to send literature. Their department has an older network—large file-sharing problems and no extranet capability. Ready for new systems. Work with Lauren Whitney, his assistant, and submit to Mr. Allan for final approval. G.C. builds and manages shopping centers nationwide.

Contact Screen

Account 11:	International Studios	Address:	5698 Hollywood Blvd.
Contact:	Mr. Robert G. Kelly	E-mail:	rgk@internstudio.com
Phone:	415-555-3456	City:	San Jose
Fax:	415-555-3481	State:	CA
Title:	President	ZIP Code:	95131
Dear:	Robert		

Sales Process Stage–Last Results: Needs Analysis

ID/Status:	Prospect		
Firm Size:	400 People	Network Need:	LAN, Consolidation
Network Now:	3 Novell	Likelihood:	0.80
Workstations:	300	Dollar Amount:	$25,000
Account Code:	Distributor	Date Close:	1/31

Notes Screen

11/29: Bob immediately asked about Ralph. I forgot to review my notes just before meeting with Bob and I couldn't remember. Ouch!

The needs discovery went well. They need only an upgraded, integrated network system to get started, combine three existing networks and servers. Next will be the e-commerce site and network connection. Camila did an excellent job reviewing their needs, I'm sure glad she's on my team. They seemed almost ready to order their new network during the needs discovery. Camila is so good with those probing and matching them up with need-satisfaction questions. Not unusual for her clients to find their solution during her needs discovery.

11/11: Bob. Nice. Supportive. Started off telling me I should contact Ralph Johnson—even looked up Ralph's phone number. International Studios distributes videos globally. Huge facility. Has 30 people managing order entry and fulfillment. Needs a network to tie together all company functions and to operate an e-commerce website for people around the world to order videos.

Bob's from Grand Rapids, MI. Knew Bill Bryan in college. Bill, he says, introduced Bob to his wife.

Contact Screen

Account 12: Johnson and Associates   Address: 6286 Evergreen Drive
Contact: Mr. Ralph Johnson   Suite 210
Phone: 650-555-3212   E-mail: rjohnson13@mchsi.com
Fax: 650-555-2135   City: San Jose
Title: Engineer   State: CA
Dear: Ralph   ZIP Code: 95133

Sales Process Stage–Last Results: Qualified

ID/Status: Prospect
Firm Size: 150 People   Network Need: LAN, Consolidation
Network Now: 5 Various   Likelihood: 0.99
Workstations: 120   Dollar Amount: $125,000
Account Code: Engineering   Date Close: 12/31

Notes Screen

11/11: Morning call to Ralph. He had a moment. Mentioned Bob Kelly again. Ralph says Bob is the nicest guy Ralph knows—"would give you the shirt . . . ." Ralph and Bob once were partners in a design firm. They sold and moved on. Bob's hobby is model railroading.

11/02: Good guy, but busy. A director. Structural engineering firm. Have buildings across the country. Does bridges too. They need a consolidated, upgraded, and integrated network. One of their people put together the five local area networks that they have now—five different networks—they need it replaced with one complete system THIS YEAR! Upgrade it to be more Web-enabled next year. Ralph suggested calling Kerri Mathers at Mercy Hospital in San Jose. He says she is a whiz in I.S.

Contact Screen

Account 13:	Lakeside Clinic	Address:	123 5th Street
Contact:	Dr. Jeff Gray	E-mail:	jgray@lakeside.com
Phone:	775-555-6600	City:	Santa Cruz
Fax:	775-555-6601	State:	CA
Title:	Manager	ZIP Code:	95060
Dear:	Jeff		

Sales Process Stage–Last Results: Needs Analysis

ID/Status:	Prospect		
Firm Size:	32 People	Network Need:	Server Upgrade
Network Now:	1 Novell	Likelihood:	0.20
Workstations:	32	Dollar Amount:	$25,000
		Date Close:	6/30

Notes Screen

11/28: Nice phone visit. Needs analysis went well. Dr. J. will be ready to accept our presentation on the 9th, at 11:00 a.m. sharp. Yes Sir! Dr. Gray went on to talk about networking in general. He didn't come right out and say it but he seems concerned that the people who manage the network, the administrators, will know more about his network than he will. I said most people in leadership positions don't want to know the "nuts and bolts," but that didn't seem to satisfy him. He also wondered how people could manage their network if they didn't know how facilities managers work. I mentioned one of our value-added benefits was training for his administrators, but stopped short of suggesting that he could sit in on that training—I sensed he might be offended. We may have a problem here with some of his people knowing more than he does. We should prepare to handle this one in our next call.

Dr. Gray says he wants to replace his current Novell server with an NT server as a first step in the process.

11/21: My whole technical sales support team, Joe, Camila, and Charlene, were meeting this morning so we reviewed Camila's proposed product configuration for Lakeside. Everyone agreed it was very well done. She proposes setting up a virtual private network within the clinic and providing access to it by the remote clinics. The other clinics could have networks for local use and the central network could tie them together. This will allow them to do key engineering, architectural, design work at HQ and share the work orders with the clinics. As the clinics make changes in their facilities, reports of the work accomplished could be transmitted back to HQ so their drawings will always be up-to-date. She included training sessions in her proposal.

We will mail proposal so Dr. Gray can review before our presentation. He wants all info in advance of anyone else and the more he has that others don't, the better he likes it. This may be the most complex application that I have worked with.

11/12: Camila just returned from their headquarters clinic. This clinic is not very large, but this is the HQ of a chain of clinics. They manage the facilities in 84 clinics nationwide. Camila met with their planners. They have a good understanding of wide-area networks and Intranets, and what they wish to accomplish. Dr. J. told Camila that he would like to stay on top of developing a shared network throughout the clinic chain. Camila will prepare her report, I will attach proposal, and it will be out by Monday afternoon.

11/03: Dr. J just called. He received and read our info already and wants someone to do a needs discovery. Camila Bleven, one of NewNet's best sales support technicians, was available so she's going out. This account could have some real potential even though the initial sale might not be that large.

11/02: Dr. Jeff is very busy director. Send info, period! Wow! This is a big, complex operation.

Contact Screen

Account 14:	Landers Engineering		Address:	606 Central Drive
Contact:	Ms. Colleen Landers		E-mail:	clanders@aol.com
Phone:	415-555-6121		City:	San Jose
Fax:	415-555-6125		State:	CA
Title:	Owner/Engineer		ZIP Code:	95165
Dear:	Colleen			

Sales Process Stage–Last Results: Qualified

ID/Status:	Prospect			
Firm Size:	10 People		Network Need:	LAN
Network Now:	None		Likelihood:	0.80
Workstations:	10		Dollar Amount:	$25,000
Account Code:	Engineering		Date Close:	12/30

Notes Screen

11/04:   Another nice visit. Need to set an appointment for a needs analysis. However, they put off decision on this for now because of revenue and cash flow problems. Thanked her for Brad Able lead. Colleen's mother's sister is married to Brad.

11/02:   Colleen is nice. Definitely an emotive. She's in a small practice. Needs a network for sharing files and Internet connection. Will be interested in buying a system by end of year—tax reasons.

Colleen suggested talking to Brad Able at Able Engineering or someone in Palo Alto. And a Bill Bryan in Redwood City.

Contact Screen

Account 15:	Media Conglomerate	Address:	987 Independence Dr.
Contact:	Mr. Joe Romera	E-mail:	Joro@media.com
Phone:	415-555-9090	City:	San Jose
Fax:	415-555-7203	State:	CA
Title:	Planner	ZIP Code:	95121
Dear:	Joe		

Sales Process Stage–Last Results: Qualified

ID/Status:	Prospect		
Firm Size:	150 People	Network Need:	Consolidation, Upgrade
Network Now:	2 Novell	Likelihood:	0.60
Workstations:	110	Dollar Amount:	$100,000
Account Code:	Video Production	Date Close:	1/31

Notes Screen

11/27: Touched base with Joe by phone. He's been busy. Reminded me he wants some testimonials from other clients of ours. He says he would like to have some names of other clients of ours with whom he could talk to get a better idea of how good we are. I asked about Bill Bryan and Joe hesitated. Seems Joe is waiting to collect on a debt from Bill for videotapes ordered by Bill's firm; however, he warned me not to say anything about this to anyone—maybe a pending lawsuit. Joe says he will be ready to order right after the first of the year. Says he doesn't need a needs analysis. I think we should at least "look over his shoulder" to confirm that they are maximizing the power of a network. I should tell him about the Langley Group. They have a network with extranet capability but no one uses it and they won't take training. Price is going to be an issue with this account.

11/09: Joe started laughing when I said Bill Bryan suggested I call. Bill and Joe go back a long way. Joe was always saving Bill's neck in college, Joe claims. Joe is emotive. Lots of humor. He's sold on upgrading their network. They have some benefits of networking, want some more. Just price, he says. They know how to maintain it, he claims. He has his own guru. Uh huh.

Contact Screen

Account 16:	Mercy Hospital	Address:	2001 Ross Avenue
Contact:	Ms. Kerri Mathers		Suite 1298
Phone:	310-555-1880	E-mail:	kmathers@mercy.com
Fax:	310-555-1811	City:	San Jose
Title:	MIS Coordinator	State:	CA
Dear:	Kerri	ZIP Code:	95122

Sales Process Stage–Last Results: Qualified

ID/Status:	Prospect		
Firm Size:	4,000 People	Network Need:	Consolidation, Workstations
Network Now:	10 Novell 3 NT	Likelihood:	0.40
Workstations:	2,000	Dollar Amount:	$250,000
Account Code:	Medical	Date Close:	3/30

Notes Screen

11/13: Brief visit with Kerri by phone. Told her I might drop in tomorrow; she said fine. By the way, she says, I should call Cheryl Castro at Modern Designs. She mentioned the success the hospital is having with their extranet, sharing medical information with doctors, nurses, and technicians in their labs, and clinics. In response to my question, she said she'd be happy to show their extranet to others.

11/02: Kerri is impressive. Talks fast, authoritatively. A directive. She has a network expansion study project under way, looking to get more out of her LAN and extranet. Very important—she invited us to send someone to sit in on their study meetings—would help us on a needs analysis. Joe would be great for this. Kerri too busy to talk now; invited me to stop in, no appointment needed.

Contact Screen

Account 17:	Modern Designs	Address:	789 Park Avenue S.
Contact:	Ms. Cheryl Castro		Suite 2190
Phone:	310-555-1098	E-mail:	ccastro@modes.com
Fax:	310-555-1533	City:	Palo Alto
Title:	Chief Engineer	State:	CA
Dear:	Cheryl	ZIP Code:	94302

Sales Process Stage–Last Results: Qualified

ID/Status:	Prospect		
Firm Size:	132 People	Network Need:	WAN, Workstations
Network Now:	3 Novell	Likelihood:	0.50
Workstations:	132	Dollar Amount:	$200,000
Account Code:	Engineering	Date Close:	8/31

Notes Screen

11/29:   Cheryl has studied wide-area networking. Glad to hear from me. She says she has talked extensively with Kerri about high-performance workstations, Internet firewalls, e-mail, and Intranet servers, and is ready to order. I took a list of her needs. Will have Joe, our tech support guru, call her and confirm that what she has specified will meet her application needs. Cheryl is more of a reflective. Her questions were pointed.

Contact Screen

Account 18:	Murray D'Zines	Address:	101 Airport Freeway
Contact:	Ms. Karen Murray		Suite 100
Phone:	310-555-1111	E-mail:	kmuray@dzines.com
Fax:	310-555-1147	City:	San Jose
Title:	Owner	State:	CA
Dear:	Karen	ZIP Code:	95166

Sales Process Stage–Last Results: Order

ID/Status:	Prospect		
Firm Size:	21 People	Network Need:	Upgrade, Workstations
Network Now:	NT	Likelihood:	1.00
Workstations:	21	Dollar Amount:	$20,000
Account Code:	Architectural	Date Close:	12/31
Order Date:	11/13	Y-T-D:	$20,000
Ordered:	20,000	Margin:	0.38
P.O.:	543244		

Notes Screen

11/13: Call her back in about 10 days—everything okay. She may need to order an upgrade to her network software and another five network workstations by the end of the year. Need to suggest this to her at some future date.

11/13: Karen called to order three NT-based workstations. She faxed the complete order within minutes of getting our quote. She thought our needs analysis was right on track. No installation or training necessary, she says. She is a directive. She knows networking, probably better than me.

Karen recommended Judith Albright as someone we should contact. Seems they play a lot of tennis together.

Contact Screen

Account 19:	Piccadilly Studio	Address:	645 North Michigan
Contact:	Ms. Judith Albright	E-mail:	jalbright@Pic.com
Phone:	408-555-3084	City:	Palo Alto
Fax:	408-555-3491	State:	CA
Title:	Owner	ZIP Code:	94309
Dear:	Judith		

Sales Process Stage–Last Results: Order

ID/Status:	Prospect		
Firm Size:	30 People	Network Need:	LAN
Network Now:	Peer to Peer	Likelihood:	1.00
Workstations:	30	Dollar Amount:	$60,000
Account Code:	Architectural	Date Close:	3/30
Order Date:	11/17	Y-T-D:	$20,000
Ordered:	20,000	Margin:	0.32
P.O.:	989472		

Notes Screen

11/17: I just received an e-mail order from Judith. Just like Karen's four NT workstations. I wish for more "sales" like this one. Our brief needs analysis sold her. I think we should have suggested more stations with 30 people working on them. I think she could also use some training and installation services to get the most out of her application.

11/17: Told her Karen referred me. Judith said she enjoys a strategic partnership with Karen and she wanted the same network configuration as Karen's. I was stunned. "You mean now?" I asked, "Yes, now," she said. She moves fast, like most emotives. Noticed some autographed photos of tennis players on her wall. Karen said something about them playing tennis.

Contact Screen

Account 20:	Quality Builders		Address:	15151 Chattanooga
Contact:	Ms. Sherry Britton		E-mail:	sherry@qbuild.com
Phone:	510-555-6886		City:	Palo Alto
Fax:	510-555-6832		State:	CA
Title:	Owner		ZIP Code:	94306
Dear:	Sherry			

Sales Process Stage–Last Results: Qualified

ID/Status:	Prospect			
Firm Size:	9 People		Network Need:	LAN
Network Now:	None		Likelihood:	0.70
Workstations:	9		Dollar Amount:	$25,000
Account Code:	Engineering		Date Close:	2/28

Notes Screen

11/18: Last night I thought about what Sherry was saying so I called her back today. I just questioned her about "keeping up" with her friends. She wants a system that's compatible with theirs. But I mentioned that her friends have spent a lot of money and she strongly agreed. She mentioned again the bad debt she's carrying and her need to budget. She definitely is looking for some special concessions—maybe we can unbundle some features. It seems she may be within range of our lowest possible price. If I discount, and I may have to in order to get this order, I won't make as much on this sale but I am actually dealing with three customers here. I wouldn't want the other two customers to know that one of them is paying less. Of course, Sherry doesn't want them to know she's having a tough time right now, either. Need to get to Casey about what we can do both ethically and legally. I think we need to do a comprehensive needs analysis to see what she needs and what she can afford.

11/17: She calls me! Says Karen told her to. Whew! She is friendly, a supportive. Sherry wants to have the same kind of system as Karen and Judith. She is not in a hurry. She'd like to budget for it first. She may need to budget more than her friends if she wants all new workstations and Internet integration. We talked for some time. Sherry's from Boise, ID, and just loves the warm weather down here. Her brother's on the Bruins football team at UCLA.

Sherry says Karen and Judith attended school together. They continue to share info, etc. I mentioned another customer, Bill Bryan, networked similarly and she paused. She knows Bill and, although she didn't come right out and say it, it sounds as though Bill or his company is in debt to Sherry for some money for a building project. Got to keep this quiet, can't say anything to anybody else!!!!

Sherry wants a network with Web integration so she can show her customers their building designs while still in progress. I mentioned private virtual network capabilities and she admitted she didn't understand. I explained. She said she'd talk with Karen about whether she needed that capability. If she does want this capability, her system will cost more than her friends.'

Appendix 3

Partnership Selling:
A Role-Play
for *Selling Today*

Source: Courtesy of Beach Resort

Appendix 3

Table of Contents

A Special Note to the Student: Use of the Role-Play Appendix

This role-play/simulation provides an opportunity to apply the principles that serve as a foundation for the four broad strategic areas of personal selling: relationship, product, customer, and presentation strategies. The activities are designed to take you from "learning about" selling to "learning to do" selling.

You will start as a convention center sales and marketing department trainee. Your sales manager will supply you with memos that will assist you in learning about your product, competition, customers, and presentations. You will be supplied with many sales tools, including photos, awards, schedules, menus, floor plans, references, company policies, electronic sales proposal/product configurators (see pp. 429–446) and sales planning worksheets.

The first memo on p. 424 provides background information about your product, company, industry, and competition. As a trainee, your first sales and marketing assignment (see memo on p. 463) will be to create an electronic sales proposal and cover sales letter. This activity will give you an opportunity to apply information presented in Chapter 6.

After successfully communicating with your first customer and being promoted to account executive, you are instructed by your sales manager in memos on pp. 464–465 to plan and conduct your first face-to-face contact with another potential customer. The primary objective of this first contact is to establish a relationship with your customer.

The next memo from your sales manager on pp. 468–469 requests that you use your questioning skills to conduct a needs analysis involving the customer you previously contacted. Your customer, who was favorably impressed as a result of your first meeting, has called and requested a meeting to talk about an important convention being planned.

The last memo on pp. 472–473 assists you in creating and presenting a proposal that meets your customer's needs. You will create a portfolio presentation using the awards, photos, price lists, menus, references, floor plans, and schedules provided.

You can access digital images of the pictures in this simulation by clicking on the www .pearsonhighered.com/manning website. You can also access an electronic sales proposal configuration to complete the customer service/sales memorandum 1 and sales memorandum 3 assignments.

Introduction

Salespeople today are working hard to become more effective in such important areas as person-to-person communications, needs analysis, interpersonal relations, and decision making. This role-play/simulation will help you develop these critical selling skills. You will assume the role of a new sales trainee employed by The Park Shores Resort and Convention Center.

PART 1 "Developing a Sales-Oriented Product Strategy" will challenge you to acquire the necessary product information needed to be an effective sales representative for the Park Shores (see Chapters 6 and 7). Your sales manager, T. J. McKee, will describe your new trainee position in an employment memorandum. Your instructions will include the study of materials featured on the following pages, viewing a video that describes the convention facilities and services provided by a competitor, and role-playing the request made in a T. J. McKee customer service/sales memorandum.

PART 2 "Developing a Relationship Strategy for Selling" is another major challenge in personal selling. An employment memorandum will inform you of a promotion to an account executive position. A sales memorandum will inform you of your assignment to accounts in a specific market segment. Part 2 also involves a role-play on the development of a relationship with a new customer in your market segment (see Chapters 3–5 and 10). Your call objective will be to acquire background information on your new customer, who may have a need for your services.

PART 3 "Understanding Your Customer's Buying Strategy" involves a needs analysis role-play (see Chapters 8 and 11). You will again meet with the customer who has indicated an interest in scheduling a business conference at your convention center. During this meeting, you will acquire information to complete Part 4, which involves preparation for the sales presentation.

PART 4 "Developing a Sales Presentation Strategy" will involve preparation of a sales proposal and a *portfolio* presentation (see Chapters 11–15). This section also involves a third role-play with the customer. During the role-play, you will reestablish your relationship with the customer, present your proposal, negotiate the customer's concerns, and attempt to close and service the sale.

Throughout completion of the role-play/simulation, you will be guided by the employment and sales memoranda (from the sales manager) and instructions and additional forms provided by your instructor.

As you complete this simulation activity, note that the principles and practices you are learning to use have applications in nearly all personal selling situations.

General Instructions for Partnership Selling Role-Playing

Overview

The primary goal of a simulation in personal selling should be to strike a balance between just enough detail to focus on the process of selling and not so much as to drown in an ocean of facts. Either too much detail or too little detail can develop anxiety in role-play participants. *Partnership Selling* is designed to minimize anxiety by including only the facts needed to focus on learning the processes involved in high-performance selling.

Some anxiety will occur, however, because you are asked to perform under pressure (in terms of building relationships, securing strategic information, changing people's thinking, and getting them to take action). Learning to perform in an environment full of genuine but non-threatening pressure affords you the opportunity to practice your selling skills so you will be prepared for real-world selling anxiety.

The following suggestions for role-playing will help you develop the ability to perform under stress.

Instructions for Salesperson Role-Plays

1. Be well prepared with product knowledge.
2. Read information for each role-play ahead of time.
3. Follow specific instructions carefully.
4. Attempt to sense both the context and the facts of the situation presented.
5. Conduct a mental rehearsal. See yourself successfully conducting and completing the role-play.
6. Be prepared to take notes during the role-play.
7. After the role-play, take note of your feelings and mentally put them into the context of what just occurred.
8. Be prepared to discuss your reaction to what occurred during the role-play.

Instructions for Customer Role-Plays

1. Read the instructions carefully. Be sure to note both the role-play instructions and the information you are about to share.
2. Attempt to sense both the context of the buying situation and the individual facts presented in the instructions.
3. Let the salesperson initiate greetings, conversations, and concluding actions. React appropriately.
4. Supply only the customer information presented in the background description.
5. Supply customer information in a positive manner.
6. Do not attempt to throw the salesperson off track.

Part One
Developing a Sales-Oriented Product Strategy

EMPLOYMENT MEMORANDUM 1

To: **New Convention Sales Center Trainees**
From: **T. J. McKee, Sales Manager**
Re: **Your New Sales Training Program—"Developing a Product Selling Strategy"**

I am extremely happy that you accepted our offer to join the Sales and Marketing Department. Enclosed is a copy of your new position description (see p. 427). Your first assignment as a trainee will be to learn about our product and what we have recently done to provide *total quality* customer service. *To apply what you are learning, I would like you to follow up on a customer service request I recently received. (See memo p. 459.)* You will use the following product information to complete the assignment. Refer also to The Park Shores Resort and Convention Center link on the www.pearsonhighered.com/manning website.

AN AWARD-WINNING UPDATE (SEE PP. 429 and 431)

We have recently completed a *$4.8 million investment in our convention center.* This customer service investment included renovating all guest rooms and suites, lobby and front desk area, meeting rooms, restaurant and lounge, and enclosure of the swimming pool. Enclosed is a copy of the "Regional Architects Award" that our facility won. We are the only facility in the Metro Area to have been presented with this award.

MEETING AND BANQUET ROOMS (SEE PP. 443–447)

The Park Shores offers convention planners just over *8,000 square feet of award-winning meeting space* in attractive, newly renovated meeting and banquet rooms. Our Central Park East and West rooms are conveniently located on the lobby level of the hotel. Each of these rooms can accommodate 180 people in a theater-style setting or 80 in a classroom-style setting. They also have a divider wall that can be retracted and, with the combined rooms, can accommodate up to 370 people.

    The Top of the Park provides a spectacular view of the city through windows that surround that ballroom. This unique room, located on the top floor, can accommodate 225 people classroom style, 350 people banquet style, or 450 people theater style. Also located in the Top of the Park is a revolving platform area that slowly moves, giving guests a 360-degree panoramic view of the city. The Parkview Room, which is also located on the top floor of the hotel, can accommodate 150 people theater style and 80 people classroom style.

    In addition for *groups booking 40 rooms or more, we provide one luxurious suite free*. This suite features a meeting room, bedroom, wet bar with refrigerator, and Jacuzzi.

    Be sure your clients understand that our meeting rooms *need to be reserved*. The first organization to sign a sales proposal for a specific date has the designated rooms guaranteed.

GUEST ROOM DECOR AND RATES (SEE P. 441)

Our recent renovation included complete redecoration of all 250 of our large and spacious guest rooms. This includes all new furniture, wall coverings, drapes, bedspreads, and carpets. Our interior designer succeeded in creating a comfortable, attractive, and restful atmosphere. *All of our rooms are designated nonsmoking.*

	REGULAR RATES	GROUP RATES	SAVINGS
Single	$169	$159	$10
Double	$199	$189	$10

A comparison of competitive room, parking, and transportation rates is presented on p. 441.

(continued)

BANQUET MEALS (SEE PP. 435–439) (*continued*)

Our executive chef, Ricardo Guido, recently won the *National Restaurant Association's "Outstanding Chef of the Year" Award* in addition to many other awards. His winning entry consisted of the three chicken entrées featured on the enclosed menus. Ricardo served as Executive Chef at the five-star rated Williamsburg Inn in Williamsburg, Virginia, before we convinced him to join us six months ago. He personally oversees all our food and beverage operations. Ricardo, in my opinion, is one of the outstanding chefs in the country. His expertise and commitment to total quality customer service will help develop long-term relationships with our customers.

The enclosed dinner selections are only suggestions. We will design a special menu for your clients if they wish. A 16 percent gratuity or service charge is added to all group meal functions.

HOTEL/MOTEL AND SALES TAXES

All room rates are subject to the *local hotel/motel room tax, which is an additional 8 percent. In addition, all billings must have a 4 percent sales tax added. (The sales tax is not added to the hotel/motel tax and does not apply to gratuities.)*

LOCATION, TRANSPORTATION, AND PARKING (SEE MAP ON P. 431)

We are located in the highly recognized Mission Beach area on the north side of San Diego. We are conveniently located just seven miles from San Diego International Airport and within easy travel distance from major San Diego attractions, including Qualcomm Stadium, PETCO Park, and the San Diego Zoo. Our beachfront location not only offers breathtaking views of Mission Beach and the Pacific Ocean, but also an excellent list of water sports and walking, hiking and running trails.

Discounted courtesy van transportation is provided to the airport as well as other attractions in the area. This service saves $7 to $14 each way for our guests who arrive by plane. Additionally, guests who will be driving to the hotel will find over 300 parking spaces available to them at no charge. Unlike other downtown properties, our free parking saves guests from $6 to $23 per day in parking fees. For security purposes, we have closed-circuit camera systems in the parking lot and underground parking areas.

VALUE-ADDED GUEST SERVICES AND AMENITIES

Our convention center owners have invested heavily in the facility to provide our clients with total quality service, unmatched by our competition. Additional value-added services and amenities include:

- A large *indoor pool, sundeck, sauna, whirlpool, and complimentary Nautilus exercise room* in an attractive tropical atmosphere (see p. 443)
- "Cafe in the Park" featuring 24-hour continental cuisine seven days a week
- "Pub in the Park" where friendly people meet, featuring *free hors d'oeuvres* Monday through Friday, 5 to 7 P.M.
- Cable television with HBO
- A.V. rental of most equipment in-house, at a nominal fee (see p. 451)
- *Free coffee and donuts or rolls* in the lobby each morning from 6 to 8 A.M.
- A team of *well-trained, dedicated, and friendly associates* providing total quality front desk, food, and guest services
- Express check-in
- Electronic key entry system
- Hair dryer, iron, and ironing board in each room
- Data port capabilities for laptop computers in each room
- Desk in each room
- Video message retrieval
- Voice mail
- On-command video (choice of 50 new release movies)

SALES LITERATURE (SEE PP. 429–457)

Included in your product training materials are photos, references, letters, room schedules, sales proposals, and other information that you will use in your written proposals and verbal sales presentations. When you move into outside sales, you should use these tools to create effective sales portfolios.

TOTAL QUALITY COMMITMENT

Our convention center is committed *to* total quality customer service. *Our Partnership Style of Customer Service and Selling* is an extension of our total quality process. The Total Quality Customer Service Glossary provides definitions of terms that describe our total quality process (see p. 428).

The hotel and convention center industry is mature and well established. Our sales and customer service plan is to *establish strong relationships, focus on solving customer problems, provide total quality customer service, and become a long-term hotel and convention center partner with our clients*. By utilizing this type of selling and customer service, your compensation and our sales revenue will both increase substantially.

TJM:ESS

Enclosures

POSITION DESCRIPTION—CONVENTION CENTER ACCOUNT EXECUTIVE

COMPANY DESCRIPTION

The Park Shores Resort and Convention Center is a total quality, full-service equal opportunity employment convention center that has recently made large investments in the physical facility, the food and beverage department, and sales department. Company culture includes an effective and enthusiastic team approach to creating *total quality*, value-added solutions for customers in a very competitive industry. The primary sales promotion tool is *Partnership Selling* with extensive marketing support in the form of photos, reference letters, team selling, and so forth. The company goal is to increase revenues 20 percent in the coming year by providing outstanding customer service.

SUCCESSFUL ACCOUNT EXECUTIVE WILL

1. Acquire necessary convention center company, product, industry, and competitive information through company training program
2. Be committed to a total quality customer service process
3. Develop a list of potential prospects in the assigned target market
4. Develop long-term, total quality selling relationships that focus on solving the meeting planner's convention center needs
5. Achieve a sales volume of $800,000 to $1 million annually

WORKING RELATIONSHIPS

Reports to: Sales Manager
Works with: Internal Support Team including Food Service, Housekeeping and Operations, Customer Service and Front Desk; External Relationships including customers, professional associations, and industry personnel

SPECIFIC REQUIREMENTS

1. Must project a positive and professional sales image
2. Must be able to establish and maintain long-term partnering relationships
3. Must be goal oriented with a plan for self-improvement
4. Must be flexible to deal effectively with a wide range of customers
5. Must be good at asking questions and listening effectively
6. Must be accurate and creative in developing customer's solutions
7. Must be clear and persuasive in communicating and negotiating solutions
8. Must be good at closing the sale
9. Must follow through on promises and assurances
10. Must have math skills necessary for figuring sales proposals

SPECIFIC REWARDS

1. Attractive compensation package that includes base salary, a commission of 10 percent of sales, bonuses, and an attractive fringe benefit package
2. Pride in working for an organization that practices total quality management in employee relations and customer service
3. Extensive sales and educational support
4. Opportunity for growth and advancement

EOE/AA/TQM

TOTAL QUALITY CUSTOMER SERVICE GLOSSARY

DIRFT—DO IT RIGHT THE FIRST TIME means being prepared, asking the right questions, selecting the right solutions, and making effective presentations. This creates repeats and referrals.

QIP—QUALITY IMPROVEMENT PROCESS means always striving to better serve our customers resulting in high-quality, long-term relationships.

TQM—TOTAL QUALITY MANAGEMENT means the commitment to support and empower people to deliver legendary customer service.

QIT—QUALITY IMPROVEMENT TEAM means a team approach to deliver outstanding customer service.

COQ—COST OF QUALITY means the ultimate lowering of cost by providing outstanding service the first time, so as to build a list of repeat and referred customers.

PONC—PRICE OF NONCONFORMANCE means the high cost of not meeting high standards. This results in correcting problems and losing customers. PONC also causes longer sales cycles and higher sales costs.

POC—PRICE OF CONFORMANCE means the lower costs of providing outstanding customer service and achieving a list of repeat or referred customers.

WIIFM—WHAT'S IN IT FOR ME means the psychic and monetary rewards in the form of personal enjoyment, higher salaries, commissions, or bonuses caused by delivering outstanding customer service.

QES—QUALITY EDUCATION SYSTEMS means internal and external educational activities designed to improve the quality of customer service.

YOU—THE MOST IMPORTANT PART OF QUALITY means the ongoing program of self-improvement that results in outstanding customer service and personal and financial growth.

Park Shores Resort and Convention Center

The all-new Park Shores Resort & Convention Center featuring an award-winning $4.8 million renovation

Source: Courtesy of Beach Resort

➡ Use the sales information on the reverse side of this page to position your convention center and the $4.8 million renovation in the mind of your customer.

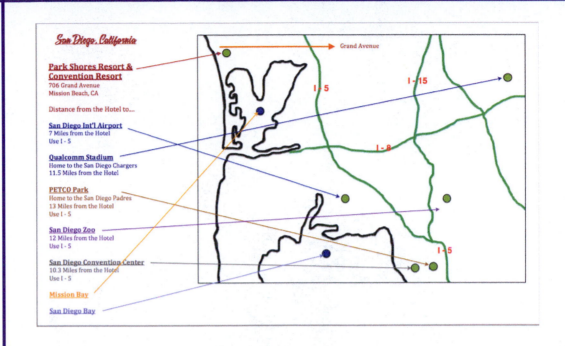

Park Shores Resort and Convention Center

*Convenient, easy-to-find beachfront location
with free on-site parking.*

*Close to all major southern California attractions.
Just 7 miles from San Diego International Airport.*

➡ Use the sales information on the reverse side of this page to illustrate the ease and convenience of your customers locating and traveling to the Convention Center in addition to highlighting all the nearby attractions.

REGIONAL ARCHITECTS
ASSOCIATION
San Diego California

EXCELLENCE IN RENOVATION DESIGN

Park Shores Resort & Convention Center

With Special Recognition for Innovative Design creating

an Outstanding Resort and Convention Complex

Patricia Bennett
Patricia Bennett, President
Regional Architects Association

Allen Rogge
Chairperson
Design Award Committee

Presented July, 2014

DESIGN
AWARD

2014

PARK SHORES RESORT & CONVENTION CENTER

Regional Architects Association
Excellence in Renovation Design

➡ Use the sales information on the reverse side of this page to demonstrate and describe the award for "Creating an Outstanding Convention Environment" and explain that it was given with regard to the quality of the meeting rooms, guest rooms, ambiance of lobby and restaurant, and the pool area.

Park Shores Resort and Convention Center

*Outstanding food service
personally supervised by award winning
Chef Ricardo Guido
National Restaurant Association
"Executive Chef of the Year"
Robert James Foundation
"Best Chef - West Coast Region"*

Source: Courtesy of Beach Resort

➡ Use the sales information on the reverse side of this page to introduce and explain the "outstanding food service" that will be personally supervised by Executive Chef of the Year Ricardo Guido.

National Restaurant Association

Executive Chef of the Year

Awarded To

RICARDO GUIDO

Executive Chef • Park Shores Resort & Convention Center • Mission Beach, CA

Presented March 2014

Chef Robert Anderson

Robert Anderson, President
National Restaurant Association

Thomas Boyce
Chairperson
Southern California Association

ROBERT JAMES FOUNDATION

Restaurant and Chef Awards

Best Chef | West Coast Region

presented to

Ricardo Guido

Executive Chef | Park Shores Resort & Convention Center | Mission Beach CA

Presented by
The Robert James Foundation

May 2014

Marsha Sweeney
Executive Director

➡ Use the sales information on the reverse side of this page to explain the benefits of having an award-winning executive chef and describe his background.

the banchetto
(menu)

BANQUET STYLE MENU

All banquet selections include the banchetto dinner salad with tossed greens, fresh California tomatoes, and choice of dressing; choice of baked, oven browned, au gratin, or garlic mashed potato; fresh vegetables; homemade rolls with butter.

All selections are accompanied with a choice of coffee, tea, iced tea, or sodas.

Desserts are extra.

CHICKEN ENTREES

Chicken Wellington | $48

Boneless Breast of Chicken Topped with a Mushroom Mixture in a Puffy Pastry Shell and Baked to a Golden Brown.

Chicken Breast Teriyaki | $48

Marinated Boneless Breast of Chicken Grilled topped with Banchetto's Special Teriyaki Sauce.

Chicken Breast New Orleans | $48

Baked Boneless Breast of Chicken Garnished with Peppers, Mushrooms, Onions and Monterey Jack Cheese.

Prices Do Not include a 16% Service Charge or Sales Tax.

BEEF ENTREES

New York Strip | $54

Center Cut New York Strip Steak Broiled to Perfection Topped with Banchetto's Seasoned Herb Butter.

Filet Mignon | $54

Center Cut Beef Tenderloin Broiled and served in a Rich Wine Sauce.

PORK ENTREES

Sliced Pork Lion w/Mustard Sauce | $58

Boneless Loin of Pork Oven Roasted and Sliced served with Mustard Sauce.

FISH ENTREES

Encrusted Chilean Sea Bass | $48

Served over Red and Black Lentils with Yellow Pepper Oil, Grilled Potatoes and Brown Sugar Baby Carrots.

Broiled Orange Roughy | $48

A Filet of Orange Roughy Broiled and covered with a Basil Lemon Sauce.

➡ Use the sales information on the reverse side of this page to explain and configure the menus available for banquet-style meals.

PARK SHORES RESORT · COMPETITIVE RATES
GUEST ROOM RATES FOR GROUPS

Source: Courtesy of Beach Resort

HOTEL/RESORT	SINGLE	DOUBLE	PARKING/DAY	AIRPORT TRANS
PARK SHORES RESORT	$159	$189	FREE	$15 Each Way
Marriott	$173	$199	$12	$22 Each Way
Sheraton	$185	$195	$16	$29 Each Way
Omni	$195	$205	$20	$19 Each Way
Hyatt	$185	$190	$22	$24 Each Way
St Regis	$175	$195	$26	$24 Each Way
Mission Terrace	$183	$185	$22	$24 Each Way
Pacific Beach Club	$171	$190	$20	$26 Each Way
Mission Bay Resort	$174	$190	$19	$24 Each Way

Recent renovation included complete redecoration of all 250 of our large and spacious guest rooms. This includes all new furniture, wall coverings, drapes, bedspreads, and carpets. Our interior designer succeeded in creating a comfortable, attractive, and restful atmosphere. The Park Shores is a smoke-free facility. Pets under 25 pounds are allowed with a $50 non-refundable cleaning fee. There is also a safe in every room and at the front desk.

Discounted *courtesy van transportation* (also known as limousine service) priced at $15/each way is provided for our overnight guests to and from the airport, as well as anywhere in the downtown area. This service saves our guests who arrive by plane from *$7.00 to $14.00 each way.*

Guests who will be driving to the hotel will find over *300 parking spaces* available to them at *no charge.* Unlike other beach properties, our free parking saves guests up to *$26.00 per day* in parking fees. For security purposes, we have closed-circuit camera systems in the parking lot and in the parking garage areas.

➡ Use the sales information on the reverse side of this page to explain and illustrate the attractive and comfortable guest rooms. Remind customers that the rooms were a major factor in receiving the Architects Award.

Also, point out the competitive room rates survey in addition to the savings on transportation and parking. Point out that the competitive room, transportation, and parking rate surveys are conducted and updated weekly.

Source: Courtesy of Beach Resort

Source: Courtesy of Beach Resort

PARK SHORES RESORT & CONVENTION CENTER

For relaxation after a day's work, take advantage of our beautiful pool overlooking the Pacific Ocean.

Take advantage of the state-of-the-art exercise equipment in our fitness center.

➡ Use the sales information on the reverse side of this page to explain and illustrate the benefits of the totally renovated and redesigned pool, with the sauna, whirlpool, sundeck, and fitness center.

PARK SHORES RESORT & CONVENTION CENTER
MEETING ROOM SET UP OPTIONS

CONFERENCE STYLE

CLASSROOM STYLE

Source: Courtesy of Beach Resort

BANQUET STYLE

U SHAPED/HOLLOW CENTER STYLE

Source: Courtesy of Beach Resort

THEATER STYLE

Source: Courtesy of Beach Resort

| U Shaped/ Hollow Square | Theater Style | Classroom Style | Conference Style | Banquet Style w/Round Tables |

➡ Use the sales information on the reverse side of this page to illustrate the attractiveness of the newly remodeled meeting rooms, which were another important factor in receiving the Architects Award. Also, use this form to explain and illustrate the various seating arrangements for meeting rooms.

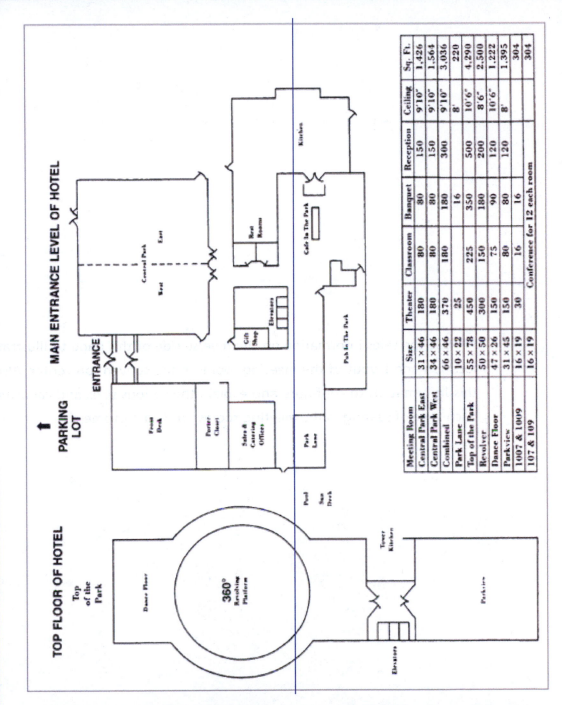

MAIN ENTRANCE LEVEL OF HOTEL

PARKING LOT

ENTRANCE

Front Desk

Porter Closet

Sales & Catering Offices

Central Park West / East

Rest Rooms

Gift Shop

Elevators

Park Lane

Cafe In The Park

Kitchen

Pub In The Park

TOP FLOOR OF HOTEL

Top of the Park

Dance Floor

360° Revolving Platform

Pool Sun Deck

Tower Kitchen

Parkview

Elevators

Meeting Room	Size	Theater	Classroom	Banquet	Reception	Ceiling	Sq. Ft.
Central Park East	31 × 46	180	80	80	150	9'10"	1,426
Central Park West	34 × 46	180	80	80	150	9'10"	1,564
Combined	66 × 46	370	180	180	300	9'10"	3,036
Park Lane	10 × 22	25		16		8'	220
Top of the Park	55 × 78	450	225	350	500	10'6"	4,290
Revolver	50 × 50	300	150	180	200	8'6"	2,500
Dance Floor	47 × 26	150	75	90	120	10'6"	1,222
Parkview	31 × 45	150	80	80	120	8'	1,395
1007 & 1009	16 × 19	30	16	16			304
107 & 109	16 × 19	Conference for 12 each room					304

PARK SHORES RESORT & CONVENTION CENTER

Meeting Rooms need to be reserved.
The first organization to sign a Sales Proposal for a specific date
has the designated room guaranteed.

Source: Courtesy of Beach Resort

➡ Use the sales information on the reverse side of this page to illustrate the location and layout of the meeting rooms in the convention center. Also, use this information to configure and explain the various sizes and capacities for each style of seating in the meeting rooms for your customers.

Rates
Meeting Room

PARK SHORES RESORT & CONVENTION CENTER MEETING ROOM RATES				
MEETING ROOM	**SQ FEET**	**4 HOURS**	**8 HOURS**	**24 HOURS**
Top of the Park	4,290	$600	$800	$1,200
Central Park - East	1,426	$200	$250	$350
Central Park - West	1,564	$190	$240	$340
Central Park - Combined	3,036	$350	$450	$600
Park Lane	220	$45	$50	$70
Revolver	2500	$500	$700	$900
Dance Floor	1222	$200	$275	$375
Park View	1395	$150	$215	$380
Room # 107	304	$80	$100	$120
Room # 109	304	$80	$100	$120
Room # 1007	304	$80	$100	$120
Room # 1009	304	$80	$100	$120

· Meeting room rental charges based on set changes at 12:00 noon, 5:00 p.m., or 10:00 p.m.
· For groups of 20 or more who are reserving 20 or more guest rooms or scheduling 20 or more banquet meals, rental rates will be waived for rooms up to 1,600 square feet for up to 8 hours of use per day.
· FOR GROUPS OF 50 OR MORE WHO ARE RESERVING 50 OR MORE GUEST ROOMS OR SCHEDULING 50 OR MORE BANQUET MEALS, RENTAL RATES WILL BE WAIVED FOR ALL ROOMS FOR UP TO 24 HOURS OF USE.

➡ Also, use the sales information at the bottom of the page to configure and explain the pricing and policies with regard to charges for use of the meeting rooms. Explain that the convention center's policies with regard to pricing and the use of meeting rooms are very competitive with the charges of other centers in the San Diego area.

Source: Courtesy of Beach Resort

PARK SHORES RESORT & CONVENTION CENTER

INTERNET CONNECTIVITY
Single Access Hardwire | $100 each connection/per day
Wireless | $50 each connection/per day
For specific bandwidth contact your Sales Associate.

TELEPHONE ACCESS
Voice, Modem or FAX Line | $200/Event

BUSINESS EQUIPMENT
Laptop Computers | $150/Event
Printers | $100/Event

MEETING EQUIPMENT
Microphone (Wireless) | $50/Event
LCD Projector | $100/Event
Rear Screen Projection | $100/Event
Video Camera | $50/Event

TECHNOLOGY ASSISTANCE
For specific technology assistance contact your Sales Associate.

➡ Use the sales information on the reverse side of this page to sell, configure, and explain the availability of audiovisual equipment to customers scheduling meetings in the convention center. This equipment must be reserved in advance of the scheduled date to guarantee availability.

Letter of Reference

December 15, 201_

Gregg Saboe, General Manager
Park Shores Resort & Convention Center
706 Grand Avenue
Mission Beach, CA 92108

Dear Gregg:

On behalf of our employees I thank you and your associates for the wonderful time we had at the Park Shores Resort & Convention Center during our convention last month. Enclosed is a check for $22,991.23 to pay the invoice for the meeting costs.

The hospitality that we received during our time there was unparalleled. The friendliness and dedication of the staff simply made our time so enjoyable we hated to leave.

The Chicken New Orleans was superb. Our heartfelt thanks to Chef Ricardo Guido for creating the best meals we have ever had at a convention.

Without reservation I will direct anyone looking for convention space to your award-winning property. The group that gave you the award certainly knew what was important to convention planners. You may count on us to return in the future.

Sincerely,

Reggie Regan

Reggie Regan, Vice President
Field Sales Division

Enclosures:
Schedule for our next eight convention dates
Check
Service Evaluation
ss

➡ Use this reference letter with customers to support the outstanding service we strive to provide to ALL of our convention center customers. Note the friendliness and dedication of the center staff, the quality of the food service, the reference to the award, and the enclosures regarding repeat business involving eight more meeting dates and the check in the amount of $22,991.23.

Client
References

REFERENCES

COMPANY/ADDRESS	TELEPHONE#	DATE OF BOOKING
Association of Business and Industry 2425 Hubbell Avenue Mr. James Warner (Director)	263.8181	July 1-2
Acme Supply 2531 Dean Avenue Linn Compiano (Training Manager)	619.265.9831 l_comp@asc.com	July 14
Rotary International 1230 Executive Towers Mr. Roger Shannon (Executive Director)	218.792.4616	July 28-29
Achway Cookie Company Boone Industrial Park Mr. Bill Sorenson (Sales Manager)	301.432.4084 bsorenson@arco.com	August 9
West College 4821 College Parkway Toni Bush (Athletic Director)	515.283.4142 tbush@west.edu	September 10-12
Travelers Insurance Company 1452 29th Mr. Richard Wiese (Training Manager)	619.223.7500 rwiese@trin.com	November 14
Meredith Corporation 1716 Locust Avenue Mrs. Carol Rains (Public Relations)	515.284.2654 crains@merco.com	November 23-24
DuPont Pioneer Hi-Bred Incorporated 5700 Merle Highway Mrs. Shari Sitterly (Meeting Planner)	641.272.3660 ssitterly@ph-b.com	December 11-12

➡ Use the sales information on the reverse side of this page to supply a list of successful businesspeople who can be contacted regarding the quality of food and service they received at previous meetings they had at the convention center.

FOOD AND BEVERAGE

| A 16 percent gratuity or service charge and applicable sales tax will be added to all food and beverage purchases.
| Any group requesting a tax exemption must submit their Certificate of Exemption prior to the event.
| There is a $25 setup fee for each meal function of 25 persons or less.

GUARANTEES

| The Convention Center will require your menu and meeting room requirements no later than two weeks before your meeting or food function.
| Convention Center facilities are guaranteed on a "first confirmed, first served" basis.
| A meal guarantee is required 48 hours prior to your function. This guarantee is the minimum your group will be charged for the function. If no guarantee is received by the Catering Office, we will then consider your last number of attendees as the guarantee. We will be prepared to serve 5 percent over your guaranteed number.

BANQUET AND MEETING ROOMS

| As other groups may be utilizing the same room prior to or following your function, please adhere to the times agreed on. Should your time schedule change, please contact the Catering Office, and every effort will be made to accommodate you.
| Function rooms are assigned by the room-number of people anticipated. If attendance drops or increases, please contact the Catering Office to ensure proper assignment of rooms.

TECHNOLOGY | MEDIA SERVICES

| A wide variety of technology services is available on a rental basis. See Technology/Media Rental Rates for details or contact your Sales Associate.

➥ Use the sales information on the reverse side of this page to carefully explain the policies and general information on the operation of the convention center. Please note the 16 percent gratuity and the $25 setup fee for certain meals. Also, note the policies and guarantees that are required for menus, meeting rooms, and meals.

CUSTOMER SERVICE/SALES MEMORANDUM 1 ROLE PLAY

To: Convention Sales Trainee
From: T. J. McKee, Sales Manager
Re: Assistance with a Customer Request

A new prospect called and requested that we immediately submit a proposal for a planned Mission Beach meeting. Please review the profile in our automated database (printed as follows).

CONTACT REPORT

Name: Graphic Forms	Address: 2134 Martin Luther King
Contact: B. H. Rivera	:
Phone: 314-619-4879	:
Title: President	City: Atlanta
Sec:	State: GA
Dear: B. H. Rivera	ZIP: 61740

◄ CONTACT SCREEN

(McKee) Visited with B. H. Rivera on the phone. Seemed very interested. Nice emotive person. Has a son, Matt, attending West College. Also knew Toni Bush of West, who is an excellent account of ours. B. H. wants a proposal ASAP to cover the following buying conditions:

1. Ten single guest rooms for two nights—Friday and Saturday
2. A meeting room for 20 people, classroom style, Friday and Saturday from 2 to 6 P.M.
3. Dinner for 20, banquet style, at 6 P.M. each night
4. Friday: Sliced Pork Loin
5. Saturday: Broiled Orange Roughy
6. A swimming pool

◄ NOTES WINDOW

Complete the following customer service/sales assignment using the material in your product sales training program and the forms on the next two pages. (See Chapters 6 and 7 on Developing a Product Strategy.)

1. *Complete the sales proposal worksheet (p. 461).*
   Our sales proposal needs to contain accurate and complete facts because, when signed, it becomes a legally enforceable sales contract. All the product and pricing guidelines have been supplied in your sales training materials. You should sign your name with your new job title "Account Executive" in the lower left-hand corner of the form. You can access an Electronic Sales Proposal Writer at www.selling-today.com.
2. *Write a sales letter (p. 462).*
   Prepare a letter that custom fits and positions the benefits that will appeal to B. H. Rivera. Be sure to list any sales literature you will be sending under the Enclosure section of your letter. (Use business letter format on p. 453 and rules on p. 120.)

Make file copies of everything you prepare so our food and beverage, housekeeping, and accounting departments will have them available.

We should send or fax the proposal, cover letter, and sales literature by tomorrow afternoon.

Thank you.

SALES PROPOSAL

Customer Name: _____ Title: _____

Organization Name: _____ Telephone: _____

Address: _____

Date(s) of Meetings: _____

Kind of Meetings: _____

Buying Conditions (What the customer needs—be specific): _____

_____

_____

A. Meal Functions Needed

	Time	Description	Quantity	Price	Total
Meal 1					
Meal 2					
Other		(Beverages, setup fees, etc.)			

Total _____

Sales Tax _____

Service Charge _____

Total Meal Cost _____

B. Meeting and Banquet Rooms and Equipment Needed (describe time, date, and cost)

Total _____

Sales Tax _____

Total Meeting/Banquet Rooms and Equipment Charges _____

C. Guest Rooms Needed

Number of Rooms Needed	Description (dates, locations, special conditions)	Group Rate per Room	Total Cost

Total _____

Room Tax _____

Sales Tax _____

Total Guest Room Charges _____

D. Total Customer Costs (from above)

A. $_____ plus **B.** $_____ plus **C.** $_____ equals **Total Charges** $_____

_____   _____

Authorized Signature   Date   Customer Signature   Date

_____   _____

Title   Title

PARK SHORES RESORT AND CONVENTION CENTER

Parts 2 to 4

EMPLOYMENT MEMORANDUM 2

To: New Convention Center Account Executives
From: T. J. McKee, Sales Manager
Re: Your New Sales Assignment

Congratulations on successfully completing your training program and receiving your new appointment. You will find three challenges as you work with your customer's buying process.

Your *first challenge will be establishing relationships* with your customers. This will require that you do strategic planning before you can call on your client for the first time. Make sure your initial meetings focus on subjects of interest to your customer. Remember, "Customers don't care how much you know until they know how much you care."

Your *second major challenge will be to gain a complete and accurate understanding of your customer's needs.* You should prepare to ask good questions, take detailed and accurate notes, and confirm your customer's and your own understanding of their need. This process is a part of our total quality management program, which strives to provide total quality customer service. "To be an effective consultative salesperson you need to seek first to understand."

Your *third challenge as an account executive will be to make good presentations.* Our industry, as most others these days, is competitive and is characterized by many look-alike products and some price cutting. Always *organize and deliver good presentations* that focus on (1) providing solutions to immediate and long-term customers' needs, (2) negotiating win-win solutions to customers' concerns, and (3) closing sales that keep our facility full. This approach will give you a competitive edge and help you maintain high-quality, long-term profitable relationships.

Attached you will find a memorandum on an account I would like you to develop. Please follow the instructions included and provide me with appropriate feedback on your progress. I look forward to working with you on this account.

P.S. I want to compliment you on your excellent work on the B. H. Rivera account. B. H. called while you were attending a training meeting and said that your proposal and letter looked very good. Their organization was impressed with our facility, the apparent quality of our food, and your letter. Their organization will be scheduling a total of *11 more meetings* at our convention center during the next 12 months if everything works the way you describe it. Each of these sales will be reflected in your *commission checks.* Great work.

Part Two
Developing a Relationship Strategy for Selling

SALES MEMORANDUM 1A/ROLE-PLAY 1A

To: **Association Account Sales**
From: **T. J. McKee, Sales Manager**
Re: **Developing the Erin Adkins YWCA Account (Call 1, Establishing a Relationship Strategy)**

My sales assistant has called Erin Adkins, chairperson of the YWCA Physical Fitness Week program (see following contact report), and set up an appointment for you on Monday at 1:00 P.M. in Erin's office. During your first sales call with Erin, your call objectives will be to (1) establish a strong relationship, (2) share an appealing benefit of our property to create customer interest, and (3) find out if your customer is planning any conventions in the future.

As we discussed during your training class, using Erin Adkins's prospect information presented below and the sales tools in your product strategy materials, your presentation plan should be to (see Chapters 3–5 and 10):

1. Use compliments, comments on observations, or search for mutual acquaintances to determine which topics Erin wants to talk about (Erin will only want to talk about three of these topics). This should set the stage for a good relationship.

2. Take notes on the topics of interest to Erin so we can add them to our customer information data bank for future calls. (Erin will share three new items of information on each topic of interest, if you acknowledge interest.)

3. Show and describe an appealing and unique benefit of our facility so we will be considered for Erin's future convention needs. (Consider using the Architects Award, p. 431.)

4. Discuss any conventions Erin may be planning.

5. Schedule a call-back appointment.

Name: YWCA	Address:	16 Ruan Center
Contact: Erin Adkins	:	
Phone: 949-245-3740	:	
Title: Chairperson, Physical Fitness Programs	City:	Anaheim
Sec:	State:	CA
Dear: Erin	ZIP:	92802

◄ **CONTACT SCREEN**

(McKee) Toni Bush, the Athletic Director of West College, supplied the following information about Erin Adkins:

1. Toni and Erin have a close relationship.
2. Erin just designed and built a new home.
3. Erin appears in local TV advertising about the YWCA.

◄ **NOTES WINDOW**

Toni reports that in Erin's office you will observe the following:

4. An autographed picture of Olympic Gold Medalist Shawn Johnson
5. A Schwinn Airdyne Fitness Cycle

Comments, Compliments, and Questions	**Notes on New Items of Interest to Customer**
(Toni Bush suggested you mention his name.)	1. (Example: Toni Bush is my cousin)
	2.
	3.
	1.
	2.
	3.
	1.
	2.
	3.

SALES MEMORANDUM 1B/ROLE-PLAY 1B

To: **Corporate Account Sales**
From: **T. J. McKee, Sales Manager**
Re: **Developing the Leigh Combs Epic Design Systems Account (Call 1, Establishing a Relationship Strategy)**

My sales assistant has called Epic Design Systems (see following contact report) and set up an appointment for you on Monday at 1:00 P.M. in Leigh's office. During your first sales call with Leigh, your call objectives will be to (1) establish a strong relationship, (2) share an appealing benefit of our property to create customer's interest, and (3) find out if your customer is planning any conventions in the future.

   As we discussed during your training class, using Leigh Combs's prospect information presented below and the sales tools in your product strategy materials, your presentation plan should be to (see Chapters 3–5 and 10):

1. Use compliments, comments on observations, or search for mutual acquaintances to determine which topics Leigh wants to talk about (Leigh will only want to talk about three of these topics). This should set the stage for a good relationship.

2. Take notes on the topics of interest to Leigh so we can add them to our customer information data bank for future calls. (Leigh will share three new items of information on each topic of interest, if you verbally or nonverbally acknowledge interest.)

3. Show and describe an appealing and unique benefit of our facility so we will be considered for Leigh's future convention needs. (Consider using the Executive Chef Award, pp. 435 and 437.)

4. Discuss any conventions Leigh may be planning.

5. Schedule a call-back appointment.

Name: Epic Design Systems	Address: 2401 West Towers
Contact: Leigh Combs	: Suite 200
Phone: 949-224-0925 X: CC:	:
Title: Customer Service Manager	City: San Diego
Sec: Rhiannon	State: CA
Dear: Leigh	ZIP: 92107

◄ **CONTACT SCREEN**

(McKee) Linn Compiano, the Training Manager at Acme Supply Company, provided the following information about Leigh Combs:
1. Leigh has been on vacation.
2. Leigh is Linn Compiano's cousin.

Linn reports that in Leigh's office you will observe the following:
1. A large picture of Napoleon Bonaparte
2. A degree from our state university
3. An extra-large bookcase containing many business books

◄ **NOTES WINDOW**

Comments, Compliments, and Questions	Notes on New Items of Interest to Customer
(Linn Compiano mentioned that Leigh Combs just returned from a very enjoyable vacation.)	1. (Example: Spent one week in New York City.) 2. 3.
	1. 2. 3.
	1. 2. 3.

ASSESSMENT FORM 1

RELATIONSHIP STRATEGY

Salesperson's Name: _____

Date: _____

Assessment Item	Excellent		Average		Poor	Did Not Do
1. Conducted good verbal introductions (shared full name, title, and company name)	10	9	8	7	6	0
2. Made good nonverbal introduction (good entrance, carriage, handshake, and seating posture)	10	9	8	7	6	0
3. Communicated call objectives (shared why salesperson was calling)	10	9	8	7	6	0
4. Verbalized effective comments and compliments (sincerely made comments and compliments on five relationship topics)	10	9	8	7	6	0
5. Kept conversation focused on customer topics (acknowledged new information provided by customer)	10	9	8	7	6	0
6. Took effective nondistractive notes (was organized and prepared to take notes)	10	9	8	7	6	0
7. Attractively showed material on convention center (was well prepared with a proof device)	10	9	8	7	6	0
8. Made specific benefit statement (made a benefit statement that appealed to customer)	10	9	8	7	6	0
9. Effectively inquired about convention needs (asked good questions about future needs)	10	9	8	7	6	0
10. Effectively thanked customer (communicated appreciation, said thank you, indicated interest in prospect future business)	10	9	8	7	6	0

Relationship Presentation: _____

Total Points

Your Name: _____

Return this form to salesperson and discuss your reaction to this presentation!

Part Three
Understanding Your Customer's Buying Strategy

To:　　**Association Account Salesperson**
From:　**T. J. McKee, Sales Manager**
Re:　　**Erin Adkins Account—phone call from customer**
　　　　(Call 2, Discovering a Customer's Buying Strategy)

Erin Adkins from the YWCA, whom you called on recently, left a message for you to stop in about a program they are planning. Congratulations on making that first call so effectively. Apparently, you established a good relationship.

As we discussed in your training program, your *call objectives* for this sales call should be to:

1. Reestablish your relationship
2. Discover specific information about Erin's buying conditions (the what, why, who, when, and what price needs), so we can custom fit a program for them
3. Set up an appointment to present your solution

Also, as we discussed, your *presentation plan* for this call should include (see Chapters 8 and 11):

1. In advance of your meeting, prepare *general survey questions* to gather facts about your customer's buying situation and to achieve your call objectives.
2. During your meeting, use *confirmation questions* to clarify and confirm Erin's and your own perception of each buying condition. Later, use *specific survey questions* to discover any special buying problems.
3. During your sales meeting, write down each of Erin's buying conditions.
4. To end your first meeting, use your notes to construct a *summary-confirmation question* to clarify and confirm all six of Erin's buying conditions.
5. Schedule a callback appointment to make your presentation and present your proposal.

　Good luck!

GENERAL SURVEY QUESTIONS	NOTES ON BUYING CONDITIONS	
(Example: Can you share with me what you had in mind?)	(Example: Needs a small meeting room)	
	1.	
	2.	
	3.	
	4.	
	5.	
	6.	

SALES MEMORANDUM 2B/ROLE-PLAY 2B

To: Association Account Salesperson
From: T. J. McKee, Sales Manager
Re: Leigh Combs Account—phone call from customer
          (Call 2, Discovering a Customer's Buying Strategy)

Leigh Combs from Epic Design Systems, whom you called on recently, left a message for you to stop in about a program they are planning. Congratulations on making that first call so effectively. Apparently, you established a good relationship.

As we discussed in your training program, your *call objectives* should be to:

1. Reestablish your relationship
2. Discover the facts about Leigh's buying conditions (the what, why, who, when, and what price needs), so we can custom fit a program for them
3. Set up an appointment to present your solution

Also, as we discussed, your *presentation plan* for this call should include (see Chapters 8 and 11):

1. In advance of your meeting, prepare *general survey questions* to gather facts about your customer's buying situation and to achieve your call objectives.
2. During your meeting, use *confirmation questions* to clarify and confirm Leigh's and your own perceptions of each buying condition. Later, use *specific survey questions* to discover any special buying problems.
3. During your sales meeting, write down each of Leigh's buying conditions.
4. To end your first meeting, use your notes to construct a *summary-confirmation question* to clarify and confirm all six of Leigh's buying conditions.
5. Schedule a callback appointment to make your presentation and present your proposal.

  Good luck!

GENERAL SURVEY QUESTIONS	NOTES ON BUYING CONDITIONS
(Example: Can you share with me what you had in mind?)	(Example: Needs a small meeting room)
	1.
	2.
	3.
	4.
	5.
	6.

ASSESSMENT FORM 2

CUSTOMER STRATEGY

Salesperson's Name: _____

Date: _____

Assessment Item	Excellent		Average		Poor	Did Not Do
1. Effectively reestablished relationship (made enthusiastic comments about information from first meeting)	10	9	8	7	6	0
2. Communicated positive body language (entrance, carriage, handshake, and seating)	10	9	8	7	6	0
3. Communicated positive verbal language (used positive words, showed enthusiasm with well-modulated voice)	10	9	8	7	6	0
4. Used customer's name effectively (used name at least three times)	10	9	8	7	6	0
5. Asked general survey questions to secure facts (seemed prepared, questions were general and open ended)	10	9	8	7	6	0
6. Verified customer needs with good confirmation questions (wanted to be correct in interpreting customer needs)	10	9	8	7	6	0
7. Asked specific survey questions to discover special problems (followed up to secure all details)	10	9	8	7	6	0
8. Appeared to take effective notes (was organized and nondistracting, used notes in confirming needs)	10	9	8	7	6	0
9. Effectively set up next appointment (requested another meeting; suggested and wrote down date, time, and place)	10	9	8	7	6	0
10. Effectively thanked customer (communicated appreciation, said thank you, indicated enthusiasm for next meeting)	10	9	8	7	6	0

Discovering Customer Needs Presentation: _____

Total Points

Your Name: _____

Return this form to salesperson and discuss your reaction to this presentation!

Part Four
Developing a Sales Presentation Strategy

SALES MEMORANDUM 3A/ROLE-PLAY 3A

To: **Association Account Sales**
From: **T. J. McKee, Sales Manager**
Re: **Your recent meeting on the Erin Adkins Account**
        (Call 3, Developing a Presentation Strategy)

Congratulations on doing such a thorough job of discovering Erin's buying conditions. I found that your list of buying conditions includes the kind of customer information important to increasing our sales and partnering with our clients. I would like to see a copy of Erin's proposal when you complete it.

Reviewing what we discussed during your training, your next call objectives are:

1. Make a persuasive sales presentation that custom fits your proposal to Erin's needs
2. Negotiate any concerns Erin may have
3. Close and confirm the sale
4. Build repeat and referral business

Also, as we discussed, your *presentation plan* for this call should be to:

1. Prepare and price a product solution that meets Erin's needs. *Complete the Sales Proposal Form* (p. 477).
2. Before your sales call, prepare a *portfolio or PowerPoint* presentation (see model on p. 476) that follows these guidelines. Also, view the PowerPoint presentation at www.pearsonhighered.com/manning.
   a. Review the relationship information and prepare for those topics you will discuss.
   b. Prepare a summary *confirmation* question that verifies the buying conditions secured in your second call. Prepare *probing* questions to discover any pain your customer may be experiencing.
   c. Select sales tools (proof devices), and create feature/benefit selling statements and *need-satisfaction questions* that appeal to Erin's buying conditions (see Chapter 12).
   d. Plan summary confirmation questions that verify Erin's acceptance of your solution to each buying condition. *Complete Strategic Sales Planning Form A* (p. 481) for items b, c, and d.
   e. Prepare to negotiate the time, price, source, and product objections. *Complete Strategic Sales Planning Form B* (p. 482) (see Chapter 13).
   f. Prepare at least four closing methods in addition to the summary of benefits. *Complete Strategic Planning Form C* (p. 483) (see Chapter 14).
   g. Plan methods to service the sale. Follow up by scheduling an appointment between now and the convention date (telephone call or personal visit) to follow through on guarantees concerning rooms and meals, suggestions about audiovisual needs, and any possible changes in the convention schedule. *Complete Strategic Sales Planning Form D* (p. 484) (see Chapter 15).
3. During the sales call reestablish the relationship and, using your portfolio presentation,
   a. Confirm all of Erin's previous buying conditions, and explore any pain being experienced
   b. Match a proof device and feature/benefit selling statement with each buying condition
   c. Confirm Erin's acceptance to each of your proposed benefit statements and need-satisfaction questions
   d. Negotiate any sales resistance
   e. Close the sale
   f. Service the sale to get repeats and referrals

Good luck!

SALES MEMORANDUM 3B/ROLE-PLAY 3B

To: **Corporate Account Sales**
From: **T. J. McKee, Sales Manager**
Re: **Your recent meeting on the Leigh Combs Account**
   (Call 3, Developing a Presentation Strategy)

Congratulations on doing such a thorough job of discovering Leigh's buying conditions. I found that your list of buying conditions includes the kind of customer information important to increasing our sales and partnering with our clients. I would like to see a copy of Leigh's proposal when you complete it.

Reviewing what we discussed during your training, your next *call objectives* are:

1. Make a persuasive sales presentation that custom fits your proposal to Leigh's needs
2. Negotiate any concerns Leigh may have
3. Close and confirm the sale
4. Build repeat and referral business

Also, as we discussed, your *presentation plan* for this call should be to:

1. Prepare and price a product solution that meets Leigh's needs. *Complete the Sales Proposal Form* (p. 477).
2. Before your sales call, prepare a *portfolio or PowerPoint* presentation (see model on p. 476) that follows these guidelines. Also, view the PowerPoint presentation at www.pearsonhighered.com/manning.
   a. Review the relationship information and prepare for those topics you will discuss.
   b. Prepare a summary *confirmation* question that verifies the buying conditions secured in your second call. Prepare *probing* questions to discover any pain your customer may be experiencing.
   c. Select sales tools (proof devices) and create feature/benefit selling statements and *need-satisfaction questions* that appeal to Leigh's buying conditions (see Chapter 12).
   d. Plan confirmation questions that verify Leigh's acceptance of your solution to each buying condition. *Complete Strategic Sales Planning Form A* (p. 481) for items b, c, and d.
   e. Prepare to negotiate the time, price, source, and product objections. *Complete Strategic Sales Planning Form B* (p. 482) (see Chapter 13).
   f. Prepare at least four closing methods in addition to the summary-of-benefits close. *Complete Strategic Planning Form C* (p. 483) (see Chapter 14).
   g. Plan methods to service the sale. Follow up by scheduling an appointment between now and the convention date (telephone call or personal visit) to follow through on guarantees concerning rooms and meals, suggestions about audiovisual needs, and any possible changes in the convention schedule. *Complete Strategic Sales Planning Form D* (p. 484) (see Chapter 15).
3. During the sales call reestablish the relationship and, using your portfolio presentation,
   a. Confirm all of Leigh's previous buying conditions, and explore any pain being experienced
   b. Match a proof device and feature/benefit selling statement with each buying condition
   c. Confirm Leigh's acceptance to each of your proposed benefit statements and *need-satisfaction* questions
   d. Negotiate any sales resistance
   e. Close the sale
   f. Service the sale to get repeats and referrals

Good luck!

ASSESSMENT FORM 3

PRESENTATION STRATEGY

Salesperson's Name: _____

Date: _____

Assessment Item	Excellent		Average		Poor	Did Not Do
1. Reestablished a good relationship (talked sincerely and enthusiastically about topics of interest to customer) Comments:	10	9	8	7	6	0
2. Confirmed needs from previous meeting Comments:	10	9	8	7	6	0
3. Made solution sound appealing (used nontechnical, customer-oriented benefit statements) Comments:	10	9	8	7	6	0
4. Used proof devices to prove sales appeals (made product sound appealing) Comments:	10	9	8	7	6	0
5. Verified customer's understanding of solution Comments:	10	9	8	7	6	0
6. Negotiated price objection (established high value to price impression) Comments:	10	9	8	7	6	0
7. Negotiated time objection (created need to sign now using empathy) Comments:	10	9	8	7	6	0
8. Negotiated source objection (knew the competition well) Comments:	10	9	8	7	6	0
9. Asked for the order, closed sale (attempted to close after each objection) Comments:	10	9	8	7	6	0
10. Serviced the sale (established relationship that would result in referrals or repeat sales opportunities) Comments:	10	9	8	7	6	0

Overall quality of sales portfolio and proof devices

Presentation Points

	25	20	15	10	5	0

Comments:

Total Points

Return this form to salesperson and discuss your reaction to this presentation!

Your Name: _____

POWERPOINT OR PORTFOLIO PRESENTATION MODEL

POWERPOINT SLIDES OR THREE-RING BINDER SUGGESTIONS

PAGE 1 Summary of Customer's Buying Conditions 1. 2. 3. 4. 5. 6. (confirmation question)	**PAGE 2** Buying Condition 1	**PAGE 3** Proof Devices (could be more than one) (state benefits, ask confirmation question)	**PAGE 4** Buying Condition 2
PAGE 5 Proof Devices (state benefits, ask confirmation question)	**PAGE 6** Buying Condition 3	**PAGE 7** Proof Devices (state benefits, ask confirmation question)	**PAGE 8** Buying Condition 4
PAGE 9 Proof Devices (state benefits, ask confirmation question)	**PAGE 10** Buying Condition 5	**PAGE 11** Proof Devices (state benefits, ask confirmation question)	**PAGE 12** Buying Condition 6
PAGE 13 Proof Devices (state benefits, ask confirmation question)	**PAGE 14** Summary of Benefits 1. 2. 3. 4. 5. 6. 7. (trial close)	**FRONT POCKET MATERIALS** Additional value-added pages as needed to overcome sales resistance and close the sale	**BACK POCKET MATERIALS** Additional value-added pages as needed to service the sale

SALES PROPOSAL

Customer Name: _____ Title: _____

Organization Name: _____ Telephone: _____

Address: _____

Date(s) of Meetings: _____

Kind of Meetings: _____

Buying Conditions (What the customer needs—be specific): _____

_____

_____

A. Meal Functions Needed

	Time	Description	Quantity	Price	Total
Meal 1					
Meal 2					
Other		(Beverages, setup fees, etc.)			

Total _____

Sales Tax _____

Service Charge _____

Total Meal Cost _____

B. Meeting and Banquet Rooms and Equipment Needed (describe time, date, and cost)

_____   _____

_____   _____

_____   _____

_____   _____

Total _____

Sales Tax _____

Total Meeting/Banquet Rooms and Equipment Charges _____

C. Guest Rooms Needed

Number of Rooms Needed	Description (dates, locations, special conditions)	Group Rate per Room	Total Cost

Total _____

Room Tax _____

Sales Tax _____

Total Guest Room Charges _____

Total Customer Costs (from above)

A. $_____ plus **B.** $_____ plus **C.** $_____ equals **Total Charges** $_____

_____   _____
Authorized Signature   Date   Customer Signature   Date

_____   _____
Title   Title

PARK SHORES RESORT AND CONVENTION CENTER

MEETING AND BANQUET ROOM SCHEDULE OF EVENTS

1ST THURSDAY OF NEXT MONTH

Central Park East
Open—Expect confirmation tomorrow

Central Park West
Open—Expect confirmation tomorrow

Park Lane
10:00 A.M. C of C Membership Committee
2:00 P.M. County Central Planning Committee

Top of the Park
Open—Expect confirmation tomorrow

Revolver
Open

Dance Floor
7:00 P.M. IBM Dinner and Dance

Parkview
Open—Expect confirmation tomorrow

1007 and 1009
11:00 A.M. Advertising Prof's Luncheon
7:00 P.M. IBM Communication Seminar

107 and 109
10:00 A.M.—Expect confirmation tomorrow

ATTENTION: Phone 949-225-0925, ext. 8512
immediately to confirm reservations.

➡ Use the scheduling information on the reverse of this page to illustrate to your customers that reservations for rooms must be scheduled as soon as possible. All guest and meeting room reservations are guaranteed on a "first come, first signed" basis with the customer's signature on a sales proposal. Once a room has been reserved on a signed sales form, it is no longer available. Upon receiving a signature, sales and marketing personnel should immediately phone, fax, or e-mail this information to the reservations department. Noting that a possible meeting may be confirmed does not constitute a signed reservation.

STRATEGIC SALES PLANNING FORM A

MATCHING BUYING CONDITIONS WITH PROOF DEVICES AND FEATURE/BENEFITS

BUYING CONDITION	PROOF DEVICE	FEATURE	SPECIFIC BENEFIT	CONFIRMATION QUESTION
You indicated you wanted . . .	*Here is . . .*	*which has (have) . . .*	*which means to you . . .*	*What do you think?*
1. _____ (number) guest rooms	A picture of one of our guest rooms (see p. 441)	Just been remodeled	Your people will enjoy clean, comfortable, spacious, and attractive surroundings	Is that what you had in mind?
2.				
3.				
4.				
5.				
6.				

Optional Role-Play 3A Instructions (see Chapters 11 and 12)

Step 1   Prepare your presentation plan by completing the above form.

Step 2   Organize your presentation plan by placing the above information on 8½″ × 11″ sheets of paper according to the portfolio or PowerPoint presentation plan on page 476. Select proof devices from the product strategy materials presented on pages 429–459 and the completed proposal on page 477.

Step 3   Using the PowerPoint or portfolio materials you have prepared, pair off with another student who will play the role of your customer. Review your customer's buying conditions, present your solutions with benefit statements, prove your sales appeals with demonstrations, secure your customer's reactions, and summarize the benefits presented. Discuss your customer's reactions to your presentation. This exercise will help you prepare for Sales Call 3.

STRATEGIC SALES PLANNING FORM B

ANTICIPATING AND NEGOTIATING SALES RESISTANCE WORKSHEET

PART I	ANTICIPATING SALES RESISTANCE	PART II	NEGOTIATING SALES RESISTANCE
Type	**What Customer Might Say**	**Methods***	**What You Will Say (include proof devices you will use)**
Time	"I would like to take a day to think over your proposal."	Indirect denial	"I understand, however" (Show p. 479, Schedule of Events.)
Price	"That price is way over my budget."		
Source	"I'm going to check with the Marriott."		
Product	"I'm concerned about the size of your meeting rooms."		

Optional Role-Play 3B Instructions

Using the preceding material you have prepared, pair off with another student who will play the role of your customer. Provide your customer with the material in Part I and instruct her to raise sales resistance in any order she chooses. Playing the role of the salesperson, you will respond with the material you prepared in Part II. Continue the dialogue until all the types of sales resistance have been successfully negotiated. Discuss with your customer her reaction to your methods of successfully negotiating the different types of sales resistance. This exercise will help you prepare for Sales Call 3.

*Method of Negotiating Sales Resistance (see Chapter 13)

- Direct denial
- Indirect denial
- Question
- Third party
- Superior benefit
- Demonstration
- Trial offer
- Feel, felt, found
- Postponement

STRATEGIC SALES PLANNING FORM C

CLOSING AND CONFIRMING THE SALE WORKSHEET

PART I	PART II	
Verbal and Nonverbal Closing Clues	**Method of Closing***	**What You Will Say** (include proof devices you will use)
Agrees with each benefit	Summary of the benefits and direct appeal	"Let me review what we have talked about. . . . May I get your signature?" (Use p. 477, Sales Proposal.)
Agrees after an objection to price, time, or source	Assumption	
Appears enthusiastic and impatient	Trial close and assumption	
Agrees with all benefits but will not under any circumstances go over budget	Special concession	

Optional Role-Play 3C Instructions

Using the preceding material you have prepared, pair off with another student who will play the role of your customer. Provide your customer with the appropriate closing clues from Part I and instruct him to provide verbal or nonverbal closing clues in any order he chooses. Playing the role of the salesperson, you will respond with the material you prepared in Part II. Continue the dialogue until you have responded to all the anticipated closing clues. Discuss with your customer his reaction to your methods of successfully closing and confirming the sale. This exercise will help you prepare for Sales Call 3.

*Method of Closing the Sale (see Chapter 14)

- Trial close
- Summary of the benefits
- Assumption
- Special concession
- Multiple option
- Direct appeal
- Balance sheet
- Management
- Impending event

STRATEGIC SALES PLANNING FORM D

SERVICING THE SALE WORKSHEET

PART I	PART II
What You Will Do to Add Value to the Sale	**What You Will Say or Write to Add Value to the Sale**
1. Schedule appointments to confirm rooms and final counts on meals. Dates Time 1 _____ 1 _____ 2 _____ 2 _____	"I would like to call to confirm . . ." (Show p. 457, Convention Center Policies)
2. Make suggestions during next meeting about audiovisual equipment, beverages for breaks, etc.	
3. Provide personal assurances concerning your continuing efforts to make the meeting an outstanding success.	
4. Prepare thank-you letter concerning Sales Call 3.	

Optional Role-Play 3D Instructions

Using the preceding material you have prepared, pair off with another student who will play the role of your customer. Using the topics identified in Part I, verbally present what you have prepared in Part II on this form. Discuss with your customer her reaction to your methods of servicing the sale. This exercise will help you prepare for Sales Call 3.

Method of Servicing the Sale (see Chapter 15)

- Follow through on promises and obligations
- Follow up to ensure customer satisfaction
- Expansion selling

GRAY ISSUES — ETHICAL DECISION MAKING IN SELLING TODAY

ANSWER KEY–PART I (SEE CHAPTER 3 ETHICS APPLICATION EXERCISES PP. 68–70)

MINI-CASE 1

Answer A (−10 points) This is a misrepresentation of the facts.

Answer B (−5 points) This is a misrepresentation of the facts, but at least you intend to clarify the information during the interview.

Answer C (+10 points) This is accurate information.

Answer D (+5 points) Listing your grade point average on the resume is an option, not a requirement.

MINI-CASE 2

Answer A (+5 points) Membership is pending so this is a good choice.

Answer B (0 points) If for some reason the membership is not approved, this option might later prove to be embarrassing.

Answer C (+10 points) An accurate description of community service activities will enhance your employment prospects.

Answer D (−10 points) This would be a misrepresentation of the facts.

MINI-CASE 3

Answer A (−5 points) This response would likely weaken your chances of getting the job.

Answer B (+10 points) The best option is to provide an accurate history of your earnings. The starting salary will, very likely, be subject to negotiation.

Answer C (−10 points) It would be a mistake to provide false information.

Answer D (−5 points) This response, like Answer A, will not enhance your chances of being hired.

MINI-CASE 4

Answer A (+10 points) The Park Shores Resort and Convention Center expects to reimburse you for actual meal expenses. You may enhance your professional image by demonstrating that you are willing to travel as economically as possible.

Answer B (−10 points) It would be wrong to request money for expenses you did not incur.

Answer C (−5 points) Although the $41.50 may cover actual out-of-pocket expenses, the Park Shore is committed to paying for actual meal expenses.

Answer D (+5 points) There is nothing wrong with this solution.

MINI-CASE 5

Answer A (−10 points) Accepting the invitation implies you are interested in working for this company.

Answer B (+10 points) Do not accept the free trip unless you are willing to consider a job offer.

Answer C (−10 points) You should not accept the free trip unless you are willing to consider a possible job offer.

Answer D (−10 points) This rationale may seem logical, but it does not justify accepting travel expenses under false pretensions.

ANSWER KEY–PART II

MINI-CASE 1

Answer A (−5 points) The customer will schedule the conference during the period when the lower rates are in effect, so it's best to use the special package rate now.

Answer B (−10 points) A major delay in providing the price quotes may result in loss of the customer.

Answer C (+10 points) The conference will be held during the time period when the lower rates are in effect. A well-established customer would likely be upset if you withheld information regarding the new rate schedule.

Answer D (−5 points) The customer should be given the accurate rate information at the time of the initial request.

MINI-CASE 2

Answer A (−5 points) There is likely some reason why you have been unable to close the sale. To discover the reason, you must make additional contacts with the customer.

Answer B (+10 points) You should make additional efforts to close the sale, but do not provide information that is not accurate.

(continued)

Answer C (−10 points) It would be unethical to provide information that is not accurate.

Answer D (−5 points) Price has already been negotiated. There are many other closing methods that should be used before considering price reduction.

MINI-CASE 3

Answer A (+10 points) You agreed to provide the special room arrangement and the menu substitution. It would be unethical to neglect these special requests.

Answer B (−5 points) It would be inappropriate to do this unless you first obtain the customer's approval for the added fees.

Answer C (−5 points) This action will likely create a customer relations problem and may eliminate any chance of repeat business.

Answer D (−10 points) This option is not only unprofessional, but will likely put an additional strain on relations with the customer.

MINI-CASE 4

Answer A (−10 points) It would be unethical to offer special concessions in order to win a bonus.

Answer B (−10 points) This action is very similar to Answer A.

Answer C (−5 points) You are very close to winning the bonus, so you should not give up.

Answer D (+10 points) If Apco decides to schedule the meeting, you will have won the bonus. If you do not sign a contract with Apco, you may sign another new account.

MINI-CASE 5

Answer A (−10 points) All of this information would be covered under a standard non-compete agreement. Therefore, it would be unethical to remove it for future use.

Answer B (−5 points) During the time this information was collected, you were on the Park Shore payroll. Therefore, the prospect list is not your property.

Answer C (+10 points) This is the most ethical course of action because all of the information is the property of Park Shore.

Answer D (0 points) This request would be denied, so it does not have merit.

Endnotes

Chapter 1

1. www.salesleadershipalliance.co.uk/sla-community-blog/inter-view-neil-rackham-the-original-spin-doctor/ (accessed February 14, 2013).
2. Adapted from Daniel H. Pink, *To Sell Is Human: The Surprising Truth about Moving Others,* (New York, NY: Penguin Group, 2012), pp. 16–19.
3. Michael R. Solomon, Greg W. Marshall, and Elnora W. Stuart, *Marketing: Real People, Real Choices,* 7th ed. (Upper Saddle River, NJ: Prentice Hall, 2012), p. 427.
4. Christian Homburg, Jan Wieseke, and Torsten Bornemann, "Implementing the Marketing Concept at the Employee-Customer Interface: The Role of Customer Need Knowledge," *Journal of Marketing*, July 2009, pp. 64–81.
5. Lucy McCauley, "Voices: The State of the New Economy," *Fast Company*, September 1999, p. 124.
6. Robert H. Bloom, "Looking around the Corner," *Salesforceexp*, November/December 2010, p. 21.
7. Stan Davis and Christopher Meyer, *Blur: The Speed of Change in the Connected Economy* (New York: Addison-Wesley, 1998), p. 9.
8. David Shenk, *Data Smog: Surviving the Information Glut* (New York: HarperEdge, 1997), pp. 27–29.
9. Michael R. Solomon, Greg W. Marshall, and Elnora W. Stuart, *Marketing: Real People, Real Choices,* 7th ed. (Upper Saddle River, NJ: Prentice Hall, 2012), p. 429.
10. Liz C. Wang, Julie Baker, Judy A. Wagner, and Kirk Wakefield, "Can a Retail Web Site Be Social?" *Journal of Marketing*, July 2007, pp. 143–157.
11. Michael Hammer, *The Agenda* (New York: Three Rivers Press, 2003), p. 6.
12. Gary L. Frankwick, Stephen S. Porter, and Lawrence A. Crosby, "Dynamics of Relationship Selling: A Longitudinal Examination of Changes in Salesperson–Customer Relationship Status," *Journal of Personal Selling and Sales Management*, Spring 2001, p. 135.
13. Greg Ip, "Why High-Fliers, Built on Big Ideas, Are Such Fast Fallers," *Wall Street Journal*, April 4, 2002, p. A–1.
14. Julia Chang, "Faker or Deal Maker," *Sales & Marketing Management*, December 2003, p. 30; Kris Maher, "A Job Where Golf Comes to the Fore," *Wall Street Journal*, June 29, 2004, p. B6; Kris Maher, "Sales Chief Is Called For," *Wall Street Journal*, May 20, 2003, p. B10.
15. "The 500 Largest Sales Forces in America," *Selling Power*, October 2015, pp. 58–60.
16. "Sales Jobs in Demand; Sales Reps at a Premium," http://www.economicmodeling.com/2014/06/27 (accessed January 13, 2016).
17. Howard Stevens and Theodore Kinni, *Achieve Sales Excellence* (Avon: Platinum Press, 2007), p. 18.
18. Gabrielle Birkner, "Who Says Titles Don't Matter?" *Sales & Marketing Management*, July 2001, p. 14.
19. "The Best- And Worst-Paying Sales Jobs Right Now," http://www.forbes.com/sites/jacquelynsmith/2013/06/04/the-best-and-worst-paying-sales-jobs-right-now/#2715e4857a0b1db799742d99 (accessed January 13, 2016).
20. "The 30 Highest-Paying Jobs in America," http://jobs.aol.com/articles/2015/09/29/the-30-highest-paying-jobs-in-america (accessed Jan. 13, 2016); "Top-paying jobs," http://money.cnn.com/gallery/pf/2015/01/27/top-paying-jobs-2015/index.html (accessed Jan. 13, 2016).
21. Thomas Steenburgh and Michael Ahearne, "Motivating Salespeople: What Really Works," *Harvard Business Review*, July–August 2012, p. 71.
22. 2015 US MBD: Sales, Marketing, & Communications Survey, Mercer, June 2015.
23. Michele Marchetti, "What a Sales Call Costs," *Sales & Marketing Management*, September 2000, pp. 80–81.
24. Theodore B. Kinni, "Fast Track to the Top: How to Start Out in Sales and End Up as CEO," *Selling Power*, July/August, 2007, pp. 56–61.
25. "Women in the Labor Force: A Databook (2014 Edition)," http://www.bls.gov/opub/reports/cps/women-in-the-labor-force-a-databook-2014.pdf (accessed January 13, 2016).
26. "Top 20 Best-Paying Jobs For Women In 2012," www.forbes.com/pictures/lmj45jmhi/no-19-marketing-and-sales-managers (accessed June 23, 2013).
27. Carol Hymowitz, "Women Put Noses to the Grindstone, and Miss Opportunities," *Wall Street Journal*, February 3, 2004, p. B1.
28. Bonnie Harris, "Wanted: Women in Finance, Why: Client Base Changing," *The Des Moines Register*, Monday, January 29, 2007, p. 4D.
29. Brett A. Boyle, "The Importance of the Industrial Inside Sales Force: A Case Study," *Industrial Marketing Management*, September 1996, p. 339.
30. Boone and Kurtz, *Contemporary Marketing*, 13th ed. (South-Western College Publishing, Cincinnati, OH, 2009).
31. www.travel.cnn.com/explorations/escape/worlds-tallest-hotel-reaches-dubai-810539 (accessed March 5, 2013).
32. Gerald L. Manning and Barry L. Reece, Intelecom Video Library, *Selling Today,* 9th ed.
33. Personal interview with Brad Duffy, December 22, 2007.
34. Gerald L. Manning and Barry L. Reece, Intelecom Video Library, *Selling Today,* 9th ed.
35. Ibid.
36. Ibid.
37. Donna Harris, "Asbury Sells College Graduates on Auto Retail," *Automotive News*, January 26, 2004, p. 26.
38. Ibid.
39. "History of Julian's," www.julianstyle.com/ (accessed March 12, 2013).
40. "Direct Selling in 2014: An Overview," http://www.dsa.org/docs/default-source/research/research2014factsheet.pdf?sfvrsn=0 (accessed on Jan 13, 2013).
41. www.igniteyourvision.net/files/DSN_USA_TOP_10.pdf, (accessed March 13, 2013).
42. John R. Sparks and Joseph A. Schenk, "Socialization Communication, Organizational Citizenship Behaviors, and Sales in a Multilevel Marketing Organization," *Journal of Personal Selling and Sales Management*, Spring 2006, pp. 161–180.
43. John Naisbitt, *Megatrends* (New York: Warner Books, 1982), p. 18.
44. Adapted from Daniel H. Pink, *To Sell Is Human: The Surprising Truth about Moving Others* (New York: Penguin Group, 2012), p. 21.
45. Stanley Marcus, "Sales School," *Fast Company*, November 1998, p. 105.
46. Thomas A. Stewart, *The Wealth of Knowledge: Intellectual Capital and the Twenty-first Century Organization* (New York: Random House, 2003), p-5. Thomas A. Stewart, "Knowledge, the Appreciating Commodity," Fortune, October 12, 1998, p. 18.

47. Martin Gargiulo, Gokhan Ertug, and Charles Galunic (2009), "The Two Faces of Control: Network Closure and Individual Performance among Knowledge Workers," *Administrative Science Quarterly*, 54, pp. 299–333.

48. Sudheer Gupta (2008), "Channel Structure with Knowledge Spillover," *Marketing Science*, 27(2), pp. 247–261.

49. Dennis Jenkins, "Entrepreneurial Endeavors for Sales & Marketing Professionals," *American Salesman*, August 2007.

50. Beth Belton, "Technology Is Changing Face of U.S. Sales Force," *USA Today*, February 9, 1999, p. A2.

51. Brian Tracy, *The 100 Absolutely Unbreakable Laws of Business Success* (San Francisco: Berrett-Koehler Publishers, Inc., 2000), p. 192.

52. Linda Corman, "Look Who's Selling Now," *Selling*, July–August 1996, pp. 46–53; "Everyone's a Seller," *Sales & Marketing Management*, March 2003, p. 12.

53. Carl Schramm, "Expanding the Entrepreneur Class," *Harvard Business Review*, July–August 2012, p. 40.

54. Gerry Khermouch, "Keeping the Froth on Sam Adams," *BusinessWeek*, September 1, 2003, pp. 54–56.

55. Simon J. Bell, Seigyoung Auh, and Karen Smalley (2005), "Customer Relationship Dynamics: Service Quality and Customer Loyalty in the Context of Varying Levels of Customer Expertise and Switching Costs," *Journal of the Academy of Marketing Science*, 33(2), pp. 169–183.

56. Harry Beckwith, *Selling the Invisible* (New York: Warner Books, 2012), p. 38; see also Norm Brodsky, "Street Smarts," *Inc.*, June 2004, pp. 53–54.

57. Alfred M. Pelham and Pamela Kravitz (2008), "An Exploratory Study of the Influence of Sales Training Content and Salesperson Evaluation on Salesperson Adaptive Selling, Customer Orientation, Listening, and Consulting Behaviors," *Journal of Strategic Marketing*, 16(5), pp. 413–435.

58. Heather Johnson, "Field of Sales," *Training*, July 2004, p. 34.

59. "Professional Selling Skills," https://www.collin.edu/cwed/ag/AG_Professional_Selling_Skills.pdf (accessed on Jan. 13, 2016).

60. Kristine Ellis, "Deal Maker or Breaker?" *Training*, April 2002, pp. 34–37; Michele Marchetti, "Sales Training Even a Rep Could Love," *Sales & Marketing Management*, June 1998, p. 70.

61. Henry Canaday, "In the Trenches," *Selling Power*, March 2007, pp. 25–27.

62. Terry Loe in Henry Canaday, "You Can Do It," *Selling Power*, January/February 2007, pp. 23–26.

Endnotes for Boxed Features

a. Gene Koretz, "Women Swell the Workforce," *BusinessWeek*, November 4, 1996, p. 32; Naomi Freundlich, "Maybe Working Women Can't Have It All," *BusinessWeek*, September 15, 1997, pp. 19–22; Keith H. Hammonds, "She Works Hard for the Money," *BusinessWeek*, May 22, 1995, p. 54; Anne Fisher, "Overseas, U.S. Businesswomen May Have the Edge," *Fortune*, September 28, 1998, p. 304; Carol Hymowitz, "Women Put Noses to the Grindstone, and Miss Opportunities," *Wall Street Journal*, February 3, 2004, p. B1.

b. Based on John F. Tanner and George Dudley, "How U.S. Salespeople Differ from Their Peers Overseas," *Value-Added Selling*, February 14, 2005, p. 4.

c. Based on Malcolm Fleschner, "Chief Sales Executives," *Selling Power*, April 2002, pp. 58–59.

d. Based on "A Living or a Life," *Fast Company*, January/February 2000, p. 264.

Chapter 2

1. For a comprehensive description of the distinct stages in the evolution of personal selling, see Thomas R. Wotruba, "The Evolutionary Process of Personal Selling," *Journal of Personal Selling and Sales Management*, Summer 1991, p. 4.

2. Phillip Kotler and Gary Armstrong, *Principles of Marketing*, 15th ed. (Upper Saddle River, NJ: Prentice Hall, 2013), p. 10.

3. Louis E. Boone and David L. Kurtz, *Contemporary Marketing*, 15th ed. (Mason, OH: South-Western Cengage Learning, 2012), p. 11.

4. Norihiko Shirouzu, Gregory L. White, and Joseph B. White, "Beyond Explorer Woes, Ford Misses Key Turns in Buyers, Technology," *Wall Street Journal*, January 14, 2002, p. A1.

5. Jeff Bennett, "Ford Expects Auto Industry Sales Pace to Continue," *Wall Street Journal Online*, May 2010, online.wsj.com (accessed March 7, 2013).

6. Malcolm Fleschner, "World Wide Winner—The UPS Success Story," *Selling Power*, November/December 2001, p. 58; "50 Best Companies to Sell For," *Selling Power*, November/December 2004, pp. 94–95.

7. "America's 25 Best Sales Forces," *Sales & Marketing Management*, July 2000, p. 59; "The 25 Best Service Companies to Sell For," *Selling Power*, November/December 2004, p. 95.

8. Philip Kotler and Kevin Lane Keller, *Marketing Management*, 14th ed. (Upper Saddle River, NJ: Pearson Prentice Hall, 2012), p. 25–26.

9. Andris A. Zoltners and Prabhakant Sinha, "Sales Territory Design: Thirty Years of Modeling and Implementation," *Marketing Science*, Summer 2005, pp. 313–331.

10. Robert M. Peterson, George H. Lucas, and Patrick L. Schul, "Forming Consultative Trade Alliances: Walking the Walk in the New Selling Environment," *NAMA Journal*, Spring 1998, p. 11; Beth Belton, "Technology Is Changing Face of U.S. Sales Force," *USA Today*, February 9, 1999, p. 2A.

11. Charles Gottenkieny, "Proper Training Can Result in Positive ROI," *Selling*, August 2003, p. 9.

12. Tim Smith, "Between Solution and Transactional Selling," www.wiglafjournal/selling (accessed March 7, 2013).

13. Thomas R. Wotruba, "The Evolutionary Process in Personal Selling," *Journal of Personal Selling and Sales Management*, Summer 1991, p. 4.

14. Christian Homburg, Nicole Koschate, and Wayne D. Hoyer, "Do Satisfied Customers Really Pay More? A Study of the Relationship between Customer Satisfaction and Willingness to Pay More," *Journal of Marketing*, April 2005, pp. 84–96.

15. Michael R. Solomon, Greg W. Marshall, and Elnora W. Stuart, *Marketing—Real People, Real Choices*, 7th ed. (Upper Saddle River, NJ: Prentice Hall, 2012), p. 35.

16. Robert B. Miller and Stephen E. Heiman, *Strategic Selling* (New York: Warren Books, 2005), p. 33.

17. Fergal Glynn, "Is Traditional Sales Obsolete? The Shift to Consultative Selling," https://www.salesforce.com/blog/2014/12/traditional-sales-obsolete-shift-consultative-selling-gp.html (accessed on Jan. 13, 2016); Patricia Seybold, *The Customer Revolution* (New York: Random House, 2001), p. 1.

18. Fernando Jaramillo, William B. Locander, Paul E. Spector, and Eric G. Harris, "Getting the Job Done: The Moderating Role of Initiative on the Relationship between Intrinsic Motivation and Adaptive Selling," *Journal of Personal Selling and Sales Management*, Winter 2007, pp. 59–74.

19. Keith M. Eades, *The New Solutions Selling* (New York: McGraw-Hill, 2004), pp. 9–10.

20. Marvin A. Jolson, "Broadening the Scope of Relationship Selling," *Journal of Personal Selling and Sales Management*, Fall 1997, p. 77.
21. Keith M. Eades, *The New Solutions Selling* (New York: McGraw-Hill, 2004), pp. 102–104.
22. Patricia Seybold, *The Customer Revolution* (New York: Random House, 2001), p. 1.
23. Christian Homburg, Jan Wieseke, and Torsten Bornemann, "Implementing the Marketing Concept at the Employee-Customer Interface: The Role of Customer Need-Knowledge," *Journal of Marketing*, July 2009, pp. 64–81.
24. Jagdish Sheth and Reshma H. Shah, "Till Death Do Us Part … But Not Always: Six Antecedents to a Customer's Relational Preference in Buyer–Seller Exchanges," *Industrial Marketing Management*, June 2003, pp. 627–631.
25. Erin Strout, "Fast Forward," *Sales & Marketing Management*, December 2001, pp. 37–38.
26. Amy Gallo, "The Value of Keeping the Right Customers," *Harvard Business Review*, October 2014, p. 45.
27. Gary Armstrong and Philip Kotler, *Marketing—An Introduction*, 11th ed. (Upper Saddle River, NJ: Prentice Hall, 2012), p. 23.
28. Lorrie Grant, "Radio Shack Uses Strategic Alliances to Spark Recovery," *USA Today*, January 26, 2001, p. 3–B.
29. Jonathan Hughes and Jeff Weiss, "Simple Rules for Making Alliances Work," *Harvard Business Review*, November 2007, p. 122.
30. For a discussion of strategic selling alliances that involve the sales representatives from two or more organizations, see J. Brock Smith and Donald W. Barclay, "Selling Partner Relationships: The Role of Interdependence and Relative Influences," *Journal of Personal Selling and Sales Management*, Fall 1999, pp. 21–40.
31. www.strategicaccounts.org/ (accessed March 7, 2013).
32. Gary Armstrong and Philip Kotler, *Marketing: An Introduction*, 11th ed. (Upper Saddle River, NJ: Prentice Hall, 2012), p. 16.
33. Michael Hammer, *The Agenda* (New York: Random House, 2001), pp. 38–39.

Endnotes for Boxed Features
a. Andris A. Zoltners and Prabhakant Sinha, Sally E. Lorimer, "Why Sales and Marketing Don't Get Along," *Harvard Business Review*, November 2013.
b. Philip Kotler, Neil Rackham, and Suj Krishnaswamy, "Ending the War between Sales & Marketing," *Harvard Business Review*, July/August 2006, pp. 68–78; Dave Stein, "Sales and Marketing Alignment, Take 2," *Sales & Marketing Management*, January/February 2007, p. 9.
c. Ken Le Meunier-FitzHugh and Nigel F. Piercy, "Does Collaboration between Sales and Marketing Affect Business Performance?" *Journal of Personal Selling and Sales Management*, 27(3), pp. 207–220.
d. Erin Anderson and Leonard Lodish (2006), "Leading the effective sales force: the Asian sales force management environment," working paper, pp. 7–8.
e. Based on Robert Kreitner, *Management*, 8th ed. (Boston: Houghton Mifflin, 2001), pp. 3–4.

Chapter 3
1. Daniel Goleman, *Working with Emotional Intelligence* (New York: Bantam Dell, 2006), pp. 22–28, 317; Geoffrey James, "Use Emotional Intelligence to Improve Sales," *Selling Power*, January/February 2005, pp. 43–45.
2. Daniel Goleman, *Emotional Intelligence* (New York: Bantam Dell, 2006), p. 34; Cary Cherniss and Daniel Goleman (eds.), *The Emotionally Intelligent Workplace* (San Francisco: Jossey-Bass, 2001), pp. 22–24. For more information on social competence, see Daniel Goleman, *Working with Emotional Intelligence* (New York: Bantam Dell, 2006), pp. 22–28.
3. L. B. Gschwandtner and Gerhard Gschwandtner, "Balancing Act," *Selling Power*, June 1996, p. 24.
4. "The World Is Flat: A Brief History of the Twenty-First Century," www.thomaslfriedman.com (accessed July 10, 2010).
5. Matthew McKay, Martha Davis, and Patrick Fanning, *Messages: The Communication Skills Book* (Oakland, CA: New Harbinger, 2009), p. 108.
6. O. C. Ferrell, John Fraedrich, and Linda Ferrell, *Business Ethics: Ethical Decision Making and Cases*, 5th ed. (Boston: Houghton Mifflin Company, 2002), p. 208.
7. Barry L. Reece and Rhonda Brandt, *Effective Human Relations: Personal and Organizational Applications* (Boston: Houghton Mifflin Company, 2008), pp. 125–126.
8. William M. Pride, Robert J. Hughes, and Jack R. Kapoor, *Business*, 7th ed. (Boston: Houghton Mifflin Company, 2002), p. 40.
9. Patricia Gray, "Business Class," *Fortune*, April 17, 2006, p. 336; Philip Kotler and Gary Armstrong, *Principles of Marketing*, 14th ed. (Upper Saddle River, NJ: Prentice Hall, 2011), p. 568.
10. Alan M. Webber, "Are All Consultants Corrupt?" *Fast Company*, May 2002, pp. 130–134.
11. Philip Kotler and Kevin Lane Keller, *Marketing Management*, 14th ed. (Upper Saddle River, NJ: Prentice Hall, 2012), p. 630.
12. Betsy Cummings, "Ethical Breach," *Sales & Marketing Management*, July 2004, p. 10.
13. "Ethics and Social Media: Where Should You Draw The Line?," http://mashable.com/2012/03/17/social-media-ethics/ (accessed February 5, 2016).
14. O. C. Ferrell, John Fraedrich, and Linda Ferrell, *Business Ethics*, 10th ed. (Boston: Houghton Mifflin Company, 2013), p. 183.
15. Michele Krebs, "All the Marketing Men," *Autoweek*, February 16, 1998, p. 11.
16. Joseph A. McKinney and Carlos W. Moore, "International Bribery: Does a Written Code of Ethics Make a Difference in Perceptions of Business," *Journal of Business Ethics*, April 2008, pp. 103–111.
17. Ken Brown and Gee L. Lee, "Lucent Fires Top China Executives," *Wall Street Journal*, April 7, 2004, p. A8; Carl F. Fey, "How to Do Business in Russia," *Wall Street Journal*, October 27, 2007, p. R4.
18. Steve Sack, "Watch the Words," *Sales & Marketing Management*, July 1, 1985, p. 56.
19. Jeanne C. Meister, "Increase Your Company's Productivity with Social Media," Harvard Business Review, September 2011, https://hbr.org/2011/09/increase-your-companys-productiv (accessed on February 5, 2016).
20. Michael Schrage, "Internet: Internal Threat?" *Fortune*, July 9, 2001, p. 184.
21. Mary C. Gentile, "Managing Yourself: Keeping Your Colleagues Honest," *Harvard Business Review*, March 2010, www.hbr.org/2010/03/managing-yourself-keeping-your-colleagues-honest/ar/1 (accessed February 5, 2013).
22. Rob Zeiger, "Sex, Sales & Stereotypes," *Sales & Marketing Management*, July 1995, pp. 52–53.
23. Barry L. Reece and Rhonda Brandt, *Effective Human Relations—Personal and Organizational Applications*, 10th ed. (Boston: Houghton Mifflin Company, 2008), p. 110.

24. Betsy Cummings, "Do Customers Hate Salespeople?" *Sales & Marketing Management*, June 2001, pp. 50–51.

25. Ron Willingham, *Integrity Selling for the 21st Century* (New York: Currency Doubleday, 2009), p. 1.

26. Nina Mazar, On Amir, and Dan Ariely, "The Dishonesty of Honest People: A Theory of Self-Concept Maintenance," *Journal of Marketing Research*, December 2008, pp. 633–644.

27. Ron Willingham, "Four Traits All Highly Successful Salespeople Have in Common" (audiotape presentation), Phoenix, AZ, 1998.

28. Price Pritchett, *The Ethics of Excellence* (Dallas, TX: Pritchett & Associates, Inc., n.d.), p. 14.

29. Research on how cheaters justify their actions is cited in Romy Drucker, "The Devil Made Me Do It," *BusinessWeek*, July 24, 2006, p. 10.

30. Robert Kreitner, Barry Reece, and James P. O'Grady, *Business*, 2nd ed. (Boston: Houghton Mifflin Company, 1990), pp. 647–648.

31. P. Andrew Riley, "Three Steps to Protect Your Trade Secrets," http://www.finnegan.com/resources/articles/articlesdetail .aspx?news=2bec35b7-5ea8-4cb4-9988-73824efe2cdf, September 2013 (accessed on February 5, 2013).

32. John D. Hansen and Robert J. Riggle, "Ethical Salesperson Behavior in Sales Relationships," *Journal of Personal Selling and Sales Management*, March 2009, pp. 151–166.

33. Neil Rackham and John R. DeVincentis, *Rethinking the Sales Force* (New York: McGraw-Hill, 1999), pp. 83–84. A discussion of the trust factor is included in Jacqueline Durett, "A Matter of Trust," *Sales & Marketing Management*, January/February 2007, pp. 36–37.

34. Geoffrey Colvin, "The Verdict on Business: Presumed Guilty," *Fortune*, November 15, 2004, p. 78.

35. O. C. Ferrell, John Fraedrich, and Linda Ferrell, *Business Ethics*, 9th ed. (Mason, OH: South-Western Cengage Learning, 2013), p. 7. The importance of character at the leadership level is described in Noel M. Tichy and Warren G. Bennis, "Making the Tough Call," *Inc.*, November 2007, pp. 36–38.

36. Shankar Ganesan, Steven P. Brown, Babu John Mariadoss, and Hillbun (Dixon) Ho, "Buffering and Amplifying Effects of Relationship Commitment in Business-to-Business Relationships," *Journal of Marketing Research*, April 2010, pp. 361–373.

37. NASP Membership Information, www.nasp.com (accessed February 15, 2016).

38. Nathaniel Branden, *Self-Esteem at Work* (San Francisco: Jossey-Bass, 1998), p. 35.

39. Stephen R. Covey, *The Seven Habits of Highly Effective People*, 2nd ed. (New York: Simon & Schuster, 2004), pp. 18, 92. See Adam Hanft, "The New Lust for Integrity," *Inc.*, February 2004, p. 104.

40. Jan Yager, *Business Protocol* (Stamford, CT: Hannacroix Creek Books, 2001), pp. 199–200.

41. Sharon Begley, "A World of Their Own," *Newsweek*, May 8, 2000, pp. 53–56; Jaren Sandberg, "Office Sticky Fingers Can Turn the Rest of Us into Joe Fridays," *Wall Street Journal*, November 19, 2005, p. Bl.

42. John A. Byrne, "How to Fix Corporate Governance," *BusinessWeek*, May 6, 2002, pp. 69–78.

43. Josh Freed, "Investigators: Drug Salesman Foiled Pharmacist," *The News & Observer*, August 26, 2001, p. 12A.

44. John Hagel III, John Seely Brown and Lang Davison, "The Best Way to Measure Company Performance," March 2010, https://hbr.org/2010/03/the-best-way-to-measure-compan.html, (accessed on February 5, 2016).

45. Marjorie Kelly, "Waving Goodbye to the Invisible Hand," *Business Ethics*, March/April 2002, p. 4. For a somewhat different point of view, see George Stalk, "Warm and Fuzzy Doesn't Cut It," *Wall Street Journal*, February 15, 2005, p. B2.

46. Yochi J. Dreazen, "Pressure for Sales Fostered Abuses at WorldCom," *Wall Street Journal*, May 16, 2002, p. B1. See Norm Kamikow, "Ethics & Performance," *Workforce Performance Solutions*, March 2006, p. 4.

47. Shoshana Zuboff, "A Starter Kit for Business Ethics," *Fast Company*, January 2005, p. 91.

48. Carol Hymowitz, "Management Missteps in '04 Hurt Companies, Endangered Customers," *Wall Street Journal*, December 21, 2004, p. B1; "Edward Jones Agrees to Settle Host of Charges," *Wall Street Journal*, December 21, 2004, p. C1; John Hechinger, "Putman May Owe $100 Million," *Wall Street Journal*, February 2, 2005, p. C1; Erin McClam, "Witness Tells of Coverup," *News & Observer*, January 29, 2005, p. 3D.

49. Robert Simons, Henry Mintzburg, and Kunal Basu, "Memo to: CEOs," *Fast Company*, June 2002, pp. 120–121.

50. Patrick Smith, "You Have a Job, But How About a Life?" *BusinessWeek*, November 16, 1998, p. 30.

51. Mitchell Pacelle, "Citigroup Works on Reputation," *Wall Street Journal*, February 17, 2005, p. C3.

52. Patricia B. Gray, "Business Class," *Fortune*, April 17, 2006, p. 336; Margery Weinstein, "Survey Says: Ethics Training Works," *Training*, November 2005, p. 15; "ERC Survey & Benchmarking," www.ethics.org (accessed July 6, 2010).

53. Bruce Weinstein, "If It's Legal, It's Ethical?...Right?" October 2007, http://www.bloomberg.com/bw/stories/2007-10-15/ if-its-legal-its-ethical-right-businessweek-business-news-stock-market-and-financial-advice (accessed on February 5, 2016).

54. Nancy Henderson Wurst, "Who's Afraid of Ethics?" *Hemisphere Magazine*, November 2006, pp. 120–123.

55. Carol Wheeler, "Getting the Edge on Ethics," *Executive Female*, May–June 1996, p. 47.

56. Sharon Drew Morgan, *Selling with Integrity* (San Francisco: Berrett-Koehler, 1997), pp. 25–27.

57. Ibid., pp. 27–28.

58. Tom Peters, *Thriving on Chaos* (New York: Alfred A. Knopf, 1988), p. 521.

59. Gerhard Gschwandtner, "Lies and Deception in Selling," *Personal Selling Power*, 15th Anniversary Issue, 1995, p. 62.

60. Price Pritchett, *The Ethics of Excellence* (Dallas, TX: Pritchett & Associates, Inc., n.d.), p. 18.

61. Ron Willingham, *Integrity Selling for the 21st Century* (New York: Currency Doubleday, 2003), p. 11.

Endnotes for Boxed Features

a. Michael T. Kenny, "Research, Observe Chinese Protocol to Land Sale," *Selling*, May 2001, p. 10; Jan Yager, *Business Protocol*, 2nd ed. (Stamford, CT: Hannacroix Creek Books, 2001), p. 113.

b. Based on Renee Houston Zemanski, "When the Competition Gets Tough," *Selling Power*, April 2006, pp. 17–19.

Chapter 4

1. Ron Willingham, *Integrity Selling for the 21st Century* (New York: Currency Doubleday, 2003), p. 11.

2. Daniel H. Pink, *A Whole New Mind* (New York: Riverhead Books, 2005), pp. 48–63.

3. Ilan Mochari, "In a Former Life," *Inc.*, April 2001, p. 100.

4. J.D. Power Consumer Center, September 22, 2010, www .jdpower.com.

5. *Partnering: The Heart of Selling Today* video (Des Moines, IA: American Media Incorporated, 1990).

6. Jerry Scher, *"Selling is a Process, Not an Event!"* http://albany-ceo.com/features/2011/05/selling-process-not-event/ (accessed February 6, 2016).

7. Larry Wilson, *Selling in the 90s* (Chicago: Nightingale Conant, 1988), p. 35.

8. William Keenan, Jr., "Customer Satisfaction Builds Business," *Selling*, March 1998, p. 12.

9. Tim Sanders, *Love Is the Killer App* (New York: Crown Business, 2002), p. 23.

10. Malcolm Fleschner, "World Wide Winner—The UPS Story," *Selling Power*, November/December 2001, p. 58.

11. Neil Rackham and John R. DeVincentis, *Rethinking the Sales Force* (New York: McGraw-Hill, 1999), pp. 79–83.

12. Phillip C. McGraw, *Self Matters* (New York: Simon & Schuster, 2001), pp. 69–70.

13. Sharon Begley, "Follow Your Intuition: The Unconscious You May Be the Wiser Half," *Wall Street Journal*, August 30, 2002, p. B1; Sharon Begley, "How Do I Love Thee? Let Me Count the Ways—and Other Bad Ideas," *Wall Street Journal*, September 6, 2002, p. B1.

14. Phillip C. McGraw, "Dr. Phil: Know Your Goal, Make a Plan, and Pull the Trigger," *The Oprah Magazine*, September 2001, pp. 60–61; see Barry L. Reece and Rhonda Brandt, *Effective Human Relations—Personal and Organizational Applications* (Boston: Houghton Mifflin Company, 2005), pp. 95–102.

15. McGraw, *Self Matters*, p. 73.

16. Stephen E. Heiman and Diane Sanchez, *The New Conceptual Selling* (New York: Warner Books, 1999), pp. 48–49. See Stephen R. Covey, "Win-Win Strategies," *Training*, January 2008, p. 56.

17. David Mayer and Herbert M. Greenberg, "What Makes a Good Salesman," *Harvard Business Review*, July–August 2006, p. 166. For information on how empathy training helps sales representatives improve, see Cliff Edwards, "Death of a Pushy Salesman," *BusinessWeek*, July 3, 2006.

18. Ibid.

19. Eli Jones, Jesse N. Moore, Andrea J. S. Stanaland, and Rosalind A. J. Wyatt, "Salesperson Race and Gender and the Access and Legitimacy Paradigm: Does Difference Make a Difference," *Journal of Personal Selling and Sales Management*, Fall 1998, p. 74; "Danielle Sacks, the Accidental Guru," *Fast Company*, January 2005, pp. 65–71.

20. Barry L. Reece, *Effective Human Relations—Interpersonal and Organizational Application,* 12th ed. (Mason, OH: South-Western Cengage Learning, 2013), p. 29.

21. Roy M. Berko, Andrew D. Wolvin, and Darlyn R. Wolvin, *Communicating*, 8th ed. (Boston: Houghton Mifflin Company, 2001), p. 45.

22. Ibid., p. 50.

23. Susan Bixler, *The Professional Image* (New York: Putnam Publishing Group, 1984), p. 216.

24. Barbara Pachter and Marjorie Brody, *Complete Business Etiquette Handbook* (New York: Prentice Hall, 1995), p. 14.

25. Adapted from Leonard Zunin, *Contact: The First Four Minutes* (New York: Ballantine Books, [1972] 1992), p. 109; Jerry La Martina, "Shake It, Don't Crush It," *San Jose Mercury News*, June 25, 2000, p. 4PC.

26. Deborah Blum, "Face It!" *Psychology Today*, September/October 1998, pp. 32–69; see Julia Chang, "Selling in Acting," *Sales & Marketing Management*, May 2004, p. 22.

27. Barbara Pachter and Mary Brody, *Complete Business Etiquette Handbook* (Englewood Cliffs, NJ: Prentice Hall, 1995), p. 27; "The Eyes Have It," *Sales & Marketing Management*, January 2002, p. 20.

28. Appropriate clothing for work is discussed in Christina Binkley, "Case Study: Dressing for the Naked CEO," *Wall Street Journal*, August 23, 2007, p. D8.

29. Tom Searcy, *"The New Rules on Dressing for Success,"* http://www.cbsnews.com/news/the-new-rules-on-dressing-for-success/ (accessed on February 6, 2016).

30. Margaret Webb Pressler, "Camouflage for the Cubicles," *News & Observer*, April 25, 2004, p. 4-E.

31. Susan Bixler and Nancy Nix-Rice, *The New Professional Image* (Adams Media Corporation, 1997), pp. 11–15; Barbara Pachter and Marjorie Brody, *Complete Business Etiquette Handbook* (New York: Prentice Hall, 1995), p. 72.

32. Paul Galanti, "Talking Motivates—Communication Makes Things Happen," *Personal Selling Power*, November–December 1995, p. 88.

33. Steve Ryan, *"Tips to Sound Better during Your Presentations,"* http://www.sellingpower.com/content/article/index.php?a=4582/tips-to-sound-better-during-your-presentations&page=1 (accessed on February 6, 2016).

34. Joann S. Lublin, "To Win Advancement, You Need to Clean Up Any Bad Speech Habits," *Wall Street Journal*, October 5, 2004, p. B1.

35. David E. Weliver, "My Fair CEO," *Inc.*, October 30, 2001, p. 112.

36. "Is Etiquette a Core Value?" *Inc.*, May 2004, p. 22.

37. Tim Sanders, *Love Is the Killer App* (New York: Crown Business, 2002), p. 18.

38. Stephen Covey, *The Seven Habits of Highly Effective People,* 2nd ed. (New York: Simon & Schuster, 2004), pp. 240–241.

39. Jack Canfield, *The Success Principles* (New York: HarperCollins, 2005), pp. 342–343.

40. Colleen DeBaise, "Offbeat Hobbies May Help Build Relationships with Some Clients," *Wall Street Journal*, February 9, 2005, p. B2.

41. Anne Murphy Paul, "Self-Help: Shattering the Myths," *Psychology Today*, March/April 2001, p. 64; Arnold A. Lazarus and Clifford N. Lazarus, *The 60-Second Shrink* (San Luis Obispo, CA: Impact Publishers), 1997, pp. 3–4.

42. McGraw, *Self Matters,* pp. 69–76.

43. Rick Saulle, "Honor Diversity," *Selling Power*, May 2004, p. 54.

Endnotes for Boxed Features

a. "International Snapshot," *Sales and Marketing Management*, November 2001, p. 63; Jan Yager, *Business Protocol*, 2nd ed. (Stamford, CT: Hannacroix Books, 2001), pp. 120–121.

b. Based on Andrew S. Gallan, "Bringing CARE to Your Customers," *Sales & Marketing Management*, May 2004, p. 72.

Chapter 5

1. Mike McNamee and Christopher Schmitt, "The Chainsaw Al Massacre," *BusinessWeek*, May 28, 2001, p. 48; Dennis K. Berman and Joann S. Lublin, "Restructuring, Personality Clashes Led to Lucent Executive's Exit," *Wall Street Journal*, May 17, 2001, p. B1; Charles Fishmann, "Jeff Bezos," *Fast Company*, February 2001, pp. 80–82.

2. Douglas A. Bernstein, Louis A. Penner, Alison Clarke-Stewart, and Edward J. Roy, *Psychology*, 9th ed. (Boston: Houghton Mifflin, 2011), p. 518.

3. Robert Bolton and Dorothy Grover Bolton, *People Styles at Work and Beyond*, 2nd ed. (New York: AMACOM, 2009), pp. 12–14.

4. Fernando Jaramillo, William B. Locander, Paul E. Spector, and Eric G. Harris, "Getting the Job Done: The Moderating Role of Initiative on the Relationship between Intrinsic Motivation and Adaptive Selling," *Journal of Personal Selling and Sales Management*, Winter 2007, pp. 59–74.

5. David W. Merrill and Roger H. Reid, *Personal Styles and Effective Performance* (Radnor, PA: Chilton Books, 1981), p. 1.

6. For a more complete description of *The Versatile Salesperson* training program, visit the Wilson Learning website, www.wilsonlearning.com (accessed March 4, 2016).

7. Robert J. Sternberg, *Thinking Styles* (New York: Cambridge University Press, 1997), p. 8.

8. Robert Bolton and Dorothy Grover Bolton, *People Styles at Work and Beyond*, 2nd ed. (New York: AMACOM, 2009).

9. Geoff James, "Inside the Psychology of Selling," *Selling Power*, January/February 2004, pp. 25–28.

10. The dominance factor was described in an early book by William M. Marston, *The Emotions of Normal People* (New York: Harcourt, 1928). Research conducted by Rolfe LaForge and Robert F. Suczek resulted in the development of the Interpersonal Checklist (ICL), which features a dominant–submissive scale. A person who receives a high score on the ICL tends to lead, persuade, and control others. The Interpersonal Identity Profile, developed by David W. Merrill and James W. Taylor, features a factor called "assertiveness." Persons classified as being high in assertiveness tend to have strong opinions, make quick decisions, and be directive when dealing with people. Persons classified as being low in assertiveness tend to voice moderate opinions, make thoughtful decisions, and be supportive when dealing with others.

11. David W. Johnson, *Reaching Out—Interpersonal Effectiveness and Self-Actualization*, 11th ed. (Boston: Pearson, 2012), p. 83.

12. The research conducted by LaForge and Suczek resulted in identification of the hostile–loving continuum, which is similar to the sociability continuum. Their Interpersonal Checklist features this scale. L. L. Thurstone and T. G. Thurstone developed the Thurstone Temperament Schedule, which provides an assessment of a "sociable" factor. Persons with high scores in this area enjoy the company of others and make friends easily. The Interpersonal Identity Profile developed by Merrill and Taylor contains an objectivity continuum. A person with low objectivity is seen as attention seeking, involved with the feelings of others, informal, and casual in social relationships. A person who is high in objectivity appears to be somewhat indifferent toward the feelings of others. This person is formal in social relationships.

13. Pierce J. Howard and Jane M. Howard, "Buddy, Can You Paradigm?" *Training & Development*, September 1995, p. 31.

14. Barry L. Reece, *Effective Human Relations: Interpersonal and Organizational Applications*, 12th ed. (Mason, OH: South-Western College Pub, 2013), p. 59. Sam Deep and Lyle Sussman, *Close the Deal* (Reading, MA: Perseus Books, 1999), p. 157.

15. Len D'Innocenzo and Jack Cullen, "Chameleon Management," *Personal Selling Power*, January/February 1995, p. 61.

16. "A Global Profiling Tool," (Eden Prairie, MN, Wilson Learning,1999).

17. Tom Ritchey, *I'm Stuck, You're Stuck* (San Francisco: Berrett-Koehler Publishers, Inc., 2002), p. 5.

18. Ron Willingham, *Integrity Selling for the 21st Century* (New York: Currency Doubleday, 2003), pp. 20–21.

19. Stuart Atkins, *How to Get the Most from Styles-Based Training* (Beverly Hills, CA: Stuart Atkins, 1996), p. 1.

20. Gary A. Williams and Robert B. Miller, "Change the Way You Persuade," *Harvard Business Review*, May 2002, p. 65.

21. Robert Bolton and Dorothy Grover Bolton, *People Styles at Work and Beyond*, 2nd ed. (New York: AMACOM, 2009), p. 8.

22. David Merrill and Roger Reid, *Personal Styles and Effective Performance* (Radnor, PA: Chilton Books, 1981), p. 2.

23. Roger Wenschlag, *The Versatile Salesperson* (New York: John Wiley & Sons, 1989), pp. 165–171.

24. Nina Munk, "How Levi's Trashed a Great American Brand," *Fortune*, April 12, 1999, p. 85.

25. "The Top 25 Managers of the Year," *BusinessWeek*, January 14, 2002, p. 65.

26. Stuart Atkins, *How to Get the Most from Styles-Based Training* (Beverly Hills, CA: Stuart Atkins, 1996), p. 3.

27. Ron Willingham, *Integrity Selling* (New York: Doubleday, 1987), pp. 21–23.

28. Eric F. Douglas, *Straight Talk* (Palo Alto, CA: Davies-Black Publishing, 1998), p. 92.

29. Ron Willingham, *Integrity Selling for the 21st Century* (New York: Currency Doubleday, 2003), p. 37.

30. David W. Merrill and Roger H. Reid, *Personal Styles and Effective Performance* (Radnor, PA: Chilton Books, 1981), pp. 134, 135.

31. Stuart Atkins, *The Name of the Game* (Beverly Hills, CA: Ellis & Stewart, 1981), pp. 49–50.

Endnotes for Boxed Features

a. Andy Cohen, "Is This Guy for Real?" *Sales & Marketing Management*, May 2001, pp. 36–44.

b. Based on Christopher Caggiano, "Psychopath," *Inc.*, July 1998, p. 83.

c. "Selling in Canada," *Sales & Marketing Management*, May 2002, p. 64; Jan Yager, *Business Protocol*, 2nd ed. (Stamford, CT: Hannacroix Creek Books, 2001), p. 112.

d. Based on "The Platinum Rule®," www.platinumrule.com (accessed March 4, 2016).

Chapter 6

1. Interview with Amy Vandaveer on March 13, 2016. For additional information regarding *Texas Monthly* magazine, visit www.texasmonthly.com (accessed June 29, 2016).

2. Paul Nolan, "Are you Committing These B2B Sales Sins," *Saleforceexp,* November/December 2010, p. 6.

3. Keith M. Eades, *The New Solution Selling* (New York: McGraw-Hill, 2004), pp. 4–5.

4. Geoffrey James, "Solution Selling," *Selling Power,* May 2006, pp. 45–48. This article is based on an interview with Keith Eades, author of *The New Solution Selling*.

5. Michael R. Solomon, Greg W. Marshall, and Elnora W. Stuart, *Marketing: Real People, Real Choices*, 7th ed. (Upper Saddle River, NJ: Prentice Hall, 2012), p. 219.

6. Noel M. Tichy, "No Ordinary Boot Camp," *Harvard Business Review*, April 2001, p. 6.

7. Dana Hedgpeth, "The Changing Role of the Travel Agent," *Roanoke Times*, May 26, 2002, pp. B1, B2.

8. Brent Adamson, Mathew Dixon, and Nicholas Toman, "The End of Solution Sales," *Harvard Business Review*, July/August 2012, p. 62.

9. Neil Rackham and John R. DeVincentis, *Rethinking the Sales Force* (New York: McGraw-Hill, 1999), p. 79.

10. Emily Nelson, "Too Many Choices," *Wall Street Journal*, April 20, 2001, p. B1; "Monthly Review of Mutual Funds," *Wall Street Journal*, June 3, 2002, pp. R1–R16.

11. Karen E. Starr, "Simple Solutions," *Selling Power*, July/August 2001, p. 22.

12. Christopher Whittier, "Quotation Management: The Revolution Is Here to Stay," www.crmresultsonline.com (accessed on July 6, 2010).

13. Based on John Fellows, "A Decent Proposal," *Personal Selling Power*, November/December 1995, p. 56.

14. Based on John Fellows, "A Decent Proposal," *Personal Selling Power*, November/December 1995, p. 56. See Neil Rackham, "Seven Rules for Creating Winning Sales Proposals," *Value-Added Selling* 21, December 16, 2003, p. 20.

15. "Feeling Under the Gun? Check Your Proposal," *Selling*, October 2001, p. 3.

16. Neil Rackham, "Seven Rules for Creating Winning Sales Proposals," *Value-Added Selling* 21, December 16, 2003, p. 20.

17. "What Kind of Rep Is Most Trustworthy?" *Sales & Marketing Management*, February 2001, p. 90.

18. Robert W. Palmatier, Lisa K. Scheer, and Jan-Benedict E. M. Steenkamp, "Customer Loyalty to Whom? Managing the Benefits and Risks of Salesperson-Owned Loyalty," *Journal of Marketing Research*, May 2007, pp. 185–199.

19. Tom Peters, *Re-Imagine! Business Excellence in a Disruptive Age* (London: Dorling Kindersley Limited, 2003), p. 224.

20. "Company Ambassadors," www.patagonia.com/web/us/patagonia.go?assetid=2897&ln=81 (accessed March 4, 2016).

21. Roland T. Rust, Christine Moorman, and Peter R. Dickson (2002), "Getting Return on Quality: Revenue Expansion, Cost Reduction, or Both?" *Journal of Marketing*, 66(3), pp. 7–24.

22. "Sea Ray," *Fortune*, April 5, 2004, p. S8.

23. Betsy Cummings, "Welcome to the Real Whirled," *Sales & Marketing Management*, February 2001, pp. 87–88.

24. Ian Gelenter, "Build Satisfaction with a Service Contract," *Selling*, May 1998, p. 7.

25. Tom Reilly, "Should You Set Prices," *Selling*, August 2000, pp. 1, 14.

26. Gerhard Gschwandtner, "ROI Selling," *Selling Power*, November/December 2004, p. 10.

27. William M. Pride, Robert J. Hughes, and Jack R. Kapoor, *Business*, 8th ed. (Boston: Houghton Mifflin Company, 2005), pp. 456–457.

28. Michael Ahearne, C. B. Bhattacharya, and Thomas Gruen, "Antecedents and Consequences of Customer-Company Identification: Expanding the Role of Relationships Marketing," *Journal of Applied Psychology*, May 2005, pp. 574–585.

29. http://fortune.com/best-companies/ (accessed March 4, 2016).

30. Michael L. Eskew, "What I Know Now," *Fast Company*, November 2005, p. 108.

31. Michael R. Williams and Jill S. Attaway, "Exploring Salespersons' Customer Orientation as a Mediator of Organizational Culture's Influence on Buyer–Seller Relationships," *Journal of Personal Selling and Sales Management*, Fall 1996, pp. 33–52.

32. "Dealer Merchandising Portfolio," *Views: The Inner Circle News*, Winter 2000, p. 10.

33. "Grassroots Problem Solving," *Inc.*, March 1996, p. 92.

34. Jim Dickie, "Lowest Price Isn't the Answer," *Selling*, August 2000, p. 14.

35. See Brian Tracy, "Analyzing the Competition," *Value-Added Selling* 21, September 16, 2003, p. 2.

36. Bob Mundson, "A Personal Blend," *Training*, February 2004, p. 11.

37. Ashwin W. Joshi, "Salesperson Influence on Product Development: Insights from a Study of Small Manufacturing Organizations, *Journal of Marketing*, January 2010, pp. 94–107.

38. www.patagonia.com (accessed March 4, 2016).

39. Margery Weinstein, "Selling Points," *Training*, June 2007, p. 51.

40. Raj Agnihotri, Adam Rapp, and Kevin Trainor, "Understanding the Role of Information Communication in the Buyer–Seller Exchange Process: Antecedents and Outcomes," *Journal of Business & Industrial Marketing* July 2009, pp. 474–486.

41. Jill Rosenfeld, "Unit of One," *Fast Company*, April 2000, p. 98.

42. www.consultingsales.com/tips/Using_Features_Advantages_Benefits.html (accessed March 4, 2016).

43. Neil Rackham, *The SPIN Selling Fieldbook* (New York: McGraw-Hill, 1996), pp. 149–152; *Value-Added Selling* 21, December 26, 2006, p. 4.

44. Gary Hamel, *Leading the Revolution* (Boston: Harvard Business School Press, 2000), p. 87; Neil Rackham, "Improve This Skill and Boost Sales Up to 27 Percent," *Value-Added Selling* 21, March 2, 2004, p. 1; *Value-Added Selling* 21, December 26, 2006, p. 4.

Endnotes for Boxed Features

a. "International Snapshot," *Sales & Marketing Management*, March 2000, p. 72; Jan Yager, *Business Protocol*, 2nd ed. (Stamford, CT: Hannacroix Creek Books, 2001), p. 111.

Chapter 7

1. Peter Egan, "The Best of All Worlds Bunch," *Road & Track*, July 2002, pp. 52–78; "2005 Geneva: Lexus Finesses Next IS Sport Sedan," www.autoweek.com (accessed March 4, 2016); Greg Kable, "Audi A4 Debuts at Frankfurt," *Autoweek*, September 3, 2007, p. 10; Joe Rusz, "Saab 9–3 & XWD," *Road & Track*, October 2007, p. 60.

2. Wayne S. Desarbo, Rajdeep Grewal, and Crystal J. Scott (2008), "A Clusterwise Bilinear Multidimensional Scaling Methodology for Simultaneous Segmentation and Positioning Analyses," *Journal of Marketing Research*, June 2008, pp. 280–292.

3. Michael R. Solomon, Grey W. Marshall, and Elnora W. Stuart, *Marketing: Real People, Real Choices*, 7th ed. (Upper Saddle River, NJ: Pearson Education, 2012), p. 201.

4. D. Lee Carpenter, "Return on Innovation—The Power of Being Different," *Retailing Issues Letter*, May 1998, p. 3.

5. Brian Tracy, "Keeping the Customers You Make," *Selling*, November 2003, pp. 1, 4.

6. James Allen, "Living Differentiation," *Harvard Business Review*, March/April 2012, p. 21.

7. Philip Kotler and Gary Armstrong, *Principles of Marketing*, 14th ed. (Upper Saddle River, NJ: Prentice Hall, 2012), p. 212.

8. Tom Leverton, "Five Questions," *Sales & Marketing Management*, July 2004, p. 13.

9. Theodore Kinni, "The Value Proposition," *Selling Power*, July/August 2005, p. 75.

10. Michael Arndt, "Built for the Long Haul," *BusinessWeek*, January 30, 2006, p. 66.

11. Carl K. Clayton, "Sell Quality, Service, Your Company, Yourself," *Personal Selling Power*, January/February 1990, p. 47.

12. Elaine Parker, "How I Made the Sale," *Value-Added Selling* 21, June 17, 2003, pp. 1–2.

13. Suein L. Hwang, "It Was a WOMBAT for the Meatware, but It Was a Good Sell," *Wall Street Journal*, May 15, 2002, p. B1.

14. Ronald W. Lane, Karen Whitehill King, and Tom Reichert, *Kleppner's Advertising Procedure*, 18th ed. (Upper Saddle River, NJ: Prentice Hall, 2011), pp. 93–109.

15. Kevin Zheng Zhou and Kent Nakamoto, "How Do Enhanced and Unique Features Affect New Product Preference? The Moderating Role of Product Familiarity," *Journal of the Academy of Marketing Science* February 2007, pp. 53–62.

16. Lawrence B. Chonko and Eli Jones, "The Need for Speed: Agility Selling," *Journal of Personal Selling and Sales Management*, September 2005, pp. 371–382.

17. Mark Leslie and Charles A. Holloway, "The Sales Learning Curve," *Harvard Business Review*, July/August 2006, p. 121.

18. Jess McCuan, "Reeling In the Big One," *Inc.*, August 2004, pp. 43–44; "What Is IntraLinks?" www.Intralinks.com (accessed March 4, 2016).

19. Information was taken from *Report to Policyholders 2004*. This 24-page report was published by New York Life in 2005.

20. Michael R. Solomon, Grey W. Marshall, and Elnora W. Stuart, *Marketing: Real People, Real Choices*, 7th ed. (Upper Saddle River, NJ: Pearson Education, 2012), p. 322.

21. Carlos Tejada, "The Allure of Bundling," *Wall Street Journal*, October 7, 2003, p. B1.

22. Michael Treacy, "You Need a Value Discipline—But Which One?" *Fortune*, April 17, 1995, p. 195.

23. Robert Shulman and Richard Miniter, "Discounting Is No Bargain," *Wall Street Journal*, December 7, 1998, p. A30.

24. Andy Cohen, "Survey Says: Service Beats Price Online," *Sales & Marketing Management*, July 2002, p. 18.

25. Geoffrey James, "Solution Selling," *Selling Power*, May 2006, p. 46.

26. Adopted from a model described in "Marketing Success Through Differentiation—Of Anything," *Harvard Business Review*, January/February 1980.

27. Theodore Levitt, "Marketing Success Through Differentiation—Of Anything," *Harvard Business Review*, January/February 1980.

28. Ted Levitt, *Marketing Imagination* (New York: The Free Press, 1983), p. 80.

29. Neil Rackham, "Boost Your Sales 20 Percent by Improving This Skill," *Value-Added Selling* 21, June 17, 2003, pp. 1–2.

30. Beth Davis-Sramek, Cornelia Droge, John T. Mentzer, and Matthew B. Myers, "Creating Commitment and Loyalty Behavior Among Retailers: What Are the Roles of Service Quality and Satisfaction?" *Journal of the Academy of Marketing Science* October 2009, pp. 440–454.

31. Thomas A. Stewart, "A Satisfied Customer Isn't Enough," *Fortune*, July 21, 1997, pp. 112–113.

32. Martin Reimann, Oliver Schilke, and Jacquelyn S. Thomas, "Customer Relationship Management and Firm Performance: The Mediating Role of Business Strategy," *Journal of the Academy of Marketing Science* 2009, pp. 326–346.

33. "Business Bulletin," *Wall Street Journal*, September 24, 1998, p. A1.

34. Chuck Salter, "On the Road Again," *Fast Company*, January 2002, pp. 50–58.

35. "Study: What Really Matters to Your Customers," *Value-Added Selling* 21, February 14, 2005, p. 4.

36. Ted Levitt, *Marketing Imagination* (New York: The Free Press, 1983), p. 84.

37. Rebecca Smith, "Beyond Recycling: Manufacturers Embrace 'C2C' Design," *Wall Street Journal*, March 3, 2005, p. B1.

38. Neil Rackham and John R. DeVincentis, *Rethinking the Sales Force* (New York: McGraw-Hill, 1999), p. 89.

39. Ibid., pp. 89–90.

40. Ibid., p. 90.

Endnotes for Boxed Features

a. Adapted from discussion in Leonard L. Berry, A. Parasuraman, and Valerie A. Zeithaml, "The Service-Quality Puzzle," *Business Horizons*, September/October 1988, pp. 35–43; Robert Kreitner, *Management*, 5th ed. (Boston: Houghton Mifflin Company, 1992), pp. 613–614.

b. Based on Ernest Beck, "How I Did It," *Inc.*, October 2004, pp. 120–122.

c. Based on Rhonda M. Abrams, "Problem for Pros: Knowing How Much to Charge," *Des Moines Register*, January 16, 1998, p. 2-B.

Chapter 8

1. Robert H. Bloom, "Sales Management in 2011 and Beyond," *Salesforceexp*, November/December, p. 22.

2. "Nighttime Reading for Daytime Success," *Sales & Marketing Management*, May 2007, p. 44.

3. Michael Hammer and James Champy, *Reengineering the Corporation: A Manifest for Business Revolution* (New York: HarperBusiness, 1993), p. 18.

4. Keith M. Eades, The *New Solution Selling* (New York: McGraw-Hill, 2004), pp. 32–33.

5. Tom Peters and Nancy Austin, *A Passion for Excellence* (New York: Random House, 1985), p. 71.

6. http://thecustomerblog.co.uk/2012/12/14/skeptical-musings-on-treating-different-customers-differently-and-the-expertise-of-business-gurus/ (accessed on March 23, 2016).

7. Philip Kotler and Gary Armstrong, *Principles of Marketing*, 16th ed. (Upper Saddle River, NJ: Prentice Hall, 2016), p. 196.

8. Michael R. Solomon, Greg W. Marshall, and Elnora W. Stuart, *Marketing: Real People, Real Choices*, 7th ed. (Upper Saddle River, NJ: Prentice Hall, 2012), p. 170.

9. Gary Armstrong and Philip Kotler, *Marketing: An Introduction, 6th ed.* (Upper Saddle River, NJ: Prentice Hall, 2003), pp. 191–192, 215.

10. Michael R. Solomon, Greg W. Marshall, and Elnora W. Stuart, *Marketing: Real People, Real Choices*, 7th ed. (Upper Saddle River, NJ: Prentice Hall, 2012), p. 168.

11. Ibid., pp. 168–169.

12. Philip Kotler and Gary Armstrong, *Principles of Marketing*, 16th ed. (Upper Saddle River, NJ: Prentice Hall, 2016), pp. 201–202.

13. FedEx, www.fedex.com (accessed March 23, 2016).

14. Philip Kotler and Gary Armstrong, *Principles of Marketing*, 16th ed. (Upper Saddle River, NJ: Prentice Hall, 2016), p. 182.

15. Ibid., p. 152.

16. S. Sajeesh and Jagmohan S. Raju (2010), "Positioning and Pricing in a Variety Seeking Market," *Management Science*, 56(6), pp. 949–961.

17. Ibid., pp. 145–146.

18. Keith M. Eades, *The New Solution Selling* (New York: McGraw-Hill, 2004), pp. 32–33; Betsy Cummings, "Proving the Sale Process," Sales & Marketing Management, June 2006, p. 12.

19. Keith M. Eades, *The New Solution Selling*, p. 31.

20. Stephen E. Heiman and Diane Sanchez, *The New Conceptual Selling* (New York: Warner Books, 1999), pp. 190–191.

21. Research reported in Tom Atkinson and Ron Koprowski, "Sales Reps' Biggest Mistakes," *Harvard Business Review*, July–August 2006, p. 1. This research indicates that 26 percent of the business-to-business buyers say salespeople "don't follow my company's buying process."

22. Philip Kotler and Gary Armstrong, *Principles of Marketing*, 14th ed. (Upper Saddle River, NJ: Prentice Hall, 2012), p. 152.

23. Neil Rackham and John R. DeVincentis, *Rethinking the Sales Force* (New York: McGraw-Hill, 1999), p. 66.

24. Bill Stinnett, "Reverse-Engineer the Buying Process," *Selling*, December 2004, p. 16.

25. Neil Rackham and John R. DeVincentis, *Rethinking the Sales Force* (New York: McGraw-Hill, 1999), p. 68.

26. Monika Kukar-Kinney and Angeline G. Close (2010), "The Determinants of Consumers' Online Shopping Cart Abandonment," *Journal of the Academy of Marketing Science* 38, pp. 240–250.

27. Hean Tat Keh and Jun Pang (2010), "Customer Reactions to Service Separation," *Journal of Marketing*, 74(2), pp. 55–70.

28. Ibid., p. 69.

29. Neil Rackham and John DeVincentis provide extensive coverage of these three selling modes in *Rethinking the Sales Force*. Also see "Let the Customer Define Value—and Sales Will Rise," by Neil Rackham and John DeVincentis, *Value-Added Selling* 21, January 13, 2004, pp. 1–2.

30. Neil Rackham and John DeVincentis, *Value-Added Selling* 21, January 13, 2004, pp. 1–2.

31. Ken Brown, "Little-Known Avaya Tackles Cisco in Internet Calling Gear," *Wall Street Journal*, October 26, 2004, p. B1.

32. Neil Rackham and John R. DeVincentis, *Rethinking the Sales Force* (New York: McGraw-Hill, 1999), p. 74.

33. Philip Kotler and Gary Armstrong, *Principles of Marketing*, 10th ed. (Upper Saddle River, NJ: Prentice Hall, 2004), p. 28.

34. Stan Davis and Christopher Meyer, *Blur: The Speed of Change in the Connected Economy* (New York: Addison-Wesley, 1998), p. 16.

35. Leilei Gao, S. Christian Wheeler, and Baba Shiv (2009), "The 'Shaken Self': Product Choices as a Means of Restoring Self-View Confidence," *Journal of Consumer Research*, 36(1), pp. 29–38.

36. www.tcnewsonline.wordpress.com/2012/04/12/selling-to-the-four-generations/ (accessed March 23, 2016).

37. William M. Pride and O. C. Ferrell, *Marketing*, 10th ed. (Boston: Houghton Mifflin Company, 1997), pp. 143–148.

38. Douglas A. Bernstein, Alison Clark-Stewart, Louis A. Penner, and Edward J. Roy, *Psychology*, 6th ed. (Boston: Houghton Mifflin Company, 2003), p. 648.

39. C. Page Moreau and Kelly B. Herd (2010), "To Each His Own? How Comparisons with Others Influence Consumers' Evaluations of Their Self-Designed Products," *Journal of Consumer Research*, 36(5), pp. 806–819.

40. Philip Kotler and Gary Armstrong, *Principles of Marketing*, 14th ed. (Upper Saddle River, NJ: Prentice Hall, 2012), pp. 139–140.

41. Douglas A. Bernstein, Alison Clark-Stewart, Louis A. Penner, and Edward J. Roy, *Psychology*, 6th ed. (Boston: Houghton Mifflin Company, 2003), p. 21.

42. Philip Kotler and Gary Armstrong, *Principles of Marketing*, 16th ed. (Upper Saddle River, NJ: Prentice Hall, 2016), pp. 167–168.

43. Louis E. Boone and David L. Kurtz, *Contemporary Marketing*, 16th ed. (Mason, Ohio: South-Western Publishing, 2013), p. 150.

44. Roger Hart, "Luxury, VW's Way," *Autoweek*, December 27, 2004, pp. 18–19; Tom Reilly, "All Sales Decisions Are Emotional for the Buyer," *Selling*, July 2003, p. 13.

45. Roy Chitwood, "Hidden Buyer Motives: Handle Them with Care," *Value-Added Selling* 21, April 2, 2007, p. 4.

46. Phil Kline, "Dominant Buying Motive Is the Result of Strong Emotions," *Marketing News*, May 24, 1993, p. 4.

47. Stan Davis and Christopher Meyer, *Blur: The Speed of Change in the Connected Economy* (New York: Addison-Wesley, 1998), p. 52.

48. Hakkyun Kim, Kiwan Park, and Norbert Schwarz (2010), "Will This Trip Really Be Exciting? The Role of Incidental Emotions in Product Evaluation," *Journal of Consumer Research*, 36(6), pp. 983–991.

49. Robert McGarvey, "The Buyer's Emotional Side," *Selling Power*, April 2006, p. 35.

50. Ibid., p. 36.

51. Gary Armstrong and Philip Kotler, *Marketing: An Introduction*, 6th ed. (Upper Saddle River, NJ: Prentice Hall, 2003), p. 216; Sid Chadwick, "New Twists in Price vs. Perceived Value," *Sales and Marketing Advisory Magazine*, July/August 2001, p. 6.

Endnotes for Boxed Features

a. Based on Dave Stein, "Selling Across Generation Gaps," Sales & Marketing Management, October 2007, p. 9.

b. Based on Sam Walker, "Can Nascar Take Manhattan?" Wall Street Journal, March 8, 2002, p. W6.

c. Erin Anderson and Leonard Lodish (2006), "Leading the effective sales force: the Asian sales force management environment," working paper, pp. 7–8.

Chapter 9

1. Gerhard Gschwandtner, "Thoughts to Sell By," *Personal Selling Power*, 15th Anniversary Issue, 1995, p. 122.

2. Personal Interview, Duane Manning, former Director of Business Development, Parker Aerospace. March 12, 2016.

3. Dorothy Leeds, "Where Are the Real Decision Makers?" *Personal Selling Power*, March 1993, p. 62; Gerhard Gschwandtner, "Getting Squeezed," *Selling Power*, May 2002, p. 10.

4. Terry Hill, "How Do You Sustain and Grow Your Customer Relationships?" *American Salesman*, October 2007, p. 26.

5. For additional information on Joe Girard, see "Joe Girard on Becoming the World's Greatest Salesperson," *Harvard Business Review*, July/August 2006, p. 25.

6. Gerhard Gschwandtner, "The Funnel Concept," *Personal Selling Power*, 15th Anniversary Issue, 1995, p. 23.

7. Joel R. Pecoraro, "Panning for Gold," *Sales & Marketing Management*, November 2004, p. 56.

8. "Skills Workshop," *Selling Power*, October 2000, p. 54.

9. Geoffrey James, "How to Earn Customer Referrals," *Selling Power*, July/August 2004, pp. 25–28.

10. *Business Network International*, www.bni.com (accessed March 23, 2016).

11. "Prospecting with social media," http://www.examiner.com/article/prospecting-with-social-media (accessed March 23, 2016); "Social Media Prospecting: Every Sale Starts with a Conversation," http://www.krusecontrolinc.com/automotive-social-media-prospecting-every-sale-starts-conversation/ (accessed March 23, 2016); "Sales Prospecting Using Social Media," https://social123.com/salestipsguide/sales-prospecting-using-social-media/ (accessed March 23, 2016); "The 5 Dos and Don'ts of Social Media Prospecting," http://marketmesuite.com/blog/the-5-dos-and-donts-of-social-media-prospecting/ (accessed March 23, 2016); "3 Things to Warm Up Your LinkedIn Prospecting."

12. Thomas Petzinger Jr., "Selling a 'Killer App' Is a Far Tougher Job Than Dreaming It Up," *Wall Street Journal*, April 3, 1998, p. B1.

13. Daniel Tynan, "Tricks of the Trade Show," *Sales & Marketing Management*, January 2004, p. 27.

14. Ron Donoho, "Steering New Sales," *Sales & Marketing Management*, November 2001, pp. 31–35.

15. Henry Canaday, "Carefully Composed," *Selling Power*, May 2007, pp. 44–46.

16. Ibid., pp. 45–46.

17. Henry Canaday, "Zeroing In on Prospects," *Selling Power*, March 2006, p. 82.

18. Ibid., pp. 84–85.

19. Andy Cohen, "Man About Town," *Sales & Marketing Management*, June 2000, p. 29.

20. John Boe, "Selling Is a Contact Sport: Keys to Effective Phone Calling," *American Salesman,* January 2008, p. 26. For more information on cold calls, see Scott Stears, "Cold Calls Have Yet to Breathe Their Last Gasp," *Wall Street Journal*, December 14, 2006, p. D2.

21. Nicole Gull, "Warming Up to Cold Calls," *Inc.*, November 2004, pp. 41–43.

22. Maxwell Maltz, Dan S. Kennedy, William T. Brooks, Matt Oechsli, Jeff Paul, and Pamela Yellen, *Zero-Resistance Selling* (Paramus, NJ: Prentice Hall, 1998), p. 167.

23. Wendy Kaufman, "A Successful Job Search: It's All About Networking," February 3, 2011, http://www.npr .org/2011/02/08/133474431/a-successful-job-search-its-all-about-networking (accessed March 23, 2016).

24. Tuba Üstüner and David Godes, "Better Sales Networks," *Harvard Business Review*, July/August 2006, pp. 102–112.

25. Michele Marchetti, "Do You Have the Knack for Networking?" *Sales & Marketing Management*, January 1996, p. 30; Deb Haggerty, "Successful Networking Begins as a State of Mind," *Selling*, December 2004, p. 13.

26. Maxwell Maltz, Dan S. Kennedy, William T. Brooks, Matt Oechsli, Jeff Paul, and Pamela Yellen, *Zero-Resistance Selling* (Paramus, NJ: Prentice Hall, 1998), pp. 179–180.

27. Steve Atlas, "Trouble Connecting?" *Selling Power*, September 2001, p. 27.

28. "Are You Generating and Using Quality Leads?" *Value-Added Selling* 21, September 16, 2003, p. 4.

29. Thomas R. Watruba, "The Evolution of Selling," *Journal of Personal Selling and Sales Management*, Summer 1991, p. 7.

30. This example was adopted from "Skills Workshop" by William F. Kendy, *Selling Power*, January/February 2000, p. 26.

31. Mitchell Pacelle, "Former SEC Chairman Levitt Decries Business Ethics in U.S.," *Wall Street Journal*, June 17, 2002, p. C7; Shoshana Zuboff, "A Starter Kit for Business Ethics," *Fast Company*, January 2005, p. 91.

32. Rick Page, *Hope Is Not a Strategy* (Atlanta, GA: Nautilus Press, 2002), pp. 69–71.

33. "Senior Execs Share Insider Tips," *Selling*, March 2000, pp. 1, 14; Tom Reilly, "Selling to Mr. Big Is Tough, But," *Selling*, February 2001, pp. 1, 12.

34. Henry Canaday, "Fishing for Big Ones," *Personal Selling Power* (Source Book 2008), p. 46.

35. Jim Dickie and Barry Trailer, "Proactive Sales Intelligence: The New Requirement for Getting into the Game," Salesforce.com, 2007.

36. www.salesforce.com/company/news-press/press-releases/2011/03/110330.jsp (accessed March 23, 2016).

37. www.salesforce.com/data/overview (accessed March 23, 2016).

38. Ibid., pp. 46–47.

39. H. F. Mackenzie et al., *Sales Management in Canada* (Toronto, ON: Pearson Education Canada, 2008), p. 140.

40. Tony Parinello, "Keeping Track of Prospects," www.entre-preneur.com/article/0,4621,306013,00.html, January 13, 2003 (accessed March 23, 2016).

41. Don Thomson, *Keeping the Funnel Full* (French Creek, BC: Mardon Publishing, 2004), p. 7.

42. H. F. Mackenzie et al., p. 141.

Endnotes for Boxed Features

a. Based on Sarah Lorge, "The Best Way to Prospect," *Sales & Marketing Management*, January 1998, p. 80.

b. Barbara Siskind, *Seminars to Build Your Business* (North Vancouver, BC: Self-Counsel Press, 1998), pp. 9–12; Sheldon Gordon, "Punch Up Your Profits," *Profit*, May 1999, pp. 17–22.

c. Barbara Pachter and Marjorie Brody, *Complete Business Etiquette Handbook* (Upper Saddle River, NJ: Prentice Hall, 1995), p. 278; "International Snapshot," *Sales & Marketing Management*, August 2001, p. 64; Jan Yager, *Business Protocol*, 2nd ed. (Stamford, CT: Hannacroix Books, Inc., 2001), pp. 116–117.

Chapter 10

1. Malcolm Fleschner, "Too Busy to Buy," *Selling Power*, March 1999, p. 36.

2. Gina Rollins, "Prepped to Sell," *Selling Power*, September 2006, pp. 74–77.

3. Bradford Agry, "Every Client Meeting Provides a Dynamic New Opportunity," *Selling*, April 2002, pp. 1, 4.

4. Malcolm Fleschner, "Anatomy of a Sale," *Selling Power*, April 1998, p. 76; Gina Rollins, "Prepare for the Unknown," *Selling Power*, July/August 2003, pp. 26–30.

5. Tom Reilly, "Prepare Like a Pro," www.TomReillyTraining.com (accessed March 23, 2016).

6. "Set the Agenda," *Personal Selling Power*, May/June 1995, p. 79.

7. Donna Fenn, "Because His Family Business Makes an Art of Customer Service," *Inc.*, April 2005, p. 94; telephone interview with Pamela Miles, staff member at Mitchells/Richards, March 22, 2005.

8. Philip Kotler and Gary Armstrong, *Principles of Marketing*, 16th ed. (Upper Saddle River, NJ: Prentice Hall, 2016), pp. 471–472.

9. Rick Page, *Hope Is Not a Strategy* (Atlanta, GA: Nautilus Press, 2002), p. 25.

10. Betsy Cummings, "Group Dynamics," *Sales & Marketing Management*, January/February 2007, p. 8.

11. James F. O'Hara, "Successful Selling to Buying Committees," *Selling*, February 1998, p. 8.

12. George R. Franke and Jeong-Eun Park, "Salesperson Adaptive Selling Behavior and Customer Orientation: A Meta-Analysis," *Journal of Marketing Research*, November 2006, pp. 693–702; Leroy Robinson, Jr., Greg W. Marshall, William C. Moncrief, and Felicia G. Lassak, "Toward a Shortened Measure of Adaptive Selling," *Journal of Personal Selling and Sales Management*, Spring 2002, pp. 111–119.

13. The role of confidence in adaptive selling is discussed in Leroy Robinson, Jr., Greg W. Marshall, William C. Moncrief, and Felicia G. Lassak, "Toward a Shortened Measure of Adaptive Selling," *Journal of Personal Selling and Sales Management*, Spring 2002, pp. 111–119.

14. Neil Rackham and John R. Vincentis, *Rethinking the Sales Force* (New York: McGraw-Hill, 1999), p. 217.

15. Graham Roberts-Phelps, "How to Add Value to Every Sales Call," *Selling Power,* March/April 2010, p. 19.

16. Ibid.

17. Thomas A. Freese, *Secrets of Question-Based Selling* (Naperville, IL: Sourcebooks, Inc., 2003), p. 114.

18. Based on John Fellows, "Your Foot in the Door," *Selling Power*, March 1996, pp. 64–65.

19. Adapted from Art Sobczak, "Please, Call Me Back!" *Selling*, March 1999, p. 12.
20. Ibid.
21. Deborah Dumaine, "Managing Customers with E-Mail," *Selling Power*, March 2004, p. 94.
22. Rachel Zupek, "Reply All and Other E-Mail Gaffes," Business.com, September 2007, p. 26.
23. Susan Bixler and Nancy Nix-Rice, *The New Professional Image* (Holbrook, MA: Adams Media Corporation, 1997), p. 3.
24. Steve Atlas, "How to Cultivate New Turf," *Selling Power*, January/February 2003, p. 26.
25. Maxine Clayton, "60 Seconds on Small Talk," *Fast Company*, November 2004, p. 43.
26. Dean A. Goettsch, "Make Your First Meeting Count," *Selling*, July 2004, pp. 1, 4.
27. Melissa Campanelli, "Sound the Alarm," *Sales & Marketing Management*, December 1994, pp. 20–25.
28. Carolee Boyles, "Prewarm Cold Calls," *Selling Power*, July/August 2001, p. 30.
29. Abner Littel, "Selling to Women Revs Up Car Sales," *Personal Selling Power*, July/August 1990, p. 50.
30. "Six Great Upselling Questions," *Personal Selling Power*, April 1993, p. 44.
31. Linda Richardson, "The Richardson Sales Excellence Review™," http://blogs.richardson.com/2012/09/05/challenger_sale_missing_link/ (accessed March 23, 2016).
32. Theodore Kinni, "How to Identify and Remove the Problems Underlying Call Reluctance," *Selling Power*, November/December 2004, pp. 69–71; "Types of Call Reluctance," *Value-Added Selling* 21, February 14, 2005, p. 4.
33. Alan Farnham, "Are You Smart Enough to Keep Your Job?" *Fortune*, January 15, 1996, pp. 34–42.
34. "The Disappointment Trap," *Selling Power*, January/February 1999, p. 14.
35. Roy Chitwood, "Still Trying to Slip Past Gatekeepers? Forget It." *Value-Added Selling* 21, December 16, 2003, pp. 1–2.

Endnotes for Boxed Features

a. Based on Jay Winchester, "Ripe for Change," *Sales & Marketing Management*, August 1998, p. 81.
b. "International Snapshot," *Sales & Marketing Management*, February 2001, p. 92; Jan Yager, *Business Protocol*, 2nd ed. (Stamford, CT: Hannacroix Books, Inc., 2001), pp. 114–115.
c. Byran Ziegler, "Your Business Card Can Be a Powerful Tool," *Des Moines Register*, August 2, 1999, p. 17-B; Kemba J. Dunham, "Here's My Card," *Wall Street Journal*, May 14, 2002, p. B12.

Chapter 11

1. Olaf Ploetner, "The Development of Consulting in Goods-Based Companies," *Industrial Marketing Management* 37, February 6, 2008, p. 329.
2. V. Kuman, Rajkuma, Rajkuman Venkatesan, and Werner Reinartz, "Performance Implications of Adopting a Customer-Focused Sales Campaign," *Journal of Marketing* 72, September 2008, p. 50.
3. *Going the Distance: The Consultative Sales Presentation* (Pasadena, CA: Intelecom); "The Amgen Difference," www.amgen.com (accessed July 30, 2013).
4. Louis E. Boone and David L. Kurtz, *Contemporary Marketing*, 16th ed. (Mason, Ohio: South-Western Publishing, 2013), p. 12; Geoffrey James, "Consultative Selling Strategies," *Selling Power*, April 2004, pp. 17–20.
5. Jack R. Snader, "Developing Consultative Sales Skills," *Pace*, October 1985, p. 49.
6. Jeff Thull, *The Prime Solution*, (Chicago, IL: Dearborn Publishing, 2005), p. 35.
7. Othman Boujena, Wesley J. Johnston, and Dwight R. Merunka, "The Benefits of Sales Force Automation: A Customer's Perspective," *Journal of Personal Selling and Sales Management*, 24, Spring 2009, p. 137.
8. Duane Sparks, Questions—*The Answer to Sales* (Minneapolis, MN: The Sales Board, 2005), p. vii.
9. Rose A. Spinelli, "Listening—A Priority in Shopping for Others," *Chicago Tribune*, November 30, 2003, p. 55.
10. Gerhard Gschwandtner, "What Makes Sales Relationships Work?" *Selling Power*, May/June 2010, p. 9.
11. Research for the SPIN model was conducted in the late 1970s and early 1980. Neil Rackham, *SPIN Selling* (New York: McGraw-Hill, 1988); www.huthwaite.com.au/research-ip.html (accessed June 8, 2010).
12. Geoffrey James, "Driving the High-Stakes Sales," *Selling Power*, May 2007, p. 51.
13. "What Do Good Salespeople Have in Common?" *Training*, December 1984, p. 21.
14. Research for the Professional Selling Skills model was conducted in the late 1960s and early 1970s. "Professional Selling Skills," http://www.achieveglobal.be/en/research-success-stories/sales/ (accessed April 1, 2016).
15. Michael D. Hargrove, "Using the Socratic Selling Method," http://bluinc.com/socratic-selling-method/ (accessed April 1, 2016).
16. Geoffrey James, "Driving the High-Stakes Sales," p. 52.
17. Robert Jolles, *Customer-Centered Selling: Mastering the Art of Urgency*, 2nd ed. (New York: The Free Press, 2009), pp. 105–106.
18. Ann Demarais and Valerie White, *First Impressions—What You Don't Know About How Others See You* (New York: Bantam Books, 2004), pp. 68–69.
19. Fernando Jaramillo and Douglas B. Grisaffe (Spring 2009), "Does Customer Orientation Impact Objective Sales Performance?" *Journal of Personal Selling and Sales Management*, 24(1), p. 167.
20. Barry L. Reece, *Effective Human Relations: Interpersonal and Organizational Applications*, 12th ed. (Mason, OH: South-Western Cengage Learning, 2013), p. 33.
21. Ibid., p. 34.
22. Demarais and White, *First Impressions*, p. 70.
23. Abner Little, "Are You Listening," *Selling Power*, May–June 2010, p. 34.
24. William F. Kendy, "The Silence Play," *Selling Power*, July/August 2007, pp. 29–30.
25. Matthew McKay, Martha Davis, and Patrick Fanning, *Message: The Communication Skills Book* (Oakland, CA: New Harbinger, 2009), p. 17; Susan Scott, *Fierce Conversation* (New York: Viking, 2002), p. 157.
26. William F. Kendy, "How to Be a Good Listener," *Selling Power*, April 2004, p. 43.
27. Tom Reilly, *Value-Added Selling* (New York: McGraw-Hill, 2003), p. 130.
28. Adam Rapp, Raj Agnihotri, and Lukas P. Forbes (Fall 2008), "The Sales Force Technology–Performance Chain: The Role of Adaptive Selling and Effort," *Journal of Personal Selling and Sales Management*, 28(4), p. 335.
29. Olaf Ploetner, "The Development of Consulting in Goods-Based Companies," p. 329.

30. Geoffrey James, "How to Use the Intuitive Model to Sell," *Selling Power*, May–June 2010, p. 40.
31. Decorating Den Interiors, www.decoratingden.com/meet-our-decorators.html (accessed April 1, 2016).
32. Tom Reilly, *Value-Added Selling*, pp. 17, 167.
33. Kerry L. Johnson, "The Things Sales Masters Do," *Value-Added Selling* 21, April 16, 2007, p. 3.
34. Aptean, http://www.aptean.com/ (accessed April 1, 2016).
35. Big Machines, www.bigmachines.com/salesforce.php (accessed April 1, 2016).
36. Rapp, Agnihotri, and Forbes, "The Sales Force Technology–Performance Chain: The Role of Adaptive Selling and Effort," p. 335.
37. Willem J. Verbeke, Frank D. Belschak, Arnold B. Bakker, and Bart Dietz (July 2008), "When Intelligence Is (Dys)Functional for Achieving Sales Performance," *Journal of Marketing*, 72, p. 44.
38. Paul F. Roos, "Just Say No," *Selling Power*, October 2003, p. 50.
39. Neil Rackham and John DeVincentis, *Rethinking the Sales Force* (New York: McGraw-Hill, 1999), p. 17.
40. Ibid., p. 9.

Endnotes for Boxed Features

a. Based on Peter Elkind, "The Man Who Sold Silicon Valley on Giving," *Fortune*, November 27, 2000, pp. 182–190.
b. Duane Sparks, *Questions—The Answer to Sales* (Minneapolis, MN: The Sales Board, 2005), p. vi; "CARQUEST Cares," http://www.carquest.com/ (accessed April 1, 2016).

Chapter 12

1. "Presentation-Wise, We've Lost Our Tails," *Sales & Field Force Automation*, July 1999, p. 4.
2. Jan Wieseke, Christian Homburg, and Nick Lee, "Understanding the Adoption of New Brands Through Salespeople: A Multilevel Framework," *Journal of the Academy of Marketing Science,* July 7, 2007, p. 278.
3. Franklin J. Carter and Ravindra Chitturi (Winter 2009), "Segmentation Based on Physician Behavior: Implications for Sales Forecasting and Marketing-Mix Strategy," *Journal of Personal Selling and Sales Management*, 29(1), p. 81.
4. Dean A. Goettsch, "Guidelines for Rethinking Sales Presentations," *Selling*, October 2001, p. 14.
5. Ryan Kibacki, "The Changing Role of the Sales Professional," *Selling Power,* May/June 2010.
6. "Communicating Technical Ideas Persuasively." This article originally appeared in the May-June 1998 issue of the *Journal for Management in Engineering,* published by the American Society of Civil Engineers (accessed April 1, 2016).
7. Gary A. Williams and Robert B. Miller, "Change the Way You Persuade," *Harvard Business Review*, May 2002, p. 6; Renee Houston Zemanski, "Subtlety Can Sell," *Selling Power*, January/February 2007, pp. 42–44.
8. Mike Coyne, "How I Made the Sale," *Value-Added Selling* 21, August 12, 2003, pp. 1, 4.
9. John M. Hawes, "Leaders in Selling and Sales Management," *Journal of Personal Selling and Sales Management,* November 5, 1985, p. 60.
10. Randall Murphy, "The Consultative Approach to Selling," *Selling Power*, March/April 2010, p. 32.
11. Fernando Jaramillo and Douglas B. Grisaffe (Spring 2009), "Does Customer Orientation Impact Objective Sales Performance?" *Journal of Personal Selling and Sales Management*, 29(2), p. 167.
12. Lambeth Hochwald, "Simplify," *Sales & Marketing Management*, June 1998, pp. 66–67; "Company Information," www.bellhelicopter.textron.com (accessed April 1, 2016).
13. Steve Heimoff, "Taking the Road Less Traveled," *Wine Spectator*, October 31, 1990, pp. 67–70; Jeff Morgan, "Geyser Peak's Turnaround," *Wine Spectator*, November 15, 1995, pp. 37–40; "Eberle Winery," www.eberlewinery.com (accessed May 1, 2016).
14. Cindy Waxer, "The Lighter Side," *Selling Power*, January/February, 2005, p. 91.
15. Douglas A. Bernstein, Alison Clarke-Stewart, Edward J. Roy, and Louis A. Penner, *Psychology*, 6th ed. (Boston: Houghton Mifflin Company, 2003), pp. 373–374.
16. Malcom Fleschner, "Funny You Should Say That," *Personal Selling Power,* May/June 2010, pp. 14–16.
17. James C. Anderson, James A. Narus, and Wouter van Rossum, "Customer Value Proposition in Business Markets," *Harvard Business Review*, March 2006, pp. 1–9.
18. Ibid.
19. Corbin Ball, "Avoiding Death by PowerPoint," www.corbinball.com/assets/docs/PowerPointDeath.pps (accessed April 1, 2016).
20. "Communicating Technical Ideas Persuasively." This article originally appeared in the May-June 1998 issue of the *Journal for Management in Engineering,* published by the American Society of Civil Engineers (accessed April 1, 2016).
21. Gerhard Gschwandtner, "What Makes Relationships Work?" *Selling Power,* May/June 2010, p. 9.
22. Kevin D. Bradford and Barton A. Weitz (Winter 2009), "Salespersons' Management of Conflict in Buyer–Seller Relationships," *Journal of Personal Selling and Sales Management,* 29(1), p. 25.
23. Robert B. Cialdini, "Harnessing the Science of Persuasion," *Harvard Business Review*, October 2001, p. 74.
24. Ibid, p. 9.
25. Stephanie G. Sherman and V. Clayton Sherman, *Make Yourself Memorable* (New York: AMACOM, 1996), pp. 58–59.
26. Willem J. Verbeke, Frank D. Belschak, Arnold B. Bakker, and Bart Dietz, "When Intelligence Is (Dys)Functional for Achieving Sales Performance," *Journal of Marketing,* 72, July 2008, p. 44.
27. John Grossmann, "Location, Location, Location," *Inc.*, August 2004, p. 83.
28. Rich Mesch, "Spinning Yarns–Seven Tips for Using Stories to Enhance Simulations and Learning," *SPBT Focus*, Spring 2007, pp. 42–46.
29. Carol Burke, "How to Create and Deliver a Winning Group Presentation," www.salesvantage.com (accessed April 1, 2016). For more information, see Joann S. Lublin, "Improv Troup Teaches Managers How to Give Better Presentation," *Wall Street Journal*, February 6, 2007, p. B1.
30. Cindy Waxer, "Light Is Right," *Selling Power*, January/February 2007, pp. 100–102.
31. Cindy Waxer, "Shine On," *Selling Power*, April 2007, p. 98.
32. Cindy Waxer, "Light Is Right," *Selling Power*, January/February 2007, p. 102.
33. Joseph B. White, "New Ergonomic Chairs Battle to Save the Backs of Workers, for Big Bucks," *Wall Street Journal*, June 8, 1999, p. B4B.
34. Rick Page, *Hope Is Not a Strategy* (Atlanta, GA: Nautilus Press, 2000), p. 126.
35. Geoffrey James, "Flight to Profit," *Selling Power*, September 2004, p. 74.

36. Lambeth Hochwald, "Simplify," *Sales & Marketing Management*, June 1998, pp. 65–66; Closetmaid, www.closetmaid.com/en-US/Pages/Default.aspx (accessed April 1, 2016).

37. Ginger Trumfio, "Ready! Set! Sell!" *Sales & Marketing Management*, February 1995, pp. 82–84; Downing Retail, http://downingretail.com/ (accessed April 1, 2016).

38. Landy Chase, "Master the Art of Brochure Selling," *Selling*, March 2005, pp. 8–9; "Colors of Corian," E.I. du Pont de Nemours and Company, 2002.

39. David Ranii, "Dermabond's Debut Disappoints," *News & Observer*, July 31, 1999, p. D-1.

40. "Three Guides to Using Your Catalog as a Sales Tool," *Value-Added Selling* 21, June 17, 2003, p. 4.

41. "The Presentation Paper Trail," *Sales & Marketing Management*, March 1995, p. 49.

42. Heather Baldwin, "Star Light Star Bright," *Selling Power Source Book*, 2002, p. 55.

43. Heather Baldwin, "Up Your Powers," *Selling Power*, October 2001, pp. 88–92.

44. Kevin Ferguson, "Reinventing the PowerPoint," *Inc.*, March 2004, p. 42; "Avoiding Death by PowerPoint," Corbin Ball Associates, www.corbinball.com/assets/docs/PowerPointDeath.pps (accessed April 1, 2016); Stacy Straczynski, "PowerPoint and Beyond," *Training,* October 2006, p. 46.

45. Gerald L. Manning and Jack W. Linge, Selling-Today.Com (Upper Saddle River, NJ: Prentice Hall, 2004), pp. 26–30.

46. Cindy Waxer, "Presenting the Power," *Selling Power Source Book*, 2005, pp. 70–71; Cindy Waxer, "Wired to Sell," *Selling Power*, June 2007, pp. 88–90.

47. Renee Houston Zemanski, "Play It Back," *Selling Power*, September 2007, p. 43.

48. Rick Page, *Hope Is Not a Strategy* (Atlanta, GA: Nautilus Press, 2002).

Endnotes for Boxed Features

a. Based on Betsy Cummings, "Selling Around the World," *Sales & Marketing Management*, May 2001, p. 70.

b. Based on Chad Kaydo, "Becoming the Face of the Brand," *Sales & Marketing Management*, February 2000, p. 14.

c. Based on "International Snapshot," *Sales & Marketing Management*, April 2000, p. 70; Jan Yager, Business Protocol, 2nd ed. (Stamford, CT: Hannacroix Books, 2001), p. 120.

d. Based on Philip Kotler and Gary Armstrong, *Principles of Marketing*, 12th ed. (Upper Saddle River, NJ: Prentice Hall, 2008), p. 467.

Chapter 13

1. *Selling Power*, June 2007, p. 32.

2. Geoff James, "The Art of Sales Negotiation," *Selling Power*, March 2004, pp. 25–28.

3. Tom Reilly, *Value-Added Selling* (New York: McGraw-Hill, 2003), p. 17.

4. Hal Lancaster, "You Have to Negotiate for Everything in Life, So Get Good at It," *Wall Street Journal*, January 27, 1998, p. B1.

5. Joydeep Srivastava and Dipankar Chakravarti (2009), "Channel Negotiations with Information Asymmetries: Contingent Influences of Communication and Trustworthiness Reputations," *Journal of Marketing Research*, 46(3), pp. 557–572.

6. Ron Willingham, *Integrity Selling for the 21st Century* (New York: Currency Doubleday, 2003), p. 154.

7. Brian Tracy, *The 100 Absolutely Unbreakable Laws of Business Success* (San Francisco: Berrett-Koehler Publishers, Inc., 2000), p. 235.

8. Ron Willingham, *Integrity Selling for the 21st Century*, p. 153.

9. Brenda Goodman, "The Art of Negotiation," *Psychology Today*, January/February 2007, pp. 64–65.

10. Richardson, www.richardson.com/Who-We-Are/Thought-Leadership/Best-Practices-in-Sales-Negotiations/ (accessed on April 1, 2016).

11. Michael Soon Lee, "Common Negotiating Mistakes That Cost You Thousands," *The American Salesman*, August 2007, pp. 25–28.

12. Rob Walker, "Take It or Leave It: The Only Guide to Negotiating You Will Ever Need," *Inc.*, August 2003, p. 81.

13. Robert H. Schuller, "Preparing to Negotiate," in *The Only Negotiating Guide You'll Ever Need: 101 Ways to Win Every Time in Any Situation* by Peter B. Stark and Jane S. Flaherty, Chapter 10 (New York, Random House, 2003), pp. 81–85.

14. Deepak Malhotra and Max H. Bazerman, *Negotiation Genius* (New York: Random House, 2007), p. 102.

15. Klaus Backhaus, Jenny van Doorn, and Robert Wilken (2008), "The Impact of Team Characteristics on the Course and Outcome of Intergroup Price Negotiations," *Journal of Business-to-Business Marketing*, 15(4), pp. 365–396.

16. Peter B. Stank and Jane Flaherty, *The Only Negotiating Guide You'll Ever Need* (New York: Broadway Books, 2003), p. 84.

17. Deepak Malhotra and Max H. Bazerman, *Negotiation Genius* (New York: Random House, 2007), pp. 20–23.

18. Ibid.

19. P. V. Balakrishnan, Charles Patton, and Phillip A. Lewis (1993), "Toward a Theory of Agenda Setting in Negotiations," *Journal of Consumer Research*, 19(2), pp. 637–654.

20. Peter B. Stank and Jane Flaherty, *The Only Negotiating Guide You'll Ever Need* (New York: Broadway Books), p. 79.

21. Nicholas G. Paparoidamis and Paolo Guenzi (2009), "An Empirical Investigation into the Impact of Relationship Selling and LMX on Salespeople's Behaviors and Sales Effectiveness," *European Journal of Marketing*, 43(7/8), pp. 1053–1075.

22. David Stiebel, *When Talking Makes Things Worse!* (Dallas: Whitehall & Nolton, 1997), p. 17.

23. For details, see Deepak Malhotra and Max H. Bazerman, *Negotiation Genius* (New York: Random House, 2007), pp. 59–64, 82.

24. Don Maruska, *Value Added Selling* 21, April 30, 2007, p. 2.

25. Robert Wilken, Markus Corneliben, Klaus Backhaus, and Christian Schmitz (2010), "Steering Sales Reps Through Cost Information: An Investigation into the Black Box of Cognitive References and Negotiation Behavior," *International Journal of Research in Marketing* 27, pp. 69–82.

26. Joseph Conlin, "Negotiating Their Way to the Top," *Sales & Marketing Management*, April 1996, p. 62; Neil Rackham, "Winning the Price War," *Sales & Marketing Management*, November 2001, p. 26.

27. Deepak Malhotra and Max H. Bazerman, *Negotiation Genius* (New York: Random House, 2007), p. 175.

28. Lain Ehman, "Not a Done Deal," *Selling Power*, November/December 2003, pp. 42–44; "Negotiate the Right Price Despite Customer Pressure," *Selling*, July 2004, p. 2.

29. William F. Kendy, "Solving the 'Friendship Buying' Problem," *Selling Power*, November/December 2001, pp. 40–44.

30. Sarah Mahoney, "Competing Against a Long-Term Supplier," *Selling*, June 1998, p. 10.

31. Marc Freeman, "Say It and Sell It," *Sales & Marketing Management*, November/December 2006, p. 13.

32. William F. Kendy, "The Price Is Too High," *Selling Power*, April 2006, pp. 30–33.

33. Ibid.

34. Jeff Keller, "Objections? No Problem," *Selling Power*, September 1996, pp. 44–45.

35. Adapted from Nanci McCann, "Irate over Rates," *Selling*, July/August 1996, p. 25.

36. Tom Reilly, *Value-Added Selling* (New York: McGraw-Hill, 2003), p. 189.

37. See Neil Rackham, *The SPIN Selling Fieldbook* (New York: McGraw-Hill, 1996), pp. 127–145.

38. David Jobber and Jeff Lancaster, *Selling and Sales Management*, 7th ed. (Prentice Hall/Financial Times, 2006), p. 261.

39. Arnaud De Bruyn and Gary E. Bolton (2008), "Estimating the Influence of Fairness on Bargaining Behavior," *Management Science*, 54(10), pp. 1774–1791.

40. William F. Kendy, "The Price Is Too High," *Selling Power*, April 2006, p. 30.

41. Tom Reilly, *Value-Added Selling* (New York: McGraw-Hill, 2003), pp. 191–192.

42. Joseph Conlin, "Negotiating Their Way to the Top," *Sales & Marketing Management*, April 1996, p. 58.

43. William F. Kendy, "The Price Is Too High," *Selling Power*, April 2006, pp. 30–33.

44. Sam Deep and Lyle Sussman, *Close the Deal: Smart Moves for Selling* (Reading, MA: Perseus Books, 1999), p. 225.

45. Tom Reilly, http://tomreillytraining.com/writings-and-recordings/articles/crush-price-objections/ (accessed on April 1, 2016)

46. William F. Kendy, "Negotiation Tactics," *Selling Power*, September 2006, p. 31.

47. Based on Homer Smith, "How to Cope with Buyers Who Are Trained in Negotiation," *Personal Selling Power*, September 1988, p. 37.

48. Ibid.

49. Robert Adler, Benson Rosen, and Elliot Silverstein, "Thrust and Parry," *Training & Development*, March 1996, p. 47.

50. Homer Smith, "How to Cope with Buyers Who Are Trained in Negotiation," *Personal Selling Power*, September 1988, p. 37.

Endnotes for Boxed Features

a. "Getting to Yes, Chinese Style," *Sales & Marketing Management*, July 1996, pp. 44–45; Sam Deep and Lyle Sussman, *Close the Deal* (Reading, MA: Perseus Books, 1999), pp. 279–281; James K. Sebenius, "Six Habits of Merely Effective Negotiators," *Harvard Business Review*, April 2001, p. 90.

b. Hal Lancaster, "You Have to Negotiate for Everything in Life, So Get Good at It," *Wall Street Journal*, January 27, 1998, p. B1; Amy Lindgren, "Want a Raise? Don't Daydream; Polish Your Negotiating Skills," *Des Moines Register*, April 26, 1998, p. IL; "The Karrass Story," www.Karrass.com (accessed April 1, 2016).

c. Based on Timothy Aeppel, "A Factory Manager Improvises to Save Jobs in a Downturn," *Wall Street Journal*, December 27, 2001, pp. A1, A14.

Chapter 14

1. *On the Dotted Line: Closing the Sale* (Pasadena, CA: Intelecom); "Special Events and Meetings," http://themeparks.universalstudios.com/index.php (accessed on April 1, 2016).

2. Subhra Chakrabarty, Gene Brown, and Robert E. Widing II (2010), "Closed Influence Tactics: Do Smugglers Win in the Long Run?" *Journal of Personal Selling and Sales Management*, 30(1), pp. 23–32.

3. Ron Willingham, *Integrity Selling for the 21st Century* (New York: Currency Doubleday, 2003), p. 179.

4. Sergio Roman and Dawn Iacobucci (2010), "Antecedents and Consequences of Adaptive Selling Confidence and Behavior: A Dyadic Analysis of Salespeople and Their Customers," *Journal of the Academy of Marketing Science*, 38(3), pp. 363–382.

5. Gene Bedell, *Three Steps to Yes* (New York: Crown Business, 2000), pp. 72–80.

6. Tom Reilly, *Value-Added Selling* (New York: McGraw-Hill, 2003), p. 176.

7. Andy Cohen, "Are Your Reps Afraid to Close?" *Sales & Marketing Management*, March 1996, p. 43.

8. Michele Marchetti, "Make Process a Sales Priority," *Sales & Marketing Management,* September 2006, p. 16; see John Graham, "How to Profit from Customer Buying-Cycle Basics," *The American Salesman,* May 2007, pp. 19–23.

9. Susan Creco, "The Need for Speed—How to Rev Up Your Sales Cycle," *Inc.,* April 2007, p. 38.

10. Graham Denton, "The Single Biggest Closing Mistake," Graham Denton Skills Center, www.members.fortunecity.com/salesman2/salescom/closing/thesingl.html (accessed September 26, 2010), p. 1.

11. Ray Dreyfock, "Is the Buyer Ready?" *Selling Power*, January/February 2002, p. 52.

12. Ralph W. Giacobbe, Donald W. Jackson Jr., Lawrence A. Crosby, and Claudia M. Bridges, "A Contingency Approach to Adaptive Selling Behavior and Sales Performance: Selling Situations and Salesperson Characteristics," *Journal of Personal Selling and Sales Management*, Spring 2006, pp. 115–142.

13. "The Closing Moment," *Personal Selling*, October 1995, p. 48; Lain Ehman, "How to Read Hidden Signals," *Selling Power*, June 2004, pp. 36–38.

14. Ron Karr, "Expert Advice—The Titan Principle," *Selling Power*, October 2001, p. 32.

15. Richard G. McFarland, Goutam N. Challagalla, and Tasadduq A. Shervani, "Influence Tactics for Effective Adaptive Selling," *Journal of Marketing*, October 2006, pp. 103–117.

16. Jenny McCune, "Closing Sales with a Splash," *Selling*, September 2004, p. 15.

17. "Selling Tips," *Selling*, May 1999, p. 13.

18. Ron Willingham, *Integrity Selling* (New York: Doubleday, 1987), p. 133.

19. Jeffrey Gitomer, "Did You Get the Order? If You Didn't, Here's Why," *Business Record*, May 7, 2007, p. 36.

20. Tom Reilly, *Value-Added Selling*, p. 179.

21. Ron Willingham, *Integrity Selling for the 21st Century* (New York: Currency Doubleday, 2003), p. 184.

22. Jenny C. McCune, "The Brief Story of Underwear's Stupendous Success," *Selling*, March 2000, p. 15.

23. Joan Leotta, "The Management Close," *Selling Power*, November/December 2001, pp. 26–28; Megan Sweas, "Heavyweights on Call," *Sales & Marketing Management*, December 2003, p. 14.

24. Ron Willingham, *Integrity Selling for the 21st Century*, pp. 185–187.

25. George R. Franke and Jeong-Eun Park, "Salesperson Adaptive Selling Behavior and Customer Orientation: A Meta-Analysis," *Journal of Marketing Research*, November 2006, pp. 693–702.

26. Richard Ruff, http://salestrainingconnection.com/2014/05/05/sales-role-plays-do-them-right-then-they-work/ (accessed on April 1, 2016).

27. T. J. Becker, "That Queasy Feeling," *Chicago Tribune*, July 21, 2002, p. W1.

28. Betsy Wiesendanger, "When a Sale Goes South," *Selling Power,* November/December 2003, pp. 65–67.

29. Betsy Cummings, "Done Deal—How One Sales Pro Closed a Big Customer," *Sales & Marketing Management,* September 2006, p. 13.

Endnotes for Boxed Features

a. Based on Barbara Hagenbough, "Economics Majors Build Brand Name with Unmentionables," *USA Today,* May 20, 2002, p. 3-B.

b. "International Snapshot," *Sales & Marketing Management,* October 2001, p. 70; Jan Yager, *Business Protocol,* 2nd ed. (Stamford, CT: Hannacroix Books, 2001), pp. 116–117.

Chapter 15

1. Bob Johnson, "Loyalty Lessons from the Pros," *Customer Support Management,* July/August 1999, p. 115; Ranjay Gulati and James B. Oldroyd, "The Quest for Customer Focus," *Harvard Business Review,* April 2005, pp. 92–97.

2. Ibid.

3. Gary Armstrong and Philip Kotler, *Marketing—An Introduction,* 6th ed. (Upper Saddle River, NJ: Prentice Hall, 2003), p. 533.

4. Don Peppers and Martha Rogers, "Customer Loyalty: A Matter of Trust," *Sales & Marketing Management,* June 2006, p. 22.

5. Theodore Levitt, *The Marketing Imagination* (New York: Macmillan, 1983), pp. 117–118; Tahl Raz, "The '4 + 2 Formula' for Success," *Inc.,* August 2003, p. 42.

6. Brett Boyle, F. Robert Dwyer, Robert A. Robicheaux, and James T. Simpson (1992), "Influence Strategies in Marketing Channels: Measures and Use in Different Relationship Structures," *Journal of Marketing Research,* 29(4), pp. 462–473.

7. See Tom Reilly, "Value-Added Service Is a Team Sport," Tom Reilly Training, www.tomreillytraining.com (accessed April 1, 2016).

8. Geoffrey Brewer, "The Customer Stops Here," *Sales & Marketing Management,* March 1998, pp. 31–33; see Ron Zemke and Chip Bell, *Service Magic* (Chicago, IL: Dearborn Trade Publishing, 2004).

9. James Digby, http://returnonbehavior.com/2010/10/50-facts-about-customer-experience-for-2011/ (accessed on April 1, 2016); Collin Burke, www.insightsquared.com/2015/04/100-customer-service-statistics-you-need-to-know/ (accessed April 1, 2016).

10. Tom Peters, *The Circle of Innovation* (New York: Vintage Books, 1997), p. 464; "Customers for Life," http://www.sewelllexus-fw.com (accessed April 1, 2016).

11. Bill Gates, *Business @ the Speed of Thought* (New York: Warner Books, 1999), p. 67.

12. Ruth Maria Stock and Wayne D. Hoyer (2005), "An Attitude-Behavior Model of Salespeople's Customer Orientation," *Journal of the Academy of Marketing Science,* 33(4), pp. 536–552.

13. Michael Ahearne, Ronald Jelinek, and Eli Jones, "Examining the Effect of Salesperson Service Behavior in a Competitive Context," *Journal of the Academy of Marketing Science,* Spring 2007, p. 13.

14. Daniel H. Pink, *A Whole New Mind: Moving from the Information Age to the Conceptual Age* (New York: Riverhead Books, 2005), pp. 48–53.

15. Frederick Hong-kit Yim, Rolph E. Anderson, and Srinivasan Swaminathan (2004), "Customer Relationship Management: Its Dimensions and Effect on Customer Outcomes," *Journal of Personal Selling and Sales Management,* 24(4), pp. 263–278.

16. Steve Ham, "Oracle—Why It's Cool Again," *BusinessWeek,* May 8, 2000, pp. 115–119.

17. Jack Mitchell, *Hug Your Customers* (New York: Hyperion, 2003), pp. 129–132.

18. Maxim Sytch and Ranjay Gulati (2008), "Creating Value Together," *MIT Sloan Management Review,* 50(1), pp. 12–13.

19. Scott Wolfe Jr., www.zlien.com/articles/credit-department-v-sales-departments-how-everyone-can-get-along/ (accessed on April 1, 2016).

20. Sally J. Silberman, "An Eye for Finance," *Sales & Marketing Management,* April 1996, p. 26.

21. Benson P. Shapiro, V. Kasturi Rangon, and John J. Sviokla, "Staple Yourself to an Order," *Harvard Business Review,* July/August 2004, pp. 162–171.

22. Daryl Allen, "Relationship Selling Is Key to Success," *Selling,* March 2002, p. 12.

23. Dave Kahle, "Protecting Your Good Accounts," *The American Salesman,* June 2007, p. 12.

24. Gary L. Frankwick, Stephen S. Porter, and Lawrence A. Crosby (2001), "Dynamics of Relationship Selling: A Longitudinal Examination of Changes in Salesperson-Customer Relationship Status," *Journal of Personal Selling and Sales Management,* 21(2), pp. 135–146.

25. Tom Reilly, "Create Satisfied Customers: Always Be Sure to Exceed Their Expectations," *Selling,* January 2001, p. 3; Mary Salafia, "Reassessment Planning," *Selling Power,* May 2004, p. 56.

26. Tom Reilly, *Value-Added Selling* (New York: McGraw-Hill, 2003), p. 117.

27. Andrea Nierenberg, "Eight Ways to Stay Top of Mind," *Selling,* April 1998, p. 7.

28. Queena Sook Kim, "For Sale: Super-Model Home," *Wall Street Journal,* August 6, 2002, p. D1.

29. Melinda Ligos, "The Joys of Cross-Selling," *Sales & Marketing Management,* August 1998, p. 75.

30. Tom Reilly, *Value-Added Selling,* pp. 124–125.

31. William F. Kendy, "Add-Ons Add Up," *Selling Power,* January/February 2007, p. 30.

32. William F. Kendy, "Skills Workshop," *Selling Power,* June 2000, pp. 33–34.

33. Jo Ann Brezette, "Smart Answers to Clients' Questions," *Window Fashions Design & Education Magazine,* September 2001, p. 120; Lain Ehman, "Upsell, Don't Oversell," *Selling Power,* January/February 2004, pp. 30–32.

34. John Hagedoorn (2006), "Understanding the Cross-Level Embeddedness of Interfirm Partnership Formation," *Academy of Management Review,* 31(3), pp. 670–680.

35. "Inspirations from Michele," *Inspiring Solutions,* February 1999, p. 3.

36. Jahyun Goo, Rajiv Kishore, H. R. Rao, and Kichan Nam (2008), "The Role of Service Level Agreements in Relational Management of Information Technology Outsourcing: An Empirical Study," *MIS Quarterly,* 33(1), pp. 119–145.

37. Bob Johnson, "Loyalty Lessons from the Pros," *Customer Support Management,* July/August 1999, p. 115.

38. Barry L. Reece, *Effective Human Relations: Interpersonal and Organizational Applications,* 12th ed. (Mason, OH: South-Western Cengage Learning, 2013), pp. 195–196.

39. Bradley E. Wesner, "From Complaint to Opportunity," *Selling Power,* May 1996, p. 62.

40. Tony Hsieh, "How I Did It: Zappos's CEO on Going to Extremes for Customers," *Harvard Business Review,* July–August, 2010.

Gerald A. Michaelson, "When Things Go Wrong, Make It Right," *Selling*, March 1997, p. 12.

41. Michael Abrams and Matthew Paese, "Wining and Dining the Whiners," *Sales & Marketing Management*, February 1993, p. 73.

42. "How to Diffuse a Customer Problem," *Sales & Marketing Management*, May 2000, p. 14.

Endnotes for Boxed Features

a. Based on Jeff Barbian, "It's Who You Know," *Training*, December 2001, p. 22.

b. "Relationships with Customers Must Be Job Number 1," *Food-Service Distributor*, July 1989, p. 74; Joan O. Fredericks and James M. Salter II, "Beyond Customer Satisfaction," *Management Review*, May 1995, pp. 29–32.

c. Jan Yager, *Business Protocol*, 2nd ed. (Stamford, CT: Hannacroix Books, 2001), p. 123; "Selling in Russia," *Sales & Marketing Management*, March 2002, p. 60; Carl F. Fey and Stanislow Shekshnia, "How to Do Business in Russia," *Wall Street Journal*, October 27, 2007, p. R4.

d. Byran Ziegler, "Your Business Card Can Be a Powerful Tool," *Des Moines Register*, August 2, 1999, p. 17-B; Kemba J. Dunham, "Here's My Card," *Wall Street Journal*, May 14, 2002, p. B12.

Chapter 16

1. Dana Ray, "The Secret of Success," *Personal Selling Power*, November/December 1995, pp. 80–83.

2. Julio Melara, www.juliomelara.com (accessed April 17, 2016).

3. Renee Houston Zemanski, "A Matter of Time," *Selling Power*, October 2001, p. 82.

4. Bernd Skiera and Sonke Albers (2008), "Prioritizing Sales Force Decision Areas for Productivity Improvements Using a Core Sales Response Function," *Journal of Personal Selling and Sales Management*, 28(2), pp. 145–154.

5. Eugene Greissman, "Seven Characteristics of High-Achieving Salespeople," *Value-Added Selling* 21, March 16, 2004, p. 4.

6. Betty Cummings, "Increasing Face Time," *Sales & Marketing Management*, January 2004, p. 12.

7. Thomas P. Reilly, "Three Tips for Effective Time Management," http://www.sellingpower.com/content/article/?a=8350/three-tips-for-effective-time-management (accessed on April 17, 2016).

8. If you are interested in how to break bad habits and form good ones, see James Claiborn and Cherry Pedrick, *The Habit Change Workbook* (Oakland, CA: New Harbinger Publications, 2001).

9. See Alison Stein Wellner, "The Time Trap," *Inc.*, June 2004, pp. 42–44.

10. Brian Tracy, *The 100 Absolutely Unbreakable Laws of Business Success* (San Francisco: Berrett-Koehler Publishers, Inc., 2000), pp. 40–47.

11. Charles R. Hall, "Create Excitement, Get Motivated Through Planning," *Selling*, February 2000, p. 13.

12. Ed Brown, "Stephen Covey's New One-Day Seminar," *Fortune*, January 1999, p. 138.

13. Betsy Wiesendanger, "Time to Spend," *Selling Power*, November/December 2003, pp. 28–32.

14. Hyrum W. Smith, *The 10 Natural Laws of Successful Time and Life Management* (New York: Warner Books, 1994), p. 108.

15. Thomas E. Weber, "Meetings in Cyberspace May Soon Be as Routine as the Conference Call," *Wall Street Journal*, June 4, 2001, p. B1.

16. Michele Marchetti, "Territories: For Optimal Performance, Segment Your Customer Base by Industry," *Sales & Marketing Management*, December 1998, p. 35.

17. Ken Grant, David W. Cravens, George S. Low, and William C. Moncrief (2001), "The Role of Satisfaction with Territory Design on the Motivation, Attitudes, and Work Outcomes of Salespeople," *Journal of the Academy of Marketing Science*, 29(2), pp. 165–178.

18. Lain Chroust Ehmann, "In the Details," *Selling Power*, September 2007, p. 34.

19. Rajkumar Venkatesan, V. Kumar, and Timothy Bohling (2007), "Optimal Customer Relationship Management Using Bayesian Decision Theory: An Application for Customer Selection," *Journal of Marketing Research*, 44(4), pp. 579–594.

20. V. Kumar, Rajkumar Venkatesan, Tim Bohling, and Denise Beckmann (2008), "The Power of CLV: Managing Customer Lifetime Value at IBM," *Marketing Science*, 27(4), pp. 585–599.

21. Ibid., p. 36.

22. Ken Liebeskind, "Where Is Everyone?" *Selling Power*, March 1998, p. 35; Marie Warner, "Take Careful Steps When Redefining Territories," *Selling*, June 2001, p. 10.

23. Alison Smith, "Plan Your Territory," *Selling Power*, March 2003, pp. 37–38.

24. Daryl Allen, "Maximize Your Territory Coverage, Increased Sales and Higher Profits Will Follow," *Selling*, June 2001, p. 10.

25. Paul Clark, Richard A. Rocco, and Alan J. Bush (2007), "Sales Force Automation Systems and Sales Force Productivity: Critical Issues and Research Agenda," *Journal of Relationship Marketing*, 6(2), pp. 67–87.

26. Henry Canaday, "Automated Reports Boost Sales Productivity," *Selling Power*, June 2007, p. 13.

27. "Maintaining Perspective by Keeping Good Records," *Value-Added Selling* 21, August 20, 2007, p. 4.

28. Jeffrey E. Lewin and Jeffrey K. Sager (2008), "Salesperson Burnout: A Test of the Coping-Mediational Model of Social Support," *Journal of Personal Selling and Sales Management*, 28(3), pp. 233–246.

29. Bruce Cryer, Rollin McCraty, and Doc Childre, "Pull the Plug on Stress," *Harvard Business Review*, July 2003, pp. 1–2.

30. Paul Hemp, "Death by Information Overload," *Harvard Business Review*, September 2009, pp 82–87.

31. "More Useful Tips for Running Your Home Office," *Selling*, January 2001, p. 11; "Home Office Etiquette," *Sales & Marketing Management*, January 2000, p. 74.

32. Patricia Sellers, "Now Bounce Back," *Fortune*, May 1, 1995, p. 57.

33. Martin Seligman, *Learned Optimism* (New York: Knopf, 2001), p. 4; Annie Murphy Paul, "Self-Help: Shattering the Myths," *Psychology Today*, March/April 2001, p. 64; Arnold A. Lazarus and Clifford N. Lazarus, *The 60-Second Shrink* (San Luis Obispo, CA: Impact Publishers, 1997), pp. 3, 4.

34. Caleb T. Hayes and Bart L. Weathington (2007), "Optimism, Stress, Life Satisfaction, and Job Burnout in Restaurant Managers," *Journal of Psychology*, 141(6), pp. 565–579.

35. Sandra Lotzs Fisher, "Stress—Will You Cope or Crack?" *Selling*, May 1996, p. 31.

36. Geoffrey Brewer, "Person-to-Person," *Sales & Marketing Management*, December 1995, p. 29.

Endnotes for Boxed Features

a. Amy Finnerty, "Bill Blass, A Designer with Class," *Wall Street Journal*, June 18, 2002, p. D9; Susan Orlean, *The Bullfighter Checks Her Makeup* (New York: Random House, 2002), pp. 177–187.

b. Based on Michael Adams, "Family Matters," *Sales & Marketing Management*, March 1998, pp. 61–65.

c. Based on "Selling in Belgium," *Sales & Marketing Management*, August 2002, p. 58.

Chapter 17

1. Jan Wieseke, Michael Ahearne, Son K. Lam, and Rolf van Dick (2009), "The Role of Leaders in Internal Marketing," *Journal of Marketing*, 73(2), pp. 123–145.

2. Robert Kreitner and Carlene M. Cassidy, *Management*, 12th ed. (OH: South-Western Cengage Learning, 2011), p. 394.

3. "Stephen Covey Talks About the Eighth Habit: Effective Is No Longer Enough," *Training*, February 2005, pp. 17–19.

4. Michael R. Solomon, Greg W. Marshall, and Elnora W. Stuart, *Marketing—Real People, Real Choices*, 7th ed. (Upper Saddle River, NJ: Prentice Hall, 2012), p. 436.

5. Jack Falvey, "Fly by Night, Sell by Day," *Wall Street Journal*, June 9, 1997, p. A18.

6. Lisa Gschwandtner, "What Makes an Ideal Sales Manager," *Selling Power*, June 2001, p. 54.

7. William Keenan Jr., "Death of the Sales Manager," *Sales & Marketing Management*, April 1998, pp. 72–79.

8. "Measuring Sales Management's Coaching Impact," http://sales-management.org/web/uploads/pdf/8fa9799a465268debbc7a352a46b7e94.pdf (accessed on April 17, 2016).

9. These dimensions are described in Edwin A. Fleischman, *Manual for Leadership Opinion Questionnaire* (Chicago: Science Research Associates, 1960), p. 3. The dimensions of consideration and structure are also described in Robert Kreitner and Carlene M. Cassidy, *Management*, 12th ed. (OH: South-Western Cengage Learning, 2011), p. 399.

10. Dale Kahle, "It Takes More Than Just Compensation to Unleash a Sales Force!" *The American Salesman,* October 2007, p. 5.

11. Brian Tracy, *The 100 Absolutely Unbreakable Laws of Business Success* (San Francisco: Berrett-Koehler Publishers, Inc., 2000), pp. 19–20.

12. Jared Sandberg, "Overcontrolling Bosses Aren't Just Annoying; They're Also Inefficient," *Wall Street Journal*, March 30, 2005, p. B1.

13. Sarah Lorge, "In the Box," *Sales & Marketing Management*, April 1998, p. 15.

14. Ken Blanchard, "Three Secrets of the One-Minute Manager," *Personal Selling Power*, March 1993, p. 48.

15. Robert Kreitner and Carlene M. Cassidy, *Management*, 12th ed. (OH: South-Western Cengage Learning, 2011), p. 399; Paul Hersey, *The Situational Leader* (Escondido, CA: Center for Leadership Studies, 1984), pp. 29–30.

16. Ron Zemke, "Trust Inspires Trust," *Training*, January 2002, p. 10; Barry L. Reece, *Effective Human Relations: Interpersonal and Organizational Applications* (OH: South-Western Cengage Learning, 2013), p. 110; Noel M. Tichy and Warren G. Bennis, "Making the Tough Call—Great Leaders Recognize When Their Values Are on the Line," *Inc.*, November 2007, pp. 36–37.

17. Scott Edinger, "How Great Sales Leaders Coach," http://www.forbes.com/sites/scottedinger/2013/06/25/how-great-sales-leaders-coach/#2eef6ef9194b (accessed on May 8, 2016).

18. Anne Fisher, "In Praise of Micromanaging," *Fortune*, August 23, 2004, p. 40; Brian Tracy, "Coaching for Success," *Sales & Marketing Management*, July/August 2007, p. 6.

19. Anne Fisher, "Essential Employees Called Up to Serve," *Fortune*, October 2000, p. 210.

20. Willem J. Verbeke, Frank D. Belschak, Arnold B. Bakker, and Bart Dietz (2008), "When Intelligence Is (Dys)Functional for Achieving Sales Performance," *Journal of Marketing*, 72(2), pp. 44–57.

21. Dana Telford and Adrian Gostick, "Hiring Character," *Sales & Marketing Management*, June 2005, pp. 39–42.

22. Andy Cohen, "What Keeps You Up at Night?" *Sales & Marketing Management*, February 2000, pp. 44–52.

23. Henry Canaday, "Search Smarts," *Selling Power Source Book*, 2008, pp. 64–68.

24. "Sales Achievement Predictor," portal.wpspublish.com/pls/portal/url/page/wps/W-311 (accessed May 8, 2016).

25. "Caliper Profile," www.calipercorp.com (accessed May 8, 2016).

26. Henry Canaday, "Search Smarts," *Selling Power Source Book*, 2008, pp. 64–68.

27. Shikhar Sarin, Trina Sego, Ajay K. Kohli, and Goutam Challagalla (2010), "Characteristics that Enhance Training Effectiveness in Implementing Technological Change in Sales Strategy: A Field-Based Exploratory Study," *Journal of Personal Selling and Sales Management*, 30(2), pp. 143–156.

28. Philip Kotler and Gary Armstrong, *Principles of Marketing,* 12th ed. (Upper Saddle River, NJ: Prentice Hall, 2008), p. 460.

29. Alan J. Dubinsky, Francis J. Yammarino, Marvin A. Jolson, and William D. Spangler, "Transformational Leadership: An Initial Investigation in Sales Management," *Journal of Personal Selling & Sales Management*, Spring 1995, p. 27.

30. Skip Corsini, "The Great (Sales) Training Robbery," *Training*, February 2005, p. 14.

31. Barry L. Reece, *Effective Human Relations: Interpersonal and Organizational Applications* (Mason, OH: South-Western Cengage Learning, 2013), p. 148.

32. Ibid.

33. Noah Lim, Michael J. Ahearne, and Sung H. Ham (2009), "Designing Sales Contests: Does the Prize Structure Matter?" *Journal of Marketing Research*, 46(2), pp. 356–371.

34. Audrey Bottjen, "Incentives Gone Awry," *Sales & Marketing Management*, May 2001, p. 72.

35. Lain Chroust Ehmann, "A Team of Winners," *Selling Power*, November/December 2006, pp. 40–43.

36. William H. Murphy, Peter A. Dacin, and Neil M. Ford (2004), "Sales Contest Effectiveness: An Examination of Sales Contest Design Preferences of Field Sales Forces," *Journal of the Academy of Marketing Science*, 20(10), pp. 1–17.

37. Julie Chang, "Trophy Value," *Sales & Marketing Management*, October 2004, p. 26.

38. Carol Hymorwitz, "When Meeting Targets Becomes the Strategy, CEO Is on Wrong Path," *Wall Street Journal*, March 8, 2005, p. B1; Carol Hymowitz, "Readers Share Tales of Jobs Where Strategy Became Meeting Target," *Wall Street Journal*, March 22, 2005, p. B1.

39. Michael Schrage, "A Lesson in Perversity," *Sales & Marketing Management*, January 2004, p. 28.

40. Michael Segalla, Dominique Rouzies, Madeleine Besson, and Barton A. Weitz (2006), "A Cross-National Investigation of Incentive Sales Compensation," *International Journal of Research in Marketing* 23, pp. 419–433.

41. Eilene Zimmerman, "Quota Busters," *Sales & Marketing Management*, January 2001, pp. 59–63.

42. "Sales Compensation Practices," http://www.wilsongroup .com/wp-content/uploads/2013/12/Wilson-Group-Sales-Compensation-Practices-Survey-Report-2012-2013.pdf (accessed on May 8, 2016).

43. Dominique Rouzies, Anne T. Coughlan, Erin Anderson, and Dawn Iacobucci (2009), "Determinants of Pay Levels and Structures in Sales Organizations," *Journal of Marketing*, 73(4), pp. 92–104.

44. "Point Incentive Sales Programs," *SBR Update*, vol. I, no. 4; Christopher Hosford, "A Carrot That Works," *Sales & Marketing Management,* November/December 2007, p. 10.

45. Donald W. Jackson Jr., John L. Schlacter, and William G. Wolfe, "Examining the Bases Utilized for Evaluating Salespeople's Performance," *Journal of Personal Selling & Sales Management*, February 1995, p. 57.

46. "Survey of Sales Evaluation Process—What Works, What Doesn't," *Selling Power*, September 1999, p. 115.

47. Lisa Holton, "Look Who's in on Your Performance Review," *Selling*, January/February 1995, pp. 47–55; Barry L. Reece and Rhonda Brandt, *Effective Human Relations: Personal and Organizational Applications* (Boston: Houghton Mifflin Company, 2005), p. 195; "Customer Ratings Are Misleading," *Selling*, November 1996, p. 1.

Endnotes for Boxed Features

a. Personal interview with Tom Gunter, vice president of sales, ConAgra Foods, conducted by Lisa Violo, Brock University MBA student, November 4, 2005; personal interview with H. F. (Herb) MacKenzie, August 9, 2015.

b. Douglas J. Dalrymple and William L. Cron, *Sales Management: Concepts and Cases* (New York: John Wiley & Sons, 1998), pp. 344–347; William Keenan, "Time Is Everything," *Sales & Management,* August 1993, p. 61.

c. Erin Anderson and Leonard Lodish (2006), "leading the effective sales force: the asian sales force management environment", working paper, pp. 8–10; Stella Lai Man So and Mark W. Speece (2000), "Perceptions of relationship marketing among account managers of commercial banks in a Chinese environment," *International Journal of Bank Marketing*, 18(7), 315–327; Roger Bennet (1999), "Guanxi and sales force management practices in China" in Malcolm Warner (ed), *China's Management Revolution*, Frank Cass Publishers: London, pp. 73–93.

d. Roger Bennet (1999), "Guanxi and sales force management practices in China" in Malcolm Warner (ed), *China's Management Revolution*, Frank Cass Publishers: London, pp. 73–93.

Glossary

3-D Product Solutions Selling Model Illustrates the product, company, and salesperson features available to satisfy the customer's potential 3-D cluster of satisfactions.

account analysis Estimates the sales potential for each prospect.

account or business development The process of identifying and developing potential customers in the business-to-business (B2B) market. Is also referred to as prospecting.

action objective Something that you want the customer to do during the sales presentation, such as provide specific financial information, schedule a visit to your manufacturing plant, agree to a trial use of your product, agree to a follow-up meeting, or place an order.

active listening The process of sending back to the person what you as a listener think the individual meant, both in terms of content and in terms of feelings. It involves taking into consideration both verbal and nonverbal signals.

adaptive selling Used to describe sales training programs that encourage salespeople to adjust their communication style to accommodate the communication style of the customer.

advantages Characteristics of the product (features) that can be used or will help the buyer.

approach The first contact with the prospect, either face-to-face or by telephone. The approach has three objectives: to build rapport with the prospect, to capture the person's full attention, and to generate interest in the product you are selling.

assumptive close After the salesperson identifies a genuine need, presents solutions in terms of buyer benefits, conducts an effective sales demonstration, and negotiates buyer resistance satisfactorily, the assumption is that the prospect has already bought the product. The closing activity is based on the assumption that a buying decision has already been made.

balance sheet close A closing method that appeals to customers who are having difficulty making a decision. The salesperson draws a T on a sheet of paper and places captions on each side of the crossbar: reasons for buying now (left) and reasons for not buying now (right).

balanced funnel Enables salespeople to know how many prospects and how much revenue will be needed at each stage in the sales process to meet sales projections and quotas.

BATNA Best Alternative to Negotiated Agreement: what alternative(s) will be acceptable to you if your negotiation does not succeed.

benefit A feature that provides the customer with personal advantage or gain. This usually answers the question, "How will the customer benefit from owning or using the product?"

bridge statement A transitional phrase that connects a statement of features with a statement of benefits. This method permits customers to connect the features of your product to the benefits they will receive.

business buyer behavior Refers to the organizations that buy goods and services for use in the production of other products and services that are sold, rented, or supplied to others.

business casual Clothing that allows you to feel comfortable at work, but looks neat and professional.

business ethics Comprises principles and standards that guide behavior in the world of business.

buyer's remorse Feelings of regret, fear, or anxiety that a buyer may feel after placing an order.

buyer resolution theory A selling theory that recognizes a purchase will be made only after the prospect has made buying decisions involving specific affirmative responses to the following five items: need, product, source, price, and time.

buying center A cross-functional team of decision makers who often represent several departments.

buying conditions Circumstances that must be available or fulfilled before the sale can be closed.

buying motives An aroused need, drive, or desire that initiates the sequence of events that may lead to a purchase.

buying process A systematic series of actions, or a series of defined, repeatable steps intended to achieve a result.

call report A written summary that provides information from a sales call to people in the sales organization, so that follow-up action will be taken when necessary.

canned presentation Refers to a standard set of steps that ignores the unique needs of each customer, and is presented in the form of a repetitive speech given to all customers interested in a particular item.

character Your personal standards of behavior, including your honesty and integrity. Your character is based on your internal values and the resulting judgments you make about what is right and what is wrong.

closed questions Questions that can be answered with a yes or no, or a brief response.

closing clue An indication, either verbal or nonverbal, that the prospect is preparing to make a buying decision.

coaching An interpersonal process between a sales manager and a salesperson in which the manager helps the salesperson improve performance in a specific area.

cold calling A method of prospecting in which the salesperson selects a group of people who may or may not be actual prospects and then calls on each one.

communication style Patterns of behavior that others observe.

communication-style bias A state of mind we often experience when we have contact with another person whose communication style is different from our own.

compensation plans Pay plans for salespeople that combine direct monetary pay and indirect monetary payments such as paid vacations, pensions, and insurance plans.

complex buying decision Decisions that are characterized by a high degree of involvement by the consumer.

confirmation questions A type of question used throughout the sales presentation to find out if the message is getting through to the prospect. It checks both the prospect's level of understanding and the prospect's agreement with the presentation's claims.

confirmation step Reassuring the customer after the sale has been closed, pointing out that he has made the correct decision. This may involve describing the satisfaction of owning the product.

consideration Sales managers displaying consideration are more likely to have relationships with salespeople that are characterized by mutual trust, respect for the salesperson's ideas, and consideration for their feelings.

consultative selling An approach to personal selling that is an extension of the marketing concept. Emphasis is placed on need identification, need satisfaction, and the building of a relationship that results in repeat business.

consumer buyer behavior The buying behavior of individuals and households who buy goods and services for personal consumption.

contract A promise or promises that the courts will enforce.

cooling-off laws Laws that give customers an opportunity to reconsider a buying decision.

cost-benefit analysis This involves listing the costs to the buyer and the savings to be achieved. This method is a common approach to quantifying the solution.

cross selling Selling products to an established customer that are not directly related to products the customer has already bought.

culture The arts, beliefs, institutions, transmitted behavior patterns, and thoughts of a community or population.

customer relationship management (CRM) The process of building and maintaining strong customer relationships by providing customer value. A modern CRM program relies on a variety of technologies to enhance customer responsiveness.

customer service All those activities enhancing or facilitating the sale and use of a product or service, including suggestion selling, delivery and installation, assistance with warranty or service contract, securing credit arrangements, and making post-sale courtesy calls.

customer service representative These people process reservations, accept orders by phone or by other means, deliver products, handle customer complaints, provide technical assistance, and assist salespeople.

customer strategy A carefully conceived plan that will result in maximum responsiveness to the customer's needs. The salesperson should develop an understanding of a customer's buying process, understand buyer behavior, and develop a prospect base.

differentiation Refers to your ability to separate yourself and your product from that of your competitors.

direct appeal close Involves simply asking for the order in a straightforward manner. It is the most direct closing approach.

direct denial Involves refuting the prospect's opinion or belief. The direct denial of a problem is considered a high-risk method of negotiating buyer resistance.

direct salesperson An independent contractor who represents manufacturers and the Internet.

directive style A communication style that displays the following characteristics: appears to be businesslike, displays a serious attitude, and voices strong opinions.

dominance Reflects the tendency to influence or exert one's will over others in a relationship. Each of us falls somewhere on this continuum.

ego drive An inner force that makes the salesperson want and need to make the sale.

elevator presentation A 30-second message that summarizes what you want people to know about you, your company, and your product line.

elevator speech Focuses on the benefit of working with the salesperson and is used to open the door and establish credibility to meet a need.

emotional buying motives Motives that prompt the prospect to act as a result of an appeal to some sentiment or passion.

emotional intelligence The capacity for recognizing our own feelings and those of others, for motivating ourselves, and for managing emotions well in ourselves and in our relationships.

emotional links The connectors that link the salesperson's message to the customer's internal emotions and increase the chance of closing a sale—for example, quality improvement, on-time delivery, service, and innovation.

emotive style A communication style that displays the following characteristics: appears to be quite active, takes the social initiative in most cases, likes to encourage informality, and expresses emotional opinions.

empathizer Someone who has the ability to imagine oneself in someone else's position and understand what that person is feeling.

esteem needs The desire to feel worthy in the eyes of others, to develop a sense of personal worth and adequacy, or a feeling of competence and importance.

expected product Everything that represents the customer's minimal expectations.

external motivation Action (taken by another person) that involves rewards or other forms of reinforcement, which causes the worker to behave in ways to ensure receipt of the reward.

feature Anything that a customer can feel, see, taste, smell, or measure to answer the question, "What is it?" Features include technical facts about such aspects as craftsmanship, durability, design, and economy of operation.

feature dump The process of talking all about the great things product X or service Y has without enabling a customer to see what it means to him or her.

field salesperson A salesperson employed by a manufacturer who handles well-established products that require a minimum of creative selling. The position usually does not require a high degree of technical knowledge.

full-line selling This selling approach, sometimes called *suggestion selling*, is the process of recommending products or services that are related to the main item sold to the customer.

general survey questions They help the salesperson discover facts about the buyer's problem and existing situation, and are often the first step in the partnership-building process.

generic product Describes only the basic substantive product being sold.

global account manager (GAM) The GAM is an account manager who is specialized on a specific product portfolio and not on a given customer or geography.

group influences Buyer behavior is influenced by the people around us. Group influences are the forces that other people exert on buying behavior.

habitual buying decisions Decisions that usually require very little consumer involvement and brand differences are usually insignificant.

impending event close Refers to making positive use of a negative point.

incremental commitment When working on a large, complex sale, some form of commitment should be obtained during each step in the multicall sales presentation.

indirect denial Often used when the prospect's concern is completely valid, or at least accurate to a large degree. The salesperson bends a little and acknowledges that the prospect is at least partially correct.

information economy The period in which our economy began shifting from an emphasis on industrial activity to an emphasis on information processing.

informative presentation Emphasizes factual information that is often taken from technical reports, company-prepared sales literature, or written testimonials from people who have used the product.

inside salesperson A salesperson employed by a wholesaler who solicits orders over the telephone. In addition to extensive product knowledge, the inside salesperson must be skilled in customer relations, merchandising, and suggestion selling.

integrity What you have when your behavior is in accordance with your professed standards and personal code of moral or artistic values. It is part of your character.

internal motivation An intrinsic reward that occurs when a duty or task is performed.

key account manager (KAM) The KAM is responsible for the coordination and management of a company's prioritized accounts.

knowledge workers Individuals whose work effort is centered around creating, using, sharing, and applying knowledge.

logrolling In a formal negotiation, using a customer's concern to form an alternate solution.

management close Involving the sales manager or a senior executive to assist with the close.

marketing concept A belief that the business firm should dedicate all its policies, planning, and operation to the satisfaction of the customer; a belief that the final result of all business activity should be to earn a profit by satisfying the customer.

marketing mix The combination of elements (product, promotion, place, and price) that creates continuing customer satisfaction for a business.

mental imagery The ability to visualize an object, concept, or action that is not actually present.

missionary, or detail, sales The situation where the end user is a business rather than an individual consumer; with services, where the end user is either a consumer or business user.

missionary salespeople Those persons, also known as "detail salespeople," who serve to develop goodwill, provide information, and stimulate demand for the manufacturer's products.

modified rebuy A situation where the customer wishes to modify product specifications, change delivery schedules, or renegotiate prices.

multiple options close With the multiple options close, the salesperson gives the prospect several options to consider and tries to assess the prospect's degree of interest in each.

national account manager (NAM) The NAM is responsible for recruiting and negotiating various business transactions, and signs on new regional and national retailers.

need discovery The salesperson establishes two-way communication by asking appropriate questions and listening carefully to the customer's responses.

need-satisfaction questions Designed to move the sales process toward commitment and action. These are questions that focus on the solution.

negotiation Working to reach an agreement that is mutually satisfactory to both buyer and seller.

networking The practice of making and using contacts. It involves people meeting people and profiting from the connection.

new-task buy A first-time purchase of a product or service.

nonverbal messages "Messages without words" or "silent messages." These are messages we communicate through facial expressions, voice tone, gestures, appearance, and posture.

open questions Questions that require the prospect to go beyond a simple yes/no response.

opportunity management A four-dimensional process consisting of time management, territory management, records management, and stress management.

organizational culture A collection of beliefs, behaviors, and work patterns held in common by people employed by a specific firm.

outside salesperson A salesperson, employed by a wholesaler, who must have knowledge of many products and be able to serve as a consultant to the customer on product or service applications. This position usually requires an in-depth understanding of the customer's operation.

partnering A strategically developed, high-quality relationship that focuses on solving the customer's buying problem.

patronage buying motives A motive that causes the prospect to buy a product from one particular company rather than another. Typical patronage buying motives include superior service, attractive decor, product selection, and competence of the salesperson.

personal digital assistants (PDAs) Small pocket-sized organizers that offer many features common to laptop computers.

personal selling Involves person-to-person communication with a prospect. It is a process of developing relationships; discovering customer's needs; matching appropriate products with these needs; and communicating benefits through informing, reminding, or persuading.

personal selling philosophy Involves three things: full acceptance of the marketing concept, developing an appreciation for the expanding role of personal selling in our competitive national and international markets, and assuming the role of problem solver or partner in helping customers to make complex buying decisions.

personality The thoughts, feelings, and actions that characterize someone.

persuasion The act of presenting product appeals so as to influence the prospect's beliefs, attitudes, or behavior.

persuasive presentation A sales strategy that influences the prospect's beliefs, attitudes, or behavior, and encourages buyer's action.

physiological needs Primary needs or physical needs, including the need for food, water, sleep, clothing, and shelter.

pipeline analytics The ability to conduct sophisticated data analysis and modeling; found in most CRM systems.

pipeline dashboards At-a-glance visualizations that define, monitor, and analyze the relationships existing in the pipeline.

pipeline management The process of managing all the prospects in the salesperson's sales funnel to ensure that sales objectives are being met.

platinum rule Provides each of us with the motivation we need to treat others the way they want to be treated.

portfolio A portable case or loose-leaf binder containing a wide variety of sales-support materials. It is used to add visual life to the sales message and to prove claims.

positioning Refers to decisions, activities, and communication strategies that are directed toward trying to create and maintain a firm's intended product concept in the customer's mind.

postpone method When selling a complex product, it is often necessary to postpone negotiations until you can complete the needs assessment or acquire additional information regarding such things as final price or delivery dates.

potential product Refers to what may remain to be done, that is, what is possible.

preapproach Activities that precede the actual sales call and set the stage for a personalized sales approach, tailored to the specific needs of the prospect. This involves the planning necessary for the actual meeting with a prospect.

presentation strategy A well-conceived plan that includes three prescriptions: establishing objectives for the sales presentation, preparing the presale presentation plan needed to meet these objectives, and renewing one's commitment to providing outstanding customer service.

probing questions Helps you uncover and clarify the prospect's buying problem and the circumstances surrounding the problem.

product One element of the marketing mix. The term "product" should be broadly interpreted to encompass goods, services, and ideas.

product buying motives Reasons that cause the prospect to buy one particular product brand or label over another. Typical product buying motives include brand preference, quality preference, price preference, and design or engineering preference.

product configuration If the customer has complex buying needs, then the salesperson may have to bring together many different parts of the company's product mix in order to develop a custom-fitted solution. The product selection process is often referred to as product configuration.

product development Testing, modifying, and retesting an idea for a product several times before offering it to the customer.

product information management (PIM) Helps manage digital assets such as images.

product life cycle Stages of a product from the time it is first introduced to the market until it is taken off the market, including the stages of introduction, growth, maturity, and decline.

product strategy A well-conceived plan that emphasizes acquiring extensive product knowledge, learning to select and communicate appropriate product benefits that will appeal to the customer, and configuring value-added solutions.

promotional allowance A price reduction given to a customer who participates in an advertising or sales support program.

proof devices A proof device can take the form of a statement, a report, a testimonial, customer data, or a photograph.

prospect Someone who has three basic qualifications. First, the person must have a need for the product or service. Second, the individual must be able to afford the purchase. Third, the person must be authorized to purchase the product.

prospect base A list of current and potential customers.

prospecting A systematic process of identifying potential customers.

psychic income Consists of factors that provide psychological rewards; helps to satisfy these needs and motivates us to achieve higher levels of performance.

qualifying Examining the prospect list to identify the people who are most apt to buy a product.

qualitative criteria One of the two ways managers assess the productivity of their salespeople. This includes attitude, product knowledge, communication skills, personal appearance, customer goodwill generation, selling skills, initiative, and team collaboration.

quality control The evaluation or testing of products against established standards. This has important sales appeal when used by the salesperson to convince a prospect of a product's quality.

quantifying the solution The process of determining if a sales proposal adds value. Quantifying the solution is especially important in situations where the purchase represents a major buying decision.

quantitative criteria One of the two ways managers assess the productivity of their salespeople. This includes sales volume in dollars, sales volume compared with previous year's sales, sales volume by product or product line, number of new accounts opened, amount of new account sales, net profit on each account, and number of customer calls.

quantity discount A price reduction made to encourage a larger volume purchase than would otherwise be expected.

rational buying motives Motives that prompt the prospect to act because of an appeal to the prospect's reason or better judgment, including profit potential, quality, and availability of technical assistance. Generally these result from an objective review of available information.

reciprocity A mutual exchange of benefits; for example, when a firm buys products from its own customers.

reference group Two or more people who have well-established interpersonal communications and tend to influence the values, attitudes, and buying behaviors of one another. They act as a point of comparison and a source of information for a prospective buyer.

referral A prospect who has been recommended by a current customer or by someone who is familiar with the product.

regional account manager (RAM) Part of a larger sales team and acts as direct client contact and manager of a number of business accounts.

reflective style A communication style that displays the following characteristics: controls emotional expression, displays a preference for orderliness, tends to express measured opinions, and seems difficult to get to know.

relationship selling Result when salespeople work hard to build and nourish long-term partnerships. They rely on a personal, customized approach to each customer.

relationship strategy A well thought-out plan for establishing, building, and maintaining quality relationships.

reminder presentation Sometimes called the *reinforcement presentation*. This assumes that the prospect has already been involved in an informative or persuasive presentation. The customer understands at least the basic product features and buyer benefits.

return on investment (ROI) A formula used to determine the net profits or savings from a given investment. It is a common way to quantify the solution.

role A set of characteristics and expected social behaviors based on the expectations of others. All the roles we assume may influence our buying behavior.

sales call plan A plan developed with information taken from the routing and scheduling plan. The primary purpose of the plan is to ensure efficient and effective account coverage.

sales call reluctance Includes the thoughts, feelings, and behavioral patterns that conspire to limit what a salesperson can accomplish.

sales data The information seen in most CRM systems, including the contact name, title, address, phone number, e-mail, and so forth.

sales intelligence Gives salespeople access to insights into the prospects' marketplace, their firm, their competitors, even about the prospects themselves.

sales management The process of planning, implementing, and controlling the personal selling function.

sales process model The total set of accounts being pursued at any given time.

sales territory A geographic area where prospects and customers reside.

satisfactions The positive benefits that customers seek when making a purchase. Satisfactions arise from the product itself, from the company that makes or distributes the product, and from the salesperson who sells and services the product.

seasonal discount Adjusting prices up or down during specific times of the year to spur or acknowledge changes in demand.

security needs Needs that represent our desire to be free from danger and uncertainty.

self-actualization The need for self-fulfillment; a full tapping of one's potential to meet a goal; the need to be everything one is capable of being. This is one of the needs in Maslow's hierarchy.

self-concept The bundle of facts, opinions, beliefs, and perceptions about yourself that are present in your life, every moment of every day.

self-talk An effort to override past negative mental programming by erasing or replacing it with conscious, positive new directions. It is one way to get rid of barriers to goal achievement.

Selling 2.0 Describes the use of personal computers; mobile phones; smartphones; Web sites; customer relationship management applications with cloud computing; e-mail; instant messaging; blogging; social media including Facebook; YouTube; Twitter; etc.; along with innovative sales practices to create value for both the buyer and seller by improving the speed, collaboration, customer engagement and accountability of the sales process.

showmanship Defined as an interesting and attractive way of communicating an idea to others.

situational leadership This leadership approach is based on the theory that the most successful leadership occurs when the leader's style matches the situation.

six-step presentation plan Preparation involving consideration of those activities that will take place during the sales presentation.

sociability Reflects the amount of control one exerts over emotional expressiveness. People who are high in sociability tend to express their feelings freely, while people who are low on this continuum tend to control their feelings.

social class A group of people who are similar in income, wealth, educational background, and occupational prestige.

social needs Needs that reflect a person's desire for affection, identification with a group, and approval from others.

social network Your set of direct and indirect contacts.

solution A mutually shared answer to a recognized customer problem. In many selling situations, a solution is more encompassing than a specific product.

solution selling A process by which the salesperson uncovers and clarifies a customer's problem, works with the customer to create a vision of how things could be better, and then develops a plan for implementing the vision.

special concession close Offers the buyer something extra for acting immediately.

specific survey questions These are designed to give prospects a chance to describe in more detail the problem, issue, or dissatisfaction they are experiencing from their point of view.

stall Resistance related to time. A stall usually means the customer does not yet perceive the benefits of buying now.

straight rebuy A routine purchase of items needed by a business-to-business customer.

strategic account management A strategic selling alliance.

strategic account manager (SAM) The SAM executes an enterprise-wide sales strategy for growth profitability, customer loyalty, and customer-driven innovation.

strategic planning A managerial process that matches the firm's resources to its market opportunities. It takes into consideration the various functional areas of the business that must be coordinated such as financial assets, workforce, production capabilities, and marketing.

strategies The things that salespeople do as the result of pre-call planning to ensure they call on the right people, at the right time, and with the right tactics to achieve positive results.

stress The response of the body or mind to demands on it, in the form of either physiological or psychological strain.

structure Sales managers clearly define their own duties and those of the sales staff. They assume an active role in directing their subordinates.

style flexing The deliberate attempt to adjust one's communication style to accommodate the needs of the other person.

subculture Within many cultures, the groups whose members share ideals and beliefs that differ from those held by the wider society of which they are a part.

summary-confirmation questions Questions used to clarify and confirm buying conditions.

summary-of-benefits close Involves summarizing the most important buyer benefits; reemphasizing the benefits that will help bring about a favorable decision.

superior benefit A benefit that will, in most cases, outweigh the customer's specific concern.

supportive style A communication style that displays the following characteristics: appears quiet and reserved, listens attentively to other people, tends to avoid the use of power, and makes decisions in a thoughtful and deliberate manner.

survey questions Questions used to collect information about the buyer's exiting situation and any problems.

systems selling A form of strategic alliance that appeals to buyers who prefer to purchase a packaged solution to a problem from a single seller, thus avoiding all the separate decisions involved in a complex buying situation.

tactics Techniques, practices, or methods salespeople use during face-to-face interactions with customers.

telemarketing The practice of marketing goods and services through telephone contact.

telesales The process of using the telephone to acquire information about the customer, determine needs, suggest solutions, negotiate buyer resistance, close the sale, and service the sale.

trade selling The sale of a product or service to another member of the supply chain.

transactional selling A type of selling that most effectively matches the needs of the value-conscious buyer who is primarily interested in price and convenience.

trial close A closing attempt made at an opportune time during the sales presentation to encourage the customer to reveal readiness or unwillingness to buy.

trial offer Involves giving the prospect an opportunity to try the product without making a purchase commitment.

unconscious expectations Certain views concerning appropriate dress.

upselling An effort to sell better quality products that will, in many cases, add value.

unbundling A strategy used to reduce the price by eliminating some items.

value-added product Product that exists when salespeople offer the customers more than they expect.

value-added selling A series of creative improvements within the sales process that enhance the customer experience.

value-added product-selling model Made up of four "possible" products: the generic product, the expected product, the value-added product, and the potential product.

value proposition The set of benefits and values that the company promises to deliver to customers to satisfy their needs.

value reinforcement This strategy involves getting credit for the value you create for the customer.

values Deep personal beliefs and preferences that influence your behavior.

variety-seeking buying decisions Decisions characterized by low customer involvement, but important perceived brand differences.

versatility Describes our ability to minimize communication style bias.

visualize To form a mental image of something you want to succeed at.

Web site A collection of Web pages maintained by a single person or organization. It is accessible to anyone with a computer and a modem.

written proposals A specific plan of action based on the facts, assumptions, and supporting documentation included in the sales presentation. Written proposals vary in terms of format and content.

ZOPA Zone of Possible Agreement: the space between the seller's walk-away point and the buyer's highest willingness to pay.

Name Index

Subject Index